The Allyn & Bacon Sourcebook for College Writing Teachers

Second Edition

James C. McDonald
University of Southwestern Louisiana

Allyn and Bacon
Boston · London · Toronto · Sydney · Tokyo · Singapore

A Pearson Education Company
160 Gould Street
Needham Heights, Massachusetts 02494

Internet: www.abacon.com

ISBN 0-205-31603-4

Printed in the United States of America

10 9 8 7 6 5 4 3 2 1   03 02 01 00

Contents

DESIGNING, RESPONDING TO, AND EVALUATING WRITING ASSIGNMENTS

FOREWORD

My first day in a composition class was as a teaching assistant instructing first year students in 1976, just four months after I had been an undergraduate myself. After two days of orientation, I was teaching two classes and relying on my textbooks, even more than my students would, to make sense of my subject. At the beginning of my first class a student came up to my desk, introduced herself as a sister of a friend of mine, and returned a paper of mine that the friend had once borrowed to—well—plagiarize. It was not a good start.

I wasn't comfortable in my role as a teacher, and I didn't know much about how to teach a classroom of writing students. I knew nothing about the writing process movement then well underway, and next to nothing about scholarship on teaching writing. At best I can only vaguely recall some arguments in my weekly teaching practicum course about *Students' Right to Their Own Language,* only recently endorsed and published by the Conference on College Composition and Communication. My students were bright and well prepared for college English, however, and being supportive of their young instructor, they made up for a lot of the weaknesses in my teaching.

I occasionally looked at scholarship on teaching composition as I worked towards my masters degree, buying a copy of Mina Shaughnessy's *Errors and Expectations* after a semester of teaching basic writing, and attending the 1978 CCCC meeting as I searched for a job. But it wasn't until I was an adjunct instructor at another school, and facing four first-year composition classes full of unprepared students, that I realized how inadequate my teaching approaches were. Then I began to look seriously beyond my textbooks to articles and presentations on composition for help in understanding the myriad of problems my students and I were encountering in class. I began to rethink my approach to teaching, really trying to analyze what I was doing for the first time. My reading was not well focused, and finding the time and energy to read articles about composition while instructing over a hundred students a semester was difficult. Improving my teaching was frustratingly slow at first. I began to improve at a quicker pace when I joined a group of adjuncts and teaching assistants at another university a few years later. There we began developing a new first-year writing course for unprepared students, basing our approach on scholarship about writing and composing by such scholars and teachers as Janet Emig, Donald Murray, Peter Elbow, Nancy Sommers, and James Kinneavy.

Those memories as graduate student or adjunct instructor, and the hope of improving the learning curve for others with experiences like mine, have guided me as I put together this collection. I want *The Allyn & Bacon Sourcebook for College Writing Teachers* to serve as a useful collection of writings on important theories and pedagogies in composition studies. To select the articles I thought would be most useful, I kept thinking back on my struggle to teach too many poorly prepared students while trying to learn more about composition. *The Allyn & Bacon Sourcebook for College Writing Teachers* is directed especially to composition teachers early in their careers who face their first teaching position or are re-examining their teaching goals and methods. At the same time I hope that experienced teachers will find this material informative.

The first group of selections describes general perspectives about composition teachers and students and historical and theoretical trends in composition studies, including basic writing instruction. The following sections discuss important dimensions of writing instruction--addressing audiences, using peer groups, composing process theories, pre-writing and revising, the integration of critical thinking and reading instruction into composition classes, using computers, and argumentation theory. Those selections are followed by sections about teaching matters of form: organization, style, and grammar. The final group of selections describe approaches to designing and sequencing assignments, responding to student writing, and grading. These articles certainly do not cover every topic important in writing instruction, no more than a composition teacher in a single course can cover everything that writers need to develop their craft. There are suggested readings at the end of each section and at the end of the book if you want to read further about a topic or read about topics that are not covered here.

Acknowledgments. I have a number of people to thank for their assistance with this book. Elsa Rogers, Eileen Barton, Laurie Dever Hook, Beth Maxfield, Mary Alice Trent, and Mary White did some of the library work for the first edition and helped me sort out selections. Ann Dobie, Nicole Greene, and Patricia Kilroe made helpful suggestions for the selections and suggested readings. Leslie Schilling scanned the articles for the second edition. Patrick Bizzaro, East Carolina University; Thomas Deans, Kansas State University; and Rodney Keller, Ricks College, provided useful reviews of the first edition that helped me decide what changes to make in the second edition, and I received a great deal of useful feedback about the first edition from the graduate students in my Teaching of College English classes. I thank Doug Day for recommending me for this project and Bill Lalicker for helping to give me a shot at it. And finally I thank my editors: Allen Workman for the first edition, who brought this project to me, and Joe Opiela, who asked me to do a second edition. Both worked to make my work easier and were patient with a busy writing teacher who couldn't always make his deadlines.

James C. McDonald

Mutual Friends: What Teachers Can Learn From Students and What Students Can Learn From Teachers

Edward P. J. Corbett

Edward P. J. Corbett, who died in 1998, was one of the most influential teachers, scholars, and historians in rhetoric and composition for over forty years. As head of the rhetoric program at Ohio State University, editor of College Composition and Communication, *author of* Classical Rhetoric for the Modern Student, *and teacher of many of today's leading rhetoric and composition scholars, Corbett played a crucial role in the development of the discipline of composition studies. In this 1991 essay, originally published in* Balancing Acts: Essays on the Teaching of Writing in Honor of William F. Irmscher, *Corbett reflects on his classroom experiences and argues that teachers need to learn from their students and put themselves in the place of beginning learners.*

We do not always recognize that teaching is a two-way street. Like another familiar analogy—that of the pitcher and the catcher in baseball—the teaching process is often viewed as one in which one of the parties involved in the transaction is doing all of the transmitting and the other party is doing all the receiving. The common concept of the writer-reader relationship is similar: the writer does all the work; the reader just sits back and absorbs—or falls asleep.

Because I am a slow learner, it took me a long time to realize that teaching is a reciprocal process. A lot of sweating goes on on both sides of the podium. Moreover, a lot of learning ensues on both sides of the podium. For a long time, I thought I was the only one in the classroom who was expressing moisture through the pores and the only one in the classroom who was dispensing knowledge. Because I

A shorter version of this paper was delivered at the Young Rhetoricians' Conference in Monterey, California, 22–24 June 1989.

was a slow learner, it took me most of my professional career to realize that all along my students had been teaching me steadily and profusely. It is too late for me to radically alter my own attitudes and methods in the light of the epiphany I have experienced, but I can make some reparation for my persistent myopia by passing on to younger teachers the instant insights I have gained from my revelation.

I might start out by talking first about the dividends that students can reap from contact with the teacher. After all, since most of us think of the teacher-student relationship as a one-way conduit, we might start with the obvious: the teacher has something to give the student.

The simplest and most general answer to the question "what can students learn from the teacher?" is that students can learn whatever the teacher knows that they do not know. Students may regard what the teacher knows as not worth the time or the effort required of them to gain that knowledge. But we all know that the judgments of young people about what is worth acquiring are sometimes erroneous. Even we senior citizens frequently misjudge the worth of the fruits that the world dangles before our eyes, so we cannot fault inexperienced youth for their misappraisals. But what we can say is that if students are not receptive to what the teacher has to offer simply because they have misjudged the value of the plum, they are the losers.

Until they learn otherwise, however, students should always presume that the teacher knows something that they do not know. After all, there are circumstances that warrant the presumption: usually the teacher has met certain certification standards; most of the time, the teacher is older and more experienced than the students. Part of the Oriental students' great reverence for the Teacher is due not only to the official certification of the teacher's wisdom but also to the respect that their culture has for older people.

From my vantage point now as an elderly person, I can honestly say that I never had a teacher who made my classroom experience a complete waste of my time and attention. I was frequently bored by a teacher. I was often baffled by a teacher. I was sometimes disenchanted by a teacher. And although today I still know who my memorable teachers were and still can tell you which ones I learned the most from, I still cannot say that I ever came away empty-handed from any teacher I ever had. On the contrary, I could tick off for you many experiences in my life where I felt I had been cheated of the expected dividends—experiences such as reading a book or seeing a play or going on a trip or viewing a television program.

I acknowledge that the teacher is not the font of all knowledge. The teacher is mainly a conveyor of knowledge and skills and just one of many repositories of knowledge. The big buzzing world around us may be the premier font of knowledge. But we desperately need a guide through the maze of that big buzzing world. There are many guides available to us—parents, clergy, and close friends. But maybe the most reliable of the guides for hire is the teacher. We can thank whatever gods that be that in our culture a certain number of years of education are mandatory for all young people and that there are paid, certified teachers to conduct that education. And if those teachers know even a little bit more than we know, our relationship with them is bound to be profitable.

The point I have been trying to make is that we stand to learn something from any relationship where the other party knows something that we do not know. What we learn may be more or less valuable to us. And admittedly there will be times when what we learn from the other party will be deleterious to us. The person, for instance, who knows about and introduces us to the euphoric sensations of a chemical drug, may ultimately prove to be a baneful influence on us. But at least we expect teachers to have only good goods to dispense to their charges. There can be some guarantee that the goods dispensed by the teacher will be good if the teacher has the kind of ethos we traditionally associate with the pedagogue.

It is that pedagogical ethos which leads me to a discussion of the second general benefit that students can derive from their contact with a teacher. The second benefit is the set of values—intellectual or cultural or moral values—that a teacher can convey to the students. I do not mean to suggest that teachers should be deliberate proselytizers. Teachers should exemplify values, not harangue their students about them. Teachers, like other professionals, go through a crucible in order to practice their profession. They want to win the privilege of standing in front of a room full of eager or apathetic students and engaging those students in some sort of intellectual exploration.

Teaching is the most private of the professions. Other professionals—doctors, lawyers, engineers—are exposed ultimately to public scrutiny and assessment. But once the teacher closes the door of the classroom, only God and the students—and maybe the teacher—know what goes on behind the closed door. That situation places a tremendous responsibility on teachers. Their integrity—and maybe the ultimate welfare of the students—is on the line. Mind you, they should not take advantage of that closed arena and indoctrinate their students verbally about any particular brand of religion or politics or way of life. However, they can hardly help transmitting some set of values just by their demeanor, their dress, their carriage, their speech patterns, and their mere presence on the podium. For that reason, they must be what Quintilian said the ideal orator must be: a good man (or woman) skilled in speaking.

To my mind, being a genuinely good person is the greatest challenge for the teacher. All of us, merely because we are human, are fallible and peccable—and we frequently fall from grace. Nevertheless, when the genuinely good person falls from grace, there is somehow always a residue of nobility and inspiration. I am not suggesting that teachers have to be untarnished saints. Some of the great ones I have known have occasionally cussed like a sailor's parrot when their sensibilities were outraged. But I am asserting that teachers must be unswervingly conscientious, honest, and fair in their dealings with students.

That is the challenge: to be invariably conscientious, honest, and fair in dealing with students. Meeting that challenge may strike some of you as being an easy task, but for most of us, meeting that challenge is the hardest task of all. When I recollect my own practices as a teacher, I simply cringe at the thought of the many times in my career when I was not conscientious or honest or fair in dealing with my students. But I have known a few teachers who hewed unswervingly to that standard.

You have all read or heard somebody's testimony about a person who had profoundly affected his or her life. I have been amazed to discover how often the influential person mentioned in those testimonies has been a former teacher. I have more often heard that it was a teacher rather than a parent or a minister or a boss that turned somebody's life around.

I want all of you now to ask yourselves who had a great influence on the course of your life. Who pushed you in the direction that you eventually took? Who made you what you are today—for better or for worse? I wonder how many of you would answer, as I would, "A teacher."

In my case, it was a teacher of Greek whom I had in high school for at least one class all four years. I want to talk a bit about him because he exemplifies the kind of beneficent ethos I am talking about. He was a Ph.D. who preferred to teach in high school rather than in the university. He was filled with his subject, classical Greek, and he loved it as no other teacher I have ever been exposed to has loved the subject he or she was teaching. An elderly man in his early sixties, he walked two and a half miles to school every morning, and on the way he would recite to himself the hundreds of lines from Homer's *Iliad* or from Xenophon's *Anabasis* that he had committed to memory. If you think that we callow youth were not edified by this display of commitment to learning, you are sadly mistaken. In the breaks between classes, we would frequently exclaim to one another about the wonders of this man's stunning erudition.

This extraordinarily learned man gave us ridiculously high grades on our report cards, not because he was indifferent to intellectual standards but because he had learned along the way that high grades were a powerful incentive for young men to study their Greek. And he was right. We studied harder in that class than we did in the classes where we barely squeaked by with a B-minus. Maybe we *earned* those high grades because we studied hard.

And he was a good man, an exemplary man. I pronounce that judgment about him not because he was a priest but because he fairly exuded, unpretentiously but genuinely moral and intellectual integrity. What an inspiration he was to us all! He did not preach to us, but by the example of his ethos he made us aspire to be solidly learned, and he made us ashamed of ourselves if we mortally or venially fell from grace in our personal lives. How can one measure what effect such a teacher had on the lives and the fortunes of his students? All I can say is that the effect was as profound as it was unmistakable.

Those are the principal things that students can learn from a teacher: a thirst and a respect for knowledge and a sterling set of intellectual and moral values. I wish I could give you the formula for how a teacher succeeds in promoting those objectives, but the formulation of such a procedure is the subject for another paper, a paper that I am not qualified to present. Instead, let us now consider the other side of the teacher-student relationship: what teachers can learn from students.

I can give a formula that will prepare teachers to learn whatever is to be learned from their students. The formula is easy to articulate but difficult to effectuate, but here it is: attune yourselves to the mind-set of your students. Anyone who has taught for even a few years has had the unsettling experience of alluding in the classroom to some putatively familiar event or personage and meeting with a scrim of glassy-eyed responses from the students. And the older you get as a teacher, the more often you meet with those blank responses. I remember how shocked I was the first time I got that kind of blank response from my students when I alluded to an event that was etched indelibly in my memory: Jack Ruby shooting Lee Harvey Oswald on live television. Now if you were to mention that 1963 world-class event in your classroom, you would not only have to describe the event but have to identify the two men involved in it.

I mention this common experience that teachers have of unresponsive responses from their students because it is the classic example of teachers broadcasting on a frequency quite different from the one their students are tuned to. The frequency metaphor is an apt one here because the baby boomers—and now their children—are, as Marshall McLuhan once reminded us, more "ear-oriented" than "eye-oriented." The private libraries of many of the college students of my generation were stocked with books. The private libraries of most students today are stocked with record albums or compact discs. The difference in what the different generations of college students treasure makes a profound difference in what students readily respond to. I won't go into the different cognitive dispositions brought on by one's repeated exposure to what McLuhan called the "hot media" and the "cool media," but I will mention that if teachers today just want to gain the attention of students in the classroom so that the students can be infused with the instruction prescribed by the syllabus, they are more likely to succeed if they resort to the medium of sound than to the medium of print. Even a message printed in billboard size is not going to distract teenagers from the enchantment of the Walkman cooing in their ears. I do not mean to suggest that older teachers have to abandon what edifies or enchants them and adopt what educates and entertains their young charges, but they do have to make an effort to discover and understand what turns their students on.

It is as natural for a gulf to develop between teachers and students as it is for a gulf to develop between parents and children. But if we do not strive to narrow that gulf, we will diminish our effectiveness as teachers and will foreclose any chance we might otherwise have of learning what our students have to teach us.

Again, I was a slow learner on this score, and I shouldn't have been, because by the time I was ten years into my teaching career, I had had considerable acting experience. It is a commonplace that one of the skills actors have to develop is the ability to put themselves into the shoes of the character they are playing and to act and think the way that character would. I did have some success in making that transformation of personalities on the stage, but it was a number of years before I realized that I had to make a similar kind of transformation in the classroom: I had to make an effort to put myself into the shoes—or, if you don't like that metaphor, into the disposition—of my students and to imagine how they were responding to what I was preaching or teaching. For a number of years, I kept exclaiming to my students about the mellifluous voice of Bing Crosby emanating from my old 78 rpm records, while they were responding to the rockabilly rhythms and gyrations of Elvis Presley on television. Just the fact that my students and I danced to a different rhythm created a gulf between us.

How do we get on our students' frequency? The surest way I know of is to have frequent conferences with the students. Many teachers, I am sure, have adopted the policy of inviting their students to their office for a conference about anything connected with the class. Some teachers have better luck with that policy than I have had. I have an office across the corridor from a colleague who gets a steady stream of students in response to that kind of standing policy. I must strike my students as an ogre; they do not come to confer with me in my office unless they are absolutely desperate for help.

There are some writing programs in this country that require instructors to hold a specified number of conferences with their students during the term. Don Murray's program at the University of New Hampshire mandated conferences with students on even, writing assignment. A teacher in that program told me that when he first began teaching at the University of New Hampshire, he was skeptical about the efficacy of mandated conferences, but now he says that he cannot conceive of teaching a writing course in any other way. I discovered the efficacy of mandated conferences when I began teaching our technical writing course about ten years ago. The curriculum demanded that we require our students to confer with us at least twice in connection with the major report they have to write. I find these conferences so exhausting that I do not set up more than four of them on any one day of the school week.

But I have found these conferences so rewarding for me that I encourage my students to visit me more than twice during the term, and I would definitely establish a system of mandated conferences for any writing course I taught if such a system were not set by the director of the course. What makes these conferences rewarding for me is that they enable me to get a fix on my students: I learn a great deal about their backgrounds, about their strengths and weaknesses in several areas, about their problems, not only in connection with the assignment but in connection with their other classes and commitments, about their aspirations, about their personal lives—although I do not press any of my students for information about their personal lives if they do not want to talk about such matters. One would suppose that the succession of relatively brief conferences with students would soon blur in one's memory, but I have been surprised by how much I remember about each student right up to the end of the term. And best of all, I get so attuned to the mind-set of my students that I no longer exclaim in the classroom about the wonders of Bing Crosby's crooning when they are at that stage of their life where they are turned on by the singing of Madonna.

Another way to get attuned to your students' psyche is to put yourself in a situation where you are once again a beginning learner. Once we ourselves get away from being a student in the classroom, it is very easy for us to forget how baffling and frustrating a teacher's lecture or assignment can be for the neophyte. I had an awakening a number of years ago when I decided that I was going to learn how to play the banjo. Instead of going to a music teacher, I decided that I was going to get a book on how to play the banjo and hole up in my room to learn the intricacies of this glorious stringed instrument. I discovered that I had to start at square zero. I had everything to learn and only an instruction book to teach me. I went through a lot of trials and made a lot of errors, and my progress in acquiring the skill was slow and uncertain. I still haven't learned to play the banjo well enough to play for my friends.

But the chief fruit of that humbling experience is that I came to realize how students feel when they venture into a new area of learning, whether it be a class in literature or composition or chemistry or economics. And when I realized the bewilderment and frustration of the beginning learner, I was better able to adjust the level of my teaching to the temper of my audience.

Mimi Schwartz, who teaches at Stockton State College in New Jersey, reported in the Staffroom Interchange section of the May 1989 issue of *College Composition and Communication* about her experience in taking two creative writing courses for credit at Princeton University, one in fiction writing, the other in poetry writing. Like me, she had some salutary epiphanies as a result of becoming a student again. She said about her experience:

> I was surprised at my own vulnerabilities as a writer. Many of my fears, confusions, and needs were not so different from my younger counterparts' as I would have predicted. Remembering "what it was like" as a student writer—and recording in my journal what worked and didn't work for me and for my classmates—has altered my teaching as well as my writing. (203–4)

Already a good teacher of writing, Mimi Schwartz has become a better teacher as a result of her experience, a teacher more sensitive to the needs, the insecurities, the bewilderments of her students. But we don't have to enroll in a formal class in order to renew the experience of a student having to write a paper. We can do what has been frequently recommended in journal articles and in convention talks: we can sit down and write the papers we assign to our students.

Another form of re-experiencing the role of the student is described by Patrick Dias in an article in *English Education.* Dias reported on an experiment in which he teamed up groups of two or three university pre-service teachers with groups of two or three secondary school students and required the pre-service teachers to work collaboratively—as students, not as teachers—with the students on all assignments. The results of that experiment were amazing to Dias, to his pre-service teachers, and to the high school students. Dias concluded that "a view of the act of teaching from the perspective of what teachers do needs to be complemented by an understanding and an experience of how that teaching is received by students. It is the students who teach us about teaching" (208). One of the fruits, Dias claims, of the collaborative experience that he set up is that it forced the pre-service teachers "to recall and re-evaluate their past experiences as students" (207).

At one time, we all were needful, insecure, bewildered students. Furthermore, as students, most of us were far from being hotshots. We handed in some of our papers late: we sometimes gave our homework only a lick and a promise; we were often too proud to ask our teacher to clarify an assignment when we were baffled by it. Since it is easy for us to forget that when we were enrolled in elementary or secondary or college classes, we were no great shakes as students, we would do well to occasionally renew our sympathy and our empathy with our students by really or vicariously projecting ourselves back into the status of students. And then we will have disposed ourselves to learn what the students can teach us.

Our students can give us a new perspective on what we already know and can present us with enticing vistas of other worlds. They can remind us that studying is hard work, that all work and no play is stultifying, that stultification rots the mind. They can make us aware that mercy is frequently a restorative virtue, that intransigence is sometimes nothing more than unconscionable rigidity, and that a mere pat on the back can often be the impetus that impels one toward the finish line. But if we have kept our sensibilities sharp, we already *know* those truisms; we just have to be reminded of them—and our students are great reminders, if we will just pay attention to them. And if we pay attention to them they can also open up new vistas for us. It is easy for all of us to get locked up in our little circumscribed worlds. One of the ways to break out of those circumscribed worlds is to travel. Another way is to read about other worlds. Still another way for teachers to break out of their circumscribed worlds is to force themselves to become acquainted with the many diverse worlds that their students inhabit. As Terry Dean said in a recent article in *College Composition and Communication*, "Multicultural Classrooms, Monocultural Teachers," "With increasing cultural diversity in classrooms, teachers need to structure learning experiences that both help students write their way into the university and help teachers learn their way into student cultures" (23). Shirley Brice Heath was speaking of much the same thing when she said in her book *Ways with Words*,

> Unless the boundaries between classrooms and communities can be broken and the flow of cultural patterns between them encouraged, the schools will continue to legitimate and reproduce communities of townspeople who control and limit the potential progress of other communities who themselves remain untouched by other values and ways of life. (369)

In short, what students can teach their teachers is the paramount lesson that a rhetorician has to learn: that of all the elements which play a part in the communication process, audience is the most important. Teachers are defined by their students. What do I mean by that curious statement? Well, there are a number of ways in which it is true to say that students define their teachers. For instance, the successes of our students help to validate us as teachers. It is common for people to say of someone who has achieved some honor, "She was a student of so-and-so." That so-and-so teacher not only basks in the glory of that student but acquires a special kind of certification as a teacher.

But teachers are defined also by their ordinary students and by their remedial students. If we remain sensitive to the aspirations that our students entertain, to the stock of knowledge that they command, and to the cognitive skills that they possess, we will be disposed to make those adjustments in our teaching necessary to accommodate their expectations and their capacities. If we don't remain sensitive to the particular population of students that we have in the classroom in a particular semester, we will make unrealistic assignments, we will season our lectures with a sprinkling of jargon, and we will probably make a lot of wounding comments about our students' responses and performances.

What kinds of teachers are we? Our students can define us from the way we manifest ourselves in a particular class of a particular year. It is too bad that we can't eavesdrop on our students when they define us for other students outside the classroom. Hearing some of those definitions might help us to amend our ways. If we don't reach them, if we don't inspirit them, if we don't edify them, all our crudition, all our degrees, all our honors go for naught. We have to observe them, to listen to them, to intuit them. Remember what Patrick Dias said: "It is the students who teach us about teaching." If we keep our antennae tuned to their frequency, we can learn much from them that could convert us from being merely competent teachers to being great teachers. That's what mellowing is—the process whereby ordinariness matures into brilliance. Ripeness is all.

Recently I saw the movie *Dead Poets Society,* in which Robin Williams plays the part of a teacher of English in a New England prep school who uses some very unorthodox methods of teaching. In one scene, he jumps up on his desk in the classroom and asks the students. "Why am I standing up here?" When one of the students answers, "Because you want to be taller." Williams responds that he is standing on his desk not because he wants to be taller but because he wants to get a new perspective on the classroom and on his students. Then he jumps down from the desk and invites all of his students to jump up on the desk in turn and from that perch take a fresh look at the classroom and at their fellow students. Maybe the secret of maximizing the lessons that teachers can learn from students and the lessons that students can learn from teachers is for both parties to change perspectives on each other occasionally so that they can put themselves in a receptive disposition for learning and can become, to use the wonderful tautology, mutual friends.

Teaching Writing: The Major Theories

Anne Ruggles Gere

Ann Ruggles Gere is an English professor at the University of Michigan and a former president of the Conference on College Composition and Communication. She is the author of numerous books and articles in composition studies, including Writing Groups: History, Theory, and Implications *and* Into the Field: Site of Composition Studies. *In this 1986 article, Gere gives a brief history of first-year writing courses and examines the four dominant approaches to teaching writing in the twentieth century: current-traditional instruction, rhetorical instruction, expressivist instruction, and "New Rhetoric." Although Gere condemns current-traditional instruction's narrow, dogmatic formalist approach to writing, she argues that none of the four approaches has a sound philosophical foundation and calls for a composition theory and pedagogy built on a philosophical exploration of the relationship between language, reality, and thought.*

When the editors of this Yearbook asked me to write a chapter on current models of composition pedagogy, an image came immediately to mind. I would portray the dominant model as King Kong standing on the Empire State Building. Like the beast who swats biplanes away as if they were flies, this model remains impervious to the challenges of other approaches, dispatching them with the brutish power born of preeminence. Or so I thought before I began looking more closely at discussions of what goes on in the majority of composition classes today. First there was the problem of what to call this dominant model. In discussions of research, classes employing experimental procedures are usually contrasted with the "traditional" class, and names for these traditional classes include "formalist," "discipline-centered," and "current-traditional."

Each of these names has a slightly different origin and meaning. The formalist approach was described by Richard Fulkerson, who, moved by Charles Silberman's description of mindlessness in education,[1] considered how to address composition instructors who "either fail to have a consistent value theory or fail to let that philosophy shape pedagogy [and who are] in Silberman's terms ... guilty of mindlessness."[2] As might be expected of one trained in English studies, Fulkerson

---

Ann Ruggles Gere. "Teaching Writing: The Major Theories" from *The Teaching of Writing: Eighty-fifth Yearbook of the National Society for the Study of Education, Part II*, edited by Anthony R. Petrosky and David Bartholomae.

turned to literary theory for a model and settled upon M. H. Abrams's four theories of literature,[3] claiming that "since the elements in an artistic transaction are the same as those in any communication. It seemed that Abrams's four theories might also be relevant to a composition."[4] Fulkerson shifts Abrams's "objective" criticism to a "formalist" approach. According to Fulkerson's definition, this approach emphasizes certain internal forms, the most commonly valued form being grammar. For the formalist, good writing is "correct" writing at the sentence level. In the classroom, one studies errors of form in order to avoid them. But forms other than grammatical can also be the teacher's key values. I have heard of metaphorical formalists, sentence-length formalists, and topic-sentence formalists, to name a few.[5]

Fulkerson names two major figures in composition (Francis Christensen and E. D. Hirsch) who exemplify the formalist position. Fulkerson offers no evaluation of formalists' effectiveness, but I argue that they take an extremely narrow view of writing. While correctness or at least adherence to conventions makes writing accessible to readers, a model that looks only at this dimension cannot help students see language as a means of communicating with others or as a source of delight.

William Woods takes a slightly broader view as he places composition pedagogy within the context of educational theory. As Woods sees it, two general pedagogical theories—one student-centered and one discipline-centered—have dominated American education since the nineteenth century. Woods claims that discipline-centered teaching accounts for more of the composition curriculum, and he divides this discipline-centered approach into three subcategories emphasizing rhetoric, logic, and language. This leads to a description of three discipline-centered composition pedagogies, one of which is the "discipline-centered/language-based" approach. As Woods describes it, the "discipline-centered/language-based" model

> gives rise to stylebooks, manuals, handbooks and workbooks concerned with grammar, syntax, diction, usage, and style. Two extensions of this theory are the "educational technology" approach, which tends to produce autoinstructional texts, and the approach to teaching writing through various uses of exemplary prose passages.[6]

Woods arrives at this and his other descriptions of discipline-centered and student-centered teaching as a way of describing composition textbooks. According to Woods, each text represents a certain approach to the teaching of writing, and one of the instructor's tasks is to decide which one appeals and choose a text that fits the approach.

The term "current-traditional paradigm" was coined by Richard Young to describe what he saw as a tacit theory dominating composition pedagogy for most of the twentieth century. Borrowing his term from what Daniel Fogarty calls "current-traditional rhetoric."[7] Young described the features of the current-traditional paradigm as

> emphasis on the composed product rather than the composing process; the analysis of discourse into words, sentences, and paragraphs; the

> classification of discourse into description, narration, exposition, and argument, the strong concern with usage (syntax, spelling, punctuation) and with style (economy, clarity, emphasis), and preoccupation with the informal essay and the research paper.[8]

Although he draws on Thomas Kuhn for the "paradigm" concept, the name for and substance of Young's description derive from the features Daniel Fogarty ascribes to current-traditional rhetoric. Fogarty distinguishes between "a teaching rhetoric and the philosophy of rhetoric" in Aristotle's work.[9] The philosophy includes thought-thing-word relationships, abstraction, definition, logic, and dialectic, while the teaching rhetoric is exemplified in Aristotle's *Rhetoric*. In Fogarty's view, current-traditional rhetoric is essentially Aristotelian, but "time and expediency" have added elements of grammar, syntax, spelling, punctuation, and mechanics; modes of discourse; qualities of style; communication; divisions of words, sentences, and paragraphs; and specialized forms.[10] Fogarty goes on to note that students of Aristotle's day could have easily integrated philosophical concerns with their study of rhetoric, yet "today it is not only quite possible, but quite likely, that the average college student may never make the connection between his philosophy and his composition."[11]

Young does not address the distinction between philosophical and teaching rhetorics, but he identifies as a problem the lack of attention to invention in the teaching rhetoric. For Young, both the delineation of the problem and its solution lie in paradigmatic terms, and he devotes considerable energy to demonstrating the applicability of the paradigm concept to composition or, as Fogarty calls it, the teaching rhetoric.

James Berlin appends the term "positivist" to "current-traditional," arguing that the epistemological basis for the current-traditional model is positivistic because it assumes that writing should assume an uncomplicated correspondence of the faculties and the world in order to "provide the language which corresponds either to the objects in the external world or to the ideas in his or her own mind—both are essentially the same—in such a way that it reproduces the objects and the experience of them in the minds of the heaters."[12] According to Berlin, the current-traditional model "demands that the audience be as 'objective' as the writer; both shed personal and social concerns in the interests of the unobstructed perception of empirical reality."[13] Further, he states that "in current-traditional rhetoric the writer must focus on experience in a way that makes possible the discovery of certain kinds of information—the empirical and rational—and the neglect of others—psychological and social concerns."[14]

These different origins—literary theory versus rhetorical history/ philosophy of science versus educational theory versus intellectual history—for describing "formalist," "discipline-centered/language-based," and "current-traditional" demonstrate the difficulty of seeing the currently dominant model as a monolith. Satisfyingly dramatic as it is, the King Kong image does not work because the current model is more complex than this colossus suggests.

Closer examination of the definitions offered by Fulkerson, Woods, Young, and Berlin illustrates some of the complexities inherent in the current approach. Fulkerson can be commended for insisting that composition avoid the "value-mode confusion"[15] that results for both instruction and evaluation when instructors fail to think carefully about what they value in composition. And we can thank Fulkerson for recognizing the need to articulate values that have remained inchoate, but his method for solving the problem creates further value conflicts. Rather than looking directly at composition instruction to determine its nature and values, Fulkerson imports literary theory to describe four postures. The awkwardness of this borrowing is evident in the extent to which Fulkerson redefines and renames Abrams's terminology. Abrams' "mimetic" does not mean that "a clear connection exists between good writing and good thinking."[16] and the translation of Abrams' "pragmatic" and "objective" to Fulkerson's "rhetorical" and "formalist" obscures more than it reveals.

Part of the problem with Fulkerson's terminology resides in its sources because terms borrowed from literary criticism fail to capture the essence of composition instruction. The limited definition Fulkerson assigns to formalism bespeaks, however, a greater problem. By concentrating exclusively on issues of form, Fulkerson omits concern with what produces the forms, thereby removing any possibility of connecting this model of instruction with a philosophy of rhetoric.

William Woods has a much less ambitious goal than Young or Fulkerson in that he considers only text selection rather than larger instructional questions. His attempt to connect composition instruction with educational trends such as "life adjustment theory," "academic reform," and the counterrevolution of the Dartmouth Conference suggests the importance of looking at composition instruction in larger terms, but Wood's analysis does not extend far enough into history. He claims, for example, that "college teaching of writing in America had its official baptism in 1949, when the NCTE founded the Conference on College Composition and Communication."[17] Nor does he explore the educational movements fully enough to demonstrate their philosophical roots.

To the extent that he draws on Fogarty's discussion of rhetorical history, Young offers a useful perspective on current-traditional composition pedagogy, but his attempt to place composition instruction within the scientific tradition is problematical. As Robert Connors has explained so well,[18] there is serious question about the applicability of the paradigm concept to composition, and Young, like others in composition, may have been unduly attracted to the glitter of science. The more serious problem with Young 's approach is that it ignores the division between philosophy and composition. Even though he borrows Fogarty's "current-traditional" term, Young fails to develop the philosophy-composition division that Fogarty delineates. In turning to the philosophy of science. Young compounds this neglect.

James Berlin comes closest to making a connection between philosophy and composition pedagogy because he searches for the rhetorical theory underlying the model. In beginning this research Berlin notes that conceptions of writers, reality, audience, and language all contribute to the definition of a model: "To teach writing is to argue for a version of reality, and the best way of knowing and communicating it."[19] As he continues, however, Berlin moves to an advocacy position, claiming superiority for what he calls new rhetoricians, and his argument veers in the direction of intellectual history.

What Fulkerson, Woods, Young, and Berlin share, then, is a failure to connect what Fogarty terms the teaching rhetoric with a philosophy. This is not a problem unique to these four theorists; it has been the continuing problem of composition pedagogy. Because the teaching rhetoric has remained separate from a philosophy of rhetoric, it has been vulnerable to the ravages of "time and expediency."[20] The dominance of mechanical features (syntax, spelling, modes, style, and punctuation) in today's instruction derives from the lack of a coherent philosophy guiding composition pedagogy. When a discipline lacks a coherent philosophy, it can be shaped by the most anti-intellectual forces, and this is precisely what has happened to composition pedagogy over the years.

At the college level, composition instruction began with the introduction of a prescribed full-year freshman course and a half-year sophomore course at Harvard in 1874. These courses, like their predecessors, were stimulated by President Charles Eliot, who at his inaugural in 1869 lamented "the prevailing neglect of the systematic study of the English language"[21] and sought every opportunity to redress this neglect. Francis James Child, Harvard's Boylston Professor of Rhetoric and Oratory when composition courses were first introduced, could have played a major role in articulating the philosophy of these courses, but he did not. Rather, Child resented the composition courses he was asked to teach and devoted his energies to finding a way to escape them. Child's real interest was English literature, and he became this nation's first professor of English in 1874. Child's successor, Adams Sherman Hill, likewise did little to unite the teaching of writing with a philosophy of rhetoric, but he did succeed in building a composition program in the face of significant faculty resistance.

In the 1870s Latin and Greek were the dominant languages on college campuses, and Harvard's faculty, like faculties everywhere, was resistant to English studies. Hill was successful in overcoming this resistance and in instituting a required freshman composition course, English A, in 1885. Hill's influence extended beyond Harvard through his textbooks. The most popular of these, *The Principles of Rhetoric and Their Application,* was published in 1878 and was still in use in the 1930s. This text demonstrates the schism between the teaching rhetoric and a philosophy of rhetoric. Hill's text substituted manner for originality of matter. He borrowed directly from the Scottish rhetoricians Blair, Campbell, and Whately, simply putting their ideas in more accessible form. While his material was not original and therefore did not profit from new philosophical insights, Hill adopted a dogmatic tone that contributed to the popularity of his text. Pronouncements such as "From the point of view of clearness, it is always better to repeat a noun than to substitute for it a pronoun which fails to suggest that noun"[22] admit no ambiguity and reassure uncertain students and instructors.

Hill's dogmatic tone may have increased the popularity of his text, but it did little to unite philosophy with composition pedagogy. In fact, it worked in the opposite direction. Until very recently teachers of composition at all levels have received no formal training. College composition instructors may have themselves taken a freshman English course, but they had no direct instruction in composition pedagogy, and the same has been true for secondary and elementary school teachers. For example, in 1952, Harold Allen could find only five graduate-level courses on composition in this country, and not all of the five were offered regularly.[23] What composition teachers learned, therefore, came through what I have called the informal curriculum.[24] This informal curriculum, a combination of self-sponsored reading, orientation meetings, and conversations with other instructors, depended heavily upon textbooks. Hill therefore influenced composition pedagogy much more substantially than would have been the case if composition pedagogy had developed its own philosophical and intellectual foundations. Instead, composition instructors, pressured by "time and expediency," clung gratefully to pronouncements about usage and emphasized these in their classes because they discouraged student questions, making teaching easier.

Hill's text was not alone in allowing "time and expediency" to create the current-traditional model of composition pedagogy. There was, in addition, the ongoing resistance of Harvard faculty. When English A became a required course in 1885, the rest of the Harvard curriculum was adopting the German university model of electives, so the one required course stood out. Further, college enrollments expanded over 60 percent during the 1890s, so this requirement directed a high proportion of Harvard's resources toward composition instruction. Predictably, this allocation of resources disgruntled faculty and administrators, leading Harvard's Board of Overseers, in 1891, to appoint a committee to investigate English A.

This committee, composed of three people from outside the academic community, issued the first of three "Harvard Reports." This report proposed a simple solution to college composition: It should be taught by high schools. The report stated:

> It is obviously absurd that the College—the institution of higher education—should be called upon to turn aside from its proper functions and devote its means and the time of its instructors to the task of imparting elementary instruction which would be given even in ordinary grammar schools, much more in those higher academic institutions intended to prepare select youth for a university course.[25]

The committee went on to recommend that admission requirements be raised to eliminate students underprepared in composition and to suggest that if schools did not devote more time to teaching writing, they could not expect their students to be accepted at Harvard. While this report may have helped solve Harvard's immediate problems, it had a negative long-term effect on composition instruction in this country,

Harvard's prestige led many other colleges to follow the recommendations of this and the other Harvard Reports. Not only did colleges emulate the position that they should have little responsibility for composition instruction, they also accepted the Committee's narrow definition of writing. This definition was characterized by statements such as it is "little less than absurd to suggest that any human being who can be taught to talk cannot likewise be taught to compose. Writing is merely the habit of talking with the pen instead of with the tongue."[26] This narrow view also emphasizes mechanical correctness in writing above all else. The 1892 report contains many negative comments about students' poor usage and gives special attention to neatness and handwriting. Because composition instructors had no coherent philosophy against which to evaluate such statements, these limited views gained currency and shaped ensuing instruction.

Since a narrow view of writing dominated college composition pedagogy and fostered the development and maintenance of the current-traditional model, it is not surprising that composition pedagogy in secondary and elementary schools followed the same direction. Secondary schools took seriously Harvard's warning that they must prepare students to write mechanically correct papers. Texts used in secondary schools mirrored Hill's *Principles of Rhetoric* in their emphasis on dogmatic statements about correctness, and common school teachers, like their college counterparts, relied on the informal curriculum of texts for their training in the teaching of writing. The nagging Miss Fidditch commonly described as hounding composition classes with details of mechanical correctness can trace her ancestry to the Harvard Reports.

The colossus of current-traditional instruction developed, then, not out of a clearly articulated philosophical tradition but in the absence of same. A convergence of administrative, demographic, and prestige concerns created the climate in which composition instructors turned their attention to issues of form, style, and correctness. The aphilosophical emergence of the current-traditional model has been matched by an equally aphilosophical maintenance of it. The extent to which other models have and have not been allowed to coexist or have been partially included by the current-traditional model has resulted from aphilosophical concerns.

One of the earliest challenges to current-traditional instruction emerged in the 1890s. Fred Newton Scott, professor of rhetoric at the University of Michigan from 1889 to 1927, attempted to develop a philosophy of composition pedagogy by drawing on linguistics, psychology, and sociology as well as rhetoric.[27] In trying to foster a fuller conception of rhetoric, one that gave it intellectual breadth as well as social importance, Scott portrayed writing in terms of function rather than mere correctness. According to one of his students, Scott saw correctness as necessary but not the chief purpose of writing. Rather, he "looked on words as a cabinet maker looks on his tools—things that just must be right and unabused throughout or the work will be bad."[28] Although Scott had some brief successes during the reform period of the 1890s, Kitzhaber explains that "most of his ideas were too new, his recommendations for change too fundamental to be generally accepted. Rhetorical instruction fell in behind the Harvard group instead."[29] According to Kitzhaber, composition pedagogy in this country "until well into the 1930s became, for all practical purposes, little more than instruction in grammar and the mechanics of writing, motivated almost solely by the ideal of superficial correctness."[30] The reform movement of the 1890s was followed by a conservative, science-oriented shift in the early decades of this century, and Scott's model could not flourish in this hostile climate.

Had Scott's challenge been successful, the current-traditional colossus might never have reached its current status. Lacking an intellectual base, the current-traditional model fed on Harvard's prestige and grew out of proportion to other models. Scott's work did, however, provide the basis from which models of future generations developed. The contemporary model that owes most to Scott's work has been variously termed "rhetorical" (by Fulkerson), "discipline-centered-rhetoric-based" (by Woods), and neo- Aristotelian or classicist (by Berlin). Richard Young's whole paradigmatic critique of the current-traditional approach derives from his concept of rhetoric, both classical and modern, as including invention as one of its central parts.

Fulkerson describes the rhetorical approach as claiming that "good writing is writing adapted to achieve the desired effect on the desired audience. If the same verbal construct is directed to a different audience, then it may have to be evaluated differently."[31] For Woods the discipline-centered-rhetoric-based approach manifests itself in texts that "reproduce the features of classical rhetoric ... [that offer] a fully developed alternative to classical theory."[32] Berlin explains neo-Aristotelian as "primarily concerned with the provision of inventional devices"[33] and notes that few textbooks adhere closely to this model. Young describes the desired rhetoric as one that "begins with the perception of a social problem and ends with changes in an audience's beliefs and behaviors."[34] Throughout Scott's work, three dimensions—communicator, audience, and language—receive continuing attention, and this emphasis laid the foundation for the contemporary rhetorical model of composition pedagogy. Scott even placed mechanical correctness in a rhetorical context in his textbook: "Presented as a means of meeting definite social needs more or less effectively, of winning attention and consideration, the various devices of grammar and rhetoric make an appeal to self-interest which pupils can understand."[35] Scott's attempt to reconnect the teaching rhetoric with a philosophy of rhetoric failed to succeed because it competed with an aphilosophical and mechanical model in a period when the growing dominance of science reinforced mechanics over philosophy.

Another factor contributing to the eclipse of Scott's model was the separation of rhetoric from English departments, a separation to which Scott himself contributed. Scott sought to create a separate department of rhetoric at the University of Michigan, and in 1903 he succeeded. This move was emulated on many campuses during the next few decades, and in 1914 these shifts were institutionalized by the formation of the Speech Association of America. The majority of these new departments of rhetoric were motivated by the resentments of rhetoricians who felt snubbed and/or overpowered by their colleagues in literature.

Composition pedagogy remained in English departments, isolated from the classical rhetoric that could give it intellectual depth. This separation not only impoverished the philosophical basis of composition pedagogy, but it also contributed to major distinctions between speaking and writing. Composition pedagogy and rhetoric remained distant from one another until the early 1960s.

Writing instruction in the common schools followed a similar pattern. Texts emphasized mechanical correctness, and all but a few exceptional teachers proffered formulaic advice about topic sentences and five-paragraph themes to their students. Compounding philosophical limitations were time constraints which sandwiched writing instruction into a curriculum crowded with language and literature studies. As recently as 1968, a study of exemplary English programs revealed that only 15.7 percent of class time was spent on writing instruction, and most of that was devoted to correcting completed papers.[36] The teaching of writing in secondary schools shared with college classes the liabilities of separating philosophical and teaching rhetorics.

Rhetoric reentered college English departments during the 1940s via the literary criticism developed at the University of Chicago by Richard S. Crane and Richard McKeon. Subsequent to this reentry, a philosophical rhetoric began to exert influence on composition pedagogy. One of the first manifestations of this influence appeared in 1957 in Richard Weaver's textbook, *Composition,* which brought classical rhetoric's enthymeme and topics to the teaching of writing.[37]

This text was followed in 1962 by *Rhetoric: Principles and Usage.* Authors Albert P. Duhamel and Richard E. Hughes made their intentions explicit by stating: "Perhaps the most significant difference between our book and those currently used in composition and rhetoric courses is our attempt to introduce the art of rhetoric as a systematic body of knowledge."[38] Accompanying this text and Edward P. J. Corbett's *Classical Rhetoric for the Modern Student,* which followed in 1965,[39] was a growing intellectual ferment among a small number of composition instructors. The Rhetoric Society of America was founded in 1968 by directors including Edward P. J. Corbett, Wayne Booth, William Irmscher, Ross Winterowd, Richard Larson, Robert Gorrell, Richard Hughes, Harry Crosby, and Owen Thomas. For these individuals and their peers, the reintegration of classical rhetoric and composition pedagogy offered a successful challenge to the current-traditional model.

One offshoot of the revival of classical rhetoric was the development of a modern rhetoric of composition pedagogy. The most notable example appears in the tagmemic theory of Kenneth Pike and his associates, *Rhetoric: Discovery and Change,* the text Pike wrote with Alton Becker and Richard Young,[40] demonstrates how tagmemic linguistics can be used with effect in composition classes. Although the nine-cell matrix of particle, wave, and field combined with contrast, distribution, and variation of tagmemics draws on modern physics, it owes a great deal to Aristotle's topics.

For the majority of composition instructors, however, this reintegration and the resulting scholarship made little difference, and the current-traditional colossus continued its dominance. This lack of effect derived, in large measure, from the training of these composition instructors. The educational expansion of the 1960s gave way to constriction in the 1970s, and secondary and elementary teachers trained in the 1960s were the last group hired in significant numbers. The innovative programs and courses in rhetoric introduced by people such as members of the Rhetoric Society of America had little influence on a stable and aging population of teachers. Courses in the teaching of writing instituted in the past decade have produced college composition instructors who make the intellectual traditions of rhetoric and composition available to future generations of instructors, but the paucity of teaching positions at all levels prevents rapid adoption of this model.

Because training in the rhetorical model has been unavailable to the majority of composition instructors in this country, the informal curriculum has continued to serve as the dominant means of transmitting composition pedagogy. This means that textbooks continue to educate most writing instructors. The small number of textbooks representing the rhetorical tradition and their marginal commercial success demonstrate the relatively small impact of this approach. A second edition of *Rhetoric: Principles and Usage* was issued in 1967, and the book was out of print ten years later. A text such as *Classical Rhetoric for the Modern Student* remains in print, not because it is widely used by composition instructors, but because it is used in courses for graduate students in composition and rhetoric. The rhetorical model of composition pedagogy is not one easily adopted by instructors relying entirely on their own resources. To be effectively assimilated, it requires grounding in an intellectual tradition, something not available in the informal curriculum.

In his discussion of forms of invention, Richard Young separates the tagmemic approach from the rhetorical, explaining:

> classical invention is concerned with finding arguments likely to induce psychological changes in the audience; prewriting, on the other hand, is concerned with the discovery of ordering principles and with changes in the writer. Tagmemic invention is concerned with both. It conceives of invention as essentially a problem-solving activity, the problems being of two sorts: those arising in one's own experience of the world and those arising out of a need to change others.[41]

To make this claim, Young minimizes the ethos of classical rhetoric and emphasizes the individual's experience in tagmemic invention. He also creates two other categories of invention: dramatistic (based on Kenneth Burke's work) and prewriting (to be discussed below). As long as these four—rhetorical, tagmemic, prewriting, and dramatistic—are described as systems of invention, there is no problem, but they are frequently extended to delineate models of composition pedagogy. David Harrington et al., for example, discusses composition texts in terms of Young's four categories, and this discussion waivers between emphasis on invention and immersion in a whole model.[42] For example, in the discussion of texts that adapt principles of classical rhetoric to the teaching of writing, Harrington et al. include not only works such as those by Duhamel and Corbett, but also books "that adapt principles of classical rhetoric for the teaching of writing."[43] This adaptation includes everything from overviews of principles of invention to a book in which "invention survives, lurking in a chapter on 'Development'."[44]

The range of Harrington's inclusions suggests the confusion that results when approaches to invention are substituted for pedagogical models, and this confusion has contributed to the maintenance of the current-traditional model. As

Harrington et al. describe it, for example, some texts have adapted principles of classical rhetoric to devices for paragraph and essay development.[45] The focus on paragraph and essay signals a concern with form, an issue much more important to the current-traditional model than to classical rhetoric.

Prewriting, another of Young's categories of invention, has likewise been appropriated by the current-traditional model. As originally described by D. Gordon Rohman,[46] prewriting uses journal writing, meditation, and metaphorical thinking to stimulate writing. The logical pedagogical model for prewriting is the expressivist approach. As Fulkerson describes it, expressivists emphasize the writer and cover a wide range, "from totally accepting and nondirective teachers, some of whom insist that one neither can nor should evaluate writing, to much more directive, experiential teachers who design classroom activities to maximize student self-discovery."[47] Further, expressivists "value writing that is about personal subjects ... [and] desire to have writing contain an interesting, credible, honest, and personal voice."[48]

The most obvious source of the expressivist model is the Dartmouth Conference of 1966. This meeting of American and British educators on the teaching of English brought new theories to this country. As Arthur Applebee puts it, "What the British offered the Americans was a model for English instruction which focussed not on the 'demands' of the discipline but on the personal and linguistic growth of the child."[49] The American educators present at this conference were profoundly affected, and their consequent activity helped shape the expressive model of composition pedagogy.

William Woods places the expressivist approach in his "student-directed" category and explains it in terms of a "maturationist" theory of development:

> [H]umankind has in it the seeds of its perfection, which will flower if allowed to grow naturally, uninhibited and unharmed by social or environmental constraints. . . . [A]ll aspects of the communication triangle are treated as extensions of the writer's experience. . . . Teaching methods guided by this theory encourage such activities as observing, recording, expressing, listening, and reacting.[50]

As this description makes clear, the roots of the expressivist model of composition pedagogy extend past the Dartmouth Conference to the progressive education movement during the first decades of this century. John Dewey, generally credited with giving voice to what became known as the progressive movement, emphasized the learner's experience, interest, and motivation and encouraged teaching that centered on the student rather than on the discipline. Dewey's views influenced many teachers, but the groups shaping the English curriculum, groups such as the Committee of Ten (established in 1892) and the National Conference on Uniform Entrance Requirements in English (active at the turn of the century), operated from the current-traditional model.

The Dartmouth Conference, then, gave new vigor to a progressive movement that had lain dormant for several decades, and it targeted the insights of the progressives toward English instruction specifically. When seen from this perspective, the expressive approach is less tied to the 1960s and is more directly related to larger currents in education. Because the expressive approach has not always been identified with a major educational and intellectual tradition (and sometimes even when it has), it has been subject to appropriation by the current-traditional approach.

One of the terms most commonly appropriated from the expressivist approach is "prewriting." As originally conceived, prewriting denoted methods of enabling writers to explore their own minds. When appropriated by current-traditionalists, however, prewriting has come to mean any activity that occurs at the beginning stages of writing. Accordingly, many current-traditional textbooks include sections on prewriting, but what these sections contain has nothing in common with prewriting as described by expressivists. For example, one text describes prewriting as asking students to make a list of topics they intend to include in their writing. This activity, much closer to outlining than to the kind of exploration described by Rohman, demonstrates the confusions that can result when a practice of one approach is appropriated by practitioners of another approach.

These three approaches—current-traditional, rhetorical, and expressivist—are categories on which theorists such as Young, Woods, Fulkerson, and Berlin agree. There is, however, a fourth category which nearly every theorist expresses differently. Fulkerson borrows Abrams's term "mimetic" to describe instruction that emphasizes correspondence with reality. According to Fulkerson, one manifestation of this approach "says that a clear connection exists between good writing and good thinking. The major problem with student writing is that it is not solidly thought out."[51] The pedagogical solution to this problem is to emphasize the teaching of reasoning and logic as a basis for good writing. Another manifestation of the mimetic approach as Fulkerson describes it is to assume that students do not write well because they do not know enough. Mimetic solutions to this problem include (a) encouragement of more research during the early stages of writing, (b) emphasis on discovery procedures, and (c) having students read authors who take different perspectives on the same topic. The result will be writing that is closer to the "real situation."

William Woods' discipline-centered-logic-based approach has much in common with Fulkerson's mimetic category. The emphasis as Woods describes it is on "the art of straight thinking."[52] Texts in this category emphasize the "reciprocal or 'dialectical' relationship between thought and language, the ways in which thought travels back and forth moving from observation to classification, and from generalization back again to specification, in the process of developing and sequencing ideas."[53] Woods explains that texts following the logic-based approach rarely give much space to audiences for writing or to processes of writing, but they focus considerable attention on the dialogue between language and thought in writing.

James Berlin assigns the term "New Rhetoricians" to his version of this fourth category, explaining that it presumes that "knowledge is not simply a static entity available for retrieval. Truth is dynamic and dialectical, the result of a process involving the interaction of opposing elements. It is a relation that is created, not pre-existent and waiting to be discovered."[54] In this view, then, writing aids discovery because writers use language to converse with themselves and, thereby, discover new ideas. Berlin shares Woods's view that Ann Berthoff's *Forming/Thinking/Writing*[55] exemplifies the New Rhetoricians' approach, but he puts the Young, Becker, and Pike text in the same category. And he argues that audience plays a significant role in the New Rhetoricians' approach. The roots of this fourth approach—New Rhetoricians', mimetic, or logic-based—lie in logic, and the paucity of texts in this category suggests the limited number of instructors who use it. Of the major theories of composition instruction, the New Rhetoricians' logic-based approach is the least widely employed. Perhaps this is because the long-standing split between philosophical and teaching rhetorics has reduced logic's accessibility to composition instructors.

Throughout this discussion I have avoided describing "the writing process" as a model of composition pedagogy. The term "writing process," derived from descriptions of what writers do as opposed to the written products they produce, does not describe a model so much as a way of proceeding within that model. Elements of the writing process, whether they are called prewriting, drafting, and revising or incubating, writing, and reworking, can be adapted to any model discussed here. Indeed, many currently available textbooks graft writing process terminology onto current-traditional, rhetorical, and expressive models.

This grafting has the benefit of reducing emphasis on products in writing, but it also exemplifies one of the problems with current models of composition pedagogy. As the preceding discussion has shown, there is little agreement about the terminology for or exact shape of any of these models. These models can and have been stretched almost beyond recognition because of the continuing separation of the teaching rhetoric from a philosophy of rhetoric. While articulating the shape of models helps reduce vulnerability to the charge of mindlessness, the fact of articulating does not develop a philosophy.

Likewise, attempts to circumvent the issue by drawing on the theoretical foundations of another discipline will only confuse the issue. Richard Young's use of science's "paradigm," for example, finally confounds more than it helps because this term cannot be used accurately with reference to composition studies. Moreover, using such borrowed terminology weakens the models to which it is being applied. Fitting a borrowed term onto an aphilosophical model involves two translations, one from the borrowed field to composition, and a second within the model itself. Just as translations of translations (the King James Bible from the Latin Vulgate, for example) lose accuracy, so models of composition pedagogy lose their integrity when philosophies of another discipline are applied.

When models lose their integrity, they develop fissures into which foreign organisms intrude, and this explaining why it has been so easy for each of the models discussed to borrow from one another and why it is so difficult to find a textbook that adheres to one model exclusively. Another result of operating with aphilosophical models is that arguments about central questions become clouded by extraneous issues. Among the questions facing composition pedagogy recently have been those of grammar instruction, Black English, and remedial studies. Each of these has been dominated by issues of time and expediency because the philosophical basis of existing models remains uncertain.

Grammar instruction, for example, has been dismissed by many theorists and researchers as useless for improving the quality of writing,[56] but it has remained prominent in composition pedagogy, particularly in the current-traditional model. And there are those who take the position that grammar instruction actually does lead to improved writing. What has been lost in this debate is attention to the relationship between language and reality, to ways of knowing the world. Instead, issues of time (teaching grammar is or is not a waste of time) and expediency (grammar instruction does or does not produce better writing) have been argued.

Discussions of Black English have occupied considerable energy in composition pedagogy, and these discussions have likewise strayed from central questions of what constitutes knowledge and the relationship of thought to language. The Black English debate stems from the pragmatic issue of how composition instructors should treat nonstandard dialects. Linguists such as William Labov have demonstrated that nonstandard dialects such as Black English follow a definite grammar of their own. Those who use Black English, therefore, are not erratic or illogical; they simply follow a different system than do users of the standard dialect. An ensuing debate among composition instructors has wrestled with how to respond to nonstandard dialects.

Some people argue that children's concepts of reality are tied to their home dialects and that teachers, especially teachers of composition, need to acknowledge the importance of such dialects. This view is elaborated in a publication of the Conference on College Composition, *Students' Right to Their Own Language.*[57] Opponents, however, argue that students who use Black English will not be able to succeed in a world that assigns negative connotations to dialects other than standard English.

Likewise, following the model of the Harvard Reports, definition of and response to remedial studies have been shaped almost entirely by questions of time and expediency rather than by philosophical considerations of how students might best arrive at knowledge. Economic incentives, more than philosophical considerations, govern schools' policies. Open admissions programs of colleges in the 1960s resulted from an expanding economy and led to expanded remedial programs, particularly in writing. Secondary schools emulated this expansion by introducing elective programs in writing, among other things. The economic constriction of the late 1970s and early 1980s led to a general shrinking in education and in writing courses particularly. Colleges began to define their missions more narrowly, excluding remedial instruction. Secondary schools likewise retreated from electives to the former pattern of combining composition with language and literature study.

This dominance of time and expediency in composition pedagogy will continue as long as models of instruction fail to have a philosophical basis. Developing such a basis does not require scrapping all current models; it simply means asking different questions about them. These questions should include issues such as thought-word-thing relationships, abstraction, definition, and logic. Put another way, when the teaching rhetoric and philosophy are united, the following questions will become central to each model:

1. What relationship exists between language and reality?
2. What relationship exists between thought and language?
3. How does this model define "truth" or "knowledge"? What system of logic does this model employ to arrive at "truth"?

When such questions are asked and answered, models of composition pedagogy will become more unified and thereby more effective.

NOTES

1. Charles Silberman, *Crisis in the Classroom* (New York: Random House, 1970).
2. Richard Fulkerson, "Four Philosophies of Composition," *College Composition and Communication* 30 (December 1979): 347.
3. Meyer Howard Abrams, *The Mirror and the Lamp: Romantic Theory and the Critical Tradition* (New York: Oxford University Press, 1953).
4. Fulkerson, "Four Philosophies of Composition," p. 343.
5. Ibid., p. 344.
6. William F. Woods, "Composition Textbooks and Pedagogical Theory 1960–1980," *College English* 43 (April 1981): 396.
7. Daniel Fogary, *Roots for a New Rhetoric* (New York: Russell and Russell, 1959), p. 118.
8. Richard Young, "Paradigms and Problems: Needed Research in Rhetorical Invention," in *Research on Composing: Points of Departure,* ed. Charles R. Cooper and Lee Odell (Urbana, Ill.: National Council of Teachers of English, 1978): p. 31.
9. Fogarty, *Roots for a New Rhetoric,* p. 117.
10. Ibid., p. 120.
11. Ibid., p. 122.
12. James Berlin, "Contemporary Composition: The Major Pedagogical Theories," *College English* 44 (December 1982): 770.
13. Ibid., p. 775.
14. Ibid., p. 775–76.
15. Fulkerson, "Four Philosophies of Composition," p. 347.
16. Ibid., p. 345.
17. Woods, "Composition Textbooks and Pedagogical Theory 1960–1980," p. 393.
18. Robert Connors, "Composition Studies and Science," *College English* 45 (January 1983): 1–20.
19. Berlin, "Contemporary Composition: The Major Pedagogical Theories," p. 766.
20. Fogarty, *Roots for a New Rhetoric,* p. 120.
21. Charles W. Eliot, *Educational Reform: Essays and Addresses* (New York: Century, 1898): p. 2.
22. Adam Sherman Hill, *The Principles of Rhetoric and Their Application* (New York: Harper, 1878): p. 84.
23. Harold Allen, "Preparing the Teachers of Composition and Communication-A Report," *College Composition and Communication* 3 (May 1952): 3–13.
24. Anne Ruggles Gere, "Teaching Writing Teachers." *College English* 47 (January 1985): 58–65.

25. *Reports of the Visiting Committees of the Board of Overseers of Harvard College* (Cambridge, Mass.: Harvard University Press, 1902): p. 119.
26. Ibid., p. 155.
27. Fred Newton Scott and Joseph Villiers Denney, *Elementary English Composition* (Boston: Allyn and Bacon, 1900).
28. Shirley Smith, "Fred Newton Scott as a Teacher," *Michigan Alumnus,* 1933: p. 279.
29. Albert Kitzhaber, "Rhetoric in American Colleges 1850–1900" (Doct. diss., University of Washington, 1953): p. 114.
30. Ibid., p. 120.
31. Fulkerson, "Four Philosophies of Composition," p. 346.
32. Woods, "Composition Textbooks and Pedagogical Theory 1960–1980," p. 396.
33. Berlin, "Contemporary Composition: The Major Pedagogical Theories," p. 769.
34. Young, "Paradigms and Problems," p. 42.
35. Scott and Denney, *Elementary English Composition,* p. iv.
36, James R. Squire and Roger Applebee, *High School English Instruction Today* (New York: Appleton, 1968): p. 42.
37. Richard M. Weaver, *Composition: A Course in Writing and Rhetoric* (New York: Holt, 1957).
38. Richard E. Hughes and Albert P. Duhamel, *Rhetoric: Principles and Usage* (Englewood Cliffs, N.J.: Prentice Hall, 1962), p. v.
39. Edward P. Corbett, *Classical Rhetoric for the Modern Student* (New York, Oxford University Press, 1965)
40. Richard Young, Alton Becker, and Kenneth Pike, *Rhetoric: Discovery and Change* (New York: Harcourt, 1970)
41. Young, "Paradigms and Problems," p. 39.
42. David V. Harrington, Philip M. Keith, Charles W. Kneupper, Janice A. Tripp, and William F. Woods, "A Critical Survey of Resources for Teaching Rhetorical Invention," *College English* 40 (February 1979): 641—61.
41 Ibid., p. 643.
44. Ibid., p. 644.
45. Ibid.
46. D. Gordon Rohman, "Pre-Writing: The Stage of Discovery in the Writing Process," *College Composition and Communication* 16 (May 1965): 106–112a.
47. Ibid., p. 345.
48. Ibid., p. 345.
49. Arthur Applebee, *Tradition and Reform in the Teaching of English: A History* (Urbana, Ill.: National Council of Teachers of English, 1974): p. 229.
50. Woods, "Composition Textbooks and Pedagogical Theory 1960–1980," p. 397.
51. Fulkerson, "Four Philosophies of Composition," p. 345.
52. Woods, "Composition Textbooks and Pedagogical Theory 1960–1980," p. 396.
53. Ibid., p. 408.
54. Berlin, "Contemporary Composition," p. 774.
55. Ann Berthoff, *Forming/Thinking/Writing* (Montclair, N.J.: Boynton/Cook, 1978).
56. See, for example, Richard Braddock, Richard Lloyd-Jones, and Lowell Schoer, *Research in Written Composition* (Urbana, Ill.: National Council of Teachers of English, 1963).
57. "Students' Right to their Own Language," special issue of *College Composition and Communication,* Fall 1974.

Instructional Practices: Toward an Integration

Janice M. Lauer

As director of the rhetoric program at Purdue University and of Purdue's Summer Seminar in Rhetoric and Composition, Janice M. Lauer, now retired, has been a major figure in establishing the discipline of composition studies. With J. William Asher, she co-authored Composition Research: Empirical Designs, *and she has published many articles on rhetorical theory and history and on composition research and pedagogy. This selection, which appeared in the first issue of* Focuses *in 1988, draws on rhetorical history and recent composition research to argue for the integration of four different, often conflicting approaches to teaching writing: teaching writing as an art that provides writers with practical knowledge and strategies to guide their writing, nurturing students' natural composing processes, engaging students in intelligent practice, and exposing students to good models for them to analyze and imitate. All four approaches are effective, Lauer writes, but the most successful pedagogies have integrated all four approaches.*

Composition teaching has taken at least two directions in its effort to avoid a pedagogy restricted to grammatical rules and skills, modes of discourse as ends, and stylistic prescriptions. Two alternative pedagogies have been advocated—teaching writing as an art and nurturing natural processes (Young). As extreme and exclusive positions, however, they do not provide the most effective means of helping students to develop as writers who strive dialogically to forge new understanding in a range of discourse communities. I want to argue here that integrating these two pedagogies together with two others, imitation and practice, offers a more stimulating and supportive context in which students can learn to write and write to learn.

Each of these four teaching approaches offers important advantages to students and requires certain teaching skills. Teaching writing as an art gives students practical strategies and rhetorical knowledge to guide them during their writing and to accompany them beyond the classroom, when the instructor and peers will no longer be present to motivate and respond to their natural processes at work. Art stresses the value of using "plans up front," which help engender confidence and independence (Perkins 190–219). Teaching writing as an art requires that the teacher study the processes and acts of effective writers in order to develop or make use of

Janice M. Lauer. "Instructional Practices: Toward an Integration," *Focuses* 1.1, 1988. Reprinted by permission of the author.

helpful heuristics which will facilitate these acts. Such teaching is most effectively done using the environmental mode of instruction in which students are situated to use strategies collaboratively in solving genuine writing problems.

Natural process pedagogy emphasizes the role of what David Perkins calls "plans down deep" (162–89) and highlights the importance of attitude and cognitive style in individual writers. This pedagogy involves motivating students and giving them responses to their developing texts. Consequently, instructors engaged in natural process pedagogy need the ability to set compelling contexts and to be sensitive to individual difference, in order to find "zones of proximal development" for inexperienced writers.

Practice, especially in classroom writing workshops and writing centers, insures that writers learn to apply their art appropriately in a variety of situations and that they develop habits as writers. Engaging students in intelligent practice requires the patience to cope with approximate texts, a tolerance of mistakes, and a willingness to withhold evaluation as portfolios expand.

The use of *imitation* expands students' awareness of effective processes and good prose. For the teacher or writing center director, it entails searching for models that exemplify processes as well as products, providing exemplars that students can emulate, and modeling the struggles and satisfactions in the instructor's own writing.

Integrating these instructional practices requires a strong commitment to work toward a creative pedagogy that fits one's students and one's own teaching style. No one way of integration exists; it requires time, dedication, and study on the part of the instructor and/or tutors. At least two kinds of evidence support this goal of integration: empirical and historical.

George Hillocks' recent meta-analysis of experimental research on five focuses and three modes of instruction demonstrates that some improvement in writing was achieved by students in classes using each of these four pedagogies: inquiry skills (art and practice), sentence combining (art and practice), criteria (art and imitation), models (imitation), and free writing (natural process and art). The only focus that produced negative results was grammatical instruction. His study also concludes that both the environmental mode of instruction (which includes art) and natural process pedagogy had more positive influences on student writing than did presentational instruction. Since each of these pedagogies accounted for a portion of improvement, how much more development could be fostered by combining the best features of each so that their strengths could complement each other. Integrated, they offer a way of situating students in richer contexts for reaching and sharing new understanding.

Each of the four pedagogies also has an impressive historical pedigree in rhetoric. Most classical rhetoricians speak of their importance in educating a maker and sharer of meaning, but rank their relative merits differently.

Aristotle highlights *art*, defining it in the *Metaphysics* as principles or theories gleaned from expert performance that explain the nature of this performance and serve as a source of strategies to guide communicators. Aristotle considers art to be a type of practical knowledge in the communicator and a set of principles in a discipline (499–500). This kind of "practical" knowledge, which is designed for performance, contrasts with scientific knowledge, which exists for its own sake. He begins his treatise on rhetoric by classifying it as an art:

All men attempt to discuss statements and to maintain them, to defend themselves and to attack others. Ordinary people do this either at random or through practice and from acquired habit. Both ways being possible, the subject can be plainly handled systematically, for it is possible to inquire the reason *why* some speakers succeed through practice and others spontaneously; and everyone would agree that such an inquiry is the function of art. (19)

Here Aristotle posits a dynamic relationship between good performance and art. Art's principles and strategies are not formulated in a vacuum—they are drawn from observation and analysis of effective communicators. Moreover, Aristotle explains that the possessor of an art is a mastercraftsman who has an advantage over the mere performer, the handicraftsman, because the mastercraftsman understands what he is doing and therefore can teach others. He not only models good performance but also can explain it (*Metaphysics* 499–500).

Aristotle cautions that an art is not a formula which guarantees success. The communicator, the rhetor, can only discover the means of "coming as near such success as the circumstances of each particular case allow" (*Rhetoric* 9–10). In other words, discoursers have to learn to apply appropriately their repertoire of strategies to genuine rhetorical situations. This concept of situatedness is an important concomitant of art. A dynamic interaction exists between art and act, the right time or the appropriate situational context. Art supplies principles that apply across many situations. *Kairos* grounds those principles in individual circumstances (see Kinneavy for a discussion of *Kairos*). Each discourse context holds for the rhetor both the old and the new. A successful communicator is one who learns by practice and imitation to choose wisely from an artistic repertoire for a particular occasion. In writing as art, writers do not face every task totally unprepared; they have strategies to help them reach new understanding in each case, but their art must be resituated.

The Roman treatise *Rhetorica ad Herennium*, which influenced education to the Renaissance, contends that all four instructional practices are necessary. It maintains that art reinforces talent and develops natural advantages, making the strongly talented exceptional and the average stronger (28–29). It explains, however, that theory (art) without continuous practice is of no avail. It also advocates the use of models to illustrate the skillful application of principles.

In Cicero's *De Oratore,* Crassus, echoing Isocrates, discusses the relative merits of these four pedagogies, privileging natural ability:

> This is then my opinion . . . that in the first place, natural talent is the chief contributor to the virtue of oratory; and indeed in those writers on the art, of whom Antonius spoke just now, it was not the principles and method of oratory that were wanting, but inborn capacity. . . I do not mean that art cannot in some cases give polish—for well I know that good abilities may through instruction become better, and that such as are not of the best can nevertheless be, in some measure, quickened and amended. (81)

Crassus has some disdain for unenlightened practice used alone: "most students . . . merely exercise their voices (and that in the wrong way) . . . and whip up their rate of utterance, and revel in a flood of verbiage. This mistake is due to their having heard it said that it is by speaking that men as a rule become speakers" (103). Antonius also emphasizes the pre-eminent role of natural ability:

> Since . . . three things are necessary to discovery of arguments, first acuteness, secondly theory, or art, as we may call it if we like, and thirdly painstaking, I must needs grant pride of place to talent, though talent is itself roused from lethargy by painstaking, painstaking, I repeat, which is always valuable. . . . Indeed between talent and painstaking there is very little room left for art. (305–07)

Quintilian comments on Antonius' position: "Some would have it that rhetoric is a natural gift though they admit that it can be developed by practice. So Antonius in the *de Oratore* of Cicero styles it a *knack derived from experience*, but denies that it is an art" (I: 327–29). Quintilian then takes issue with this view:

> [Certain persons] make it their boast that they speak on impulse and owe their success to their native powers. . . . Further, owing to their contempt for method, when they are meditating on some future effusion, they spend whole days looking at the ceiling in the hope that some magnificent inspiration may occur to them, or rock their bodies to and fro, booming inarticulately as if they had a trumpet inside them. . . . The least unreasonable of them devote their attention not to the actual case but to their purple patches, in the composition of which they pay no attention to the subject-matter, but fire off a series of isolated thoughts just as they happen to come to hand. . . . Nonetheless they do occasionally strike out some good things. . . . Why not? and if we are to be satisfied with this sort thing, then goodbye to any theory [art] of rhetoric. (I: 281–83)

Quintilian argues instead for an integration of the four approaches: "Without natural gifts . . . rules [art] are useless. Gifts, on the other hand, are of no profit in themselves unless cultivated by skillful teaching, persistent study, and continuous and extensive practice" (I: 19). He maintains that "the average orator owes much to nature while the perfect orator owes more to education" (I: 349). For Quintilian, art is a "power reaching its ends by a definite path, that is, by ordered methods" and is based on examination and practice (I: 345). About the art of invention he asserts: "We owe a debt of gratitude to those who have given us a short cut to knowledge. For thanks to them the arguments discovered by the genius of earlier orators have not got to be hunted out and noted down in detail" (II: 269). He cautions, however, against an excessive reliance on art, calling those who have only book knowledge of the topics "possessors of a dumb science" because "the discovery of arguments was not the result of the publication of text-books. . . . The creators of the art were the orators" (II: 269–70). He ridicules those who plod through entire lists of topics "knocking at the door of each with a view to discovering whether they may chance to serve to prove our point" (II: 269). He does not, however, rule out methodical invention, but reserves it for learners (II: 269–70), recommending that communicators develop a sense of appropriateness by applying strategies in real situations, not in practice exercises.

What happened to this integrated view of instruction in discourse? At least two major complex developments have bought us to a condition of exclusion and extreme emphasis on one or the other type of pedagogy. First, the concept of art changed. Second, different periods valorized one or the other of these instructional practices.

When Aristotle or Quintilian speak of the art of rhetoric, they refer to principles and strategies for invention, arrangement, and style. But in the medieval period, as Richard McKeon has explained, the concept of art is narrowed because the art of invention is gradually driven out of rhetoric to play an underground role in the formation of the scholastic and scientific methods. During this period, another curious development occurs: art and natural ability start to polarize, almost reify, into two positions. The first is that of Aquinas, who treats art as a body of formal principles, intellectualizing the art and changing its orientation to subject matter and to problems of inquiry and understanding. The second is that of Bonaventure, who considers art as knowledge in the artist, leading to a preoccupation with the relationship between morals and eloquence and to a view of rhetoric as virtue (189).

By the Renaissance, the concept of art has become ambiguous. On the one hand, according to Sister Miriam Joseph, the Aristotelian meaning still prevails: "The Elizabethan literary critics and poets, no less than the rhetoricians and logicians, insisted on the importance of precepts and theory in the creation of literature. . . . Art . . . is assumed to rest on a body of precepts derived from nature" (7). On the other hand, Ramus narrows the scope of rhetorical art, transferring invention and arrangement to dialectic and reducing the art of rhetoric to style. The Ramian tests do more than narrow the scope of art; they distort it. Walter J. Ong examines the complex meanings of "method" that Ramus inherits, shrinks, and transmits, showing that Ramus changes the concept of art from that of action guided by principles and strategies to that of a rigid method of analysis. The student produces discourse not by learning and applying principles and strategies but by analyzing and imitating texts. This transformation manifests itself in Ramus' discussion of invention as part of dialectic. Ong translates Ramus as saying:

> Logical analysis the process by which a given example of discourse already composed is examined in terms of the laws of the art, the question is extracted, then the invention studied, and the place from which the argument was drawn looked for. This is the analysis of invention. (263–64)

Ong explains that

> analysis, for Ramus, is thus at root a way of operating didactically upon a text. It belongs not to an art but to *usus* or exercise, and is complemented by *genesis* or composition, for, once the schoolboy has broken down a sample of discourse—written discourse, for analysis is here growing out of the humanist approach to language through the written word—he can assemble the parts in configurations of his own, which according to Ramus, is what one does in composing. (264)

Moreover, instead of explaining principles and strategies in terms of their nature, purpose, and appropriateness in different contexts, the Ramian treatises print geometric models of logic, schemes, and tropes, stripped of context.

In the eighteenth century Hugh Blair reiterates this reduction of art, proclaiming: "With respect to [invention], I am afraid it is beyond the power of art to give any real assistance. Art cannot go so far as to supply a speaker with arguments... though it may be of considerable use in assisting him to arrange and express those which his knowledge of the subject has discovered" (117). Blair emphasizes natural processes: "Whether nature or art contribute most to form an orator, is a trifling inquiry. In all attainments whatever, nature must be the prime agent" (129). In the nineteenth century, Richard Whately skeptically describes the prevailing view:

> Many, perhaps most persons, are inclined to the opinion that Eloquence, either in writing or speaking, is either a natural gift, or at least, is to be acquired by mere practice, and is not to be, attained or improved by any system of rules. And this opinion is favored not least by those . . . whose own experience would enable them to decide very differently; and it certainly seems to be in great deal practically adopted . (287)

CURRENT PRACTICES

At the present time, three divergent conceptions of art have emerged: 1) art as natural process, 2) art as heuristics, and 3) art as prescription. The first is the opposite of the classical conception. William Stafford describes art as "an interaction between object and beholder. . . . One doesn't learn how to do art, but one learns that it is possible by a certain adjustment of consciousness to participate in art—it's a natural activity for one not corrupted by mechanical ways" (48). John Barth expresses a similar view of art and its consequences for teaching:

> Given the inclination and the opportunity, those with any aptitude for it at all surely hone what skills they have, in the art of writing as in any other art, craft, skill. It gets learned . . . first, by paying a certain sort of attention to the experience of life as well as merely undergoing it; second, by paying a certain sort of attention to the works of their great and less great predecessors in the medium of written language, as well as merely reading them; third, by practicing that medium themselves, usually a lot; . . . and fourth, by offering their apprentice work for discussion and criticism by

> one or several of their impassioned peers, or by some more experienced hand, or both. (36)

For Barth art has turned into natural processes, imitation, and practice to the exclusion of the classical concept of art.

The second contemporary meaning of art is articulated by those who advocate the use of heuristics to guide composing. *Heuristics* for them has the same meaning as the classical concept of art: "explicit strategies for effective guessing. Heuristic procedures are not to be confused with rule-governed procedures . . . there are few rule-governed procedures possible in rhetoric. . . . A heuristic procedure provides a series of questions or operations whose results are provisional. Although explicit and more or less systematic, heuristic search is not wholly conscious or mechanical; intuition, relevant knowledge, and skill are also necessary" (Young 57). The purpose and value of these heuristics is discussed by Christina Murphy in a recent dialogue:

> Allowing students to wander through rhetorical mazes unassisted in search of insights into the riddles of compositional strategies and outcomes that have already been demystified and resolved seems largely an inefficient practice. . . Strategies of inquiry free many students to understand in the fullest sense what the creative process at the heart of composition is all about. (14)

The third view of art is a rule-governed one whose roots go back to Roman times. From the Roman period to the Renaissance, technical rhetorics appeared, crowded with topics that had been endlessly subdivided and with lengthy prescriptions for parts of the discourse. These bloated and mechanistic versions of art were perpetuated by the encyclopedic treatises of the medieval period and deteriorated into the lists of the Renaissance. Learning hundreds of directives for invention, arrangement, and style, became an end, not a means. Such a version of art prevails today, in textbooks, particularly handbooks, which present rules of style and arrangement as invariant, true for any context or type of discourse. Classrooms based on this version of art teach isolated prescriptions, formulae like the five-paragraph theme and the features of good style.

In addition to the existence of divergent conceptions of art, another force is contributing to a lack of integration in our current instructional practices: an overemphasis on one or the other of the four types of instruction. Some champions of natural process assert its preeminence to the exclusion of art, considering a knowledge of principles and strategies not only ineffective but obstructive to writers. Cy Knoblauch and Lil Brannon claim:

> Teaching, from this vantage point, no longer stresses giving people a knowledge they did not previously possess, but instead involves creating supportive environments in which a competence they already have can be nurtured to yield increasingly mature performance. . . . Progress toward

> excellence is a function of increasing experience more than objective understanding of principles. . . . Highlighting "strategies" . . . seems more distracting than helpful. (4, 15, 37)

An overreliance on imitation can be seen in the dominance of collections of readings in composition classrooms. Although some instructors use these collections interactively with the other pedagogies, a high percentage of teachers devote the majority of class time to reading and analyzing essays, with the assumption, as Gordon Rohman expresses it, "that if we train students how to recognize an example of good prose (the rhetoric of the finished word), we have given them a basis on which to build their own writing abilities" (17). Practice too has its zealots, who base their pedagogy on the maxim: "a theme a day keeps illiteracy away." Finally, overenthusiasm for art can be seen in instructors who present heuristics as ends to be mastered rather than as means to meaningful discourse, who proliferate heuristics so that learning then consumes writers' energies, who lecture on strategies rather than encourage collaborative engagement in using them purposefully, or who convert heuristics into formulae that are claimed to guarantee good writing.

These overemphases obscure the goal of integration that I argue for here—classrooms or writing centers that draw on the strengths of each of the four instructional practices: setting motivating contexts in which writers can raise and answer their own compelling questions, offering students guiding strategies, engaging students collaboratively in writing in a range of discourse communities, and presenting models of students, teachers, and professional writers planning and revising texts.

Works Cited

Aristotle. *Metaphysics*. Great Books of the Western World. Ed. Robert Hutchins. Chicago: Encyclopedia Britannica, 1952.

——. *The Rhetoric and The Poetics of Aristotle*. Trans. W. Rhys Roberts. New York: Modern Library, 1954.

Barth, John. "Writing: Can It Be Taught?" *New York Times Book Review* 16 June 1985: 1, 36–37.

Blair, Hugh. *Lectures on Rhetoric and Belles Lettres: The Rhetoric of Blair, Campbell, and Whately*. Ed. James L. Golden and Edward Corbett. New York: Holt, 1968.

Cicero. *De Oratore*. Trans. E. W. Sutton. Cambridge: Harvard UP, 1942.

Hillocks, George. "What Works in Teaching Composition: A Meta-analysis of Experimental Treatment Studies." *American Journal of Education*. 93 (1984): 133–70.

Kinneavy, James L. "The Relationship of the Whole to the Part in Interpretation Theory and in the Composing Process." *Linguistics, Stylistics, and the Teaching of Composition*. Ed. Donald McQuade. Akron, OH: L & S Books, 1979. 292–312.

Knoblauch, C. H., and Lil Brannon. *Rhetorical Tradition and the Teaching of Writing*. Upper Montclair, NJ: Boynton/Cook, 1984.

McKeon, Richard. "Rhetoric in the Middle Ages." *The Province of Rhetoric*. Ed. Joseph Schwartz and John Rycenga. New York: Ronald, 1965. 172–212.

Miriam Joseph, Sister. *Rhetoric in Shakespeare's Time*. New York: Harcourt, 1962.

Murphy, Christina, and Bonnie Dickinson. "If You Meet the Buddha with a Rosetta Stone: A Dialogue on Strategies of Inquiry and The New Rhetoric." *Freshman English News* 14 (1985): 13–18.

Ong, Walter J. *Ramus, Method, and the Decay of Dialogue*. Cambridge: Harvard UP, 1958.

Perkins, David. *The Mind's Best Work*. Cambridge: Harvard UP, 1981.

Quintilian. *The Institutio Oratoria of Quintilian*. Trans. H. E. Butler. Vols. I and II. Cambridge: Harvard UP, 1920.

Ramus, Peter. *The Logike of the Moste Excellent Philosopher P. Ramus, Martyr: Translated by Roland MacIlmaine (1574)*. Ed. Catherine Dunn. Northridge, CA: San Fernando Valley State College, 1969; Dudley Fenner. *The Artes of Logike and Rhetorike, plainlie set foorth in the Englishe tounge*. Ed. Robert Pepper. Gainesville, FL: Scholars' Facsimiles, 1966.

Rhetorica ad Herennium. Trans. Harry Caplan. Cambridge: Harvard UP, 1954.

Rohman, D. Gordon, and Albert Wlecke. *Pre-Writing: The Construction and Application of Models for Concept Formation*. U. S. Office of Education Cooperative Research Project No. 2174. East Lansing: Michigan State UP, 1964.

Stanford, William. *Writing the Australian Crawl*. Ann Arbor: The U of Michigan P, 1978.

Whately, Richard. *Elements of Rhetoric: The Rhetoric of Blair, Campbell, and Whately*. Ed. James L. Golden and Edward P. J. Corbett. New York: Holt, 1968.

Young, R. E. "Arts, Crafts, Gifts, and Knacks: Some Disharmonies in the New Rhetoric." *Reinventing the Rhetorical Tradition*. Ed. A. Freedman and I. Pringle. Urbana, IL: NCTE, 1980. 53–60.

POMO BLUES: STORIES FROM FIRST-YEAR COMPOSITION

Lee Ann Carroll

Feminism, Freire, cultural studies, Bakhtin, critical pedagogy, Foucault, border theory, Burke, gay and lesbian studies, Barthes, intertextuality, Cixous, deconstruction, Rorty, social constructionism, Lyotard, dialogic learning, Lacan, post-structuralism, post-process, post-modernism—recent composition books and articles are rife with terms and names from the many, often conflicting postmodern theories influencing academic thought and the culture in general. Many writing instructors are working out the implications of postmodernist thought for composition instruction, their different approaches reflecting not only the range of postmodern theories but also the range of their institutions and of their own subjectivities as well as those of their students. In this 1997 article from College English, *Lee Ann Carroll, professor of English and writing center director at Pepperdine University, explains five key positions that she has taken from her study of postmodernist theory and describes how they affect how she structures her first-year composition classes and how she designs assignments and responds to student writing.*

I begin my essay with some examples of fairly conventional, but, I believe, effective student responses to some typical writing assignments. These do not represent a startling new pedagogy, but should sound familiar to those who actually teach writing to first-year students rather than those who like to think about how others should do it. A postmodernist perspective, now permeating composition studies, challenges us to rethink what we are doing when we read, write, and talk our way through projects like the ones I will describe. What difference does it make to think of the stories students tell not as the authentic reflections of autonomous individuals but as verbal artifacts heavily structured by the cultural and institutional

---

Lee Ann Carroll is a professor of English at Pepperdine University, where she teaches composition and rhetoric and directs the Writing Center. She chairs the Advisor, Board of the California Writing Project and codirects the CD-ROM Portfolio Project, a longitudinal study of college student learning across disciplines. Her current work, based on data from the Portfolio Project, examines how institutional practices and student experiences interact to shape student writing.

contexts in which they are produced? What do first-year students need to know about decentering the subject, the multivocal text, and the interrelations of discourse and culture? The classroom is our second home, and our writing assignments can seem like natural, fairly straightforward transactions between a teacher and students. But playing in the background is what Lester Faigley at the 1993 CCCC called the "Pomo Blues." We have read Faigley's *Fragments of Rationality: Postmodernity and the Subject of Composition,* Harkin and Schilb's *Contending With Words: Composition and Rhetoric in a Postmodern Age,* Susan Miller's *Textual Carnivals: The Politics of Composition,* and articles drawing on postmodernist theory by Kurt Spellmeyer, James Berlin, Gary Olson, and others. These sources examine the work of postmodern thinkers in philosophy, literature, and political theory and argue for the impact they might have on the practice of teaching writing.

At the heart of the postmodernist shift in the classroom is a shift in the conception of the teacher and the student writer. In the past, both might be seen as fairly stable, autonomous individuals drawing on skills within themselves, acting independently to teach and to produce original pieces of writing. From a post-modernist perspective, teachers and students might be seen to be acting with much less autonomy. Their "selves," their teaching, and their writing are much more constructed by culture and language, bits and pieces pulled together provisionally to act in expected ways. Lester Faigley, for example, demonstrates how the "authentic voice of the student writer is "discursively produced and discursively bounded" *(Fragments* 129), and David Bartholomae has repeatedly shown us ways that students attempt to "invent the university;" Susan Miller argues that the "self" that the freshman in the composition classroom is imagined to be is often a "presexual, preeconomic, prepolitical person" (87). This "infantilized" student is "taught by those described in class schedules as 'staff'" (102). The "selves" of staff are equally shaped by cultural and political forces, as Nancy Welch shows in a critique of a teacher training program with a postmodernist agenda. After reviewing several new approaches to composition theory and pedagogy, Kathryn Flannery concludes, "To really understand the import of postmodern challenges to the originary subject means to rethink the dominance, the persistence of such notions as authenticity and authority in the composition classroom" (711–12).

What does it mean actually to play this tune day to day in the classroom? Faigley points out that the composition community generally has come to accept a postmodern view of knowledge and discourses of all kinds as socially and politically constructed, but, he adds, "where composition studies has proven least receptive to postmodern theory is in surrendering its belief in the writer as an autonomous self" *(Fragments* 15). The questioning of belief in an autonomous self can be liberating, like surviving a disastrous love affair or improvising new versions of old songs. Yet without this belief, a house just isn't a home. I don't feel like my "self" any more. And what do we tell the kids? The news of postmodernism may strike students the way news of a divorce strikes children of an unhappy marriage. They may prefer the myths and stories that have shored up their familiar realities and, certainly, resist threats to their sense of "autonomous selves."

In this essay, I do not want to suggest an oversimplified "Postmodernism's Greatest Hits" approach to first-year composition; however, I do want to show how some key postmodern ideas about texts force me and my students to rethink some typical writing assignments and typical student responses. I will begin by describing the assignments rather straightforwardly, then consider how they invite the same type of postmodernist critique we might apply to texts of literature, popular culture, and the academic disciplines. I suggest, following John School, that we should "involve students as co-inquirers into the ramifications of cultural studies and postmodernism even though the issues raised may "discompose" students (187). I will argue that we and our students live in a postmodern world and are already "discomposed" by the competing discourses that play in our heads. The Pomo Blues suggest that we give up grandiose, romantic notions that Freshman Comp can fix students either personally or politically. Instead, we come back more modestly to consider what kinds of stories it is possible for us to tell in English I, what it means to tell such stories "effectively," and what is at stake in playing different variations of the same tune.

Here are some of the assignments that have discomposed me and my students:

Assignment One: Following a Script

For a placement exam for Honors English, incoming first-year students are asked to write about any book that they particularly remember reading and tell why this book was especially memorable for them. The responses of these bright, imaginative students fall into several categories:

> I was lost and now I am found. I thought I was going to hate *The Old Man and the Sea.* It seemed like a boring story of an old man and a fish but through my English class I came to see what a great book it is.
>
> A book was my therapist. *Prince of Tides* gave me greater insights into the problems in my own family.
>
> There is no frigate like a book. *Bridge to Terabithia* took me to another world at a time when I was under a lot of stress in my own life.

Assignment Two: Writing as Re-Writing

Maria, in my advanced composition class, is student teaching in a sixth-grade classroom with a literature-based, whole language curriculum. Her students are reading novels and historical accounts about slavery. She asks them to write journals as though they were escaping slaves, imagining what they would feel. For my class, she tries completing this assignment herself and is disappointed with the result. She is able to write a technically competent journal, but it is flat, only remotely suggesting the pain and terror of slavery.

Assignment Three: Problematizing Experience

In the fall, my students and I begin a first-year composition course with an assignment sequence adapted from Bartholomae and Petrosky, *Ways of Reading*. We have read Freire's "The 'Banking' Concept of Education" and now students are writing a first draft about an experience they might "problematize." The assignment, sophisticated and complex like most of the suggestions for writing in *Ways of Reading*, reads in part:

> For this assignment, locate a moment from your own recent experience (an event or chain of events) that seems rich or puzzling, that you feel you do not understand but that you would like to understand better (or that you would like to understand differently). Write a first draft of an essay in which you both describe what happened and provide a way of seeing or understanding what happened. (744)

For this assignment, Alex writes a first draft about how his grandfather's illness taught him the true meaning of Christmas. Carolyn tells how she was rejected by her first-choice college and how this has made her a better person. Ray produces a lengthy, rambling essay that details his complaints about a roommate whom he sees as a snobby, spoiled rich kid.

Assignment Four: Making Stories Academic

For her last essay in the same first-year composition class, Laura writes "An Analysis of Our Homeless." She has been working collaboratively with other students to read and review a book they selected about children and poverty; Now she is completing an "I-Search" reporting on a topic related to the book and her own experience. She and her group are also preparing an oral presentation. Her essay begins:

> When you are raised in Santa Barbara, California, homelessness is something nearly impossible to ignore. Throughout the majority of my life I have been faced with the typical scenes of the homeless: the drunk old man, the hippie playing his guitar, and the mentally disturbed lady yelling at something that simply isn't there. As a teenager I participated in school functions helping to gather canned food for the homeless during Thanksgiving and helped my church feed the hungry in their annual Christmas dinner. These things were all a part of growing up in Santa Barbara and I never thought that homelessness would be different in any other places in America.
>
> My first trip to Inner city Los Angeles was a shocking one. I could hardly keep the tears out of my eyes as I viewed the depressing sights around me. The unforgettable stench of LA enveloped me the instant we hit Main Street, but what was truly shocking to me was the sidewalks. Up and down Main Street to the right and to the left I saw tents, sleeping bags and cardboard boxes lining every available inch of space. Old men, young children, mothers, and wives lined the streets, curled up inside their small

sidewalk palaces. I never knew this many homeless people existed and the reality of this shocked me in a powerful way.

Laura goes on to outline the questions that were raised in her mind by this experience. She focuses on the connection between homelessness and mental illness. In her essay, she uses a variety of statistics, examples, and cases to show how one might become homeless in America. She moves considerably beyond the stereotypes in her first two paragraphs.

As a new school year begins, what can I tell my students about these assignments and their responses to them? The question is not merely speculative because it is the end of August, hot and desert dry, and I need to plan my English 101 course. I envision the class as a space: a time blocked out to meet, a room set aside for the purpose, a grid of blank squares like the squares on the calendar I use to map out the semester. I scribble and erase, trying to make the imagined class fit exactly the number of squares allotted for it. Soon school will start and experience—mine, my students', that of the world at large—will overflow the squares. Within those squares, my students and I tell stories like the ones I have described in my examples-stories about books we have read, about illness, college, slavery, homelessness. Although students will write in many forms—essays, magazine articles, arguments, book reviews, poems, research reports—I think of all of these primarily as stories, tales made up by captive Scheherazades for the interest and amusement of their teacher, attempts to make sense of overflowing experience through language. At the risk of a kind of vulgar, homogenized postmodernism, I list five key postmodernist ideas about texts that I will include in my syllabus. I want to explain these to my students as key themes that we will return to again and again during the semester. I want to "make strange" the seemingly natural transaction of a teacher requiring writing and a student fulfilling those requirements. Many students sense already that their writing for the classroom is "artificial" and that what they say "doesn't really matter" as long as they give the teacher "what she wants." I want to examine this perception of their "job" as students, not erase the ways they and I are constructed by our institutional and cultural roles. At the same time, I want to suggest that we can be more conscious of how all of our experiences are rhetorically constructed and consider why it might "matter" to tell our stories one way rather than another. In this process, however, I hope I will not simply impose on students my own stories and the kind of selves I think they should be, insist that their "postmodernist" songs be correctly liberal, multicultural, sensitive to class distinctions, and free from gender bias.

I take seriously Lynn Worsham's and Victor Vitanza's warning that in attempting to tame theory, we are in danger of recreating the same limited views of self, language, and culture that postmodernist theorists have tried to explode. However, I agree with Gary Olson, who argues that the activity of theorizing "can lead us into lines of inquiry that challenge received notions or entrenched understandings that may no longer be productive" (54). With the Pomo Blues playing in the background, we cannot conduct business as usual. In the rest of my essay, I explore how the five key postmodernist ideas from my syllabus play out over my typical writing assignments.

1. THE STORIES WE TELL ARE THE STORIES THAT ARE CULTURALLY AVAILABLE TO US TO TELL.

When they are singing the Pomo Blues, my students are apt to find this idea depressing. James Berlin noted that, at times, "students and teachers are at odds with each other" in a curriculum at Purdue that tries to "problematize students' experiences, requiring them to challenge the ideological codes they bring to college by placing their signifying practices against alternatives" ("Poststructuralism" 31–32). I am not surprised that students are discomposed. My student, Alex, presents the positive story of his grandfather's illness as a sincere account of his family's individual and unique experience. He writes well and would be angry to have either his originality or his sincerity challenged. He certainly does not want to see himself as a "cultural dope," determined by made-for-television movies and self-help books that persistently ennoble pain and deny suffering. He struggles to find the language that fits his experience and the task, writing his first essay for a college class. But Alex is not finished after writing his first draft. The "problematizing" assignment asks students to write another draft of their narrative, working on passages "that seem to be evidence of the power of language to dominate, mystify, deceive, or alienate" (747) and telling the story in a "different" way, changing, perhaps, the perspective, the details reported, the language, and the intended effect on a reader. This assignment is meant to be more than the parlor trick of describing your dorm room in two different ways for your Aunt Bessie and your best friend Josh. In class, as we look at published narratives, including literacy stories by writers as different as Malcolm X and Helen Keller, we consider how these stories are familiar and what other stories the writers might have told. We notice how the writers construct both themselves and readers, working with and against cultural stereotypes and values. James Slevin suggests that this kind of critical literacy "can make all of us as writers aware that our voice is not necessarily our own, that it is not simply one possibility among a repertoire of private, personal voices; rather, it is, or can be an imposed voice, constructed not by us but for us" (71). In class workshops, I ask students to be critical readers of their own texts.

The class sympathizes with Alex's positive account of his experience and hesitates to critique his story. when Alex says he wants help revising, they notice that the positive version of his story seems weak in details. Writing of Christmas Day visiting Grandpa in the hospital, Alex says, "Even though we had a store bought dinner, it was still nice because we all were together. We all had a lot on our minds so we did not talk much, but we still managed to make a couple jokes every now and then to try to lighten the mood." Alex decides that one way he can work against the typical heart-warming story of illness is to write a more "negative" version of his experience. He speaks in a slightly different voice when he writes:

> Christmas dinner is supposed to be a great time filled with laughter, excitement, and, of course, a turkey and all the fixings, but this year my mind was wandering too much to even enjoy the store-bought dinner that we had got. Though nothing was mentioned of it, we knew everyone of our minds was wrestling with the thought that this may be the last Christmas that we would be lucky enough to have my Grandfather with us. We tried to lighten the atmosphere with small jokes and stories. Although we managed to make small smiles across our faces, nothing could have changed the pain that we all felt deep in our hearts.

Alex begins in this draft to bring in some of the grief his family experienced. Is this a "problematized" version of his story? Alex, in his self-analysis of this assignment, writes, "The language I used to tell the story was quite different in the two narratives." He points out some examples of differences, then concludes, "The event may have been the same in both narratives, but I feel that the mood they convey to the reader is completely different." Alex changes the language of his narrative, but, as he says, the "event" stays "the same." He still learns a lesson about "the true meaning of Christmas." I know other discourses about illness, families, and Christmas that Alex might incorporate into his own, but has Alex gotten the assignment wrong because he has not written Susan Sontag's *Illness as Metaphor* or recognized how both illness and Christmas are commodified, because he has "problematized" the rhetoric of his narrative, but not a primary "ideological code"? A postmodernist perspective suggests that there is no essential experience to be narrated first, and then problematized. Neither version of Alex's story is necessarily more authentic. In class, we discuss why different versions of stories matter and examine the idea that the way we map experience in language is important because it can change how we act both individually and as a society. The writing class has value because it is a place to play around with language, with different discourses. School authorizes the teacher to insist that Alex swap one discourse for another, even an unfamiliar discourse of philosophical or political critique. So Alex is not wrong in seeing his main job at the beginning of English I as largely a rhetorical problem, constructing a story that will be acceptable to his teacher, but also to himself and his peers. In any version of his story, Alex will be constructing an artifact out of the bits and pieces culturally available to him, including our class readings and discussions, an academic discourse that we have had only three weeks to examine. The desire for mastery; for language to construct a coherent, familiar narrative, works powerfully against the directive of the teacher-reader to disrupt this narrative with another type of "story."

And Alex does learn something from this assignment about how texts are constructed. He explains that his work "illustrates the importance of reading everything objectively, because sometimes people are not even aware that they are slanting what they tell, but they are. It is up to the reader to get their information from a variety of different sources to be sure that they are receiving the whole story" Alex maintains the Enlightenment concept that there is a whole story out there somewhere that the readers can piece together if they can only read enough sources "objectively."

And he says he especially enjoyed this assignment because it allowed him to "write more from my heart."

The second key idea, however, continues to challenge the notion that writing comes primarily "from the heart," rather than from familiar cultural narratives.

2. THE CONVENTIONS AND DETAILS OF MANY OF THE STORIES WE TELL ARE, IN A SENSE, ALREADY WRITTEN AND READ BY THE CULTURE.

From a teacher's perspective, this idea helps Maria and me analyze the slave narrative assignment for sixth graders. Maria knows writing process pedagogy; so she has led her students through a prewriting exercise brainstorming how they would feel if they were planning to escape from slavery and what might happen to them. At first this seems like an exercise in empathy, one self putting itself in the place of another. Few of us could truly enter into the fear and pain of slavery, and one might fear trivializing suffering through encouraging a spurious empathy. But actually writing the imagined journal calls for quite different skills. Most of us can quickly imagine the elements sixth graders will incorporate in their narratives, the "moves" they might make in telling such a story; These may vary somewhat depending on each student's prior knowledge but will likely include hiding in a field or barn, following the north star, crossing a river, being pursued by slave catchers, and so forth. In that sense, each student's narrative is already written in the teacher/reader's head before the student begins. The student's skill is not empathy but the ability to pick up the appropriate discourses from reading and to reproduce them. We are only now analyzing the competing discourses in original slave narratives. These are reinterpreted and conventionalized again in the mass media and materials for school children. It takes extraordinary ability—one thinks of Toni Morrison's *Beloved*—to reinvent this story.

This is not to say that teachers should not give this sort of assignment. Entering into a discourse of slavery does focus children's attention on this experience. Maria's own narrative of slavery is best seen as one way of integrating and reporting what she has learned. While teachers might look for creativity in students' imaginary journals, often the papers judged most creative are those that recreate in the greatest detail and variety the sources the child is familiar with. A teacher of immigrant children in East Los Angeles complained to me of her fourth graders' lack of creativity in writing about the sights, sounds, and smells of Christmas. When she described to me the kinds of details that might show creativity, she suggested the fragrant pine tree, the crackling fire, the roasting turkey, and the other accouterments of an idealized Dickensian Christmas. Again, the text was in a sense already written and read, and students' success measured by their ability to manipulate conventions which, in this case, were not part of their experience. And it would not be enough merely to expect children to substitute within the frame of the Christmas story details of their experience, turkey with *mole* rather than with stuffing. Many of these children who may manipulate language creatively in other contexts have limited backgrounds in reading and storybooks and do not share the teacher's implicit understanding of the basic moves one might make in telling such a story.

Though first-year college students often have more extensive repertoires of rhetorical moves, the classroom context continues to shape how students manipulate these conventions.

3. THE STORIES WE CAN TELL ARE CONSTRAINED BY THE CONTEXT IN WHICH WE TELL THEM, WITH MUCH LEFT OUT OR SUPPRESSED.

This third key idea says more than that we consciously shape our texts to fit our audience and purpose. It should be obvious that the situation in which we write powerfully shapes the stories we tell, and yet the constraints of writing for a college class may seem so normal to teachers and students that they become invisible. On a global level, I think we have a very limited perception of how time, physical arrangements of classes, institutional structures, and daily procedures work to form our perceptions of what kind of writing is appropriate or possible in the classroom. Here, I would simply consider some of the constraints that are easier to make visible to students and ourselves. Ray's complaining essay about his roommate seemed at first merely disorganized and confusing. But in a conference, Ray explained that he was gay and he believed that was why his roommate was treating him with such disdain and hostility Suppressing this information that he did not want to include in a classroom essay limited Ray to a conventional story of roommate problems but contributed to an emotional tone that seemed out of proportion to arguments about who left dirty socks on the floor. Yet Ray wanted to tell this story. Encouraged by the "problematizing" assignment to experiment with other voices, he took the unusual step of recasting his entire story as an opera set in student days in a mythical Italian Renaissance university town. This frame, certainly unconventional for the classroom, revealed Ray, a music major, to be highly creative and skilled in drawing on the operas he knew and in manipulating those elements to produce a text that allowed him to maintain the privacy he wanted while more nearly capturing the drama he was experiencing. (He later also found a roommate he perceived to be more humane.)

Ray's struggle with this assignment and Alex's difficulty in reframing his family story might suggest that we should avoid writing about personal experience, which is often fraught with conflicts over what to reveal, what to suppress. But constraints operate on less personal stories, too. When we analyzed the Honors English placement test, which we no longer give, we were struck by the way the texts were, again, in a sense already written and read. They fell into predictable types and were invariably positive. Even a student who had been tortured by studying *Hamlet* for an entire semester would cheerfully conclude that this had been a good experience. What other story could you tell if you were a college freshman wanting to be in Honors English and writing under time pressure for an audience of professors? When we ranked these placement essays, the best were able to create the appearance of sincerity with much relevant detail and a restrained tone, not too effusive, either serious or gently self-mocking. Now I do not mean to say that none of these stories were "true." Good English students are often students who like books and that is one of the reasons we asked about their reading. But the best essay is not the "truest"; it is one that rings most true for the readers.

Relentlessly insisting on a positive outcome and maintaining that gently self-mocking tone is a constraint that many students seem to apply to their classroom writing. Carolyn's first draft about being rejected by several other colleges suppressed her resentment of affirmative action plans that she felt favored some of her friends and worked against her. For Carolyn, the problematizing assignment does prompt her to rethink the choices she has made in writing. Retelling her story allows Carolyn to acknowledge that there is a "problem" in the way students are selected for college and that this problem has significantly affected her own life. The process of retelling is an antidote to some students' belief that they have told their own true story in the one and only way possible and there is nothing left to say. As Judith Summerfield notes, "currently fashionable constructs of plurality and relativity are implicated in recent narrative theories: we know that there is no one story of an event, but there are stories; no history, but histories" (180). This may be less obvious to students.

When students simply reproduce cultural commonplaces, teachers complain that these students "can't think critically." But critical thinking is not an attribute students have or lack; it is an active process. Trying to recover what the constraints of particular story lines pressure us to leave out is a way of thinking more critically. In my classroom, we accept the cultural commonplace and, indeed, applaud those who can reproduce these well, with lots of specific detail and what the handbooks call "effective word choice." These are powerful stories. Instead of forbidding them, we want to examine the sources of their power. To do this, in one assignment I encourage students to write a "publishable" article on a topic related to language issues that we have been studying and that they will continue to research. Their task is to mimic as much as possible the way that topics like communication between women and men or censorship are discussed in women's magazines or the daily paper or the nightly news. Students are frequently adept at relaying the common sense wisdom of the mass media, complete with appealing layouts, typefaces, and illustrations. Sam, an international student from Singapore, joins a peer writing group studying gender and language, saying he wants to understand more about "what's going on with women" and also to represent the "male" point of view. He models his publishable writing on an actual column that offers readers of a male-oriented magazine advice about flirting-including the tip that pro-choice rallies might be a good place to meet sexually active women. Sam, in turn, offers advice to women in his article entitled "Sexism? Let's Say Something Boys." After many suggestions from his writing group and his writing center tutor about tone, style, examples, and overall effect, Sam's final draft begins with a magazine-type anecdote:

> "Men are all chauvinist pigs," proclaimed a silver-tongued young lady who was sitting with a couple of her friends, who were all, like her, in their twenties in a cafe. She continued her bashing on men and their stereotypical name-calling on women, which are directed on their "oinkers." Sitting on a table next to them, I could clearly hear—or shall I say—listen tentatively and feel a little unjustified. I, as a superior sex,

> would want to defend our fellow kinsmen from the attack and come out victorious again, like how it should be. But this time, I just sat down. Are we that despised that we should be called a filthy animal? The answer from the three million people reading this article is a clear "No." But why is the claim? I am not writing to deny the fact that we, men, are in a certain degree, sexist. The point I am trying to say to you, women out there, is, "Hey, calm down a little will you? We are often being treated unfairly too."

Finding models of published articles to imitate for this assignment leads students to consider different ways they might structure information. They can make their case as young Republicans or radical feminists, but they need to find forums where their case can be made. This is an opportunity to speak in the voice of Rush Limbaugh, the editors of the *Los Angeles Times;* or *Cosmopolitan* magazine. Surprisingly, perhaps, in these articles, I seem to read fewer comments that strike me as egregiously sexist, racist, or homophobic than I find in students' more conventional classroom essays. In those classroom essays, students may believe they are conveying simply their own non-negotiable personal opinions. On the other hand, in his "publishable" article, Sam, despite his sometimes twisted syntax and shaky sense of audience, discovers through imitating a model and through the responses of his peers and tutor that he can, and indeed must, be entertaining as well as persuasive for the mass market. He becomes more conscious of shaping his opinions in language, what he leaves in and what he leaves out. The constraints of mainstream popular publications may push students to more bland, homogenized expressions of opinion and information at the same time as their writing becomes more "colorful."

In a second piece of writing based on the same topic as their publishable imitation, students include more material from their research and their own experience that is added, left over, or reshaped from their earlier article. The structure of this text, though modeled on the familiar I-Search paper, is flexible. Instead of struggling to find "smooth transitions" from one discourse to another, Sam uses sub-heads to lay out what he can say at this point. He writes about how he got interested in the topic of gender and language and what he learned from reading Dale Spender's *Man Made Language* and other sources. The sections of his paper include "The Down Side," "The Complaints," "The Need for Inclusive Language," "Teaching of Inclusive Language," and "Some Alternative Names." while this is not a well-formed academic essay, it does display some of the competing discourses Sam has encountered in this project and one way of putting these together. In more formal academic writing, under the constraints of time and the expectation that all school writing must be "well-organized," students frequently reach for those texts that are easiest to reproduce and suppress everything that does not fit. What we take as critical thinking is another type of discourse, a learned way of talking about social problems and popular culture-the staple topics of first-year composition courses. The "critical" texts that teachers have already written and read in their heads may be as unfamiliar to many freshmen as the Dickensian Christmas stories were to East Los Angeles fourth graders.

Compelled to write in new genres in their college classes, students express the frustration most writers feel in trying to connect what they experience in day-to-day life, what they think in their heads, and what they are able to express on paper. The fourth key idea is another way of thinking about those connections and contradictions that Sam and other students may sense but must often suppress to produce acceptable, coherent classroom texts.

4. NON-NARRATIVE FORMS ARE OFTEN CLOSELY RELATED TO SUPPRESSED PERSONAL NARRATIVES.

Traditional academic writing informed by Western rationalism encourages students to adopt a guise of objectivity. This version of critical thinking assumes a stable self free to sift through competing arguments and choose those that are logically most compelling. Expository writing, argumentation, and research reports have traditionally been seen as distinct from autobiography, narrative, and imaginative fiction. The postmodernist perspective blurs this distinction, and as James Berlin points out, "The postmodern turn has put rhetoric back on the agenda of virtually all of the human sciences" ("Poststructuralism" 172). In history, anthropology, psychology, biology, and other disciplines, we now question whether we can separate the knower from what is known.

In three different pieces of writing, Carolyn moves from her positive account of not getting into her first-choice college to a second narrative showing herself as a victim of affirmative action to a third, researched report about changes in affirmative action policies at our university and others in California. Laura reads a book about children living in poverty, writes a book review, and constructs a personal narrative that she sees as related to her reading. For each student, her analytical writing is shaped in part by her understanding of her own experience. Developing writing assignments that persistently rule out narrative obscures the situated nature of texts. Writing again becomes distorted by the stories we are trying not to tell. In individual conferences, in peer groups, and in the Writing Center, I point to passages in student writing and like all teachers ask, "How do you know?" "What does this mean?" "Is this what you really think?" "Why?" There are, disconcertingly, elements of psychotherapy, which I am not licensed to practice, here. Perhaps I do think it is "healthier" for Carolyn not to "repress" her pain and anger. Certainly, there is social engineering, which I feel ethically committed to practice, in asking Laura to problematize her idea of homelessness. But I am not, in fact, trying to uncover some essential version of students' thoughts and experiences.

Of course, students will measure conflicting stories against their lived experience, the more or less coherent narratives we all construct about our lives. On the other hand, privileging what we believe we have learned from personal experience as more true than what we learn from secondary sources is also a distortion. Students can cocoon in a private world they feel is real, rather than venture into a public world over which they feel they have little control. I suggest to Carolyn and Laura, aware of the force of teacher's "suggestions," that there are other "stories" about affirmative action and homelessness that can be told by our admissions officers, by other students, by statistics, editorials, books in the library, screen after screen of material on the Internet. In book reviews, summaries, and reading responses students try to honor the voices of their sources, to analyze the "stories" that other writers tell and, perhaps, the stories they are trying not to tell. Students often take on the role of the objective, critical selves that I presume they need to practice in their academic classes.

It is not that students know too few stories, but that they know too many. Students experience every day how the lines between genres are blurred—in news presented as entertainment, docudramas, shock-jockey talk shows as the most public forums for political debate. Contrasting different forms over the course of a semester makes clearer how conventions both permit and constrain us to speak in different ways. In class, we work on reading all texts rhetorically, as situated in particular times, places, and experiences. Students are also rhetoricians, not obliged to transcribe a predetermined reality, but invited and commanded by English I to put together provisional accounts of their subjects that will be persuasive to their teacher-reader, peers, and other audiences we might imagine. The composition classroom should be a space where we can play around with rhetorical conventions and mix various forms of writing. Don Bialostosky, in *Contending with Words,* suggests, "Such a class can modify the terms of disciplinary education in the students' favor by letting them in on the secrets of genre and convention that the disciplines silently observe" (16). For undergraduates, it might be developmentally appropriate to ask them more often to explain how they came to know than to insist they present an argument or a body of knowledge as objective experts.

It is a delicate balancing act, to construct an academic self that seems open to the voices of others and that, at the same time, evaluates, saying, "Yes, I agree," or "No, that's not how it goes." This balancing act is at the heart of the Pomo Blues, a sense of doubleness, the need to balance a vision of a world created by language, a world of endlessly competing discourses, against a lived experience that requires judgment and action. This is the task of the teacher as well as the student and brings us to a final key idea.

5. ALL TEXTS ARE "INTERESTED"—NONE ARE INHERENTLY "NORMAL" OR "NEUTRAL."

The last verse of the Pomo Blues is the most frustrating for students who want to know the "right" version of the song. You can play around, trade one discourse for another, love them and leave them, but that bed is awfully cold at night when you don't even have your "self" to keep you warm. Students get tired of the endless play of texts. Sooner or later, preferably sooner, they want to finish the paper, get the grade, and go home with some credits in their pockets. The values of the business transaction structure much of what goes on in the classroom. Students pay for credits and, in this sense, are customers, consumers of what the teacher can offer. On the other hand, it is not a simple exchange of money for credits. Students must also "earn" the credits through the work they do. In the composition class, they must tell stories, make arguments, construct analyses. Students are not wrong in supposing that it is in their self-interest to construct stories, arguments, and analyses that accommodate the teacher's values, beliefs, and experiences. Although Freirian pedagogy has taught ways to restructure power relationships in the classroom, as long as grades are given, the transaction of trading papers for grades will strongly influence how students and teachers construct themselves and their writing. This is perhaps the first way and the deepest level at which students recognize that their texts are not "neutral" accounts of self-evident truths. Their "normal" way of writing must be shaped to meet "what the teacher wants."

If postmodernist theory challenges students' sense of an authentic self, it also challenges teachers' claims of objectivity. While it might be frightening for teachers to give up the claim of objectivity, it is more threatening to students who, rightly, do not want to be graded capriciously. Like many teachers, I try to construct a classroom self that I would describe as tolerant and fair, invoking what I understand to be conventional academic standards for evaluating thinking and writing, negotiating these as openly as I can with students, and, by using portfolios, reducing the emphasis on grading during the semester. That we are all operating in good faith is a story that most of my students and I struggle to tell ourselves.

Looking at how cultural discourses are constructed means shifting the focus from how good a story or argument is to asking what is at stake in telling or arguing it in this way. Certainly, we are interested in whether a piece of writing "works," but we are also interested in what it works for. Laura, for example, in her writing considers what difference it makes how she tells the story of "the homeless." Her topic, "the homeless," is one the culture has defined, a category to structure and simplify our thinking about complex persons and events. Postmodernist theory shifts us away from asking primarily whether Laura is telling the "right" story, whether this is defined as the most logical or most persuasive or most politically sensitive or most sincere. Instead the focus is on what kinds of stories she can tell and what is at stake in each of those different possibilities. I can't be sure if I am giving her text the "right" reading since I am also subject to the stories culturally available to me. But I can reflect back to her what I think is at stake in our possible writings and readings. Laura and her research group consider what beliefs and values lead us to write of those who live in the streets and parks as colorful characters or helpless victims. How is our treatment of those we describe as having made poor choices different from our treatment of those we describe as mentally ill? Whose interests are served in constructing the story of those without permanent homes as "others" or "just like you and me," as ill or lazy or addicted or simply unlucky or any of the other explanations we might offer? Of course, we can and do ask the same kind of questions about affirmative action, books students read, slave narratives, and stories of personal experience. In giving up claims to neutrality and objectivity, writers and readers acknowledge how much they are determined by cultural values, attitudes, and beliefs. Annette Patterson, an Australian educator who applies this critical approach to teaching literature in secondary schools, describes her goals as follows: "I want my students to be able to analyse the construction of readings and to consider what is at stake in the disagreement between readings; to make visible the gaps and silences of texts and to examine what particular interpretations support in terms of values they affirm. I want my students to be able to challenge dominant versions of texts and to construct new readings" (144).

I would like to say that my class meets Patterson's goals, but the postmodernist perspective resists closure. So I construct several different endings for my essay and ask you to consider each.

In the first ending, although I have suggested postmodernism favors the blues over more catchy tunes, I find almost irresistible the pull to construct a happy teaching story. In this ending, five oversimplified ideas about postmodernism help not just Laura but most of my students to question the stories they read and write, to identify some key cultural narratives, and to resist those that are especially limited or harmful. They feel freer to write their own stories in new ways that lead to ethical action. But the blues reassert themselves. The dilemma of postmodernism is that all discourses are limited, and there is no outside place to stand to judge what is harmful or what is good. As Peter McLaren and Colin Lankshear conclude in *Critical Literacy: Politics, Praxis, and the Postmodern,* the challenge is "to steer an ethical and political course in times of shifting theoretical boundaries and unstable systems of meaning and representation" (412). The danger lies in being paralyzed by competing discourses and unable to make ethical choices.

Another ending then, is the reading of my more conservative colleagues who see a postmodernist pedagogy as an attack on traditional, Western values and who see Laura and others as being "brainwashed" into political correctness. Why not go back to a more "neutral," unpoliticized curriculum? That debate is too well known and too large to take up here, except to say that once you have seen the Wizard behind the screen, once you see how we all make language and reality together, you know there is no neutral space into which you can retreat. To quote loosely from Thomas Wolfe, Dorothy, and Gertrude Stein: You can't go home again. We're not in Kansas any more. There is no there, there.

So, no. Not that ending.

Then there is the analysis from the radical left, which I find more persuasive. Academic postmodernism, like academic Marxism, is a ploy of post-sixties liberals, many of whom are closet humanists. New theories merely repackage old ideas and teach Laura and company to critique cultural ideas with safe, academic politeness. These "theories" do not lead to real change, fit neatly into current classroom structures, and ultimately are designed to produce the next labor force for late capitalism. This upper cadre of workers will be "brainwashed" to be flexible, open to new ideas, and somewhat capable of dealing with abstract concepts. (See Mas'ud Zavarzadeh and Donald Morton for an elaboration of this argument.) Yes, of course. University professors are unlikely to discard humanist values of justice and rationality, and just as unlikely to give up privileged positions to advocate true revolution. Of course, universities supported by public and private moneys produce socialized workers. So, consider this ending.

But all three of these endings indicate a measure of arrogance. The stories students read, write, and listen to in English I are only a small part of the universe of discourse that surrounds them and that they help to construct. Intro to Pomo Blues as performed by the composition establishment is just one tune playing in the background of student lives. My university strongly identifies itself as a Christian university The master narrative of the Christ story is a guide to core values and behavior for those who share Christian belief and gives students like Laura and Alex a way of evaluating what is at stake in their stories and a reason for committing themselves to one course of action or another, even though they may each interpret and apply the Christian story differently. Other students bring to the classroom the narratives of their own religious, cultural, and political beliefs. The classroom is only one arena in which these stories play out. Kurt Spellmeyer critiques theories that have "presupposed the existence of determining laws or codes that operate 'behind the back' of those subject to them." He argues, "what disappears from the 'behind-their-backs' tradition is any sense of how human subjects struggle to preserve their life-worlds against the imposition of alien values. This struggle, arguably the central issue of education, is nothing less than the central issue of postmodernity itself" (270–71). The university is implicated in the creation and maintenance of a post-modern world, but should neither underestimate nor overestimate its power.

Students are living postmodernism, not merely studying it. Some few are sure of their stories; most are, in my students' words, stressed, though scarcely able to articulate all the forces that are stressing them. Bombarded by so many tunes, the listener hears only noise. With few fixed reference points, many continue to struggle with the question, how is one to act ethically? Others—cynical, bored, alienated from community, education, and their own experience—do not ask the question.

Those who are successful in doing school manage the balancing act of post-modernism. Allison articulates the struggle between school and the sense of an authentic self as she writes in a self-analysis:

> When I think about writing, my mind conjures two images. Writing for school is a form of imprisonment. There are certain rules and guidelines to follow and a non-negotiable due date. There is pressure to finish it and I usually dread it so much that I don't do it until the night before, so it is sloppy and unorganized. But writing for pleasure is the exact opposite. It is freedom. I can write whatever I want, whenever I want, and not have to worry about it being judged (or "graded") or even read if I don't want it to be. I can release pent up frustration by letting my pen fly on its own. It is a form of therapy for me.

Allison goes on to testify that she is "learning to find a middle ground, to combine the two," especially through the process of revision. She credits feedback from her peers, writing center tutors, and me in changing her writing. Most importantly, she says explaining her ideas to international students in our class helped her "discover other ways I could take the paper, because during my explanations, new ideas would pop into my mind."

Allison's three-page self-analysis is thoughtful, detailed, sincere, and even amusing as she reviews her trials over the semester. It sounds like a happy ending. But then Allison figuratively winks at me and adds:

> The funny thing is that, as I reread this letter, I could see how I slanted it. I tried to portray myself as the hardworking student who is trying her very best to write well. And guess what? IT'S ALL TRUE! So I definitely deserve an A on this assignment!

And Allison is exactly right. It is all true. She is a hard-working student, and she has produced a polished portfolio of writing, and I have helped her do this. And she is making up her story to persuade me to give her an A. And I do give her the A.

This is the conclusion I am looking for. I think Allison gets what we have said about postmodernism all semester. English I is about telling stories, about the stories we tell students and the stories they tell us and the stories we construct together. At the same time, IT'S ALL TRUE, not because stones map a unified reality but because stories do have consequences, though I am not always as sure as Allison what these consequences are. Any ending I construct will have the same doubleness as Allison's conclusion. I sometimes lose the delicate academic balance and identify too strongly with the cynical, bored, and alienated who cannot muster Allison's enthusiasm. I wonder why I am standing in the front of the classroom. I cannot make romantic claims for the particular consequences of any one story, and I am skeptical of others who say they are able both to respect students' experience and to change their lives during a few months of Freshman Comp. I know something about language and something about rhetoric and writing that I can teach students. This is the theme of my song. Beyond that I struggle with issues of authenticity and authority. I improvise a postmodern tune.

Please feel free to sing along.

WORKS CITED

Bartholomae, David. "Inventing the University." *When a Writer Can't Write: Studies in Writer's Block and Other Composing Problems.* Ed. Mike Rose. New York: Guilford, 1985. 134–65.

Bartholomae, David, and Anthony Petrosky, eds. *Ways of Reading: An Anthology for Writers.* 2nd ed. Boston: Bedford, 1990.

Berlin, James A. "Postmodernism, Politics, and Histories of Rhetoric." Pre/Text 11 (1990): 170–87

——. "Poststructuralism, Cultural Studies, and the Composition Classroom: Postmodern Theory in Practice." *Rhetoric Review* 11(1992): 16–33.

Bialostosky, Don H. "Liberal Education, Writing, and the Dialogic Self." Harkin and Schilb 11–22.

Clifford, John, and John Schilb, eds. *Writing Theory and Critical Theory.* New York: MLA, 1994.

Faigley, Lester. *Fragments of Rationality: Postmodernity and the Subject of Composition.* Pittsburgh: U of Pittsburgh P, 1992.

——. Pomo Blues." Conference on College Composition and Communication. San Diego, April 1993.

Flannery, Kathryn. "Composing and the Question of Agency." *College English 53* (1991): 701–13.

Harkin, Patricia, and John Schilb, eds. *Contending with Words. Composition and Rhetoric in a Postmodern Age*. New York: MLA, 1991.

McLaren, Peter L., and Cohn Lankshear. "Critical Literacy and the Postmodern Turn." *Critical Literacy: Politics, Praxis, and the Postmodern.* Ed. Peter McLaren and Colin Lankshear. Albany: SUNY P, 1993. 379–419.

Miller, Susan. *Textual Carnivals: The Politics of Composition.* Carbondale: U of Illinois P, 1991.

Olson, Gary. "Theory and the Rhetoric of Assertion." *Composition Forum* 6 (1995): 53–61.

Patterson, Annette. "Individualism in English: From Personal Growth to Discursive Construction." *English Education* 24 (1992): 131–46.

Schilb, John. "Cultural Studies, Postmodernism, and Composition." Harkin and Schilb 173–88.

Slevin, James E. "Reading and Writing in the Classroom and the Profession." Clifford and Schilb 53–72.

Spellmeyer, Kurt. "'Too Little Care': Language, Politics, and Embodiment in the Life-World." *College English* 55 (1993): 265–83.

Summerfield, Judith. "Is There a Life in This Text? Reimagining Narrative." Clifford and Schilb 179–94.

Welch, Nancy. "Resisting the Faith: Conversion, Resistance, and the Training of Teachers." *College English* 55 (1993): 387–401.

Worsham, Lynn. "Writing against Writing: The Predicament of *Ecriture Féminine* in Composition Studies." Harkin and Schilb 82–104.

Vitanza, Victor J. "Three Countertheses: Or, A Critical In(ter)vention into Composition Theories and Pedagogies." Harkin and Schilb 139–72.

Zavarzadeh, Mas'ud, and Donald Morton. "A Very Good Idea Indeed: The (Post) Modern Labor Force and Curricular Reform." *Cultural Studies in the English Classroom.* Ed. James A. Berlin and Michael J. Vivion. Portsmouth, NH: Boynton/Cook. 66–86.

Toward a Social-Cognitive Understanding of Problematic Reading and Writing

Glynda Hull and Mike Rose

Glynda Hull and Mike Rose have published extensively, separately and together, about literacy and developmental English students. Hull's articles have appeared in such journals and books as CCC, Written Communication, Perspectives on Research and Scholarship in Composition, *and* Facts, Artifacts and Counterfacts. *Rose, a member of the faculty at UCLA, is best known for* Lives on the Boundary: The Struggles and Achievements of America's Underprepared *and* Possible Lives: The Promise of Public Education in America, *as well as two books about writer's block. This article appeared in* The Right to Literacy, *a collection of presentations from MLA's landmark Right to Literacy Conference in 1988. Hull and Rose's analysis of a paper written by Tanya, a student in a basic reading and writing class, reveals some of the complexities behind the writing problems of basic writing students and suggests ways to teach students like Tanya more effectively.*

All about us we hear news of a literacy crisis in America: the technicians who cannot read manuals, the unemployed workers who must struggle to fill in the blanks on a job application, the fathers who fail to decode the printed stories in their children's primers—all sorts of people, young, old, of varied races whose facility with written language is sufficiently poor to impair their functioning day to day. Associated with these reports—sometimes sensibly, sometimes not—is America's other population, one that we know intimately: that significant stratum of students (variously termed remedial, nontraditional, developmental, underprepared, nonmainstream) who enter higher education but are not prepared for the writing and reading tasks that they encounter.

Such students listen to teachers talk about sentence and paragraph structure; they fill in blanks in workbooks; they sit before material written in a language that is formal, complex, and strange. And they try to write. The small body of research that exists on what happens as such students try to write suggests that, for

---

them, composing is a slow, often derailed process that proceeds by rules and strategies that are often dysfunctional. But that is about the extent of our knowledge. Teachers receive these students' essays and try to evaluate them and make inferences about what the students learned or didn't learn, what their cognitive capacity is, whether or not they're fit for the institution that already classifies them as marginal. And teachers do so with a limited knowledge of the complex cognitive and social processes that produced the writing they read.

Clearly, we need further information on what it is that cognitively and socially defines an underprepared student as underprepared. What kind of knowledge does an underprepared student bring to the classroom? How is the teacher representing the writing process and the writing task? How is the student representing the teacher's discussion of the writing process and the writing task? What occurs between the two in the classroom as they attempt to negotiate a common understanding of the task, and in what ways might that interaction further define the student as remedial? What happens when the student sits down to write? Researchers have few answers to those questions; not a lot of research has addressed them.

We are conducting a research project on remediation at the community college, state college, and university level that, we hope, will provide some information on what it is that cognitively and socially defines an underprepared student as underprepared. The writing and reading classes we chose to study are those considered to be the most remedial in each of the institutions we visited. Students in these classes are very much at risk to succeed, and, in some ways, they present profound challenges to the stated mission of the institutions that enroll them.

We focus here on a piece of writing produced by Tanya, one of the students in a basic reading and writing class—close in level to an adult literacy program—in the urban community college we studied.[1] Tanya is nineteen years old, never finished high school, grew up in the inner city. We tutored her over a four-month period. We asked her, in the instance we focus on here, to write a paper that was more difficult than any she had done so far, one closer to the school-based writing tasks she would eventually confront if she moved closer to her goal of becoming a nurse's aide or a licensed vocational nurse. To meet her interests, we provided a simple case study written by a nurse, "Handling the Difficult Patient." The author gives a first-person account of her experiences with an ornery patient in a hospital. The nurse begins by sympathetically describing the patient—very ill, hooked to an intravenous tube, gaunt. She then details how she introduced herself and received a response of anger and rejection: "You're killing me, you XXX!" The next nine paragraphs of the article were marked up by Tanya and figured prominently in the piece of writing she did for us. Those nine paragraphs follow.

Case Study of a Difficult Patient

> "Oh, this is going to be a great day," I said to myself. "Just be patient, kind, and understanding. Maybe he only needs some TLC to alleviate his fears. He really seems more frightened than anything." With these thoughts, I began to care for him as skillfully as I could. [paragraph 4

of original text]

The day was exhausting. No matter what I did and no matter how gently I handled him, it was all to no avail. Sometimes the verbal abuse pounded and grated until it became almost physical. My nerves were frazzled; 3 P.M. just didn't come soon enough. [5]

In giving the evening nurse my report, I tried to provide a fair assessment of the situation and to prepare her for the ordeal that lay ahead. She was willing to give it a try, but if he proved too difficult, she said, she wouldn't remain on the case. [6]

My thoughts were similar, but deep down I really wanted to help him. What was the right approach? [7]

The next morning there was no night special to report. She had left the case, and the report she sent to the Registry of Nurses was so descriptive that it would be almost impossible to find a replacement. My second and third days were as terrible as the first. By the fourth day, the evening nurse decided she wouldn't take the abuse any longer and also left the case. To say I felt abandoned was an understatement; even the doctor didn't have any advice. [8]

The turning point came on my fifth day. I was attempting range of motion exercises with the patient. Despite his cursing, I explained the purpose of the therapy and told him I was doing it as gently as possible. He continued to object, and at one point I said, "I hope you understand that I'm doing this to help you." He growled sarcastically, "Oh, sure, girlie! You're doing this for me, are you? And I suppose for free, too." [9]

Well, five days of total frustration were enough. I was extremely hurt and angered. Retaliation had never been one of my methods, but this time it flowed out naturally. [10]

"You're right," I said. "I am getting paid for what I'm doing, but here's the difference: I have pride in my profession, and I earn my pay by giving my patients the best nursing care I possibly can. But I can give the minimum, too. I can sit here most of the day and still collect my 35 bucks at the end of the shift. If that's what you want, the choice is yours. So make up your mind fast, because I'm not taking any more of your abuse." [11]

Then I stopped what I was doing, picked up the newspaper, and proceeded to read it. I felt terrible about speaking that way to a patient. Never before had this happened. My confidence in my ability to keep calm was as shaky as my hands were. The patient was asleep when I left at 3 P.M. [12]

We asked Tanya to write a summary of the article, explaining to her that a summary is a short version of a reading that reports its main points. It is "what you would tell someone who hadn't read the article if they asked you, 'Tanya, what was that about?'" To gain some access to Tanya's composing process, we used a stimulated-recall procedure; that is, we videotaped Tanya as she wrote, recording the emergence of her text on the page (Rose). We then played the videotape for her to prompt her to recall what she was thinking as she wrote. The summary that Tanya wrote follows. After the whole process, we talked to her about her reading. We were satisfied that she had a general idea of what a summary is and that she understood the case study she had read.

Tanya's Summary of the Case Study

Page 1
1 The Handling About
2 difficult patient

3 this something telling about
4 a nurse ~~to~~ who won't to
5 help a patience.
6 She was a special night nurse,
7 this man had a stroke and
8 was ~~para~~ paralsis on his
9 left side. She Was really
10 doing a lot for the patience
11 She Introduced myself
12 she asked him How was
13 he feeling. remark was,"
14 XXX, can't you see 'Im in
15 pain?" he telling the nurse
16 he was in so much pain.

Page 2
17 he really didn't won't
18 to answer her. Before
19 she was ready to give
20 him his I.V. Are Anything
21 XXX "you're killing me,
22 you XXX."
23 Oh this going to Be a great
24 Day I said to myself
25 just thinking alone.
26 I have pride in What
27 I Do I am going to get
28 pad no matter what I am
29 still ~~am~~ going to collect
30 my money no matter
31 what happen I do Believe
32 and I no that In ~~my~~ mind
33 My thoughts were similar
34 but deep down.

Page 3
What was the approach?
A Registry nurse
was so descriptive.
impossible for me to
find a replacement.
My second and thirddays
she decided she ~~won~~ wouldn't
Abuse any longer and
~~Also~~ also left the case
felt Abandoned was an
understatement; even
this doctor In this case
she Really liked what she
was doing But was getting
treated Right Respect.
She had chance of getting
A another job But Don't
she wanted to But ~~I~~ then again
She wanted to.

Tanya's summary is the kind of writing that feeds everyone's worries about the consequences of illiteracy and the failure of our schools. It will also suggest to some people that this writer is somehow cognitively and linguistically deficient, that she is incoherent, can't think straight. But if we examine this piece of writing in context, taking into consideration the student's past experiences with schooling, her peculiar notions about reading and writing, the instruction she is currently receiving, her plans and goals for her future—that is, if we assume a coherence, if we assume that a learner's performance at any time has a history and, as Mina Shaughnessy taught us, a logic—we will think about this text and the student who wrote it quite differently.

Part of the seeming incoherence of Tanya's text falls away when we look at the text she was summarizing (see table 1). Tanya marked up the text she was reading, underlining and bracketing sentences and paragraphs that she considered important—paragraphs 7 and 11, for example. When we examine Tanya's summary against her marked-up source text, we see that she lifted some of these sentences and parts of sentences from the original and situated them in her summary, though not in the way we would expect. For example, lines 23 through 39 of her summary are bits and pieces drawn from disparate parts of the original text.

When we examine what Tanya takes from the case study, how she modifies those sentences and phrases, and how she situates them in her summary, we notice two things: she makes slight modifications in the original, changing a word here and there but copying whole chunks verbatim, and she juxtaposes segments of the original without connecting them each to the other. For example, a phrase taken from paragraph 11 in the original is put next to one from paragraph 7, which comes next to one from paragraph 8, with no apparent attention to the features of discourse that allow readers to construct a coherent text.

Table 1. Juxtaposing the Case Study and Tanya's Summary

Original text	*Student's summary (lines 23–39)*
"Oh, this is going to be a great day," I said to myself. [paragraph 4]	23 Oh this going to Be a great 24 Day I said to myself 25 just thinking alone.
I have pride in my profession [paragraph 11]	26 I have pride in What 27 I Do I am going to get
But I can give the minimum, too. I can sit here most of the day and still collect my 35 bucks at the end of the shift. [paragraph 11]	28 pad no matter what I am 29 still ~~am~~ going to collect 30 my money no matter 31 what happen I do Believe 32 and I no that In ~~my~~ mind.
My thoughts were similar, but deep down I really wanted to help him. What was the right approach? [paragraph 7]	33 My thoughts were similar 34 but deep down. 35 What was the approach?
. . . the report she sent to the Registry of Nurses was so descriptive that it would be almost impossible to find a replacement. [paragraph 8]	36 A Registry nurse 37 was so descriptive. 38 impossible for me to 39 find a replacement.

Tanya had a patchwork approach to writing a summary, and, when we began to talk to her, we learned why. We pointed to some of the sentences she had lifted from the case study and modified slightly before patching them into her summary. For example, she changed the nurse's statement "I have pride in my profession" to "I have pride in what I do." In response to our question as to the purpose of her modifications, she answered, "I have practice from when I try not to copy. When I get a little bit from there, a teacher'll really know what I'm talking about . . . then if some parts from there I change a little bit, they know I'm not really that kind of student that would copy, 'cause another student would copy."

Tanya seems to be operating with two intentions here: to display and convey knowledge ("a teacher'll really know what I'm talking about") and to show she's "not. . . that kind of student that would copy." Tanya wants to be a successful student this time around, so displaying knowledge is for her a powerful and understandable signal of her good academic citizenship. What is intriguing here, though, is the procedural rule she invokes when writing her summary: change a few words so as not to copy. This injunction against plagiarism is probably a holdover from some past instruction. The thing that interests us about this rule is that it is a good reminder what a powerful hold negative injunctions can have on students; it also recalls for us that school has been mainly punitive for Tanya. In our formal interviews with Tanya, in our talks with her after class, in her essays and writings throughout the semester, we heard many variations on this theme: being kicked out of five high schools during her senior year, being hit on the hand with rulers, being chastised in the middle of reading class for not coming to school, feigning sleep for fear of being called on. Here is an example:

> **TANYA:** I was scared a lot.
> **INTERVIEWER:** Just scared of reading out loud or. . .?
> **TANYA:** 'Cause see, the only reason I was scared was 'cause the teacher, she would look on an attendance list, and she would see who was that person reading. And she would call out that person's name and ask you, "What is your problem?" and look at my attendance and know that I ain't been coming to school. And she would get on me, and that's what I would be scared of. 'Cause she'd call my name out, have me to come up here and just stop everything. (interview, 6 Oct.)

We heard so many negative memories of schooling and literacy instruction from Tanya and other students that we began to appreciate anew the power of directives like "Don't plagiarize," even when they aren't explained or aren't contextualized or in some other way don't make sense to students.

Another rule that seemed to govern Tanya's construction of the summary had to do with selection. Remember that she had marked up the case study, picking out things that interested her. We learned from our interviews with her that she changed whole sentences around not only because she wanted to avoid plagiarism hut because "the parts about the nurse are something about me. . .you see 'I have pride,' you see, I can read that for me." In her construction of the summary, then, she seemed to privilege propositions that related to herself. While some of the details she included in her summary contained its gist, she tended to choose details not because they were important to the original text but because they were important to her; their placement, therefore, had more a personal than a textual relevance.

We saw this again and again in both her reading and her writing. Texts sometimes didn't appear to have a coherent identity apart from Tanya as a reader; the importance of the text tended to be in direct relation to its importance to her. This practice led some of her teachers to think she was a flake, but we should also recall that the practice resembles the kind of reading strategies that teachers may encourage her to use, that actually resemble expert ones: interact with the text, relate it to your own experiences, derive your own meaning from it. In fact, Tanya's reading teacher encouraged all her students to take what she called star notes—notes that would make them star readers. These notes were a dialogue that students were supposed to have with the author of the text.

Another way to understand Tanya's penchant for privileging propositions that related to herself is to read this strategy as an interesting assertion of her own self-worth in relation to a life and a school history that had left her feeling that she wasn't worth much. A theme that rises, phoenixlike, from our many pages of transcripts of tutoring sessions and interviews is Tanya's assertion that she can do it, she can make it, she can learn and succeed.

> "I'm going to get a little bit better in my reading and my math. All the test I think I'm capable of doing." (9 Sept., first interview statement)
>
> "I can do that, too [write a comparison-contrast essay]. I can do a lot of things." (20 Oct.)
>
> "I know I can do it. I know I can do it. That's what I really need [to improve her writing and math]." (27 Oct.)

The way Tanya aggressively appropriates the meaning of a text to suit her own interests parallels for us the chorus she repeats over and over again: I can make it, I have pride and confidence in myself, I really am going to be a nurse. Such goals and dreams allow her to identify with the nurse in the case study, and it is likely that they orient, to a disproportionate extent, her construction of that reading and writing task and perhaps other school literacy tasks as well. Tanya had a lot of strikes against her: kicked out of school, on the outs with her mother and an overbearing stepfather, living on her own in a drug-infested apartment complex, pulled by a legion of boyfriends—"the only thing good in my life," she once said. Tanya has got to hold on for dear life to the idea that she can be a nurse, that she is important, that she can succeed.

Tanya's bizarre word salad is, perhaps, not so bizarre after all. Still, one's heart sinks when one places Tanya's statements about her hopes and dreams next to a text that, though now better understood, is still exceptionally flawed mechanically, grammatically, and orthographically. Her errors are the stigma of illiteracy. What is a teacher to do? First, we want to recall that Tanya's essay is a first draft, and our experience with her has shown us that, with instruction to revise and proofread, she would most likely correct some of her punctuation, capitalizing, and spelling errors. Still, a revised version would be littered with many errors, and it would be hard to ignore them. One of the rewards, though, that comes from working with marginal students is that they force you again and again to scrutinize your own reactions, to question your received assumptions about literacy and pedagogy, about cognition, and about the purposes of discourse. After wrestling with our own concerns about the errors in Tanya's written language, about all those markers of illiteracy, it struck us that something profoundly literate is going on here. A fundamental social and psychological reality about discourse, oral or written, is that human beings continually appropriate each other's language to establish group membership, to grow, and to define themselves in new ways. Socially oriented linguists discuss the way this impulse plays itself out in speech, but it can occur as well with written discourse (see Bartholomae; Lanham; Witte).[2] Tanya's appropriation of the nurse's text, with enough words changed to signal that she's not the kind of student who would copy, is related to her desire to redefine her life, to make it, to be a nurse's aide or a licensed vocational nurse. Tanya is trying on the nurse's written language and, with it, the nurse's self.

A powerful pedagogic next move with Tanya would be to temporarily suspend concern about errors and pursue, full tilt, her impulse to don the written language of another. What she seems to need at this point in her reentry into the classroom is a freewheeling pedagogy of imitation, one that encourages her to try on the language of essays like the nurses's case study, essays related to health care that are accessible and tie in with Tanya's hopes for herself. Then, gradually, the teacher could begin calling attention to certain sentence patterns through a focused imitation; could help Tanya make and develop discourse patterns, like the chronological one she's trying to follow in the summary we presented; could show her some simple ways to effect coherent transitions from one bit of language to another; could teach her a few conventions that would enable her to use the texts of others in ways that show she's not copying. The teacher could, in short, help Tanya shape her writing in the way the nurse and other such authors are shaping theirs.

At the same time that we outline a pedagogy to move Tanya toward a conventional discourse, we are aware of what her unconventional performance can teach us. We are struck by her "plagiarism," for example, not only because it is a startling departure from traditional ways of using a source text but because it puts into the foreground what is often an unquestioned practice in the Western essayist tradition. We academic writers internalize rules and strategies for citing source texts, for acknowledging debts to previous scholarship, for separating what we can claim as our own ideas from the intellectual property of others. And we do so, once we have learned the tricks of our trade, almost without thinking, producing essays that seem to mark clearly where other people's ideas end and ours begin. Such clearly documented writing may let us forget or even camouflage how much more it is that we borrow from existing texts, how much we depend on membership in a community for our language, our voices, our very arguments. We forget that we, like Tanya, continually appropriate each other's language to establish group membership, to grow, and to define ourselves in new ways and that such appropriation is a fundamental part of language use, even as the appearance of our texts belies it.

We have given one snapshot of some of the social and cognitive variables surrounding one piece of writing from one of the students we studied in a community college. As we and those working on the project with us continue to examine our data—texts, videotapes of classroom interaction, audiotapes of tutorial sessions, speak-aloud and stimulated-recall sessions—we hope that our research will provide answers to the following questions:

1. What productive and counterproductive strategies, habits, rules, and assumptions tend to characterize the writing and reading skills of underprepared students?
2. How are these strategies represented in the students' minds, and what personal, social, and historical forces may have influenced these current representations?
3. What tends to happen to these strategies, rules, and assumptions during instruction?
4. What mismatches or points of convergence tend to occur between pedagogies or programs and the students' background knowledge, experiences, and goals?
5. What are the social and institutional processes whereby students like Tanya are defined as deficient or remedial or substandard?

We are hoping to bring to bear several layers of information on the problem of underpreparation in reading and writing. By comparing the data we collect in our three sites—the community college, the state college, and the university—and by making sure that our work is many-layered, we hope to construct rich descriptions of the knowledge, assumptions, and behaviors that characterize and influence underprepared students' creation and use of texts. In the process we hope to devise a social and cognitive framework for analyzing the discourse produced by underprepared students, a framework that allows us to go beyond merely describing textual features, to understanding the production of those features. Moving from textual features, whether written or oral, to a description of those knowledge structures that yielded those features and moving from a description of those knowledge structures to an understanding of their origins in a broader context is the tough problem that we want to work on. We hope, finally, to construct a set of vivid examples that may be used in teacher or tutor training, examples that illustrate dysfunctional reading and writing strategies and reveal the social and cognitive factors influencing them. We hope these vignettes will provoke some epiphanies, that they will move us all toward a different and richer representation of literacy instruction for underprepared students—toward a redefinition of *remedial*, away from the deficit orientation it currently has and toward a richer, more informed, and generative conception.[3]

NOTES

1 This piece of writing is also discussed in Hull, "Literacy, Technology and the Underprepared." In that essay Tanya was identified by the different pseudonym of Ariel, a rather literary name used to capture what seemed to be her essence, a mischievousness and a wonderful lightness of being in the face of difficult circumstances.

2 Our thanks go to Stephen Witte for helping us shape this discussion.

3 An extended version of this essay appears in *Written Communication* 16 (Apr.1989):139–54.

We would like to thank our colleagues for their assistance at various stages of this project: Kay Losey Fraser, Marisa Garrett, Peter Simon, Susan Thompson-Lowry, Smokey Wilson, and Stephen Witte. Our work has been supported by the Spenser Foundation, the Center for the Study of Writing, and the James S. McDonnell Foundation's Program in Cognitive Studies for Educational Practice.

WORKS CITED

Bartholomae, David. "Inventing the University." *When a Writer Can't Write.* Ed. M. Rose. New York: Guilford, 1985. 134–65.

Hull, Glynda A. "Literacy, Technology and the Underprepared: Notes toward a Framework for Action." *Quarterly of the National Writing Project and the Center for the Study of Writing,* 10 (1988): 1–3, 16–25.

Lanham, Richard A. *Style: An Anti-Textbook.* New Haven: Yale UP, 1974.

Rose, Mike. *Writer's Block: The Cognitive Dimension.* Carbondale: Southern Illinois UP, 1984.

Shaughnessy, Mina. *Errors and Expectations.* New York: Oxford UP, 1977.

Witte, Stephen P. "Some Contexts for Understanding Written Literacy." Right to Literacy Conference. Columbus, Ohio, Sept. 1988.

SUGGESTED READINGS: GENERAL THEORIES AND PERSPECTIVES

Adler-Kassner, Linda, Robert Crooks, and Ann Watters, eds. *Writing the Community: Concepts and Models for Service-Learning in Composition.* Washington: AAHE, 1997.

Berthoff, Ann E. *The Making of Meaning: Metaphors, Models, and Maxims for Writing Teachers.* Upper Montclair, NJ: Boynton/Cook, 1981.

Bishop, Wendy, and Hans Ostrom, eds. *Genre and Writing: Issues, Arguments, Alternatives.* Portsmouth, NH: Boynton/Cook, 1997.

Bleich, David. *Know and Tell: A Writing Pedagogy of Disclosure, Genre, and Membership.* Portsmouth, NH: Boynton/Cook, 1998.

Bizzell, Patricia. *Academic Discourse and Critical Consciousness.* Pittsburgh: U of Pittsburgh P, 1992.

Bullock, Richard, John Trimbur, and Charles Schuster, eds. *The Politics of Writing Instruction: Postsecondary.* Portsmouth, NH: Boynton/Cook, 1991.

Connors, Robert J., Lisa S. Ede, and Andrea A. Lunsford, eds. *Essays on Classical Rhetoric and Modern Discourse.* Carbondale: Southern Illinois UP, 1984.

Coles, William E., Jr. *The Plural I—and After.* Portsmouth, NH: Boynton/Cook, 1988.

Cooper, Marilyn M., and Michael Holzman. *Writing as Social Action.* Portsmouth, NH: Boynton/Cook, 1989.

Covino, William A., and David A. Jolliffe, eds. *Rhetoric: Concepts, Definitions, Boundaries.* Boston: Allyn & Bacon, 1995.

Crowley, Sharon. *Composition in the University: Historical and Polemical Essays.* Pittsburgh: U of Pittsburgh P, 1998.

Donahue, Patricia, and Ellen Quandahl, eds. *Reclaiming Pedagogy: The Rhetoric of the Classroom.* Carbondale: Southern Illinois UP, 1989.

Elbow, Peter, ed. *Landmark Essays on Voice and Writing.* Davis, CA: Hermagoras, 1994.

Enos, Theresa, and Stuart C. Brown, eds. *Professing the New Rhetorics: A Sourcebook.* Englewood Cliffs, NJ: Blair, 1994.

Faigley, Lester. *Fragments of Rationality: Postmodernity and the Subject of Rationality*. Pittsburgh: U of Pittsburgh P, 1992.

Foster, David. *A Primer for Writing Teachers: Theorists, Issues, Problems*. 2nd ed. Portsmouth, NH: Boynton/Cook, 1992.

Flower, Linda. *The Construction of Negotiated Meaning: A Social Cognitive Theory of Writing*. Carbondale: Southern Illinois UP, 1994.

Freedman, Aviva, and Peter Medway, eds. *Learning and Teaching Genre*. Portsmouth, NH: Boynton/Cook, 1994.

Fulwiler, Toby. *College Writing: A Personal Approach to Academic Writing*. 2nd ed. Portsmouth, NH: Boynton/Cook, 1997.

Halasek, Kay. *A Pedagogy of Possibility: Bakhtinian Perspectives on Composition Studies*. Carbondale: Southern Illinois UP, 1999.

Helmers, Marguerite H. *Writing Students: Composition Testimonials and Representations of Students*. Albany: SUNY P, 1994.

Jensen, George H., and John K. DiTiberio. *Personality and the Teaching of Composition*. Norwood, NJ: Ablex, 1989.

Kinneavy, James L. *A Theory of Discourse*. New York: Norton, 1971.

Lindemann, Erika. *A Rhetoric for Writing Teachers*. 3rd ed. New York: Oxford UP, 1995.

Malinowitz, Harriet. *Textual Orientations: Lesbian and Gay Students and the Making of Discourse Communities*. Portsmouth, NH: Boynton/Cook, 1995.

Moffett, James. *Teaching the Universe of Discourse*. Portsmouth, NH: Boynton/Cook, 1983.

Murphy, James J., ed. *A Short History of Writing Instruction: From Ancient Greece to Twentieth-Century America*. Davis, CA: Hermagoras, 1990.

Neman, Beth S. *Teaching Students to Write*. 2nd ed. New York: Oxford UP, 1995.

Newkirk, Thomas, ed. *Nuts and Bolts: A Practical Guide to Teaching College Composition*. Portsmouth, NH: Boynton/Cook, 1993.

Rankin, Elizabeth. *Seeing Yourself as a Teacher: Conversations with Five New Teachers in a University Writing Program*. Urbana, IL: NCTE, 1994.

Shepard, Alan, John McMillan, and Gary Tate, eds. *Coming to Class: Pedagogy and the Social Class of Teachers*. Portsmouth, NH: Boynton/Cook, 1998.

Simons, Elizabeth Radin. *Student Worlds, Student Words: Teaching Writing Through Folklore*. Portsmouth, NH: Boynton/Cook, 1990.

Smith, Maggy. *Teaching College Writing*. Boston: Allyn & Bacon, 1995.

Spellmeyer, Kurt. *Common Ground: Dialogue, Understanding, and the Teaching of Composition*. Englewood Cliffs, NJ: Prentice Hall, 1993.

Sternglass, Marilyn S. *Time to Know Them: A Longitudinal Study of Writing and Learning at the College Level*. Mahwah, NJ: Lawrence Erlbaum, 1997.

Williams, James D. *Preparing to Teach Writing: Research, Theory, and Practice*. 2nd ed. Mahwah, NJ: Lawrence Erlbaum, 1998.

Winterowd, W. Ross, with Jack Blum. *A Teacher's Introduction to Composition in the Rhetorical Tradition*. Urbana, IL: NCTE, 1994.

Young, Richard E., Alton L. Becker, and Kenneth L. Pike. *Rhetoric: Discovery and Change*. New York: Harcourt, Brace and World, 1970.

SUGGESTED READINGS: BASIC WRITING

Bartholomae, David. "Inventing the University." *When a Writer Can't Write: Studies in Writer's Block and Other Composing-Process Problems*. Ed. Mike Rose. New York: Guilford, 1985.

Bartholomae, David. "The Tidy House: Basic Writing in the American Curriculum." *Journal of Basic Writing* 12 (1993): 4-21.

Delpit, Lisa D. "The Silenced Dialogue: Power and Pedagogy in Educating Other People's Children." *Harvard Educational Review* 58 (1988): 280–98.

DiPardo, Anne. *A Kind of Passport: A Basic Writing Adjunct Program and the Challenge of Student Diversity*. Urbana, IL: NCTE, 1993.

Enos, Theresa. *A Sourcebook for Basic Writing Teachers*. New York: Random, 1987.

Horner, Bruce, and Min-Zhan Lu. *Representing the "Other": Basic Writers and the Teaching of Basic Writing*. Urbana, IL: NCTE, 1999.

Kasden, Lawrence N., and Daniel R. Hoeber, eds. *Basic Writing: Essays for Teachers, Researchers, Administrators*. Urbana, IL: NCTE, 1980.

Laurence, Patricia, Peter Rondinone, Barbara Gleason, Thomas J. Farrell, Paul Hunter, and Min-Zhan Lu. "Symposium on Basic Writing." *College English* 55 (1993): 879–903.

Moran, Michael G., and Martin J. Jacobi, eds. *Research in Basic Writing: A Bibliographic Sourcebook*. Westport, CT: Greenwood, 1990.

Rose, Mike. "The Language of Exclusion: Writing Instruction at the University." *College English* 47 (1985): 341–59.

Rose, Mike. "Narrowing the Mind and the Page: Remedial Writers and Cognitive Reductionism." *CCC* 39 (1988): 267–302.

Shaughnessy, Mina P. *Errors and Expectations: A Guide for the Teacher of Basic Writing*. New York: Oxford UP, 1977.

More Meanings of "Audience"

Jack Selzer

Jack Selzer, a professor in the English department at Penn State University, has written numerous articles on rhetorical theory and scientific writing as well as the popular composition textbook Conversations. *This 1992 article, originally published in* A Rhetoric of Doing: Essays on Written Discourse in Honor of James L. Kinneavy, *summarizes the major theories in rhetoric and literary studies about the reader or audience as well as other related theories. Selzer attempts to reconcile theories of "addressed audiences" (the people who actually read the text) and "invoked audiences" (the readers imagined by the writer or implied by the text) to explain the complicated relationship between writer and audience.*

A major source of frustration—and fascination—within English studies these days is that certain basic concepts once regarded as givens within the profession have come into dispute. *Author, text, literature, genre:* in a postmodern, poststructuralist time, all these terms have become problematic. A quarter century after Roland Barthes in *Image Music Text* declared the "author" dead; two decades after reader-response critics declared the text an event (not an entity) and genre critics found conventional forms to be dynamic organisms rather than static containers; ten years after everyone from Stanley Fish to Terry Eagleton to Robert Scholes concluded that distinctions between *literature* and *nonliterature* cannot survive critique—now all these terms have become the occasion for discussion, dispute, confusion, and loads of commentary.

And so it is with *audience.* Once a stable referent, *audience* has become fractured into *audiences,* into a not-always-peaceable and too-often-fragmented kingdom of terms, complete with colorful relatives, feuding rivals, strange bedfellows, and new arrivals turning up each month. What exactly are the differences and relationships between "evoked" and "invoked" audiences? Or between "narratees" and "implied readers"? Or between "demographic" and "fictionalized" audiences? Or between "fictionalized," "intended," "ideal," "inscribed," and "universal" audiences? What is the difference between "audience" and "discourse community"? What do technical writing textbooks mean by "multiple audiences"? Is it useful to conceive of audiences and readers as distinct entities? How do texts signal

---

the differences among all of these characters? And how does one devise a pedagogy for "audience" that would improve reading and writing? The aim of this essay is to address these questions, to straighten out some of the current confusion that has converged about the term *audience.* I certainly do not expect to succeed completely in that endeavor—the issues are complex and slippery—but I do hope to clarify some matters, especially for people who teach rhetoric and writing. Failing that, perhaps I can at least throw into relief the ambiguities involved in understanding the meanings of audience.

Not that there hasn't already been considerable progress made on the question of audience. In the field of rhetoric and composition, two articles have especially clarified and stimulated my own thinking on the subject: Lisa Ede and Andrea Lunsford's "Audience Addressed/Audience Invoked: The Role of Audience in Composition Theory and Pedagogy" and Douglas Park's "The Meanings of 'Audience.'"[1] Chiefly in order to influence pedagogical practice, Ede and Lunsford identify, explicate, and finally synthesize the two basic schools of audience study, which they term (after the example of Henry Johnstone) *audience addressed* and *audience invoked.* Those people (often associated with speech departments) who envision audience as "addressed," Ede and Lunsford explain, emphasize the concrete reality of "real people" who receive messages, while those who consider audience as "invoked" (often literary theorists) stress the "fictional" audience present in the text itself. Take the case of a recent article in the *Wall Street Journal* by Milton Friedman entitled "An Open Letter to William Bennett," on the subject of legalizing drugs (see the Appendix; I will return to this example throughout this essay). Readers of the *Wall Street Journal* article, including Bennett himself, for instance, are real people—an audience addressed. But the "William Bennett" in the "open letter" itself is a fictional character created by Friedman—an audience invoked. For rhetorical purposes—to win the assent of real readers—writers invoke or create within their texts fictional readers (who correspond to fictional authors, sometimes called "implied authors" or "narrators" or "personae"). Walter Ong and Wayne Booth, among others, contend that all discourse contains invoked (or "fictionalized" or "created" or "implied") audiences cast by means of textual cues into a role that real readers are then invited to assume.

Ede and Lunsford strive for a "synthesis" of the two perspectives that will be useful in the composing process. They seek "a fully elaborated view of audience" that will "balance the creativity of the writer with the creativity of the reader" (169):

> The addressed audience, the actual ... readers of a discourse, exists outside of the text. Writers may analyze these readers' needs, anticipate their biases, even defer to their wishes. But it is only through the text, through language, that writers embody or give life to their conception of the reader. In so doing, they do not so much create a role for the reader—a phrase which implies that the writer somehow creates a mold to which the reader adapts—as invoke it.

Douglas Park's essay, written two years before Ede and Lunsford's, works from their same central distinction and contains their same interest in pedagogy. According to Park, there are "two general directions of meaning of 'audience'—outside the text and back into the text" (250)—which Park then divides into four more specific meanings: (a) anyone who happens to read a given discourse; (b) external readers or listeners as they are involved in the rhetorical situation; (c) the set of conventions that shape the discourse as something to be heard; (d) an ideal conception shadowed forth in the way the discourse itself defines and creates contexts for readers. The first two specify "real" readers outside the text; the last two refer to fictional readers created within the text. While Park does mention the first two, does acknowledge real "people-as-they-are-involved in a rhetorical situation" (244), his main interest is in exploring the latter two, which he claims are "obviously the most important" (250). In his difficult but stimulating analysis, he therefore tends to treat audience essentially as "a metaphor" (252) for the set of conventions, contexts, and aspects of knowledge that writers use to create meaning. He would "replace the idea of 'audience' with a set of questions as to how the work ... establishes or possesses the contexts that make it meaningful" (252). And when he calls for a more systematic and precise "map of the territory of audience" (256), he really means a map of the audience *in the text.*

I want to provide some of this mapping that Park calls for; I want to contribute to "the fully elaborated view of audience" that Ede and Lunsford seek. By way of a general thesis, let me provide a map of my own (fig. 1), a chart of the "meanings of *audience*" as I understand them and as those meanings might relate to each other and as I will discuss them in this essay. My catalogue of the meanings

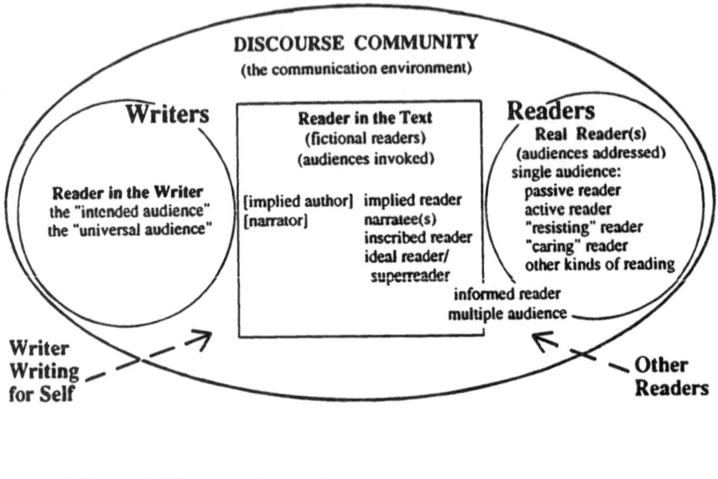

Figure 1 The meanings of <u>audience</u> for and in a given document

of *audience* includes both the *audiences invoked* in the text ("the reader in the text") and the *audiences addressed* outside it ("real readers"). But audiences in the text may be distinguished: as I will explain, there are implied readers, narratees, inscribed readers, informed readers, and ideal readers (to name some of them). "Real" audiences outside the text may be distinguished, too: there are single (or homogeneous) and multiple (heterogeneous) audiences. But in neither case are real audiences the same thing as a *discourse community,* a broader concept synonymous with *culture* or *environment* or *social setting.* Finally, there is also such a thing as a reader in the writer (the intended audience). Even this short overview should make my general aim clearer. I mean to rehabilitate some of the elements deemphasized by Park and to problematize some of the constructs used by Ede and Lunsford in their pedagogically oriented synthesis. I work from their basic distinction between the reader in the text and the reader outside the text (I prefer *reader* to *audience* to make clear that I am discussing audience only in terms of written discourse), but I also consider the reader in the writer as well. Furthermore, I treat audience and reader not as monoliths: I want to call attention to the multiplicity of readers inside and outside the text because puzzling out the distinctions enriches our sense of audience. And I want to clear up some misconceptions about audience, chiefly in connection with the term *discourse community,* that have arisen since Park and Ede and Lunsford wrote. Thus, while my ultimate aim is similar to theirs—to subdue the meanings of audience for the sake of teaching—my perspective is somewhat broader and more abstract. My hope is that this essay might come to be read as a supplement—it is not a correction—to Park and Ede and Lunsford, a gloss and an extension, if you will.

The Reader in the Writer: "The Intended Reader"

In all the recent interest in real audiences and in created audiences within texts, it should not be forgotten that audience can also be seen as a writer-based concept. From the writer's point of view, *audience* may have little to do with the identities of the actual people who later actually read the document. An intended audience, in fact, may never even see the document; conversely, some of those who do see the document (e.g., teachers or editors or supervisors or someone in the distant future yet unborn) may not be intended readers. For *intended audience* denotes the mental construct in the writer that aids the act of invention and directs the features of the developing text; it denotes the more or less concrete representation of readers that the writer conceives during composition and then uses to condition his or her developing work. For instance, Milton Friedman's sense of "the people who read the *Wall Street Journal*" was very likely one influence on the composition of his letter. Friedman's internal sense of William Bennett's personality and beliefs may have been another such influence; whether Bennett ever actually read the letter or not, his image may well have affected Friedman during the acts of invention, arrangement, and revision. The same could be true of the Alabama clergymen mentioned in King's famous "Letter from Birmingham Jail": whether those clergymen ever read King's letter or not, they almost certainly served as some of King's intended readers—

readers whose image stimulated King during the act of composing. King may have had other readers in mind as well as he planned and drafted and revised.

For we know that writers conceive of audiences as they write; we know that the intended audience[2] does influence the creative process—even if the resulting texts are never actually read. Mikhail Bakhtin insists, for example, that "the listener and his (or her) response are regularly taken into account when it comes to everyday dialogue and rhetoric, but every other sort of discourse as well is oriented toward an understanding that is 'responsive.' Responsive understanding is a fundamental force, one that participates in the formulation of discourse" (280). More empirically, Carol Berkenkotter has documented through protocol analysis that a sense of audience influences writers in the process of composition, that "the internal representation or mental sketch a writer makes of the audience is an essential part of the writing process" (396). Peter Elbow concurs: his "argument for ignoring audience" during composing recognizes both implicitly and explicitly that people do regard audience as they write; Elbow would simply advise writers to push audience into the background at certain points in the creative act and especially to disregard any threatening or intimidating audiences that impede the composing process or that diminish the value of writing for the writer. From the perspective of developmental psychology, Barry Kroll, Bennett Rafoth, and Donald Rubin and Gene Piche document how children learn to "decenter"—to consider the perspective and personalities of others—as they grow as writers. My own favorite example of the writer-based nature of audience comes from the testimony of the eminent British evolutionary biologist John Maynard Smith. He claims that he keeps two readers in mind as he writes: "an intelligent but ignorant 16-year-old ... [i.e.,] myself when young" and "an even more ignorant British Civil Servant, bent on improving his mind" and modeled on "an actual person, [a relative] of mine." In any case, there is plenty of reason to support the writing teacher's perennial exhortation to students, "Consider your audience as you write!"

And there is additional theoretical support for the notion as well, since no less an authority than Chaim Perelman argues that "an orator wishing to persuade a particular audience must of necessity adapt himself to it" (20). Perelman, who gives primary emphasis to the canon of invention, conceives of audience—particularly his "universal audience"—as a speaker- or writer-based construct. According to Perelman, audience determines the direction and substance that an argument will take. Three such audiences are possible:

> The first such audience consists of the whole of mankind, or at least, of all normal, adult persons; we shall refer to it as the *universal audience.* The second consists of the single *interlocutor* whom a speaker addresses in a dialogue. The third is the *subject himself* when he deliberates or gives himself reasons for his actions. (Perelman 30; quoted in Ray)

Perelman sees audience—and particularly the *universal audience,* a theoretical collection of rational people whose values and beliefs are grounded on rational thought—as more than a real object to which a rhetor directs arguments. It becomes "an active participant in the argumentation process" (Anderson 40), "a mental concept of the speaker" (Ray 363).[3]

The problem is, *how do* and *how should* writers think of audience? Do writers (and should writers) think of concrete persons as they write—as for example Maynard Smith's relative? Or is the representation of audience in the writer's mind an idealization, a creation-like Maynard Smith's "intelligent but ignorant 16-year-old"? Can audience in the writer be "universal" and philosophical, as Perelman maintains? (King's rational, philosophical "Letter" might imply an affirmative answer to that question.) Or is the reader in the writer something more abstract—something like Berkenkotter's "mental sketch"? Or something more abstract still—something closer to the "conventions" of text discussed by Park? Is it, in short, the experience of writers with real readers that tells writers what to include and how? Or is it the experience of writers with reading—with what the reading experience comprises—that enables writers to write, since writing assumes a system of shared conventions?

There is evidence for all these senses of audience within writers. Charlotte Thralls and her colleagues, for instance, found both "real" and "implied" audiences simultaneously in the minds of writers. Their protocol analyses turned up "exophoric referents" that pointed to real readers in the minds of writers as well as "endophoric referents" that pointed to readers as conventional features of texts. Robert Roth found the same range in his student writers' sense of audience as they wrote: some students projected themselves as readers; others incorporated the viewpoints of different (sometimes several) real readers; others had only indefinite and largely text-based senses of audience. Not only that, Roth's students revised their sense of audience as they composed. Audiences expanded, or grew more concrete (or less distinct), or became more realistic or more idealized or more (or less) like their authors or more implicated in the developing text. Like texts themselves in the process of construction, "audience is subject to revision" (Roth 53).

The Reader in the Text

Whatever the status of the reader in the writer, the presence of the intended reader is ultimately manifested in the text itself. In the case of spoken rhetoric, audiences are nearly always "real"—real people on hand for the occasion of the speech. But in the case of writing, audiences are textual presences as well as intended or real ones. But just how are audiences realized in the text?

Answering that question has occupied the energies of several reader-response critics over the past several decades. Walker Gibson and Wayne Booth in the 1950s noticed the presence in fiction of what they called "the mock reader" or "the implied reader"; later, Walter Ong contended that "the writer's audience is always a fiction" no matter what the genre: "the historian, the scholar or scientist, and the simple letter writer all fictionalize their audiences, casting them in a made-up role" (17). According to Gibson, Booth, and Ong, not only does a rhetorical transaction involve a real writer and a real audience; it also involves an implied author distinct from the real author and an implied reader distinct from the real reader—an implied reader created in the text by means of textual conventions. Just as the implied author or persona of this essay is distinct from the "real" Jack Selzer, so the implied reader is distinct from real readers. In Booth's words: "The author creates ... an image of himself and another image of his reader; he makes his reader [i.e., the implied reader], as he makes his second self" (*Rhetoric of Fiction* 138). The implied reader of a particular text, who is distinct from the reader implied by other texts, is known through the background knowledge and assumptions and values and other human characteristics implied by the language of that text. The implied reader created in the first sentences of Friedman's letter, for instance, is an American citizen (implied by the phrase "our foreign policy") who accepts the freemarket assumptions apparent in paragraphs three and six, shares the sense of crisis apparent in the second half of the piece, sympathizes with "innocent" victims of current drug policy (paragraphs five, six, and nine), sees the drug problem more pragmatically than morally (note the reference to Billy Sunday), and has the historical knowledge to understand references to "Oliver Cromwell," "Billy Sunday," and "the prohibition of alcoholic beverages." The implied reader, the "we" and "our" and "us" of the letter, has something in common with the "you" and "Bill Bennett," but (as will become further apparent in a moment) is quite distinct nevertheless. By creating implied readers and implied authors like this, authors enact conversations that real readers listen in on.

Implied readers invite a reading behavior that real readers may accept, if they so choose. Gibson, Booth, and Ong all assert that real readers *must* take on the roles implied by a well-written text: they are "called on ... to play the role assigned" (Ong 17); they must "subordinate [their] mind and heart to the book" (Booth, *Rhetoric of Fiction 138).* But that is surely an overstatement. Real readers may or may not identify with the implied reader. Wolfgang Iser's account of the implied reader accordingly allows for more flexible reading behavior on the part of real readers. Though not without its problems (Iser at times conflates the real reader and the reader in the text), his formulation allows for an active reader who may well choose to remain quite distinct from the role suggested by the implied reader: "the concept of the implied reader is ... a textual structure anticipating the presence of a recipient without necessarily defining him [or her]" (*Act of Reading* 34). It is this active yet text-based view of reading and this view of the implied reader that Iser has demonstrated and popularized in his analyses of fiction. And it is this view of reading and the reader in the text that Ede and Lunsford subsume under their heading "audience invoked."

However, the fictional audience created by a text need not be monolithic. In fact, a common mistake is to confuse or conflate the implied reader with other fictional readers that may be created in a text. To put the matter another way, readers may exist in a text in other forms in addition to the implied reader; and real readers therefore might at times be not so much listening in on a conversation between an implied author and implied reader as witnessing a full-fledged drama—a sort of implicit Socratic dialogue—complete with multiple and conflicting speakers and readers representing a range of views. Everyone agrees that a real author can be distinguished from the implied author, and the implied author at times from a dramatized narrator such as Nick Carraway; so, too, a real reader can be distinguished from the implied reader, and the implied reader from other fictional readers. Gerald Prince calls these other fictional readers "narratees," by analogy to the equally fictional narrator.

Narratees rival narrators in their diversity. Prince cites as examples the caliph in *A Thousand and One Nights,* whose threat to execute Scheherazade shapes the stories-within-the-larger-story that we listen in on, and the comrades aboard the *Nellie* who listen to Marlowe tell the events of *Heart of Darkness;* and I immediately think of Chaucer's pilgrims, who listen with all their biases to the Canterbury tales, or of Shreve and Quentin, who swap the roles of narrator and narratee in the course of *Absalom, Absalom!* Friedman's letter in the Appendix can also clarify how fictional audiences in the text can differ from implied readers. I have mentioned how Bennett *might* have figured as one of Friedman's intended readers and how Friedman's "letter" creates an implied reader with certain values and attitudes and knowledge. But the letter also includes a fictional character "Bill Bennett" (distinct from the implied reader and distinct from the real William Bennett), a "you" whose values comprise the straw man created in the opening and closing paragraphs and whose points of view are dismantled in the essay. Or think again of King's "Letter from Birmingham Jail." King creates an implied reader in his text with the values of justice and tolerance, a knowledge of biblical and theological and political texts, and the attitudes of sympathy and generosity; it is this implied reader that King invites his real readers to identify with. But he also creates other fictional readers: the "white moderates" referred to late in the essay that King hopes his real readers will *not* identify themselves with; and of course the eight Birmingham clergymen addressed in the salutation and throughout the essay. Whether those eight clergymen "really" exist is beside the point: almost all real readers know them only as the fictional characters created by King, characters with values at odds with those of the text and those of the implied reader.[4]

Like the intended reader, therefore, and like any other fictional character, narratees and implied readers can be based on real people, can be idealizations of real people, or can be pure creations. Not that every text makes dramatic use of narratees, of course: in Wendell Harris's formulation, "there is always a narrator speaking at least to an assumed narratee, just as there is always an implied author and an implied reader, but in some cases the narrator and implied author and/or the implied reader and narratee are indistinguishable while in other cases ... the members of each pair are quite separate. In these [latter] cases, the implied author seems almost to be speaking to the implied reader over the heads of the narrator and narratee."

Besides implied readers and narratees, other readers in the text have been identified and described. One is the "inscribed" reader associated with the work of Jonathan Culler. While implied readers and narratees often have a presence in a text that is as concrete as the presence of other "characters" in it, the inscribed reader is something more abstract, something more general: the system of shared conventions and codes and formal devices (what Iser refers to in *The Act of Reading* as the text's "repertoire") that writers and readers deploy to make meaning, the implicit rules that allow a writer to create a text and a reader to comprehend it.[5] "It is his [or her] experience of reading, his [or her] notion of what readers can and will do," says

Culler, "that enables the author to write, for to intend meanings is to assume a system of conventions and to create signs within the perspective of that system" ("Prolegomena" 50). The inscribed reader is therefore something close to Park's conception of audience: the "set of conventions ... that shape the discourse," the "totality of the assumptions the discourse makes about context" (251), whether those conventions are generic, lexical, or rhetorical. Inscribed readers are not at all specific or "real"; they are impersonal, a collective. For Culler, "the question is not what actual readers happen to do but what an ideal reader must know implicitly in order to read" *(Structuralist Poetics* 24).

The "ideal reader" is therefore also a textual feature, a set of assumptions inscribed within a document, a fiction implied by the very being of a text but impossible for someone to become in reality. Like many linguistic concepts (Culler here is speaking as a structuralist, after all), the ideal reader is a generalized construct assumed by and in a text; competent in every way, the ideal reader has instantaneous recognition of every rule and convention and signal necessary for deciphering a text. The ideal reader is a "superreader" who is hypersensitive to every formal nuance, who has encyclopedic knowledge to bring to bear on every textual move. As Chomsky puts it in the famous opening paragraphs of *Aspects of the Theory of Syntax,* "linguistic theory is concerned primarily with an ideal speaker-listener, in a completely homogeneous speech community, who knows its language perfectly and is unaffected by such grammatically irrelevant conditions as memory limitations, distractions, shifts of attention and interest, and errors ... in applying his knowledge in actual performance" (3).[7]

More concrete, less theoretical, and more on the way to "real readers" is the *informed reader,* a term suggested by Stanley Fish to denote "neither an abstraction nor an actual living reader but a hybrid—a real reader (me) who does everything within his power to make himself informed" (49). On the one hand, the informed reader is something of a textual ideal that presupposes a general competence ("competence" in Chomsky's and Culler's sense) in the language of the text, an acute awareness of the formal features of all texts, and experience with the properties of every specific kind of discourse, "including everything from the most local of devices (figures of speech, and so on) to whole genres" (48). On the other hand, the informed reader is quite real and quite actively engaged in understanding a particular text—someone living and breathing who is fully involved in becoming what a specific text asks its readers to become ("the informed reader of Milton will not be the informed reader of Whitman"), doing "everything within his [or her] power to make himself [or herself] informed." "Each of us," says Fish, "if we are sufficiently responsible and self-conscious can ... become the informed reader" (49). The informed reader is at once a communal reader predisposed by the linguistic codes and conventions agreed on by an interpretive community and an individual reader in the world who is seeking to understand those codes completely. Or to put it in the terms of linguistic theory, the informed reader is a real reader striving to bring performance into conformity with competence.[8] Informed readers, therefore, like the other fictional readers distinguished in this section, are in one sense literally embodied in texts. But they offer a link with real readers, too. In fact, the text in general (and any sort of reader within that text) may be described as a place where real authors and real readers may meet.

Real Readers

Real readers truly exist. They are a temporal fact, not simply a textual one. Experience with real readers, and experience being real readers, tells writers what to say in a given piece and how to say it; and the actions and responses of real readers provide a most important gauge to the success of any document. When teachers exhort novices to "analyze your audience," therefore, it is to real readers that they are referring. And it is well known that such teachers have a repertoire of techniques to recommend to their novices for the purpose of turning up specific demographic and attitudinal information on real audiences.

Nevertheless, understanding the nature of real readers is by no means uncomplicated. For one thing, real readers may or may not be the ones "intended" by the real author or even the ones "invoked" by the text. All sorts of people may actually read a document who were never "intended" to read it; think of a copyeditor, for instance, or the twentieth-century readers of Keats's letters, or your first reading of the "Letter to Bill Bennett" here. All sorts of people may also read a text who are not "invoked" by it, either; think of that same copyeditor, for example, or recall your first confusing encounter with a Socratic dialogue or medieval allegory or legal brief or some other text whose conventions seemed at first quite alien. To put the matter another way, not all real readers are audiences from the writer's or text's perspective; nor do intended or implied or inscribed audiences always become realized in the flesh.

Nor are real readers any more monolithic than are the readers in the text; in fact, they are so various as to defy any complete classification. It may be useful, however, to consider first a basic distinction between multiple (or heterogeneous) audiences and single (or homogeneous) ones, a distinction commonly made in technical communication to distinguish the readers of documents in complex organizations.[9] Multiple audiences, I would suggest, are not to be defined by their various physical characteristics or by their different places in organizations or by their various roles in relation to the writer or by the different cultural and sexual roles that distinguish real people. They have to do with the multiple *tasks* or *multiple reading behaviors*—that various readers may require of a text, whether those behaviors are implied in texts or assumed in fact by real, empirical readers. That is why in figure 10.1 the term *multiple audience* cuts across boundaries between text and real reader.

Let me try to clarify by means of an example or two. Consider first the booklet that describes employee benefits at a university or some other large organization. Such a booklet may have multiple uses, may be read in multiple ways: it can be a recruiting device that attracts new employees; once the new employee signs on, it can be read for several informative purposes (as a way of finding out if a particular situation is covered by insurance, for instance, or as a way of learning how to make an insurance claim); it can serve as a model for writers constructing similar documents; or it can become the object of analysis for English teachers and students in a technical writing class. All of these multiple roles are legitimate, of course. Some of them may be implied by the text or intended by the authors; some of the roles perhaps *should* be implied by the text (or should have been intended by the authors), but aren't (that's one reason why people have to phone for additional information on their benefits); and some of those roles are brought to the text "from outside," if you will, sanctioned neither by text nor by authors. A second example: the Friedman letter can intend and invoke a single real audience, but it cannot guarantee that real readers will sit still for a single role. Real readers cannot be completely controlled by a text, though authors may certainly seek such control.[10] Friedman's letter addressing *Wall Street Journal* readers may also be read by social scientists trying to understand the *Wall Street Journal,* for instance, or by someone preparing a biographical essay on Friedman, or by a historian a generation from now, long after the question of legalizing drugs has been resolved. Thus multiple audiences-heterogeneous audiences—can consist of many individuals; or a multiple audience can be one individual who assumes multiple, even conflicting roles over time.

Conversely, even if very different readers (different in a demographic sense) come to a text for the same reason, they may be considered single, not multiple. Single or homogeneous audiences are worth discussing, since they, too, are hardly monolithic. That is, even if a reader approaches a particular text "single-mindedly," that does not imply that the same reader will approach another text in the same way. Readers adjust their reading not only in response to textual cues but also as a result of their own needs and idiosyncracies.

Sometimes readers are "passive"; in the terminology of communication theory, they are "receivers," uncritical receptacles for taking in messages. In one sense, this view of communication sees messages as objects to be consumed and digested in the same way that a computer dispassionately takes in and stores information. In another sense, this view sees writing as a script and reading as a process of accepting cues spelled out, implicitly or explicitly, by a text. Whatever the metaphor, the reader becomes one who passively "processes" a piece of writing. While recent developments in critical theory, reading, and cognitive psychology have quite properly undermined this view of reading, it remains true that to read relatively passively remains an option for readers in certain circumstances. At times it makes sense to subordinate oneself to the text, to try to "process" the text as much as possible. Just think about how you typically read a biology textbook or cookbook, for instance (especially if you are an inexperienced biologist or cook), or any other kind of routine instructions or militantly expository prose.

But most often, of course, readers and reading are more active. The text may be a script, but the actor/reader still has plenty to do, even in the face of the most dictatorial implied author. At the very least, reading means bringing to the text knowledge and experience that enable people to recognize connections and fill in omitted information. At most, reading means shaping the outcome of an encounter with a text—not "processing" but "making meaning." Someplace in the middle it means negotiating meaning—*negotiating* in both senses of the term—with the author through the text." A reader of Friedman's essay, for instance, may be taking in the text relatively passively, or tentatively, if he or she is unfamiliar (or unconcerned) with the controversy over legalizing drugs. Or the reader might be actively engaged with the argument, taking mental notes, posing possible objections, imagining Bennett's possible responses, supplying analogues or counterinstances, and ultimately being convinced. Or the reader might resist the argument from the outset and examine each sentence with a jaundiced eye.

The use of the word *resist* in connection with the Friedman argument brings to mind people who not only resist the roles set out for them but who resist the entire ideology of a text. Though the term *resisting reader* derives from feminist critical theory[12] and strictly speaking refers to the experience of women readers who resist the masculine ideology of certain texts, the notion of the resisting reader may be implicit in the very notion of persuasion in our culture, a notion that assumes readers who carefully guard—resist—ideological positions that are under siege by a rhetor. Resisting readers resist every kind of textual move; they move through discourse with a kind of skepticism or suspicion, implicitly counter the text at every opportunity, and finally may subjugate it to personal proclivities or counterideologies. It is perhaps a response to this notion of resistance that prompts so many "new rhetoricians" to move toward less agonistic versions of persuasion; consider Burke's concept of identification, Booth's "rhetoric of assent," the notion of "Rogerian" argument, and so forth.

And perhaps that is the motive behind Patrocinio Schweikart's invention of a "caring reader." In an attempt to resolve dualities (is meaning in the text or in the reader? is reading an interaction or a negotiation? are readers "active" or "passive"? is the text a repository of truth or of power?), Schweikart proposes a new model for the reading process that is based on Nel Noddings's work in ethics and education. The caring reader is absorbed by the text but not effaced by it, gains a dual perspective through reading both the self and the text in question, and enacts a reciprocal relationship—an "interanimation"—among author, text, and reader that is mutually respectful and liberating. Schweikart's caring reader has enormous possibilities as a model for writing teachers engaged themselves with student texts and for those who stress collaboration; that is why I emphasize it here. But it can also describe a way of reading a range of other documents in a range of circumstances as well with student texts and for those who stress collaboration; that is why I emphasize it here. But it can also describe a way of reading a range of other documents in a range of circumstances as well.

The possibility of a caring reader does not preclude the existence of resisting readers or of active or passive readers, for that matter. Styles of reading on the part of real audiences are quite various, and those styles may be assumed or discarded, quite legitimately, at different times by the same reader (even in the course of reading a single document) or at the same time by different readers. Whatever the specific facts of a particular reading experience, however, it does seem clear that there is no generic Real Reader, only temporal and situated real readers of various abilities and motivations and backgrounds who exist in differing and dynamic relationships to the texts they are working with.

One last point. A real audience is not the same thing as a discourse community—though *audience* and *discourse community* are sometimes used as synonyms.[13] A discourse community, however it is defined (see Porter, Nystrand, and Fish for definitions), essentially denotes the setting or culture that enables communication within it. As figure 10.1 implies, it refers to the system of rules, conventions, constraints, and beliefs that readers and writers share, and draw upon during the process of communicating. Directing and subtly directed by the whole discourse, the discourse community amounts to the dynamic "rules of the system governing discourse production within [a] community" (Porter 244). As such, a discourse community is something broader than audience, for particular audiences (like particular writers) nearly always exist within a discourse community. (An exception might be a reader who "eavesdrops" for some reason on the conversations, written or oral, of another community.) Many members of a discourse community will never be among the intended or implied or real audience for particular documents. The discourse community for Friedman's letter on drugs, for example, is everyone capable of reading it; but the audience for the letter, as I have noted, consists of those Friedman "intended" it for or those "created" within it or those who really encounter it. To appropriate Roman Jakobson's famous distinction, an *addressee* for a piece of writing should not be confused with the *context* for that writing (see Kinneavy 58–59).

Conclusion

Where does all of this leave the teacher in search of the meanings of *audience*? After all these distinctions have been made among various kinds of audiences and readers, it might be best to end by smoothing over the distinctions a bit. For though it might be useful for teachers or critics or theoreticians to distinguish among the readers in the writer, the readers in the text, and the readers in the real world, in practice, of course, those readers cannot be so nearly separated. In practice the concept of audience is dynamic: it is their experience with addressing real readers and reading real texts that tells writers what to include and how; it is in terms of the reader in the text and the author's intention that real audiences situate themselves (usually) during the act of reading; and it is with reference to real people and to accomplish authorial aims that texts create their fictional readers. Intention and understanding are two ends of the act of reading that meet in a text. Each of those ends, in the words of Stanley Fish, necessarily "stipulates (includes, defines, specifies) the other. To construct the profile of the informed or at-home reader [or any other kind of audience, I would add] is at the same time to characterize the author's intention and vice versa, because to do either is to specify the contemporary conditions of utterance" (161). Writer and audience and text are inextricably patterned in the creation of meaning through discourse. What is needed in understanding discourse, therefore, is what is needed in understanding audience: a tolerance of complexity and a commitment to a pluralism that does justice to the multiple senses of *reader* and *audience*.

Acknowledgments

For their helpful suggestions on this essay in an earlier form, thanks to the members of my seminar on Reader-Response Criticism at Penn State in the spring of 1990, and to those who responded to my presentation on the subject at the Conference on College Composition and Communication in Chicago, 1990. Thanks also to Cynthia Miecznikowski, who served as a research assistant for this project.

Milton Friedman's "Open Letter to Bill Bennett" is reprinted with permission of the *Wall Street Journal*, copyright (c) 1989, Dow Jones and Company, Inc. All rights reserved.

Appendix

An Open Letter to Bill Bennett (*Wall Street Journal*, 19 Sept. 1989)
Dear Bill:

In Oliver Cromwell's eloquent words, "I beseech you, in the bowels of Christ, think it possible you may be mistaken" about the course you and President Bush urge us to adopt to fight drugs. The path you propose of more police, more jails, use of the military in foreign countries, harsh penalties for drug users, and a whole panoply of repressive measures can only make a bad situation worse. The drug war cannot be won by those tactics without undermining the human liberty and individual freedom that you and I cherish.

You are not mistaken in believing that drugs are a scourge that is devastating our society. You are not mistaken in believing that drugs are tearing asunder our social fabric, ruining the lives of many young people, and imposing heavy costs on some of the most disadvantaged among us. You are not mistaken in believing that the majority of the public share your concerns. In short, you are not mistaken in the end you seek to achieve.

Your mistake is failing to recognize that the very measures you favor are a major source of the evils you deplore. Of course the problem is demand, but it is not only demand, it is demand that must operate through repressed and illegal channels. Illegality creates obscene profits that finance the murderous tactics of the drug lords; illegality leads to the corruption of law enforcement officials; illegality monopolizes the efforts of honest law forces so that they are starved for resources to fight the simpler crimes of robbery, theft and assault.

Drugs are a tragedy for addicts. But criminalizing their use converts that tragedy into a disaster for society, for users and non-users alike. Our experience with the prohibition of drugs is a replay of our experience with the prohibition of alcoholic beverages.

I append excerpts from a column that I wrote in 1972 on "Prohibition and Drugs." The major problem then was heroin from Marseilles; today, it is cocaine from Latin America. Today, also, the problem is far more serious than it was 17 years ago: more addicts, more innocent victims, more drug pushers, more law enforcement officials; more money spent to enforce prohibition, more money spent to circumvent prohibition.

Had drugs been decriminalized 17 years ago, "crack" would never have been invented (it was invented because the high cost of illegal drugs made it profitable to provide a cheaper version) and there would today be far fewer addicts. The lives of thousands, perhaps hundreds of thousands of innocent victims would have been saved, and not only in the U.S. The ghettos of our major cities would not be drug-and-crime-infested no-man's lands. Fewer people would be in jails, and fewer jails would have been built.

Colombia, Bolivia and Peru would not be suffering from narco-terror, and we would not be distorting our foreign policy because of narco-terror. Hell would not, in the words with which Billy Sunday welcomed Prohibition, "be forever for rent," but it would be a lot emptier.

Decriminalizing drugs is even more urgent now than in 1972, but we must recognize that the harm done in the interim cannot be wiped out, certainly not immediately. Postponing decriminalization will only make matters worse, and make the problem appear even more intractable.

Alcohol and tobacco cause many more deaths in users than do drugs. Decriminalization would not prevent us from treating drugs as we now treat alcohol and tobacco: prohibiting sales of drugs to minors, outlawing the advertising of drugs and similar measures. Such measures could be enforced, while outright prohibition cannot be. Moreover, if even a small fraction of the money we now spend on trying to enforce drug prohibition were devoted to treatment and rehabilitation, in an atmosphere of compassion not punishment, the reduction in drug usage and in the harm done to the users could be dramatic.

This plea comes from the bottom of my heart. Every friend of freedom, and I know you are one, must be as revolted as I am by the prospect of turning the United States into an armed camp, by the vision of jails filled with casual drug users and of an army of enforcers empowered to invade the liberty of citizens on slight evidence. A country in which shooting down unidentified planes "on suspicion" can be seriously considered as a drug-war tactic is not the kind of United States that either you or I want to hand on to future generations.

Milton Friedman
Senior Research Fellow
Hoover Institution
Stanford University

NOTES

1. For other accounts of recent work on audience, see Allen; Coney; Keene and Barnes-Ostrander; Kroll ("Writing for Readers").
2. Peter Rabinowitz, speaking of literary discourse, prefers the term *authorial audience:* authors "design their books rhetorically for some more or less specific *hypothetical* audience, which I call the *authorial audience.* Artistic choices are based upon ... assumptions—conscious or unconscious—about readers" *(Before Reading* 21). Though his interest is in narrative art, Rabinowitz's general classification of audiences as *authorial, narrative,* and *actual* roughly correspond to

my own classification of audiences as *intended, textual,* and *real.* Gerald Prince's term for the intended reader is the *virtual reader:* the reader the author believes himself or herself to be writing to.

3. For critiques of Perelman's contentions, see Ray and Ede.
4. King's "Letter" was not really written to or for the eight Alabama clergymen; we know that from its publication history. The "Letter" was never posted to the clergymen but was instead quickly printed by the American Friends Service Committee and later collected in *Why We Can't Wait.* The clergymen are fictions, "narratees": creations used by King to focus his comments and to define his implied audience against. No doubt they were also useful in the process of creating the essay, as I mentioned above. For a discussion of the circumstances of King's "Letter" that is coincidentally quite relevant to a discussion of audience, see Fulkerson.
5. Many of those conventions are catalogued in Kinneavy's *Theory of Discourse.*
6. *Superreader is* Michael Riffaterre's term. Though still a structuralist committed to careful analysis of textual conventions, Riffaterre does move beyond strict textual formalism by acknowledging that the superreader brings to the text cultural and historical awareness, not merely a mastery of textual and generic conventions. In that sense, Riffaterre moves beyond strict structuralisms, and in that sense his superreader can be distinguished from the ideal reader assumed by the structuralists.
7. Quoted in Fish 246. For a helpful short account of distinctions to be made among ideal readers, informed readers, and superreaders, see Iser, *Act* 26–32.
8. *Ideal* readers and *real* readers—i.e., *competent* and *performative* readers, to continue with the terms of linguistic theory—are also combined in Dell Himes's concept of "communicative competence."
9. The term *multiple audience* is associated with Mathes and Stevenson.
10. See Roland Barthes's S/Z. Barthes classifies texts according to how much they attempt to control the responses of readers.
11. Reader-response critics may be distinguished according to how "active" they see or sanction the process of reading. Ong, Booth, Prince, and Gibson see the text as giving directions to a relatively passive reader; Norman Holland and David Bleich lease relatively more control to active readers than to the texts they experience; and Iser would be in a middle position, with the text providing fixed guides but plenty of gaps, or "indeterminacies," and the reader reducing the indeterminacies. Rather than try to adjudicate among their positions, I would rather see the level of "activity" in a reader as "rhetorically" constrained—as contingent on text and reader and circumstance in a given case.
12. The term seems to have been coined by Judith Fetterley. Feminist readers are not necessarily resisting readers, of course. For a survey of the range of possibilities involved in feminist reader-response theory, see Elizabeth Flynn and Patrocinio Schweikart's *Gender and Reading,* particularly the essays by Flynn and Schweikart themselves.
13. See, for example, James E. Porter, "Reading Presences in Texts: Audience as Discourse Community." It is not just Porter's title that conflates audience and discourse community; throughout the essay the two are treated as ultimately synonymous. I cite Porter not because his is the most egregious example—I could cite many others—but because his essay remains for me a most thoughtful discussion of the term *discourse community* and its implications, a discussion that I recommend most heartily to others.

WORKS CITED

Allen, Jo. "Breaking with a Tradition: New Directions in Audience Analysis." *Technical Writing: Theory and Practice*. Ed. Bertie Fearing and W. Keats Sparrow. New York: MLA, 1989. 53–62.

Anderson, John R. "The Audience as a Concept in the Philosophical Rhetoric of Perelman, Johnstone, and Natanson." *Southern Speech Communication Journal* 38 (1972): 39–50.

Bakhtin, Mikhail M. *The Dialogic Imagination: Four Essays*. Ed. Michael Holquist; trans. Caryl Emerson and Michael Holquist. Austin: U of Texas P, 1981.

Barthes, Roland. *Image Music Text*. New York: Hill and Wang, 1977.

——. S/Z. Trans. Richard Miller. New York: Hill and Wang, 1974.

Berkenkotter, Carol. "Understanding a Writer's Awareness of Audience." *CCC* 32 (1981): 388–99.

Bleich, David. *Subjective Criticism*. Baltimore: Johns Hopkins UP, 1978.

Booth, Wayne. *Modern Dogma and the Rhetoric of Assent*. Notre Dame, IN: U of Notre Dame P, 1974.

——. *The Rhetoric of Fiction*. Chicago: U of Chicago P, 1961.

Chomsky, Noam. *Aspects of the Theory of Syntax*. Cambridge: MIT P, 1965.

Coney, Mary. "Contemporary Views of Audience: A Rhetorical Perspective." *Technical Writing Teacher* 14 (1987): 319–36.

Culler, Jonathan. "Prolegomena to a Theory of Reading." *The Reader in the Text*. Ed. Susan R. Suleiman and Inge Crosman. Princeton: Princeton UP, 1980. 46–66.

——. *Structuralist Poetics*. Ithaca: Cornell UP, 1975.

Ede, Lisa. "Rhetoric Versus Philosophy: The Role of the Universal Audience in Chaim Perelman's *The New Rhetoric*. " *Central States Speech Journal* 32 (1981): 118–25.

Ede, Lisa, and Andrea Lunsford. "Audience Addressed/Audience Invoked: The Role of Audience in Composition Theory and Pedagogy." *CCC* 35 (1984): 155–71.

Elbow, Peter. "Closing My Eyes as I Speak: An Argument for Ignoring Audience." *College English* 49 (1987): 50–69.

Fetterley, Judith. *The Resisting Reading: A Feminist Approach to American Fiction*. Bloomington: Indiana UP, 1978.

Fish, Stanley. *Is There a Text in This Class?* Cambridge: Harvard UP, 1980.

Flynn, Elizabeth, and Patrocinio Schweikart, eds. *Gender and Reading*. Baltimore: Johns Hopkins UP, 1986.

Fulkerson, Richard. "The Public Letter as a Rhetorical Form: Structure, Logic, and Style in King's 'Letter from Birmingham Jail'" *Quarterly Journal of Speech* 65 (1979): 121–36.

Gibson, Walker. "Authors, Speakers, Readers, and Mock Readers." *College English* 11 (1950): 265–69.

Harris, Wendell. *A Dictionary of Concepts in Literary Criticism and Theory*. Westport, CT: Greenwood, 1992.

Himes, Del. "On Communicative Competence." *Sociolinguistics: Selected Readings*. Ed. J.B. Pride and Janet Holmes. Harmondsworth: Penguin, 1972.

Holland, Norman. *The Dynamics of Literary Response*. New York: Oxford UP, 1968.

Iser, Wolfgang. *The Act of Reading: A Theory of Aesthetic Response*. Baltimore: Johns Hopkins UP, 1978.

——. *The Implied Author: Patterns of Communication in Prose Fiction from Bunyan to Beckett*. Baltimore: Johns Hopkins UP, 1974.

Johnston, Henry W. *Validity and Rhetoric in Philosophical Argument*. University Park, PA: Dialogue Press of Man and World, 1978.

Keene, Michael, and Marilyn Barnes-Ostrander. "Audience Analysis and Adaptation." *Research in Technical Communication: A Bibliographic Sourcebook.* Ed. Michael Moran and Debra Journet. Westport, CT: Greenwood, 1985. 163–91.

Kinneavy, James. *A Theory of Discourse.* Englewood Cliffs, NJ: Prentice Hall, 1971.

Kroll, Barry. "Cognitive Egocentrism and the Problem of Audience Awareness in Written Discourse." *Research in the Teaching of English* 12 (1978): 268–81.

——. "Writing for Readers: Three Perspectives on Audience." *CCC* 35 (1984): 172–85.

Mathes, J.C., and Dwight Stevenson. *Designing Technical Reports.* New York: Bobbs-Merrill, 1976.

Maynard Smith, John. Letter to the Author. 17 Sept. 1989.

Noddings, Nel. *Caring: A Feminine Approach to Ethics and Moral Education.* Berkeley and Los Angeles: U of California P, 1984.

Nystrand, Martin. "Rhetoric's 'Audience' and Linguistic's 'Speech Community': Implications for Understanding Writing, Reading, and Text." *What Writers Know.* Ed. Martin Nystrand. New York: Academic, 1982. 1–28.

Ong, Walter. "The Writer's Audience Is Always a Fiction." *PMLA* 90 (1975): 6–2 1.

Park, Douglas. "The Meanings of 'Audience. '" *College English* 44 (1982): 247–57.

Perelman, Chaim, and L. Olbrechts-Tyteca. *The New Rhetoric: A Treatise on Argumentation.* Trans. John Wilkerson and Purcell Weaver. Notre Dame, IN: U of Notre Dame P, 1969.

Porter, James E. "Reading Presences in Texts: Audience as Discourse Community." *OldspeaklNewspeak: Rhetorical Transformations.* Ed. Charles W. Kneupper. Arlington, TX: Rhetoric Society of America, 1985. 241–56.

Prince, Gerald. "Introduction to the Study of the Narratee. " *Poetique* 14 (1973): 177–93.

Rabinowitz, Peter. *Before Reading: Narrative Conventions and the Politics of Interpretation.* Ithaca: Cornell UP, 1987.

——. "Truth in Fiction: A Reexamination of Audience." *Critical Inquiry* 4 (1977): 121–4 1.

Rafoth, Bennett. "Audience Adaptation in the Essays of Proficient and Nonproficient Freshman Writers." *Research in the Telling of English* 19 (1985): 237–53.

Ray, John W. "Perelman's Universal Audience." *Quarterly Journal of Speech* 64 (1978): 361–75.

Riffaterre, Michael. "Describing Poetic Structures: Two Approaches to Baudelaire's 'Les chats.'" *Yale French Studies* 36-37 (1966): 200–242.

Roth, Robert. "'The Evolving Audience: Alternatives to Audience Accommodation." *CCC* 38 (1977): 47–55.

Rubin, Donald, and Gene Piche. "Development in Syntactic and Strategic Aspects of Audience Adaptation Skills in Written Persuasive Discourse." *Research in the Teaching of English* 15 (1979): 293–316.

Schweikart, Patrocinio. "Reading, Teaching, and the Ethic of Care." *Gender in the Classroom: Pedagogy and Power.* Ed. Susan L. Gabriel and Isaiah Smithson. Champaign: U of Illinois P, 1990.

Thralls, Charlotte, Nancy Blyler, and Helen Ewald. "Real Readers, Implied Readers, and Professional Writers." *Journal of Business Communication* 25 (1988): 47–65.

Consensus Groups: A Basic Model of Classroom Collaboration

Kenneth Bruffee

Collaborative learning among students has a long history in writing instruction, but in the 1980s a series of articles and a textbook by Kenneth A. Bruffee, a professor of English at Brooklyn College of the City University of New York, helped to make peer group work a central part of writing instruction. Bruffee's theories of collaborative learning draw heavily on pragmatism, social constructionist theory, and research on group dynamics, and they received a great deal of critical attention in the late 1980s from such scholars as John Trimbur, Greg Myers, and Donald Stewart. In this selection from Collaborative Learning: Higher Education, Interdependence, and the Authority of Knowledge, *a 1993 book that promotes student group work in all disciplines, Bruffee explains some of the purposes of collaborative learning and lays out a number of practical principles for guiding student groups and designing group activities.*

One model of collaborative learning, although by no means the only one, is classroom consensus groups. In consensus groups people work collaboratively on a limited but open-ended task, negotiating among themselves what they think and know in order to arrive at some kind of consensus or agreement, including, sometimes, agreement to disagree. In organizing these groups, teachers typically do four things:

- They divide a large group—the class—into small groups.
- They provide a task, usually designed (and, preferably, tested) ahead of time, for the small groups to work on.
- They reconvene the larger group into plenary session to hear reports from the small groups and negotiate agreement among the group as a whole.
- They evaluate the quality of student work, first as referee, then as judge.

Organizing small consensus groups is not hard to do. But satisfactory results require college and university teachers to behave in their classrooms in ways that strike many who are used to traditional teaching as at best unusual. The nitty-gritty of this process of social organization can look trivial on the page. But it adds up to fairly sophisticated expertise that includes some familiarity with the research on "group dynamics," some forethought, some sensitivity to social situations and relationships, a somewhat better-than-average understanding of what is being taught, and self-control.

This chapter describes what happens in a typical consensus-group class and outlines some of the relevant research. It explains what goes into designing a good collaborative learning task. It explains how teachers draw a collaborative class back together to develop a consensus of the whole. And it explains how they evaluate students' individual contributions to the class's conversation through the students' writing.

A collaborative class using consensus groups goes something like this:

After explaining what's going to happen, the teacher divides students into groups of five or six. This usually means that the teacher acts a bit like a social director at a vacation resort or summer camp, counting students off, wading in to help them rearrange chairs, separating groups to minimize noise from other conversations, and encouraging group members to draw close enough together to hear one another over the din and to make the group more likely to cohere.

Then the teacher gives students a sheet with a task and instructions on it. An alternative is to pick out a passage of text as it appears in a book that all the students have at hand and write questions and instructions on the blackboard. (Later in this chapter I will explain what is distinctive about collaborative learning tasks and offer suggestions for designing them.)

Once students are settled in their groups, teachers ask them to introduce themselves (if necessary) and decide on a recorder, a member of the group who will take notes on the group's discussion and report on the consensus the group has reached when the work is over. As the small-group work starts, the teacher backs off. Emphatically, the teacher does not "sit in" on consensus groups, hover over them, or otherwise monitor them. Doing that inevitably destroys peer relations among students and encourages the tendency of well-schooled students to focus on the teacher's authority and interests.

If a teacher's goal is productive collaboration among peers, closely monitoring student small-group discussion is self-defeating. That is because the message that teachers deliver when they monitor student small-group discussion is a foundational message: that students should first and foremost be striving to use the language of the teacher's discipline, the teacher's own community of knowledgeable peers. This is a foundational message because it reinforces dependence on the teacher's authority and unquestioning reliance on the authority of what the teacher knows. Students fear that they will "get it wrong." Teachers fear that discussion will "get out of hand"—that is, go in some direction that the teacher has not anticipated and thereby cast doubt on the teacher's classroom authority and the authority of the teacher's knowledge.

While students are at work, the teacher's main responsibility is keeping time. Time is a nonrenewable natural resource. The teacher's job is to conserve it. The length of time that students spend on a task depends on the complexity of the task and on how accustomed students are to working together. Depending on how much time is available, the teacher sets a time limit for the work or simply asks each group at some point how much more time they think they will need. When most groups have completed the task, the teacher asks the recorder in each group to report and, acting as recorder for the class as a whole, writes out the results on the blackboard or asks the recorders to write their results on the board themselves. If most groups have been able to complete only part of the task, the task the teacher has assigned was too long or complex for the time available. Recorders report on the part the group has been able to complete and leave the rest for another time.

When the small-group work is finished, the teacher referees a plenary discussion in which the class as a whole analyzes, compares, and synthesizes the groups' decisions, negotiating toward an acceptable consensus. Here, the teacher serves as recorder for the class as a whole, not only writing out and revising the consensus as the discussion proceeds, but also pointing out gaps, inconsistencies, and incoherence. Finally (as we shall see later in this chapter), the teacher compares the class's consensus with the current consensus in the knowledge community that the teacher represents.

Throughout this process—group work toward local consensus plus reports, followed by plenary discussion toward plenary consensus—alert teachers will expect some awkwardness at first. During the small-group work, teachers and students alike may have to adjust to the noise produced by several excited conversations going on at once in the same room. Classroom noise is partly a matter of room size and sound-absorbing materials. Sensitivity to classroom noise is largely a matter of expectation. Teachers who normally think that students should sit quietly and take notes or speak only after they have raised their hands find that the din of conversation in a smoothly running collaborative classroom takes a lot of getting used to. Most college and university teachers and students have not experienced classes where active, articulate students are the norm. They decidedly are the norm within the protective security of collaborative consensus groups. With experience, some teachers even become so acutely sensitive to the register of sounds generated by consensus group conversation that they can tell by the tone of the din whether or not things are going well.

Teachers and students alike may also be disturbed at first by what they feel as the chaos of collaborative classes. This feeling of chaos is also a matter of expectation. As Chapter 4 explains, classroom social interaction of the sort that goes on in collaborative learning is rare in the classrooms that most college and university teachers are used to. Traditional teaching places teachers at the center of the action and makes teachers the center of attention. Conversation goes on between the teacher and each individual student in the room. Traditional lecturers seem to be speaking to a socially coherent group of people. Actually they are speaking one to one, to an aggregate set of isolated individuals among whom there are no necessary social relations at all. Even when discussion among students in the class does occur, it tends to be a performance for the teacher's benefit, just as the teacher is performing for the students' benefit.

In place of this traditional pattern of one-to-one social relations, collaborative learning substitutes a pattern in which the primary focus of students' action and attention is each other. Teachers teach for the most part indirectly, through reorganizing students socially and designing appropriate tasks. Students converse among themselves with the teacher standing by on the sidelines, for the time being mostly ignored. Once consensus-group collaborative learning finally "takes" in a class, even when teachers lecture and conduct drills and recitations (as they almost inevitably must do once in a while), the negotiated understanding among the students changes the lecturer's position relative to the class. Teachers no longer lecture to a set of aggregated individuals. The fact that the students have become a transition community of people who know one another well means that whatever the teacher says takes its place in the context of an ongoing conversation among the students to which the teacher is not entirely privy. Empowered by their conversation, students are less likely to be wowed into passivity by whizbang lectures. They are more likely to question actively and synthesize what the teacher has to say.

So, both in organizing consensus groups and in lecturing to classes in which students have worked together collaboratively, teachers used to traditional classroom organization may at first feel that a collaborative learning class is desperately out of control—that is, out of the teacher's control. It may well be out of control if the collaboration is successful, but from the point of view of nonfoundational teaching it is comfortably and productively so. And the teacher's initial feeling of lost control tends to dissipate as students and teachers alike understand and accept the unaccustomed social structure of collaborative learning.

Much of the research on the negotiations that go on in collaborative learning consensus groups was done in the 1950s and 1960s, although in recent years there has been some resurgence in this research. Because to date most research has studied "decision-making groups" in businesses, government, and the military, some of it is only marginally related to college and university teaching. The relevant work is nevertheless important to collaborative learning, and awareness of it can be useful to teachers organizing consensus groups. It has mainly to do with group composition (effective group size relative to the type of task and the effects of heterogeneity and homogeneity), the quality of decisions made (number of options considered or variables accounted for), the phases of work through which groups pass in negotiating decisions (openings, transitions, endings; resistance to authority, internalization of authority), barriers to effective group decision making (authority-dependency problems, effects of reticent and dominating personalities), the nature of consensus, and the effects and fate of dissent.[1]

Studies suggest that the optimum size for decision-making groups (such as classroom consensus groups) is five. More than five will not change the social dynamics much but will dilute the experience, negligibly in groups of six but significantly in groups of seven and eight, and almost totally in groups of nine, ten, and more. Fewer than five in a group will change the dynamics in fairly obvious ways. Groups of four tend to subdivide into two pairs; groups of three tend to subdivide into a pair and an "other"; and groups of two (called "dyads") tend to sustain levels of stress sharply higher than those of any other group size. In contrast to consensus or decision-making groups, however, working groups (students doing research projects together for several days, weeks, or months, for example) seem to be most successful with three members. Long-term working groups larger than three often become logistically cumbersome.

Degree of heterogeneity or homogeneity is another issue in group composition. In general, heterogeneous decision-making groups work best because, as we saw in Chapter 1, differences tend to encourage the mutual challenging and cancellation of unshared biases and presuppositions that Abercrombie observed. Groups that are socially or ethnically too homogeneous (everyone from the same home town, neighborhood, family, or fraternity; close friends, teammates, clique members) tend to agree too soon, since they have an investment in maintaining the belief that their differences on basic issues are minimal. There is not enough articulated dissent or resistance to consensus to invigorate the conversation. Worse, homogeneous groups tend to find the differences that do arise difficult to endure and are quick to paper them over. On the other hand, members of decision-making groups that are too heterogeneous may have no basis for arriving at a consensus—or no means for doing so: they find that they cannot "come to terms" because they "don't speak the same language."

This inability to come to terms can be literally the case in some highly diverse student populations in which many people are struggling with English as a second language. Too much heterogeneity can also occur when the different languages in question are community dialects of standard English (ethnic, regional, or neighborhood) that students bring with them to class. But difficulty in coming to terms does not of course afflict only students. Lawyers, physicians, accountants, and members of the academic disciplines have "community dialects," too. For example, ask a group composed of otherwise cooperative, well-disposed faculty members from a half-dozen different disciplines (say, biology, art, mathematics, English literature, cultural anthropology, and history) to arrive at a consensus on the definition and proper use of the word "natural," and the only resulting agreement is likely to be an agreement to disagree.

Some of the most troublesome differences that teachers organizing consensus groups may encounter are ethnic differences, often masked by stereotyping (including self-stereotyping) or by superficial conformity. Difficulties arise because collaborative learning requires students to do things that their ethnic background may not have taught them to do or that it actively disposes them not to do.

Some ethnic groups (indeed, some families) accustom people to negotiating decisions that affect all members of the group. Students with this kind of background tend to be comfortable with collaborative learning and know how to go about it. In other ethnic groups (and families), decisions are made autocratically by one person or by a small in-group. Negotiation is unknown. Dissent is forbidden and punished.

Students with this kind of background tend to feel uncomfortable in collaborative learning, don't know how to do it, and resist it.

In still other cases—typically among adolescents—the pressure to maintain the coherence of cliques or gangs can curtail participation in other relationships, such as working collaboratively in classroom consensus groups. Classroom collaboration on tasks that excite interest can threaten clique values and, by cutting across clique loyalties, weaken them.

On the average, most students take well to collaborative learning, but many still have something to learn about it. Many students working together in small groups go through a fairly predictable process of adaptation in which they relate to each other differently at different times during their collaboration. Studies of people working together tend to identify two such "phases of work," dependence and interdependence, and two "major events" that challenge people's preconceptions, one at the beginning of each phase.[2]

Each phase of work displays a characteristic source of disruptive stress. In the first phase, the source of stress is stereotyped attitudes toward authority that people bring with them into a group. *Authority* here refers to feelings about the way power is distributed in the group: who makes the decisions and how those decisions are enforced. The major event that precipitates an authority crisis in consensus groups is withdrawal of the acknowledged external authority. It may happen in collaborative learning, for example, if the teacher leaves the room.

The second source of stress comes into play in the second phase, as the group develops interdependence. It is the stereotyped attitudes toward intimacy that people bring with them into a group. *Intimacy* here means how people normally get along with their peers. The event that precipitates an intimacy crisis is being asked as peers to exercise authority with regard to one another. In collaborative learning, typically, it happens when the teacher asks students to evaluate one another's work.

Teachers organizing consensus groups have to keep all these variables in mind—degree of heterogeneity, group size, ethnic background, phases of work, and so on. When collaborative learning "just doesn't work," any number of forces may be in play. The first few times students work together at the beginning of a term the principal agenda may have to be, for some students, learning how to negotiate effectively. For others, it may be feeling comfortable negotiating at all. Sometimes, when teachers find that some students need to learn how to work together productively, they may have to teach them what they need to know through role playing or modeling. Very occasionally, teachers may have to suggest some basic rules for respecting others in conversation. Some students may have to be told explicitly not to interrupt when others are talking, to maintain dissent firmly but not obstreperously if they continue to believe in it, and to expect that negotiation and consensus building may involve compromise—giving up something you want in order to get something else you need or want more.

Students may also resist consensus group work or other kinds of collaborative learning simply because social engagement can be hard work. It calls upon a range of abilities that many college and university students may not yet have developed fully or refined: tact, responsive listening, willingness to compromise, and skill in negotiation. But it is usually a lot better for teachers to assume until they find out otherwise that their students have learned at least some rudimentary skills of the craft of interdependence and are socially mature enough to work together productively. Most college and university students, whatever their age and background, have had a lot more informal experience working collaboratively than most teachers give them credit for. Only when ethnic background, personal incompatibility, or social immaturity gets in the way of working on the task will it help for teachers to call attention to the process as opposed to the task. Even then, usually, the best way to do it is to turn the way the group is working together—the way people are helping or not helping get the task done—into a task like any other task for the group to work on collaboratively.

Partly because of the many variables involved in successful collaboration, many teachers find that, over time, changing the makeup of consensus groups from class hour to class hour tends to ease classroom tensions. Change in group makeup helps students enlarge their acquaintance, escape aversions and entrenched enmities, dissolve entrapment in cliques, and acquire new interests and abilities by working with a variety of student peers. In any case, the teacher's goal is to create a collaborative class as a whole, not an aggregate of loosely federated mini-classes coherent in themselves but unrelated to all the others.

On this issue of regularly changing the composition of consensus groups, as in the other practical matters, there is room for disagreement among teachers who have had experience with collaborative learning. Peter Hawkes argues, for example, that social coherence among students working in small groups may be time-consuming to achieve, and achieving it may be demanding and complex for the students involved. In that case, keeping students in the same small groups all term may be more efficient than mixing them up from class to class. A teacher's decision on this score may be in part a function of institutional conditions such as size, composition of the student body, whether students are in residence or commute, and so on.

Besides composing students into consensus groups, teachers who organize collaborative learning also set the tasks that students work on together. Designing effective exercises, problems, or tasks for people to undertake collaboratively requires forethought and practice. Tasks may be questions to be answered by arriving at a consensus, or they may be problems to be solved to the satisfaction of all members of the group. A closed-ended question with a yes-or-no answer is in most cases of little value, although an open-ended task that requires groups to agree on a rationale for a yes-or-no answer can be very valuable indeed. That is, collaborative learning tasks do not ask, Yes or no? But they may ask, Why yes or why no?

In general, collaborative learning tasks differ significantly from textbook, problem-set tasks, which are usually foundational in nature. Foundational tasks are what Richard Rorty calls "jigsaw puzzles." They have a predetermined right answer that students must arrive at by a predetermined acceptable method. Their solution requires, as Rorty puts it, a tidy "inferential process . . . starting with premises formulated in the old vocabularies," the accepted disciplinary languages and method, leading to the discovery of "a reality behind the appearances, . . . an undistorted view of the whole picture with which to replace myopic views of its parts."[3]

In contrast, collaborative learning tasks are nonfoundational, constructive, tool-making tasks. They do not presuppose either one right answer or one acceptable method for arriving at it. As Chapter 4 suggests, these tasks draw students into an untidy, conversational, constructive process in which, because they do not yet know "the old vocabularies," they create new ones by adapting the languages they already know. The result is not an undistorted view of a reality presumed to lie behind appearances. The result is a social construct that students have arrived at by their own devices and according to their own lights.

Foundational and nonfoundational tasks are, of course, alike in some ways. Usually both are unambiguous about initial procedures and starting points. But unlike foundational tasks, nonfoundational tasks are ambiguous about methods and goals. That is, they tell students how to begin, but they are designed so that neither teacher nor students can predict with much accuracy where the discussion will go from there.

A nonfoundational, tool-making task may look at first like a foundational task, a jigsaw puzzle. It may look as if it requires students to fit together old vocabularies in order to discover "the right answer." But even if it has this traditional appearance, a nonfoundational task is designed so that, as students work through it, it turns into an eccentric, ill-fitting puzzle. They may find out that there are not enough pieces included in the task to complete the puzzle, so that they have to hunt up or invent some. Or they may find that some of the pieces are the wrong shape for the holes they seem intended for. In some cases, there may be too many pieces, so that students have to select among them. Or the pieces of the puzzle may turn out to be inappropriate, so that students have to translate them, changing their shape in order to make them fit.

In practical terms, therefore, there are two basic types of nonfoundational tasks that can be used in consensus-group collaborative learning. The purpose of both is to generate focused discussion directed toward consensus. They are both "open-ended," but in different ways.

One kind of collaborative learning task, which we might call Type A, asks a question to which there is no clear and ready answer. The purpose of this kind of task is to generate talk about the kinds of consensus that students might reach in response to the question asked. The instructions tell groups to arrive at a consensus that completes the task in a way that satisfies most members of the group and to discuss the possible reasons for differences of opinion among members of the group or dissent from the group's consensus.

An example of a Type A task, one that I have sometimes used in demonstrating collaborative learning, is to ask people working in consensus groups to consider a key sentence of the Declaration of Independence:

> We hold these Truths to be self-evident, that all men are created equal, that they are endowed by their Creator with certain unalienable Rights, that among these are Life, Liberty, and the pursuit of Happiness.

The instructions for this task ask people to reach a consensus on the definition of several words in the sentence (such as *truths, self-evident, created equal, unalienable rights, life, liberty,* and *happiness)* and to write, collaboratively, a sentence that paraphrases the passage in their own words. What makes this task a nonfoundational, constructive, tool-making exercise and not a foundational jigsaw-puzzle task is that several crucial terms in the sentence are, to say the least, somewhat vague, while other terms, most notoriously the reference to "men," contradict popularly held current views.

The other kind of collaborative learning task, which we might call Type B, asks a question and does provide an answer to it—an answer that is accepted by the prevailing consensus in the disciplinary community that the teacher represents. The instructions tell groups to arrive at a consensus about how (or why) the larger community may have reached that answer.

The purpose of this kind of task is to generate talk about what the small group would have to do to reach the consensus reached by the larger community. The task might pose a textbook problem in mathematics or the natural sciences, give the accepted answer to that problem, and ask the group to explain two or more ways to reach that answer. Or it might quote an authoritative scholar's interpretation of a poem or historical event and ask the group to explain how they suppose the critic arrived at that interpretation.

Peter Hawkes has described one example of a Type B task. In teaching *Huckleberry Finn,* he points out that the way the novel ends—by humiliating the runaway slave, Jim—seems inconsistent with earlier passages in which Huck and Jim become reconciled as human beings. He asks students working in groups to arrive at a consensus in response to the major questions that critics discuss: how do they explain "Huck's 'forgetting' what he learned about Jim on the raft," whether they think the ending "undercuts all the meaning developed in the main body of the novel," and how they think the novel should end (what the "right ending" would be).[4]

So far, the task differs little from a Type A task. What turns it into a Type B task is that Hawkes then asks students to compare the positions they have taken with "positions staked out by various critics." He introduces them to the critical opinions of major writers on the novel, such as Ernest Hemingway, Lionel Trilling, and T. S. Eliot. The students may then discover that some of the positions they have taken correspond to positions that the critics have taken. When they do not correspond, the students' task is to try to determine how a critic might have arrived at such a position. In the process, the students have joined a conversation that has gone on among members of the community that the teacher represents, rather than being merely outsiders looking in. They are not talking about literary criticism. They are being literary critics.

Mathematics, the sciences, and technical subjects also offer opportunities for both Type A and Type B collaborative learning tasks. In an introductory college or university physics course, a Type A task might ask students to address the question, How do we think about things we can't touch and don't have an instrument to measure, such as quarks and supernova? Arnold B. Arons exemplifies a Type B task, in which the teacher provides minimum guidance by asking questions and eliciting suggestions. In introducing the laws of inertia, for example, Arons places a 50-pound block of dry ice on a level glass plate and asks students, working in groups, to answer questions such as, How does the block behave once it is moving? What action on our part is necessary to make the object move faster and faster, that is, accelerate continuously? Suppose the block is moving: what actions change the *direction* of its motion? and so on. Questions such as these are designed to help students "notice systematic changes," "impose systematic alterations on a configuration and predict or interpret the resulting effects," and "invent interesting and fruitful configurations of their own." Like Abercrombie's medical students, it is up to these physics students, working in small groups, to "suggest, try, argue, and interpret in their own words, carefully avoiding any, so far undefined, technical vocabulary."[5]

Both kinds of open-ended, collaborative learning tasks have a consistent, long-run educational purpose and a clear, short-run criterion for success. The purpose in both cases is to help students organized collaboratively to work without further help from the teacher toward membership in the discourse community that the teacher represents. The criterion for success is that students have created the tools they need to solve the somewhat eccentric puzzle that the task presented them with.

Besides being appropriately nonfoundational and constructive in design, the degree of difficulty of consensus-group collaborative learning tasks should be appropriate to the students in the class and to the point in the course that the class has reached. When a task is too easy, students get bored. There is not enough to talk about, the conversation is trivial and unchallenging, and the groups solve the problem too quickly. If a task is too hard, it stymies students from the start and throws them back into dependency on the teacher's authority. Then both students and the teacher have no choice but to rely once again on direct instruction. This reversion to type puts the whole process at risk. Effective consensus group tasks engage the collective labor and judgment of the group and keep students' interest focused long enough and sharply enough for the job to get done. They therefore fall within a band of complexity and difficulty defined by each class's collective "zone of proximal development."

"Zone of proximal development" is a term invented by the Russian psychologist L. S. Vygotsky to refer to understanding that lies just beyond current knowledge and ability: what we cannot learn on our own at the moment, but can learn with a little help from our friends. For any of us individually, the zone of what we are capable of learning next, between what we already know and what we can't make sense of for love nor money, can often be somewhat narrow: what I am ready to understand working alone may be fairly limited. But in a heterogeneous group that includes diverse experience, talent, and ability, people's "zones of proximal development" overlap. The distance between what the group as a whole already knows and what its members as a whole can't make sense of for love nor money—the area of what as a whole they can learn next—is likely to be fairly broad. As a result, I may be ready to understand a good deal more as a member of a working group than I would be ready to understand by myself alone.[6]

One thing that students learn in consensus group collaboration, therefore, is that they can accomplish the task at hand by analogizing, generalizing, or extending what they know—the knowledge and abilities they have acquired in other social, conceptual, or practical contexts—so as to complement other people's strengths and limitations in unexpected ways. Teachers design collaborative learning tasks to help students transform the knowledge that everyone brings to class and apply it to the new problems and conditions imposed by the task.

For example, suppose the task were to examine the political or sociological problems involved in installing a new sewer system without killing business on Main Street. In that case, what one student knew about how to address a complex audience (learned, say, working in a factory job trying to talk simultaneously to the boss, the shop steward, and fellow workers) might enlighten another student who could provide expertise in efficient work planning and division of labor (learned in dividing household tasks equitably among several children in order to gain time for work or study or in assigning responsibilities to a television production team).

Or if the task were to understand a love poem by John Donne, a student who was a dictionary or encyclopedia freak might rustle up definitions and background; another who has learned to read aloud effectively in a speech class or on the campus radio station might provide insights through emphasis and tone of voice; still another might call upon an unusual wealth of personal experience in affairs of the heart. What one person knew about how to put together a carburetor, a banjo, or a sales campaign might complement what another knew about the personal tensions among people on a basketball team, in a church vestry, or on a construction crew. In examining the effects of inertia on a block of dry ice, students may be able to bring to bear what they have learned rowing a boat, biking, driving, or moving their luggage into the dorm.

The teacher's job is to design tasks that help people discover and take advantage of group heterogeneity and thus, by expanding the group's collective "zone of proximal development," to increase the potential learning power of every individual in the group. In order to help students discover these collective resources, tasks often include an element of "polling" sometime early in the process. After one student in each group reads the whole task aloud (to get the issue as a whole "on the table" and break the ice), the task requires each person in the group to give his or her off-the-cuff definition of key words in the passage being discussed. Later tasks may include an element of writing and collaborative editing. Typically, toward the end of a group-work period the group asks its recorder to read aloud a draft of the report. Listening to its recorder rehearse the report to be given to the class as a whole, the group then suggests ways to make it more complete and represent more accurately the group's discussion and consensus.

The way that task design can foster constructive conversation may be illustrated by my own experience a number of years ago in a freshman course intended to introduce undergraduates to reading fiction. The goal was to acquaint students with a few well-known stories in a standard anthology, help them interpret those stories in a relatively sophisticated way, and introduce them to some basic critical issues. In planning the course and in devising collaborative tasks for it, I returned to the tried-and-true source of critical principles, Aristotle's *Poetics.* I followed the Aristotelian emphasis on "action" or "plot" as first in importance among the elements of fiction, followed closely by "character."

I divided the analytical tasks for collaborative work into a set of questions that focused the students' attention on these aspects of several short stories I had assigned. The students dealt collaboratively with one task each class hour. The first task asked them to identify the central action in one of the stories (What "happens" in the story?) and its central character (Who does it? or, To whom is it done?). The second task asked students to identify the story's central action and central character as generic "types" (action: falling in love, the end of a career; character: ingenue, old man). The third task was to explain how the story distinguishes the central action and central character from that "type." That is, it asked what expectations the story raised and how the story met, fulfilled, frustrated, or changed those expectations.

What I learned from posing these deceptively simple, apparently unsophisticated generic questions to the consensus groups I organized in that class is that even relatively naive, untutored students can be trusted to generate many important disciplinary (in this case, literary-critical) problems and even some classic solutions. Of course, the better prepared students are, the more complex and sophisticated the resulting consensus may be.

But even when students start such a set of tasks from scratch, their first and persisting problem, as Abercrombie discovered, is to unearth the presuppositions and biases that each of them brings to the task and to resolve conflicts between them resulting from those presuppositions and biases. Being required to arrive at a position that the whole group can "live with" can hurl students headlong into the knottiest and most sophisticated issues of almost any discipline. It can therefore lead to a firmer and more sophisticated grasp of subject matter. That's what happened in the course I have just described. Eventually, the students began to understand this particular set of short stories in considerable depth. They also began to read fiction in general with greater understanding and talk and write more effectively about it.

There is no foolproof method for devising consensus tasks. I have written plenty of tasks that I believed would work perfectly and wound up revising every one of them again and again. I have nevertheless found that the following set of principles, devised by Peter Hawkes, covers the basic issues in collaborative learning task design.[7]

1. **Head every worksheet with the same general instructions.** This eliminates the time groups may spend interpreting new directions. One heading that works well is this:

> *Instructions.*
>
> *Once the groups have been formed, please introduce yourselves to each other. Then agree on one person to record the views expressed in the group, including both the decisions the group makes collaboratively and significant dissent. The recorder will speak for the group. For each*

question, decide on one answer that represents a consensus among the members of the group.

2. If the task asks students to discuss a written passage (a primary, secondary, or student-written text), in the first instruction following the general instructions **ask one member in each group to read the whole task aloud.** To encourage participation, the person reading the task aloud should not be the recorder.

3. Because arriving at a consensus can be time consuming, **make the material to be analyzed short.** A single short paragraph or even just a sentence or two is plenty—often more than enough—for a thirty- or forty-minute discussion.

4. For the same reason, **limit the number of questions that the task asks students to address**. In most cases one question is enough. More than two or three can be overwhelming.

5. **Make the questions short and simple**. Conversation leads students in most cases into as much profundity and complexity as they can handle and in some cases more than the teacher bargained for.

6. **Make the questions concrete and clearly expressed.** Otherwise, students are stymied and throw the questions back. That is, the task becomes figuring out the terms of the question and the teacher's intent, not dealing with the substantive issue.

7. **Sequence the questions within each task, and sequence tasks from class to class and week to week.** The general direction should be from low-involvement, nonthreatening questions and tasks to high-demand questions and tasks.

For example, a task might begin by asking students to explain to one another their first impressions of a topic, problem, or text, or to survey how each student in the group would define key terms (that is, do some "polling"). Then it might ask an analytical question. Finally, the task might ask a broad question that requires students to synthesize the material and their answers in order to climb a few rungs on the abstraction ladder. A whole semester of tasks could be developed on this general sequence.

8. **Ask questions that have more than one answer.** Different responses ensure that recorders' reports do not become repetitive and will provide issues for debate. In a composition course, for example, "What's wrong with sentence five?" is less effective than "How would you improve the weakest sentence in this essay?" If the task is to analyze material drawn from a subject matter

textbook, the questions should go beyond "What does it say?" to "What does it assume?"

9. In some tasks **ask controversial questions.** Some of these can be based on issues raised by prominent authorities in the field but not yet satisfactorily resolved. After the groups have made their decisions and the class has discussed them, the teacher can read aloud some of the published controversy for comparison and further discussion.

10. In some tasks **ask students to analyze short passages concretely.** These passages can be typed out or reproduced from the printed page, or the task can refer to a page in a book that everyone brings to class. Make the questions directing students' analysis pointed: ask about specific words and phrases, what they mean, their relation to other specific words and phrases, their significance in the whole passage, and so on.

11. **Whenever the task asks students to generalize, ask them to support their generalizations with particulars.** For example, if the task is to evaluate a student essay, also ask the groups to specify, say, three examples from the essay that support their opinion. If the task is to discuss a substantive issue, don't just ask "What are the implications of the passage?" Ask "Where exactly—with which words—does the passage imply what you think it implies?"

Teachers have to be prepared for the fact that faulty tasks often provide an occasion for students to draw the teacher into the small-group discussion. Even under the best conditions and with the best-designed tasks, traditional dependence on a teacher's authority exerts a powerful undertow on students and teachers alike. It sometimes leads to "performance" questions—requests for information or clarification made in the belief that the student role demands it. These apparently innocent requests take the form of "What does X mean?" or "How are we supposed to do Y?" Teachers handle questions like these best by turning them back to the students to decide in group discussion what they think X means or how they think they should do Y, and then go on with the task.

For example, sometimes a task turns out to be ambiguous in a way that the teacher hadn't noticed or fails to supply a basic item of information. When that happens, in addition to apologizing, teachers can redirect students' appeal for help or information in several ways. One way is to ask if any group has found the necessary information, in the textbook or elsewhere, or has discovered a way to clarify the ambiguity or work around it. Another is to provide the whole class with the necessary information or clarification. A third is to ask the groups to stop discussing the question asked in the task and begin discussing instead how they would go about getting the information they need in order to answer the question, or how they would debug the task.

The payoff for teachers who turn questions back to consensus groups in this way is that the teacher is likely to get an unusually precise (and sometimes dismaying) estimate of just how much students really understand so far about the course material, in contrast to an estimate of the native student ability to parrot answers. This new awareness has been known to undermine college or university teachers' previously unquestioned belief in the imperative of "coverage," because it tends to explore the tacit but widely held notion that (as Elaine Mamion has aphoristically put it) "I know I've taught it, because I've heard myself say it." Asking students to question the task can sometimes also sow healthy, unanticipated doubts in the minds of the most sell-confident college and university teachers about their own grasp of the subject matter and the universality of some of their discipline's least questioned, most authoritative truths.

The third responsibility taken on by teachers who organize consensus groups, or any other kind of collaborative learning, for that matter, is to evaluate the quality of students' work, both individual and collaborative. Teachers fulfill this responsibility in two ways, or rather, during two phases of the process: as referees while the work is going on and as judges after the work is over.

Every social relation that involves differences of opinion requires a referee. Someone has to represent, not the interests of one party or another, but the values and mores of the larger community that has a stake in the peaceable, profitable outcome of negotiations that go on in the subcommunities it encompasses. Even in sandlot baseball games, kids know the importance of nominating someone in the group to call strikes, balls, and outs. In jury trials, defense and prosecution lawyers represent the defendant and the state, respectively. The jury represents the local community of the defendant's peers. The judge referees, representing the legal system as a whole: the larger community that includes all of us who agree to live by the rule of law.

Consensus-group collaborative learning also needs a referee. Whenever small groups of students negotiate toward consensus, there are, within groups and among them, both resolvable differences of opinion and unresolvable dissent. When students disagree on the main point of a paragraph because they understand a key word differently, for example, they may be able to resolve their difference by resorting to a dictionary. But if two factions in the discussion disagree because they are making different assumptions, based, say, on ethnic, gender, or class differences, the disagreement may not be so easy to resolve. One faction may dissent from the consensus being forged by the other members of the group and refuse to be budged. In this case, the group agrees to disagree. That is its consensus. That agreement (and an account of what led to it) is what its recorder reports in the plenary session.

Throughout this stage of the process, teachers typically remain uninvolved in any direct way. Once the small-group work is over, however, teachers become more actively and directly involved, not by taking sides but as referees who organize and moderate a plenary discussion based on the reports delivered to the class as a whole by the groups' reporters. Whether or not they understand every aspect of their agreements and differences, most student consensus groups will be prepared, and usually eager, to maintain their position against different positions arrived at by other groups. The teacher's role in plenary discussion is to help the class synthesize reports of the groups' work and draft a synthesis that draws together major points in those reports, if possible helping to construct a consensus that represents the views of the whole class.

Here dissent becomes especially important. In collaborative learning, teachers should make it clear that dissent is welcome and actively encourage recorders to mention in their reports dissenting views that were expressed during the group's discussion. By a "dissenting view" I do not mean only a hard-line, entrenched position. I mean any opinion or view expressed by anyone in any group, anytime during the discussion, perhaps only in passing, perhaps incompletely formulated, that could not be completely assimilated into the group consensus.

Dissent is important in collaborative learning for at least two reasons. First, it may frequently happen that dissent in one group turns out to be the essence of another group's consensus. A split opinion within or between groups may be just what is needed to disrupt complacent or trivial decisions arrived at by the rest of the class. It can also happen, even more strikingly, that one lonely voice of dissent in a class can eventually, in the course of plenary discussion, turn the whole class around, leading it out of a quandary and toward a more satisfactory consensus of the whole or toward a more correct or acceptable view—that is, toward the view that is currently regarded as correct or acceptable by the teacher's disciplinary community.

Another reason for ferreting out dissent is that part of the point of collaborative learning is to teach the craft of interdependence to students who face a world in which diversity is increasingly evident, tenacious, and threatening. Plenary discussions may therefore explore the sources of dissent in ethnic, gender, class, and other "background" differences. Part of the lesson in that case, as John Trimbur has argued, is that understanding why people dissent can be as important to reaching accord as understanding the dissenting opinion itself.

In order to achieve a larger consensus of the class as a whole when the issue is divided, teachers direct student energies in the plenary discussion toward debating two (or more) sides of the issue. The debate ends when the differing parties arrive at a position that satisfies the whole class, or when they agree to disagree and understand the reasons for their disagreement. Occasionally, of course, a lone dissenter or small faction of dissenters will hold out against the class as a whole, taking a position that would not be regarded as correct or acceptable by the teacher's discipline. In that case, wise teachers trust the negotiating process over time either to bring the dissenters within the boundaries of what is currently regarded as acceptable, or (rarely, but also possible) to move the teacher's own and the discipline's current view of what is acceptable in the direction of the dissenters' position.

The teacher's role changes once again once the class reaches a plenary consensus—some sort of agreement that most members of the class as a whole can "live with," including perhaps, for some members, an agreement to disagree. At this stage in the process teachers act for the first time directly and overtly as representatives of the larger community they are members of and that their students hope to join. That community may be a disciplinary one, a community of mathematicians, historians, chemists, sociologists, or whatever, depending on the course and teacher's field of expertise. Or it may be the larger community of those who write, and who expect to read, standard written English organized in certain conventional ways. In speaking for the community at large at this stage of collaborative work, teachers are in the educationally fortunate position of not having to label the consensus formed by the class as merely right or wrong. Rather, the teacher's role is to tell the class whether or not its consensus corresponds to or differs from the prevailing consensus of the larger community.

If the class consensus is more or less the same as the consensus of the larger community, in most cases that's that. Next task. But if the consensus reached by the class differs from the consensus of the larger community in a significant way, then the issue becomes "Why?" To answer that question, teachers usually send the class back to small-group discussion. The task is to examine the process of consensus making itself. How did the class arrive at its consensus? How do the students suppose that the larger community arrived at a consensus so different from their own? In what ways do those two processes differ?

Here the teacher's job, although quite a bit different from the job of a baseball umpire, still looks a lot like the job of a judge in a court of law. Umpires do not explain their decisions to players. But judges often explain their decisions in terms of precedents: the existence of similar decisions in other cases, arrived at by other members of the judge's community of knowledgeable peers. That is, they show that their views are consistent with the views of the community they represent. When they do that, judges are acting a lot like college and university teachers who organize collaborative learning.

Teachers do not tell students what the "right" answer is in consensus-group collaborative learning, because the assumption is that no answer may be absolutely right. Every "right" answer represents a consensus for the time being of a certain community of knowledgeable peers: mathematicians, historians, chemists, sociologists, or whatever—or perhaps only some mathematicians, historians, chemists, sociologists, or whatever. The nature of the answer depends on the nature of the reasoning conversation that goes on in differently constituted communities. And the authority of the answer depends upon the size of the community that has constructed it and the community's credibility among other, related knowledge communities. Once the teacher has shown the class the relation between its own process of negotiation and the negotiations that go on in larger, professional communities, it is poised to take an important step beyond reliance upon external authority toward learning more about the process by which ideas, values, and standards are constructed, established, and maintained by communities of knowledgeable peers.

Comparing the class consensus with that of the larger community is one way to evaluate students' work. The other way is by judging the work that students do individually, based on their collaborative work. That is, teachers evaluate the degree to which students have internalized the language of the conversation that has gone on both in small-group discussion and in the plenary discussions. In this capacity, college and university teachers do not usually judge the quality of students' social behavior in class or how effectively they work with each other in collaborative groups, although (rarely) they may find it appropriate to do that. They evaluate the quality of students' contributions to the class's conversation in its displaced form, writing.

Writing enters the collaborative process at several points. In the first place, conversation in consensus groups prepares students to write better on the topic at hand by giving them an opportunity to rehearse and internalize appropriate language. Recorders write reports, and the groups they represent help edit them. Teachers can ask students to write their own essays or reports on the basis of consensus group conversation, or to revise what they have already written based on it. And (as Chapter 3 explains in detail) teachers can ask consensus groups to undertake tasks that increase students' ability to talk effectively with one another about writing itself and to help one another revise. As a result, after students have begun to acquire language appropriate to peer evaluation—that is, as they begin to learn how to talk effectively with one another about writing—teachers can ask students to begin writing peer reviews of one another's writing and then evaluate the helpfulness, incisiveness, and tact of their remarks.

But in the end, it is the writing that students produce individually as a result of this process that counts in evaluating them. It is with their writing, after all, that students apply for official membership in the communities—of chemists, lawyers, sociologists, classicists, whatever—that are larger, more inclusive and authoritative than any plenary classroom group, reaching well beyond the confines of any one college or university campus.

One reason for judging the quality of students' written contributions to the working conversation among peers is that, as agents of the institution, teachers must satisfy the college or university's grading requirements in order to maintain institutional records. A more important reason is that judging the quality of students' output helps students understand the responsibility they accept when they join a community of knowledgeable peers. The process fosters in students the responsibility to contribute to that community, to respect the community's values and standards, to help meet the needs of other members of the community, and to produce on time the work they have contracted to produce. When students join the community of those who write standard English organized in conventional ways, for example, they accept responsibility on terms agreed to by that community for the writing and reading that they do. They write so that others in the community can understand what they have written. And they read one another's work carefully enough so that if they were to report on what they have read, the writer would agree that that indeed was what was intended.

In this chapter we have followed a class of college or university students discussing an appropriately limited issue through a series of nested consensus groups: small groups, the class as a whole, and the disciplinary community that the teacher represents. Each group in the series constructs knowledge in conversation with knowledgeable peers. That is, the knowledge that group members wind up with was not "given" to them directly by the teacher. They constructed it in the course of doing the task that the teacher supplied. So at first their new knowledge, the knowledge they have constructed, does not have the same degree of authority—or "clout"—as the knowledge that teachers "give" students in a traditional class. There, the authority of knowledge is understood to vary according to the preparation of the teacher. In a class organized for collaborative learning, authority of knowledge varies according to the size and complexity of the groups of students that, with the teacher's guidance, construct it. In the sequence we have followed, the knowledge constructed by small consensus groups has less authority than the knowledge that, based on the reports of those groups, the class as a whole constructs. The knowledge that the class as a whole constructs has this greater authority not only because the class is larger than the small groups, but also because it contains the small groups nested within it.

The knowledge constructed by each small consensus group has only the authority of a group of five students. Nevertheless, the authority of these small groups is greater than the authority of any individual student in the group before the group reached consensus. Small groups increase the authority of their knowledge when they compare their results with the consensus that other groups have arrived at and negotiate a consensus of the class as a whole (of, say, twenty-five students). In that way they increase the authority of the knowledge they have constructed from that of one student to that of twenty-five.

The final step in constructing knowledge and increasing its authority occurs when the class as a whole compares its consensus on the limited issue addressed in the task with the consensus on that issue of the immeasurably larger and more complex disciplinary or linguistic community (such as chemists, historians, or writers of standard English) that the teacher represents. If the two match, the authority of the knowledge that the students have constructed increases once again. The small knowledge community of the class as a whole, with its still smaller discussion groups nested in it, has itself become nested, on one issue, within that much larger community. The students in the class have joined, with respect to that issue, the community that they aspired to join by taking the course.

An example of the process would be the way a class might analyze the key sentence in the Declaration of Independence. Four or five small groups might arrive at quite different definitions of, say, the term "unalienable Rights." These definitions would be the knowledge (or "understanding") that each group constructed and would have the authority implicit in a consensus arrived at among five people. The teacher would ask the class as a whole, after hearing reports from each group, to work toward a single consensus, acknowledging differences. That consensus would then be the understanding of the term that the class as a whole has constructed. It might be similar to some of the definitions constructed by the small groups, or, as a result of further discussion, it might be quite different. It would have greater authority than the definition arrived at by any one student or any one small group: it would have the authority implicit in an agreement among twenty-five people as opposed to just one or five.

Finally, the teacher might ask the class, perhaps working again in small groups, to compare the whole-class consensus with relevant passages from Supreme Court decisions that, speaking for a still larger community, define which benefits or privileges American citizens enjoy by "inalienable right" and which ones may be limited or eliminated entirely. The Court's understanding of the term would of course have a lot more authority than the class's understanding of it. And if the class's consensus matches the Court's, the knowledge the class constructed would have the authority of the whole community that the Court represents, the community of American citizens, in which the class-community is nested. If its consensus does not match that larger community's consensus, the teacher asks students to return to small-group discussion. Their task now is not to decide why their consensus was "wrong." Their task is to try to reconstruct the reasoning by which the Justices of the Court might have arrived at a different consensus and compare it with the reasoning by which the class arrived at theirs.

As we shall see in Chapter 7, this process models the collaborative process by which the authority of all knowledge increases, assuming that all knowledge is socially constructed. Communities of knowledgeable peers construct knowledge in an ongoing negotiation to consensus that involves increasingly larger and more complex communities of knowledgeable peers, a conversation in which, as Richard Rorty says in *Philosophy and the Mirror of Nature,* community members socially justify their beliefs to one another.

In describing knowledge in this nonfoundational way, Rorty generalizes Thomas Kuhn's description, in *The Structure of Scientific Revolutions,* of the way scientists construct scientific knowledge, a description that in their two-year study of the Salk Institute, *Laboratory Life: The Social Construction of Scientific Facts,* Bruno Latour and Steve Woolgar corroborate. Scientists, they say, construct knowledge in conversation about their work over lab benches and in hallways and offices and by revising what they think in the course of that conversation. This is the conversation of "conjoined intelligence. . . made by confluent, simultaneously raised human voices, explaining things to each other" that Lewis Thomas hears on the beach at the Woods Hole Marine Biological Laboratory in *Lives of a Cell.*[8]

But constructive conversation among members of communities of knowledgeable peers takes different forms. Community members engage in direct, face-to-face conversation: they talk, as college and university students do in small consensus-group discussion and as scientists do on the beach at Woods Hole. More importantly, Latour and Woolgar show, they engage in indirect, displaced conversation: they write to each other. In the next chapter we will discuss the important role that writing plays in the craft of interdependence.

Notes

1. For a more thorough survey of this research see "Developing a New Group Service: Strategies and Skills" in Gitterman and Shulman.
2. This and the next two paragraphs are loosely based on Bennis and Shepard.
3. Rorty, *Contingency* 11–12.
4. Hawkes, 141; Hawkes explains this task in helpful detail.
5. Arons, 61–32, 171.
6. Vygotsky, *Mind* 84–87.
7. Edited version republished by permission of Peter Hawkes.
8. Thomas, 15, 73.

Works Cited

Ambercrombie, M.L.J. *The Anatomy of Judgment.* Harmondsworth, England: Penguin, 1969; New York: Hutchinson, 1960.

Arons, Arnold B. *A Guide to Introductory Physics Teaching.* New York: Wiley, 1990.

Bennis, Warren G., and Herbert A. Shepard, "A Theory of Group Development." *Human Relations* 9 (1956): 415–37.

Gitterman, Alex, and Lawrence Shulman, eds. *Mutual Aid Groups, Vulnerable Populations, and the Life Cycle.* New York: Columbia UP, 1993. Also *Mutual Aid Groups and the Life Cycle*, Itasca, IL: Peacock, 1986.

Hawkes, Peter. "Collaborative Learning and American Literature." College *Teaching* 39 (1991): 140–44.

——. *The Structure of Scientific Revolutions.* 2nd ed. Chicago, IL: U Chicago P, 1970.

Latour, Bruno, and Steve Woolgar. *Laboratory Life: The Construction of Scientific Facts.*Princeton: Princeton UP, 1986.

Rorty, Richard. *Contingency, Irony, and Solidarity.* Cambridge: Cambridge UP, 1989.

——. *Philosophy and the Mirror of Nature.* Princeton: Princeton UP, 1979.

Thomas, Lewis. *The Lives of a Cell: Notes of a Biology Watcher.* New York: Bantam, 1975

Trimbur, John. "Collaborative Learning and Teaching Writing." *Perspectives on Recent Research and Scholarship in Composition.* Ed. Ben W. McClelland and Timothy R. Donovan. New York: Modern Language Association, 1985

——. "Consensus and Difference in Collaborative Learning." *College English* 51 (1989): 602–16

Vygotsky, L. S. *Mind in Society: The Development of Higher Psychological Processes.* Ed. Michael Cole, Vera John-Steiner, Sylvia Scribner, and Ellen Souberman. Cambridge: Harvard UP, 1978.

SUGGESTED READINGS: AUDIENCE AND PEER GROUPS

Bishop, Wendy. "Helping Peer Writing Groups Succeed." *Teaching English in the Two-Year College* 15 (1988): 120–25.

Bruffee, Kenneth A. "Collaborative Learning and the 'Conversation of Mankind.'" *College English* 46 (1984): 635–52.

Bruffee, Kenneth A. *Collaborative Learning: Higher Education, Interdependence, and the Authority of Knowledge*. Baltimore: Johns Hopkins UP, 1993.

Cain, Mary Ann. *Revisioning Writers' Talk: Gender and Culture in Acts of Composing*. Albany: SUNY P, 1995.

Ede, Lisa S., and Andrea A. Lunsford. "Audience Addressed/Audience Invoked: The Role of Audience in Composition Theory and Pedagogy." *CCC* 35 (1984): 155–71.

Ede, Lisa, and Andrea Lunsford. *Singular Texts/Plural Authors: Perspectives on Collaborative Writing*. Carbondale: Southern Illinois UP, 1990.

Elbow, Peter, and Pat Belanoff. *Sharing and Responding*. 2nd ed. New York: McGraw-Hill, 1995.

Gere, Anne Ruggles. *Writing Groups: History, Theory, and Implications*. Carbondale: Southern Illinois UP, 1987.

Grimm, Nancy. "Improving Students' Responses to Their Peers' Essays." *CCC* 37 (1986): 91–94.

Harris, Joseph. "The Idea of Community in the Study of Writing." *CCC* 40 (1989): 11–22.

Kirsch, Gesa, and Duane H. Roen. *A Sense of Audience in Written Communication*. Newbury Park, CA: Sage, 1990.

Lunsford, Andrea A., and Lisa S. Ede. "Rhetoric in a New Key: Women and Collaboration." *Rhetoric Review* 8 (1990): 234–41.

Myers, Greg. "Reality, Consensus, and Reform in the Rhetoric of Composition Teaching." *College English* 48 (1986): 154–74.

Park, Douglas B. "Analyzing Audiences." *CCC* 37 (1986): 478–88.

Porter, James E. *Audience and Rhetoric.* Englewood Cliffs, NJ: Prentice Hall, 1992.

Reagan, Sally Barr, Thomas Fox, and David Bleich, eds. *Writing With: New Directions in Collaborative Teaching, Learning, and Research.* Albany: SUNY P, 1994.

Stewart, Donald. "Collaborative Learning and Composition: Boon or Bane?" *Rhetoric Review* 7 (1988): 58–83.

Trimbur, John. "Consensus and Difference in Collaborative Learning." *College English* 51 (1989): 602–16.

Youga, Jan. *The Elements of Audience Analysis.* New York: Macmillan, 1989.

Composing Processes: An Overview

Patricia Bizzell

Patricia Bizzell is a professor of English at the College of the Holy Cross and author of Academic Discourse and Critical Consciousness. *With her husband, Bruce Herzberg, she is co-editor of* The Rhetorical Tradition, *an important anthology of readings in the history of rhetoric. This 1986 article provides an excellent survey of process-centered theories of writing since the 1960s and discusses their practical implications for teaching. As the writing process movement developed, Bizzell writes, different theories of writing processes emerged, some stressing the development of a personal style, some building on research into cognitive processes, and others arguing that the nature of composing processes depends on writers' cultural and rhetorical contexts. While we still have much to learn about composing in writing, Bizzell argues that we now realize that there is no one composing process that works for all writers and situations, that each writer employs several processes for different types of writing, and that writing is a recursive process that cannot be divided neatly into isolated stages of pre-writing, drafting, and revising.*

What Is "Composing"?

Composition scholars agree that the composing process exists or, rather, that there is a complex of activities out of which all writing emerges. We cannot specify one composing process as invariably successful. Current research in the field is beginning to draw a detailed picture of these composing processes.

"Composing" usually refers to all the processes out of which a piece of written work emerges. During composing, the writer may spend some time musing, rereading notes or drafts, or reading the texts of others, as well as actually putting words on the page herself In composition research, "writing" usually refers precisely to the scribal act. One focus of composition research examines the extent to which composing occurs during writing, as opposed to the composing that takes place while other tasks, such as those I just listed, are being performed.

Simply to acknowledge that composing processes exist is something of a gain for modern composition studies. My undergraduate students would like to deny

---

Patricia Bizzell. "Composing Processes: An Overview," from *The Teaching of Writing: Eighty-Fifth Yearbook of the National Society for the Study of Education, Part II,* edited by Anthony R. Petrosky and David Bartholomae, pp. 49–70.

this premise: they prefer the fantasy that when they finally become "good writers," they will be able to sit down at the desk and produce an "A" paper in no more time than it takes to transcribe it. Nor are my students alone in this fantasy of instant text production. It is part of a more general notion in our culture, a sort of debased Romantic version of creativity wherein verbal artifacts are supposed to be produced as easily and inevitably as a hen lays eggs. This more general fantasy affects Americans' judgment of political orators, for example; we value as "good speakers" those who can think on their feet, apparently producing eloquence in no more time than it takes to utter the words.

The classical rhetoricians knew better. Greek and Roman teachers of effective writing and speaking elaborated a five-stage composing process: invention, or finding ideas; arrangement, or putting the ideas into persuasive order; style, or dressing the ideas in persuasive language; memory, or memorizing the text of the speech thus prepared; and delivery, or delivering the speech with the most effective use of voice, gesture, and so on. No one supposed that brilliant orators simply opened their mouths and let it flow.

Many of my students, however, have not encountered anything like the classical composing process in school. Until very recently, most language arts instruction in American schools had lost a sense that composing requires complex processes. Instead, students brought their finished products to the teacher for correction and evaluation. The composing of these products was something students had to manage on their own. Whatever processes they used remained a "black box" to the instructor: the assignment went in at one end, and out came the final paper at the other.

Given that classical rhetoric did emphasize process, how is it that we have inherited such a product-oriented pedagogy? The history is too long to recount here in detail, but let me summarize by saying that over the centuries rhetoric was shorn of four of the five classical stages of composing. In the Renaissance, Ramist rhetoricians, because they sought to develop a purely objective discourse in which to conduct the researches of the new science, redefined invention and arrangement as matters of logic. Rationality, rather than persuasiveness, would be the new standard for judging the soundness and order of ideas. Much later, as English departments were formed in late nineteenth-century American colleges, their avowed focus on literature—on texts to be read—made the study of memory and delivery unnecessary (these elements continued to be studied in the departments of speech which, not coincidentally, split off from English departments at about this time).

As a result of these changes, the study of rhetoric came to focus on only one stage in the classical composing process: style. The tasks of the English department were to analyze the style of canonical literary works, for the purpose of interpreting these works' enduring human values; and to analyze the style of student essays, for the purpose of correcting their errors and encouraging the writers toward the beauties discovered in the canonical works. From the students' viewpoint, the English department thus devoted to the study of style certainly encouraged the fantasy that there are no composing processes. Only finished products were treated in class, whether the accomplished works of literary masters or the mediocre ones of the students themselves. Evidently one could not learn how to compose more effectively, since this was never taught. Evidently one either possessed the inborn ability to produce good texts, or one was out of luck: a cat can't lay eggs.

Rediscovering Composing

Dissatisfaction with this product-centered pedagogy has arisen periodically at least since the early twentieth century in the Progressive Education movement. But a surge of interest in composing developed in the 1960s. It probably received its single greatest impetus from the change in the school population that began to be evident at that time. To summarize this change crudely: more and more students were unable to bring to their teachers essays that needed only stylistic revision. More and more students were producing essays full of errors that were supposed to disappear in the earlier grades and of ideas so ill considered as to call into question the students' cognitive development. Drastic action seemed called for to help these student writers to improve.

It was largely in response to the perceived new needs of students and teachers—that composition studies began to emerge in the 1960s as an area of specialization within English studies. Literary critics, too, were dissatisfied with the New Criticism's focus on style and began the theoretical debates over a replacement paradigm that have continued to the present. The entire discipline of English studies, in other words, has been undergoing some radical changes. But while literary scholars have focused on problems of reading literary texts, composition scholars have turned to examining writing, the process of composing texts, and particularly the texts of student writers and others who are not literary masters.

Most of the research that shapes our current knowledge of composing has been published since 1970. Composition specialists in the 1960s saw themselves primarily as teachers of writing, not as researchers. Nevertheless, their work has strongly influenced current research, not only in what it tells us about composing but also in the professional agenda it establishes for composition studies.

These first of the modern scholars in composition found themselves at odds with the academy from the beginning. Many academics (not to mention administrators and parents) assumed that the solution to the problem of student writing was simply to correct the ever-more-numerous errors, until by dint of the drill students finally learned not to splice commas, split infinitives, and so on. This assumption informed many early professional decisions made by senior academics about their colleagues in composition. For instance, if teaching grammar need be the only content of the writing class, writing teachers would not require advanced academic training. It became customary (as it still is to this day) to staff the bulk of a school's writing courses with teachers reassigned from other disciplines, voluntarily or not, with graduate students, or with people no longer actively seeking terminal degrees and teaching part-time by choice or necessity. These writing teachers found themselves gaining little professional respect, except, perhaps, that due the person who undertakes a necessary but unpleasant job that nobody else wants. Their senior colleagues assumed, moreover, that there was no serious scholarly work to be done in the field of composition studies, so that the way to professional advancement lay in escape from the writing classroom.

But writing teachers became increasingly convinced, on the basis of their classroom experience, that the initial assumption on the need for grammar drills simply was wrong. Attending closely to the problems students had in writing their papers, rather than merely to the problems that appeared in their finished products, writing teachers became convinced that students needed a better understanding of the whole process of working on a piece of writing, to give adequate time to the task and to make the time spent more productive. To gain this understanding, writing teachers began to work through this along with their students and to try to determine what contributed to a successful, or unsuccessful, writing process.

Some early fruit borne by such study was the model of composing introduced by Gordon Rohman and Raymond Wlecke.[1] Rohman and Wlecke found that successful college-level writers typically traverse three stages in composing: pre-writing, writing, and editing. Most significant here is the concept of "pre-writing," that is, degenerating activities that provide essential preparation for drafting. This was perhaps the first intimation that we needed to study a whole complex of composing processes, of which the actual writing of the paper was only one. Moreover, Rohman suggested that prewriting activities such as journal keeping and meditation could be taught—that composing processes, rather than grammar drills, could become the actual content of the writing course.

Some academics opposed such activities, however, on grounds that they were not likely to foster the writing of good academic expository prose. This objection was met with even stronger resistance from writing teachers. During this same era, the academy itself began to seem discredited, in the eyes of many students and teachers, by political developments in the nation at large. For one thing, the academy was reluctant to incorporate new methods of responding to these developments, preferring its traditional subjects and methods of inquiry. For another, this reluctance was seen as enforcing discriminatory social sorting, with white middle-class men being educated for positions of power and all others being disenfranchised. Academic expository prose, the mastery of which was a prerequisite for traditional academic work, was implicated in the indictment of the academy as an institution of political oppression.

Hence, many writing teachers came to argue that students could not write good academic expository prose because academic expository prose was bad in itself—it was verbose, indirect, and impersonal to the point of hypocrisy. Instead of forcing students to master it, and the concomitant complexities of formal Standard English, writing teachers began to believe that they should be helping students to free themselves from its baleful influence if ever their writing were to improve. Students should forget their anxieties about correctness, stop trying to sound like someone else, and work to discover and refine their own personal, authentic writing styles.

The study of composing thus came to serve the liberation of each student's personal style, a way of writing that would dearly and sincerely convey her perspective on the world, as uniquely valuable as the student's own humanity. As I have tried to suggest, a combination of professional and historical circumstances made the development of a pedagogy of personal style something of a political crusade for many writing teachers. By fostering students' own styles, instead of forcing conformity to an oppressive institutional standard, writing teachers could feel they were making their own contribution to the reform of oppressive academic and political institutions.

Since the standard for judging a personal style could come only from within the student, who alone could certify its ability to represent her perspective on the world, the pedagogy of personal style aimed mainly to remove barriers to students' perceptions of what they had achieved in their writing. Close-reading, a technique of literary New Criticism, in which many writing teachers were trained, could be adapted for this purpose. Working as a group, teacher and students focused on student writing as the principal text for the course, and by detailed analysis helped each student writer to see whether her choice of words adequately expressed her thoughts. Given the original political agenda of personal-style pedagogy, this process typically worked to eliminate oppressive vestiges of academic writing. A student's personal style was to be characterized by comfortable use of the first person; by focus on a topic the student knows at first hand, typically personal experiences rather than academic subjects and by exposition relying far more heavily on a detailed account of the writer's perceptions and feelings than on analysis and generalization. Peter Elbow's influential textbook, *Writing Without Teachers,* emphasizes the open-endedness of the composing processes necessitated by the search for a personal style.[2]

The pedagogy of personal style thus established that composing processes are complex and often lengthy and, hence, that a substantial phenomenon exists for scholarly study. The Rohman-Wlecke model of composing has been faulted for its linearity, that is, for assuming that the successful writer typically moves through the composing process without backtracking or omitting any stage. But, in general, personal-style pedagogy, with its emphasis on rewriting, encouraged the view of composing processes as recursive, which has been confirmed by contemporary research.

In addition to these influential assumptions about composing, personal-style pedagogy helped shape contemporary research through its assumptions about what should go on in the writing classroom: that students and teacher should democratically discuss each student's work, with the teacher acting not as authoritative director but as knowledgeable collaborator and with the goal being each student's accomplishment of self-selected writing tasks. Students should not be sidetracked in their search for personal styles by emphasis on standards of correctness set by others, such as the rules of formal Standard English. The teacher's main function, in addition to participating in the class writing workshop, should be to protect students from the academy's oppressive requirements.

Since the great majority of composition scholars have adhered at some time to personal-style pedagogy, it is not surprising that its pedagogical assumptions, as well as its assumptions directly bearing on composing, have influenced our sense of what research projects are worth undertaking. Moreover, this influence is not pernicious, both because all research can only occur under the guidance of assumptions and because these assumptions have guided us toward some fruitful research. It might not be too much to say that we owe all our current knowledge of composing to the early decisions of beleaguered composition scholars to resist the pedagogical agenda being set for them by senior academics, namely teaching grammar, and to seek a pedagogy more responsive to student needs. This pedagogy, in helping students develop their personal styles, brought their composing processes into the classroom and hence into the domain of scholarly inquiry. Moreover, the emphasis of this pedagogy on the personal, on the creative power of the individual writer's mind, helped to legitimate voices silenced in the traditional English classroom, voices of women, ethnic minorities, and other oppressed groups, and so did help to make the academy more responsive to contemporary political issues.

Under the influence of personal-style pedagogy, the first school of thought on composition research, which continues to flourish, encouraged the study of what goes on inside the individual writer's head. Such research is now often referred to as cognitive analyses of composing, because it has borrowed some methods and assumptions from the social sciences. The work of this school has been valuable, as I will explain below; unfortunately, however, until recently, composition research was limited to work in this school by personal-style pedagogy's assumptions about the individual nature of writing ability.

The problem was—and still is, to some extent—that personal-style pedagogy sees the political conflict in schools as between an oppressive institution and individual creative talents. In this view, what the student writer needs to do is to strip away all "outside" influences, such as academic standards of correctness, in order to get down to the thoughts and language that are uniquely, authentically hers. The kind of first-person narrative elicited in personal-style classes was assumed to be such "authentic" writing. The problem with this assumption, however, is illustrated by the fact that this "antiacademic" writing is actually a well-recognized belletristic essay style in itself, as exemplified in writers such as George Orwell and E.B. White, favorites for personal-style classroom reading. To heighten the irony, this style comes much more easily to white middle-and upper-class students than to others, thus preserving in personal-style pedagogy the very social discrimination it sought to combat.

What this example illustrates, however, is not the culpability of writing teachers for failing to free themselves from class-based attitudes, but rather the impossibility of doing so. No one uses language autonomously. One's speaking, reading, and writing are always shaped by one's social and cultural background and by the political relations this background creates with audiences of similar or very different backgrounds. This shaping is as much a matter of what the writer knows as of what she does. For example, a student may fail to produce an acceptable personal-style essay because she comes from a social group that does not value the sort of intense introspection such an essay calls for. Hence, she may either be simply too unfamiliar with introspection to produce it, or too wary with classmates (and teacher) from other social groups to produce it for them to read. As I have argued elsewhere, research into the social and cultural contexts from which the writer's knowledge comes and in which she is addressing an audience is as necessary to our understanding of composing as is research into what goes on in the writer's head.[3] Recently, more research into these contexts of composing has been forthcoming, as I will explain below.

Cognitive Analyses of Composing

The contemporary moment of research on composing may be said to begin with the work of James Britton and Janet Emig. Working independently, but aware of each other's work, Britton and Emig developed strikingly similar pictures of students' composing processes. Perhaps the greatest insight they share is that composing processes vary with the kind of writing the student is doing. Britton distinguishes three kinds: "poetic," which produces literary artifacts; "expressive," in which the student explores a subject and her own feelings about it, for an audience of herself or an intimate friend; and "transactional," in which the student seeks to convey information or argue for a position, for an audience of the teacher in the role of examiner.[4] Emig names two kinds of writing: "reflexive," very similar to Britton's expressive; and "extensive," very similar to Britton's transactional.[5] Britton and Emig agree that student writers' composing processes typically are most truncated and least successful in transactional/extensive writing and most elaborated and most successful in expressive/reflexive writing. Britton and Emig conclude that students should be offered far more opportunities in school for expressive/reflexive writing.

Britton and Emig formed these conclusions about composing by looking at student work, not literary masterpieces. Britton and his colleagues read about 2000 essays by British school children between the ages of eleven and eighteen. Emig interviewed eight American, high school seniors while they composed and produced a case study of one of these writers. This methodology has been widely influential, without being followed to the letter. Although not all researchers base their conclusions on a sample of student essays or on case studies, there is general agreement that composing is best investigated by looking at writers at work.

Emig's and Britton's conclusion, that students need more opportunities in school for expressive/reflexive writing, has also been widely influential, even when their terminology is not used. Indeed, this conclusion formed one of the assumptions of the pervasive pedagogy of personal style. The work of Emig and Britton was thus welcomed because it appeared to provide empirical justification for personal-style pedagogy's political indictment of academic writing. Britton and his colleagues, however, do not see the conflict in terms of academic writing versus individual styles, although their language is sometimes misleading. Rather, it is a battle between the language-using practices of the privileged social class and those of other social classes attempting to gain legitimacy in school. The underlying political agenda of Britton et al. is thus much more radical than that of personal-style pedagogy, calling for a class-based reversal of what constitutes good style rather than for a democracy of styles.

Preferring a focus on the personal, American composition research developed first along lines indicated by Emig, to explore what goes on in the individual writer's head. Some researchers have attempted to make the examination of working writers more rigorous by borrowing methodology from the social sciences. Composition scholar Linda Flower and her colleague, cognitive psychologist John R. Hayes, have pioneered the use of protocol analysis, a cognitive psychology research technique, for studying composing. Flower and Hayes ask writers to describe their thought processes aloud while they are composing. The transcript of what they say is the protocol, which the researchers then analyze for regular features of a composing process.

The Flower-Hayes model divides composing into three main parts: one, the "task environment," subdivided into "rhetorical problem" and "text produced so far"; two, the "writing process," subdivided into "reviewing" (further subdivided into "revising" and "evaluating"), "translating," and "planning" (further subdivided into "generating," "goal-setting," and "organizing"); and three, the "writer's long-term memory." "Task environment" encompasses the immediate context of a composing situation, such as a school assignment for which a written product must be completed; "long-term memory" encompasses the larger social context for composing to be found, for example, in the writer's knowledge of genre. In the Flower-Hayes model, however, these contexts of composing are treated largely as a ground or frame for the main area of interest, namely the "writing process" (note the much greater number of subdivisions in this part of the model). "Writing process" encompasses activities taking place inside the writer's head.[6]

The most influential arguments propounded in the Flower-Hayes model are, first, that the writer can "access" task environment and long-term memory and switch from one writing subprocess to another at any time while composing: in other words, the composing process typically is recursive, not linear. For instance, the writer typically does not plan first and, that done, go on to write without ever reconsidering her plans. Second, although there is no single natural order in which composing activities do or should occur, there is a sort of natural relationship among them such that some activities are, or should be, subordinated to other activities: in other words, the composing process typically is hierarchical.

The Flower-Hayes model seeks to be comprehensive, that is, to describe all possible composing behaviors, although Flower and Hayes have been careful to point out that not every act of composing will—or should—employ every possible behavior. But in spite of this model's important arguments, which I just mentioned, it can be critiqued precisely on grounds of its claim to comprehensiveness. The problem is that some composition specialists have been prompted by this claim to attempt to explain the differences between successful and unsuccessful writers in terms of how fully they make use of the cognitive activities described in the model. Such research might lead to use of the Flower-Hayes model as a Procrustean bed for students' necessarily diverse composing processes.

For example, some researchers influenced by the Flower-Hayes model have argued that poor writing results from neglecting the recursive quality of the composing process, as did the poor writers in Pianko's study who failed to pause for reflecting on what they were writing.[7] Other researchers have held that poor writing results from misranking activities in the process hierarchy. The poor writers studied by Sondra Perl accorded inordinate importance and time to editing for errors in grammar, spelling, and mechanics.[8] The single most important factor in successful writing, Perl has argued, is to allow the recursive quality of composing by rereading the text as one produces it and waiting for a "felt sense" of structure to emerge and guide planning.[9]

The new importance given to the recursive quality of composing has led some researchers to focus exclusively on revision. Nancy Sommers has argued that the whole composing process, rightly understood, is a process of revision in which the writer does not simply polish her style but, more important, develops her ideas. "Revision" comes to mean the whole complex of activities of rereading, evaluating, and making small-scale and large-scale changes in the text as one produces it. Unsuccessful writers, Sommers argues, do not so understand revision, saving it for the end of the composing process and using it only to make small-scale changes such as in word choice.[10] It follows that the most effective writing pedagogy will be that which creates a climate for continual revising in the classroom, as described, for example, by Lil Brannon.[11]

Interest in revision and a desire to correct some problems with protocol analysis by adapting Emig's case-study method for research on composing have led researchers such as Carol Berkenkotter[12] and Mimi Schwartz[13] to follow the progress of a single text through multiple revisions. This research has emphasized that successful writing, whether by accomplished professionals or beginning students, emerges from recursive composing processes. There must be adequate time for rethinking; a willingness to respond to hunches, word associations, and other seemingly random techniques to trigger revision; and a recurring strong sense of the audience for whom one is writing.

Schwartz, Donald Graves, and others have argued that these factors influence revision even in very young children's writing.[14] Children have a natural proclivity for composing, according to Glenda Bissex and other researchers into the genesis of writing ability.[15] Graves argues in his influential book *Writing: Teachers and Children at Work* that it is vitally important for schools not to stifle children's natural desire to write by constraining them with assignments they are not interested in and intimidating them with constant corrections.[16] Rather, children should be given many opportunities to write on topics they choose and offered help with any aspect of composing only when such help seems necessary to the successful completion of a particular writing project and when it can be offered in such a way as not to make the child feel that she is no longer in control of her own writing. Although Shirley Brice Heath, David Olson, and others have argued that students' readiness to develop their writing in school is greatly influenced by their social and cultural backgrounds, most researchers into children's writing agree that Graves's pedagogy is the most helpful for all students.[17]

It is interesting to note how these various kinds of cognitive research on composing, like the work of Britton and Emig, echo some assumptions of personal-style pedagogy. The work of Pianko, Perl, and Sommers leads to the conclusion that something very like personal-style pedagogy is still the best: the main classroom activity is group revision of student texts, students rewrite to achieve their own expressive goals rather than to satisfy academic requirements, and any insistence on formal correctness is taboo. Graves recommends a similar pedagogy for elementary-school children, with the additional personal-style assumption that the resources they will call on in writing are mainly innate abilities, not knowledge gained in school. Thus, the kind of pedagogy emerging from current cognitive research on composing is open to the same objection that was leveled against personal-style pedagogy, namely, that this new pedagogy does not lead to mastery of academic writing. Personal-style pedagogues, as I noted earlier, were inclined to answer this charge by arguing that mastery of academic writing was undesirable anyway. Those advocating the new pedagogy, however, generally argue that it offers the best route to eventual mastery of academic writing and any other kind of writing the student chooses to do. This view is still open to debate; we have no research evidence that students educated according to this pedagogy develop into more accomplished academic writers than those educated by other means, though the student excerpts typically quoted in works advocating this pedagogy suggest they are accomplished at other kinds of writing. The fact is, however, that curricula designed according to this pedagogy generally do not teach academic writing directly, whatever abilities may be expected of students afterwards.

Research on the Social and Cultural Contexts of Composing

Although, as I suggested earlier, the first contemporary school of thought on composition research focused on the individual writer's mind, more recently a second school has developed to research the social and cultural factors that influence the individual writer's performance. These researchers have been motivated in part by a reluctance to accept the conclusion, forced by personal-style and cognitive-based analyses of composing, that differences in individual performance are due to differences in individual talent. This reluctance sprang from the scholars' observation that performance differences seemed to correlate with social groups; it seemed logical, therefore, to assume that social and cultural, as well as individual, factors influence composing. Moreover, poor performance seemed to correlate with relatively less privileged social groups. Retaining a sympathy with these groups consistent with some assumptions of personal-style pedagogy, these scholars wished to save them from the stigma of personal failure and to seek a pedagogy specific to their needs.

For many of these researchers, mastery of academic writing has become once more an acceptable goal of composition pedagogy, but not as it was traditionally taught. Once, the course teaching academic writing simply laid down its laws, and those who would not or could not conform simply left the academy. Now, composition scholars seek to serve these students particularly—the ones who have trouble mastering academic writing—so as to give them equal access to the knowledge generated and maintained by the academy. Some scholars may hope that, if academic writing is still a weapon of political oppression, students who master it may be able to turn the weapon against the oppressors. At any rate, many students are now asking for help in mastering academic writing, and writing teachers are responding, just as we responded fifteen years ago when they asked for help in mastering nonacademic, personal styles.

Another influence on the interest in social and cultural contexts of composing has been the new interest in classical rhetoric among composition specialists. Classical rhetoric began to be recovered for English studies in the 1960s, when new collections of original classical texts became available and E.P.J. Corbett's influential Classical *Rhetoric for the Modern Student* suggested contemporary pedagogical applications.[18] At first, classical rhetoric's most important contribution was its multistage composing process, particularly its emphasis on invention, which reinforced the movement in personal-style pedagogy to develop "pre-writing" or idea-generating techniques.

The classical model of composing has been faulted on grounds of excessive linearity. C.H. Knoblauch and Lil Brannon have blamed classical rhetoric, not as recently rediscovered but as embedded in American schooling since the nineteenth century, for influencing teachers to vitiate new pedagogical techniques, such as those encouraging personal style, by inserting them into a curriculum dominated by this linear model of composing.[19] In this way the techniques become mere moments in a rigid progression of stages of composing, rather than, as they should be, periodically useful tools in an open-ended and recursive process. But there is more to the story of classical rhetoric's relevance for the modern student.

As composition specialists have begun to turn to research on the contexts of composing, they have become aware that perhaps the most important contribution of classical rhetoric is precisely its focus on context. Classical rhetoric assumes that the function of writing is not to express oneself but to effect change in the human community in which one lives. Hence, the ability to suit one's style to the particular audience, rather than addressing all in one "personal" register, becomes art, not hypocrisy. Classical rhetoric invites discussion of the social and political uses of writing in ways that personal-style pedagogy, for all its political agenda, never could.

As composition specialists' interest in the contexts of composing has emerged, two seminal theorists have been Ann Berthoff and Mina Shaughnessy. They take two very different approaches, without much reference to each other, but both insist on the crucial connection between individual writer and "outside world." Berthoff has made this point in the strongest terms: human beings use language to make sense of themselves and their world.[20] Hence, if we want to understand composing, we must look at that world with which the writer is in a dialectical relationship, as well as at the writer's individual talents. Berthoff does share some assumptions with personal-style pedagogy concerning all students' innate meaning-making powers. But because she also looks at the context of composing, the world in which and on which they work, she realizes that student writers can be taught to make more personally satisfying use of their meaning-making powers in language—that is, she favors a more directive pedagogy than the personal-style, one that offers what she calls "assisted invitations" to composing. These "invitations" aim not to liberate student writing from the influence of others' styles, but to make students constructively self-conscious about the resources available to their own writing in their society's repertoire of styles. For example, instead of merely keeping a personal journal, Berthoff's students might be encouraged to maintain a "double-entry notebook" in which they periodically reread and critique their own earlier observations. Thus they are made students of their own language-using practices.

While Berthoff's approach is intended, I believe, to be universally applicable, that is, to describe the universal human experience with making meaning in language, Shaughnessy confined her study specifically to the academic community.[21] In her analysis of successive drafts of papers by extremely unskilled college writers, Shaughnessy has found attempts at meaning making where there appears to be no order at all. She understands the composing process as a socialization process, in which gradually bringing one's writing into line with the discourse conventions of one's readers also brings one to share their thinking, their values, in short, their world view. Shaughnessy has argued that student writers are least successful when most ignorant of academic discourse conventions: how the academic audience evaluates evidence, what allusions strike it as elegant, what personae it finds credible, and so on. Shaughnessy has suggested a philosophical critique of personal-style pedagogy in her repudiation of the "honest face" persona for student writers. Nowhere, including the academy, does clear, sincere self-expression win assent unaided.

Shaughnessy's work gave composition specialists a new perspective on student writing problems. Her analysis allows us to retain the best element of personal-style pedagogy, namely, its sense that students' relationship with the academy is agonistic and requires our mediation if social justice and common humanity are to be served. But she also allowed us to step back from the position that bad student writing was caused by the imposition of bad academic standards on natural creativity. Rather, if no writing is autonomous, if all writing is situated in some language-using community, then bad student writing, according to Shaughnessy, should be understood as the output of apprentices or initiates into the academic community. The pedagogy they need is not one that excoriates academic discourse, but rather one that mediates their introduction to it while remaining respectful of the language-using practices they bring to school.

Research into the social, cultural, and political influences on composing, particularly as they bear on students attempting to master academic writing, has taken several directions, exploring writing across the curriculum, basic writing, collaborative learning, and reading/writing connections. Questions which remain problematic for this research include the extent to which social, cultural, and political factors determine composing as opposed to merely influencing it, and the pace at which students should be urged toward mastery of academic writing. Assumptions from personal-style pedagogy can be seen playing their part in this school of research, as much as in the cognitive research that this school often seeks to correct or oppose. For example, recommendations for workshop classrooms in which students pursue self-selected writing goals often emerge from this research, as my brief overview will show. Nevertheless, the emphasis on contexts of composing is an essential and unique contribution.

Writing across the curriculum began as a pedagogical movement in Great Britain in the late 1960s. It was fostered by James Britton, Nancy Martin, and their colleagues in response to the discovery, made in the course of their composing process research, that students wrote very little outside the English classroom. Believing that students would write better if given more opportunities to write in school, particularly opportunities for expressive writing, the British researchers published a series of pamphlets explaining how to integrate expressive writing into a wide range of academic disciplines. In effect, these pamphlets argue for teaching a composing process which would begin with expressive writing, for example in class journals, and only later issue in finished academic essays. The British researchers envision a classroom in which much student writing and talking do not issue in finished work at all, but are nevertheless essential for their heuristic value.[22]

Toby Fulwiler[23] and Lil Brannon and C.H. Knoblauch[24] are among the American composition scholars who have adapted for American colleges the work of Britton et al., which is aimed at elementary and secondary level students. In arguing for the efficacy of a journal-centered composing process in college-level academic disciplines, these proponents of writing across the curriculum have focused the British methods more directly toward the production of finished essays, while maintaining that better papers grow from personal interest in the topic that students develop through their journals. This pedagogy, too, has argued that student composing processes may be idiosyncratic and no single composing process can be assumed to be successful for everyone.

Other American work in writing across the curriculum moves away from this focus on the individual writer to look more directly at the academic context and its demands. Composition scholars such as Elaine Maimon have sought to respond to Shaughnessy's call for a taxonomy of academic discourse conventions.[25] Maimon's focus is not merely on formal features of texts, such as laboratory report format. Rather, she analyzes the intellectual framework suggested by the laboratory report and asks: What do the discourse conventions reveal about how scientists define and interact with the world? What kind of thinking does this kind of writing ask students to do or actually make them do as they write? Maimon's work suggests that there may be epistemological constraints on composing. A writer's varying degrees of success with different kinds of writing may not be due to a simple dichotomy of personal writing (good) versus academic writing (bad). Rather, the different kinds of thinking demanded in different disciplines may cause the student's composing process to vary as a function of the different distances between these ways of thinking and that with which the student is originally comfortable.

Thus these two different approaches to writing across the curriculum typically issue in different pedagogies. The centered approach, once again, endorses something very similar to personal-style pedagogy. The classroom is a workshop, students generate their own writing topics and stylistic goals, and emphasis on correctness is avoided. The teacher is likely, however, to encourage writing projects that involve something like traditional academic inquiry—for instance, a topic requiring library research. Moreover, it is not unusual for such a writing course to be linked with a course in some other discipline, so that the students prepare their papers for that course with the aid of the journal-centered pedagogy of the writing course. Typically, however, journal-centered pedagogy spends relatively little time on formal academic expository writing.

In contrast, the approach centered on academic discourse conventions gives first priority to mastery of academic writing and the formal Standard English it employs. Students may well be encouraged to begin front journals and other forms of pre-writing associated with personal-style pedagogy, but they will be urged along more quickly to the production of finished academic essays. Students will be helped to meet academic English standards in the final stages of composing, on grounds that to do so is to observe what counts as polite behavior in the community they are seeking to enter. The classroom atmosphere is likely to be more directive, with the teacher actively seeking to explain academic writing conventions and to demystify the kinds of thinking they make possible.

The academic context has particularly marked effects on students who are least familiar with its discourse conventions and ways of thinking—the students known as "basic writers" who are at the very beginning stages of being able to produce successful academic writing. Much research on the composing processes of basic writers has focused on the extent to which their difficulties are due to the academic context. Mike Rose has argued that a truncated or blocked composing process can result from overly rigid internalization of advice given in writing instruction, rather than from some deficiency in the student's innate ability to compose.[26] David Bartholomae, extending the work of Shaughnessy, has explained the discourse of basic writers as an approximation of the academic discourse whose conventions and world view are unfamiliar to them, rather than merely as a tissue of errors.[27] These readings of the work of basic writers suggest that their composing processes must include a considerable amount of trial-and-error experimentation as they gradually discover how to use academic discourse for their own purposes.

Teaching academic discourse to basic writers has become a particularly sensitive issue because their difficulties with academic writing tend to be a function of the social distance between the academy and their home communities. That is, basic writers typically come from less privileged social groups, where the language-using practices are most unlike those of the academy, which reflect the practices of the privileged groups in our society. Hence, basic writers appear to be in more danger than others of being alienated from their home communities by mastery of academic discourse. Literacy researchers Walter Ong[28] and Thomas J. Farrell[29] have argued in favor of such alienation or assimilation, on grounds that the ways of thinking enabled by the language-using practices of such students' home communities are cognitively inferior to those of the academy. Other scholars, however, see such arguments as unjustly enforcing the social privileges of academic writing.[30] We do not know whether academic ways of thinking are in fact cognitively different from, or superior to, those of other communities; nor do we know to what extent assimilation is unavoidable for basic writers.

As research on writing across the curriculum and on basic writing has emphasized students' adapting to new ways of thinking, many composition researchers have been led to focus on the extent to which learning to compose is a socialization process, a process of initiation into the discourse community's world view. Such a focus immediately brings to the foreground the extent to which composing is a collaborative process. More broadly, the ways we "compose" experience are culturally conditioned. More particularly, all writers are influenced in their composing processes by other writers, other writing, more experienced mentors, and so on. For the student, these are the influences of academic discourse, teachers, and peers. Kenneth Bruffee, a specialist in the "collaborative learning" of writing, has explored these influences and concludes that students who understand something of the academic world view and its discourse are often more effective than teachers in mediating other students' introduction to the academy.

Bruffee has developed a method of training students to tutor their peers that helps them all to become conscious of what they already knew about academic discourse and to improve their knowledge through attention to their own composing processes. Bruffee's writing workshop resembles the personal-style classroom in procedure, with the difference that the main goal is not discovery of one's inmost honest feelings, but rather articulation of a public voice that will allow participation in the academic intellectual community.[31] The greatest contribution of work on collaborative learning is to emphasize that composing is always in some sense a social process.

Intellectual socialization may be accomplished not only by interacting with people, but also by encountering the writing of others. Thus research on connections between reading and writing also speaks to our knowledge of composing processes. That the writer must be able to read her own text while composing it, we know from such work as that of Sommers and of Flower and Hayes. But Anthony Petrosky and Mariolina Salvatori have suggested that the ability to read the works of others also affects a writer's composing process. Petrosky argues that the successful reading of a literary text is a "transaction" in which the reader must work to make the text meaningful in terms of her own experience, a view influenced by reader-response literary theory. Writing from these perceived correspondences between personal and literary experience helps student writers to elaborate their composing processes where it is most needed: in the linking of adequate illustrations to the generalizations that frame their arguments.[32] Similarly, Salvatori has argued that student writers develop intellectually more complex composing processes as they learn to link moments of reading comprehension into larger patterns of meaning and to relate these in turn to their own experience for comparison or critique.[33] In effect, for these researchers, the texts of others become collaborators in the students' composing processes, stimulating critical reflection on composing in much the same way as do peer tutors or the conventions of academic discourse itself, self-consciously viewed.

What We Know: Curricular Implications

We know that the act of composing through writing is a complex process. Although we are beginning to identify characteristic moments or stages in this process, we cannot say exactly what are the relationships of these stages one to another. We can say that we know such relationships exist, that is, the composing process is hierarchical, and also that they are not necessarily ordered serially, that is, the composing process is recursive. We cannot say that there is one composing process invariably successful for all writers, for all purposes. Rather, we know that composing processes vary both as the same writer attempts different kinds of discourse and as different writers attempt the same kind of discourse, and that such variations may be necessary to success in composing. The current state of our knowledge of composing permits the limited generalizations that successful composing results more often from attention to the thinking required by a piece of writing than to its adherence to standard conventions of grammar, spelling, and so on; and that successful composing results more often from a process that allows for rereading, rethinking, and rewriting than from one in which time limitations or other pressures force a rush to closure. I believe that we can also conclude—although this is perhaps more debatable—that "successful" composing results in writing that participates actively in the language-using practices of a particular community, without slavishly imitating them.

This limited understanding of composing processes nevertheless permits some broad recommendations on curriculum. First, learning to write requires writing. Students cannot be expected to master such complex processes if they only practice them two or three times in a school term, or without a teacher's guidance. It follows, then, if students are to be writing frequently and receiving frequent responses from the teacher, that classes in which writing is taught (whether in English or some other discipline) must be kept small. The teacher must be able to get to know the students in order to respond consistently to the thinking they develop in their writing. Moreover, if the emphasis in writing is to be on developing thinking, it follows both that the curriculum should be structured to encourage recursive composing processes and that institutionalized testing of student writing should not set a counteragenda for the writing class, such as mastering a certain number of features of formal grammar.

But in this small class in which students are writing and rewriting frequently, what should they be writing? What should the classroom activities be? These questions, it seems to me, are more open to debate. Some answers can be found in the Position Statement on teaching composition recently promulgated by the Commission on Composition of the National Council of Teachers of English.[34] This document suggests that students should be encouraged "to make full use of the many activities that comprise the act of writing," presumably including various pre-writing and editing techniques as well as the actual drafting of papers. The document also states that writing assignments should reflect the wide variety of purposes for writing, including expressive writing, writing across the curriculum, and writing that would have a place in "the world beyond school." The writing classroom, according to the document, should be organized as a workshop in which students write for each other, as well as for the teacher, and in which writing is used as "a mode of learning" rather than merely "reporting on what has been learned." To accomplish these ends, class size should not be larger than twenty students, and student writing should be the principal text. Tests should allow students "to demonstrate their writing ability in work aimed at various purposes" and should encourage the development of students' self-critical abilities.

The recommendations on class size, testing, and teaching a full range of composing activities, which would necessitate much attention to substantive revision, may be the most politically sensitive of the recommendations, since they at once ask the public for more money for education (more teachers to keep class size small) and deny the public the kind of testing in writing skills that it seems to desire. Yet current research suggests that it is essential to implement these recommendations if student writing is to improve.

It is not equally evident, however, that for good writing to ensue students must always write for each other and make their own writing the principal text. If the curricular goal is to foster mastery of academic discourse, such a classroom organization will not be very productive unless many of the students have already achieved the desired goal and so can teach the others. But it appears that today's students typically do not have enough prior knowledge of academic discourse conventions to help each other to mastery of them. More guidance from the teacher and more reading materials that illustrate and elucidate these practices may be needed (without, however, returning to the traditional, authoritarian classroom).

The Position Statement may be recommending what amounts to a personal-style classroom because the value of this approach is widely acknowledged among composition specialists, while the goal of mastering academic discourse is more problematic. The Commission also finesses the issue of academic discourse by taking a pluralistic view of the kinds of writing assignments it recommends, all the way from personal-style pedagogy's favored expressive writing to some kind of business or technical writing (for "the world beyond school"). In fact, there is no consensus on what kinds of writing students should be doing. Recent anthologies of college student writing, published as textbooks, suggest that personal-style essays still enjoy an edge; indeed, if they did not, there would be no point in publishing such anthologies.[35] But, as I suggested earlier, various kinds of academic writing are mounting a strong challenge. I believe, however, that it is salutary for teachers and students to discuss the problem of what constitutes "good" writing. Thus there is no way to escape the fact that course content choices, with the kinds of writing they valorize, will have political consequences with which we must deal.

Indeed, perhaps the most important conclusion to be drawn from this overview of research on composing is that research results alone not only should not dictate a curriculum, they cannot dictate it. Notice how persistently composition researchers have interpreted their results in light of personal-style pedagogical assumptions, whether about classroom organization or political agenda. But we could not do otherwise. Scholars writing up their research, like students struggling with their first essay assignments, must work within the language-using practices of a particular community, which are in turn shaped by its social, cultural, and political circumstances. The challenge is to be an active participant, to change the community in light of the values that make one's commitment to education professionally and personally meaningful.

FOOTNOTES

1. D. Gordon Rohman, "Pre-Writing: The Stage of Discovery in the Writing Process," *College Composition and Communication* 26 (May 1965): 106–12.
2. Peter Elbow, *Writing Without Teachers* (New York: Oxford University Press, 1973).
3. Patricia Bizzell, "Cognition, Convention, and Certainty: What We Need to Know about Writing," *PRE/TEXT* 3 (Fall 1982): 213–44.
4. James Britton, T. Burgess, N. Martin, A. Mcleod, and H. Rosen. *The Development of Writing Abilities (11–18)* (London: Macmillan Education, 1975).
5. Janet Emig, *The Composing Processes of Twelfth Graders* (Urbana, Ill.: National Council of Teachers of English, 1971).
6. Linda Flower and John R. Hayes, "A Cognitive Process Theory of Writing," *College Composition and Communication* 32 (December 1981): 365–87.
7. Sharon Pianko, "A Description of the Composing Processes of College Freshman Writers," *Research in the Teaching of English* 13 (February 1979): 5–22.
8. Sondra Perl, "Composing Processes of Unskilled College Writers," *Research in the Teaching Of English* 13 (December 1979):317–36.
9. Sondra Perl, "Understanding Composing," *College Composition and Communication* 31 (December 1980): 363–69.
10. Nancy Sommers, "Revision Strategies of Student Writers and Experienced Adult Writers," *College Composition and Communication* 31 (December 1980): 378–88.
11. Lil Brannon, Melinda Knight, and Vera Neverow-Turk, *Writers Writing* (Montclair, N.J.: Boynton/Cook, 1983).
12. Carol Berkenkotter and Donald Murray, "Decisions and the Planning Strategies of a Publishing Writer, and Response of a Laboratory Rat—or Being Protocoled," *College Composition and Communication* 34 (May 1983): 156–72.
13. Mimi Schwartz, "Two Journeys through the Writing Process," *College Composition and Communication* 34 (May 1983):188–201.
14. Donald Graves, "An Examination of the Writing Processes of Seven-Year-Old Children," *Research in the Teaching of English* 9 (Winter 1975): 227–41; Linda Leonard Lamme and Nancy M. Childers, "Composing Processes of Three Young Children," *Research in the Teaching of English* 17 (February 1983): 31–50.
15. Glenda L. Bissex, *Gnys at Work: A Child Learns to Write and Read* (Cambridge, Mass.: Harvard University Press, 1980).
16. Donald H. Graves, *Writing: Teachers and Children at Work* (Portsmouth, N.H., and London: Heinemann Educational Books, 1983).
17. Shirley Brice Heath, *Ways With Words: Language, Life, and Work in Communities and Classrooms* (Cambridge, Eng.: Cambridge University Press, 1983); David R. Olson, "The Language of Instruction: The Literate Bias of Schooling," in *Schooling and the Acquisition of Knowledge,* ed. Richard C. Anderson, Rand J. Spiro, and William E. Montague (Hillsdale, N.J.: Lawrence Erlbaum Associates, 1977), pp. 65–90. For a dissenting view, see Margaret Donaldson, "Speech and Writing and Modes of Learning," in *Awakening to Literacy. The University of Victoria Symposium of Children's Response to a Literate Environment: Literacy before Schooling,* ed. Hillel Goelman, Antoinette A. Oberg, and Frank Smith (Exeter, N.H., and London: Heinemann Educational Books, 1984), pp. 174–84.
18. Edward P.J. Corbett, *Classical Rhetoric for the Modern Student,* 2nd edition (New York: Oxford University Press, 1971).
19. C.H. Knoblauch and Lil Brannon, *Rhetorical Traditions and the Teaching of Writing* (Montclair, N.J.: Boynton/Cook, 1984).

20. Ann E. Berthoff, *The Making of Meaning: Metaphors, Models and Maxims for Writing Teachers* (Montclair, N.J.: Boynton/Cook, 1981).

21. Mina P. Shaughnessy, *Errors and Expectations: A Guide for the Teacher of Basic Writing* (New York: Oxford University Press, 1977).

22. Nancy Martin, editor, *Writing across the Curriculum: Pamphlets from the Schools Council/London Institute of Education W.A.C. Projects* (Montclair, N.J.: Boynton/Cook, 1984).

23. Toby Fulwiler, "The Personal Connection: Journal Writing across the Curriculum," in *Language Connections: Writing and Reading across the Curriculum,* ed. Toby Fulwiler and Art Young (Urbana, Ill.: National Council of Teachers of English, 1982), pp. 15–32.

24. C.H. Knoblauch and Lil Brannon, "Writing as Learning through the Curriculum," *College English* 45 (September 1983): 465–74,

25. Elaine Maimon, "Maps and Genres: Exploring Connections in the Arts and Sciences," in *Composition and Literature: Bridging the Gap,* ed. Winifred Bryan Homer (Chicago: University of Chicago Press, 1983) pp. 110–25.

26. Mike Rose, "Rigid Rules, Inflexible Plans and the Stifling of Language: A Cognitivist Analysis of Writer's Block," *College Composition and Communication* 31 (December 1980): 389–400.

27. David Bartholomae, "The Study of Error," *College Composition and Communication* 31 (October 1980): 253–69.

28. Walter J. Ong, "Literacy and Orality in Our Times," in *Composition and Literature: Bridging the Gap,* ed. Horner, pp. 126–140.

29. Thomas J. Farrell, "I.Q. and Standard English," *College Composition and Communication* 34 (December 1983): 470–84.

30. See rebuttals to Farrell by Karen Greenberg, Patrick Hartwell, Margaret Himley, and R.E. Stratton in *College Composition and Communication* 35 (December 1984): 455–77.

31. Kenneth A. Bruffee "Collaborative Learning and the 'Conversation of Mankind,' " *College English* 46 (November 1984): 635–52.

32. Anthony R. Petrosky, "From Story to Essay: Reading and Writing," *College Composition and Communication* 33 (February 1982): 19–36.

33. Mariolina Salvatori, "Reading and Writing a Text: Correlations between Reading and Writing," *College English* 45 (November 1983): 657–66.

34. Commission on Composition of the National Council of Teachers of English, "Teaching Composition: A Position Statement," (Urbana, Ill.: National Council of Teachers of English, 1983). I should note that as a member of the Commission I participated in the drafting of this document and endorsed its publication.

35. See, for example, William E. Coles, Jr., and James Vopat, editors, *What Makes Writing Good: A Multiperspective* (Lexington, Mass., and Toronto: D.C. Heath Co., 1985); Nancy Sommers and Donald McQuade, editors, *Student Writers at Work: The Bedford Prizes* (New York: Bedford Books of St. Martin's Press, 1984).

Rhetorical Invention

W. Ross Winterowd

W. Ross Winterowd, professor of English at the University of Southern California, has been writing about rhetoric, literacy, and the teaching of writing since the 1960s. His books include The Culture and Politics of Literacy, The English Department: A Personal and Institutional History, A Teacher's Introduction to Composition in the Rhetorical Tradition, *and* Encountering Student Texts *(co-edited with Bruce Lawson and Susan Sterr Ryan). Disagreeing with those who hold that thinking cannot be taught, Winterowd, in this chapter from his book* Composition/Rhetoric: A Synthesis, *argues that invention should be at the heart of composition instruction. Invention systems like those based on classical rhetoric, Kenneth Burke's pentad, and tagmemic theory tap into the creative powers of the mind, Winterowd explains, and provide writers with perspectives for viewing and "problematizing" the world.*

Aristotle and Extrapolation

In *The Philosophy of Composition* (1977), E.D. Hirsch, Jr. argued that composition and rhetoric are separate fields, and it was this argument that led Hirsch into what I have called neo-Ramism, the exclusion of invention from composition. In fact, Hirsch's "philosophy" reduced composition to stylistics. But as practitioners, we know positively that style is not all, not even our central concern when we teach composition.

Favorable or unfavorable, each of our responses to student texts falls into one of four categories: content, organization, style, or editing. We react to logic, semantic intention, development of ideas; to the order in which the ideas are presented; to sentence structure, figurative language, tone; and to "mechanics" such as punctuation and verb agreement. If this spectrum does represent what we can say about a text, then we must have methods for teaching *invention, arrangement, style,* and *mechanics*.

The traditional departments of rhetoric are invention, arrangement, style, delivery, and memory, but since we are dealing with written discourse, not spoken, delivery and memory become irrelevant.

Obviously, then, composition and rhetoric are *not* identical, in just the

---

same way that cardiology and medicine are not: one is a branch of the other. Just as a cardiologist must be a physician, so a compositionist must be a rhetorician. Aristotle and his successors wrought better than they could have imagined. Much better.

A schematic of the field of composition/rhetoric appears on the next page. I will use the diagram—which captures something of the elegance of rhetoric, either traditional or modern—as the basis for this and the two subsequent chapters.

Rhetorical invention concerns the generation of subject matter: any process-conscious or subconscious, heuristic or algorithmic—that yields something to say about a subject, arguments for or against a case. Inartificial arguments are simply the facts of the "case," discoverable through research if they are not immediately obvious. (Aristotle lists such evidence as contracts, testimony of witnesses, statements under torture and so on.) Artificial arguments are more subtle, arising from the character of the speaker *(ethos),* the nature of the audience *(pathos),* or the integrity of the argument itself *(logos).* And, of course, logical arguments can be either deductive or inductive.

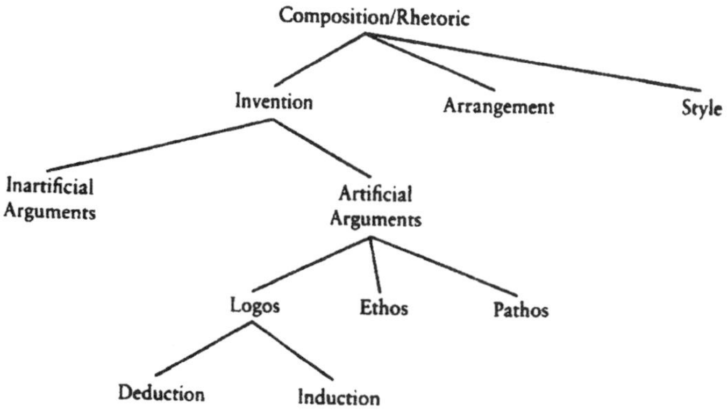

"Brain, Rhetoric, and Style" (pp. 129–57) is, in fact, a contemporary reaction to the deduction-induction dichotomy in rhetoric and logic. It is perhaps dangerous to boil the argument down to its simplest terms, but for the sake of clarity: the left hemisphere of the brain works deductively, and the right hemisphere works inductively. Western rationalist that he was, Aristotle had little to say about induction, the mode of reasoning most congenial to the "intuitive" right hemisphere, and rhetoric throughout its history has not paid attention to the alternative, right hemispheric processes of logos. Currently, however, the situation is changing: a great deal of work in rhetoric proper, linguistics, psychology, neurophysiology, anthropology, and other fields is concerned with cognitive and discourse modes of the right hemisphere, and certainly this work will be a major influence on composition theory and teaching in the next decades. (See Benderly, 1981; Emig, 1978; Freed, 1981; Glassner, 1981; Miner, 1976.)

It is a useful oversimplification to point out that in literary criticism, mimetic theories focus on "truth" value (logos); expressive, on the poet (ethos); pragmatic, on the reader (pathos); and objective, on the text itself (arrangement and style). However, as chapters 2 and 3 should have demonstrated, a theory of language, a hermeneutic method, or a set of evaluative criteria will be unsatisfactory unless it squares with the classical theory of rhetoric, dealing with all factors as they interrelate. Thus, it can be argued that a literary theory (or any other theory of discourse) will be adequate just to the degree that it squares with the classical theory of rhetoric. (See "The Three R's: Reading, Reading, and Rhetoric," pp. 253–63.) I am not claiming that modern rhetoric is simply a new application of the same old stuff, though I would argue strongly that modern work in linguistics, psycho-linguistics, speech act theory, anthropology, and other fields gives a more penetrating conception of the triad ethos-pathos-logos, but does not supersede it.

Invention, Lost and Found

As composition became a massive, if not respectable, enterprise in American schools and universities, the emphasis was squarely on style and structure, to the virtual exclusion of invention. (See Berlin, 1984.)

Inside the front cover of my edition of *The Foundations of Rhetoric, by* Adam Sherman Hill, Boylston Professor of Rhetoric and Oratory in Harvard University (Harper and Brothers Publishers, 1897)—owned once by Julian U. Siegel of Baltimore—are these ghostly wisps of humor: "Shake well before using!" and "Take in small doses!" This, from the preface:

> Differ as good writers may in other respects, they are all distinguished by the judicious and the skillful placing of words. They all aim (1) to use no word that is not established as a part of the language, in the sense in which they use it, and no word that does not say what they wish it to say so clearly as to be understood at once, and either so strongly as to command attention or so agreeably as to win attention; (2) to put every word in the place fixed for it by the idiom of the language, and by the principles which govern communication between man and man—the place which gives the word its exact value in itself and in its relations with other words; (3) to use no more words than are necessary to effect the purpose in hand. If it be true that these simple principles underlie all good writing, they may properly be called *The Foundations of Rhetoric.*

In short for A.S. Hill as for E.D. Hirsch, Jr., almost a century later, stylistics was virtually the all.

The Foundations of Rhetoric is by no means a bad book; it is not schlock mindlessly and quickly produced to capitalize on a G.I. Bill or a Baby Boom or a Sputnik. For our purposes, it is merely a typical book, and the highest praise we can give it is to say it is an admirable example of an era that stretched from the latter part of the nineteenth century to, roughly, 1964, when Rohman and Wlecke published their landmark study of invention: *Pre-Writing: The Construction and Application of Models for Concept Formation in Writing.* It was the genius of these scholars to understand that the compositionist must deal with substance, for a composition has meaning as well as style and structure. No doubt Adam Sherman Hill would have agreed, but he was caught in a rhetorical paradigm which implied that his colleagues in the substantive fields had a comer on the content market, Brothers Hunt who, in the educational marketplace, controlled logos: "Save the fuss; leave the thinking to us."

A kind of antiquarian passion leads me from one old composition text to another, those solidly bound, magisterial books with now-fading notations of students from generations ago; the ignominy of the old texts—none of them classics, all of them forgotten—is a melancholy but salubrious commentary on the profession that we share. Our best works, composition texts that do give students the ability to write (and hence a powerful tool of cognition), are as doomed as is *Composition and Rhetoric,* by Alfred M. Hitchcock (Henry Holt, 1923; copyright 1906, 1908, 1909, 1913, 1914, 1917). In the margin on page 270 (chapter 21 "Adjectives and Adverbs"), is the penciled enigmatic word "Lymerick." What drowsy lecture inspired Rina White, 849 Genesee Ave. (telephone Wasatch 7079), to make the inscription? We can be certain that on that day in the 1910s or 1920s—in Salt Lake City—there was a lecture in the composition class, and probably some exercises on adjectives and adverbs. And looming somewhere was a theme for Rina to compose; when it was turned in, the lecturer would become a correcter. (A Saturday afternoon in May. The trees are lacy green, and the peonies are almost ready for their Memorial Day duty. The lecturer-correcter sits at her dining-room table, "marking" papers. She is unmarried, necessarily so, lest students in her high school think of—fantasize about—her libido, thus losing respect for the virginal purity of her nunlike mediation between the doctrine according to Saint Alfred Hitchcock—presumably no relation—and their imperfect attempts to achieve correctness.) No doubt this digression is invidious, but let it stand. As a corrective, assume that Hitchcock, lecturer-correcter, and Rina were decent, intelligent folk doing the best they knew how within the paradigm and educational system that they inherited. Assume the same about us and our students. With this healthier, at least more charitable, attitude, let us proceed with our delineation of the enlightened present, hoping that our successors will be at least as mellow as we.)

After a long, disastrous hiatus, composition once again became rhetorical, starting, as I have said, in about 1964 with the Rohman-Wlecke study. *(Writing Instruction in Nineteenth-Century American Colleges,* by James A. Berlin [1984], is essential reading.) In 1965, Edward P.J. Corbett reintroduced students and teachers to the tradition with *Classical Rhetoric for the Modern Student,* and second and third editions of even the most conservative texts began to include sections on prewriting and invention. William Irmscher's enormously successful *Holt Guide to English* (1972) included an extensive introduction to Kenneth Burke's Pentad.

In his important essay "Invention: A Topographical Survey" (1976), Richard Young outlines current "methodologies": neo-classical invention, adapted from the classical tradition, as in Corbett (1965); Burke's dramatism, as in Irmscher

(1972); prewriting (Rohman and Wlecke, 1964); and tagmemic invention, as in Young, Becker, and Pike (1970); to which I would subjoin the variety of heuristics to be found in the second edition of my own textbook (1981).

Heuristics

In "'Topics' and Levels in the Composing Process" (1973), I have explained a system for classifying and evaluating heuristics; however, my purpose now is to discuss their usefulness for composition teachers.

We find ourselves uncomfortably on the spot when we claim that we're trying to teach people to think or to think creatively, for we are hardly philosophers or psychologists, and yet we find ourselves equally in an uncomfortable position (since being on the spot whether we are standing or sitting is not an optimum sort of repose) when we must respond to student texts with "You need to develop your ideas" or "Your ideas are unoriginal"—though, of course, in more tactful ways, less scarifying terms, for we attempt to give sympathetically helpful reactions to texts that we must, as teachers, take seriously. As teachers! What are we to advise students? "Think, and you'll discover ideas!" "Be original, and you'll be original!" We are constrained, in fact, to teaching thinking or methods thereof.

The fashionable word "heuristics" is broad enough to cover the field of methods available to the comp teacher faced with the problem of a student who either seems unable to generate ideas concerning a topic or inscribes platitudes—and my dour tone here simply obscures my respect for every student's potential to write amply and originally, though I find myself, for the strategic purposes of this essay, too often assuming the negative stance, which, of course, is always disastrous in teaching: the sort of attitude that implies bare tolerance of the acne-essays submitted by our composition students, the bubble-gum writings of juveniles who will never mature to the suave literacy and keen thinking of their mentors. As mentors, nonetheless, we must respect our charges enough to believe that maturity and a healthy diet will cure the acne and that our guidance will overcome the taste for bubble gum.

In his 1976 essay, Richard Young provides an apposite account of heuristics:

> It is important to distinguish between rule-governed procedures (i.e., algorithms) and heuristic procedures lest we make the error of thinking that because invention is a systematic activity it is necessarily a mechanical one. A rule-governed procedure specifies a finite series of steps which can be carried out consciously and mechanically without the aid of intuition or special ability and, if properly carried out, infallibly produces a correct result—for example, the procedure for making valid inferences in syllogistic reasoning. A heuristic procedure provides a series of questions or operations whose results are provisional; it helps us guess more effectively—for example, the procedure used by journalists for gathering information for an article, the familiar who? what? when? where? how? and

> why? It does not infallibly lead to a comprehensive and useful account but it makes data gathering more efficient and increases the likelihood that the account will be adequate. Although systemic, heuristic search is neither purely conscious nor mechanical, intuition, relevant experience and skill are necessary for effective use. The use of heuristic procedures is, by implication, an acknowledgment that the psychological processes involved in invention are too unpredictable to be controlled by rule-governed procedures. (p. 2)

In more homely terms, heuristics are procedures that encourage the writer to "walk around" his or her subjects, viewing them from different angles—the problem with invention frequently being the head-on, unwavering approach that the writer takes.

The subject of heuristics is properly a branch of creativity theory, the literature of which is massive, fascinating and sometimes fatuous, often commonsensical but frequently outlandish, useful to some degree though often just plain esoteric. "Creativity and the Comp Class" (pp. 205–20) provides an entry into the field and a bibliography.

If I were asked to recommend the single best discussion of heuristics in general, I would unhesitatingly cite Chapter 7, "Plans Up Front," from *The Mind's Best Work*, by D.N. Perkins (1981). In three propositions, Perkins sums up his points regarding heuristics:

> The broad organization of behavior does not necessarily take care of itself once contributing performances are mastered. Both particular heuristic advice and the more general heuristics of managerial strategies may be helpful. Most of all, one's big plans for conducting various activities deserve critical scrutiny and creative revision. (p. 200)

> People often modify considerably the heuristics they are taught. But they may gain anyway, by improving poor heuristics, learning to think about how they think, and in many other roundabout ways. (p. 106)

> Of course, one needs particular knowledge and experience to function at all in a field. But beyond that, knowing the informal rules of the game is more important than knowing very general heuristics. (p. 213)

The "translation" of these propositions for composition teachers yields productive advice and an understanding of what heuristics can be expected to do (or not to do).

Heuristics are obviously prompts, aids to "natural" cognitive processes in problem solving. We would expect, then, that various procedures—such as brainstorming, clustering, the Pentad, the tagmemic grid—would have differing appeal and utility for various writers working on various topics. In other words, we have strong reason to believe that some writers prefer and are more successful with some heuristics than with others, and we know for a fact that heuristics function well or poorly, depending on the subject matter. (See Adams, 1979, pp. 83–101.) And, of course, hemisphericity is a factor. In discussing cerebral organization and function, Jerry Levy (in Wittrock, ed., 1980) might well have been presenting an argument in favor of heuristics:

> Neither the nature of stimuli, choices, nor responses, or even actual hemispheric capacity, determines hemispheric dominance. Rather a hemisphere's propensity to control behavior seems to be a function of how it perceives the cognitive requirements for a given task. If those requirements call for literal encoding of sensory information or visualization of spatial relations, the right hemisphere assumes and maintains control, even if it turns out that the particular task is poorly processed by the controlling hemisphere. If there appears to be a requirement for speaking, phonetic analysis, semantic decoding of words, or for the derivation of conceptual categories, the left hemisphere assumes and maintains control, even if on the particular task, the right hemisphere is as competent as the left. (p. 258)

We are, of course, interested in teaching skills—for instance, those of syntactic fluency and accessibility in style. The Christensen (1967) free modifiers (illustrated on pp. 52–53) are a heuristic for the development of style, giving students possibilities to elaborate their sentences; in Perkins' terms, the system of free modifiers constitutes "particular heuristic advice." However, the ability to elaborate sentences is one thing, and knowing when to do so is quite another, a decision that might be facilitated by "the more general heuristics of managerial strategy"—for instance, Roman Jakobson's schema for the discourse act, which places style in relation to purpose (emotive, referential, phatic, and conative), which imply various relationships with audiences. (Jakobson, 1960; see Winterowd, 1981, pp. 86–93.)

In a sense, heuristics such as the Jakobson schema, the Pentad, and the tagmemic procedure are what Kenneth Burke calls "terministic screens." If you view the world through the Pentad, all acts are dramas—scenes, purposes, agents, and agencies being foregrounded—whereas tagmemics brings one to look at features, contrasts, processes, organizations. It seems obvious that the Pentad is more useful as an instrument for understanding literature but that tagmemics could be valuable for developing a critique of, say, an organization such as a college cafeteria.

When Perkins talks about "knowing the informal rules of the game," he is getting at one of the central points of language skills learning. By and large, we acquire those skills—i.e., do not learn them through conscious effort—and our knowledge of them is tacit. (See pp. 95–101; also "Developing a Composition Program," pp. 281–97; and "From Classroom Practice to Psycholinguistic Theory," pp. 299–306.) Heuristics can help us acquire them by calling them to our attention, and can help us bring them into performance once acquired. You could never teach students to write expository essays by using heuristics alone; writers gain a sense of genre only through immersion in it, acquiring the informal rules of the game, but once some acquisition has taken place, heuristics can be extremely useful as teaching methods. For instance, I find the Jakobson schema helpful when I am attempting to help a student create a satisfactory essay. Using the schema as a guide, I can teach the student to ask questions about *audience,* the *writer* and his or her intentions, the *content* of the piece, its *structure,* its *format*, and its *style*. In Chapter 9 (pp. 104–6), I give an extended example of how this heuristic works.

These sets of questions are no panacea, but they do provide useful points of departure for instruction, and they do make students aware of the manifold problems involved in producing a successful text. The heuristic itself is of no value, however, if students have not at least partially internalized the informal rules of the game. Perkins summarizes:

> This might seem to say that general heuristics are useless. Indeed to a degree it says just that. There is no substitute for knowledge—experience, familiarity with a field, knowing the ins and outs, the rules of the game, whether explicit or tacit. Yet for all that, general heuristics have their place. When genre-specific principles are used, general strategies can add to their power. Moreover, we do not always operate in familiar problem domains. In fact, we encounter new kinds of problems constantly not only as we explore novel subject areas but as we go further in a familiar field. General strategies provide an initial approach that will give way to genre-specific understanding as experience accumulates. Finally, remember that the deliberate search for and use of genre-specific strategies can itself be a potent general strategy. (p. 213)

It is important to realize, however, that Perkins is talking about heuristics in specialized fields such as mathematics or botany. In composition, we are concerned with those areas of knowledge that constitute liberal education; the thinking and writing that we are interested in is nonspecialist; we attempt to create *bricoleurs,* not engineers. Perkins deals with the use of heuristics for "engineers"; we are concerned about the analytic and inventive abilities of "bricoleurs." (Obviously, I am not talking about specialized composition courses, such as technical writing or proposal writing.) In fact, I completely agree with George Dillon (1981) when he says,

> The expository essay as here understood has a rhetorical purpose beyond "conveying information"; it attempts to convince the reader that its model of experience or the world is valid. It does not seek to engage the reader in a course of action, however, but rather in the process of reflection, and its means of convincing are accordingly limited to the use of evidence [including, from my point of view, the non-logical proofs that I characterize as "appositional"] and logical proof and the posture of open-mindedness. These methods are also associated with the liberally educated person, who is meditative, reflective, clear-headed, unbiased, always

> seeking to understand experience freshly and to find things of interest in the world. (p. 23)

Eureka, the Textbooks

Among textbooks, we can take *Forming, Thinking, Writing: The Composing Imagination,* by Ann E. Berthoff (1978), as the Alpha in regard to heuristics and Young, Becker, and Pike's *Rhetoric: Discovery and Change* (1970) as the Omega.

Berthoff is enormously suspicious of "recipes" such as the tagmemic grid, believing that composition is an organic process which begins with

> ... meaning, not with thought ("Think of what you want to say ...") or language("Choose the words which you feel would fit your idea best ..." we will never get the two together unless we begin with them together. The making of meaning is the work of the active mind, or what used to be called the *imagination*—that power to create, to discover, to respond to form of all kinds. My guiding philosophical principle is that this form-finding and form-creating is a natural activity; the book's central pedagogical principle is that we teach our students *how* to form by teaching them *that* they form. Man is the forming animal, the *animal symbolicum,* as the philosopher Ernst Cassirer puts it. (p. 2)

Berthoff's claim seems to be that in the discovery of meaning, students will find the forms to embody it (provided, I assume that the substratum of competence, gained from reading, is there). We must enthusiastically grant the premise that for follows purpose (see Shuy, 1981), and we know painfully that "dry-run" exercises are the bane of composition classes.

In regard to tagmemic heuristics, I can do no better than quote from and paraphrase a review (1975) that I did of *The Tagmemic Discovery Procedure: An Evaluation of Its Uses in the Teaching of Rhetoric,* by Richard E. Young and Frank M. Koen (1973). (In order to avoid cluttering the text, I will not indicate direct quotes.)

Tagmemic theory postulates that in order to know any "thing" (including abstract concepts), one must understand (1) how it contrasts with everything else in its class, (2) how much it can change and still be itself, and (3) its distribution within the larger system of which it is a part. In other words, one must perceive (1) *contrast,* (2) *variation*, and (3) *distribution.*

Furthermore, any "thing" can be viewed from three perspectives: (1) as an unchanging static entity, (2) as a process, and (3) as a system made up of parts. In other words, borrowing from physics, tagmemicists give us the perspectives of (1) particle, (2) wave, and (3) field.

Finally, a particle, wave, or field can be viewed from the standpoints of contrast, variation, and distribution. Thus, a nine-item set of topics or, in other words, a heuristic emerges. (For its diagrammatic realization, see table following.)

Table The Tagmemic Matrix

	Contrast	***Variation***	***Distribution***
Particle	(1) View the unit as an isolated, static entity. What are its contrastive features, i.e., that differentiate it from similar things and serve to identify it?	(4) View the unit as a specific variant form of the concept, i.e., as one among a group of instances that illustrate the concept. What is the range of physical variation of the concept, i.e., how can instances vary without becoming something else?	(7) View the unit as part of a larger context. How is it appropriately or typically classified? What is its typical position in a temporal sequence? In space or geographical array? In a system of classes?
Wave	(2) View the unit as a dynamic object or event. What physical features distinguish it from similar objects or events?	(5) View the unit as a dynamic process. How is it changing?	(8) View the unit as part of a larger dynamic context. How does it interact and merge into its environment? Are its borders clear-cut or indeterminate?
Field	(3) View the unit as an abstract multidimensional system. How are the components organized in relation to one another? More specifically, how are they related by class, in class systems, in temporal sequence, and in space?	(6) View the unit as a multidimensional physical system. How do particular instances of the system vary?	(9) View the system as an abstract system within a larger system. What is its position in the larger system? What systematic features and components make it a part of the larger system?

It seems to me that the tagmemic grid is so complex as to be opaque, and I have found it a hindrance in my composition classes. However, it appears obvious to me that questions implied by the perspectives are valuable and, indeed, I have found them to be so. The tagmemic perspectives give students a way to analyze and move toward an understanding of problematic situations. From the grid, I have drawn the following set of questions:

What are the item's FEATURES?
What are the parts of the SYSTEM?
How does the item OPERATE?
What is the DISTRIBUTION of the item—i.e., how does it fit into the larger system(s) of which it is a part?
How does the item CONTRAST with others in its class?
How can the item be CHANGED?

These questions—and their implications and elaborations—encourage students to "walk around" their subject, viewing it from a variety of angles, and this in itself is a useful function of the heuristic.

In the 1973 study, Young and Koen asked of the procedure, "Does it work?" And the answer to that question:

> The results of the experiments provide clear support for the proposition that strong personal involvement in an intellectual activity and substantial knowledge of the subject tend to improve the quality of what is written. Even though no formal instruction was provided in conventional rhetorical and composition skills (such as usage, sentence and paragraph development, logic, methods of persuasion, and arrangement), English teachers regularly rated final essays more acceptable than initial ones. Students also improved in their ability to analyze problematic situations and state problems; and the results of their explorations of problematic data were more complex and varied; they became more sophisticated in taking hypotheses for adequacy; and they wrote essays that were more understandable and more persuasive at the end of the course.
>
> The experiment, however, did not establish that the improved ability to explore problematic data was directly related to the nine-cell discovery procedure. In addition, the tests did not indicate that the theory as presently formulated and the course as it was taught increased students' sensitivity to problematic situations. (pp. 49–50)

Perkins (1981, pp. 195–96) would agree that there is no hard, fast evidence that heuristics create versatility or originality in thinking.

In rhetorical invention, as in the other departments of our complex art, we have no absolute certainty, but that situation, after all, is not such a disadvantage, for it gives us the freedom to follow our own intuitions and hard-won experiential knowledge, but also the responsibility for knowing what is available, to be sensitively tested in our scene, the composition classroom. Our methods come from our knowledge of the field and its resources and the scholarship and theories behind them, as well as from our own quotidian observant and caring practice with students.

Writing Topics and "Problematization"

I would like to put heuristics into the framework of what Paulo Freire (1982, p. 76) has called "problematization":

> Human existence cannot be silent, nor can it be nourished by false words, but only by true words with which men transform the world. To exist, humanly, is to *name* the world, to change it. Once named, the world in its turn appears to the namers as a problem and requires of them a new *naming.* Men are not built in silence, but in word, in work, in action-reflection.

We hear continually—I heard just yesterday—that students do not read widely enough to gain either background or the ability to think critically. Surely students (and most professors, for that matter) do not read extensively or critically, and surely reading is central to a liberal education—not specialized reading in textbooks or scientific reports, but general reading in books of all kinds, in magazines and newspapers. In our composition classes, we cannot supply the deficit of years, though we can do a great deal to encourage reading and to help students read better. We can help students view their world as a series of problems that invite analysis and discussion, and we can do that with heuristics.

To take a specific example of a problem we all face: We want to judge writing—especially holistically scored finals—on the basis of both form and content. One way to "control" for content is to assign a group of readings—on atomic power, gun control, capital punishment, legislative reapportionment, entitlements, or whatever—and then gear writing prompts to those topics: "In a brief but carefully thought-out essay, analyze the problem of entitlement and propose a solution." But there is another way, provided students have learned to "problematize" their worlds. Assign a topic that all of them have in common, regardless of reading backgrounds. For example, the university itself is a microcosm of the difficulties of any society, with the super-addition of its own particular quirks: inadequate parking, professors who remain isolated from students, dorms, tuition, course requirements, student voice in university governance, adjusting to academic life . . . None of these is trivial and can result in thoughtful writing if students learn how to recognize and analyze problems.

Obviously, I believe that problematization is the central concern of composition; that being the case, heuristics, properly used, are the most important "methods." After all, Paulo Freire was speaking of peasants just gaining literacy, not of the graduates of Brazil's fancier academies.

References

Adams, James L. (1979). *Conceptual Blockbusting: A Guide to Better Ideas.* New York: W.W. Norton.

Benderly, Beryl Lieff (1981). "The Multilingual Mind." *Psychology Today.* (March), 9–12.

Berlin, James A. (1984). *Writing Instruction in Nineteenth-Century American Colleges.* Urbana, Ill.: NCTE.

Berthoff, Ann E.. (1978). *Forming, Thinking, Writing: The Composing Imagination.* Rochelle Park, N.J.: Hayden.

Burke, Kenneth (1969). *A Grammar of Motives.* Berkeley: University of California Press.

——. (1969). *A Rhetoric of Motives.* Berkeley: The University of California Press.

Christensen, Francis (1967). *Notes Toward a New Rhetoric.* New York: Harper & Row.

Corbett, E.P.J. (1965). *Classical Rhetoric for the Modern Student.* New York: Oxford University Press.

Dillon, George F. (1981). *Constructing Texts: Elements of a Theory of Composition and Style.* Bloomington: Indiana University Press.

Emig, Janet (1978). "Hand, Eye, Brain: Some 'Basics' in the Writing Process." Cooper and Odell, eds. *Research on Composing: Points of Departure.* Urbana, Ill.: NCTE.

Freed, Richard (1981). "Using the Right Brain." *WLA Newsletter.* No. 17 (Spring), 3–4.

Freire, Paulo (1982) [1970]. *Pedagogy of the Oppressed.* Trans. Myra Bergman Ramos. New York: Continuum.

Glassner, Benjamin (1981). "Writing as an Integrator of Hemispheric Function." Kroll and Vann, eds. *Exploring Speaking/Writing Relationships: Connections and Contrasts.* Urbana, Ill: NCTE.

Hill, Adam Sherman (1897). *The Foundations of Rhetoric.* New York: Harper & Brothers.

Hirsch, E.D., Jr. (1977). *The Philosophy of Composition.* Chicago: University of Chicago Press.

Hitchcock, Alfred M. (1923). *Composition and Rhetoric.* New York: Henry Holt.

Irmscher, William (1972). *The Holt Guide to English.* New York: Holt, Rinehart and Winston.

Jakobson, Roman (1960). "Linguistics and Poetics." Thomas A. Sebeok, ed. *Style in Language.* Cambridge, Mass: MIT Press.

Levy, Jerre (1980). "Cerebral Asymmetry and the Psychology of Man." M.C. Wittrock, ed. *The Brain and Psychology.*

Miner, Earl (1976). "'That Literature Is a Kind of Knowledge." *Critical Inquiry.* 2 (Spring), 487–518.

Perkins, D.N. (1981). *The Mind's Best Work.* Cambridge, Mass.: Harvard University Press.

Rohman, D. Gordon, and Albert O. Wlecke (1964). *Pre-Writing: The Construction and Application of Models for Concept Formation in Writing.* East Lansing: Michigan State University.

Winterowd, D. Ross (1973). "'*Topics*' and Levels in the Composing Process." *College English.* 34:5 (Feb.), 701–09.

——. (1975). Review of *The Tagmemic Discovery Procedure: An Evaluation of Its Uses in the Teaching of Rhetoric,* by Richard Young and Frank M. Koen. *Philosophy and Rhetoric.* 8:3 (Summer), 183–87.

——. (1981). *The Contemporary Writer.* Second Edition. New York: Harcourt Brace Jovanovich.

Wittrock, M.C., ed. (1977). *The Human Brain.* Englewood Cliffs, N.J.: Prentice-Hall.

Young, Richard (1976). "Invention: A Topographical Survey." Gary Tate, ed. *Teaching Composition: Ten Biographical Essays.* Fort Worth: Texas Christian University.

——, Alton L. Becker and Kenneth L. Pike (1970). *Rhetoric: Discovery and Change.* New York: Harcourt Brace Jovanovich.

——, and Frank M. Koen (1973). *The Tagmemic Discovery Procedure: An Evaluation of Its Uses in the Teaching of Rhetoric.* Ann Arbor: University of Michigan.

Recognition, Representation, and Revision

Ann E. Berthoff

Ann E. Berthoff, professor emeritus at the University of Massachusetts at Boston, has been a writing teacher for over forty years and is the author of many books and articles on rhetorical theory and writing instruction, including The Making of Meaning, Forming/Thinking/Writing, Reclaiming the Imagination: Philosophical Perspectives for Writers and Teachers of Writing, *and* Richards on Rhetoric, *a collection of essays by I. A. Richards. This article first appeared in the* Journal of Basic Writing *in 1981 and later was included in Berthoff's* The Sense of Learning. *Berthoff objects vigorously to linear models of the composing process and proposes instead a theory of composing and revising that is consistent with a "pedagogy of knowing" that emphasizes the importance of seeing relationships in thinking, knowing, and writing. Revision, she writes, "is not a stage but a dimension" of composing. Instructors need to teach students "to take advantage of the allatonceness of composing, to assure that they continually rediscover how forming, thinking, and writing can be simultaneous and correlative activities."*

We should not be surprised that our students so often consider revision as a chance to get "it" right the second time around.[1] Despite recent attempts to differentiate editing and rewriting, most English teachers probably continue to instill the idea that revision is like taking another swing at the ball or shooting again for the basket. The idea of revision as correction is, like readability formulas and sentence combining, consonant with a view of language as, merely, a medium for the communication of our views of a reality *out there:* we have ideas and we put them into language. (Sometimes we might get the wrong slot: try again.) Language is often seen as a window which keeps us from enjoying an immediate vision. The pedagogical corollary is that the best we can do is to teach window washing, trying to keep the view of what is "really there" unobstructed by keeping the prose clean and

First published in *Journal of Basic Writing,* 3 (Fall–Winter, 1981). Reprinted in *A Sourcebook for Basic Writing Teachers,* ed. Theresa Enos (New York: Random House, 1987).

clear. Revision, in this view, is polishing. I argue in the following that we can learn to teach revision as itself a way of composing if we consider it analogous to acts of mind whereby we make sense of the world.

One rainy afternoon last fall I stopped by to browse among some miscellaneous journals in the gaudy reading room of a graduate school library where, as it turned out, I witnessed a basic writer at work. He sat in a low-slung, purple velour settee, a pad of lined paper on his knee, a nice new yellow pencil and a pack of cigarettes at the ready, and a Dixie Cup of coffee to hand. He seemed prepared for the labors of composition. He would write a sentence or two, light a cigarette, read what he had written, sip his coffee, extinguish the cigarette—and the two sentences. He had pretty much worn out the eraser by the time I left. (That would be an interesting research index: How long does the eraser last, if it is not bitten off in momentary despair?) My eyes glazed over more quickly than usual as I leafed through *Research in the Teaching of English* because my mind was otherwise engaged in formulating what I would have said to this earnest graduate student, if I had had the nerve. Something like this:

> You need to get some writing down on paper and to keep it there long enough so that you can give yourself the treat of rewriting. What you need is a ballpoint pen so you can't erase and some cheap paper so you can deliberately use a lot of it—and one very expensive sheet of creamy foolscap for your inventory of glosses: it's a sensuous pleasure to write on a beautiful surface after you've been scratching away on canary pads. But wait a minute! Where are your notes to yourself? Where are your lists? Where are your points of departure? Where are your leads? Where is your lexicon? Where are your quoted passages? Where is your chaos? Nothing comes of nothing! Here you are in this spaceship pod of a chair, this womb, with essentials like coffee and cigarettes, but without the essential essential—language! How can you know what you think until you hear what you say? see what you've written?

I think it is instructive to consider how the "writing behaviors" of this graduate student resemble those of our basic writers. There is, of course, a difference: whereas the graduate cannot get beyond the compulsive readjustment of the (doubtless) insubstantial and formless generalization he has begun with, our students hate even to start—for a dozen reasons which have been carefully formulated and studied in recent years—and once they do have something down, they are loath to touch it: those few words are hard-won and therefore precious, not to be tampered with. The graduate destroys by restatement because he does not know how to get the dialectic going; the undergraduate cannot conceive of adjustment or development because his fragile construct might collapse. But insofar as neither knows how to make language serve the active mind, they both are basic writers: they do not understand rewriting because they do not understand how writing gets written in the first place.

My tendentious claim is that the same is often true also of their teachers: revision is poorly taught, or is not taught at all, because composition teachers and composition textbook authors often do not know how writing gets written. Without a substantial understanding of composing as a dialectical process in which the *what* and the *how* continually inform one another—a nonlinear process motivated by both feedback and what I.A. Richards calls "feedforward"—there will be no way for teachers to differentiate between revision and editing, no way to teach revision not as a definite phase, a penultimate stage, but as a dimension of composing. Revision is, indeed, reseeing and it goes on continually in the composing process.

There is, of course, a great deal of talk currently about "the composing process," but there are very few pedagogies which are consonant with the kind of process composing actually is. I have elsewhere discussed the reasons for this state of affairs: current rhetorical theory has provided little guidance for our classroom practice because it has no philosophically sound way of accounting for how words work. There is no understanding in current rhetorical theory that in composing everything has to happen at once or it does not happen at all. If there is not something to think about, if there are not ideas to think *with,* if language is not in action, if the mind is not actively engaged, no meanings can be made. The pedagogical challenge is to help students take advantage of *allatonceness,* to see it as a resource, not the mother of dilemmas.

The linear sequence by which "the composing process" is commonly represented—prewriting, writing, rewriting—is antithetical to the "audit of meaning," I.A. Richards' term for dialectic. Instead of allatonceness, it suggests that there is a nonreversible order, a sequence of activities which unfold in a predetermined manner. The interrelationships of the triad are obscure; the notion, for instance, that pre and re have anything to do with one another, logically or psychologically, seems unheard of. If prewriting is, in many instances, presented as a matter of amassing the slottables, rewriting is considered a matter of checking out what has been slotted. "Think of what you want to say" in prewriting is matched by such instructions as these for rewriting: "Go back over what you have written. Are there any unnecessary words? Does everything you say refer to your thesis? Is your main point at the end of the paragraph? Are they any mechanical errors?" These questions are only transformations of the old imperatives: "Do not use unnecessary words. Assure that all statements support your thesis. Avoid mechanical errors." Get law and order. Plant a tree. Love your mother. People who have done a lot of writing themselves frequently consider it a self-evidently sensible thing to teach the use of this kind of checklist to inexperienced writers. What they leave out of account is that the experienced writer has criteria which are brought into play by asking such questions: that's what it means to have "experience."

I think it is fair to say that the linear model of composing as prewriting, writing, rewriting fosters a pedagogy of exhortation. Now, if we are to undertake to teach composing as a dialectical process of which revision is not a stage but a dimension, how can we prevent what was earlier described, the write—erase—write again—erase it all syndrome? The short answer is, as I have noted, to teach students to take advantage of the allatonceness of composing, to assure that they continually rediscover how forming, thinking, and writing can be simultaneous and correlative activities. Beginning writers need the experience of seeing how it is that consciousness of the *what* leads to understanding the *how*. This is what Paulo Freire means by "conscientization," the chief principle of his "pedagogy of knowing." If a pedagogy of knowing is to be the successor to the pedagogy of exhortation, we will need as models of knowing those acts of mind which are logically and psychologically analogous to writing, namely, perception and concept formation.

Taking perception as a model for writing lets us exploit the ancient wisdom that seeing and knowing are radically alike. Our word *idea* derives from the Greek *oida,* which meant both *I have seen* and *I know*. The eye is not a passive recorder; Ruskin's notion of "the innocent eye" has been superseded by that of "the intelligent eye."[2] When we see, we compose. Rudolf Arnheim lists as the operations involved in visual perception the following: "Active exploration, selection, grasping of essentials, simplification, abstraction, analysis and synthesis, completion, correction, comparison, problem-solving, as well as combining, separating, putting in context" (*Visual* 13). Is there any aspect of the composing process not represented in that list?

From Arnheim, E.H. Gombrich, R.L. Gregory, and other philosophers and scientists, we can learn that perception involves matching and reordering, from the molecular level on up: *Vision* is through and through a matter of *revision.* Indeed, seeing is actually contingent on reseeing. To clarify this fascinating fact, I have students read Owen Barfield's explanation of how it is that cognition depends on recognition. He asks the reader to suppose that

> he is standing in the midst of a normal and familiar environment ... when suddenly he is deprived by some supernatural stroke of every vestige of memory—and not only of memory, but also of all those assimilated, forgotten experiences which comprise his power of recognition. He is asked to assume that, in spite of this, he still retains the full measure of his cognitive faculty as an adult. It will appear, I think, that for the first few moments his consciousness—if it can bear that name—will be deprived not merely of all thought, but even of all perception. It is not merely that he will be unable to realize that that square, red and white object is a "house" ...; he will not even be able to see it as a square, red and white object (*Reclaiming* 39–40).

Seeing the point, my students speak of "Barfield's meaningless man." We can make meaning because we see in terms of what we have seen. Without remembered forms to see with, we would not see at all. Seeing is thus the primal analogizing in which thinking has its origin.

Now these philosophical principles of perception—seeing is knowing, seeing is contingent on reseeing, the intelligent eye forms by analogizing—provide the foundation for a pedagogy of knowing. How can we use what we can learn about perception in order to make observation not a preliminary exercise but a model of the composing process?

The allatonceness of composing is well represented by looking and writing in tandem. Since learning to record observations has a self-evident usefulness for everybody from nuclear physicists to nurses, from parents to doctors, and since observing our observations *requires* language, assignments which involve looking and looking again can rationally involve writing and writing again. Exercises which make recording and commenting correlative and virtually simultaneous have an authenticity which is unusual in composition assignments. One procedure which helps writers enact revision as a mode of composing is what I call a dialectical notebook: notes, lists, statements, critical responses, queries of all sorts are written on one side; notes on these notes, responses to these responses are written on the facing page. The inner dialogue which is thinking is thus represented as a dialectic, the beginning of thinking about thinking. This double-entry journal encourages a habit which is of immediate usefulness, since this format is the best there is for taking notes on lectures and reading. And it is easily adapted to what Dixie Goswami calls a "speculative draft," a procedure for writing papers which allows students to take advantage of allatonceness by keeping notes and queries, formulations and reformulations in continual dialogue on facing pages.

The dialectical notebook teaches the value of keeping things tentative. Without that sense, the allatonceness of composing is dangerous knowledge that can cause a severe case of writer's block. Unless students prove to themselves the usefulness of tentativeness, no amount of exhortation will persuade them to forego "closure," in the current jargon. The willingness to generate chaos; patience in testing a formulation against the record; careful comparing of proto-statements and half-statements, completed statements and restatements: these are all expressions of what Keats famously called "negative capability," the capacity to remain in doubt. The story is told of a professor of internal medicine who brought home to his students the value of this attitude in diagnosis with the slogan: "Don't just DO something: Stand there!"

Along with the value of tentativeness, practice in observation teaches the importance of perspective and context, which become ideas to think *with* as students practice observing natural objects, for instance, and observing their observations. A shell or pebble on the beach has one kind of appearance; if you bring it home, it has another. Such facts call for recognition, formulation, and articulation. In the practice of looking and looking again, of writing and writing again, as students learn to compare kinds of appearances, they are also learning that perception depends on presuppositions, remembrances, anticipations, purposes, and so on. In my own teaching, I hand out weeds and grasses, seeds and bones because natural forms are themselves compositions, pedagogically useful emblems of historical process. Friends and colleagues have occasionally argued that nature is an alien point of departure and that such an exercise as Ira Shor's examination of the contents of a wastebasket is more likely to engage the attention of basic writers. Detective work or archaeology is certainly as useful a metaphor for interpretation as nature study: the point is to make the transformation of the familiar to the strange and the strange to the familiar an exemplification of what goes on in all interpretation; to foreground the process of "reading," of construing, of making sense of whatever is under observation, from different perspectives, in different contexts.

Freire shows us how. The peasants in his culture circles, who are learning *how* they make meaning and *that* they make meaning simultaneously with learning to recognize words and sounds, study pictures depicting familiar scenes, reading them as texts, translating and interpreting them, and interpreting their interpretations in dialogue. What Freire calls "problematizing the existential situation" is a critical act of mind by which historical contexts for objects and pictures are developed: careful observation of what is depicted works together with the interpretation of its significance. Perception thus provides the point of departure for a pedagogy of knowing because it is through and through conceptual.

Problematic symbols and problem-posing pictures at one end; organic structures in the middle; at the other end, abstract designs and diagrams which we can ask students to observe, translating in the process from pictorial to verbal language. I.A. Richards, in a valuable essay called "Learning and Looking," suggests just how challenging that translation can be *(Design)*. He is ostensibly discussing the problems of literacy training in societies in which depiction is not thought of as representational, but in the course of demonstrating how "reading" certain diagrams exercises the translation-transformation capacity necessary for handling the graphic code, he does much more. For one thing, he shows how comparing depends on the principle of opposition, which is essential to all critical inquiry into "what varies with what while the rest is treated as remaining constant." Even more important, he provides demonstrations of how perspective and context function heuristically. Careful looking and experimental translation teach the observer to use oppositions to limit the range of choices. Just as learning to keep things tentative is an all-important support structure for the concept of the allatonceness of composing, so learning the use of limits is essential if beginning writers are to understand that composing necessarily involves choosing. Limits are their means of defining and controlling choices; unless we teach the function of limits, no amount of exhortation will persuade our students to tolerate the risks which revision entails.

By keeping looking and writing together, we can teach revision as analogous to recognition in perception. If we can keep thinking and writing together, our students can learn how revision is analogous to the representation which language makes possible. Language has, of course, an indicative function, but it is its power to represent our interpretations of experience which is vital for a pedagogy of knowing. No thinking—no composing—could happen if we had no means of stabilizing images of what we have seen, of recalling them as forms to think about and to think *with*. Language is our means of representing images as forms: *forming* is our means of seeing relationships from one or another perspective and in different contexts.

Writing teachers have not, generally speaking, taken advantage of this power of language and mind—it was once called *imagination*—because linguistics, as institutionalized by current rhetorical theory, has no way of accounting for it. The conventional notion of thinking finds no room for the dialectic which language makes possible. It is based, rather, on the dichotomy of induction/deduction: either, it is thought, we go from "the data" to one or another principle, or we go from "high level abstractions" to the substantiating particulars. If teachers want to benefit from the fact that everything that happens when we think is analogous to what we do when we compose, they will need to form the concept of forming.

The logical ground for the analogy of thinking and writing is *forming*—seeing relationships, recognizing and representing them. Understanding that principle can show us how to start with thinking and writing together, and if we start with them together we will be more likely to keep them together. The way to bridge from so-called personal writing to so-called expository writing, from creative to critical writing, and, I will argue, from writing to rewriting is not to allow a separation in the first place. I want to concentrate now on one particular implication for classroom practice and course design of the premise that thinking and writing involve us in *seeing relationships:* how that can help us to teach revision not as a definite phase but as a dimension of the composing process.

From the idea that composing is a matter of seeing relationships, we might profitably conclude that at the pedagogical center of any composition course there should be not the grammatical unit of the sentence but the rhetorical unit of the paragraph.[3] Sentences depend on how they relate to other sentences; it is therefore easier to construe several sentences than it is one. The writer as reviser is a writer reading. Reading a paragraph, he has many points of entry; if he does not see a relationship as he starts to read, he might catch hold of another as he goes on. He can then reread and apprehend the earlier sentence. Because it articulates a structure of relationships, the paragraph provides a more appropriate focus for learning revision than the single sentence does. Apprehending the logical and rhetorical relationships of sentences in a paragraph is analogous to perception and concept formation in a way that apprehending those relationships articulated according to grammatical conventions *within* the sentence is not. That is why Gertrude Stein is right: "So paragraphing is a thing that anyone is enjoying and sentences are less fascinating."

Seeing relationships, as an idea to think with, can help offset the effects of certain theories of learning which, taking motor activity as the model, lead to the idea that because we must walk before we can run, we must therefore study sentences before paragraphs. Surely first things come first, but wherever language is concerned that will always mean that complexity comes before the allegedly simple. That is because meanings are not elements but relationships. It is by virtue of its complexity that the paragraph is simpler to take hold of than the sentence. This kind of paradox is central to the pedagogy of knowing. I do not mean that we ignore sentence structure when we teach revision. My point is that although errors are best identified in isolation, sentences are best revised in context, in the relational terms which the paragraph provides or which the would-be paragraph can be brought to the point of supplying. We are taking advantage of the allatonceness of making meaning when we teach our students to compose paragraphs in the course of revising sentences.

Along with the dialectical notebook, "glossing" paragraphs can raise consciousness of the interdependence of saying and intending. I ask students to summarize their paragraphs in oppositional form, to represent in a double phrase in the margin what is being set over against what. Thus identified, the logical structure of the paragraph can be used as an Archimedean point from which to survey the individual sentences. If it is impossible to formulate a gloss, that will tell a student more than exhortatory comments on incoherence ever could. Or it may be that in the process of glossing the student will express a hitherto unspoken intention which the paragraph can use. In that case, the gloss can be revised in sentence form and incorporated. Invention of needed sentences is contingent on recognizing the need, in my opinion, that recognition is inspired not by asking empty questions about what the audience needs to know but by seeing what the paragraph needs to say. To discover logical and rhetorical needs is to discover purpose, a process which is at once more complex and more manageable than trying to ascertain audience needs directly. They, of course, must be hypothesized and considered in conjunction, dialectically, with purposes. But to instruct the student to determine "the audience's needs" is frequently only an updated version of asking him to ask himself "What am I trying to say?" That is not, I think, a heuristically useful inquiry.

A way to encourage students to ask what a paragraph needs—what their argument or explanation or description or narrative needs—is to have them read their own paragraphs (a day or so after they have been written) a sentence at a time with the remaining sentences covered, anticipating at each period what the next sentence will be, will do, by writing one in its place. The writer can do this on his own, of course, but it is best done in conference or in company with other readers, dialogue being the best model of dialectic there is. The newly framed sentence can then be compared with the original sentence, of which it may, of course, be a replica: having two ways of saying to work with, or one way twice, is important in the practice of revision. The choice can be made, then, of which serves better in answering the perhaps newly felt need, but nothing should be thrown away, since the paragraph might well require the old original sentence in a new setting.

Developing a sense of rhetorical and logical form is in large part a matter of anticipating what comes next, of knowing what is needed, recognizing its emergence. That is not a "skill" but a power of mind, and it is exactly comparable to recognition in perception and representation with language. We do not need to teach this power, but we should assure that it is exercised. These simple techniques of paragraph review can serve that purpose because they keep the dialectic of intending and forming lively. Glossing and anticipating can help students see to it that the "what I mean" does not remain an amorphous, ghostly nonpresence but is embodied over and over again. To find out if you have said what you meant, you have to know what you mean and the way to determine that is to say "it" again.

Only when a paragraph has been reviewed in the light of its gloss, the various sentences abandoned or rewritten, restored, and reordered according to emerging criteria, is it time to work on sentence correction. Error identification is often tantamount to error correction and, as I have noted, that is best carried out if the sentence can be "heard" in isolation from its support system, the context which makes meaning rather than grammatical structure predominate. The procedure I recommend is to read the paragraph backwards aloud, sentence by sentence—an old proofreader's trick. If the student stumbles or hesitates, that is a sign of recognition and actual rewriting can begin. Nothing will come of this or any other such procedure, of course, if the student cannot recognize a faulty sentence when he hears one. By assuring that there are occasions for reading good prose closely, carefully, and frequently aloud, we can help our students to develop an "ear" for syntax, like an "ear" for music, to expect the way a sentence will go or can go so that when it goes awry, they can hear the error. The remedy for a deficient "ear" is hearing good prose, and that means that student writing will not be the exclusive "text" in a well-designed composition course.

When it is a simple matter of agreement, pronoun reference, tense consistency, or punctuation (in some cases), grammatical instruction can be useful. But sentences which fail because of pleonasm, faulty parallelism, misused idiom, or mixed constructions are, generally speaking, a different matter. They will yield to our grammatical analysis or the student's, but that analysis will serve no heuristic function.

Take, for instance, the following sentences:

> The elemental beach and the music of the sea was more preferable than that other summer beach.
>
> North Carolina is a state where the long straight roads that lead to small quiet places has an unusually loud bunch of inhabitants.
>
> I have always seen that as a silver lining behind the cloud.
>
> Teachers judge the quality of the student's performance much like that of the farmer's grading his beef.

In my opinion, the best way to work with sentences like these is for everybody in a small group, or for both student and tutor in conference, to revise the sentence by means of composing several interpretive paraphrases, using the parent paragraph as a sounding board. Restating, representing is a way to recognize intention: interpreting by means of paraphrase, rather than tinkering with the incorrect sentence as it stands, allows a student to call upon the resources he has for making meaning which are independent of any explicit knowledge of grammatical laws. I do not mean that rhetorical and logical forms are simply "generated": written discourse is not natural in the way that speech, in a social setting, is. I have no faith that well-formed intentions will surface from the deep if only grammarians will step aside. Returning to intention is a hard journey, but it is profitable because of what can be learned on the way about the making of meaning.

Syntactical structures are linguistic forms which find conceptual forms: making them accessible to our students is one of our chief duties. Kenneth Koch's experiments are important to us all because they remind us of the value of teaching syntactical structures as generative forms rather than as slots to be filled or inert elements to be combined. We can learn from Koch and others how to make syntax itself a heuristic. The procedure I have found most useful is called "persona paraphrase," in which a specific passage is selected, illustrating a particular kind of structure. Students then copy its structure, phrase by phrase, sentence by sentence, substituting completely different subject matter.[4] Kenneth Burke's conception of recalcitrance explains the principle on which persona paraphrase is based: "A statement is an attitude rephrased in accordance with the strategy of revision made necessary by the recalcitrance of the materials employed for embodying this attitude" *(Permanence 255)*. Insofar as it recognizes the dialectics of recalcitrance, the paradox that complexity is simple, the fact that concept formation is dynamic, the fact that saying and intending inform one another—insofar as persona paraphrase is a technique which can teach revision as a mode of composing, it is the antithesis of sentence combining. This is not surprising. It presupposes a philosophy of language entirely foreign to the conceptions which underlie the manipulations of sentence combining.

Revising at this level in these ways means slowing things down: allatonceness always does. Composing a persona paraphrase can take a full hour; composing interpretive paraphrases for a single conceptually faulty sentence can take up the entire class or conference time. It is time well spent, but there is a very difficult pedagogical challenge in seeing to it that this necessarily slow, deliberate pace is not the only one at which the composition course moves. Others have probably long since discovered the paradox I have been slow to come to, namely, that allatonceness requires a double track, if not a triple focus. Students should work independently on a long-term project for which the dialectical notebook is the enabling means of making meaning; they should continually be revising paragraphs with their fellow students; every day, in class or out, they should focus on the analysis and correction of a single sentence. The difference between the 101 section for basic writers, the noncredit course required of graduate students, and the Continuing Education workshops in writing should be a matter not of which elements are included but only of the ratios among them and the pace at which the entire course proceeds.

If we reject the linear model of composing and the pedagogy it legitimates—teaching the allegedly first things first; subskills before skills; the *know how* before the *know what;* walking (sentences) before running (paragraphs)—we will be free to invent courses which are consonant with the idea of the composing process as a continuum of forming. I have been claiming that recognition and representation, as the central operations of perception and concept formation, provide the models of forming which can help us teach revision as a way of composing.

NOTES

1. This finding is reported by Susan V. Wall and Anthony R. Petrosky in "Freshman Writers and Revision: Results from a Survey," *Journal of Basic Writing,* 3 (Fall–Winter 1981).
2. Richard Coe brought my attention to the fascinating book with this title by R.L. Gregory. Coe's textbook, *Form and Substance* (New York: Wiley, 1981), is one of the few which present perception as profoundly conceptual, as an act of mind as well as of brain.
3. I agree with those who argue that the paragraph is a rhetorical convention and that a single sentence may constitute a paragraph. See "The Logic and Rhetoric of Paragraphs," *Forming/Thinking/Writing* 215ff. For the time being, I use the term to mean a sentence sequence which displays logical coherence.

4. Phyllis Brooks, "Mimesis: Grammar and the Echoing Voice," *College English,* 35 (November 1973),161–68. As Brooks notes, persona paraphrase is highly adaptable. I have described certain uses which my students have made of it in *Forming/ Thinking/Writing* 211–15.

SUGGESTED READINGS: COMPOSING AND REVISING

Belanoff, Pat, Peter Elbow, and Sheryl I. Fontaine, eds. *Nothing New Begins with N: New Investigations of Freewriting.* Carbondale: Southern Illinois UP, 1991.

Berthoff, Ann E. *Forming/Thinking/Writing: The Composing Imagination.* 2nd ed. Portsmouth, NH: Boynton/Cook, 1988.

Britton, James, et al. *The Development of Writing Abilities* (11–18). New York: Macmillan, 1975.

Cooper, Charles R., and Lee Odell, eds. *Research on Composing: Points of Departure.* Urbana, IL: NCTE, 1978.

Crowley, Sharon. *The Methodical Memory: Invention in Current-Traditional Rhetoric.* Carbondale: Southern Illinois UP, 1990.

Elbow, Peter. *Writing with Power: Techniques for Mastering the Writing Process.* New York: Oxford UP, 1981.

Emig, Janet. *The Composing Processes of Twelfth Graders.* Urbana, IL: NCTE, 1971.

Faigley, Lester. "Competing Theories of Process: A Critique and a Proposal." *College English* 48 (1986): 527–42.

Faigley, Lester, and Stephen Witte. "Analyzing Revision." *CCC* 32 (1981): 400–14.

Flower, Linda, et al. "Detection, Diagnosis, and the Strategies of Revision." *CCC* 37 (1986): 16–55.

Flower, Linda, and John R. Hayes. "A Cognitive Process Theory of Writing." *CCC* 32 (1981): 365–87.

Flower, Linda, and John R. Hayes. "Problem-Solving Strategies and the Writing Process." *College English* 39 (1977): 442–48.

Flynn, Elizabeth A. "Composing as a Woman." *CCC* 39 (1988): 423–35.

Fulwiler, Toby. *The Journal Book.* Portsmouth, NH: Boynton/Cook, 1987.

Hairston, Maxine. "Different Products, Different Processes: A Theory about Writing." *CCC* 37 (1986) 442–52.

Harrington, David V., et al. "A Critical Survey of Resources for Teaching Rhetorical Invention: A Review-Essay." *College English* 40 (1979): 641–61.

Harris, Muriel. "Composing Behaviors of One- and Multi-Draft Writers." *College English* 51 (1989): 174–91.

Kneupper, Charles W. "Revising the Tagmemic Heuristic: Theoretical and Pedagogical Considerations." *CCC* 31 (1980): 160–68.

Laib, Nevin. "Conciseness and Amplification." *CCC* 41 (1990): 443–58.

Lanham, Richard. *Revising Prose*. 3rd ed. New York: Macmillan, 1992.

LeFevre, Karen Burke. *Invention as a Social Act*. Carbondale: Southern Illinois UP, 1987.

Murray, Donald M. "Write Before Writing." *CCC* 29 (1978): 375–82.

Murray, Donald M. *Learning by Teaching: Selected Articles on Writing and Teaching*. Portsmouth, NH: Boynton/Cook, 1982.

Perl, Sondra, eds. *Landmark Essays on Writing Processes*. Davis, CA: Hermagoras, 1994.

Rohman, D. Gordon. "Pre-Writing: The State of Discovery in the Writing Process." *CCC* 16 (1965): 106–12.

Rose, Mike, ed. *When a Writer Can't Write: Studies in Writer's Block and Other Composing Problems*. New York: Guilford, 1985.

Rose, Mike. *Writer's Block: The Cognitive Dimension*. Carbondale: Southern Illinois UP, 1984.

Sommers, Nancy. "Revision Strategies of Student Writers and Experienced Adult Writers." *CCC* 31 (1980): 376–88.

Wall, Susan V. "The Languages of the Text: What Even Good Students Need to Know about Re-Writing." *Journal of Advanced Composition* 7 (1987): 31–40.

Welch, Nancy. *Getting Restless: Rethinking Revision in Writing Instruction*. Portsmouth, NH: Boynton/Cook, 1997.

Willis, Meredith Sue. *Deep Revision: A Guide for Teachers, Students, and Other Writers*. New York: Teachers & Writers Collaborative, 1993.

Young, Richard E., and Yameng Liu, eds. *Landmark Essays on Rhetorical Invention in Writing*. Davis, CA: Hermagoras, 1994.

Zoellner, Robert. "A Behavioral Pedagogy for Composition." *College English* 30 (1969): 267–320.

A Relationship Between Reading and Writing: The Conversational Model

Charles Bazerman

With Ph.D. degrees in English and physics, Charles Bazerman, a professor at the University of California, Santa Barbara, is well known for his scholarship on reading and writing in the academic disciplines, especially in the sciences. His publications include Shaping Written Knowledge: The Genre and Activity of the Experimental Article in Science, Textual Dynamics of the Professions: Historical and Contemporary Studies of Writing in Professional Communities *(co-edited with James Paradis), and the textbook* The Informed Writer, *which reflects the approach to teaching reading and writing outlined in this selection. "A Relationship Between Reading and Writing" first appeared in* College English *in 1980 and later was included in Bazerman's 1994 book,* Constructing Experience. *"Each piece of writing," Bazerman states, is "a contribution to an ongoing written conversation." Writers need to consider what others have written, and their response should consider the circumstances behind these earlier statements. To prepare students for writing in their major disciplines and in other forums, Bazerman argues, "we must cultivate various techniques of absorbing, reformulating, commenting on, and using reading." He proposes a sequence for writing instruction that first teaches students to comprehend texts, then to respond to them, to evaluate them, and finally to define issues and informed positions in their reading and writing.*

The connection between what a person reads and what that person then writes seems so obvious as to be truistic. And current research and theory about writing have been content to leave the relationship as a truism, making no serious attempt to define either mechanisms or consequences of the interplay between reading and writing. The lack of attention to this essential bond of literacy results in part from the many disciplinary divorces in language studies over the last half century: *speech* has moved out taking *rhetoric* with it; *linguistics* has staked a claim to all skilled language behavior but has attended mostly to spoken language; *sociology* and *anthropology* have offered more satisfactory lodgings for the study of the social context and meaning of literacy; and *English* has gladly rid itself of basic *reading* to concern

Charles Bazerman. "A Relationship Between Reading and Writing: The Conversational Model," *College English,* February 1980.

itself purely with the higher reading of *literary criticism.* Writing in its three incarnations as basic composition, creative writing, and the vestigial advanced exposition, remains an unappreciated houseguest of *literature.* All these splits have made it difficult for those of us interested in writing to conceive of writing in terms broad enough to make essential connections: our accommodation has been to focus on the individual writer alone with the blank piece of paper and to ignore the many contexts in which the writing takes place. This essay will review developments in composition in light of this difficulty, propose a remedy in the form of a conversational model for the interplay of reading and writing, and then explore the implications of the model for teaching.

One of the older views, with ancient antecedents, held that a neophyte writer was an apprentice to a tradition, a tradition the writer became acquainted with through reading. The beginning student studied rules and practiced set forms derived from the best of previous writing; analysis and imitation of revered texts was the core of more advanced study of writing. The way to good writing was to mold oneself into the contours of prior greatness. Although current composition theory largely rejects this tradition/apprentice model as stultifying, teachers of other academic disciplines still find the model attractive, because writing in content disciplines requires mastery of disciplinary literature. The accumulated knowledge and accepted forms of writing circumscribe what and how a student may write in disciplines such as history, biology, and philosophy.

Recent work in composition has chosen instead to emphasize the writer's original voice, which has its source in an independent self. The model of the individual writer shaping thought through language informs recent investigations into the composing process, growth of syntactic maturity, and the source of error. We have aided the student in the struggle to express the self by revealing the logic of syntax, by asking for experiential and personal writing, and by offering techniques for prewriting and invention to help the student get closer to the wellsprings of thought that lie inside. Even traditional rhetoric finds its new justification in the reflection of organic psychological realities. By establishing the importance of the voice of the writer and the authority of personal perception, we have learned to give weight to what the student wants to say, to be patient with the complex process of writing, to offer sympathetic advice on *how to* rather than *what not to,* and to help the student discover the personal motivations to learn to write.

Yet the close observation of the plight of the individual writer has led us to remember that writing is not contained entirely in the envelope of experience, native thought, and personal motivation to communicate. Communication presupposes an audience, and deference to that audience has led to a revived concern for the forms of what is now called standard written English. E.D. Hirsch, in *The Philosophy of Composition,* locates the entire philosophy in readability, that is, concern for the audience. We have also noticed that most writing our students do during college is in the context of their academic studies; interest in writing across the curriculum has been the result. In the most thoughtful study coming out of this approach, *The Development of Writing Abilities (11–18)*, James Britton and his colleagues begin to notice that students use readings, but in personal and original ways, in order to write for their academic courses. "Source-book material may be used in various ways involving different levels of activity by the writer" (23).

We may begin to understand those "various ways" and "different levels of activity" Britton refers to if we consider each piece of writing as a contribution to an ongoing, written conversation. Conversation requires absorption of what prior speakers have said, consideration of how earlier comments relate to the responder's thoughts, and a response framed to the situation and the responder's purposes. Until a final statement is made or participants disengage themselves, the process of response continues. The immediacy of spoken conversation does, I must admit, differ significantly from the reflectiveness of written conversation, but the differences more illuminate the special character of writing than diminish the force of the model. Speech melody, gestural communication, rapidly shifting dynamics, and immediate validation on one side are set against explicitness, development, complexity, contemplation, and revision on the other. The written conversation also may bring together a more diffuse range of participants than the spoken one, although the examples of an exchange of office memos or the closed circle represented in professional journals indicate that such is not always the case. Further, in spoken conversation the makers of previous comments are more likely to be the auditors of the response. But again the counterexamples of the teacher who turns one student's question into the occasion for a lecture to the entire class, or the printed back and forth of a literary war, suggest that this distinction should not be oversimplified.

The conversational model points up the fact that writing occurs within the context of previous writing and advances the total sum of the discourse. Earlier comments provide subjects at issue, factual content, ideas to work with, and models of discourse appropriate to the subject. Later comments build on what came before and may, therefore, go farther. Later comments also define themselves against the earlier, even as they dispute particulars, redefine issues, add new material, or otherwise shift the discussion.

If as teachers of writing we want to prepare our students to enter into the written interchanges of their chosen disciplines and the various discussions of personal and public interest, we must cultivate various techniques of absorbing, reformulating, commenting on, and using reading. In the tradition/apprentice model, such skills were fostered only implicitly under the umbrella assignment of the research paper, but they were not given explicit, careful attention. Only access to the tradition (information gathering) and acknowledgement of the tradition (documentation) were the foci of instruction. In the newer model of the voice of the individual self, assignments such as the research paper are superfluous, remaining only as vestiges of former syllabi or as the penance imposed on a service department. The model of the conversation, however, suggests a full curriculum of skills and stages in the process of relating new comments to previously written materials. The following partial catalog of stages, skills, and assignments points toward the kinds of issues that might be addressed in writing courses. The suggestions are in the form of a framework rather than of specific lessons in order to leave each teacher free to interpret the consequences of the model through the matrix of individual thoughts, experiences, and teaching styles. Similarly, the teacher will need to interpret the model through those conversations that are most familiar and important to students. Given the diversity of existing written conversations and the variety of individual responses, it is not profitable to prescribe a single course for everyone.

Intelligent response begins with *accurate understanding of prior comments,* not just of the facts and ideas stated, but of what the other writer was trying to achieve. A potential respondent needs to know not just the claims a writer was making but also whether the writer was trying to call established beliefs into question or simply add some detail to generally agreed-upon ideas. The respondent needs to be able to tell whether a prior statement was attempting to arouse emotions or to call forth dispassionate judgment. The more we understand of the dynamics as well as the content of a conversation, the more we have to respond to. Vague understanding is more than careless; it is soporific. Particular writing assignments can help students become more perceptive readers and can help break down the tendency toward vague inarticulateness resulting from purely private reading. Paraphrase encourages precise understanding of individual terms and statements; the act of translating thoughts from one set of words to another makes the student consider exactly what was said and what was not. Summary reveals the structure of arguments and the continuity of thought; the student must ferret out the important claims and those elements that unify the entire piece of writing. Both paraphrase and summary will also be useful skills when in the course of making original arguments, the student will have to refer to the thoughts of others with some accuracy and efficiency. Finally, having students analyze the technique of writing in relation to the writing's apparent purpose will make students sensitive to the ways writing can create effects that go beyond the overt content. Analysis of propaganda and advertising will provide the extreme and easy cases, but analysis of more subtle designs, such as that of legal arguments or of reports of biological research, will more fully reveal the purposive nature of writing.

The next stage, *reacting to reading,* gives students a sense of their own opinions and identity defined against the reading material. As they try to reconcile what they read with what they already think, students begin to explore their assumptions and frameworks of thought. At first their responses may be uninformed, either fending off the new material or acquiescing totally to what appears to be the indisputable authority of the printed word. But with time and opportunities to articulate their changing responses, students can become more comfortable with the questions raised by their reading; they enter into a more dialectical relationship with those who have written before. Prior assimilated reading becomes grist for processing new reading. Three kinds of exercise encourage the development of more extensive and thoughtful reactions: marginal comments on reading, reading journals, and informal reaction essays. From early in the semester, teachers should encourage students to record their thoughts about the reading in marginal notes. The teacher must be careful to distinguish this kind of reaction annotation from the more familiar study-skills kind of content annotation, perhaps by suggesting that content annotations go on the inside margin and reactions go on the wider outside margins. This reaction in the margins increases the student's awareness of moment-by-moment responses to individual statements and examples. Reading journals written after each day's reading give the student additional room to explore the immediate responses at greater length and to develop larger themes. Again the teacher must insist on the distinction between content summaries and reactions, no matter how tentative the latter may at first be. Finally, the informal response essay allows the student to develop a single reaction at length, perhaps drawing on a number of related, more immediate responses. Here the teacher should make sure that the response maintains contact with issues growing out of the reading and does not become purely a rhapsody on a personal theme unrelated to the reading. For all three types of assignment, the teacher can refer the student to previously held opinions, experiences, observations, and other readings as starting points for reactions. As students become more sensitive to their responses to reading, they will spontaneously recognize likely starting points.

Developing reactions leads to more formal *evaluation of reading*, measuring what a book or article actually accomplishes compared to its apparent ambitions, compared to reality, and compared to other books. The evaluative review, if treated as more than just a notice covered with a thin wash of reaction, is an effective exercise, for it requires the student both to represent and to assess the claims of the book or article. The reader's reaction to the book is also significant to the evaluation, for if the reader finds him- or herself laughing when he or she should be nodding in assent, the book has failed to meet at least some of its purposes. Another kind of evaluative essay measures the claims of the reading against observable reality. The data the student compares to the book's claims may be from prior experience, new observations, formal data gathering using social science techniques, or technical experiments. Here the teacher may discuss the variety of purposes, criteria, and techniques of data gathering in different academic disciplines as well as other human endeavors. Finally, students may be asked to compare the claims and evidence of a number of different sources. In this kind of exercise, the students have to judge whether there is agreement, disagreement, or merely discussion of different ideas; then students must identify on what level the agreement or disagreement occurs, whether of simple fact, interpretation, idea, or underlying approach; and finally, they must determine how the agreements can be fitted together and the disagreements reconciled or adjudicated. Conflicts cannot, of course, always be resolved, but students become aware of the difficulties of evaluation. Comparison of matched selections, reports requiring synthesis, reviews of literature, and annotated bibliographies are all assignments compatible with this last purpose. Reviews of literature and annotated bibliographies also give the student a coherent picture of how previous comments add up in pursuit of common issues.

Students can then begin to define those *issues* they wish to pursue and to develop *informed views* on those issues. Two kinds of exercise, definitions of problem areas and research proposals, require the students to identify some issue he or she would like to know more about, to assemble the prior statements relevant to the issue, and to indicate the limitations of those sources. The proposal requires the further task of planning how the gap of knowledge in the literature can be overcome. Problem definition and proposals are early stages of the familiar assignment of the research paper. Also familiar is the teacher's disappointment upon receiving a derivative research report instead of an original, informed view in the form of a research essay. The use of preparatory assignments—not just the proposal, but also progress reports, reflections on the evidence, hypothesis testing, and idea sketches—will help remind the student of the original goal of the work while encouraging creative and detailed use of the source material. Prior instruction in the skills discussed above will also insure that the student knows how to use reading to form independent attitudes toward the sources and so facilitate the development of original theses. Other, more specific exercises that set the conditions for the development of informed views involve setting factual and theoretical sources against each other. Three case studies can be compared to elicit general patterns, or one writer's theories can be measured against another's factual material. These two assignments are, in fact, forms of critical analysis using a coherent set of categories derived from a theoretical standpoint to sort out specifics. Such exercises show the student the many uses of source material beyond simple citation of authority in support of predetermined opinion.

The independent, critical standpoint the student develops with respect to reading other people's works can also help the student frame and revise his or her own writing to be a purposeful and appropriate contribution to an ongoing conversation. Consideration of the relationship to previous statements will help the student decide what techniques are likely to serve new purposes. Will a redefinition of basic concepts, the introduction of a new concept, or the close analysis of a case study best resolve confusion? Or perhaps only a head-on, persuasive argument will serve. Further, knowledge of the literature likely to have been read by an audience helps a writer determine what needs to be explained at length and what issues need to be addressed.

The model of written conversation even transforms the technical skills of reference and citation. The variety of uses to be made of quotation, the options for referring to others' ideas and information (e.g., quotation, paraphrase, summary, name only), and the techniques of introducing and discussing source materials are the tools that allow the accurate but pointed connection of one's argument to earlier statements. The mechanics of documentation more than being an exercise in intellectual etiquette, become the means of indicating the full range of comments to which the new essay is responding.

When we ask students to write purely from their selves, we may tap only those prior conversations that they are still engaged in and so limit the extent and variety of their thinking and writing. We can use reading to present new conversational opportunities that draw the students into wider public, professional, and academic communities. Thus, the students will learn to write within the heavily literate contexts they will meet in college and later life. Whether writing tasks are explicitly embedded in prior written material—a review of literature, a research paper, or a legal brief—or whether they are only implicitly related to the thought and writing of others, as in critical analyses or matters of public debate, if students are not taught the skills of creating new statements through evaluating, assimilating, and responding to the prior statements of the written conversation, we offer them the meager choice of being parrots of authority or raconteurs stocked with anecdotes for every occasion. Only a fortunate few will learn to enter the community of the literate on their own.

Works Cited

Britton, James T., Martin N. Burgess, A. Mcleod, and H. Rosen. *The Development of Writing Abilities* (11–18).(London: Macmillan Education,1975).

Hirsch, E.D., Jr. *The Philosophy of Composition.* (Chicago: University of Chicago Press, 1977).

Five Ways of Interpreting a Text

John Peters

In this chapter from The Elements of Critical Reading, *John Peters describes five perspectives or strategies for reading and analyzing texts "that apply across the disciplines and that form the basis of even specialized critical discussions." The social perspective considers a text's relation to culture. The emotional or psychological perspective examines the text's emotional appeals and conflicts. The rhetorical perspective focuses on the work's form and style. The logical perspective analyzes its reasoning. And the ethical perspective examines the moral and political values discussed and implied in the text. Peters provides brief sets of questions to help students apply each interpretive strategy.*

Interpretation can be frustrating if you don't know where to begin. Suppose you're in a classroom or other meeting place where a text is being discussed. Maybe the target is an essay or a chapter or a formal report of some kind. Though you've read the material as closely as others have, you feel awkward talking about it. You remember most of what you have read, but when it comes to commenting on its

---

NOTE [from the author's "Preface"] This is a book about reading and elementary criticism. It is addressed to college undergraduates who must learn traditional ways of analyzing, discussing, and evaluating what they are assigned to read. In a wider sense, however, this book is for anyone—in college or out—who must read often and who is in some doubt as to what "critical reading" means.

[From the introduction to Chapter 2 :]: .... In order to demonstrate the five critical perspectives, we shall need to refer often to ... three sample texts ... as models for practice. Besides, those three texts—Lincoln's Gettysburg Address, Joan Didion's "On Going Home," and Lewis Thomas's "Making Science Work"—are good examples of the kinds of writing which college students and other critical readers nowadays find themselves interpreting. Those three texts represent respectively the "classic" document of historic reputation, the contemporary personal memoir, and the expository or argumentative essay. The skills you develop in discussing those kinds of texts will help prepare you for future critical reading across the disciplines.

---

meaning or importance, you don't know where to start. You hear other people saying things, and you know you're expected to say something too. All of a sudden, the professor or discussion leader turns to you and asks, "What's your view?"

Silence descends. Faces stare at you. After catching your breath, you stammer a few words as chill perspiration bedews your forehead. Then the discussion moves on to someone else while you sit frozen, trying to recall what you said. You hope it sounded reasonable, but you're not sure. Could it be that you didn't have a "view" at all?

Nonsense! You probably had plenty of views, but you weren't used to organizing or expressing them effectively. What you lacked was a means of approach that would allow you to bring your ideas together.

In this chapter we review five ways of approaching a text of any kind. These are ways that apply across the disciplines and that form the basis of even specialized critical discussions. Even though we shall be reviewing them here in brief and somewhat simplified terms, you'll find that they can be adapted easily to more advanced circumstances, depending on your needs and interests.

THE SOCIAL PERSPECTIVE

Using the social perspective means discussing the text in relation to society. Just about everything you read has some social relevance. Invitations, legal contracts, letters, and advertising are obvious examples. In the case of essays, nonfiction books, and other demanding texts, you can begin to take a social perspective by answering a few key questions:

What Social Concerns Does the Text Reveal?

One way to answer this question is simply to think about what general function or usefulness the text may have. Magazine articles, for example, may be reporting on new trends, showing people how to do things, or giving opinions on subjects of popular interest. On the other hand, some texts have less obvious social relevance. A mathematics textbook may not reveal social concerns directly; but if you consider how necessary applied math is to technology we use, the social significance of polynomials or differential equations should be evident. Thinking about how a text is used by others is one way to discover its relation to society.

Another way of answering the question is to think about any problems or conflicts that the text may address. Because all writing involves contrast, you can reexamine a given text's contrasts to see if any of them is social in nature. Ordinary reading material may present obvious social contrasts, as when a magazine ad tries to convince you of the difference between the wise people who own a given product and the fools who don't. But in longer texts, the social contrasts may have to do with anything from family tensions to class conflict, generation gaps, professional rivalries, political differences, or even war.

If you have read the three sample texts reprinted in the Appendix, try to summarize the social issues raised within each. You may discover that in Lincoln's

Gettysburg Address the most obvious social conflict is the Civil War, for as Lincoln reminds his audience: "We are met on a great battle-field of that war." But other social concerns are detectable as well. One student summarized them this way:

> The author is also concerned about the continuing struggle for equality and the preservation of our nation, which is "dedicated to the proposition that all men are created equal."

The question of whether a government "of the people" will survive or perish is certainly a social issue, and so is the issue of slavery—a matter not directly discussed in the speech itself but implied by the allusion to the Civil War.

As for the other two models in the Appendix, you may find that Joan Didion's essay reveals social concerns having to do with family identity and the meaning of "home," while Lewis Thomas's essay focuses on the social uncertainties brought about by twentieth-century science. Is the American family what it used to be? Is technology our friend or our enemy? These are matters which Didion and Thomas address respectively. The social perspective allows you to focus on those issues as you discuss their essays.

Not everyone will agree on exactly how a text's social concerns should be summarized. But to make the effort is to begin using the social perspective as an approach to the text. When you've discovered what you believe are the key social issues, you can move on to another question that the social perspective calls for:

How Does the Text Relate to the Past?

In considering whatever social concerns a text reveals, you might ask how the text relates to the times during which it was written. Newspaper articles are an obvious example of how nonfiction depends on the world around it. In the case of books, essays, and other less "news"-oriented texts, the relation of text to history may be more subtle. Yet most writing does reflect the author's awareness of his or her times. Scientific writing, for example, may not always seem concerned with the society around it, but the scientist's findings will be influenced by the current state of research in his or her century. More personal writing, such as memoirs and autobiographies, often comments on social trends that the author has witnessed.

Consider again the three texts in the Appendix. Joan Didion's "On Going Home" is a product of the 1960s. The author takes her times into account by speculating on whether she is a member of "the last generation to carry the burden of 'home,' to find in family life the source of all tension and drama" (par. 2). Lewis Thomas, whose essay appeared in the early 1980s, also takes history into account by surveying the past 300 years of science in contrast to the rapid developments of the past half century (par. 2). And, of course, we can't overlook Abraham Lincoln's famous allusions to historical events as he saw them in 1863: the founding of the nation "four score and seven years ago"; the battle at Gettysburg; and the unresolved fate of the nation during the Civil War. If you ask yourself whether a given text has something to say about the times before or during which it was written, the answer will often be *yes*—maybe even a *great deal*!

There is still another question you can ask from a social perspective, and it is this:

How Does the Text Relate to Right Now?

Important as it is to consider how a text relates to the past, even more important may be how it relates to the present. If you've just read this morning's newspaper, the relation between the text and "right now" may seem obvious. In college, however, much of what you read may have been written months, years—even centuries ago. For that reason you should be ready to ask whether social concerns raised by a text still affect us.

This question may cause you to emphasize matters that earlier audiences might have found less central to the text. For example, the crowd listening to Lincoln's 1863 speech probably felt that the key concern was whether the Civil War could be won by the Union forces. Today we know the answer to *that* question, and so we may choose to focus on broader concerns raised by the speech, such as freedom and the aims of government. Is the Gettysburg Address still relevant to American society in the late twentieth century? Here is what one student said:

> I find this speech very moving. The racial issue was a powerful and destructive force then—it still is. As a nation, we've come a long way. As a world, we have so far to go in matters of race, religion, and gender. For our nation, it seems the march was openly begun with this war, with this speech.

If you agree that Lincoln's words still challenge us to preserve democracy, you'll have a basis for discussing how this old text addresses the present.

What about works of more recent vintage, such as essays or books written within the past few decades? Here the question may be whether the social concerns raised by the text still reflect current behavior or practice in matters of custom, social activity, fashion, science, business, or whatever the subject may be. You may have to do some sifting to decide what still applies. In the case of Lewis Thomas's essay, you might be aware that scientific funding from business and government has increased since the essay was written, but still find timely the author's point about the continuing need for basic research. And in considering Joan Didion's "On Going Home," you might find the allusion to a girl dancing topless on crystal a bit dated; nevertheless, you could still find the author's uncertainty about the meaning of "home" relevant to the 1990s.

Summary

Discussing things from a social perspective allows us to view a text in relation to the world around it. By focusing on a text's social concerns as they apply to both the past and "right now," we may find that we already have plenty to say. But there are at least four other useful ways of approaching what we've read.

THE EMOTIONAL PERSPECTIVE

A second way of looking at a text is from a psychological viewpoint, or what we might simply call the emotional perspective. Though some texts seem emotionless (a legal contract, for example), most writing appeals to human feelings in one way or another. Focusing on a text from an emotional perspective can reveal new areas for interpretive discussion.

Does the Text Contain Objects of Emotion?

First, look for objects that the text invests with strong emotional significance. In the Bible, for example, such objects include the apple that tempts Adam, the Ark of the Covenant, and the Cross in the New Testament. While poetry and other kinds of imaginative literature are usually rich in emotive symbols, even nonfiction will sometimes display objects of emotion to signify moods or attitudes within the text.

In Joan Didion's "On Going Home," we come across several such objects: the contents of a drawer (par. 3), the telephone (par. 4), the vandalized cemetery (par. 4), and the sundress from Madeira (final par.). In context, those objects become associated with moods of nostalgia, uncertainty, dread, and hope—or, at least, those are general terms that might be used to describe their effects on the author. We can see that Didion is using those objects as symbols to intensify the emotional dynamics of her very personal essay. Consider also this from paragraph 3: "Paralyzed by the neurotic lassitude engendered by meeting one's past at every turn, around every corner, inside every cupboard, I go aimlessly from room to room." This eerie and rather discomforting sentence suggests that the ordinary objects in the house are for Didion more than mere objects of sentiment. They become associated with a "lassitude" that slows her down as she moves among them.

The more impersonal the writing, the fewer objects of emotion we might expect to find. However, if you look closely at Lewis Thomas's "Making Science Work," you'll notice how the author describes scientific discoveries as moments of "surprise" (final par.). Also, early in the essay he calls attention to the hostile emotions of those who distrust science itself:

> Voices have been raised in protest since the beginning, rising in pitch and violence in the nineteenth century during the early stages of the industrial revolution, summoning urgent crowds into the streets. . . .

Here the author deliberately uses emotion-charged terms—"protest," "violence," "urgent crowds"—to characterize science's detractors as being like an angry mob. Fair or not, this characterization dramatizes the contrast Thomas wants to draw between his opponents and scientists like himself.

Finally, consider the Gettysburg Address. Here Lincoln underscores the solemnity of the occasion by alluding to a single object—the battlefield. It has become "a final resting place for those who here gave their lives." For Lincoln the field is a symbol of sacrifice, but also, he tells us, a point of departure from which the living can take "increased devotion."

Naming and discussing the objects of emotion found in a text should help you to develop an interpretive analysis. But there is more to the emotional perspective than identifying a few key objects and the moods associated with them. Often there are several contrasting emotions to deal with, and for that reason we should pay attention to any emotional conflicts within the text.

Do You Find Evidence of Conflicting Emotions?

Since contrast is necessary to the structure of any text, we may well find that part of the contrast is emotional. In the Biblical story of Eden, for example, the apple may at first seem to signify temptation. But once Adam has sinned, the emotional picture grows very complicated. If we study the Eden story from an emotional perspective, we find many conflicts being raised: desire versus loyalty, pleasure versus pain, innocence versus guilt, and so forth. By recognizing those emotional contrasts we can learn something about the emotional *range* of the text.

When Abraham Lincoln tells his Gettysburg audience that "in a larger sense, we can not dedicate—we can not consecrate—we can not hallow—this ground," he is introducing an emotional conflict of sorts. The respect for the dead soldiers is so profound that the mourners are incapable of enacting that respect merely by dedicating the cemetery. The soldiers have already consecrated the ground "above our poor power," as Lincoln puts it. He then *resolves* that emotional conflict by turning from the dedication of the cemetery to a greater alternative: the dedication of ourselves: "It is rather for us to be here dedicated to the great task remaining before us. . . ." In other words, we must turn from mourning to a spirit of new commitment. Lincoln's appeal to his audience thus moves from one emotional plane to another, challenging the audience to share in a transition from sadness to hope.

Sometimes the emotional conflicts within a text are left unresolved. In "Making Science Work," Thomas contrasts the "surprise" of pure scientific discovery with the desire of society for predictable technological advances. The author cannot tell us where this conflict of interests will lead, exactly, but he does assure us that the surprises won't stop coming: "... we will not be able to call the shots in advance" (final par.). Similarly, in "On Going Home," Joan Didion describes emotional tensions between her husband and her family, between her two senses of "home," and between one generation and another. But she does not tell us how those tensions will be resolved.

It's important to realize that many texts do leave emotional conflicts unresolved, sometimes because they must. A text isn't a failure or poorly written just because it doesn't offer a solution to every problem it poses. Emotional conflict within writing is known as *irony* (a literary term for the balancing of opposites), and many fine works are full of emotional ironies. We can't as readers be expected to resolve all of those ironies any more than we can expect the author to do it for us, but we can share the author's awareness of conflict and thereby move closer to a sympathetic understanding of the text.

What Is the Tone of the Author?

The word "tone" refers to the attitude of the author toward the subject he or she is writing about. Even when particular objects in the text become associated with particular emotions, and even when the text contains emotional conflicts, we may find that the overall work takes on a tone which we may infer as characteristic of the author. Thus, for example, we might say that Lincoln has a "solemn" tone throughout the Gettysburg Address, that Joan Didion writes "wistfully" about her family home, or that Lewis Thomas's writing conveys a tone that is serious but lively.

Characterizing tone is bound to be a subjective exercise on the part of the reader. That is because we infer tone from our personal responses to the subject matter of the text. Also, when we describe tone we allow ourselves to generalize about what are really many separate aspects of the writing: content, diction, prose style, and so forth. But even though describing the author's tone may be risky, no discussion of a text from an emotional perspective can be complete without our taking the chance. For of all the emotions that may be present in the text, it is the author's own that are likely to affect us most.

Summary

The emotional perspective considers whatever objects of emotion may be present, any emotional conflicts that may arise within the text, and finally the author's overall tone. It's important to remember that sometimes the emotions of a text vary, and that we cannot always expect emotional conflicts to be neatly resolved.

THE RHETORICAL PERSPECTIVE

Rhetorical analysis takes as its focus the form and style of the writing. Here, rather than concerning yourself with the social and emotional issues that might be raised, you give your attention to *how* a text is constructed. If you want to learn to write well, you can benefit from applying the rhetorical perspective. That is because rhetoric has to do with skills employed by writers to achieve desired effects. By looking carefully at the form and style of particular texts, you can discover ways to advance your own writing skills. In fact, you will find yourself appreciating more fully the *art* of writing.

Here are some questions you can ask to begin using the rhetorical perspective:

How Can the Text's Form Be Described?

Describing form means recognizing categories to which the text may belong. For example, you can begin by asking yourself whether the text is nonfiction or imaginative literature. If you know it's nonfiction, go on to categorize it by *genre.* Is it an essay, a speech, a biography, an editorial, a technical operations manual, or what? If it is a work of imagination, is it poetry, drama, or prose fiction? More specifically, is it a lyric poem, an epic, a short story, a novel, a tragedy, a comedy, or what? If you are in doubt as to the definitions of the various genres and subgenres, you can consult a handbook of literary terms for help. To know why a text belongs to a particular category, you need first to know how that category is defined.

The term *essay,* for example, denotes a short, nonfictional prose work that comments on some aspect of reality. As a form, the essay goes back at least as far as the sixteenth-century *essais* of Michel de Montaigne. That French author asked himself, "What do I know?" His many essays become answers to that question, commenting on subjects from war and politics to religion and literature. Today the essay is a popular means of exploring what *we* know about the various disciplines and experiences that affect our lives. In general, we come upon two kinds of essays: those that are *personal,* involving reminiscences about the author's own past; and those that are *impersonal,* containing little or no reference to the author's private life.

Joan Didion's "On Going Home" is an example of a personal essay, while Lewis Thomas's "Making Science Work" is an impersonal one—at least in terms of its subject matter. We find that Didion's essay refers often to her family, her home(s), her special memories, and her own identity in relation to what she has witnessed. By contrast, Lewis Thomas's essay tells us nothing about the author's private life; instead, the focus is on a public controversy having to do with science and technology. What Thomas writes does of course reflect his personal views and judgment, but his own personality is not the focal point of the essay.

Another subgenre of nonfiction is the speech, or what is more precisely called *oration.* Speeches, too, can be either personal or impersonal, though the historic ones tend to be the latter. Lincoln's Gettysburg Address is not about Lincoln himself, after all, but about the future of the nation. If you look up a definition of *oratory* in a handbook or encyclopedia, you'll find that a classical oration contains three parts: an *exordium,* which appeals to the traditions or customs of the audience; an *argument,* which sets forth the main message and offers reasons for agreeing with the speaker; and a *peroration,* or summing up, that heightens or message. The Gettysburg Address is an unusually short oration, but it does contain all three parts if you look closely. The first sentence invokes the nation's past; the rest, except for the last sentence, argues on behalf of renewed dedication to national principles; and the last sentence serves as the peroration. In other words, this very short speech does follow the form of classical oratory.

Once you've identified the overall form of a text—as being a personal essay, a classic oration, or whatever—you are ready to go on with a more detailed analysis of the text's rhetoric.

Which Rhetorical Modes Do You Find in the Text?

We use the term *rhetorical modes* to describe methods of organizing writing to serve particular functions. Those functions may include describing, narrating, defining, comparing, contrasting, classifying, illustrating, summarizing, as well as persuading. All texts make use of at least some rhetorical modes, and the text's overall form may determine the kinds being used.

The kinds of rhetorical modes found in an essay, for example, may depend on whether that essay is personal or impersonal. Because Joan Didion's "On Going Home" is a personal essay, we might expect to find modes that help make her personal experience vivid. Those modes include *description* and *narration.* Describing means providing sense impressions having to do with sight, sound, taste, touch, and/or scent. Narrating means telling about a sequence of events. We find that both of those modes are used throughout Didion's essay:

> ... I drive across the river to a family graveyard. It has been vandalized since my last visit and the monuments are broken, overturned in the dry grass. Because I once saw a rattlesnake in the grass I stay in the car and listen to a country-and-Western station. Later I drive with my father to a ranch he has in the foothills.

Notice that the quoted passage contains both descriptive images (the broken monuments, the dry grass, etc.) and narrative (visiting the cemetery, listening to the radio, etc.). Personal writing often blends description and narration artfully so that the reader can experience an event and at the same time become aware of the setting. Precise narrative-descriptive detailing is almost a necessity in personal essays, though other rhetorical modes may be present as well.

On the other hand, impersonal essays tend to employ rhetorical modes suited to research reporting. Those include *definition, summary, classification, illustration, process analysis,* and *comparison/contrast* (see the Glossary for further explanations of those terms). In Lewis Thomas's "Making Science Work," for example, we find *summary* occurring in the essay's opening sentence: "For about three centuries we have been doing science, trying science out, using science for the construction of what we call modern civilization." Elsewhere, Thomas makes use of *classification* when he reviews scientific developments in fields from biology to social science (pars. 4–11), and again when he discusses the types of institutions that support basic research (pars. 12–16). This sort of formal distinguishing among types or categories is characteristic of impersonal essays, or what we call expository prose. The aim is to expose differences and distinctions that help explain a problem and/or point to its possible solution.

If you look carefully at Lincoln's Gettysburg Address, you may find the chief rhetorical modes to be contrast (i.e., between past and present), definition (i.e., the greater meaning of *dedicate),* and summary (i.e., of the events leading up to the dedication ceremony). You may find others, too.

By identifying which rhetorical modes appear in a text, you can reveal what functions the text is performing. That is true not only of essays but of all kinds of writing. In analyzing fiction, for example, you'll probably find plenty of narration and description, just as you will in personal essays, for the aim of fiction is to bring you close to the lives of imaginary characters. Business documents, textbooks, and other kinds of expository nonfiction may be given to other modes, especially classification, definition, process analysis, and summary.

How Can the Author's Style Be Described?

As E.B. White once pointed out, style is always something of a mystery: "Who can confidently say what ignites a certain combination of words, causing them to explode in the mind?" We can analyze the grammar of a text's sentences for clues, and we can talk about the "tone" of the author's voice. But style, like personality, is likely to remain more than the sum of its parts. Our efforts to describe an author's style probably won't succeed completely. But that doesn't mean we shouldn't try.

A graceful prose style often reflects a writer's keen awareness of grammar. Smooth parallel structures—known as parallelism or coordination—are often regarded as virtues of style, whereas misplaced modifiers, mixed metaphors, and verbosity are usually seen as flaws. (See the Glossary for more about those terms.) Analyzing the grammar of sentences can teach you a great deal about what works and what doesn't.

Some prose styles can be described as highly "formal." That is, they're marked by evenly balanced sentence structures resembling the fine cadences of classical music. The Gettysburg Address has that kind of polished formality. Consider this sentence: "The world will little note, nor long remember, what we say here, but it can never forget what they did here." Obviously, we *do* remember what Lincoln said here, partly because he said it so well. The sentence shows fine coordination as he balances the rise and fall of clauses on either side of the conjunction *but.* The verb phrases are parallel in form (i.e., "little note"—"long remember" —"never forget"). Furthermore, the repeating of the word "here," which otherwise might seem verbose, works like a resounding chord because of the rhythmic spacing.

Less formal styles are often called "conversational" because they come closer to the varied rhythms and loose structure of everyday speech. That doesn't mean, however, that an informal style isn't carefully done. Consider this passage from Lewis Thomas's "Making Science Work":

> We will solve our energy problems by the use of science, and in no other way. The sun is there, to be sure, ready for tapping, but we cannot sit back in the lounges of political lobbies and make guesses and wishes; it will take years, probably many years, of research. Meanwhile, there are other possibilities needing deeper exploration.

Here, as in conversation, the language moves forward unevenly. The lengths of the three sentences vary, and within those sentences some clauses are much shorter than others. There is a sort of stop-and-go urgency that gives emphasis to certain terms. Notice how Thomas writes "it will take years, probably many years, of research." The double stress on *years* seems deliberate, but also a bit hesitant. We seem to be hearing someone thinking aloud, letting his style reflect the natural course of his reasoning.

Often you'll find that a prose style falls somewhere between the high formality of Lincoln and the more conversational quality of Thomas. If you consider Joan Didion's style, for example, you'll find her a bit closer to Lincoln when it comes to balanced phrases within sentences, but much closer to Thomas when it comes to varying the lengths of sentences themselves. Notice how her essay ends:

> I would like to give her more. I would like to promise her that she will grow up with a sense of her cousins and of rivers and of her great-grandmother's teacups, would like to pledge her a picnic on a river with fried chicken and her hair uncombed, would like to give her *home* for her birthday, but we live differently now and I can promise her nothing like that. I give her a xylophone and a sundress from Madeira, and promise to tell her a funny story.

If you're tempted to say that the personal subject matter and the pronoun "I" make this style less formal than Lewis Thomas's, look again. The long sentence is far more oratorical than conversational, building rhythmically on a series of parallel phrases. But you'd be right in saying that, like Thomas, Didion sharply varies the sentence lengths and thereby brings her prose style closer to the normal pacing of everyday speech.

Let's say that you've now looked at the form, rhetorical modes, and style of the text. There is still another matter to consider when you are using the rhetorical perspective:

What About Ambiguity?

As philosophers from Francis Bacon to Jacques Derrida have reminded us, language is ambiguous. The same word or term can be understood to mean different things to different readers or listeners. The word "pride," for example, suggests healthy self-respect to some persons, but to others it connotes the sin of overestimating what we deserve. Thus saying that someone is a "proud person" could be taken as a compliment or a rebuke, depending on the intent of the speaker and on the understanding of the audience. Dictionaries can supply us with general definitions, called denotations. But each reader also interprets terms according to personal connotations—meaning his or her own previous experiences with those terms. As the semanticist S.I. Hayakawa once pointed out, if we hear the phrase "Bessie the cow," we are all likely to think of different cows. The full implications of this problem are far reaching. If all language is potentially ambiguous, no two readers will read a text in quite the same way, and even the same reader may read a text differently on different occasions.

If you accept the notion that any word may be ambiguous, finding ambiguities in texts should be fairly simple. All you have to do is point to any line and say, "This can be read in different ways." You'd be right. But as a practical matter, we can't pause to challenge every word or term we read. What we need to look for are those words whose ambiguity raises serious questions about the meaning of the whole text.

In considering this problem we should first distinguish between ordinary—or "bad"—ambiguity that results from stylistic faults, and a literary—or "good"—kind that enhances the quality of the text. Ambiguity of the ordinary "bad" kind can be caused by mixed metaphors, misplaced modifiers, equivocation, imprecise translation from a foreign language, or by verbosity (refer to listings in the Glossary). Ambiguity of the literary or "good" kind is another matter. Here the reader's uncertainty as to the meaning isn't caused by poor writing but, on the contrary, by the ability of the author to heighten or intensify words in a way that creates new levels of possible meaning for them.

One way to find these "good" ambiguities is to look for terms that the author stresses as being hard to define. Sometimes a text will begin to raise questions about its own key words. Consider, for example, this passage from Joan Didion's "On Going Home":

> I am home for my daughter's first birthday. By "home" I do not mean the house in Los Angeles where my husband and I and the baby live, but the place where my family is, in the Central Valley of California. It is a vital although troublesome distinction.

Here the author gives us two connotations for the word "home." She tells us that she will be using the second one—home as the place where her family is—in this essay. But she also says that the distinction between the two senses of "home" is troublesome. Later in the essay, we find that Didion is still uncertain as to what "home" means:

> Sometimes I think that those of us who are now in our thirties were born into the last generation to carry the burden of "home," to find in family life the source of all tension and drama. The question of whether or not you could go home again was a very real part of the sentimental and largely literary baggage with which we left home in the fifties; I suspect that it is irrelevant to the children born of the fragmentation after World War II.

In this second passage, the author no longer uses "home" to stand for her childhood house in the Central Valley of California. Now she associates the word with abstract ideas such as "burden" and the "tension and drama" of family life. But Didion cannot be sure that this wider, more abstract meaning still holds true for a post-World War II generation. Thus the meaning of "home" remains a problem throughout the essay.

The author may be saying that one's sense of "home" depends on one's age and viewpoint, but that the ultimate meaning may be undecidable. In any case, we need to recognize that special ambiguity of the word "home" in this essay, for the difficulty of knowing what "home" means is largely what the essay itself is about.

The two other texts reprinted in the Appendix also raise questions about some of their own key terms. Lewis Thomas's essay is largely concerned with what "science" has come to mean in the modern world. He admits that part of the meaning remains unclear:

> Illumination is the product sought, but it comes in small bits, only from time to time, not ever in broad, bright flashes of public comprehension, and there can be no promise that we will ever emerge from the great depths of the mystery of being.

Science may not be only a matter of proving things, Thomas suggests, but also of living with uncertainty. As one example of that uncertainty, he points to the word "cell":

> For a while things seemed simple and clear; the cell was a neat little machine, a mechanical device ready for taking to pieces and reassembling, like a tiny watch. But just in the last few years it has become almost imponderably complex, filled with strange parts whose functions are beyond today's imagining.

Here, Thomas shows us that a scientific term like "cell" can be as ambiguous as an everyday term like "home." But by facing up to that ambiguity, the essayist can address not only the question of what the word has meant—but also the question of what it is coming to mean. The reader is invited to wonder right along with the author.

Consider, finally, the Gettysburg Address. Here the word "dedicate" is surely a key term. In one sense, the dedication of the cemetery is a social ritual for which the audience has gathered. But Lincoln quickly challenges that ordinary sense of "dedicate." In a larger sense, he says, "We can not dedicate ... this ground." The brave soldiers, he reminds us, have already done so. Setting aside the dedicating of the cemetery, therefore, Lincoln instead uses "dedicate" in other contexts: for example, being "dedicated to the proposition that all men are created equal," and being a "nation ... so dedicated." If we look carefully at Lincoln's repeated use of "dedicate" within the speech, we realize that he is doing more than just reviewing familiar connotations of the word. He is creating new meaning:

> It is rather for us to be here dedicated to the great task remaining before us—that from these honored dead we take increased devotion to that cause for which they here gave the last full measure of devotion—that we here highly resolve that ... this nation, under God, shall have a new birth of

> freedom—and that, government of the people, by the people, for the people, shall not perish from the earth.

Here Lincoln has given new meaning to the word "dedicate." That new meaning inspires a commitment to ideals that transcend the hour of mournful commemoration. Being dedicated in the newer sense is a matter of "increased devotion." But the full sense of what Lincoln means by "dedicate" may be indefinable—a sublime ambiguity. For it remains a word among others, and those other words—"unfinished work," "task remaining," "new birth of freedom"—all point to an uncertain future when the present act of dedication must be fulfilled.

Ambiguity is thus an important issue in rhetorical analysis. Sometimes the question of what a text means comes down to the question of what a particular word means. If that word is important within the text but treated by the author as having different connotations, chances are that deciding what that word means is a challenge that the text itself is facing.

Summary

The rhetorical perspective allows us to discuss a text's form, its rhetorical modes, its style, and its words. Once we have considered those matters, we should have a pretty fair idea of how the text is constructed.

THE LOGICAL PERSPECTIVE

The logical perspective takes into account the reasoning used by an author to reach a conclusion. Sometimes that reasoning can be very complicated, as in, say, a treatise on physics or a detailed legal brief At other times, logic may seem to have been suspended altogether, as in a fairy tale where things happen by magic. But in the course of reading standard nonfictional material, you'll need to look carefully at the text's logic as a basis for deciding whether or not you agree with the views expressed. Here are some questions you might ask.

What Debatable Issue Is Raised by the Text?

A debatable issue is one that allows for controversy. It is a problem whose solution has not been agreed upon by everyone before the text was written. Sometimes a text will raise several such issues, though all of them will usually cluster around a central problem.

What is at issue in the Gettysburg Address? Lincoln puts it very succinctly: "Now we are engaged in a great civil war, testing whether that nation, or any nation so conceived, and so dedicated, can long endure." For the audience listening at Gettysburg in 1863, the question of whether the United States could survive as a nation was surely an unresolved issue. The war was not yet won, nor was its outcome in sight. Many believed that the Union forces would prevail, but half of America was still in rebellion. How could the Union hope to win? Lincoln raises precisely that question.

Or consider Joan Didion's "On Going Home." Hers is a personal essay, not a work of formal argumentation. But Didion does raise a controversial issue when she speculates on whether she is part of "the last generation to carry the burden of home, to find in family life the source of all tension and drama." At issue here is whether American values changed after World War II in such a way that the "tension and drama" of family life lost much of its former importance. Obviously, not everyone would agree that such a change occurred. The issue is open for debate, as Didion recognizes.

Consider also Lewis Thomas's essay. Here the author is addressing a general readership concerned about the future of science. The author raises a controversial issue early in the essay:

> Three hundred years seems a long time for testing a new approach to human interliving, long enough to settle back for critical appraisal of the scientific method, maybe even long enough to vote on whether to go on with it or not. There is an argument. Voices have been raised in protest since the beginning. . . . Give it back, say some of the voices, it doesn't really work. . . .
>
> The scientists disagree, of course, partly out of occupational bias, but also from a different way of viewing the course and progress of science in the past fifty years.

The issue, then, is whether science does "really work." Thomas reminds us that while some people fear and distrust science, others—scientists themselves—have a different view. As readers we infer that the essay will go on to explore this controversy in more detail, and of course it does so.

What Conclusions Does the Text Reach?

After discovering what issues have been raised, you want to know what conclusions the text reaches about those issues. Logical thinking about a matter of controversy often results in a stated position which the audience is invited to share. To analyze the reasoning by which that conclusion is reached, you might begin by identifying the conclusion itself.

If the main issue raised by the Gettysburg Address is whether a "nation ... so dedicated" can long endure, the main conclusion is that survival depends on the dedication of the living to the "unfinished work" of the past. Lincoln encourages his audience to share the belief that further sacrifice to preserve "government of the people, by the people, for the people" is necessary.

And if the main issue in Didion's "On Going Home" is whether the meaning of "home" changed following World War II, the conclusion seems to be that the meaning did indeed change. At the end of the essay, the author wants to give her daughter "home" in the sense of family picnics by the river, but instead she gives her a sundress from Madeira and a promise to tell a funny story. The symbolism here may suggest that in the author's view commercialism and the promise of "fun" have become substitutes for the "tension and drama" of family life.

In the case of Thomas's essay, the issue—whether or not science works—is one upon which the author has strong opinions. The major conclusion is perhaps found in this passage:

> Science is useful, indispensable sometimes, but whenever it moves forward it does so by producing a surprise; you cannot specify the surprise you'd like. Technology should be watched closely, monitored, criticized, even voted in or out by the electorate, but science itself must be given its head if we want it to work.

Much of Thomas's essay argues that while we may distrust technology, or applied science, we should recognize that basic scientific inquiry "works" if given the freedom to produce its surprises. The key to workable science, in the author's view, is respect for the difference between science and technology.

Does the Text Contain Sufficient Evidence?

Once you've identified issues and conclusions, you need to analyze the reasoning by which conclusions are reached. In effect, you now become a bit like a jury weighing the evidence.

When you ask whether a text contains "sufficient evidence," you are really asking whether that text gives convincing reasons to show why its conclusion is valid. To answer that question, you need to take another look at the reasoning. In general, there are two possible kinds of reasons any text can offer you: those based on deduction and those based on induction. Most texts of any length offer you both kinds, though one kind may predominate. Again, let's consider the three texts in the Appendix as examples.

The Gettysburg Address, like many speeches, is primarily a work of *deductive reasoning.* Lincoln's argument for continuing the Civil War is based on general principles, and his conclusion follows from the application of those principles to the issue at hand. In effect, he reasons that only the living can complete the "unfinished work" of democracy, that "we" are the living, and that therefore only we can complete the task begun by our founding fathers. If you sketched out this line of reasoning in the form of a syllogism, it would look like this:

> *Major premise:* Only the living can save democracy.
> *Minor premise:* We are the living.
> *Conclusion:* Only we can save democracy.

Of course, Lincoln doesn't use quite those terms. But if you infer his reasoning from the speech, you can see that his argument for dedicating ourselves to the task ahead rests on the major premise that responsibility falls on the living.

The two other model texts rely mainly on *inductive* evidence to support their conclusions. Reasoning by induction means drawing conclusions from the observation of facts or data. Such reasoning is at the heart of most scientific writing. But it also shows up in more personal writing when an author sets out to interpret his or her own experience.

Joan Didion's "On Going Home" is packed with inductive evidence to show that times have changed—and with them the meaning of "home." Her writing concentrates on precise factual details: the contents of a drawer, the vandalized cemetery, the image of a girl dancing in a San Francisco bar, the telephone calling Didion back to another city, the fried-chicken picnics she remembers versus the xylophone and sundress she buys for her daughter. Contrasts between past and present occur even in the conversation she holds with her great-aunts, who no longer know where she lives. All of the essay's details contribute to a sense of loss, a hypothesis about the "fragmentation" after World War II.

It may be easy to see the validity of that hypothesis as a applied to the author's own circumstances, which are after all the subject matter of the essay. But it may be wrong to go further and say that the text contains sufficient evidence to justify a general conclusion about society as a whole. After all, Didion is reasoning from a range of facts bearing on her own family; she can only wonder whether she is a member of the last generation to carry the "burden" of home. The reader, in turn, must decide on the basis of his or her own experience whether the speculation about society rings true.

Lewis Thomas's essay is also in large part a work of inductive reasoning, though the scope of that reasoning is more impersonal. To support his hypothesis about the need for science, Thomas surveys history and specifies facts about the challenges ahead. He also comments on the various fields of science—biology, aerospace, earth science, astronomy, and so on—and suggests how each is facing new horizons. He summarizes the inductive evidence by saying this:

> The doing of science on a scale appropriate to the problems at hand was launched only in the twentieth century and has been moving into high gear only within the last fifty years. We have not lacked explanations at any time in our recorded history, but now we must live and think with the new habit of requiring reproducible observations and solid facts for the explanations.

If you find the inductive reasoning in this essay convincing, you'll probably agree that we must now live with the habit of requiring "reproducible observations"—in other words, with the habit of science.

Thomas also argues that science must remain independent of technology in order to succeed. That argument may be more deductive than inductive, for it rests on the assumption that all scientific progress occurs as "surprise" and that "basic, undifferentiated science" is what makes surprise possible. Your acceptance or rejection of that line of reasoning will probably determine whether you agree that science and technology are as different as this essay concludes.

However well reasoned the argument of a text may be, almost any conclusion remains open to question or future debate. That is because logic alone cannot account for everything. Deductive reasoning depends on premises that in turn depend on the author's personal beliefs. Inductive reasoning depends on the ability of a hypothesis to apply in all future cases. Because deductive premises are "givens" based on faith, and because inductive hypotheses can be overturned by future exceptions to the rule, argument remains a process in which opposing views are always possible.

Does the Text Take Opposing Arguments into Account?

In formal debate of the kind practiced by lawyers and college forensic teams, taking opposing views into account is always important. Often one side will summarize the opponents' reasoning, then attack it for containing errors or omissions. *Fallacies* are formal charges made against an opponent's reasoning; they include question begging, hasty generalization, stereotyping, and so on. (See the Glossary for a more complete list.) Making fallacy charges against someone else's argument is a bit like throwing punches in a boxing match, and usually there is plenty of punching from both sides.

However, most argumentative texts that you read are not structured like formal debates. There is no rule which says that an author must take into account every possible counterargument and refute it. Consequently, you may find that the attention paid to an opposing view is a minor or even nonexistent part of the text. Nevertheless, it's a good idea to search for any places where the author does allude to opposing views, for those places may give you clues as to which other lines of reasoning you might investigate on your own.

The Gettysburg Address is one example of an argument that does *not* take opposing views into account, at least not directly. Many readers have noticed how Lincoln avoids any mention of the Confederacy or of the South's argument for fighting the Civil War. One reason may be that the occasion did not call for it; another may be that Lincoln hoped to include opponents in his appeal for a "new birth of freedom." Because he does not attack Confederate logic in this speech, we can only wonder if Lincoln has his opponents in mind when he appeals to national idealism.

Texts that contain narrative writing will sometimes bring in opposing views by telling about persons who disagree—either with the author or with each other. In "On Going Home," Joan Didion presents her husband as an outsider who doesn't share her understanding of her family's home:

> Nor does he understand that when we talk about sale-leasebacks and right-of-way condemnations we are talking in code about the things we like best, the yellow fields and the cottonwoods and the rivers rising and falling and the mountain roads closing when the heavy snow comes in. We miss each other's points, have another drink and regard the fire. My brother refers to my husband, in his presence, as "Joan's husband." Marriage is the classic betrayal.

Like the reader, the author's husband hasn't shared all of her childhood experiences, and his more distant and sometimes uncomprehending view of her family home is perhaps closer to the reader's own perspective. He serves as a foil to the nostalgia that Didion feels, and his presence in the essay reminds us that there are other ways of looking at what "home" means. Late in the essay when he telephones to suggest that she "get out, drive to San Francisco or Berkeley," we are hearing a call to another way of life, a renewed involvement in the larger world beyond the family of one's childhood.

When it comes to exploring opposing views, impersonal expository essays are more likely to approximate the structure of formal debate. In Lewis Thomas's "Making Science Work," for example, the second and third paragraphs present two contrasting views of science: the first being the view that science "doesn't really work," and the second being the view of scientists who "disagree."

Though Thomas remains on the side of the scientists throughout the essay, he is careful to acknowledge the evidence cited by his opponents. At several points he draws attention to the problems and dangers that science has brought. He reminds us of the "radioactivity from the stored, stacked bombs or from leaking, flawed power plants, acid rain, pesticides, leached soil, depleted ozone, and increased carbon dioxide in the outer atmosphere." He also acknowledges that "[u]ncertainty, disillusion, and despair are prices to be paid for living in an age of science." By naming the drawbacks cited by his opponents, Thomas forces us to see the issue from two sides. He also helps his own cause by making his argument appear more objective than it otherwise might seem.

Besides introducing views opposed to his own on the question of whether science whether science works, Thomas also summarizes disagreements between business and the academic community:

> Each side maintains adversarial and largely bogus images of the other, moneymakers on one side and impractical academics on the other. Meanwhile, our competitors ... have long since found effective ways to link industrial research to government and academic science, and they may be outclassing this country before long.

Here the author does not join one side or the other, but attacks them both. By saying that each side maintains "largely bogus images of the other," Thomas in effect charges both with the fallacy of stereotyping. He also causes the reader to wonder if reasoning on the basis of "bogus images" may prove costly to the nation's future.

Summary

Taking opposing views into account thus adds new dimensions to an author's argument. As a reader, you can study those opposing views for leads to other arguments that lie beyond the scope of the essay or book you may be reading. But remember that logical analysis is first a matter of studying the author's own argument: its issues, conclusions, and reasons offered as evidence.

THE ETHICAL PERSPECTIVE

You may feel that an interpretation should be over once the social, emotional, rhetorical, and logical factors have been taken into account. But there is one more important perspective to consider, especially if the text discusses or depicts human behavior. You should not overlook the question of moral values, or what might be called the ethics of the text.

Morality is a touchy subject to discuss. For that reason it is important to respect certain ground rules as you approach the whole matter. One is that you should not attempt to impose your own moral values on the text. In other words, you shouldn't try to "read into" a text values that are not actually there. It is also important to remember that some authors do not advocate particular ethical positions but instead try to be objective or "unbiased" reporters. With those ground rules in mind, you should be ready to make use of the ethical perspective. Here are some questions to ask:

What Is the Highest Good Envisioned by the Text?

In moral philosophy the *summum bonum*—the highest good—is the ultimate ideal toward which ethical behavior is directed. Precisely what that ideal is can vary from person to person. However, the history of ethics suggests that duty, happiness, and perfection are among the most widespread concepts of the highest good. You might therefore begin by asking whether a text seems to aim at one of those three ideals, while keeping in mind that it may not.

Duty is an ancient and important ideal. When Moses carried the Ten Commandments down from the mountain, he may have brought with him the ethics of obedience. We find duty idealized by Socrates and the Greek stoics, by many religions, and by military codes throughout history. For the philosopher Immanuel Kant (1724–1804), duty is a matter of intuitive conduct. According to Kant's belief, you should "act only on that principle which you can at the same time will to be a universal law." This axiom, called the "categorical imperative," suggests that the individual should recognize intuitively what ought to be done—and then do it. Many philosophers have agreed that conscience is the basis for duty and that each person's struggle to obey the dictates of conscience leads to the highest good.

If we consider the Gettysburg Address, for example, it is easy to see that Lincoln is stressing the importance of duty. As one student put it,

> Lincoln states that the people must "resolve" to continue to fight the war for freedom. Using the word resolve imparts a sense of duty. By his ending statement—"and that, government ... shall not perish from the earth"—he implies that if people do not continue this fight, the government which they created will not last.

Though Lincoln does not use the word "duty" as such, he admonishes his audience to be "dedicated to the unfinished work" and to preserve a government formed "of the people, by the people, for the people." Since duty may be defined as fulfilling one's sense of moral obligation to a cause, the Gettysburg Address is above all an appeal to conscience and a call to duty.

Happiness as the highest good is also an ancient ideal. The ethics of happiness (also called *eudaemonistic* ethics) dates back at least as far as Aristotle. Though there have been many disputes over what "happiness" may mean in particular circumstances, we may in general say that acts or ideas are aimed at happiness if their end result would bring pleasure or a sense of well-being. In our own time, many kinds of popular texts seem aimed at happiness. Travel magazines, self-help books, and light fiction may be obvious examples, though sometimes very serious literature also has happiness as a chief concern. In some cases, an author may reveal his or her longing for happiness by depicting its absence.

Throughout her essay "On Going Home," Joan Didion alludes to moments of past happiness and reveals her desire to pass on to her daughter the pleasures of family life. "I would like to promise her that she will grow up with a sense of her cousins and of rivers and of her great-grandmother's teacups. . . ." The regret that she can promise her daughter "nothing like that" suggests how deeply the author is aware of lost happiness. In an ideal world based on this essay's nostalgic vision, the highest good might be a perfect "home" that can be passed on from generation to generation. That such a home may now be out of reach does not prevent its remaining an ideal in this essay.

Perfection as the highest good is an ideal often associated with scientific progress. Philosophers such as Condorcet (1743–1794) and Auguste Comte (1798–1857) teach that whereas happiness may be an elusive goal, we can at least contribute to social and scientific progress and thereby help create a future perfection. Texts that report on ways to improve existing knowledge are thus often aimed at perfection as an ideal.

Thomas's "Making Science Work" might be viewed as such a text. The opening paragraphs of the essay suggest that science is flawed but "just at its beginning." Give science more time, Thomas urges. Give it time to perfect itself:

> What lies ahead, or what *can* lie ahead if the efforts in basic research are continued, is much more than the conquest of human disease or the amplification of agricultural technology or the cultivation of nutrients in the sea. As we learn more about the fundamental processes of living things in general we will learn more about ourselves, including perhaps the ways in which our brains, unmatched by any other neural structures on the planet, achieve the earth's awareness of itself. It may be too much to say that we will become wise through such endeavors, but we can at least come into possession of a level of information upon which a new kind of wisdom might be based.

Like many scientists before him, Thomas looks toward a future in which new discoveries, new capabilities, and ultimately new wisdom can be realized. The price for that future may be living with uncertainty, but we can dream of a time when our work will have paid off. Rather like Lincoln in the Gettysburg Address, Thomas asks us to consider our unfinished work. But whereas Lincoln reminds us of our national heritage in order to call us to duty, Thomas reminds us of our present ignorance in order to make us desire a perfected wisdom. "It is a gamble to bet on science for moving ahead," Thomas tells us, but in his view science is "now the only game in town."

Though duty, happiness, and perfection may not encompass all possible ideas of the highest good, they do often serve as signposts marking the main ethical routes along which many texts are moving. Even so, in looking closely at the ethics of a text we need also to consider specific convictions.

What Ethical Convictions Does the Text Reveal?

If we know which highest good the text seems aimed at, we can then ask what convictions are involved in the pursuit of that ideal. An ethical conviction is a belief about the rightness or wrongness of a particular way of behaving. There are many kinds of ethical convictions, but among the major categories are those which we may respectively call altruistic, egoistic, and political.

Altruistic convictions hold that the best way to do one's duty, achieve happiness, or reach perfection is by selfless commitment. That commitment may be to other people or to a cause deemed greater than oneself. Altruists in history include St. Paul, Joan of Arc, Mahatma Gandhi, and others who gave themselves wholly to the causes in which they believed. When Abraham Lincoln in the Gettysburg Address challenges us to be "here dedicated to the great task remaining," he is expressing an altruistic conviction. If we are to fulfill our duty to the nation, Lincoln tells his audience, we must give ourselves to the cause of preserving democracy.

Egoistic convictions have in common the belief that the highest good can be achieved through self-fulfillment of the individual. *Egoism,* or the concern with one's own destiny, should not be confused with *egotism,* or mere selfishness. An "egotistical" conviction may have to do simply with one's self-importance, but an egoistic conviction has to do with how one can best come to terms with oneself. "The good or ill of man lies within his own will," said the Greek philosopher Epictetus. And according to Henry David Thoreau, "What a man thinks of himself, that it is which determines, or rather indicates, his fate."

Because personal essays, letters, and other autobiographical texts tend to focus on the author's life they can be expected to reveal some egoistic convictions. In Joan Didion's "On Going Home," for example, the author is concerned with her own identity in relation to her family and with how to face the changes in her life. Although she has an altruistic desire to give her daughter the same forms of happiness she herself experienced as a child, she comes to terms with the fact that present realities force her to behave differently. Perhaps it is just as well, Didion says, "that I can offer her little of that life." She will try instead to bring her daughter happiness in other ways, dependent on the newer circumstances of a postwar generation.

Political convictions relate the highest good to the welfare of the community. Such convictions range widely over the various ideologies that make up partisan politics and contrasting systems of government: Republicanism, Liberalism, Socialism, Monarchism, and so on. Obviously, the convictions of those political philosophies will vary with regard to specific issues. But you should at least recognize political convictions when you see them. They are different from egoistic convictions insofar as the latter stress the self working alone to fulfill ideals, whereas political convictions focus on group relations as the key to ethical behavior.

In "Making Science Work," Lewis Thomas states a political conviction when he calls for a closer partnership between industry and academic institutions:

> There needs to be much more of this kind of partnership. The nation's future may well depend on whether we can set up within the private sector a new system for collaborative research. Although there are some promising partnership ventures now in operation, they are few in number; within industry the tendency remains to concentrate on applied research and development, excluding any consideration of basic science. The academic community tends, for its part, to stay out of fields closely related to the development of new products.

Here we have a political statement that can't be neatly labeled "Democrat" or "Republican," liberal or conservative, but it is political nonetheless. Thomas is saying that if we are to perfect our science, we need closer relations between two sectors of the economy. Such closer relations might not have much to do with the politics of government, but they would have plenty to do with the politics of industry and with the academic politics of institutions. Moreover, if you were to disagree with Thomas on this matter, you would quickly find yourself involved in a controversy that could only be described as political.

Summary

The ethical perspective leads us to consider a text on the basis of ideals and convictions. Often a book or essay may present several ideals and many separate convictions. In some cases the author may boldly stress his or her own; in other cases ethical implications may be subtle. But even when the text does not seem to make an issue of ethics, the reader should search for whatever ideals may be implied—and whatever ethical convictions may be apparent.

REVIEW OF QUESTIONS TO ASK

The Social Perspective

What social concerns does the text reveal?
How does the text relate to the past?
How does the text relate to right now?

The Emotional Perspective

Does the text contain objects of emotion?
Are there emotional conflicts?
What is the tone of the text?

The Rhetorical Perspective

How can the form be described?
Which rhetorical modes do you find?
How can the author's style be described?
What about ambiguity?

The Logical Perspective

What debatable issue is raised?
What conclusions are reached?
Is there sufficient evidence?
Does the text take opposition into account?

The Ethical Perspective

What "highest good" does the text envision?
What ethical convictions are revealed?

Helping Students Use Textual Sources Persuasively

Margaret Kantz

Margaret Kantz, who teaches in the Department of English and Philosophy at Central Missouri State University, argues for teaching critical reading strategies in research paper instruction in this 1990 article from College English. *Normally, she writes, students read sources as repositories of facts, gleaning information from them to plug into their papers. Because their stance as readers grants sources an almost unassailable authority, it is often difficult for students to write argumentative research papers instead of papers that merely report and synthesize information. Kantz proposes that a problem-solving approach to teaching the research paper in which students learn to read and critique all texts as arguments. And because of the complexity of the reading and writing involved in composing a research paper, Kantz opposes a "one-shot" research paper assignment and instead urges instructors to develop a sequence of assignments that allows students to develop the reading, writing, and research abilities that a research paper requires.*

Although the researched essay as a topic has been much written about, it has been little studied. In the introduction to their bibliography, Ford, Rees, and Ward point out that most of the over 200 articles about researched essays published in professional journals in the last half century describe classroom methods. "Few," they say, "are of a theoretical nature or based on research, and almost none cites even one other work on the subject" (2). Given Ford and Perry's finding that 84% of freshman composition programs and 40% of advanced composition programs included instruction in writing research papers, more theoretical work seems needed. We need a theory-based explanation, one grounded in the findings of the published research on the nature and reasons for our students' problems with writing persuasive researched papers. To understand how to teach students to write such papers, we also need a better understanding of the demands of synthesis tasks.

As an example for discussing this complex topic, I have used a typical college sophomore. This student is a composite derived from published research, from my own memories of being a student, and from students whom I have taught at an open admissions community college and at both public and private universities. I have also used a few examples taken from my own students, all of whom share many

---

of Shirley's traits. Shirley, first of all, is intelligent and well-motivated. She is a native speaker of English. She has no extraordinary knowledge deficits or emotional problems. She comes from a home where education is valued, and her parents do reading and writing tasks at home and at their jobs. Shirley has certain skills. When she entered first grade, she knew how to listen to and tell stories, and she soon became proficient at reading stories and at writing narratives. During her academic life, Shirley has learned such studying skills as finding the main idea and remembering facts. In terms of the relevant research, Shirley can read and summarize source texts accurately (cf. Spivey; Winograd). She can select material that is relevant for her purpose in writing (Hayes, Waterman, and Robinson; Langer). She can make connections between the available information and her purpose for writing, including the needs of her readers when the audience is specified (Atlas). She can make original connections among ideas (Brown and Day; Langer). She can create an appropriate, audience-based structure for her paper (Spivey), take notes and use them effectively while composing her paper (Kennedy), and she can present information clearly and smoothly (Spivey), without relying on the phrasing of the original sources (Atlas; Winograd). Shirley is, in my experience, a typical college student with an average academic preparation.

Although Shirley seems to have everything going for her, she experiences difficulty with assignments that require her to write original papers based on textual sources. In particular, Shirley is having difficulty in her sophomore-level writing class. Shirley, who likes English history, decided to write about the Battle of Agincourt (this part of Shirley's story is biographical). She found half a dozen histories that described the circumstances of the battle in a few pages each. Although the topic was unfamiliar, the sources agreed on many of the facts. Shirley collated these facts into her own version, noting but not discussing discrepant details, borrowing what she assumed to be her sources' purpose of retelling the story, and modeling the narrative structure of her paper on that of her sources. Since the only comments Shirley could think of would be to agree or disagree with her sources, who had told her everything she knew about the Battle of Agincourt, she did not comment on the material; instead, she concentrated on telling the story clearly and more completely than her sources had done. She was surprised when her paper received a grade of C-. (Page 1 of Shirley's paper is given as Appendix A.)

Although Shirley is a hypothetical student whose case is based on a real event, her difficulties are typical of undergraduates at both private and public colleges and universities. In a recent class of Intermediate Composition in which the students were instructed to create an argument using at least four textual sources that took differing points of view, one student, who analyzed the coverage of a recent championship football game, ranked her source articles in order from those whose approach she most approved to those she least approved. Another student analyzed various approaches taken by the media to the Kent State shootings in 1970, and was surprised and disappointed to find that all of the sources seemed slanted, either by the perspective of the reporter or by that of the people interviewed. Both students did not understand why their instructor said that their papers lacked a genuine argument.

The task of writing researched papers that express original arguments presents many difficulties. Besides the obvious problems of citation format and coordination of source materials with the emerging written product, writing a synthesis can vary in difficulty according to the number and length of the sources, the abstractness or familiarity of the topic, the uses that the writer must make of the material, the degree and quality of original thought required, and the extent to which the sources will supply the structure and purpose of the new paper. It is usually easier to write a paper that uses all of only one short source on a familiar topic than to write a paper that selects material from many long sources on a topic that one must learn as one reads and writes. It is easier to quote than to paraphrase, and it is easier to build the paraphrases, without comment or with random comments, into a description of what one found than it is to use them as evidence in an original argument. It is easier to use whatever one likes, or everything one finds, than to formally select, evaluate, and interpret material. It is easier to use the structure and purpose of a source as the basis for one's paper than it is to create a structure or an original purpose. A writing-from-sources task can be as simple as collating a body of facts from a few short texts on a familiar topic into a new text that reproduces the structure, tone, and purpose of the originals, but it can also involve applying concepts from one area to an original problem in a different area, a task that involves learning the relationships among materials as a paper is created that may refer to its sources without resembling them.

Moreover, a given task can be interpreted as requiring an easy method, a difficult method, or any of a hundred intermediate methods. In this context, Flower has observed, "The different ways in which students [represent] a 'standard' reading-to-write task to themselves lead to markedly different goals and strategies as well as different organizing plans" ("Role" iii). To write a synthesis, Shirley may or may not need to quote, summarize, or select material from her sources; to evaluate the sources for bias, accuracy, or completeness; to develop original ideas; or to persuade a reader. How well she performs any of these tasks—and whether she thinks to perform these tasks—depends on how she reads the texts and on how she interprets the assignment. Shirley's representation of the task, which in this case was easier than her teacher had in mind, depends on the goals that she sets for herself. The goals that she sets depend on her awareness of the possibilities and her confidence in her writing skills.

Feeling unhappy about her grade, Shirley consulted her friend Alice. Alice, who is an expert, looked at the task in a completely different way and used strategies for thinking about it that were quite different from Shirley's.

"Who were your sources?" asked Alice. "Winston Churchill, right? A French couple and a few others. And they didn't agree about the details, such as the sizes of the armies. Didn't you wonder why?"

"No," said Shirley. "I thought the history books would know the truth. When they disagreed, I figured that they were wrong on those points. I didn't want to have anything in my paper that was wrong."

"But Shirley," said Alice, "you could have thought about why a book entitled A *History of France* might present a different view of the battle than a book subtitled A *History of British Progress.* You could have asked if the English and French writers wanted to make a point about the history of their countries and looked to see if the factual differences suggested anything. You could even have talked about Shakespeare's *Henry V,* which I know you've read—about how he presents the battle, or about how the King Henry in the play differs from the Henrys in your other books. You would have had an angle, a problem. Dr. Boyer would have loved it."

Alice's representation of the task would have required Shirley to formally select and evaluate her material and to use it as proof in an original argument. Alice was suggesting that Shirley invent an original problem and purpose for her paper and create an original structure for her argument. Alice's task is much more sophisticated than Shirley's. Shirley replied, "That would take me a year to do! Besides, Henry was a real person. I don't want to make up things about him."

"Well," said Alice "You're dealing with facts, so there aren't too many choices. If you want to say something original you either have to talk about the sources or talk about the material. What could you say about the material? Your paper told about all the reasons King Henry wasn't expected to win the battle. Could you have argued that he should have lost because he took too many chances?"

"Gee," said Shirley, "That's awesome. I wish I'd thought of it."

This version of the task would allow Shirley to keep the narrative structure of her paper but would give her an original argument and purpose. To write the argument, Shirley would have only to rephrase the events of the story to take an opposite approach from that of her English sources, emphasizing what she perceived as Henry's mistakes and inserting comments to explain why his decisions were mistakes—an easy argument to write. She could also, if she wished, write a conclusion that criticized the cheerleading tone of her British sources.

As this anecdote makes clear, a given topic can be treated in more or less sophisticated ways—and sophisticated goals, such as inventing an original purpose and evaluating sources, can be achieved in relatively simple versions of a task. Students have many options as to how they can fulfill even a specific task (cf. Jeffery). Even children can decide whether to process a text deeply or not, and purpose in reading affects processing and monitoring of comprehension (Brown). Pichert has shown that reading purpose affects judgments about what is important or unimportant in a narrative text, and other research tells us that attitudes toward the author and content of a text affect comprehension (Asche; Hinze; Shedd; Goldman).

One implication of this story is that the instructor gave a weak assignment and an ineffective critique of the draft (her only comment referred to Shirley's footnoting technique, cf. Appendix A). The available research suggests that if Dr. Boyer had set Shirley a specific rhetorical problem such as having her report on her material to the class and then testing them on it, and if she had commented on the content of Shirley's paper during the drafts, Shirley might well have come up with a paper that did more than repeat its source material (Nelson and Hayes). My teaching experience supports this research finding. If Dr. Boyer had told Shirley from the outset that she was expected to say something original and that she should examine her sources as she read them for discrepant facts, conflicts, or other interesting material, Shirley might have tried to write an original argument (Kantz,

"Originality"). And if Dr. Boyer had suggested that Shirley use her notes to comment on her sources and make plans for using the notes, Shirley might have written a better paper than she did (Kantz, "Relationship").

Even if given specific directions to create an original argument, Shirley might have had difficulty with the task. Her difficulty could come from any of three causes: 1) Many students like Shirley misunderstand sources because they read them as stories. 2) Many students expect their sources to tell the truth; hence, they equate persuasive writing in this context with making things up. 3) Many students do not understand that facts are a kind of claim and are often used persuasively in so-called objective writing to create an impression. Students need to read source texts as arguments and to think about the rhetorical contexts in which they were written rather than to read them merely as a set of facts to be learned. Writing an original persuasive argument based on sources requires students to apply material to a problem or to use it to answer a question, rather than simply to repeat it or evaluate it. These three problems deserve a separate discussion.

Because historical texts often have a chronological structure, students believe that historians tell stories and that renarrating the battle cast them as a historian. Because her sources emphasized the completeness of the victory/defeat and its decisive importance in the history of warfare, Shirley thought that making these same points in her paper completed her job. Her job as a reader was thus to learn the story, i.e., so that she could pass a test on it (cf. Vipond and Hunt's argument that generic expectations affect reading behavior. Vipond and Hunt would describe Shirley's reading as story-driven rather than point-driven). Students commonly misread texts as narratives. When students refer to a textbook as "the story," they are telling us that they read for plot and character, regardless of whether their texts are organized as narratives. One reason Shirley loves history is that when she reads it she can combine her story-reading strategies with her studying strategies. Students like Shirley may need to learn to apply basic organizing patterns, such as cause-effect and general-to-specific, to their texts. If, however, Dr. Boyer asks Shirley to respond to her sources in a way that is not compatible with Shirley's understanding of what such sources do, Shirley will have trouble doing the assignment. Professors may have to do some preparatory teaching about why certain kinds of texts have certain characteristics and what kinds of problems writers must solve as they design a text for a particular audience. They may even have to teach a model for the kind of writing they expect.

The version of Shirley's problem, which Flower calls "writer-based prose," occurs when Shirley organizes what should be an expository analysis as a narrative, especially when she writes a narrative about how she did her research. Students frequently use time-based organizing patterns, regardless of the task, even when such patterns conflict with what they are trying to say and even when they know how to use more sophisticated strategies. Apparently such common narrative transitional devices such as "the first point" and "the next point" offer a reassuringly familiar pattern for organizing unfamiliar material. The common strategy of beginning paragraphs with such phrases as "my first source," meaning that it was the first source that the writer found in the library or the first one read, appears to combine a story-of-my-research structure with a knowledge-telling strategy (Bereiter and Scardamalia, *Psychology*). Even when students understand that the assignment asks for more than the fill-in-the-blanks, show-me-you've-read-the-material approach described by Schwegler and Shamoon, they cling to narrative structuring devices. A rank ordering of sources, as with Mary's analysis of the football game coverage with the sources listed in an order of ascending disapproval, represents a step away from storytelling and toward synthesizing because it embodies a persuasive evaluation.

In addition to reading texts as stories, students expect factual texts to tell them "the truth" because they have learned to see texts statically, as descriptions of truths, instead of as arguments. Shirley did not understand that nonfiction texts exist as arguments in rhetorical contexts. "After all," she reasoned, "how can one argue about the date of a battle or the sizes of armies?" Churchill, however, described the battle in much more detail than Shirley's other sources, apparently because he wished to persuade his readers to take pride in England's tradition of military achievement. Guizot and Guizot de Witt, on the other hand, said very little about the battle (beyond describing it as "a monotonous and lamentable repetition of the disasters of Crecy and Poitiers" [397]) because they saw the British invasion as a sneaky way to take advantage of a feud among the various branches of the French royal family. Shirley's story/study skills might not have allowed her to recognize such arguments, especially because Dr. Boyer did not teach her to look for them.

When I have asked students to choose a topic and find three or more sources on it that disagree, I am repeatedly asked, "How can sources disagree in different ways? After all, there's only pro and con." Students expect textbooks and other authoritative sources either to tell them the truth (i.e. facts) or to express an opinion with which they may agree or disagree. Mary's treatment of the football coverage reflects this belief, as does Charlie's surprise when he found that even his most comprehensive sources on the Kent State killings omitted certain facts, such as interviews with National Guardsmen. Students' desire for truth leads them to use a collating approach whenever possible, as Shirley did (cf. Appendix A), because students believe that the truth will include all of the facts and mill reconcile all conflicts. (This belief may be another manifestation of the knowledge-telling strategy [Bereiter and Scardamalia, *Psychology*] in which students write down everything they can think of about a topic.) When conflicts cannot be reconciled and the topic does not admit a pro or con stance, students may not know what to say. They may omit the material altogether, include it without comment, as Shirley did, or jumble it together without any plan for building an argument.

The skills that Shirley has practiced for most of her academic career—finding the main idea and learning content—allow her to agree or disagree. She needs a technique for reading texts in ways that give her something more to say, a technique for constructing more complex representations of texts that allow room for more sophisticated writing goals. She also needs strategies for analyzing her reading that allow her to build original arguments.

One way to help students like Shirley is to teach the concept of rhetorical situation. A convenient tool for thinking about this concept is Kinneavy's triangular diagram of the rhetorical situation. Kinneavy, analyzing Aristotle's description of rhetoric, posits that every communicative situation has three parts: a speaker/writer (the Encoder), an audience (the Decoder), and a topic (Reality) (19). Although all discourse involves all three aspects of communication, a given type of discourse may pertain more to a particular point of the triangle than to the others, e.g., a diary entry may exist primarily to express the thoughts of the writer (the Encoder); an advertisement may exist primarily to persuade a reader (the Decoder). Following Kinneavy, I posit particular goals for each comer of the triangle. Thus, the primary goal of a writer doing writer-based discourse such as a diary might be originality and self-expression; primary goals for reader-based discourse such as advertising might be persuasion; primary goals for topic-based discourse such as a researched essay might be accuracy, completeness, and mastery of subject matter. Since all three aspects of the rhetorical situation are present and active in any communicative situation, a primarily referential text such as Churchill's *The Birth of Britain* may have a persuasive purpose and may depend for some of its credibility on readers' familiarity with the author. The term "rhetorical reading," then (cf. Haas and Flower), means teaching students to read a text as a message sent by someone to somebody for a reason. Shirley, Mary, and Charlie are probably practiced users of rhetorical persuasion in non-academic contexts. They may never have learned to apply this thinking in a conscious and deliberate way to academic tasks (cf. Kroll).

The concept of rhetorical situation offers insight into the nature of students' representations of a writing task. The operative goals in Shirley's and Alice's approaches to the term paper look quite different when mapped onto the points on the triangle. If we think of Shirley and Alice as Encoders, the topic as Reality, and Dr. Boyer as the Decoder, we can see that for Shirley, being an Encoder means trying to be credible; her relationship to the topic (Reality) involves a goal of using all of the subject matter; and her relationship to the Decoder involves an implied goal of telling a complete story to a reader whom Shirley thinks of as an examiner—to use the classic phrase from the famous book by Britton et al.—i.e., a reader who wants to know if Shirley can pass an exam on the subject of the Battle of Agincourt. For Alice, however, being an Encoder means having a goal of saying something new; the topic (Reality) is a resource to be used; and the Decoder is someone who must be persuaded that Alice's ideas have merit. Varying task representations do not change the dimensions of the rhetorical situation: the Encoder, Decoder and Reality are always present. But the way a writer represents the task to herself does affect the ways that she thinks about those dimensions—and whether she thinks about them at all.

In the context of a research assignment, rhetorical skills can be used to read the sources as well as to design the paper. Although teachers have probably always known that expert readers use such strategies, the concept of rhetorical reading is new to the literature. Haas and Flower have shown that expert readers use rhetorical strategies "to account for author's purpose, context, and effect on audience ... to recreate or infer the rhetorical situation of the text" (176; cf. also Bazerman). These strategies, used in addition to formulating main points and paraphrasing content, helped the readers to understand a text more completely and more quickly than did readers who concentrated exclusively on content. As Haas and Flower point out, teaching students to read rhetorically is difficult. They suggest that appropriate pedagogy might include "direct instruction ... modeling, and ... encouraging students to become contributing and committed members of rhetorical communities" (182). One early step might be to teach students a set of heuristics based on the three aspects of the communicative triangle. Using such questions could help students set goals for their reading.

In this version of Kinneavy's triangle, the Encoder is the writer of the source text, the Decoder is the student reader, and Reality is the subject matter. Readers may consider only one point of the triangle at a time, asking such questions as "Who are you (i.e., the author/Encoder)?" or "What are the important features of this text?" They may consider two aspects of the rhetorical situation in a single question, e.g., "Am I in your intended (primary) audience?"; "What do I think about this topic?"; "What context affected your ideas and presentation?" Other questions would involve all three points of the triangle, e.g., "What are you saying to help me with the problem you assume I have?" or "What textual devices have you used to manipulate my response?" Asking such questions gives students a way of formulating goals relating to purpose as well as content.

If Shirley, for example, had asked a Decoder-to-Encoder question—such as "Am I in your intended audience?"—she might have realized that Churchill and the Guizots were writing for specific audiences. If she had asked a Decoder-to-Reality question-such as "What context affected your ideas and presentation?" —she might not have ignored Churchill's remark, "All these names [Amiens, Boves, Bethencourt] are well known to our generation" (403). As it was, she missed Churchill's signal that he was writing to survivors of the First World War, who had vainly hoped that it would be the war to end all wars. If Shirley had used an Encoder-Decoder-Reality question—such as "What are you saying to help me with the problem you assume I have?"—she might have understood that the authors of her sources were writing to different readers for different reasons. This understanding might have given her something to say. When I gave Shirley's source texts to freshmen students, asked them to use the material in an original argument, and taught them this heuristic for rhetorical reading, I received, for example, papers that warned undergraduates about national pride as a source of authorial bias in history texts.

A factual topic such as the Battle of Agincourt presents special problems because of the seemingly intransigent nature of facts. Like many people, Shirley believes that you can either agree or disagree with issues and opinions, but you can only accept the so-called facts. She believes that facts are what you learn from textbooks, opinions are what you have about clothes, and arguments are what you have with your mother when you want to stay out late at night. Shirley is not in a position to disagree with the facts about the battle (e.g., "No, I think the French won"), and a rhetorical analysis may seem at first to offer minimal rewards (e.g., "According to the Arab, Jewish, and Chinese calendars the date was really…").

Alice, who thinks rhetorically, understands that both facts and opinions are essentially the same kind of statement: they are claims. Alice understands that the only essential difference between a fact and an opinion is how they are received by an audience. (This discussion is derived from Toulmin's model of an argument as consisting of claims proved with data and backed by ethical claims called warrants. According to Toulmin, any aspect of an argument may be questioned by the audience and must then be supported with further argument.) In a rhetorical argument, a fact is a claim that an audience will accept as being true without requiring proof, although they may ask for an explanation. An opinion is a claim that an audience will not accept as true without proof, and which, after the proof is given, the audience may well decide has only a limited truth, i.e., it's true in this case but not in other cases. An audience may also decide that even though a fact is unassailable, the interpretation or use of the fact is open to debate.

For example, Shirley's sources gave different numbers for the size of the British army at Agincourt; these numbers, which must have been estimates, were claims masquerading as facts. Shirley did not understand this. She thought that disagreement signified error, whereas it probably signified rhetorical purpose. The probable reason that the Guizots give a relatively large estimate for the English army and do not mention the size of the French army is so that their French readers would find the British victory easier to accept. Likewise, Churchill's relatively small estimate for the size of the English army and his high estimate for the French army magnify the brilliance of the English victory. Before Shirley could create an argument about the Battle of Agincourt, she needed to understand that, even in her history textbooks, the so-called facts are claims that may or may not be supported, claims made by writers who work in a certain political climate for a particular audience. She may, of course, never learn this truth unless Dr. Boyer teaches her rhetorical theory and uses the research paper as a chance for Shirley to practice rhetorical problem-solving.

For most of her academic life, Shirley has done school tasks that require her to find main ideas and important facts; success in these tasks usually hinges on agreeing with the teacher about what the text says. Such study skills form an essential basis for doing reading-to-write tasks. Obviously a student can only use sources to build an argument if she can first read the sources accurately (cf. Brown and Palincsar; Luftig; Short and Ryan). However, synthesizing tasks often require that readers not accept the authors' ideas. Baker and Brown have pointed out that people misread texts when they blindly accept an author's ideas instead of considering a divergent interpretation. Yet if we want students to learn to build original arguments from texts, we must teach them the skills needed to create divergent interpretations. We must teach them to think about facts and opinions as claims that are made by writers to particular readers for particular reasons in particular historical contexts.

Reading sources rhetorically gives students a powerful tool for creating a persuasive analysis. Although no research exists as yet to suggest that teaching students to read rhetorically will improve their writing, I have seen its effect in successive drafts of students' papers. As mentioned earlier, rhetorical reading allowed a student to move from simply summarizing and evaluating her sources on local coverage of the championship football game to constructing a rationale for articles that covered the fans rather than the game. Rhetorical analysis enabled another student to move from summarizing his sources to understanding why each report about the Kent State shootings necessarily expressed a bias of some kind.

As these examples suggest, however, rhetorical reading is not a magical technique for producing sophisticated arguments. Even when students read their sources rhetorically, they tend merely to report the results of this analysis in their essays. Such writing appears to be a college-level version of the knowledge-telling strategy described by Bereiter and Scardamalia (*Psychology*) and may be, as they suggest, the product of years of exposure to pedagogical practices that enshrine the acquisition and expression of information without a context or purpose.

To move students beyond merely reporting the content and rhetorical orientation of their source texts, I have taught them the concept of the rhetorical gap and some simple heuristic questions for thinking about gaps. Gaps were first described by Iser as unsaid material that a reader must supply to/infer from a text. McCormick expanded the concept to include gaps between the text and the reader; such gaps could involve discrepancies of values, social conventions, language, or any other matter that readers must consider. If we apply the concept of gaps to Kinneavy's triangle, we see that in reading, for example, a gap may occur between the Encoder-Decoder corners when the reader is not a member of the author's intended audience. Shirley fell into such a gap. Another gap can occur between the Decoder-Reality corners when a reader disagrees with or does not understand the text. A third gap can occur between the Encoder-Reality points of the triangle if the writer has misrepresented or misunderstood the material. The benefit of teaching this concept is that when a student thinks about a writer's rhetorical stance, she may ask "Why does he think that way?" When a student encounters a gap, she may ask, "What effect does it have on the success of this communication?" The answers to both questions give students original material for their papers.

Shirley, for example, did not know that Churchill began writing *The Birth Of Britain* during the 1930s, when Hitler was rearming Germany and when the British government and most of Churchill's readers ardently favored disarmament. Had she understood the rhetorical orientation of the book, which was published eleven years after the end of World War II, she might have argued that Churchill's evocation of past military glories would have been inflammatory in the 1930s but was highly acceptable twenty years later. A gap between the reader and the text (Decoder-Reality) might stimulate a reader to investigate whether or not she is the only person having this problem; a gap between other readers and the sources may motivate an adaptation or explanation of the material to a particular audience. Shirley might have adapted the Guizots' perspective on the French civil war for American readers. A gap between the author and the material (Encoder-Reality) might motivate a refutation.

To discover gaps, students may need to learn heuristics for setting rhetorical writing goals. That is, they may need to learn to think of the paper, not as a rehash of the available material, but as an opportunity to teach someone, to solve someone's problem, or to answer someone's question. The most salient questions for reading source texts may be "Who are you (the original audience of Decoders)?"; "What is your question or problem with this topic?"; and "How have I (the Encoder) used these materials to answer your question or solve your problem?" More simply, these questions may be learned as "Why," "How," and "So what?" When Shirley learns to read sources as telling not the eternal truth but a truth to a particular audience and when she learns to think of texts as existing to solve problems, she will find it easier to think of things to say.

For example, a sophomore at a private university was struggling with an assignment that required her to analyze an issue and express an opinion on it, using two conflicting source texts, an interview, and personal material as sources. Using rhetorical reading strategies, this girl discovered a gap between Alfred Marbaise, a high school principal who advocates mandatory drug testing of all high school students, and students like those he would be testing:

> Marbaise, who was a lieutenant in the U.S. Marines over thirty years ago ... makes it very obvious that he cannot and will not tolerate any form of drug abuse in his school. For example, in paragraph seven he claims "When students become involved in illegal activity, whether they realize it or not, they are violating other students ... then I become very, very concerned ... and I will not tolerate that."
>
> Because Marbaise has not been in school for nearly forty years himself, he does not take into consideration the reasons why kids actually use drugs. Today the social environment is so drastically different that Marbaise cannot understand a kid's morality, and that is why he writes from such a fatherly but distant point of view.

The second paragraph answers the So what? question, i.e., "Why does it matter that Marbaise seems by his age and background to be fatherly and distant?" Unless the writer/reader thinks to ask this question, she will have difficulty writing a coherent evaluation of Marbaise's argument.

The relative success of some students in finding original things to say about their topics can help us to understand the perennial problem of plagiarism. Some plagiarism derives, I think, from a weak, nonrhetorical task representation. If students believe they are supposed to reproduce source material in their papers, or if they know they are supposed to say something original but have no rhetorical problem to solve and no knowledge of how to find problems that they can discuss in their sources, it becomes difficult for them to avoid plagiarizing. The common student decision to buy a paper when writing the assignment seems a meaningless fill-in-the-blanks activity (cf. Schwegler and Shamoon) becomes easily understandable. Because rhetorical reading leads to discoveries about the text, students who use it may take more interest in their research papers.

Let us now assume that Shirley understands the importance of creating an original argument, knows how to read analytically, and has found things to say about the Battle of Agincourt. Are her troubles over? Will she now create that A paper that she yearns to write? Probably not. Despite her best intentions, Shirley will probably write another narrative/paraphrase of her sources. Why? Because by now, the assignment asks her to do far more than she can handle in a single draft. Shirley's task representation is now so rich, her set of goals so many, that she may be unable to juggle them all simultaneously. Moreover, the reading technique requires students to discover content worth writing about and a rhetorical purpose for writing; the uncertainty of managing such a discovery task when a grade is at stake may be too much for Shirley.

Difficult tasks may be difficult in either (or both of) two ways. First, they may require students to do a familiar subtask, such as reading sources, at a higher level of difficulty, e.g., longer sources, more sources, a more difficult topic. Second, they may require students to do new subtasks, such as building notes into an original argument. Such tasks may require task management skills, especially planning, that students have never developed and do not know how to attempt. The insecurity that results from trying a complex new task in a high-stakes situation is increased when students are asked to discover a problem worth writing about because such tasks send students out on a treasure hunt with no guarantee that the treasure exists, that they will recognize it when they find it, or that when they find it they will be able to build it into a coherent argument. The paper on Marbaise quoted above earned a grade of D because the writer could not use her rhetorical insights to build an argument presented in a logical order. Although she asked the logical question about the implications of Marbaise's persona, she did not follow through by evaluating the gaps in his perspective that might affect the probable success of his program.

A skillful student using the summarize-the-main-ideas approach can set her writing goals and even plan (i.e., outline) a paper before she reads the sources. The rhetorical reading strategy, by contrast, requires writers to discover what is worth writing about and to decide how to say it as or after they read their sources. The strategy requires writers to change their content goals and to adjust their writing plans as their understanding of the topic develops. It requires writers, in Flower's term, to "construct" their purposes for writing as well as the content for their paper (for a description of constructive planning, see Flower, Schriver, Carey, Haas, and Hayes). In Flower's words, writers who construct a purpose, as opposed to writers who bring a predetermined purpose to a task, "create a web of purposes ... set goals, toss up possibilities ... create a multi-dimensional network of information ... a web of purpose ... a bubbling stew of various mental representations" (531–32). The complex indeterminacy of such a task may pose an intimidating challenge to students who have spent their lives summarizing main ideas and reporting facts.

Shirley may respond to the challenge by concentrating her energies on a familiar subtask, e.g., repeating material about the Battle of Agincourt, at the expense of struggling with an unfamiliar subtask such as creating an original argument. She may even deliberately simplify the task by representing it to herself as calling only for something that she knows how to do, expecting that Dr. Boyer will accept the paper as close enough to the original instructions. My students do this frequently. When students decide to write a report of their reading, they can at least be certain that they will find material to write about.

Because of the limits of attentional memory, not to mention those caused by inexperience, writers can handle only so many task demands at a time. Thus, papers produced by seemingly inadequate task representations may well be essentially rough drafts. What looks like a bad paper may well be a preliminary step, a way of meeting certain task demands in order to create a basis for thinking about new ones. My students consistently report that they need to marshal all of their ideas and text knowledge and get that material down on the page (i.e., tell their knowledge) before they can think about developing an argument (i.e., transform their knowledge). If Shirley's problem is that she has shelved certain task demands in favor of others, Dr. Boyer needs only to point out what Shirley should do to bring the paper into conformity with the assignment and offer Shirley a chance to revise.

The problems of cognitive overload and inexperience in handling complex writing tasks can create a tremendous hurdle for students because so many of them believe that they should be able to write their paper in a single draft. Some students think that if they can't do the paper in one draft that means that something is wrong with them as writers, or with the assignment, or with us for giving the assignment. Often, such students will react to their drafts with anger and despair, throwing away perfectly usable rough drafts and then coming to us and saying that they can't do the assignment.

The student's first draft about drug testing told her knowledge about her sources' opinions on mandatory drug testing. Her second draft contained the rhetorical analysis quoted above, but presented the material in a scrambled order and did not build the analysis into an argument. Only in a third draft was this student able to make her point:

> Not once does Marbaise consider any of the psychological reasons why kids turn away from reality. He fails to realize that drug testing will not answer their questions, ease their frustrations, or respond to their cries for attention, but will merely further alienate himself and other authorities from helping kids deal with their real problems.

This comment represents Terri's answer to the heuristic "So what? Why does the source's position matter?" If we pace our assignments to allow for our students' thoughts to develop, we can do a great deal to build their confidence in their writing (Terri raised her D+ to an A). If we treat the researched essay as a sequence of assignments instead of as a one-shot paper with a single due date, we can teach our students to build on their drafts, to use what they can do easily as a bridge to what we want them to learn to do. In this way, we can improve our students' writing habits. More importantly, however, we can help our students to see themselves as capable writers and as active, able problem-solvers. Most importantly, we can use the sequence of drafts to demand that our students demonstrate increasingly sophisticated kinds of analytic and rhetorical proficiency.

Rhetorical reading and writing heuristics can help students to represent tasks in rich and interesting ways. They can help students to set up complex goal structures (Bereiter and Scardamalia, "Conversation"). They offer students many ways to think about their reading and writing texts. These tools, in other words, encourage students to work creatively.

And after all, creativity is what research should be about. If Shirley writes a creative paper, she has found a constructive solution that is new to her and which other people can use, a solution to a problem that she and other people share.

Creativity is an inherently rhetorical quality. If we think of it as thought leading to solutions to problems and of problems as embodied in questions that people ask about situations, the researched essay offers infinite possibilities. Viewed in this way, a creative idea answers a question that the audience or any single reader wants answered. The question could be, "Why did Henry V win the battle of Agincourt?" or, "How can student readers protect themselves against nationalistic bias when they study history?" or any of a thousand other questions. If we teach our Shirleys to see themselves as scholars who work to find answers to problem questions, and if we teach them to set reading and writing goals for themselves that will allow them to think constructively, we will be doing the most exciting work that teachers can do, nurturing creativity.

Appendix A: Page 1 of Shirley's paper

The battle of Agincourt ranks as one of England's greatest military triumphs. It was the most brilliant victory of the Middle Ages, bar none. It was fought on October 25, 1414, against the French near the French village of Agincourt.

Henry V had claimed the crown of France and had invaded France with an army estimated at anywhere ~~between~~ from 10,000[1] ~~and~~ to 45,000 men[2]. During the seige of Marfleur dysentery had taken 1/3 of them[3], his food supplies had been depleted[4], and the fall rains had begun. In addition the French had assembled a huge army and were marching toward him. Henry decided to march to Calais, where his ships were to await him[5]. He intended to cross the River Somme at the ford of Blanchetaque[6], but, falsely informed that the ford was guarded[7], he was forced to follow the flooded Somme up toward its source. The French army was shadowing him on his right. Remembering the slaughters of Crecy and Poictiers, the French constable, Charles d'Albret, hesitated to fight[8], but when Henry forded the Somme just above Amiens[9] and was just

---

1. Carl Stephinson, Medieval History , p. 529.

2. Guizot, Monsieur and Guizot, Madame, World's Best Histories-France, Volume II, p.211.

3. Cyrid E. Robinson, England-A History of British Progress, p. 145.

4. Ibid.

5. Winston Churchill, A History of the English-Speaking Peoples, Volume I: The Birth of Britain, p. 403.

6. Ibid.

7. Ibid.

8. Robinson, p. 145.

9. Churchill, p. 403.

You footnote material that does not need to be footnoted.

Works Cited

Asch, Solomon. *Social Psychology.* New York: Prentice, 1952.

Atlas, Marshall. *Expert-Novice Differences in the Writing Process.* Paper presented at the American Educational Research Association, 1979. ERIC ED 107 769.

Baker, Louise, and Ann L. Brown. "Metacognitive Skills and Reading." *Handbook of Reading Research.* Eds. P. David Person, Rebecca Barr, Michael L. Kamil, and Peter Mosenthal. New York: Longman, 1984.

Bazerman, Charles. "Physicists Reading Physics: Schema-Laden Purposes and Purpose-Laden Schema." *Written Communication* 2.1 (1985): 3–24.

Bereiter, Carl, and Marlene Scardamalia. "From Conversation to Composition: The Role of Instruction in a Developmental Process." *Advances in Instructional Psychology.* Ed. R. Glaser. Vol. 2. Hillsdale, NJ: Lawrence Erlbaum Associates, 1982. 1–64.

——. *The Psychology of Written Composition.* Hillsdale, NJ: Lawrence Erlbaum Associates, 1987.

Briscoe, Terri. "To test or not to test." Unpublished essay. Texas Christian University, 1989.

Britton James, Tony Burgess, Nancy Martin, Alex McLeod, and Harold Rosen. *The Development of Writing Abilities* (11–18). Houndmills Basingstoke Hampshire: Macmillan Education Ltd., 1975.

Brown, Ann L. "Theories of Memory and the Problem of Development: Activity, Growth, and Knowledge." *Levels of Processing in Memory.* Eds. Laird S. Cermak and Fergus I.M. Craik. Hillsdale, NJ: Laurence Erlbaum Associates, 1979. 225–258.

——, Joseph C. Campione, and L.R. Barclay. *Training Self-Checking Routines for Estimating Test Readiness: Generalizations from List Learning to Prose Recall.* Unpublished manuscript. University of Illinois, 1978.

—— and Jeanne Day. "Macrorules for Summarizing Texts: The Development of Expertise." *Journal of Verbal Learning and Verbal Behavior* 22.1 (1983): 1–14.

—— and Annmarie S. Palincsar. *Reciprocal Teaching of Comprehension Strategies: A Natural History of One Program for Enhancing Learning.* Technical Report #334. Urbana, IL: Center for the Study of Reading, 1985.

Churchill, Winston S. *The Birth of Britain.* New York: Dodd, 1956. Vol. I of *A History of the English-Speaking Peoples.* 4 vols. 1956–58.

Flower, Linda. "The Construction of Purpose in Writing and Reading." *College English* 50.5 (1988): 528–550.

——. *The Role of Task Representation in Reading to Write.* Berkeley, CA: Center for the Study of Writing, U of California at Berkeley and Carnegie Mellon. Technical Report, 1987.

——. "Writer-Based Prose: A Cognitive Basis for Problems in Writing." *College English* 41 (1979): 19–37.

Flower, Linda, Karen Schriver, Linda Carey, Christina Haas, and John R. Hayes. *Planning in Writing: A Theory of the Cognitive Press.* Berkeley, CA: Center for the Study of Writing, U of California at Berkeley and Carnegie Mellon. Technical Report, 1988.

Ford, James E., and Dennis R. Perry. "Research Paper Instruction in the Undergraduate Writing Program." *College English* 44 (1982): 825–31.

Ford, James E., Sharla Rees, and David L. Ward. *Teaching the Research Paper: Comprehensive Bibliography Of Periodical Sources,* 1980. ERIC ED 197 363.

Goldman, Susan R. "Knowledge Systems for Realistic Goals. *Discourse Processes* 5 (1982): 279–303.

Guizot and Guizot de Witt. *The History of France from Earliest Times to 1848.* Trans. R. Black. Vol. 2. Philadelphia: John Wanamaker (n.d.).

Haas, Christina, and Linda Flower. "Rhetorical Reading Strategies and the Construction of Meaning." *College Composition and Communication* 39 (1988): 167–84.

Hayes, John R., D.A. Waterman, and C.S. Robinson. "Identifying the Relevant Aspects of a Problem Text." *Cognitive Science* 1 (1977): 297–313.

Hinze, Helen K. "The Individual's Word Associations and His Interpretation of Prose Paragraphs." *Journal of General Psychology* 64 (1961): 193–203.

Iser, Wolfgang. *The Act of Reading: A Theory of Aesthetic Response.* Baltimore: The Johns Hopkins UP, 1978.

Jeffery, Christopher. "Teachers' and Students' Perceptions of the Writing Process." *Research in the Teaching of English* 15 (1981):215–28.

Kantz, Margaret. *Originality and Completeness: What Do We Value in Papers Written from Sources?* Conference on College Composition and Communication. St. Louis, MO, 1988.

——. *The Relationship Between Reading and Planning Strategies and Success in Synthesizing: It's What You Do with Them that Counts.* Technical report in preparation. Pittsburgh: Center for the Study of Writing, 1988.

Kennedy, Mary Louise. "The Composing process of College Students Writing from Sources." *Written Communication* 2.4 (1985): 434–56.

Kinneavy, James L. *A Theory Of Discourse.* New York: Norton, 1971.

Kroll, Barry M. "Audience Adaptation in Children's Persuasive Letters." *Written Communication* 1.4 (1984): 407–28.

Langer, Judith. "Where Problems Start: The Effects of Available Information on Responses to School Writing Tasks." *Contexts for Learning to Write: Studies of Secondary School Instruction.* Ed. Arthur Applebee..Norwood. NJ: ABLEX Publishing Corporation, 1984: 135–48.

Luftig, Richard L. "Abstractive Memory, the Central-Incidental Hypothesis, and the Use of Structural Importance in Text: Control Processes or Structural Features?" *Reading Research Quarterly* 14.1 (1983): 28–37.

Marbaise, Alfred. "Treating a Disease." *Current Issues and Enduring Questions.* Eds. Sylvan Barnet and Hugo Bedau. New York: St. Martin's, 1987: 126–27.

McCormick, Kathleen. "Theory in the Reader: Bleich, Holland, and Beyond." *College English* 47.8 (1985): 836–50.

McGarry. Daniel D. *Medieval History and Civilization.* New York: Macmillan, 1976.

Nelson, Jennie, and John R. Hayes. *The Effects of Classroom Contexts on Students' Responses to Writing from Sources: Regurgitating Information or Triggering Insights.* Berkeley, CA: Center for the Study of Writing, U of California at Berkeley and Carnegie Mellon. Technical Report, 1988.

Pichert, James W. "Sensitivity to Importance as a Predictor of Reading Com- prehension." *Perspectives on Reading Research and Instruction.* Eds. Michael A. Kamil and Alden J. Moe. Washington, D.C.: National Reading Conference, 1900: 42–46.

Robinson. Cyril E. *England. A History of British Progress from the Early Ages to the Present Day.* New York: Thomas Y. Crowell Company, 1928.

Schwegler, Robert A., and Linda K. Shamoon. "The Aims and Process of the Research Paper." *College English* 44 (1982): 817–24.

Shedd, Patricia T. "The Relationship between Attitude of the Reader Towards Women's Changing Role and Response to Literature Which Illuminates Women's Role." Diss. Syracuse U, 1975. ERIC ED 142 956.

Short, Elizabeth June, and Ellen Bouchard Ryan. "Metacognitive Differences between Skilled and Less Skilled Readers: Remediating Deficits through Story Grammar and Attribution Training." *Journal of Education Psychology* 76 (1984): 225–35.

Spivey, Nancy Nelson. *Discourse Synthesis: Constructing Texts in Reading and Writing.* Diss. U Texas. 1983. Newark, DE: International Reading Association, 1984.

Toulmin, Steven E. *The Uses of Argument.* Cambridge: Cambridge UP, 1969.

Vipond, Douglas, and Russell Hunt. "Point-Driven Understanding: Pragmatic and Cognitive Dimensions of Literary Reading." *Poetics* 13, (1984), 261–77.

Winograd, Peter. "Strategic Difficulties in Summarizing Texts." *Reading Research Quarterly* 19 (1984): 404–25.

SUGGESTED READINGS: CRITICAL THINKING AND READING IN WRITING

Atkins, C. Douglas, and Michael L. Johnson, eds. *Writing and Reading Differently: Deconstruction and the Teaching of Composition and Literature*. Lawrence: UP of Kansas, 1985.

Bartholomae, David, and Anthony Petrosky. *Facts, Artifacts, and Counterfacts: Theory and Method for a Reading and Writing Course*. Portsmouth, NH: Boynton/Cook, 1986.

Berlin, James A., and Michael J. Vivion, eds. *Cultural Studies in the English Classroom*. Portsmouth, NH: Boynton/Cook, 1992.

Bishop, Ellen, ed. *Cinema-(to)-graphy: Film and Writing in Contemporary Composition Courses*. Portsmouth, NH: Boynton/Cook, 1999.

Brent, Doug. *Reading as Rhetorical Invention: Knowledge, Persuasion, and the Teaching of Writing*. Urbana, IL: NCTE, 1992.

Cain, William E. *Teaching the Conflicts: Gerald Graff, Curricular Reform, and the Culture Wars*. New York: Garland, 1994.

Corbett, Edward P. J. *The Elements of Reasoning*. Boston: Allyn & Bacon, 1991.

Corcoran, Bill, and Emrys Evans, eds. *Readers, Texts, Teachers*. Portsmouth, NH: Boynton/Cook, 1987.

Dickson, Marcia. *It's Not Like That Here: Teaching Academic Writing and Reading to Novice Writers*. Portsmouth, NH: Boynton/Cook, 1995.

Elbow, Peter. *Embracing Contraries: Explorations in Learning and Teaching*. New York: Oxford UP, 1986.

Emig, Janet. *The Web of Meaning: Essays on Writing, Teaching, Learning, and Thinking*. Ed. Dixie Goswami and Maureen Butler. Portsmouth, NH: Boynton/Cook, 1983.

Flower, Linda, et al. *Reading to Write: Exploring a Cognitive and Social Process*. New York: Oxford UP, 1990.

Horner, Winifred Bryan, ed. *Composition and Literature: Bridging the Gap*. Chicago: U of Chicago P, 1983.

Kutz, Eleanor, and Hephzibah Roskelly. *An Unquiet Pedagogy: Transforming Practice in the English Classroom.* Portsmouth, NH: Boynton/Cook, 1991.

Lindemann, Erika. "Freshman Composition: No Place for Literature." *College English* 52 (1990): 258–71.

McCormick, Kathleen. *The Culture of Reading and the Teaching of English.* Manchester, UK: Manchester UP, 1994.

Moss, Jean Dietz, ed. *Rhetoric and Praxis: The Contribution of Classical Rhetoric to Practical Reasoning.* Washington: Catholic UP of America, 1986.

Newkirk, Thomas, ed. *Only Connect: Uniting Reading and Writing.* Upper Montclair, NJ: Boynton/Cook, 1986.

Peterson, Bruce T. *Convergences: Transactions in Reading and Writing.* Urbana, IL: NCTE, 1986.

Scholes, Robert. *Textual Power: Literary Theory and the Teaching of English.* New Haven: Yale UP, 1985.

Shor, Ira, ed. *Freire for the Classroom: A Sourcebook for Liberatory Teaching.* Portsmouth, NH: Boynton/Cook, 1987.

Slevin, James F., and Art Young, eds. *Critical Theory and the Teaching of Literature: Politics, Curriculum, Pedagogy.* Urbana, IL: NCTE, 1996.

Tate, Gary. "A Place for Literature in Freshman Composition." *College English* 55 (1993): 317–21.

Young, Art, and Toby Fulwiler, eds. *When Writing Teachers Teach Literature: Bringing Writing to Reading.* Portsmouth, NH: Boynton/Cook, 1995.

SUGGESTED READINGS: WRITING RESEARCH PAPERS

Ballenger, Bruce. *Beyond Note Cards: Rethinking the Freshman Research Paper.* Portsmouth, NH: Boynton/Cook, 1999.

Booth, Wayne C., Gregory G. Colomb, and Joseph M. Williams. *The Craft of Research.* Chicago: U of Chicago P, 1995.

Ford, James E., eds. *Teaching the Research Paper: From Theory to Practice, from Research to Writing.* Metuchen, NJ: Scarecrow, 1995.

Gibaldi, Joseph. *MLA Handbook for Writers of Research Papers*. 5th ed. New York: MLA, 1999.

Kroll, Barry M. "How College Freshmen View Plagiarism." *Written Communication* 5 (1988): 203–21.

Larson, Richard L. "The 'Research Paper' in the Writing Course: A Non-form of Writing." *College English* 44 (1982): 811–16.

Macrorie, Ken. *The I-Search Paper*. Portsmouth, NH: Boynton/Cook, 1988.

Publication Manual of the American Psychological Association. 4th ed. Washington: APA, 1994.

Computer-Mediated Communication: Making Nets Work for Writing Instruction

Fred Kemp

Fred Kemp, a professor of English at Texas Tech University, is co-director of the Alliance for Computers and Writing, founder and current president of the educational software company The Daedalus Group, and founder of several electronic discussion groups on the teaching of writing. He is the author of numerous articles on computer-mediated composition instruction and co-author of award-winning computer programs for writing instruction. This selection appeared originally in 1998 in The Dialogic Classroom: Teachers Integrating Computer Technology, Pedagogy, and Research, *edited by Jeffrey Galin and Joan Latchaw. Kemp describes how networked computer classrooms and the Internet are used to teach writing in a collaborative environment and prepare students for a world in which writing normally takes place on computers. His article provides several web addresses that further discuss computer-based writing instruction.*

The commercial introduction of the microcomputer in the early 1980s gave some writing instructors the hope that what was wrong in the writing classroom could be fixed by presumably intelligent machines. During the intervening fifteen years, researchers have proposed six general computer-based instructional functions, each of which at one time or another has been promoted as what computers will principally "do" in a future of computer-dominated writing instruction. Recently, two of these functions or capabilities—computer-mediated communications (CMC), or networks, and hypertext—have become integral elements of the global supernetwork, the Internet, in ways that revive the promise of a technology-based universal learning. This essay seeks to provide an understanding of the instructional power of one of those functions—networked peer-to-peer communication. Along with a glimpse into how networking through the Internet may transform writing instruction, this essay offers a warning or two about what may be lost. The six proposed functions for computer-based instruction are that (1) computers could grade essays, (2) computers could provide self-paced drill and practice exercises, (3) computers could provide interactive invention heuristics, (4) computers could provide powerful word

---

processing capability, (5) computers, using networks, could provide much greater student-to-student interaction, and (6) computers, using hypertext, with its ability to jump between portions of documents and documents themselves, could closely mirror the associative properties of the brain (whereby an external support system facilitates internal cognitive processes). All but these last two failed to deliver on their promise to influence writing instruction, and the decision is still out on networking and hypertext. Hopes, however, are once again on the rise. Much could be written on why automated graders, self-paced drill and practice, interactive heuristic "thought processors," and word processing itself have not affected instruction as much as once believed, but research indicates that the early excitement about, and fear of, "teaching machines" revealed both an unrealistically high appraisal of what computers could do and a disturbingly low appraisal of what human teachers (and writers) had been doing all along. The idea that computers could somehow glamorize instructional tasks that were inherently dull and unproductive arose out of an appallingly reductive view of our own students as primitives who could be bought into drudgery with a few pretty trinkets.

Because computers could not (as soon became obvious) employ natural language capability and therefore could not understand what students wrote, the dream of replacing graders and even teachers with machines, even for the presumed lowest-level student-teacher interactions, faded, and by the mid-1980s, some early enthusiasts were announcing the failure of computer-assisted writing instruction altogether. Yet the problem was, as always, not the lack of ability of the computers but rather the lack of imagination of those who would use them. The failed attempts to automate what teachers *presumably* do revealed the much greater complexity of what the mind and language are and what teachers *actually* do, and this encouraged skeptics, for a brief time, to reject the process-based tenets of the "new rhetoric" and return to the comforting view that teaching was an art, writing itself was ineffable, and any attempt to mediate the learning process with technology was a reductionist pipe dream.

But in 1985, Trent Batson at Gallaudet University established a form of computer-based writing instruction that bypassed the old problem of how smart or dumb computers really were and in some ways saved computer-based writing instruction from what was promising to be a period of debilitating retrenchment. At Gallaudet, which serves hearing-impaired students, Batson concluded that one of the problems with the writing of hearing-impaired students was that they communicated in their day-to-day discourse using ASL, American Sign Language, which only incidentally employed the English language as its base. Although hearing students were required to shift from oral to written English in their essays—admittedly a difficult task—the gap for hearing-impaired students between their everyday communication and writing was much greater: "when the typical deaf child encounters print, the child most often doesn't have the same potential for linking his previous communication experience with the symbol patterns on the page" (Batson 92). Batson decided to use computer networks, then in their infancy, and software that allowed a *synchronous* movement of electronic text from user to user as a means of allowing hearing-impaired students to communicate interactively in text, a sort of written conversation. In essence students sat at networked microcomputers and typed in comments that were then visible on every computer in the room.

By 1986 Batson realized that revitalizing written communication through networks could be valuable for *all* students of writing, not just those with hearing impairments.

> Very quickly it became apparent that the move to the network was not a simple shift from signed to written English; it led to a social shift as well. My role as teacher became very different once I was but a line on a screen and not the dominating presence at the front of the room. I also could see new energies emerging in our classroom interaction that had never occurred in my classes before. (99–100)

My colleagues and I at the University of Texas at Austin in 1987 picked up on his idea and applied networking to the collaborative learning theories of Kenneth Bruffee (Kemp, "Origins of ENFI"). Bruffee's distillation of ideas centering on the authority of discourse communities and the social construction of knowledge in a writing pedagogy *(Short Course in Writing*) seemed perfect for what the electronic distribution of student texts allowed. It was in Bruffee's 1986 *College English* article, "Social Construction, Language, and the Authority of Knowledge: A Bibliographical Essay," that we began to see how networks eroded the epistemological assumptions on which the traditional classroom was based, and how the epistemological assumptions privileged by networks dovetailed nicely with the challenges to classroom positivism, formalism, and imposed authority (current-traditionalism) that Bruffee described. The question of "authority" was central to issues of revitalizing classroom instruction. Sharon Crowley states emphatically that "current-traditional rhetoric maintains its hold on writing instruction because it is fully consonant with academic assumptions about the appropriate hierarchy of authority" (66). Networks, we realized, had the *potential* to decenter the classroom and redistribute authority in dramatic ways. By introducing us to Thomas Kuhn *(The Structure of Scientific Revolutions),* Bruffee also provided some frightened upstarts the courage to chip away at the Goliath of current-traditionalism that has long dominated writing instruction. Kuhn's discussion of paradigm shifts validated in our minds what we were seeing as the seismic shifts in classroom teaching presaged by computer-mediated communications.

The principal tenets of a network-based instruction were not new, at least to students of rhetoric and composition. Writing instruction theorists such as Jim Berlin, Richard Fulkerson, and Lester Faigley had earlier presented taxonomies of instructional emphases (based more or less on the literary critical taxonomy framed by M. H. Abrams in *The Mirror and the Lamp)* in which they all stressed a principal dichotomy between a fixed, formalist concept of what language is and hence how writing should be taught, and a fluid, rhetorical concept. This dichotomy is central to an understanding of the power of a network-based writing instruction.

Outside of Bruffee himself, the distinction has perhaps been most clearly articulated by Karen Burke LeFevre in *Invention as a Social Act* (1987). After quoting Bruffee, who underscores the importance of language as "the supreme means by which communities have created and continue to create knowledge by negotiating consensus and assent" (135), LeFevre acknowledges Thomas Kuhn as "among those who argue that knowledge is constructed by means of ongoing argument, and eventually, acceptance by a consensus of a community of thinkers" (136). "The inventing self," LeFevre says, "is thus socially constituted, and what is invented is judged according to its social contexts" (139). The knowledge community is a function of its social interaction and its ability to openly negotiate its meanings and values.

Networked computer-based writing instruction is based on a rhetorical or social dynamic in writing that, as proposed by LeFevre and Bruffee (and others), asserts that a genuine act of writing requires the open negotiation of issues in a classroom, and that presumes a reader who reads for information and effect, not simply to evaluate a performance, as a teacher does. The presumption on the part of the writer that his or her reader is reading merely to grade drains the writer of authorial independence and dilutes commitment to the writing act, causing in effect a breakdown in effort and the sorts of lazy, sterile writing that instructors are all too familiar with. Writing to peer readers, however, tends (over time and with the proper structure and intensity provided by computer-mediated communications) to restore a sense of engagement to the writing act, producing, in the memorable phrase of David Bartholomae (delivered in another context), the "sign of a student for whom something is happening" (16). Student writers often value the reactions of their peers over those of a professional reader—their teacher—and show more concern for their own text when writing for an audience they understand well. Effective writing, therefore, is not a "knowledge," in the sense of mathematics, that can be incrementalized and transmitted from knower to unknower as a hierarchy of principles or formulas, but rather a complex set of behaviors and highly individual comprehensions generated from intensive rhetorical activity.

The principal skill practiced in a computer-based networked classroom is the critical reading of student text, which is often flawed text. Student readers learn not only to discover problems and areas for improvement in a text, but most important, they learn how to articulate their responses publicly. Over time, and as the result of much negotiation with peers through the network, student readers construct for themselves theories of effective and ineffective writing. As Joseph Petraglia, arguing against what he terms a "general writing skills instruction" (which I interpret as yet another term for current-traditional practices) has put it most clearly, "To the extent that rhetorical writing can be learned, it will only be so by students building individual models of how to be rhetorically effective and adapting those models to everyday situations where writing is called for and can serve a strategic purpose" ("Writing" 97). Because all student readers in a networked class are also student writers, they employ this emerging understanding as they revise their own papers. Motivated and thorough critical revising is, of course, at the heart of good writing.

But a major problem with group work and peer critiquing, as proposed by Bruffee, is managerial: distributing student texts and feedback, keeping groups on task, and keeping the always potentially disruptive psychological elements of group work to a minimum. By translating almost all peer interactions into electronic form—

both informal "discussion" and the more formal student drafts themselves—the network largely bypasses the managerial problems of extensive group work and text sharing that arise in face-to-face settings. Because the interaction occurs through computer-mediated communication, the nature of the collaborative software ("groupware") and, above all, the tasks the instructor sets, have the ability to direct the students' efforts more thoroughly than is possible in oral class discussions and group work while, paradoxically, allowing the instructor to remove himself or herself from the role of classroom traffic cop.

A significant number of teachers complained in the early years of the networked classroom, and some still do, that the drastic reduction of face-to-face encounters in the networked class deprives the classroom dynamic of an important "human" ingredient. But it has been my experience, and those of most of my colleagues who seriously employ networked peer interaction, that while some aspects of personality are inhibited by the reduction of face-to-face activity, others are privileged through the networks. For instance, some groups or individuals normally intimidated in a largely oral instructional medium engage freely in class discourse, as Jerome Bump and Lester Faigley clearly show.

In an attempt to integrate theory and practice, the group in Austin developed an overview of computer-based instruction that recommended attention to four elements: (1) the proper equipment, (2) the proper software, (3) a coherent pedagogy (instructional theory), and (4) a group of people who can combine the previous three elements with energy, enthusiasm, and dogged persistence. We had discovered through experience that those who initiate computer-based instruction in their departments often concentrate on the equipment, give small attention to the software (usually choosing whatever popular form of word processing or desktop publishing software appeals to them), and ignore, often seriously, the pedagogy and the people who will use and manage the equipment and software, which generally creates what I have since called the "knowledge problem."

Of these four elements, what we lacked at the University of Texas in the mid-1980s was the software that would enable the written conversation over networks that Batson had pioneered. Batson's own work had been supported by a large grant that financed the development of special software, but the commercial version of that software was too expensive for our fledgling microlab, and the software contained instructionally unnecessary features and a troubling interface. Our efforts to link up with programmers at the university who might write local software for us failed, so three of us—Locke Carter, Paul Taylor, and I—laboriously applied our own rudimentary programming skills, first in BASIC and then in Turbo PASCAL, to produce software modules that would drive the computer-based classroom in ways that were consistent with our own research and experience as classroom teachers and with collaborative learning theories being developed by Wayne Butler and Valerie Balester, graduate students studying rhetoric. The result was a series of crude programs that were eventually more capably rewritten as a single piece of software marketed as "The Daedalus Integrated Writing Environment," or DIWE.

DIWE combines simple word processing, e-mail, and synchronous messaging with a menu-driven file management feature that allows students to turn in documents to a network and distribute them easily without fear of tampering or overwriting by other students. These capabilities of the software, and several adjunct writing heuristic and bibliography mechanisms are simple to use. The point is not so much what the software does but what the writing environment supports, and a major consideration is that the software should enable, not overwhelm, writing, reading, and peer responding.[1]

The educational software market eventually responded to an increasing enthusiasm for classroom CMC. In 1994 Norton expanded its Textra word processing software into Textra Connect, which employed functions of DIWE together with Textra's full-featured word processor, and in late 1995 Houghton Mifflin marketed software (CommonSpace) to compete with both DIWE and Connect. These products, along with the commercial version of the original ENFI software, Realtime Writer, several features of Aspects, and more generic groupware features being included in major word processing packages all support, in various ways, a "text-sharing pedagogy," or the ability of students in or out of a classroom to distribute their informal and formal writing to peer readers for extensive feedback. Comparisons of these programs, like comparisons between the Macintosh operating system and Microsoft Windows, often reveal little besides the predilections of various users; the differences pale in comparison to the similarities, which include synchronous messaging, e-mail, and document sharing.

The efforts of Batson and the Texas group to promote a network pedagogy helped produce in the early 1990s a resurgent interest in what was once called "computer-assisted instruction" (CAI) in composition, although professionals in the field generally came to refer to it as "computer-*based* instruction," having arrived at the realization that computer-mediated communications were transforming classroom instruction in the paradigmatic terms of Thomas Kuhn. Computers were no longer merely assisting precomputer instructional processes but rather providing a peer interactivity and a reading-writing arena that supported a new rhetorical base for instruction (or provided the old collaborative base with a new, enabling functionality). The "teaching-grading machine" idea that had so captured the imagination (in terms of both good and evil) early on had been replaced by the new notion that communication was the key to better writing instruction and that whatever facilitated peer-to-peer communication would improve writing instruction.

By the mid-1990s, the astonishing growth of the Internet provided a powerful push for CMC-based instruction and online group work, and the teaching community was suddenly faced with an exciting but bewildering range of techniques by which teachers could employ e-mail, e-mail discussion lists, real-time discussion (IRCs, MUDs, and MOOs), and information delivery systems (gophers and the World Wide Web) throughout the world. The tendency of instructors and administrators to tie a particular form of instruction to a specific piece of software was being belied by the new, universal networking capabilities of the Internet and the appearance of peer-to-peer collaborative pedagogy working across classroom, departmental, campus, and even national boundaries.

So what actually happens in a networked classroom? Although one can hardly present a "typical" picture of instruction that is anything *but* typical, I can describe a series of instructional tasks that some on my campus have employed over the past eight years in order to illustrate the sorts of assignments that lead to the benefits of using CMC and the Internet.

By 1996 the Computer-Based Writing Research Project at Texas Tech University, begun in 1988 and formalized in 1990, was supporting three Pentium and Performa classrooms of twenty-two to twenty-four computers each, all networked to a single local-area server and connected to the Internet. Some twenty-five instructors, mostly graduate students, were teaching full-time every semester in these rooms, serving about seven hundred to eight hundred students. Courses included composition, technical communication, literature, and creative writing. Accordingly, Texas Tech had gained considerable experience using classroom and wide-area networks for instruction, principally using DIWE.[2]

Although it would be difficult to describe in comprehensive terms all the computer-based networked tasks that teachers assign their students, in general the classes rely heavily on CMC and peer responding. Class discussions are conducted using synchronous messaging (as described previously), e-mail is sent between individuals to pursue topics further, drafts are shared online in a variety of ways, peer comments are mailed back to the writers, and both invention and responding are managed on the computer in structured and unstructured formats. Of the seventy-some instructors who had used these methods at Texas Tech through 1996, only two decided to return to the traditional classroom. What follows in the paragraphs below is a schedule of CMC-based tasks throughout an instructional unit.

At the beginning of an essay cycle (the series of student tasks that lead from prewriting to final draft), the instructor presents the class with a prompt to initiate an Interchange session (Interchange is DIWE's synchronous messaging feature). An example of such a prompt states that freshmen who live in the dorms should not be allowed to own cars. Immediately, a lively online discussion ensues, and the writer of the prompt is soundly vilified. But eventually (and this happens every time), someone posits that if freshmen didn't own cars, their studies would improve. A few others support that view. The exchange quickly evolves into a discussion of why people go to college in the first place, to play or to study. After thirty minutes or so, several conflicting points of view are supported, often by significant reasoning. It seems human nature cannot resist this sort of engagement; people discussing topics they are personally interested in will, largely on their own and especially when "protected" by the pseudo-anonymity of CMC, express contentious views. The nature of the contention encourages students to assert, support, and justify their opinions. First-time observers, sometimes teachers with many years of classroom experience, are often startled by what they characterize as the sheer "thinking" that takes place during an Interchange session.

After about thirty minutes, the instructor stops the session and asks the students to write on the word processor for ten minutes summarizing the gist of the discussion. These summaries are saved to Netmanager (DIWE's secure classroom database feature) and to the students' disks. The Interchange discussion is also saved to their disks. The students are asked to read the discussion at home or on the dorm computers and delete all but three of the most interesting points they themselves did not make. From these three points, they are to construct a thirty-line draft discussing whatever issue they have gleaned from the discussion. If they wish, they may cite their classmates in the draft.

The next class day the students read an online description of propositions (Bruffee's term for thesis statements) and are given fifteen minutes to construct adequate propositions for their own drafts. Then students e-mail their drafts to another member of the class, and the peer reader is asked to (1) comment on the quality of the proposition and (2) make general comments regarding the draft, such as how interesting it is and how it might be made more interesting. These comments are e-mailed back to the writer, who may then ask for clarification from the peer responder, either on e-mail or face to face. The instructor asks the students to revise the proposition and drafts according to feedback from the peer responder, building them to perhaps fifty lines of text.

On the third class day, the students load their second drafts into an Interchange session, almost instantly creating a classroom electronic anthology of drafts. The students spend twenty minutes skimming this anthology. (Students report that reviewing the drafts is extremely helpful in assessing their own skills and weaknesses in relation to the class.) The following comment from a student is typical:

> I hated the idea of other people reading my own writing at first. Then I realize[d] that they weren't much better than I was and that they made mistakes that I wouldn't make. I don't know why but I got a kick out of that. You [the instructor] say that reading other student papers makes us read our own differently and I really believe that now. Before [this class] I had never read anybody else's paper, and now I think I understand my own problems better.

Students are asked to freewrite about what they see as the major problems or strengths in regard to the class's writing and how their writing compares. The constant requirement to examine their own writing in terms of the class's writing encourages an awareness of writing itself and demystifies a process that many of them have been encouraged to see as purely mystical. The student quoted previously finished his evaluation by commenting, "Now I know that writing isn't just a matter of Fate," which I take as a significant realization that writing is an improvable skill—no small understanding for students who far too often assume that good or bad writing is "hard-wired" into their abilities and beyond their capacity to affect.

The students are asked to prepare a third draft for the next class period and are provided a description of various ways of supporting the essay proposition. On the fourth class day, students upload their third drafts into an Interchange session that has been broken up into groups of four students each. Each group reads the four drafts uploaded to its electronic space, and then members discuss how the writers managed to provide support for the propositions, similarities and differences in the writers' approaches, style, and so forth. The following student response illustrates this process:

> Both Jamie's and Howard's paper uses an item list to support the thesis and Robert used a chain of reasoning ["item list" and "chain of reasoning" are the instructor's terms for patterns of support]. But Howard, you should use a chain of reasoning because a thesis talking about space travel can't be supported that way. One thing has to lead to another but you just string out a bunch of ideas, not connected, . . . it's all kind of science fiction. Robert's way would fit better, I think. See how he "builds" his support and doesn't just say a bunch of unconnected things?

Such student analyses, delivered extemporaneously and online, are more effective than teacher feedback because the targeted texts are blended with interactive student commenting. The discussions are downloaded to the students' disks, and students are asked to review the discussions out of class and prepare a fourth draft of about seventy-five lines for the next class day, taking the comments of their group members into consideration.

On the fifth class day, the students turn in their drafts to Netmanager, and peers are asked to respond to the drafts using Respond, the DIWE feature that provides a structured revision heuristic, or a series of specific questions regarding the draft. Because the prompts can be written on-site, the instructor includes a number of specific queries regarding the proposition, the development of the proposition, managing support for the proposition, and so forth. (The Respond prompts increase in specificity and complexity throughout the semester, moving the students along a progressive understanding of the critical features of a student essay. I often use the Respond prompts as guides for grading my essays.) Each draft undergoes two Respond critiques, and the peer readers e-mail their Respond sessions (which include both prompts and responses) back to the writers and to Netmanager (so that the instructor can review and grade, if necessary, the quality of the peer readers' critiques).

Responding to student drafts is a learned behavior, as I well know from supervising sixty-five teaching assistants in Texas Tech's composition program. Even English graduate students often do poorly at first, so teachers should not be discouraged when first-year undergraduates struggle with the process and produce initially awkward results. But features like Respond provide the student responder with a "learning scaffold" or (an image I prefer) "training wheels" for the initial responding sessions, allowing progress to be measured and gradated. For instance, a prompt offered at the beginning of a semester received this response:

> PROMPT: Copy the proposition and judge its effectiveness.
> RESPONSE: The proposition is "So keep[ing] pets is good for a person's mental and physical well being." I like the thesis and it is arguable.

(One of the simple criteria I set for a good proposition or thesis is that it is a statement a reasonable person might disagree with.) I had asked students to provide at least four to six lines per response, and this student did not write four lines in responding to any of the six prompts. Eight weeks later, the same student responded to a slightly more difficult prompt with the following:

> PROMPT: Locate the proposition and critique how effective it is and how effectively the writer supports it.
> RESPONSE: You put down "telecommunications is ruining the agricultural base of America by allowing foreign ownership of industrial farms." This thesis makes me want to keep reading and even angers me a little, so it is good, but you describe how Japanese and Arabs own all this land and your data is good and well researched, but the telecommunications part is left out. There's one thing about global markets and satellites near the end of the paper, but almost nothing about telecommunications. You don't even describe what telecommunications is actually. The part about conference calls doesn't seem to me to be a definition of telecommunications. You need to put down a definition and then make it connect to agriculture some way.

There were twelve prompts in this later series of critiquing criteria, and all of the student's responses to them were equally detailed and almost as long. Practically all other students in this class produced commensurately longer and more detailed critiques, and I have found that the pattern generally holds true for all of my students who undergo the same process. The ability to expand the student's skill to read student texts critically lies at the heart of good writing instruction and for this, peer communication is essential.

For the last class day of the essay cycle, the writers are asked to prepare a final draft based on the critiques received, the directives of the instructor, and any relevant classroom discussions captured in Interchange. On this last day the final drafts are circulated to members of assigned groups for a rapid, last-ditch editing session in which peers can specifically point out surface errors.[3]

Those who support CMC-based instruction make strong claims that cause others to call for proof, but there is no proof that CMC provides better instruction than precomputer pedagogies, just as there is no proof that precomputer pedagogies provide any instruction at all. There is, in fact, no universally accepted substantiation for any writing pedagogy, for if there were, we would all be using it. Question of proof aside, however, there are still forces driving the transition to technology-based writing instruction that are stronger than the hallowed (if never validated) traditions of classroom instruction and the deep-seated mistrust of technology most teachers in the humanities feel. As one of my students trenchantly put it, society is "voting for technology in a big way." English teachers, with their undeniable love for the immutable truths of literature, have secretly and not-so-secretly prided themselves on escaping the vicissitudes of commercial and scientific pressures, but society's shift toward an information economy has inescapable implications: Unless we plan on transporting our students back to the nineteenth century on graduation, we must prepare them to use words in a rapidly expanding electronic environment. The Internet, especially, and the easily navigable World Wide Web, are rapidly becoming pervasive, exerting an influence on society at a speed never before seen by even the most transformative technologies. How does a networked collaborative pedagogy relate to the Internet?

Of the six computer-based functions that writing instructors have hypothesized as useful to their craft in the last fifteen years, the last two seem most faithful to the character of the Internet as it has evolved: networked collaborative instruction and hypertext-based instruction. Ironically, these two points of view, once seen as mildly antithetical among scholars, have both become integral to the Internet. The collaborative emphasis is demonstrated in e-mail discussion lists (managed by distribution software such as Listserv Listproc, and Majordomo), and interactive discussion available in IRC (Internet Relay Chat) and MUD/MOO (multiple-user domains, object-oriented), two Internet features that provide synchronous messaging capability much like DIWE, Connect, CommonSpace, and other local-area programs but that allow real-time written conversation to extend throughout the world. The hypertext emphasis is dramatically displayed in the World Wide Web, a means of accessing information across the Internet in a simple interface characterized by Web browsers such as Mosaic and Netscape. Users merely click on highlighted terms that appear on their screens in order to quickly access further information located on computers anywhere in the world. Web browsers and Web servers have taken file access capabilities that have existed on the wide-area networks for decades and made them astonishingly easy to use.

Because of these capabilities on the Internet and their rapidly increasing ease of use, access to the Internet is exploding, within two years (1994–95) tripling in size to estimates of nearly 60 million users (Bournellis 47). The respected Nielsen ratings, in what *Time* magazine called "the first solid survey of the Internet," reported that 37 million Americans and Canadians were accessing the Internet by the end of 1995 (Dibbell 121). Statistics like these are important, for they show both how compelling CMC activities are to people outside instructional settings and how familiar the CMC process is becoming to increasing numbers of people. The argument, almost a given in the early 1980s, that computers and computer activities were intrinsically foreign to everyday human activities is being reversed, and we are finding more and more that, for the young, doing some daily activities *without* a computer seems strange.

The CMC activities that have been explored inside networked classrooms over the last ten years at places like Texas Tech can be employed between classes, between campuses, and between countries. Written conversations, e-mail peer responses, publishing student writing to a peer readership—all can be done over networks using connections and computers that are proliferating at a mind-boggling rate because they are increasingly being valued by the society at large, not by the education community alone. The vast amount of this traffic being moved over the Internet by the 37 million Americans and Canadians is in writing, and a large proportion of that writing is being written interactively (Kemp, "Writing Dialogically"). In a number of ways, the expansion of the Internet is restoring to North America what another issue of *Time* (July 4, 1994) called "for millions of people, a living, breathing life of letters."

In other words, CMC is bringing millions of people into writing every day, and this in a society steeped in television, VCRs, radio, Nintendo, CDs, movies, and above all else, the telephone. CMC has made writing a "living, breathing" thing once more for people who had been seduced into a dependence on audio/video media, a dependence that no doubt has led more to the United States' declining writing skills than the shortcomings of teachers and pedagogy. For our purposes, the popularity of the Internet is simply another indication of the inherent power of CMC to restore vitality to a form of expression—writing—that was in deep retreat, pushed into the fixed forms and purposeless exercises of classroom assignments.

What will happen to writing instruction when it takes to the Internet? For one thing, it will slowly lose its identity as "writing instruction." Just as word processing, following the example of the telephone and automobile, has moved from being a consciously considered process into the anonymity of being a fact of life, learning to write will be a part of writing itself, in a vastly richer writing and reading arena than now possible. Teachers will continue to make assignments, but the assignments will be directed toward a great, unknown readership out there, which, for the writer, will make all the difference. Classes from different campuses will link up and hold regular discussions online, share work, and argue principles. Students will encounter, and occasionally recoil from, the opinions of a readership they must learn to anticipate.

In the short run, pre-CMC practices will simply be extended onto the Internet and change slowly as the effects of CMC impact their current modes of operating. Writing centers, for instance, have begun to extend tutoring onto the Internet, becoming "online writing labs" (OWLs), as at Purdue, the University of Michigan, Texas Tech University, and other campuses. Students submit drafts through e-mail and tutors provide feedback. An even more adventurous process is called The Cyberspace Writing Center Consultation Project, supported by Roane State Community College and the University of Arkansas at Little Rock. Here tutors stay online in a synchronous writing environment (MOO), interacting with patrons who "drop in" at any time to talk about writing problems.

Likewise, classroom instruction is extending onto the Internet. One notable example occurred in the spring of 1993, when graduate courses at San Francisco State, the University of Texas at Austin, and Texas Tech conducted the "Interclass." The Interclass provided an e-mail discussion list for the students in the three courses. Because the courses were concerned with computers and writing, approximately ten scholars and researchers in computers and writing were invited to "present" a work-in-progress each week and then remain joined to the e-mail discussion list for that week, responding to student queries and comments, in effect creating a shared, online, living "text" for the three courses. The students were able not only to interact with well-known figures in the field (such as Cynthia Selfe, Trent Batson, Karen Schwalm, Michael Joyce, and Bill Condon), but they also engaged (sometimes heatedly) in discussions about the presentations and various points of view. The mix of students from the three campuses and the often competing agendas of the professors stimulated the colloquy in startling ways, contributing to a general feeling (admittedly not shared by all the students) that the intellectual fervor was compelling.

One graduate student commented,

> The class was simply incredible. Never in my wildest dreams had I thought I would take a class where I was able to talk with (write with, actually) the famous people whose articles I was reading, and they treated me like my ideas were as important as their own (well, sort of). It's the first time I've ever thought I might some day actually be one of them.

Instructors at Texas Tech are experimenting with combinations of Internet features, including the use of Usenet newsgroups, class meetings held principally on the MOO, various uses of e-mail discussion and submissions of writing, and communication with other classes at other schools. At least nine sections of composition, literature, and technical communication were engaged in such Internet CMC activities in the spring of 1996, with more expected in the fall. One of the reasons these classes report enthusiastic support from instructors and students is that the instructors who attempt such innovations at Texas Tech have considerable experience in local-area CMC and are usually cognizant of the perils and the preparations necessary; they know how to gauge their expectations to avoid the emotional swings that sometimes attend enthusiasm for CMC-based instruction.

Similar efforts are being conducted on campuses around the country in a technologically charged spirit of innovation that resists description in print. A principal online means of tapping into such activities in a timely fashion exists on the World Wide Web pages of the Alliance for Computers and Writing (http://english.ttu.edu/acw/). There, links can be made to the field's principal e-mail discussion lists, online journals, support organizations, OWLs, and a plethora of other sources describing K–12 and postsecondary uses of CMC. The social dynamic that drives writing engagement in CMC-based writing classes also drives professional efforts when participants in the discipline maintain continuous active contact with each other, electronically oblivious of time and space.

Although I remain, after ten years of struggling with the technology, an enthusiastic supporter of CMC-based writing instruction, I would be foolish not to recognize the downsides, and there are some serious ones. No change of the magnitude that I am suggesting in this essay occurs without severe individual costs. The most serious may be that fine teachers who have contributed decades to their profession will be unable to use computers and will find themselves shunted aside by social forces they find difficult to acknowledge. This same displacement is currently happening in every vocational setting in the United States, but teachers in the humanities have all too often blithely assumed that what *they* have to teach is protected from societal pressures, relying perhaps on the medieval perception of scholarship as purely defensive, something to protect behind monastery walls.

A few of these teachers will have been exceptional teachers who have thrived, as their students have thrived, on the sheer puissance of association. These are the teachers that we who have *become* teachers remember best and have wanted most to be like. To "decenter" the classrooms of these teachers is to deprive them of the very air they breathe and to deny their students an extraordinary experience. I would hope and would argue for administrators to recognize this dynamic and exempt such teachers from the collaborative processes described in this essay, but at the same time I understand how few in number they are and how we must not fall back on "golden age" notions of teaching as we try to provide a pedagogy for the learning of hundreds of thousands of students across North America and the globe. To ignore the diversity in human talent among teachers and mandate any particular form of instruction, even within a single facility, would be irresponsible.

There will be instructors who jump into computer-based processes simply as an escape hatch from teaching itself, thinking they see in CMC-based instruction a way to hide from their students. The danger for them is not realizing that, in order to succeed, the teachers using technology must be clever, hardworking, and ambitious. The computer-based writing classroom is a kind of learning kitchen where the heat is always on high. It is not (as often presumed) an automated assembly line on which the teacher can fade from responsibility and effort, but many teachers and many more administrators will revert to the old "teaching machine" concept and assume that computers will allow the dumbing down of teacher requirements, the increase of classroom sizes, and the shrinking of payrolls. This one issue is sure to fuel debate for decades to come, no doubt making some instructors long for the good old days when the classroom represented as fixed an activity as the pulpit.

Within many computer-based classrooms, there will be bad instruction, just as there is bad instruction in many noncomputer classrooms now, and often the technology will simply make things worse, perhaps glossing over improper training and lackadaisical effort the way that prettified laser-printed student papers can gloss over serious problems with the text. Administrators will see students clicking away at computers and assume that the technology is ensuring significant effort, an ironic reversal of the usual impression not long ago that a student at a computer was doing "nothing but typing a paper."

Many people see these problems as rationales for rejecting any intrusion of technology into the classroom. But the writing classroom is not an island separate from the society it serves and can no more preserve its own prerogatives in the face of overwhelming outside pressure than can any other element of society. Computer technology is not superfluous gimmickry that can be imposed or excluded based on individual likes and dislikes. Instructional fads come and go and the tough teacher can outlast most of them, but societal changes in information access and communication will require profound changes in the classroom and in the way most people learn. As always, the burden will rest on the classroom teacher to use the tools at hand to do the best for the students, and this requires anticipating and avoiding the pitfalls that will come with these changes.

Notes

1. For an extended description of DIWE, see Kemp's "The Daedalus Integrated Writing Environment."
2. A description of Texas Tech's computer-based research project may be obtained on the World Wide Web at `http://english.ttu.edu/`.
3. An online class that I taught may be examined through a Web browser at

`http://englısh.ttu.edu/courses/1302/kemp/sp96/.`

Works Cited

Bartholomae, David. "What is Composition and (if you know what it is) Why Do We Teach It?" *Composition in the Twenty-First Century: Crisis and Change.* Ed. Lynn Z. Bloom, Donald A. Daiker, and Edward M. White. Carbondale: Southern Illinois University Press, 1996. 11–28.

Batson, Trent. "The Origins of ENFI." *Network-Based Classrooms: Promises and Realities.* Ed. Bertram C. Bruce, Joy Kreeft Peyton, and Trent Batson. Cambridge: Cambridge University Press, 1993.

Berlin, James. "Contemporary Composition: The Major Pedagogical Theories." *College English* 44 (1982): 765–77.

Bournellis, Cynthia. "Internet '95." *Internet World* November 1995. 47–52.

Bruffee, Kenneth A. *A Short Course in Writing.* 3rd Edition. Boston: Little, Brown and Company, 1985.

——. "Social Construction, Language, and the Authority of Knowledge: A Bibliographical Essay." *College English* 48 (1986): 773–96.

Bump, Jerome. "Radical Changes in Class Discussion Using Networked Computers." *Computers in the Humanıties* 24 (1990): 49–65.

Crowley, Sharon. "Around 1971: Current-Traditional Rhetoric and Process Models of Composing." *Composition in the Twenty-First Century: Crisis and Change.* Ed. Lynn Z. Bloom, Donald A. Daiker, and Edward M. White. Carbondale: Southern Illinois University Press, 1996. 64–74.

Dibbell, Julian. "Nielsen Rates the Net." *Time* 13 November 1995: 121.

Faigley, Lester. "Subverting the Electronic Workbook: Teaching Writing Using Networked Computers." *The Writing Teacher as Researcher: Essays in the Theory and Practice of Class-Based Research.* Ed. Donald Daiker and Max Morenberg. Portsmouth, NH: Boynton/Cook, 1990.

Fulkerson, Richard. "Four Philosophies of Composition." *College Composition and Communication* 30 (1979): 343–48.

Kemp, Fred. "The Daedalus Integrated Writing Environment." *Educator's Tech Exchange* Winter (1993): 24–30.

——. "The Origins of ENFI, Network Theory, and Computer-Based Collaborative Writing Instruction at the University of Texas." *Network-Based Classrooms: Promises and Realities.* Ed. Bertram Bruce, Joy Kreeft Peyton, and Trent Batson. Cambridge: Cambridge University Press, 1993.

——. "Writing Dialogically: Bold Lessons From Electronic Text." *Reconceiving Writing, Rethinking Writing Instruction.* Ed. Joseph Petraglia. Mahwah, NJ: Lawrence Erlbaum, 1995. 179–94.

LeFevre, Karen Burke. *Invention as a Social Act.* Carbondale: Southern Illinois University Press, 1987.

Petraglia, Joseph. "Writing as an Unnatural Act." *Reconceiving Writing, Rethinking Writing Instruction.* Ed. Joseph Petraglia. Mahwah, NJ: Lawrence Erlbaum, 1995. 79–100.

Online Reading between the Lines: Searching for and Evaluating Internet Information[1]

Ellen Strenski

Because publishers, editors, and librarians have screened most of the print sources available to students, teachers have often given little attention to teaching students strategies for evaluating sources in their research. As a result, students often simply grab several books and journals off library shelves without worrying about the accuracy and authority of their sources. As students conduct more and more of their research on the Internet, which has no screening mechanism, close reading and evaluation of sources is becoming a greater priority. Ellen Strenski, who teaches in the Electronic Rhetoric Project at the University of California, Irvine, suggests that evaluating websites should be an extension of instruction in the close reading of print texts. Her article, which appeared in the August 1998 issue of The ACE Journal, *a publication of the NCTE Assembly on Computers in English, describes ways in which students can find and evaluate sources on the World Wide Web and suggests several useful websites developed by librarians to help teachers and students evaluate web pages.*

"What is the Internet but a form of reading?" John Updike

All English instructors who use technology to teach introductory literature, argument, or research writing courses should include specific instruction in searching for and assessing Internet sources. Faculty recalcitrance about bibliographic instruction, to borrow English professor, G. W. Thompson's title phrase, must be overcome, especially as students turn increasingly to the Internet for any kind of information, school-sponsored or not (Lubans). Students are increasingly

[1] I am indebted for inspiration, information, and encouragement to my colleagues, Lisa Haefele, James Zeigler, and Jenny Williams, in our Electric Rhetoric Project at UC Irvine, `http://eee.uci.edu/faculty/strenski/er/`, to Catherine Palmer, UC Irvine Humanities Librarian, and to Stephen D. Franklin and David G. Kay of UC Irvine's Department of Information and Computer Science.

Ellen Strenski, "Online Reading between the Lines: Searching for and Evaluating Internet Information,"by ellen Sprenski, *Assembly on Computers in English Journal* 1.3 (1998): 56–69. ISSN 1094–2106. Reprinted with permission.

snowed, in many senses, by the blizzard of undifferentiated data they encounter on any foray into online databases or the WWW. Without adequate guidance, they misuse inappropriate sources. To help them, we can do what English teachers have always done: teach the critical thinking skills of reading between the lines. Reading lines that appear on a monitor, as opposed to paper, presents a slightly different challenge, but the educational goal is the same: discerning readers able to exercise judgment by applying principles of inference and interpretation. To foster this information literacy, we can join forces with our traditional allies—librarians. Librarians are equally dedicated, in the words of one, "to help students become efficient users of information—i.e., how to identify the information need and then how to find, evaluate, and select the best information to meet that need" (Tiefel 320). Nor is their mission of library user education novel. Librarian Tiefel points out that it is "a very old service predating even reference service" (319). If none of this is essentially new, however, the eruption of technological change is nonetheless confusing as the Internet explodes the traditional definitions of "the library" and "information source" and "classroom" far beyond concrete objects and physical spaces, and as institutions challenge their various departments and programs to develop and provide correspondingly appropriate instruction. Computer Science Departments (Cunningham), as well as library user education programs, are responding, sometimes redundantly or at cross-purposes. At the least, then, the impact on the undergraduate curriculum of these technological changes merits our present attention in order to clarify the academic division of labor in the immediate, ongoing partnership between librarians and English instructors, and to confirm the continuing, even increasing, value of this partnership by recognizing the distinctive professional contribution each group makes to this common goal of information literacy.

Librarians, on the one hand, are increasingly characterized as "information managers" or "information scientists." These experts know about information architecture (for example, the relationships between various collections of databases) and corresponding search strategies (for example, applying Boolean logic to concept terms for locating desired data). English teachers, on the other hand, know about texts—reading them and writing them. Both groups contribute in a complementary fashion to students' critical thinking skills of evaluating sources. The differences are primarily ones of sequence and of scale. Essentially, librarians engage students in an earlier evaluation of potential sources from among a vast array in order most efficiently to locate (that is, in Tiefel's words above, "to find, evaluate, and select") the most promising ones for later. Then, applying reading practices taught by English teachers, students further evaluate each of their selected sources—the "reading between the lines" in the present title—in order to use the information in each as theme or evidence in their own writing, or to discard the source. Librarians teach students to find, read critically, and evaluate information records, whether catalog or data base citations or URLs, in order to select those, from among potential sources, that merit further study. Note the sequence: "find, evaluate, and select." English teachers teach students to read beyond the record, to examine critically the selected sources in order to understand the information in them for discussion and use in their own writing.

Although in principle separate, these evaluative practices overlap and offer opportunities for fruitful reinforcement. The main obligation for English teachers is explicitly to show students how the reading skills taught in traditional English classes—using their imaginations to make inferences about meanings in printed stories, plays, poems, and essays—translate to reading online. One way to do so is for English teachers to use, build on, and follow up on various checklists that librarians have prepared to help students practice these evaluative skills of "quality filtering." This essay will explain how specific examples of online reading activities can be incorporated into the English curriculum to engage students' creative imaginations productively in such Internet search and evaluation.

Consider how, when students begin searching for Web information on the literally millions of existing pages, they have only their imaginations and Internet search engines as resources for help, and how different this is from using a traditional library. A library sifts through and prearranges information for readers through three or four means. Physically, information is collected in various places, for instance, "current periodicals," "stacks," "archives," that in turn reflect its accumulation and sedimentation, and thereby its processing and testing over time. Information comes into the library in newspapers and periodicals, which readers and writers recycle back into the library as journal articles and books, which more readers and writers ultimately codify and recycle back into the library as references and encyclopedias. Similarly, library information is classified and indexed according to Dewey Decimal or Library of Congress cataloguing systems by human beings. All of these means situate, stabilize, and help certify library information.

On the Internet, however, students are on their own; all they have for help is their own perspicuity and robot software search engines to face a collection of information which differs in four major ways from that in the traditional library. First, it is undifferentiated, with legitimate, useful data listed arbitrarily among trash, for example, the offensive pornographic sites pulled up with an unwary student's search on the topic of school uniforms, an observation that does not need laboring. Second, it is overwhelmingly immense. For example, American tobacco companies recently posted 27 million documents on the WWW, the exact same number, 27 million, as volumes in the University of California library, one of the largest in the world. Third, Internet information is decontextualized. It is automatically presented literally out of the ether. Finally, particularly because of pressures exerted by the last two qualities, it encourages the accelerated processing of a speedy reading—a quick glance, search for clues, and then on to a link, which is necessarily superficial and therefore less thoughtful.

Gone, then, are the days when to find information all that was needed was the *Library of Congress Subject Headings*. In the old days, a student researcher would look up his or her topic in this big red multi-volume index located conveniently by the card catalogue (whether in drawers of paper index cards. on celluloid, or in a computer data base). Consider the UC Irvine student who proposed a research paper on the environmental topic of recycling household garbage. In those old days, not so long ago, he might have started by looking up "Recycling" in an encyclopedia and found that there are three basic ways to recycle: buy-back centers, drop-off centers, and curbside collecting programs. However, searching for library information using the word "curbside" as a subject, turned up nothing. Nothing is catalogued under "curbside" although such sources might exist in the library. Nor is anything listed under the subject "garbage." To determine which terms are official subject headings used to catalogue library information, a researcher consults the reference book, *Library of Congress Subject Headings.* When the researcher looks up "garbage," he or she is there advised to "USE Refuse." All the pertinent library information is catalogued under "refuse."

Now, however, no such index exists to the WWW, although some search engines, such as *Excite!,* will mindlessly suggest related terms, some of which may actually be useful. Now a student researcher must literally dream up a group of possible terms under which the sought-for information might be retrieved by the robot spiders that collect Web information for the various search engines. Sometimes this is a matter of straightforward synonyms: **ascorbic acid or Vitamin C,** or **euthanasia or "mercy killing.**" However, more often it requires students to imagine family relationships and build a network of keywords by empathetically free-associating connections.

For instance, the student interested in ways to get people to recycle their household garbage had to dream up a group of terms including **recycling, curbside, collection, energy conservation, green politics, litter, trash, refuse, garbage, waste, incentive.** Moreover, creating these associations is often, literally, a stretch of the imagination. For example, WWW information on "electric cars" is most easily retrieved and accessed through the search term "battery" a related term which is not immediately obvious.

Stimulating the imagination through literature has always been a goal of the English curriculum. The student interested in recycling and about to create a search strategy for sources could be well-advised to read A. R. Ammons' poem, Garbage, not in this case for the incidental shared frustration of the researcher, who obviously did not consult the Library of Congress Subject Headings:

. . . I punched
out Garbage at the library and four titles
swept the screen, only one, Garbage Feed,

seeming worth going on to; and that was about
feeding swine right: so I punched Garbage Disposal
and the screen came blank—nothing! all those
titles, row on row, of western goodies, mostly
worse than junk, but not a word on Disposal: I
should have looked, I suppose under Waste Disposal
but, who cares, I already got the point: I know garbage is being
"disposed" of . . . . (49)

but, rather, for the vivid evocation of concrete details that could prompt and inspire the student reader's imagination, that suggest possible keyword terms and concepts, and that thereby prepare him for a productive search:

> dew shatters into rivulets on crunched cellophane
> as the newly-started bulldozer jars a furrow
> off the mesa, smoothing and packing down:
> flattening, the way combers break flat into
> speed up the strand: unpleasant food strings down
> the slopes and rats' hard tails whirl whacking
> trash . . . . (35)

Note how the details in this passage suggest to the imagination a number of evocative associations: water pollution, environmental degradation of the physical landscape caused by landfill, food surplus, and medical sanitation and threats to public health. So, too, do many other passages work this way in Ammons' poem, which typifies this imaginative, associative, function of literature.

Once students have found and selected suitable data to work with, these data must be evaluated, a complicated process of applying specific criteria such as credibility, provenance and sponsorship, accountability, recency, in order to judge the reliability of specific pages, and then students must make inferences and connections among these WWW pages. Consider how search engines deliver lists of potentially valuable URL's. The electronic interface reduces all information to the same stream of digitized bits. The URL for a Web site denying the Holocaust may be sandwiched in with URLs for more respected sites, and the page itself may look in many ways similar to any other Web site. These URL's are presented in some percentile order of relevancy as determined by a mindless robot search engine spider, but they are stripped of context. An analogy would be being shown part of a chapter in a book without the cover, title page, table of contents or index. For example, a UC Irvine student researching the problem of legalized gambling in California was randomly presented the URL `http://www.capitolresource.org/b_gamb.htm`, which linked to an essay, "Gambling in California: Win or Lose" (Thomasson). This document is quite compelling with its footnotes, and even its unpleasantly small, hard-to-read, and hence somewhat academic-looking font. Moreover, its frame features the Capitol dome. Altogether, it looks seriously legislative and immediately credible. However, like all Web pages it has no context. The diligent researcher must click on the home link to find that this page's sponsor, Capitol Resources, is an organization "dedicated to the principles of traditional families, parental rights, limited government, and citizen responsibility." This very clear social agenda is not, in itself, bad, but the agenda certainly does color the information in the essay on legalizing gambling, and is only minimally identified on the essay through a link to the organization's home page.

This medium of computer technology and its screen interface, coupled with the immense number of potential, decontextualized sources, challenge students who are both unsettled by the resulting leveling effect of Web pages and unprepared to distinguish quality among them, that is, unprepared for the task of "quality filtering," in librarians' words. English teachers, whose essential job is to teach close reading and its associated critical thinking skills, are ideally situated to help students learn these new survival skills by transferring their abilities from reading conventional literary texts on paper to reading Web pages on screen. This process involves two steps. The first step, borrowed from the librarians, is to apply specific criteria to an Internet site in order to identify it, "identify" in the sense of locate and contextualize it. This step involves sensing equivalents of both physical arrangements in space (for example, in an academic collection or not, to start with, and then in current periodicals, a pamphlet file, newspaper data base, archives, government documents, or elsewhere) and classification schemes (for example, by genre—advertising, editorial, research report—or by cataloguing system, like the Library of Congress). Obviously, only trained specialists can recognize well these kinds of equivalents of print and other media. However, students nonetheless need to know that these equivalents do exist and are suggested by specific clues on Web pages, for example, the components in a URL, and to practice using their imaginations to sense what these equivalents might be. The next step is to connect the inferences from this application of the checklists to arrive at a judgment of quality and usefulness.

A number of librarians have developed WWW-specific, checklist criteria for evaluating Web pages. One of the first, from mid- 1995, was UCLA's Esther Grassian's "Thinking Critically about World Wide Web Resources, "`http://www.ucla.edu/campus/computing/bruinonline/trainers/critical.html`. Grassian's criteria derive from three main categories: Content & Evaluation, Source & Date, and Structure. More recently, UC Irvine instructors have found the criteria developed by Susan M. Beck of the New Mexico State University Library `http://lib.nmsu.edu/susabeck/eval.html` to be particularly helpful. In her classification scheme, "The Good, the Bad, & the Ugly," Beck suggests these categories: Accuracy, Authority, Objectivity, Currency, Coverage.

These kinds of criteria are usually combined into question and answer checklists. For instance, Grassian's checklist asks questions like "When was the Web item produced?" "When was the Web item last revised?" "Are there blind links, or references to sites which have moved?" "Is contact information for the author or producer included in the document?" Beck asks these, among other questions: "Is there any advertising on the page?" "Is the page dated?" "Is the author qualified? An expert?" "Is there a link to information about the author or the sponsor?" These checklists or rating sheets tend to be of the "yes" or "no" variety and on their own do not guarantee that students will be able to infer meaningful quality from the totality of their answers so that they can assert, for instance, that a particular page is worthless or might perhaps be good for some purpose, but not necessarily for their own particular project.

The more effective checklists, like Susan Beck's, are supplemented in two ways. First, they are available on the World Wide Web with hyperlinked examples of their criteria. Second, they are the basis of ready-made exercises whereby students can practice developing their evaluative skills. These checklists are valuable but alone they are not enough. English teachers can build on these criteria, checklists, and online exercises in order to push students further in several ways, first, by following up these questions with additional and more probing interpretive questions, and, second, by providing a context—other readings in the course at whatever level—for comparative analysis.

Note first the surface similarity of these prompting questions to those typically asked in freshman anthology *Readers,* like *The Blair Reader* (Eds. Kirszner and Mandell) assigned in freshman composition at UC Irvine. The genre is immediately recognizable. For example, here are several typical questions that Kirszner and Mandell ask students about George Orwell's essay "Politics and the English Language": "Why does Orwell title his essay 'Politics and the English Language'?" (205). Or, "What cause-and-effect relationship does Orwell discuss in Paragraph 2?" (206). Some of these questions, such as "To what 'certain topics' does Orwell refer in Paragraph 4?" (206), have relatively simple fill-in-the-blank answers, similar to the checklists.

However, more typically, such an answer is only the first part of the students' responses. Students are then pushed to reflect further. About Orwell's title, they are first asked, "Why does Orwell title his essay 'Politics and the English Language'?" and then they are pushed further: "What connections does he draw between the two?" (205). About the cause-and-effect relationship in Paragraph 2 they are first asked, "What cause-and-effect relationship does Orwell discuss in Paragraph 2?" then prompted further: "Explain the reasoning behind his analysis and decide whether you agree" (206). English teachers' typical "Discussion Questions" like these go beyond "yes"-"no" answers to generate exploration and practice in inference and interpretation:

Additionally, English courses offer the convenience of a ready-made, built-in context for comparative analysis. Librarian Susan Beck, for instance, offers an excellent online comparative exercise to judge WWW sites whereby the viewer is asked to compare and contrast sets of three sites about such topics as "Smoking & Tobacco" or "Immigration." However, these sites are arbitrarily chosen to exhibit different features that correspond to Beck's criteria, for example, advertising, an identified sponsor, "zombie" links, or omitted date of construction. A typical English course, on the other hand, provides a context that makes such comparative analysis more salient: a difference with a meaningful distinction, not just a difference. For instance, Kirszner and Mandell ask students a typical two-part question, "Why do you think Orwell chose a verse from *Ecclesiastes* for his parody? Could another kind of quotation have served as well?" (206). Students can answer this question by distinguishing cases, not just by describing differences, because in their English courses they have presumably been studying other works, studying other artists' strategies of quotation, and studying their own developing, self-conscious techniques of providing quotations from other texts.

In UC Irvine's Internet-enhanced freshman composition classes, three kinds of follow-up classroom activities, that is following up the librarians' checklists, lend themselves especially well to helping students develop these inference skills and interpretive sensitivities. These three kinds of assignments require students, first, to respond to parody sites; second, to provide links to authoritative sites on their own Web pages; and, third, to engage in problem-solving case studies.

Parody, first, has the benefit of providing humor, but also runs the risk of confusing students who do not "get it," who don't get the irony and therefore do not get the point of the exercise. For example, UC Irvine instructors have designed several assignments based on reading two parody Web sites. Typically, after students have discussed criteria like librarian Susan Beck's, they are led through a site like "The True But Little Known Facts about Women and Aids" (Henderson), linked off Beck's collection. This page begins with a logo from the University of Santa Anita and the caption "Serving the largest metropolitan area in the United States with no major institution of higher learning." Santa Anita is quite close to UC Irvine, and is well known locally not for any university, but for its racetrack. Instructors pause and ask students to reflect on this statement and on this affiliation. Finally, in the baffled silence someone has a Eureka experience and laughs. Students are then asked to consider the authority of the author, a Dr. Juatta Lyon Fueul, and some of her facts like the claim that "Married women can reduce their risk from AIDS by 73.8% if they do not share their toothbrushes with their husbands," or that the spread of AIDS in Europe is linked to sharing elevators with Haitian nuns. UC Irvine instructors, like the real librarian author, John R. Henderson of Ithaca College, use this site to implore students to "Think about it."

A follow-up exercise to this group analysis of a parody site requires students to read another parody site on their own and then to send a minimum of two sentences to a class listserv about it. This particular site, "Feline Reactions to Bearded Men" `http://www.improb.com/airchives/cat.html`, is one of several sites illustrating librarian Beck's criterion of "Authority." It parodies a report of a lab experiment, making outrageous claims, such as the laboratory assistant was anaesthetized during the procedure so as not to influence unduly the cat subjects, and including footnotes from Arnold Schwartzenegger, Doctor Seuss, and Madonna Louise Ciccone, among other experts. Inevitably, some students cannot detect the joke at all. They struggle typically to assert such observations as "The procedure and results of the study all had appropriate headings that told you what exactly you were reading." "It was organized, easy to understand." "I believe I would use this as a source myself if prompted to." "Maybe other related links posted on the page might make it more worthwhile." Too few see the humor: "I found the study to be quite hysterically funny and I laughed so hard my family gave me strange looks."

Parody Web exercises, then, require some tact and discretion on the instructor's part, and can backfire unpleasantly. Such a pedagogical challenge is, of course, nothing new, and affects any English teacher's attempt to engage students' ability to recognize irony in whatever they are reading. The World Wide Web does, however, make the challenge more urgent. Consider another site in this respect. Dream Technologies International at `http://www.d-b.net/dti/` goes beyond parody to an awesome fictional construction of a parallel commercial reality. DreamTech purports to be a company, the first and largest of its kind, that provides human (and animal) cloning services. This astonishing Web collection includes testimonials from satisfied clients, a price list, an order form, and even a job ad for microbiologists to work in the head laboratory on Vanuatu featuring attractive photos of the labs on this tropical island. DreamTech also includes "Cloning News," a page with many current links, which claims: "The news stories given here are authentic and have not been adulterated in any way. At DreamTech we give top priority to accuracy of reproduction." Some of these links, for instance, to a Reuters' report of the stand taken by the American Medical Association on the congressional moratorium on cloning, are truly useful and credible sources of up-to-date and reliable information. This collection, in other words, dramatizes the challenge facing our students, who are vulnerable readers, uncertain about how to read such an aestheticized object. It also intimates the pleasurable rewards and useful gratifications from skillful reading of such a clever textual artifact. So, too, the DreamTech site challenges us correspondingly as English teachers to help our students accomplish this goal.

Requiring students to provide authoritative, credible links on their own pages is a second, less charged assignment. In some composition classes at UC Irvine, as elsewhere, students are required to publish their final papers as components of group collections on related topics. Students can include links that they deem useful on their own pages in three ways. First, they can ensure that any of their conventional "Works Cited" citations to Internet sources are hot linked. Second, they can feature links to central sites that inform their papers as background. For instance, students writing about issues related to California's recent smoking ban in bars and restaurants can link to and thereby feature for the Web reader the online text of the legislative bill prohibiting such tobacco use. Third, students can include lists of recommended sites for further reading. These lists can be annotated or not. In all cases, student must work through a critical evaluation of possible candidate sites in order to select the ones to include as links in their own Web texts.

Finally, a third kind of assignment to teach students the online critical thinking skills of reading between the lines is a mini-case study requiring students to solve a realistic problem. One such case study at UC Irvine `http:/eee.uci.edu/98w/21358/cat.html` involves a real, 15-year-old cat, Zelda, suffering from hyperthyroidism. Students put themselves in the position of Zelda's owner who must decide how Zelda will be treated for this potentially fatal condition. Zelda's veterinarian has pointed out that all three treatments (surgery, medication, and radioactive iodine) have drawbacks. The last treatment, radioactive iodine is so new that very little has been published in print about it. So students must search for, and in the process evaluate, information on the WWW in order to decide on the best treatment. Specifically, students are instructed to

- first, find out about Zelda's ailment, and the three current ways of treating it, by searching for information about it on the WWW.

- decide what you do want done to help Zelda, and why you would not want the other two treatments.

- explain what it is about the sources you consulted that convinced you about this course of action. What impressed you about these sources? When you answer this question, make sure you refer to specific URLs you have examined and to the specific criteria (accuracy, relevance, currency, sponsorship, credibility, etc.) that we have been studying so far.

In the process of completing this assignment, students must make a number of strategic decisions: determine which search engines to use and how to search with the synonym "feline" for "cat"; which veterinary encyclopedia to consult for a general overview of feline hyperthyroidism; how to follow up links to determine sponsorship or other affiliation; how to exclude sites because they are out of date or commercially biased; even how to value an award-winning site ostensibly written by a cat, "Callie," on a server with an "edu" domain.

These activities and exercises reinforce and extend librarians' instruction in the technicalities of strategic online searches and their checklists. Such a valuable partnership has dramatically demonstrated to instructors involved in UC Irvine's Internet-enhanced composition classes an institutional and pedagogical imperative to emphasize these critical reading skills in our own classrooms and to encourage our colleagues to do likewise. English teachers must conspicuously assert our own professional expertise and responsibility to teach these new Internet survival skills, which are really not that new: digital literacy transfers some of the traditional imaginative and interpretive practices of reading literary texts on paper to reading between the lines on a computer screen.

Works Cited

Ammons, A. R. *Garbage.* New York: Norton, 1993.

Beck, Susan M. "The Good, the Bad, & the Ugly: or, Why It's a Good Idea to Evaluate Web Sources." 7 July 1997. `<http://lib.nmsu.edu/staff/susabeck/eval.html>`.

The Blair Reader (Annotated Instructor's Edition). Eds. Laurie G. Kirszner and Stephen R. Mandell. Englewood Cliffs, NJ: Prentice Hall, 1992.

Cunningham, Sally Jo. "Teaching Students to Critically Evaluate the Quality of Internet Research Resources." *SIGCSE Bulletin: A Quarterly Publication of the Association for Computing Machinery Special Interest Group on Computer Education* 29.2 (June 1997): 31–34, 38.

Henderson, John R. "The True But Little Known Facts about Women and Aids." 3 Oct.1997 <http://147.129.1.10/library/lib2/AIDSFACTS.html>.

Lubans, John, Jr. "How First-Year University Student Use and Regard Internet Resources." 8 Apr. 1998 <http://www.lib.duke.edu/staff/orgnztn/lubans/firstyear.html>.

Tiefel, Virginia M. "Library User Education: Examining Its Past, Projecting Its Future." *Library Trends* 44.2 (Fall 1995): 318–338.

Thomasson, Randy. "Gambling in California: Win or Lose." *Capital Resource Institute.* <http://www.capitolresource.org/b_gambling.htm>.

Thompson, G. W. "Faculty Recalcitrance about Bibliographic Instruction." In *Bibliographic Instruction in Practice: A Tribute to the Legacy of Evan Ira Farber*. Eds. L. Hardesty, J. Hastreiter, and D. Henderson. Ann Arbor, MI: Pierian Press, 1993. 103–105.

Updike, John. "A Writer at Large," *New Yorker* 29 Sept. 1997: 31–32.

SUGGESTED READINGS: COMPUTERS AND WRITING

Bolter, Jay David. *Writing Space: The Computer, Hypertext, and the History of Writing*. Hillsdale, NJ: Lawrence Erlbaum, 1991.

Galin, Jeffrey R., and Joan Latchaw, eds. *The Dialogic Classroom: Teachers Integrating Computer Technology, Pedagogy, and Research*. Urbana, IL: NCTE, 1998.

Hawisher, Gail E., and Cynthia L. Selfe, eds. *Passions, Pedagogies, and 21st Century Technologies*. Urbana, IL: NCTE, 1999.

Lanham, Richard A. *The Electronic Word: Democracy, Technology, and the Arts*. Chicago: U of Chicago P, 1993.

Reiss, Donna, Dickie Selfe, and Art Young, eds. *Electronic Communication Across the Curriculum*. Urbana, IL: NCTE, 1998.

Selfe, Cynthia L., and Susan Hilligoss, eds. *Literacy and Computers: The Complications of Teaching and Learning with Technology*. New York: MLA, 1994.

Tornow, Joan. *Link/Age: Composing in the Online Classroom*. Logan: Utah State UP, 1997.

Tuman, Myron C., ed. *Literacy Online: The Promise (and Peril) of Reading and Writing with Computers*. Pittsburgh: U of Pittsburgh P, 1992.

Teaching Argument: A Theory of Types

Jeanne Fahnestock and Marie Secor

Jeanne Fahnestock, professor of English at the University of Maryland, and Marie Secor, professor of English at Penn State University, are co-authors of Readings in Argument *and, with Richard Larson, of* A Rhetoric of Argument, *and they have published widely on the theory of argumentation as well as the history of rhetoric, scientific writing, text structure, stylistics, and the teaching of writing. In this article, which first appeared* in College Composition and Communication *in 1983, Fahnestock and Secor briefly describe three basic approaches to teaching argumentative writing: logical/analytical (teaching argument by teaching principles of formal logic), content/problem-solving (teaching argument by having students write arguments that develop out of assigned readings or case studies), and the approach Fahnestock and Secor believe is the most effective, rhetorical/generative (teaching argument by teaching invention). Fahnestock and Secor explain the four types of proposition that an argument may make, each addressing a different question. Categorical propositions address the question "What is this thing?" Causal statements answer "What caused it or what effects does it have?" Evaluations address "Is it good or bad?" And proposals answer "What should be done about it?" Fahnestock and Secor explain an invention process and structure for each type of argument as well as problems that students often have with each type.*

The climax of many composition courses is the argumentative essay, the last, longest, and most difficult assignment. An effective written argument requires all the expository skills the students have learned, and, even more, asks for a voice of authority and certainty that is often quite new to them. Aware of the difficulty and importance of argument, many composition programs are devoting more time to it, even an entire second course. At Penn State, for example, the second of our required composition courses is devoted entirely to written argument, out of our conviction that written argument brings together all other writing skills and prepares students for the kinds of writing tasks demanded in college courses and careers.

We know what we want our students to do by the end of our second course: write clear, orderly, convincing arguments which show respect for evidence, build in refutation, and accommodate their audience. The question is, how do we get them to

---

Jeanne Fahnestock and Marie Secor. "Teaching Argument: A Theory of Types," *College Composition and Communication*, February 1983.

do it? What is the wisest sequence of assignments? What and how much ancillary material should be brought in? The composition teacher setting up a course in argument has three basic approaches to choose from: the logical/analytic, the content/problem-solving, and the rhetorical/generative. All of these approaches teach the student something about argument, but each has problems. Our purpose here is to defend the rhetorical/generative approach as the one which reaches its goal most directly and most reliably.

The teacher who uses the logical/analytic approach in effect takes the logic book and its terminology into the classroom and introduces students to the square of opposition, the syllogisms categorical and hypothetical, the enthymeme, the fallacies, induction and deduction. It has not been demonstrated, however, that formal logic carries over into written argument. Formal logic, as Chaim Perelman and Stephen Toulmin have pointed out, is simply not the same as the logic of discourse;[1] students who become adept at manipulating fact statements in and out of syllogisms and Venn diagrams still may not have any idea how to construct a written argument on their own.

Another supposed borrowing from logic is the distinction between induction and deduction as forms of reasoning and therefore as distinct forms of written argument. Induction and deduction are sometimes seen to be as different as up and down, induction reaching a generalization from particulars and deduction affirming a particular from a generalization. Actually the exact distinction between the two is a matter of some controversy. In his *Introduction to Logic* Irving M. Copi defines the two not as complementary forms of reasoning, but as reasoning toward a certain conclusion (deduction) and reasoning toward a probable conclusion (induction).[2] And Karl Popper in *Conjectures and Refutations* obliterates the distinction by showing that induction, as traditionally defined, is not valid.

> But in fact the belief that we can start with pure observations alone, without anything in the nature of a theory, is absurd; as may be illustrated by the story of the man who dedicated his life to natural science, wrote down everything he could observe, and bequeathed his priceless collection of observations to the Royal Society to be used as inductive evidence. This story should show us that though beetles may profitably be collected, observations may not.
>
> Twenty-five years ago I tried to bring home the same point to a group of physics students in Vienna by beginning a lecture with the following instructions: 'Take pencil and paper; carefully observe, and write down what you have observed!' They asked, of course, *what* I wanted them to observe. Clearly the instruction, 'Observe!' is absurd. . . . Observation is always selective. It needs a chosen object, a definite task, an interest, a point of view, a problem. And its description presupposes a descriptive language, with property words; it presupposes similarity of classification, which in its turn presupposes interests, points of view and problems.[3]

Thus according to Popper, the observations that supposedly lead to a conclusion are, in fact, controlled by a prior conclusion. There is no pure form of reasoning which goes "example + example = conclusion," as it is represented in many rhetorics. We cannot reason "x chow is vicious + y chow is vicious + z chow is vicious = most chows are vicious" unless we assume "Chows x, y and z are typical chows." The conclusion of a so-called inductive argument depends not on the number of examples but on their typicality. The reasoning in such an argument does not leap from particular to general but proceeds from an assumption of typicality and particular evidence (in this case three examples of vicious chows) to a conclusion. This process is not essentially different from deduction. Students are misled if they think their minds work in two gears, inductive forward and deductive reverse, or if they believe it is possible to argue purely from evidence without assumptions. But students who recognize the necessity for typical evidence can fruitfully consider whether their audience will accept their evidence as representative or whether they must explicitly argue that it is.

Another continually attractive if indirect way of teaching argument in the composition classroom is the content/problem-solving approach, which assumes that students will absorb the principles and methods of written argument simply by doing it. In such content-based courses, which may use a casebook (now rare) or a group of related readings or even the lectures and readings of another course, the instructor may not even define the writing as argument. Instead, students write papers with "theses" which grow naturally out of their readings or are suggested by the instructor. Another variety of this approach is the problem-solving method, as in *Cases for Composition* (by John P. Field and Robert H. Weiss, Boston: Little, Brown & Co., 1979), which frames assignments not only by specifying topics but also by defining rhetorical situations. Students write their way out of problems, arguing in letters, memos, reports, and brief articles.

The content/problem-solving approach effectively approximates real-life writing situations which supply both purpose and content. Moreover, a course that teaches writing this way is attractive because the instructor can present for discussion a coherent body of material from philosophy, sociology, psychology or even literature; if such a course works well, invention is not a problem because students are directly stimulated by the content, and they do practice writing arguments. And at best students may learn a method of problem-solving which they can apply to other writing situations when their instructor is no longer suggesting topics nor the controlled reading stimulating invention. However, the content in such courses tends to crowd out the writing instruction or, increasingly, it is given away to the real experts in other departments and the composition teacher reduced to an overseer of the revision process, a police officer with a red pencil.

The composition course which does not organize itself around a body of content can take what we will call the "rhetorical/generative" approach and explicitly teach invention. Now the composition course devoted entirely to argument can turn to the classical sources which are still the only scheme of invention purely for argument. These sources (definition, comparison, cause and effect, and authority) do help students find premises for the proposals and evaluations they usually come up with when left on their own to generate theses for arguments. But the sources are less help when we ask students to take one step further back and support the very premises which the sources have generated. If, for example, the student wants to argue that "the federal government should not subsidize the airlines," thinking about definition might yield a premise like "because airline subsidies are a form of socialism," and thinking about cause and effect might yield a premise like "because once an industry is subsidized, the quality of its service deteriorates." But how is either of these premises to be supported? How does one actually argue for a categorization such as the first or a cause and effect relationship such as the second? To tell the student to continually reapply the four sources is rather discouraging advice. Thus while the classical sources are powerful aids to invention in the large-scale arguments that evaluations and proposals require, they do not help students construct smaller-scale supporting arguments.

It is possible to give students more specific aid in inventing arguments if we begin by distinguishing the basic types of arguments and the structures characteristic of each. We derived this approach when confronted by the variety of propositions our students volunteered as subjects for argument. After collecting scores of these, we found they could be sorted into four main groups answering the questions 1. "What is this thing?" 2. "What caused it or what effects does it have?" 3. "Is it good or bad?" and 4. "What should be done about it?" Propositions which answer these questions are, respectively, categorical propositions, causal statements, evaluations, and proposals. The thesis of any argument falls into one of these categories. The first two, which correspond to the classical sources of definition and cause and effect, demand their own forms of argument with distinctive structures. Arguments for the third and fourth, evaluations and proposals, combine the other two. If we take students through these four types of argument, from the simpler categorical proposition to the complex proposal, we have a coherent rationale for organizing a course in argument.

Any statement about the nature of things fixed in some moment of time can be cast as what logicians call a categorical proposition (CP), a sentence which places its subject in the category of its predicate. The pure form of a CP is

Subject	*Linking Verb*	*Predicate*
All art	is	an illusion
Caligula	was	a spoiled brat
Ballet dancers	are	really athletes

Statements about the nature of things do not always come in such neat packages, but even a proposition without a linking verb, like "Some dinosaurs cared for their young," is still a CP which could be recast into pure form, "Some dinosaurs were caring parents."

Whenever a CP is the thesis of an argument, it makes certain structural demands. Since supporting a CP is always a matter of showing that the subject belongs in the category of or has the attributes of the predicate, that predicate must be defined whenever its meaning cannot be assumed, and evidence or examples must be given to link the subject up with that predicate. The arguer for a CP, then, works under two constraints: the definition of the predicate must be acceptable to the audience and the evidence or examples about the subject must be convincing and verifiable. We can see these two constraints operating on the arguer constructing support for a CP like "America is a class society." For most audiences, the definition of "class society" cannot be assumed. If our arguer defined a "class society" as one in which people live in different sized towns, he or she could produce plenty of evidence that Americans do indeed live in towns small, medium, and large, but "class society" has been defined in what speakers of English would intuitively recognize as a completely unacceptable way. It may be a vague term, but there are some meanings it cannot have. On the other extreme, the writer could define "class society" more acceptably as "a society structured into clearly defined ranks, from peasantry to nobility," but where could he or she find the non-metaphoric American duke or serf? Obviously, the arguer must construct a definition which is acceptable to its audience while it fits real evidence.

But suppose a student writes a brief argument supporting a CP like "My roommate is generous." He or she will bypass definition and go straight to examples of the roommate's generosity: the lending of money, clothes, shampoo, and time. The student can go right to such evidence because he or she has a clear definition of "generous" in mind and cannot imagine any audience having a different one. Still a definition of "generous," whether or not articulated in the argument, controls the choice of examples. It was not the roommate's behavior which led to the label "generous," but a definition of "generous" which led to the categorization of the behavior. Because we tend to forget the controlling power of definition, we delude ourselves into thinking that the examples come first and lead inductively to the thesis when in fact the process goes the other way.

Once the student understands that definition and specific evidence are the structural requirements of a CP argument, several organizational options become available. The controlling definition can sit at the beginning of the argument, can emerge at the end, or can have its elements dispersed.[4] In this last option, the definition of the predicate is broken down into components, each supported, with appropriate evidence. Take a CP like "Wilkle Collins's *Armadale* is a sensation novel." An arguer for this proposition might specify a multi-part definition of "sensation novel" which would supply the whole structure of the paper: "a sensation novel is characterized by its ominous setting, grotesque characters, suspenseful plot, and concern with the occult." Each of the elements from this definition becomes the predicate of its own CP (again requiring definition where necessary) and the topic sentence of its own paragraph, e.g. "*Armadale* has grotesque characters," "Collins dabbles in the occult in *Armadale*."

Once students have learned the fundamentals of the CP argument, they have the tools to support a comparison or a contrast as well. An arguer for a single comparison, "Kissinger is like Metternich," for instance, find one or more traits that the two subjects have in common. "Both Kissinger and Metternich had no chauvinistic pride." This is simply a CP with a compound subject which can be divided into two simple CPs ("Kissinger had no chauvinistic pride," "Metternich had no chauvinistic pride"), each supported, as much as the audience requires, by definition and evidence.

A second type of proposition needs quite a different kind of argument. An assertion of cause and effect adds the dimension of time and is therefore not supported with definition but with another kind of ruling assumption, that of *agency,* a basic belief about what can cause what. Just as users of the same language share a set of definitions, so do people in the same culture share many causal assumptions. We have a commonsense understanding, for instance, of such natural agencies as light, heat and gravity, as well as many accepted human agencies whose operation we believe in as readily as we believe in the operation of physical law. Philosophers, psychologists, anthropologists and social scientists debate about what to call these agencies—motives, instincts, or learned patterns of behavior. But we recognize a believable appeal to the way human nature works, just as we recognize an appeal to the way physical nature works; we no more accept happiness as a motive for murder than we would accept the power of rocks to fly.

Definition and agency, then, are the warrants (to use Toulmin's term) behind the two basic kinds of arguments.[5] If we make a claim about the nature of things (a CP), we rely on an assumption about the nature of things, a definition. If we make a claim about causal relations, we rely on an assumption about what can cause what, an agency. And whether or not we articulate agency in a causal argument depends largely on audience. For example, if we argue that a significant cause of teenage vandalism is violence on TV, the agency between these two is imitation. Since most audiences will readily accept imitation as a human motive, we would not have to stop and argue for it. But if we claimed that wearing a mouth plate can improve athletic performance *(Sports Illustrated,* 2 June 1980), we will certainly have to explain agency. (The article did.)

Students have two problems with causal argument. First, they need help thinking up the possible causes of an event. Students tend to overlook the complex interaction of factors, conditions, and influences that yield an effect; they will seize on one cause without understanding how that cause works in connection with others. We have to teach them to think backwards along the paths of known causal agencies, and we can help them do this by introducing the existing terminology of causality. Causes can be identified as necessary and sufficient, as remote and proximate, or as conditions and influences acted on by a precipitating cause. Or sometimes any linear model of causality is a falsification and we have to look at causes and effects as reciprocal, as acting on each other; inflation urges pay raises and higher wages fuel inflation. And, oddly enough, students have to consider what was missing when they think about causes, for an event can take place because a blocking cause was absent. Finally, whenever people are involved in a consideration of causes, the question of responsibility arises. We look for whoever acted or failed to act, or at the person in charge, as causes (usually with the ribbon of praise or the stigma of blame in our hands). In the aftermath of the Three Mile Island reactor breakdown, for instance, the operators in the control room, the engineers who designed the reactor, and even the Nuclear Regulatory Commission officials whose safety regulations controlled its operation were all considered in varying degrees as causes of the accident. Students who are familiar with these possible frames or sets of causes, from necessary cause to responsible cause, can put together models of how causes interacted to bring about the effect they are interested in.

Convincing an audience that a particular cause did in fact operate is the second problem students need help with. The writer of a causal argument can choose from several tactics for presenting evidence that two events are connected as cause and effect. A remote cause, for instance, can be linked to an effect by a chain of causes. NASA provides us with a good example of this technique in their argument claiming that sunspots caused Skylab's fall. Sunspots are storms on the sun which hurl streams of electromagnetic particles into space; these streams, the solar wind, heat up the earth's outer atmosphere. The heated atmosphere expands into Skylab's orbit, increasing the drag on the craft; the craft therefore slows down and falls. Identifying such a chain of causes in effect replaces an implausible leap from cause to effect, a leap an audience is not prepared to take, with a series of small steps they are willing to follow.

Although proximity in time is by itself insufficient evidence of a causal relationship (indeed this is the *post hoc* fallacy), nevertheless, in the presence of plausible agency, time sequence is another tactic for supporting a causal assertion. So is causal analogy, a parallel case of cause and effect; we believe for instance that saccharin or red dye no. 2 causes cancer in humans because it causes cancer in animals. And in the case of a causal generalization such as "Jogging increases self-confidence," a series of individual cases, so long as agency is plausible (and in this instance a definition of self-confidence established), will lend support.

John Stuart Mill's four methods for discovering causes are also powerful aids to invention in causal argument. If the student can find at least two significantly parallel cases, one in which an effect occurred and one in which it didn't, the *single difference* between them can be convincingly nominated as a cause. Or if the same effect occurs several times, any *common factor* in the antecedent events is possibly a cause; this was the method of the health officials searching for the cause of Legionnaire's disease. Another method, that of *concomitant variation,* is the favorite of the social scientist who looks for influences and contributing factors; when two trends vary proportionately, when the hours of TV watching increase over a decade as SAT scores decline, a causal relationship is suggested, especially when a plausible agency can be constructed between the two. Mill's fourth method, *elimination,* is the ruling-out of all but one possible sufficient cause. It is the favorite of Sherlock Holmes and other detectives faced with a limited number of possible causes.

The student who uses one of Mill's methods can construct a convincing causal argument by repeating the process in writing. Take our sample proposition, "Violence on TV encourages teenage vandalism." Support may come from concomitant variation if we can document an increase in TV violence and a corresponding increase in vandalism perpetrated by teenagers. (The propositions that teenage vandalism exists and has increased along with TV violence can be supported with CP arguments, which the student knows by now require careful definition. What, for instance, precisely constitutes "violence" on TV?) And since this causal claim is a generalization, it could also be supported by citing specific acts of violence clearly inspired by similar acts on TV.

Arguments for CPs and causal statements are the two basic types. Once students have learned to construct these simpler arguments they can combine them into the more complex arguments required for evaluations and proposals. An evaluation is a proposition which makes a value judgment: e.g. "The San Diego Padres are a bad team," "*Jane Eyre* is a great novel," "The open classroom is a poor learning environment." We have to encourage our students to see such propositions as genuinely arguable, as claims which an audience can be convinced of and not merely as occasions for the expression of personal taste. The key is, once again, finding and, when necessary, articulating and defending the sharable assumptions or criteria on which the evaluation is made. Just as the CP argument rests on definition and the causal on agency, so do all evaluations rest ultimately on criteria or assumptions of value.

Students can be taught to construct evaluations by first learning to distinguish the various subjects of evaluations. We evaluate objects both natural and man-made, including the practical and the aesthetic. We also judge people, both in roles and as whole human beings, and we evaluate actions, events, policies, decisions and even abstractions such as lifestyles and institutions which are made up of people, things and actions. Constructing a good evaluation argument is a matter of finding acceptable criteria appropriate to the subject. Our students are already familiar with the typical standards behind the "consumer" evaluations of practical objects. They are far less familiar with the formal criteria used or implied in aesthetic judgments. Most challenging of all are the evaluations of people, actions, and events which require the application of ethical criteria. Students must be encouraged to see that arguing about ethics is not the exclusive province of religion or law, but that we all have beliefs about what is right, proper, or of value which an arguer can appeal to in an evaluation.

In form, an evaluation proposition looks exactly like a CP and, overall, the argument is carried on like a CP argument. Our example above places *Jane Eyre* in the class "great novel." An arguer for this proposition must construct a plausible "definition" or set of criteria for "great novel" which fits the evidence from the book. But the criteria or standard of an evaluation can easily include good or bad consequences as well as qualities, and thus evaluations often require causal arguments showing that the subject does indeed produce this or that effect. If we want to argue, for example, that it was right to bring the Shah to the U.S. for medical treatment, we could do so by classifying that decision as an humanitarian one in a CP argument; or we could argue that the decision was wrong by exploring its consequences in a causal argument. (Of course, whether a consequence can be labeled good or bad gets us right back to ethical assumptions which must be either appealed to or defended, depending on one's audience. Evaluations can lead us into an infinite regress unless we stop eventually on an appeal to shared values.)

The fourth and final type of proposition is the proposal, the call to action. The specific proposal which recommends an exact course of action requires a special combination of smaller CP and causal arguments. We can imagine this argument's structure as something like an hour glass, preliminary arguments funneling in from the top, proposal statement at the neck, and supporting arguments expanding to the base.

We can see how that structure works if we imagine ourselves carrying through an argument for a proposal such as, "Wolves should be reestablished in the forests of northern Pennsylvania and a stiff fine levied for killing them." No one will feel a desire to take action on this proposal unless first convinced that some problem exists which needs this solution; that is the work of the preliminary arguments. An opening CP argument establishes the existence of a situation, in this case the absence or extreme rarity of wolves in certain areas. But an audience may agree that a situation exists yet not perceive it as a problem; it may take a further causal argument to trace the bad consequences (i.e. deer herds are out of control) or show the ethical wrongness of the situation (i.e. a species has been removed from its rightful habitat). These opening parts amount to a negative evaluation. Another preliminary step might be a causal argument singling out the dominant reason for the problem, for ideally the proposal should remove or block this cause or causes, rather than simply patch up the effect alone. If wolves have become nearly extinct in northern Pennsylvania because of unrestricted hunting, then a ban on hunting wolves ought to take care of that.

After the specific proposal is disclosed, it can be supported with another series of CP and causal arguments. The proposal will lead to good consequences (the causal: deer population will be controlled), and it will be ethically right (CP: the balance of nature will be as it ought to be). And most important, the proposal is feasible; the time, money, and people are available (CP), and the steps to its achievement are all planned out (causal).

Just how much of this full proposal outline is actually needed for the writer to make a convincing recommendation depends entirely on audience and situation. A problem may be so pressing that preliminary arguments can be dispensed with entirely; after the last flood, the people of Johnstown did not have to be convinced they had a problem. And not every call to action requires a full proposal argument. One which ends with an unspecified plea, "We really ought to do something about this," is actually a negative evaluation. Such a vague call to awareness is really a coda resting on the widely-held assumption that if something is wrong it ought to be corrected.

In addition to dealing with the four types of arguments we have described, any course in argument must treat the two elements common to all arguments: accommodation and refutation. Consideration of audience (accommodation) and consideration of potential or actual opposition (refutation) inform all argument, affecting invention, arrangement, and style. Where do they sensibly come in a course? The only answer is first, last, and all the way through, worked into every discussion of every type of argument.

Once students have learned the necessary structures of CP and causal arguments and learned how these types combine in support of evaluations and proposals, they have not only the help they need for constructing arguments but tools for the critical analysis of argumentative discourse as well. They can recognize what type of proposition an argument is trying to support, identify the necessary structural elements both explicit and implied and, considering the argument's audience, determine whether all was skillfully done. We might illustrate how this process works by taking a brief look at James Madison's *Federalist* No. 10, reprinted in Corbett's *Classical Rhetoric for the Modern Student* and followed by a careful analysis of its logical elements and the arguments from the sources (2nd edition, New York: Oxford University Press, 1971, pp. 239–256). Madison's argument is an all but perfectly symmetrical full proposal with preliminary arguments (pars. 1–13), explicit proposal (par. 14), and supporting arguments (pars. 15–23). Given his audience and purpose, Madison needs no lengthy demonstration of the existence of a problem; he has only to appeal to "the evidence of known facts." He turns quickly, therefore, to a causal analysis of the problem and finds it in "faction," rooted in the corrupt nature of man. The ethical problem facing his audience is that of preserving two self-evident goods, the control of faction and some form of popular government. The solution which will bridle the effects (for the causes, as he cogently argues, are untouchable) is the federal union, which Madison then goes on to support by tracing the good consequences that will flow from it. Its feasibility has of course been argued elsewhere. Such an analysis is possible to the student who recognizes types of arguments and can thus identify the necessary structural elements in a given argument and even come to a satisfying understanding of why they are where they are.

The approach to argument we have outlined, then, makes it possible to teach argument coherently while avoiding some of the pitfalls of existing approaches. We can avoid extensive and unnecessary diversions into formal logic while keeping to the principles of sound reasoning. And the overall method of building from simple, basic types of argument to types requiring a combination of steps gives the student transferable structures which are suitable for any subject but are not so automatic as to preclude the student from doing his or her own thinking.

Notes

1. Chaim Perelman and L. Olbrechts-Tyteca, *The New Rhetoric: A Treatise on Argument* (Notre Dame, IN: University of Notre Dame Press, 1969), pp. 1–4; Stephen Toulmin, *The Uses of Argument* (Cambridge, England: Cambridge University Press, 1958), p. 146.
2. Irving M. Copi, *Introduction to Logic*, 5th ed. (New York: Macmillan, 1978), pp. 23–26.
3. Karl Popper, *Conjectures and Refutations: The Growth of Scientific Knowledge* (New York: Harper & Row, 1963), pp. 46–47.
4. Here perhaps is the only legitimate use of the terms "inductive" and "deductive" in written argument. They can be used to describe the organization of arguments, the deductive setting out the thesis at the beginning and the inductive disclosing it at the end.
5. Stephen Toulmin, finding the syllogism ambiguous, created a new pattern for analyzing arguments. In his terminology, a "claim" is supported by "data" linked to the claim by a "warrant." Warrants are "inference licenses," "the general hypothetical statements which can act as bridges between the data and the claim" (Toulmin, p. 98). Warrants often require backing themselves. They are not always

interchangeable with the minor premise of a syllogism, which may be either a warrant or its backing.

General Strategies of Argument

Richard Fulkerson

Richard Fulkerson, director of English Graduate Studies at Texas A & M University-Commerce, has been teaching and writing about argument for almost 30 years. His articles and his 1996 book, Teaching the Argument in Writing, *from which this selection is taken, have developed out of his study and teaching of argument, not only in composition but also in debate and logic, as well as a lifetime of arguing with friends and family. Fulkerson's teaching suggestions here combine and adapt principles of argumentation from classical rhetoric, Stephen Toulmin, and contemporary theories in composition and informal logic and reflect what has worked in his classrooms.*

In some texts on nonformal logic, the acronym GASCAP is used to help students remember six types of argument strategies:

G—Argument for a *G*eneralization
A—Argument from *A*nalogy
S—Argument from *S*ign
C—*C*ausal Argument
A—Argument from *A*uthority
P—Argument from *P*rinciple

These are major types of relationships possible between premises and claims in single argumentative steps (kernel arguments). But each can be used in larger patterns, either as sub-arguments or as broad frames; each can be diagramed (see Appendix A); each can be analyzed using the Toulmin model; each can be used both legitimately and fallaciously. In traditional logic, all are nondeductive arguments (with the possible exception of the argument from principle), because in each type, when well done, the claim follows only probably from the premises.

In a sense, the six GASCAP strategies play roles similar to what compositionists call *modes* of development—such as definition, comparison, and example. And the argument strategies bear the same relationship to the aims of argument that modes do to aims of discourse. The argument strategies, like the modes, are not ends in themselves but methods of achieving your argumentative end. Sometimes a single strategy is sufficient to make an argument, but more commonly (again, like the discourse modes), they work in combination. Nevertheless, for

---

students in introductory logic classes, the strategies are often taught separately; partly to provide help in analyzing arguments and, more important, for help in evaluation, since each of the six has its own evaluative norms.

Several of these types of arguments, the ones I judge most important to (or the most complicated for) students, will be treated at more length in Chapter 6, but it will be just as well to give an overview of all six here. If each is analyzed as a full argument, then they can all be put into the basic Toulmin formula with a general and usually unstated warranting premise that justifies the entire strategy.

1. Argument for a Generalization

WARRANT:	Whatever is true of a well-chosen sample will be true of the population it was selected from.
DATA:	The sample has trait X, and the sample is chosen or constructed in such a way as to be typical.
CLAIM:	Therefore, the larger group also has trait X.

Examples: All sorts of polls. Television Nielsen ratings. Generalizations about universities based on short visits, or about people based on first meetings, or about groups (such as student writers) based on sampling or case studies. Even reading an essay as a measure of writing skill involves generalizing from the document.

Uses: Generalizing may well be the most common form of reasoning. Whenever we meet people, we get a "sample" of their behavior and decide what we think about them. When we go to a restaurant, or leaf through a book, or listen to a politician for an hour, we are getting a sample. Quality control checks in industry involve sampling the product at intervals and generalizing to the whole. A scientific experiment is a sample of the behavior of elements of the universe; since we assume a uniformity in nature, a small sample (one experiment) is, in theory, logically sufficient.

Evaluation: Essentially by the STAR system. For a generalization to be reliable, we need a *S*ufficient number of *T*ypical, *A*ccurate, and *R*elevant instances. The poorer the sample, the more the claim needs to be qualified ("certainly," "very likely," "probably," "maybe," "possibly"). In professional polls, the criteria given in Ralph Johnson's "Poll-ution" are important, especially the margin of error.

2. Argument from Analogy

WARRANT:	Two situations that are alike in most observable ways will tend to be alike in other ways also.
DATA:	Facts about the observed similarities between the two cases.
CLAIM:	Therefore, probably, they are also alike in some further feature.

Example: Many states with financial problems have adopted state lotteries. And the lotteries seem to raise a significant amount of money, without causing severe problems. Also, they are completely voluntary. Therefore, it's a good idea for Texas to adopt a lottery. (This argument was actually accepted by the citizens of Texas during the course of my writing this monograph. Note that the argument from analogy does not mean an argument by means of a metaphoric comparison. Logical analogies involve literally similar situations, which act as precedents for the situation at issue.)

Uses: Argument from analogy is used in law (Perelman and Olbrechts-Tyteca's "rule of justice" is that essentially similar cases must be treated in essentially similar ways; see *The New Rhetoric* 218–20), where precedent is crucial. Analogy is also used in deciding future policies (governmental, educational, institutional, etc.) if similar situations can be found in which the same policy is used somewhere else at present or was in the past. In science, analogy is used as a method of generating hypotheses to be tested but isn't a method of proof.

Evaluation: An analogy is made stronger by a greater number of *relevant* similarities, and it is weakened by dissimilarities that seem relevant to the claim. Of course, deciding what makes a similarity relevant or how seriously a dissimilarity weakens an analogy are interpretive activities based on experience, insight, and intuition; they are not algorithmic, or even rule governed.

3. Argument from Sign

WARRANT:	X can be taken as a sign that Y (which is not directly observable for some reason) is the case.
DATA:	X (the sign) is the case.
CLAIM:	Therefore, Y is probably true.

Example #1: When we stopped the driver, we had seen his car weaving from side to side on the highway. He was unable to walk a straight line, and he failed a Breathalyzer™ test. From these signs we concluded that he was legally intoxicated.

Example #2: We have a letter from a prospective job applicant which opens, "Dear Sir." He also uses the word "he" to refer to an assistant he hopes to hire. And he says that he "always believe(s) in hiring the best man for the job." Such use of male pronouns is sexist language, a sign that he is not really in favor of marketplace equality for women.

Uses: We use argument by sign whenever the matter at issue is a question of fact but not directly observable. Usually, the warrant for an argument from sign is based on prior reasoning by generalization: "In our past sample, X has been a sign of Y, so we conclude that it generally is such a sign, and therefore that it is a sign of Y in this case." A lie detector takes certain bodily signs as proof that one is lying. A doctor looks for typical signs of a disease to begin her diagnosis. An expert tracker looks for signs of the beasts he is after. Body language is often taken to be a sign that can be read by someone with experience. Other people believe that handwriting is such a sign. We take high ACT and SAT scores as signs that a student will do well in college. Scientists use signs of phenomena that can't be observed directly, such as the spectrum of light coming from a distant star in order to infer what elements are in the star. English scholars working in cultural studies use television, film, advertising, literature, and pop-culture phenomena as signs of our basic belief systems or ideologies. (Note: In everyday language, we might call this *reasoning by clues.)*

Evaluation: Judging the argument depends purely on how strong the relationship is between the overt sign (the clue) and the inferred claim. That is, is it always true that a fever indicates a virus? If it were, this would be an *infallible* sign; but since it is possible to have a fever and not a virus, it is actually a *fallible* sign (the distinction goes back to Aristotle). Does rough idling and dying at intersections always show a car to have carburetor problem? Does everyone who fails a breath analysis have to be drunk? Will a student who scores high on the Daly Test of Writing Apprehension actually have trouble turning in high-quality writing on time? Criticizing such an argument usually involves explaining other ways in which the same signs can be produced and thus showing that they are fallible.

Often the STAR system can also be used here. Are there a sufficient number of relevant signs? Is the situation typical of the times the relationship has held in the past? Is the sign actually present? How relevant is that sign to the claim?

4. Causal Argument

WARRANT: If condition X and condition Y nearly always appear together, then they are causally related. (But we don't yet know the exact nature of the relation—maybe both are the result of some other factor.)

DATA: In many instances X and Y have appeared together and X has come first.

CLAIM: X causes Y, unless (rebuttal condition) there is some third common factor.

Example: I had been waking up with a painful headache off and on for several weeks. I began to examine my behavior. I soon found that each night that I read for several hours before going to sleep, I woke up with a headache. But on other nights, when I watched TV, or cleaned the garage, or played ball, I didn't have a headache. I concluded that my morning headaches were probably being caused by some sort of eyestrain the night before.

Uses: Causal reasoning is probably the most complex of the various forms. Yet it is absolutely necessary. If we want to know how to solve a disease, we need to know its cause. If we want to get a car to run, we have to know what is causing it not to. If we want to know how to teach students, we have to find out what effects various classroom practices have on them. If we want to grow crops, if we want to help the economy, if we want to predict the weather, etc. Scientists are concerned with determining the causal laws of our universe, such as those governing combustion, chemical reactions, plant growth, and gravitational attraction.

Evaluation: The big danger is reasoning *post hoc, ergo propter hoc* (Latin for "after the fact, therefore because of the fact"). If after watching pornographic films in a laboratory, 55 percent of college males said they would commit rape if they were sure they would not be caught, one might think the pornography caused the response. But we would also have to know what percentage of college males would say yes to the question without having watched any pornography. If the other percentage is 55 percent, then no causal relationship is shown. On the other hand, if only 25 percent of the "control" group answers yes, then by Mill's methods of agreement *and* difference (discussed in more detail in Chapter 6), some sort of causal connection has been shown. (But if the films the men watched also contained violence, then maybe it was the violence rather than the pornography that led to their answers.)

Other poor reasoning about causation includes claiming a partial cause is *the* cause, or the "real" cause ("the real causes of crime in our culture are poverty and ignorance"); failing to distinguish between proximate causes and distant causes, or necessary and sufficient causes; or failing to realize that both phenomena are actually caused by a third. There is a well-known and strong correlation between ice-cream sales and crime rates: they go up and down together. But it isn't that ice cream causes crime—both are influenced by weather.

Again, the STAR system is relevant. If any sort of study has been done, then sufficient, typical, accurate, relevant information must have been gathered. If no study has been done, the reasoning is largely guesswork and should be carefully qualified with *maybe* or *possibly.*

In the hard sciences, some cause-and-effect connections are absolute and one-to-one. If you heat a metal rod and do not increase the pressure on it, it will expand. If you deprive a fire of oxygen, the fire will cease. But outside the laboratory, things are rarely that simple. Will an abused child always become an abusive parent? Will trying marijuana cause you to become an addict? (Does drinking milk lead to using drugs? After all, nearly every drug user started with milk.) Will arguing against a professor cause you to get a poor grade? Answer: it all depends. On what, we aren't sure.

One of the best examples in modern life concerns the causal link between cigarette smoking and lung cancer. It isn't an absolute one-to-one relationship, so the cigarette companies still contend that no causal connection has been "proved." But the evidence is so strong now that most informed people accept the connection, granting the claim that using tobacco significantly increases one's chances of developing lung cancer, just as drinking increases one's chances of having a wreck, and poor diet and overwork increase one's chances of becoming ill.

5. Argument from Authority

WARRANT:	Whatever the expert says about X is probably correct.
BACKING:	The expert has authoritative credentials on that subject.
DATA:	The expert says that Y is the case.
CLAIM:	Therefore, Y is true.

Example: My doctor says that I am suffering from bursitis, not a strained muscle. So I have bursitis (and should treat it accordingly).

Uses: Since we live in a complex world, it is impossible to know everything we need to know in making decisions. So when we have to decide many issues that we lack adequate personal knowledge of, we rely on experts: doctors, accountants, auto mechanics, writing teachers, economists.

Evaluation: The major question is whether X is a genuine authority (whatever that means) on the issue in question. Then, is it the sort of issue that all authorities are likely to agree on? If not, use STAR. Do a sufficient number of typical authorities, who are accurately cited and who have relevant credentials, all agree? Are there equally important authorities who say otherwise? If the weight of authoritative opinion is nearly all on one side, that side is *probably* correct. But then, at one time most authorities were sure the world was flat and that Galileo was wrong about planetary motion.

6. Argument from Principle

WARRANT:	Principle X is generally regarded as true or proper.
DATA:	This is the sort of situation to which that principle applies.
CLAIM:	X is the case here.

Example #1: Since, in the U.S., we generally believe in "equality of opportunity," it is wrong to give college scholarships to high school debaters because not all students had the opportunity to be in debate. (Someone arguing for such scholarships would be likely to reason by analogy and say that debaters are, for this purpose, similar to athletes or band members who receive scholarships.)

Example #2: Since we generally believe in the right to privacy, I am not going to answer that question about my sex life as part of my election campaign.

Uses: Whenever we have to make value judgments, some general principle has been applied. Moreover, we often apply a previously identified causal connection in a predictive fashion: "Harsh criticisms of their writing generally turn students off, so if you really tell Randy that this essay is 'an absolute disaster,' he will probably just give up." The Toulmin model itself analyzes all arguments as forms of argument from principle, since the warrant is a statement of principle that applies to the data.

Evaluation: First, is the principle, in fact, generally accepted? Second, does it apply to the sort of situation in question? Third, are there commonly agreed on exceptions (such as one can take a human life if it is in self-defense)? Fourth, do other general principles lead to a different claim? Fifth, are the practical consequences of following the principle so obviously undesirable that we wish to alter the principle in the present case? Consider the principle that a child should live with its biological parents rather than its adoptive parents if the biological parents desire it. (We will return to this sort of argument in Chapter 7, under "claims of value.")

To what extent any of this material should be taught in a composition class is problematic. Certainly, it would be inappropriate to teach a given argument procedure and then assign students to write a paper illustrating it. That is a major confusion of ends and means. On the other hand, a student who understands the principles above is likely to be a better analytic reader of academic and other discourse, which is both of general value and helpful in using other texts in one's writing. Moreover, a student who is familiar with these principles may well be able to use them as criteria for revision within the context of an extended paper that joins several different types of argument, a topic I will discuss further in the next four chapters. This is another area in which classroom research is needed.

The Main Types of Claims: Lessons from Classical Rhetoric

Richard Fulkerson

Richard Fulkerson is a professor of English and the director of English Graduate Studies at Texas A&M University-Commerce. "The Main Types of Claims: Lessons from Classical Rhetoric" describes stasis theory, a heuristic and classification system from classical rhetoric to help speakers determine the main question at issue for an argument. After describing several modern adaptations of stasis theory, Fulkerson explains his own modifications for teaching argumentative writing and the thesis statement. This selection immediately follows "General Strategies of Argument" in Fulkerson's book, Teaching the Argument in Writing.

In classical Greek and Roman rhetoric, the types of discourse were three: forensic (also called judicial), epideictic, and deliberative. Forensic discourse dealt with past events and the subjects of guilt or innocence; it was the argument of the courtroom. Epideictic dealt with the present and was largely the argument of the legislative process, focusing on consequences and expediency.

Within forensic rhetoric, *stasis,* or *status,* theory arose. If a person was charged with a crime, a number of different defenses could be used, and if he or she was to be found guilty of the crime, the prosecuting rhetor would have to show that three different questions could be answered in the affirmative.[1]

1. Did the accused commit the acts in question? A question of fact.
2. Do the acts in question constitute the crime charged? A question of definition.
3. Was the act such that no unique circumstances morally justified its commission? A question of values.

These questions are still relevant in a court, but if we join them with deliberative rhetoric, about what course of action should be followed, they can constitute the basis for a modern rhetorical system of classifying argumentative discourses, a system that is complete, useful, sequential, and elegant.

Stasis theory, unlike the induction/deduction pairing and unlike the GASCAP taxonomy, classifies arguments purely on the basis of what sort of assertion about reality is made in the major claim. Thus, it applies to full or extended arguments rather than to micro-arguments. In order to classify an argument as being within a stasis, all a reader has to do is locate the major claim and identity its type. Stasis theory is thus a classification of arguments by their purposes rather than by their strategies.

Several modern scholars have presented variations of classical stasis theory, and my own presentation—while somewhat different from any of them—owes much to their work. In a valuable rhetoric/reader in 1957, Harold Graves and Bernard Oldsey presented one version of modern stasis theory, although they did not refer to its classical origins. They stressed that each piece of writing could be thought of as answering a question and that the sequence of questions is

1. Questions of fact
2. Questions of definition
3. Questions of probability
4. Questions of value
5. Questions of policy

This sequence is very close to the classical progression, if we merge questions of fact with questions of probability. Whether the accused committed the acts is in one sense a question of fact: either the accused did or did not. But since we probably cannot know with certainty, it becomes—for argumentative purposes—a question of the likelihood or probability that the accused committed the acts in question.

More recently, Caroline Eckhardt and David Stewart have argued for a very similar "Functional Taxonomy of Composition." They note that our more common ways of classifying types of writing, either the Bainian categories of description, narration, exposition, and argumentation, or the common division into modes such as illustration, comparison-contrast, details, etc., stress *means* in discourse rather than ends. They propose that a more useful taxonomy can be built around the types of purposes one can have in writing. They thus divide essays into

1. Definition
2. Substantiation
3. Evaluation
4. Recommendation

Again we see the reformulation of classical rhetoric's stasis theory. In fact, the four can easily be applied directly to judicial discourse. Definition asks what are the components of the crime in question, say battery. Substantiation asks whether the accused probably (beyond a reasonable doubt in American jurisprudence) committed the acts. Evaluation asks whether she was somehow justified in her actions. And recommendation asks what should be done with her.

Eckhardt and Stewart, however, stress that these issues are not limited to judicial questions, but actually provide a comprehensive classification of the types of claims one can argue for. We can easily illustrate from almost any general topic, for example, affirmative action:

1. *Question of definition:* What is affirmative action, and how does it differ from and relate to equal employment opportunity?

2. *Question of substantiation:* Have colleges in the past five years made significant improvements in the hiring of minority faculty members?

3. *Question of evaluation:* Is reverse discrimination in hiring (or admission) policies justified by desires to encourage diversity in faculties and student bodies? Can nonminority faculty effectively teach courses in ethnic issues?

4. *Question of recommendation:* What sort of requirements and penalties should be placed on university athletic programs in order to achieve gender equity?

Eckhardt and Stewart stress that these are sequentially progressive, meaning that to answer a question of substantiation, you have to establish definitions. To evaluate, you will need both to define and substantiate. And to recommend that something be done, you must define, then substantiate, then evaluate the situation as less than acceptable, and then propose the recommendation to remedy the substantiated problem. That progression provides a sensible cumulative way to organize a course in argumentative writing, unlike taxonomies built on modes, which have no natural order and always turn out to be inherently but erratically overlapping.

Finally, Jeanne Fahnestock and Marie Secor, in several articles and a thoughtful textbook, have proposed a variation of the taxonomy. For them the types of thesis claims are

1. Categorical propositions ("X is Y")
2. Causal propositions ("X causes or results from Y")
3. Evaluative propositions ("X is Y" where Y is an evaluative category)
4. Proposals (which answer: "What should we do about X?")

Fahnestock and Secor give a good illustration of how the various stases showed up in the trial that grew out of the government investigation known as Abscam:

> The first collision of charge and denial occurred at the stasis of fact: "You took the money"/"I did not take the money." Here the preponderance of evidence in the form of video tapes [*sic*] moved the issue to the stasis of definition: "You took a bribe"/"No, I took evidence for an investigation." As the bargaining proceeded, the defendants lost this issue, so the ground shifted to the third stasis of quality, where we can characterize the prosecution as maintaining: "You deserve censure for an act particularly reprehensible for a public official," and the defense mitigating this evaluation of the crime by answering: "I do not deserve such severe censure

> because I did not do what those who bribed me asked me to do." The final plea in the fourth stasis turns to the nature of the legal case itself and the jurisdiction of the court, the defense claiming entrapment and appealing to a higher court. Whether or not the investigation constituted entrapment is, of course, a question that takes us down to the stasis of definition again, and the two sides will continue to chase one another up and down the stases and in and out of the courts until the appeal process is exhausted. ("Toward a Modern Version of Stasis" 218)

Several newer argumentation texts also make extensive use of stasis theory, such as Ramage and Bean's *Writing Arguments*; Gage's *The Shape of Reason*; and Rottenberg's *Elements of Argument*.

These various schemes seem incredibly useful to me because they are non-overlapping and sequentially progressive, and as I hope to demonstrate in this and the next three chapters, they can serve as generative heuristics to help students create the arguments needed in a paper. Once students realize what sorts of theses they are attempting to support, then they also know a series of types of subordinate arguments which that sort of thesis requires in order to make a case that will persuade a critical reader. And these sub-arguments become heuristic questions causing the student to generate relevant information.

I'm going to modify the schemes to say that we need only three categories of thesis statement:

1. Substantiation—including
   - any needed definitions;
   - questions of fact if the facts are in doubt;
   - all categorical and comparative claims that do not involve value judgments (such as, "There are three and only three types of thesis statements that one can argue"); and
   - all causal statements that do not involve value judgments (such as, "The first-year class is getting smaller each year because of the rise of several new junior colleges in the region").

2. Evaluation—these include all claims asserting that something is good/bad, right/wrong, desirable/undesirable, valuable/worthless, moral/ immoral, effective/ineffective. Such questions make up a large division of philosophy sometimes known as *axiology* (which includes both ethics and aesthetics).

3. Recommendation—these include all theses claiming that something should be done. Such claims are nearly always signaled by the word "should" or some synonym such as "ought" or "must."

In law and competitive debate, the term *prima facie* is used to describe an argumentative presentation that deals with all of the essential features demanded by the type of proposition being argued. A prima facie case is not necessarily a convincing one, but at least on first examination it is not obviously defective. Let me illustrate with a somewhat oversimplified example from American legal practice. In a civil court (as opposed to a criminal court) it is possible for one person to sue another for damages resulting from an assault. Technically, "assault" means "a harmful or offensive offer to touch another person which causes the other to fear such a touching is imminent. In addition, the touching must be unprivileged, unconsented, and not an act of self-defense" (adapted from Brand and White 178; also, see Josephson 10–11). In order for a plaintiff to recover damages for an assault, the plaintiff's lawyer must show that each of those conditions held, merely in order to present a prima facie case. If any feature of the case is lacking, the defense may move for dismissal, and the judge may throw the case out, the defense never needing to present any counterarguments. This is not to say that just because a prima facie case has been presented, the plaintiff will necessarily win the argument, but if the case presented is not prima facie, the plaintiff will necessarily lose.

I will maintain that each of the three types of stasis claims—substantiation, evaluation, recommendation—imposes different demands on the arguer for presenting a prima facie case. If students learn what the different requirements are, then these requirements can serve both as heuristics for discovering relevant support and as revision checklists for criticizing drafts. (They can also become critical-thinking probes for reading an argumentative text thoughtfully.)

A closing lesson from classical rhetoric: it became traditional to talk about the various parts of the classical oration, parts which supposedly existed whether the discourse was forensic, epideictic, or deliberative. Classical theorists disagreed over how many parts there were and about how rigid the form was, but a typical list includes

Exordium—an introduction attracting the audience
Narration—how the topic has come up at the moment; background to the issue
Proposition—the claim to be argued for
Confirmation—the premises upon which the claim rests
Refutation—criticism of the arguments that would be advanced by someone arguing the opposing view
Peroration—a moving conclusion

The classical orators recognized that the sorts of propositions that are worth arguing are almost never certain but nearly always contingent. Hence, the confirming arguments would never be absolutely solid, and premises would always be available to argue one or more opposing views. Thus, they explicitly built into their arguments a consideration of the opposition voices. That is an exceptionally wise strategy, one that too few of our students are able or willing to use. In fact, when I first discuss with students the need to include refutation, the typical reaction, even if the paper is based on research, is, "'Why would I want to include arguments that weaken my own position?" That means my students are often willing to ignore research that conflicts with their claims and to assume that the reader will not know of it and thus will be convinced. They seem to think of argumentation and research as looking for material that supports conclusions they already believe rather than as a dialectical attempt to find answers. Such a view demeans argumentation.

I argue that such behavior is unethical. But assuming they are not likely to be persuaded by ethical principles, I further assert that ignoring the arguments against one's position is less persuasive than addressing them explicitly, conceding those one must (and raising ethos while doing it), and refuting the others (also enhancing ethos).

In a competitive debate (and other triadic situations), refutation is not part of a prima facie case because an opponent is expected to present the counterarguments, which can then be dealt with in later speeches. The same situation exists in the courtroom, where the prosecuting attorney is not expected to bring up defense arguments, since the defense attorney is charged with that task. Both of these rhetorical situations involve triadic communication in which side A deals with side B for the benefit of audience C. Here, the individual arguments presented by both (or several) sides are parts of the overall argumentation. But writing is usually not triadic. It is dyadic communication in which writer A has to address reader B and convince B of the soundness of A's position without immediate feedback from B or from opponents.[2]

I suggest that in all dyadic argumentation, no matter which stasis is involved, refutation of likely opposing arguments (especially those likely to come up in the mind of the reader) should be considered a part of the prima facie case.

Moreover, the goal of "refutation" should not be just to bring up opposing arguments in order to show that they are false. On complex issues, the opposition will surely have some solid arguments, that is, arguments that cannot be refuted. It is a good arguer's job to show that these arguments are understood and credited, but that they need not lead to rejecting the arguer's claim. Good reasons exist on both (or several) sides of questions worth arguing. And the purpose of argumentation in a free society or within a research field is to reach the best conclusion possible at the time.

Notes

1. Actually, in classical rhetoric there was a fourth stasis, which might be called a *stasis of venue*. It asked the technical question of whether the charge had been properly made and whether the court had jurisdiction. The issue is obviously still relevant in courtroom procedure, but is of little concern to composition teachers.

2. In a larger sense, writing about public issues can be seen as triadic. One arguer makes a contribution to an ongoing dialogue, not so much in hopes of convincing the opponents but to win support from the broader audience. But even in such a situation, where the opponents' voices are not immediately present, it is generally more effective to introduce them into your own argument, taking care to do so fairly.

Works Cited

Brand, Norman, and John O. White. *Legal Writing: The Strategy of Persuasion.* 2nd ed. Boston: St. Martin's, 1988.

Eckhardt, Caroline, and David Stewart. "Towards a Functional Taxonomy of Composition." *College Composition and Communication* 30 (Dec. 1979): 338–42. Rpt. in *The Writing Teacher's Sourcebook.* Ed. Gary Tate and Edward P.J. Corbett. New York: Oxford, 1981. 100–06.

Fahnestock, Jeanne, and Marie Secor. *A Rhetoric of Argument.* 2nd ed. New York: McGraw, 1990.

——. "Teaching Argument: A Theory of Types." *College Composition and Communication* 34 (Feb. 1983): 20–30.

——. "Toward a Modern Version of Stasis." *Oldspeak/Newspeak Rhetorical Transformations.* Ed. Charles W. Kneupper. Arlington, TX: Rhetoric Society of America, 1985. 217–26.

Gage, John T. *The Shape of Reason: Argumentative Writing in College.* 2nd ed. New York: Macmillan, 1991.

Graves, Harold F., and Bernard S. Oldsey. *From Fact to Judgment.* New York: Macmillan, 1957.

Josephson, Barry. *Essential Principles of Torts.* Culver City, CA: Center for Creative Educational Services, 1983.

Mill, John Stuart. *A System of Logic, Ratiocinative and Inductive, Being a Connected View of the Principles of Evidence, and the Methods of Science.* 5th ed. London: Parker, Son, and Bourn, 1862. [See Vol. II, Chapters 8 and 9.]

Perelman, Chaim, and L. Olbrechts-Tyteca. *The New Rhetoric: A Treatise on Argumentation.* Trans. John Wilkinson and Purcell Weaver. Notre Dame, IN: U of Notre Dame P. 1969.

Ramage, John D., and John C. Bean. *Writing Arguments: A Rhetoric with Readings.* 3rd ed. New York: Macmillan, 1995.

Rottenburg, Annette T. *The Elements of Argument: A Text and Reader.* 4th edition. Boston: Bedford, 1994.

Toulmin, Stephen Edelston. *The Uses of Argument.* 1st paperback ed. Cambridgeshire, England: Cambridge UP, 1964.

——. "Logic and the Criticism of Arguments." *The Rhetoric of Western Thought.* 3rd ed. Ed. James L. Golden, Goodwin F. Berquist, and William E. Coleman. Dubuque, IA: Kendall/Hunt, 1983. 391–401.

SELECTED READINGS: ARGUMENTATION

Aristotle. *On Rhetoric: A Theory of Civic Discourse.* Trans. George Kennedy. New York: Oxford UP, 1991.

Corbett, Edward P. J., and Robert J. Connors. *Classical Rhetoric for the Modern Student.* 4th ed. New York: Oxford UP, 1999.

Eckhardt, Caroline D., and David H. Stewart. "Toward a Functional Taxonomy of Composition." *CCC* 30 (1979): 338–42.

Fulkerson, Richard. *Teaching the Argument in Writing.* Urbana, IL: NCTE, 1996.

Lamb, Catherine E. "Beyond Argument in Feminist Composition." *CCC* 42 (1991): 11–24.

Perelman, Chaim. *The Realm of Rhetoric.* Trans. William Kluback. Notre Dame, IN: U of Notre Dame P, 1982.

Perelman, Chaim, and L. Olbrechts-Tyteca. *The New Rhetoric: A Treatise on Argumentation.* Trans. John Wilkinson and Purcell Weaver. Notre Dame, IN: U of Notre Dame P, 1969.

Ramage, John D., and John C. Bean. *Writing Arguments: A Rhetoric with Readings.* 4th ed. New York: Allyn & Bacon, 1998.

Toulmin, Stephen. *The Uses of Argument.* New York: Cambridge UP, 1964.

An Apology for Form; or, Who Took the Form Out of the Process?

Richard M. Coe

Richard M. Coe, who teaches at Simon Fraser University, has written often about form in writing, most notably in Toward a Grammar of Passages, *"If Not to Narrow, Then How to Focus: TwoTechniques for Focusing," and this 1987 article originally published in* College English, *as well as his textbook,* Process, Form, and Substance. *As Coe writes, process-oriented pedagogies arose in opposition to formalist instruction that emphasize outlining, the modes of discourse, and the five-paragraph theme and regard sentences and paragraphs as building blocks for the essay, which students had to learn before moving on to essay-writing. Process-oriented teachers are often uncomfortable teaching form, fearing students will approach writing in formalist, even formulaic ways. But for Coe, writing is "a forming process" where decisions about form should be made considering purpose, audience, and rhetorical situation. Forms are heuristic, helping writers conduct "structured searches" about their subjects, and they are "socially shared," reflecting communities' ways of knowing and communicating.*

> Form ... is an arousing and fulfillment of desires. A work has form in so far as one part of it leads a reader to anticipate another part, to be gratified by the sequence.
>
> (Burke, *Counter-Statement* 124)

> Desire is the presence of an *absence.*
>
> (Kojeve 134)

> Translated into terms of the composition class, "form" becomes "organization" and brings with it ... the most dismal stuff that students and teachers must deal with. And yet, the concept of form in discourse is utterly fascinating, for it concerns the way in which the mind perceives infinitely

Richard M. Coe. "An Apology for Form; or, Who Took the Form Out of the Process?" *College English,* January 1987.

complex relationships. The way, indeed, in which the mind constructs discourse.

(Winterowd 163)

I. History, Politics, and Theory

At this point in the history of our profession, the conflicts within the fold of the faithful (i.e., among adherents of "the process approach" to teaching composition) are far more significant than the opposition between process and "product" approaches. Which process emphasis one chooses matters a great deal, not only to the type of success students may achieve but also to such relationships as those between writing and humanistic education, between writers as individuals and writing as process. Certain conceptions of process (and of the relationship between form and process) prevent us from realizing the full potential of process approaches to composition.

Historically, the process approach must be understood as antithesis. At the Dartmouth Conference and elsewhere, practitioners such as John Dixon, D. Gordon Rohman, Ken Macrorie, Stephen Tchudi, Donald Graves, Donald Murray, et al. spoke and wrote from their own experiences, but also in response to a traditional way of teaching writing—proffering an antidote, if you will, to the inadequacies of that traditional approach. Their emphases, as always in an antithetical situation, were defined to some significant extent by what they were opposing. To reach a clearer understanding of writing as process, we must sublate (i.e., simultaneously transcend and conserve) this antithesis.

Before distinguishing types of process approaches, it is important to clarify the distinction between process writing and what preceded it. These days, it has become commonplace to juxtapose process writing with a so-called "product approach." Rather than defining what the traditional approach is, this inadequate and derogatory title shifts our attention to what it is not (i.e., not process). Properly termed, what the past two decades saw was a conflict between a (traditional) *formal* approach and a (renewed) *process* approach. To sublate the antithesis and avoid the simplistic choice, we must clarify the relationship between form and process, define the place of forms in the process.

Although it dabbled occasionally (and inaccurately) in process—what else is outlining?—the traditional formal approach essentially taught good form. It answered, formally, the question, "What is good writing?" Because it radically dichotomized form from "content," its answer emphasized structure: sentence structure, paragraph structure, essay structure, even the proper structures for term papers, business letters, resumes—all that Winterowd calls "dismal stuff." If the proper forms were defined, they could be described and exemplified for students. After students wrote, they could be shown where their writing failed to match the ideal forms. And then, the formalists hoped, students would correct their writing to create a better match.

Unfortunately, most students failed to do this because the formalists told them only *what* to do, not also *how* to do it. Until a few decades ago, however, this was not a major social problem because such students also failed to stay in school. Although the data vary from country to country and region to region, we may safely say that only after World War II do even half the students who start grade one complete high school. But then radical changes in the nature of work and other social realities led to declining drop-out rates and increasing postsecondary enrollment, creating a need for a pedagogy that would work with students who used to disappear before senior high school—and thus forming a historical opening for process approaches (Coe, "Literacy 'Crises'"). For any process approach, by definition, concerns itself with one or more of the *hows* formalists traditionally ignore: how writers create; how writers think, feel, and verbalize to enable writing; how writers learn while writing; how writing communicates with readers; and *how* social processes and contexts influence the shaping and interpreting of texts.[1]

There is not one process approach; there are many. All share an emphasis on process, and any process approach inevitably involves intervening in the creative process, if only by recontextualizing it. But writing comprises many processes, and the strongest pedagogical conflict is between those who emphasize writing as a learning process and those who emphasize writing as a communicative process (see Fig. 1; cf. Perelman 471–72, Faigley 527–28).

Those concerned with process writing as a means of learning tend to emphasize underlying mental processes and techniques for destructuring invention, for enabling unconscious processes (e.g., freewriting). Those concerned with writing as a process with worldly uses tend to emphasize communicative process and techniques for structuring invention, for enabling conscious planning (e.g., heuristics, nutshelling). Although there are certainly senses in which both emphases deal with writing as social, these are very different senses, and the treatment of form also differs radically between these two emphases, which I shall call Expressionist and

[1] There is, of course, a sense in which this distinction between mental and social processes is false, for our minds are themselves social as well as individual. The metaphor that equates mind with brain misleads us into locating our minds "in" our heads; but while the brain is a crucial locus of mind, we would avoid many errors if we made a radical epistemological shift and began thinking of our minds as open systems, as structures and flows of information that pass through our brains. Cf. Bateson (esp. 478–88 and 494–505). Burke makes a similar point when he locates motives.

New Rhetorical. [2]

Behind the traditional conception of form lies a long-dead metaphor—one so dead we fail to notice it—inherited from such conservative neo-Classicists as Samuel Johnson. In this metaphor, form is a *container* to be filled (hence the term *content*). If the metaphor is to make sense, our conception of the matter with which we fill forms must be sufficiently "liquid" (i.e., independent of form) to accept the outlines imposed by the shape of the form. This is not Cicero's conception of form, but it is Samuel Johnson's, which is why he can speak of language as a dress thought puts on. For neo-Classicists, ideas exist first; then we dress them in (socially conventional) words and forms. (It is highly significant that most New Critics, neo-Romantics when they deal with literature, adopt this neo-Classical conception of form when they must teach composition.)

Although advocates of Expressionist process writing are radical neo-Romantics, and thus more consistent with what was and probably still is the majority approach to literature, they continue to operate in terms of a form/content dichotomy. For them, however, form grows organically to fit the shape of the subject

[2] In evoking this antithesis, I use Berlin's terms, in part because I think they are significantly accurate, in part to avoid a proliferation of terminologies. My point, however, does not depend upon his analysis. Indeed, I disagree with parts of Berlin's analysis and recognize that any analysis of this nature reduces the complex variety of what is actually happening—that is how it achieves clarity and defines the core of the issue. But I think it is fair to assert that the two major influences on classroom practice, at least in North America, were the traditional formal approach and the Expressionist process approach.

The traditional formal approach avoided questions of substance by defining "content" as outside the field of composition, i.e., either as unteachable art (as in "inspiration") or as the proper concern of other disciplines ("content" courses, as contrasted with "skills" courses). The Expressionist process approach, taking its cue from the derivation of *education* (to lead out, to draw forth), also avoided questions of substance but by placing "content" within students, this process approach begins by removing constraints, creating contexts and processes through which students can express themselves, can articulate (hence, on another level, discover) what *they* want to say, can *ex-press* what is presumably already "inside" them.

The differences in the ways the two process approaches deal with the social aspect of process writing are consistent with their respective conceptions of form. The New Rhetorical treatment of form is radically distinct from either the traditional formal approach or the Expressionist process approach.

matter. Thus there is little need to teach form except as an afterthought (along with punctuation) late in both the teaching and writing processes. Thus the Expressionist process approach and the traditional formal approach are indeed opposites: where the traditional approach ignores content to teach form, Expressionist process writing enables content, allowing form to develop organically. Interestingly, Ken Macrorie's pragmatic description of "good form" represents the same stylistic values (and often the same particulars) as does Strunk and White's; but *Telling Writing* presents them as secondary, to be dealt with during revision, while in *The Elements of Style* they are virtually the whole ball of wax. And the very act of enabling content, of encouraging student writers to write about what concerns them, does create the potential of writing as a liberating *social* act of self-discovery (cf. Schultz).

Figure 1. The Process Approach

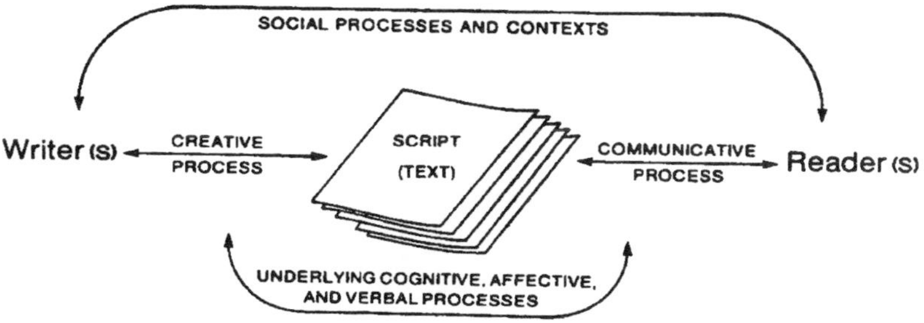

The teaching process involves *intervening* in the various processes surrounding and underlying the writing

In *The Philosophy of Rhetoric,* I. A. Richards urges us to "avoid some traditional mistakes—among them the use of bad analogies which tie us up if we take them too seriously." Some of these bad analogies, Richards asserts,

> are notorious; for example, *the opposition between form and content.* . . . These are wretchedly inconvenient metaphors. So is that other which makes language a dress which thought puts on. We shall do better to think of meaning as though it were a plant that has grown—not a can that has been filled or a lump of clay that has been molded. (12, emphasis added)

Richards reminds us that implicit in the form/content opposition is the "dead" neoclassical metaphor which makes form a container. If form is like a container, then form and "content" are relatively independent: a can hold peas (or marbles) quite as well as beans, and pouring your peas (or marbles) from one can to another does not affect their substance. Like clay, "content" is malleable, capable of adapting to any mold without changing its essential nature.

These metaphors are "inconvenient," Richards argues, because they lead us to misconceive the relation of form to (what we should *not* call) "content." There is no meaning without form: information is *formed* matter (which becomes meaningful in relation to contexts). When you trans*form* a message into a new form, as when you translate a poem, you have re*form*ulated it, thus to some extent changing the meaning. Information is made by putting data (i.e., subject matter) *in formation, by* forming. What neo-Classical formalists called "content" is unknowable in its formlessness; it becomes substantive and knowable only when formed. (And this formed matter becomes meaning—full only when someone relates it to some context—but that is another issue.)

Figure 2. Matter to Meaning

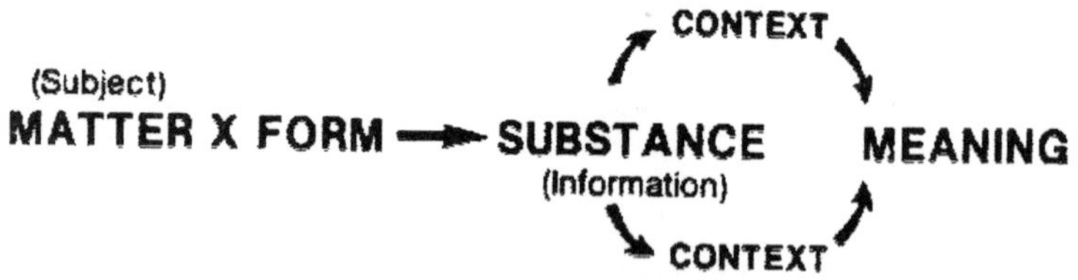

Richards' assertion, perhaps controversial when made in 1936, is now thoroughly confirmed by research in cognitive psychology, information theory, and other such disciplines. As Richards argued, perception itself is humanly impossible until sensory input has been formed (i.e., coded, juxtaposed with mental schema that allow us to perceive pattern in the thousands of "bits" of input that would otherwise overwhelm our mental capacities). As the information theorists would have it:

Noise x Code → Information

Broadly, then, we can define form in terms of its function in a process of forming. This definition is purposively tautological: whatever is used to inform—to impose pattern on noise, cosmos on chaos—is form. Even when we define form narrowly (as rhetorical forms, patterns of development, and so on), we should retain this process conception of form, which reminds us of function.

In composition, as elsewhere, the formalists promulgated a falsely static sense of form. They ignored, rather than refuted, Richards. Meanwhile, the conception we need to sublate the static form/content dichotomy awaited us in the

New Rhetoric: the theory we find in Richards and, especially, Kenneth Burke; later from practitioners such as Francis Christensen and Ann Berthoff come practical applications to teaching composition.

Frank D'Angelo summarized the concept this way in A *Conceptual Theory of Rhetoric:*

> Following Aristotle's system I take form to be closely related to the formal principle, i.e., one of the causes of a mode of being which produces discourse ... Patterns of development are not only organizational, they ... also ... serve a heuristic function. . . . They are ...dynamic organizational processes, symbolic manifestations of underlying mental processes, and not merely conventional static patterns. (56–57)

In this conception form is both generative and constraining—or, better said, generative because constraining. Form is empty, an absence. But this emptiness has shape (i.e., form). In human beings, at least, this emptiness creates a desire to find what might fill it—which is at least part of what Burke means in "Definition of Man" when he wryly defines us as "rotten with perfection" (*Language* 16 ff.).

Another aspect of Burke's point—Burke's significant points are never singular—reminds me of Donald Murray (the writer, *not* the theoretician of writing) describing invention as knowing how to sit waiting under the lightning. Murray recounted how various wordings of a particular subject struck him until, recognizing the last as a poem, he wrote it out ("Talking to Yourself"; cf. Murray's essay in Waldrep's collection).

I take his report of the process as exceptionally significant because it sublates his own theory. Somehow, Murray recognized a particular set of words *as a poem.* His selection of this version as poem was also, inevitably, a rejection/deflection of other versions (as non-poem or, at least, as inferior poem). And his recognition could only have occurred because Murray had within his mind a schema for poem, an abstract (i.e., empty) formal idea of *poem*—a "perfection" through which Murray is "rotten," far beyond his willingness to admit, *with the social.* For since this poem was later recognized by an editor (hence published) and by readers, I take it that Murray's schema of poem is shared, not idiosyncratic.

In short, we have here a shared form "provided by language," a cultural form, a social structure enabling the creative process. That Murray, like many writers, finds it useful to ignore the place of cultural/social structures in his writing process is neither here nor there—it certainly does not imply that teachers of writing should ignore the impact of such structures on the creative process.

Form, in its emptiness, is heuristic, for it guides a structured search. Faced with the emptiness of a form, a *human* being seeks matter to fill it. Form becomes, therefore, a motive for generating information. Like any heuristic, it motivates a search for information of a certain type: when the searchers can anticipate what shape of stuff they seek, generation is less free, but much more efficient; by constraining the search, form directs attention. (Heuristics, in this sense, are distinct from unstructuring discovery techniques such as freewriting.)

Consider, for example, the form we entitle "the five-paragraph essay." In my more cynical moments, I suspect that the better part of several generations of students have been socialized to believe that, at least in school, there are three reasons for (and/or three examples of) anything. Although the five-paragraph essay originates as an exercise in using the Classical *proposition + partition* to structure an essay, and although there is no reason whatsoever why it should not sometimes contain two or four or more body paragraphs, students who have memorized the form almost inevitably generate three.

In my less cynical moments, I recognize the good in this: left on their own, many of these same students would discover only one reason or example. Thus even this static school form has some liberal value. My main point here, however, is that the form, *because it contains three **empty** slots,* motivates students to continue inventing until they have discovered subject matter to fill three slots. (For a broader critique of formal tyranny in school essays, see Fort.)

In this respect, any form is like the forms we are often served by various bureaucracies (e.g., income tax forms). They move us to consider certain types of things, to search for particular information and, generally, to find something (if only "N/A") to fill every slot. And the other side of this mundane example is the sense in which all heuristics, not just the tagmemic grid but also the Pentad and the journalists' 5Ws, are empty forms whose shaped emptinesses motivate writers to generate appropriate information.

Rhetorical structures are in this sense the social memory of standard responses to particular types of rhetorical situations and subject matter.[3] Like language, form is thus social. One function of discourse communities is to provide, prescribe, and prefer forms. Learning conventional forms, often by a tacit process of

---

[3] Cf. Burke's assertion that "critical and imaginative works are answers to questions posed by situation in which they arose," that we should think of "any work of critical or imaginative cast" as "the adopting of various strategies for the encompassing of situations. These strategies size up the situations, name their structure and outstanding ingredients, and name them in a way that contains an attitude towards them. ... The symbolic act is the *dancing of an attitude*" (*Philosophy* 3, 8–9). The point I am making about rhetorical forms is Burke's point generalized—as the forms are generalized texts. Forms are synchronic structures that function as generalized memories of (diachronic) processes. For an application this conception of form to the interpretation of literature (and architecture), see Wayne's *Penshurst.*

"indwelling," is a way of learning a community's discourse, gaining access, communicating with that community. For a form implies a strategy of response, an attitude, a way of sorting factors, sizing up situations. If a text, as Burke would have it, dances an attitude, then forms are attitudes frozen in synchronicity. Insofar as a form is socially shared, adopting the form involves adopting, at least to some extent, the community's attitude, abiding by its expectations.

Readers who make up the community use these same forms to focus their attention, to anticipate as they approach and move through a text, as they use the text to reinvent meanings. Recognizing forms—both of the whole text (sonnet, editorial, term paper) and of parts within the text (definition, example, instructions)—is an important aspect of reading. Readers' abilities to recognize—even (or perhaps especially) subliminally—various kinds of formal patterns of development allow them to "process" text (i.e., to understand it) efficiently. Those who fail to recognize forms, perhaps because they are from another culture or subculture, not part of the community, often misinterpret function, hence meaning.

Writers' abilities to use formal patterns particular readers will recognize allow them to communicate accurately and effectively. In general, communication is most likely to succeed, to generate understanding rather than misunderstanding, when writer(s) and reader(s) know and use the same forms.[4] (For writers, "use" may mean reproducing or *varying* the form; in either case, recognition enables reading.)

Conventional forms, as they function in both creative and communicative processes, are a major part of what makes those processes social. And, to continue along these Burkean lines, inasmuch as an attitude is an incipient action, i.e., a potential action waiting for an activating situation, so forms are suasive, rhetorical insofar as by shaping our attitudes they guide our responses to situations.

Thus an example somewhat more interesting than the five-paragraph essay or a bureaucratic form is the form that allows us to "know" there are two sides to a question or issue even before we know what the question or issue is. The apparent motive behind this form is usually to get someone who is seeing only one side to look for another. In that sense, this is a generative form. Perhaps because it fits so neatly with binary dualism and other reductionist tendencies in modern Western culture, however, it is also a constraining form that allows us to feel fulfilled after we have discovered only two sides: how else can we explain several decades during which

[4] De Beaugrande coins the term "frame defense" to argue that a text may be "rejected or simply not understood" if it conflicts with a reader's informational or situational frame (168). Hypothetically, I would apply this notion to formal frames as well. Cf. Kinsch's argument that readers structure information within a knowledge frame they bring to the text and Goffman's notion of "primary frames" (21–39). Burke, of course, has made various comparable analyses earlier, although without using the same terminology.

otherwise intelligent Westerners looked at the Middle East and saw *only* two sides? And, worse, this form becomes the basis of Golden Mean dualism, which allows us to know that both extremes are wrong and the liberal middle correct even before we know what the issue is. (What is the Golden Mean in the conflict between rapist and victim?)

As this example indicates, form is cultural, not neutral. The sense in which conventional forms are culture-bound is most apparent; but other sorts of forms, such as those discussed by D'Angelo *(Conceptual Theory* 38–60) or those Burke calls progressive and repetitive *(Counter-Statement* 124–25), vary more from culture to culture than most of us realize.

A form may be generative insofar as it motivates a search for more information; but any form also biases the direction of the searching and constrains against the discovery of information that does not fit the form. A particular message may be very difficult (if not impossible) to communicate within the parameters of a conventional form. Literary history is filled with examples of writers who needed to invent new forms to communicate new messages. More mundanely, certain messages are hard to squeeze into a business letter, for example, because they exceed the maximum effective length of that form (i.e., two typewritten pages). A pedagogically significant example is the standard formal technique for achieving focus, which often constrains against what a student writer has set out to say (Coe, "If Not to Narrow"). Form can, in this sense, be ideological: when a particular form constrains against the communication of a message contrary to the interests of some power elite, it serves an ideological function. Insofar as form guides function, formal values may carry implicit moral/political values.

As this series of examples indicates, the nature of form is variable. If you accept the notion of form I am putting forth, one implication is that we need to study form—and forming—much more carefully and in many more contexts than we have: form as organic, as construct; as flexible, as rigid; as generative, as constraint; as an instrument of creation and meaning; as the social penetrating the personal. In order to emphasize the essential nature of form, I have in this essay been conflating distinctions that would distinguish various types of forms. For the unity is logically prior to the partition. That unity grasped, however, we do need better insights into the various functions of distinct formal principles. And while remembering Burke's warning "not to confine the explanation [of form] to *one* principle, but to formulate sufficient principles to make an explanation possible" *(Counter-Statement* 129), we could certainly do worse than to start from his discussion of progressive (syllogistic and qualitative), repetitive, conventional, and minor or incidental form.

Even without awaiting further study, we can draw certain implications from the general thesis argued here. As humanists, we should be able to explain (especially to our students) the relation of forms to functions. As rhetoricians, we should explicitly invent forms to meet new needs, new functions, as Young, Becker, and Pike formally invented Rogerian persuasion. As writing teachers we need a more articulated understanding than do writers of how form functions in the writing process.

That brings me to "Monday morning."

II. Monday Morning

If you agree with the New Rhetorical conception of form asserted here, what should you do on Monday morning?

1. You should help students learn those forms socially necessary for effective communication within the society in which they live. (This is comparable to teaching them Standard English so that they have functional access to professional jobs, power, etc.)

2. You should help them learn—and invent—forms that allow them to understand and communicate what they want to understand and communicate, what it is in their interests to understand and communicate.

3. You should help students grasp this New Rhetorical conception of form and learn how to think critically about form—but, let me add immediately, not by pontificating about form, rather by creating processes that allow them to experience both the constraining and generative powers of forms.

Learning socially significant forms—and understanding how they function, how to use them appropriately—is a key to success (sometimes even to survival) in a discourse community. This is perhaps particularly so in schools, for schools serve in part to teach such forms, or at least to weed out those who do not know them. As Frances Christie argues,

> Those who fail in schools are those who fail to master the genres of schooling: the ways of structuring and of dealing with experience which schools value in varying ways (24; cf. Heath).

So it matters that we continue to teach the basic forms which constitute a condition of access to professional discourse, and hence to professional communities, in modern societies. But it also matters that we discuss these forms, as any others, in terms of their functions in various writing processes (cf. Figure 1 above): how they serve (or limit) the creative process, how they enable (or disable) communication, how they structure what happens in our minds, how they mesh with social processes.

Like other rhetorical factors, form should be taught in context, in terms of appropriateness and effectiveness. When teaching such standard forms as the thesis paragraph (i.e., thesis statement + partition used to prefigure the argument), it matters that we explain the importance of this form in academic (and other professional) discourse. make clear why it predominates in certain types of discourse (academic, scientific, professional—and textbooks). We should validate (and limit) this form by showing that it makes a certain type of critical reading easier because proofs can be evaluated more easily if readers know in advance what they purportedly prove, because information can be taken in more efficiently if one knows in advance the outline of what is to be learned. In this way, we should put whatever forms we teach in functional rhetorical context.

Figure 3. Basic Patterns of Arrangement

	SYNCHRONIC PATTERNS	PROGRESSIVE PATTERNS
REPORT PATTERNS	Description	Narration
EXPLANATORY PATTERNS	Comparison/contrast Classification and division Definition Analogy and exemplification	Process-analysis Causal explanation Logical progression

Though we might wish to emphasize patterns relevant to our students' educational, professional and humane purposes, we can begin with the standard formal *patterns of development,* largely on the hypothesis that they correspond with basic patterns of thought (cf. D'Angelo, *Conceptual Theory* 28–29, 42–47, 53–59; Berthoff 38–45). The main innovation is to treat the formal patterns as representing mental functions and to place them functionally within the creative process.

I start with narration and description, modes in which the structure of the text is ordinarily shaped to a significant extent by the chronology of the story being narrated or the arrangement of what is being described. Studies in contrastive rhetoric demonstrate that even narrative and description are not simple reflections of reality; on the contrary, they vary significantly from one culture to another. (To cite just one example, place is very important in the stories of aboriginal Australians, but it is stated near the end; when those stories are translated for Anglo Australians, the translators generally move the statement of place to the beginning, where English narrative form demands it.) There is, nonetheless, a sense in which the arrangements of narrative and description are shaped by the structure of their subject matter to a greater extent than are the arrangements of more abstract modes. The cognitive task of arrangement is, therefore, easier in these modes, and so I do start with them.

Thence I follow traditional pedagogy to comparison/contrast, the thought structure of which may be represented by the grid in Figure 4. Obviously, this structure focuses attention, hence invention, toward a particular task (i.e., toward comparing and contrasting). Students instructed to compare and contrast generate different substance than would students instructed to, say, describe and exemplify. Thus teaching this pattern of development teaches a heuristic technique; already the formalists' static conception of form is sublated. (Is not the grid in Figure 4 just as much a heuristic as the tagmemic grid?)

Figure 4. Comparison/Contrast.

	Subject A	Subject B
Characteristic 1:		
Characteristic 2:		
Characteristic 3:		
Characteristic 4:		
Characteristic 5:		
Characteristic 6:		
. . .		
Characteristic N:		

But there are further implications because two distinct rhetorical forms can be used to communicate comparison/contrast. In the half-and-half format, composition moves vertically down the grid: Subject A is described first, then Subject B is compared and contrasted. In the alternating characteristics format, composition moves horizontally: each characteristic of Subject A is compared and/or contrasted with Subject B before the next characteristic is raised.

How boring! No, because even in a case such as this the choice of rhetorical format may significantly affect the substance of what gets invented. Ask a writer who has used the half-and-half format to reformulate using the alternating characteristics format, and the message will sometimes change. First, the close juxtaposition of each comparison/contrast point often leads writers to notice that they have left something out. Second, and more significantly, when the rhetorical format forces close juxtaposition, writers sometimes decide that an example, or even the point, is not so strong as they thought. For an instance of what happened to one student's literary critical essay when she was assigned to reformulate it in this way, see Coe, *Form* 238–41.

A more interesting exercise of the same type involves the juxtaposition of two rhetorical forms that serve the same general purpose. For instance, one can juxtapose Classical and Rogerian persuasion. It quickly grows obvious to students that the choice of a form for persuasion affects both tone and substance. I effect the juxtaposition this way:

1. First, I ask students to pair themselves with someone with whom they can agree on a thesis for a persuasive writing. Each pair must submit a single thesis statement.

2. Working in pairs, using Aristotle's *topoi*, brainstorming, and whatever other invention techniques they wish, each pair of students invents as many arguments as they can in support of their chosen thesis.

3. One student of each pair elects to try the Classical form, the other to try the Rogerian form. Each chooses an appropriate audience, i.e., a group of potential readers who would (a) initially disagree with the thesis, and (b) effectively be addressed by whichever form that student has elected. (Note that the exercise is inevitably artificial here: in real world writing situations, writers generally know the audience first, choose an appropriate form second—and the nature of the audience is usually an important factor in the invention of arguments.)

4. Each student submits a brief audience analysis, outlining the relevant knowledge, beliefs, and vested interests of the chosen audience. On the basis of this audience analysis, each selects arguments from those the pair has invented, adds any others that might be suggested by the nature of the audience, and writes a persuasion using the elected format.

5. The persuasions are read and criticized (in terms of how well they are likely to persuade the chosen audiences). They are then revised.

6. To discover how audience and form have influenced the tone and substance, we do comparison/contrast of persuasions written from the same corpus of invented arguments to support the same thesis.

Quite a number of birds get hit by this one assignment: learning to work with another writer, at least through the stage of invention; developing the ability to empathize with and analyze an audience; learning two rhetorical forms for organizing persuasion; learning something about the relationship between audience and rhetorical structure; developing some control of tone and understanding of the relationship between audience and tone; and learning something, hands on, about the relationship between form and substance.

It is important that students understand composition *as a forming process.* As Ann Berthoff argues,

> Composing is like an organic process, not an assembly line on which some prefabricated parts are fitted together. However, plants and animals don't just "grow" mystically, developing from seed to flower and fully framed creatures, without plan or guidance or system. All organic processes are forms in action: the task of the composer is to find the forms that find forms; the structures that guide and encourage growth; the limits by means of which development can be shaped. [This] method of composing ... is a way of making meanings by using the forms provided by language to re-present the relationships we see. (153)

The curriculum and pedagogy championed by Berthoff exemplifies this emphasis. For pedagogical examples, see *forming/thinking/writing* (50–62, on classifying, and 94–100, on defining); cf. Berthoff, "The Intelligent Eye and the Thinking Hand," in Hays et al.

In North America, at least, Francis Christensen is the best-known early proponent of teaching what I call *generative form.* First on the level of the sentence, then on the level of the paragraph, and posthumously (through his followers) on the level of the whole piece of writing, Christensen taught form as "generative rhetoric." If one teaches students the form of the cumulative sentence, replete with "loose" or free modifiers, he argued, the students will generate the material to fill "empty" modifier slots in their sentences. Thus their writing will acquire what Christensen termed "texture": details, examples, reasons, qualifiers, etc. Comparable lessons on the paragraph level will motivate them to generate that form of texture writing teachers have traditionally called good or full "development." (For pedagogical examples and detailed discussion, see Christensen's articles on generative rhetoric and his *Rhetoric Program,* the cited articles by Grady, D'Angelo, Nold and Davis, and Shaughnessy's chapter, "Beyond the Sentence," in *Errors and Expectations.)*

Taking this lesson one step further, I will argue that a new form often must be created in order to express a radically new idea—and that knowing a form with which an idea can be articulated improves the likelihood of thinking that idea. Teaching a new form is a pedagogy often used to encourage a new *form of discourse.* Before reading Richards, I used to call this, "New Forms for New Content." Oppressed social groups often find it necessary to invent new forms because the socially dominant forms will not readily carry their ideas. Several examples of this kind of formal invention can be found in the work of feminists.

There is, for instance, the formula for constructive criticism, synthesized by U.S. feminists from humanistic psychology and Mao Zedung's essay on criticism/self-criticism, that I find tremendously useful in my composition classes. The formula, simply, is:

> When you _____, I feel/think _____, so I wish you would _____ instead.

> *When you* tell me my writing is "incoherent, ungrammatical and confused," *I feel* stupid, discouraged, and angry, *so I wish you would* make more specific and constructive criticisms *instead.*

This formula has two virtues: (a) it encourages constructive criticism (rather than blaming criticism) by helping to keep criticism specific, making it clear that a particular action (not the whole person) is being criticized, focusing attention on the effect of the criticized action and forcing the critic to indicate what can be done about the criticism; and (b) by providing an appropriate structure, the formula makes it easier for people to express criticisms. Indeed, if one looks at feminist assertiveness training, one sees that providing appropriate forms is one of the most important techniques for enabling a new kind of communication.

This same principle can be applied to teaching the standard rhetorical patterns of development. I have done so frequently, especially when asserting that the traditional cause-to-effect pattern should be complemented with instruction in causal explanation by constraints. Explanation by constraints focuses more attention on context as a possible locus of cause and motive, thus improving students' ability to think and communicate about organized complexity (e.g., about human motives, human societies, ecosystems).[5] A similar argument can be made that while the standard forms of Western thought are effective for thinking about stasis and essences, teaching the form of reasoning and communication embodied by the Hegelian/Marxist dialectic (or even the Taoist/Zen Buddhist dialectic) helps people think and communicate more effectively about process and change.

Though the kind of instruction I am describing is in a significant sense formal and sublates certain aspects of traditional formal curricula, it is worlds (or, more accurately, levels) away from traditional static formalism. For it places form in the context of various processes: creative, communicative, mental, social, and learning. Thus formalism is not rejected, but subordinated to process. And we create a kind of process approach that encompasses and transforms formalism, rather than simply opposing it.

What I am advocating is that we teach this New Rhetorical kind of process writing. That in part through theory, but mostly through hands-on practice, we help our students develop an awareness of form as simultaneously constraining and generative that will empower them to understand, use, and even invent new forms for new purposes.

[5] The essence of this argument is that the cause-to-effect pattern of development taught in traditional composition courses overestimates the extent to which occurrences are explainable as the result of prior events that actively "caused" them and underestimates the sense in which certain types of occurrences are better explained as responses or adaptations to contexts. The theory of evolution is an excellent example of an idea invented because its inventor stopped looking for "causes" and started looking at contexts. The increasing tendency in various practical and academic disciplines to discuss causation in terms of "parameters," "restraints," and "constraints" indicates increasing awareness that contextual factors are crucial for explaining events and decisions shaped by organized complexity. Contextual factors are qualitatively different from mechanistic causes, but it is difficult to emphasize, communicate or even think about that qualitative difference while using the cause-to-effect pattern of development. See especially Coe, "Closed System Composition," "Rhetoric 2001," and "Causation" in *Form and Substance* (300–20). C.E. Bateson (399–410), the discussion of scenic factors in Burke's *Grammar* (esp., xv-vii, 3–7, 127–70), and of order and hierarchy in Burke's *Rhetoric* (Part III).

WORKS CITED

Bateson, Gregory. *Steps to an Ecology of Mind.* New York: Ballantine, 1972.

Berlin, James A. "Contemporary Composition: The Major Pedagogical Theories." *College English* 44 (1982): 765–77.

Berthoff, Ann E. *forming/thinking/writing.* Rochelle Park, NJ: Hayden, 1978.

Burke, Kenneth. *Counter-Statement.* 1931. Berkeley: U of California P, 1968.

——. *A Grammar of Motives.* 1945. Berkeley: U of California P, 1969.

——. *Language as Symbolic Action.* Berkeley: U of California P, 1966.

——. *A Rhetoric of Motives.* 1950. Berkeley: U of California P, 1969.

——. *The Philosophy of Literary Form.* 1941. New York: Vintage, 1957.

Christensen, Francis. *The Christensen Rhetoric Program.* New York: Harper, 1966.

——. "A Generative Rhetoric of the Paragraph." *College Composition and Communication* 16 (1965): 144–56.

——. "A Generative Rhetoric of the Sentence." *College Composition and Communication* 14 (1963): 155–61.

Christie, Frances. "Language and Schooling." *Language, Schooling and Society.* Ed. Stephen Tchudi. Upper Montclair, NJ: Boynton, 1985. 21–40.

Coe, Richard M. "Closed System Composition." *ETC., A Review of General Semantics* 32 (1975): 403–12.

——. *Form and Substance.* New York: Wiley: Scott, 1981.

——. "If Not to Narrow, Then How to Focus." *College Composition and Communication* 32 (1981): 272–77.

——. "Literacy 'Crises': A Systemic Analysis." *Humanities in Society* 4 (1981): 363–78.

——. "Rhetoric 2001." *Freshman English News* 3.1 (1974): 1–13.

D'Angelo, Frank. *A Conceptual Theory of Rhetoric.* Cambridge, MA: Winthrop, 1975.

——. "A Generative Rhetoric of the Essay." *College Composition and Communication* 25 (1974): 388–96.

De Beaugrande, Robert. *Text, Discourse, and Process: Toward a Multidisciplinary Science of Texts.* Norwood, NJ: Ablex, 1980.

Faigley, Lester. "Competing Theories of Process: A Critique and a Proposal." *College English* 48 (1986): 527–42.

Fort, Keith. "Form, Authority, and the Critical Essay." *College English 33* (1971): 629–39.

Goffman, Erving. *Frame Analysis.* New York: Harper, 1974.

Grady, Michael. "A Conceptual Rhetoric of the Composition." *College Composition and Communication* 22 (1971): 348–54.

——. "On Teaching Christensen Rhetoric." *English Journal* 61 (1972): 859+

Hays, Janice N., et al., eds. *The Writer's Mind: Writing as a Mode of Thinking.* Urbana: NCTE, 1983.

Heath, Shirley Brice. *Way with Words: Language, Life, and Work in Communities and Classrooms.* Cambridge: Cambridge UP, 1983.

Kinsch, Walter. "On Modeling Comprehension." *Literacy, Society, and Schooling.* Ed. Suzanne de Castell, Allan Luke, and Kieran Egan. Cambridge, UK: Cambridge UP, 1986.

Kojeve, Alexandre. *Introduction to the Reading of Hegel.* Tran. J.H. Nichols, Jr. New York: Basic, 1969.

Macrorie, Ken. *Telling Writing.* 3rd ed. Rochelle Park, NJ: Hayden, 1980.

Murray, Donald M. "Talking to Yourself. The Reason Writers Write." Opening Sess. Wyoming Conference on Freshman and Sophomore English. Laramie, 24 June 1985.
Nold, Ellen W., and Brent E. Davis. "'The Discourse Matrix." *College Composition and Communication* 31 (1980): 141–52.
Perelman, Les. "The Context of Classroom Writing," *College English* 48 (1986): 471–79.
Richards, I.A. *The Philosophy of Rhetoric.* London: Oxford, 1936.
Shaughnessy, Mina. *Errors and Expectations.* New York: Oxford, 1977.
Shultz, John. "Story Workshop." *Research on Composing.* Ed. Charles Cooper and Lee Odell. Urbana: NCTE, 1978. 151–87.
Strunk, William, and E.B. White. *The Elements of Style.* New York: Macmillan, 1959.
Waldrep, Tom ed. *Writers on Writing.* New York: Random, 1985.
Wayne, Don E. *Penshurst: The Semiotics of Place and the Poetics of History.* Madison: U of Wisconsin P, 1984.
Winterowd, W. Ross, ed. *Contemporary Rhetoric.* New York: Harcourt, 1975.
Young, Richard, Alton Becker, and Kenneth Pike. *Rhetoric: Discovery and Change.* New York: Harcourt, 1970.

What Makes a Text Coherent?

Betty Bamberg

Coherence has been an important term in writing instruction since the 19th century when Alexander Bain defined the paragraph as a collection of sentences that possesses unity, coherence, and emphasis. In this 1983 article, first published in College Composition and Communication, *Betty Bamberg, an English professor at California State University, Los Angeles, provides an audience-centered definition of coherence based on linguistic research. Traditional instruction, she argues, confuses cohesion, a system of textual cues like transitional expressions, pronouns, and repetition of key words that connects the parts of a text, with coherence, which deals with a reader's experience of a text. While cohesive ties contribute to the coherence of a text, Bamberg argues against a formalist conception of coherence and in favor or a reader-oriented definition in which "[m]eaning and coherence . . . arise from readers' efforts to construct meaning and to integrate the details in the text into a coherent whole." Readers continually guess at the overall meaning, purpose, and structure of a text as they read, so to achieve coherence, writers must help readers in their predictions, with passages that orient audience expectations and provide a context for what the writer has to say.*

Pedagogical interest in coherence has its roots in the nineteenth century, its probable beginnings in Alexander Bain's first rule of the paragraph: "The bearing of each sentence upon what precedes shall be explicit and unmistakable."[1] By the end of the nineteenth century coherence, along with unity and emphasis, was an established canon of paragraph structure. The view of coherence in some of today's popular composition texts still closely resembles Bain's original formulation. For example, McCrimmon's *Writing With a Purpose,* one of the most widely used freshman composition texts, defines coherence as follows:

> A paragraph is coherent when the reader can move easily from one sentence to the next and read the paragraph as an integrated whole, rather than a series of separate sentences.

McCrimmon then advises writers to make paragraphs coherent by weaving sentences together with such connective devices as pronouns, repetitive structures, contrast, and transitional markers.[2]

Coherence is generally accepted as a *sine qua non* in written discourse; writing that lacks coherence will almost certainly fail to communicate its intended message to a reader. Even though most composition texts and rhetorics have routinely included a section on coherence, interest in this topic has intensified during the last five years. In part, this increased interest grows out of linguistic research, which has evolved from a focus on the sentence to a consideration of "texts," or extended sections of discourse. But the interest also arises from the renewed emphasis on writing instruction and the recognition, in writing instruction, that many problems in writing require attention at the level of the whole discourse rather than at the level of the word or sentence.

In 1975, as we began to see other evidence of a decline in students' writing skills, the National Assessment of Educational Progress (NAEP) reported that the average level of performance on one of their writing tasks had decreased significantly between 1969 and 1974. Students had been asked to write an impromptu essay describing something they knew about "so that it could be recognized by someone who has read your description." NAEP's preliminary analysis of these essays concluded that lack of coherence contributed substantially to the lower scores received by the 1974 essays.[3] Although NAEP's analysis of these essays identified coherence as a major problem, it could offer no guidelines for writing instruction because the essays had not been analyzed to determine what difficulties in the texts might be described as "lack of coherence." To identify these difficulties, I recently read over 800 essays written by thirteen- and seventeen-year-olds for the 1974 Assessment. I was particularly interested in the essays written by seventeen-year-olds because their writing was likely to be close to the level of writing of freshman composition students.

My first reading of the essays made clear that the traditional view of coherence derived from Bain was too limited to account for the coherence problems I found. This traditional view treats coherence as a phenomenon somewhat similar to what many linguists and rhetoricians now call cohesion. In *Cohesion in English,* Halliday and Hasan define "cohesion" as a relationship between two textual elements in which one is interpreted by the other. For example, in the sentence "He said so," "He" and "so" presuppose something that has gone before. We cannot interpret this sentence (as opposed to decoding it) unless we can relate "He" and "so" to words in a preceding sentence. Such relationships between words create cohesive "ties" and allow us to differentiate sentences that constitute a "text" from sequences of unrelated sentences. Halliday and Hasan define a text as "a semantic unit: a unit not of form but of meaning..." that "may be anything from a single proverb to a whole play."[4]

However, this view of "cohesion" differs from the traditional concept of coherence as presented by Bain. His formulation of "coherence" stressed between sentence connections that created tightly-structured, autonomous paragraphs which were then linked together into a larger text by transitions. As discussed by Halliday and Hasan, however, "cohesive" ties often connect adjacent sentences (or more precisely, adjacent T-units), but they may also connect "remote" rather than "immediate" sections of text. In a "remote" tie, the cohesive elements are separated by at least one t-unit and may extend across paragraph boundaries. "Cohesion," therefore, describes a linguistic system that extends through the text and binds together larger chunks of discourse, in addition to forming smaller discourse units.

Research and theory in discourse analysis now view cohesive ties as part of what makes a text coherent; however, these ties are not, by themselves, sufficient to create a coherent text. After analyzing cohesive ties in student essays, Stephen Witte and Lester Faigley differentiated between cohesion and coherence, concluding that "coherence defines those underlying semantic relations that allow a text to be understood and used" and "coherence conditions are governed by the writer's purpose, the audience's knowledge and expectations, and the information to be conveyed.[5] The text linguist T.A. van Dijk points out that cohesive ties create only "local" coherence (his term for cohesion) and are unable by themselves to create discourse-level or "global" coherence.[6] He illustrates the difference between local and global coherence in the following example:

> I bought this typewriter in New York. New York is a large city in the USA. Large cities often have serious financial problems....

Although this passage contains lexical cohesive ties—repetitions of "New York" and "large city"—readers will not consider the text as a whole to be coherent unless they can discover a broader topic that incorporates buying typewriters, large cities, and financial problems. Van Dijk further notes that essays, in addition to being unified around a theme or topic, must have an overall form or structure if readers are to find them coherent over the whole discourse.[7]

Research on artificial intelligence has found that we rely heavily on conventional structures of knowledge known as scripts, frames, or schema to organize experience and knowledge so that we can understand it.[8] A script may prescribe a sequence of actions to be followed in a particular situation. For example, in a restaurant we expect to order food from a menu, to be served by a waitress or waiter, and to pay for our meal after eating it. However, the restaurant script will vary, depending upon the type of restaurant we select. Buying a hamburger at

McDonald's follows a script different from ordering a meal at Howard Johnson's, and both differ from the script prescribed at Chasen's or Le Pavillon. Textual information also follows conventional patterns. Labov found that oral narratives could be divided into five parts: abstract, orientation, complication, resolution, and coda. More recently, a number of discourse theorists have constructed "story grammars" that describe narrative structure.[9] Scientific reports also have a predictable structure: they begin with an abstract and are then divided into introduction, method, results, and discussion. Form is more fluid in expository essays, but certain methods of development—classification, comparison/contrast—tend to provide familiar structures. Despite their different forms, all schema serve the same function: they help readers anticipate upcoming textual information, thereby enabling them to reduce and organize the text into an understandable and coherent whole.

The complexity of any inquiry into the sources of coherence is further increased by recent research on reading and on discourse comprehension, which shows that the reading process "constructs" a text and that the reader's prior knowledge—both conscious and tacit—affects the understanding of a text.[10] Meaning and coherence are not inscribed in the text, this research shows, but arise from readers' efforts to construct meaning and to integrate the details in the text into a coherent whole. Although readers are guided by textual cues, they also draw on their own knowledge and expectations to bridge gaps and to fill in assumed information. Louise Phelps argues that failures in coherence occur either because writers undercue—provide too few cues for readers to let them perceive the relationships between parts of a text or because they miscue—give conflicting or misleading cues.[11]

The interaction between text and reader and its effect on judgments about coherence can best be understood in the context of psycholinguistic reading theory. To comprehend a text, fluent readers do not read word for word, but, in what Kenneth Goodman has called a "psycholinguistic guessing game," predict meanings from graphic, semantic, and syntactic cues, sampling only enough of the text to confirm their predictions. They predict meaning from nonvisual information—their prior knowledge and expectations—as well as from the letters on the page.[12] For example, tacit knowledge of the English language (acceptable letter combinations and their relative frequency of occurrence, along with syntactic rules) helps readers predict the meanings of individual words by limiting the possible choices of meaning.[13] Similarly, a knowledge of discourse conventions helps readers predict meaning and structure. Preschool children have learned that "once upon a time" signals the beginning of a story, and experienced readers of research reports are able to read an abstract and then turn to sections of interest, perhaps skipping the review of research or description of methodology and going directly to the results and discussion.

While reading, readers draw on their tacit knowledge at the level of the sentence and of the whole discourse by using a "top-down," "bottom-up" strategy. That is, as they process individual words and sentences at the beginning of a text, they attempt to form an overall conception of the structure and meaning of the whole text into which they can fit the information that follows.[14] This anticipation of structure and meaning, in turn, directs their guesses about individual words and phrases. Clearly stated topic sentences, an obvious organizational pattern, statements of topic and purpose, and headings which indicate divisions of the text—these are all cues that facilitate a reader's integration of details in a text into a coherent whole. When such cues are missing, readers may be unable to make this integration.

Theoretical discussions of coherence—whether of sentences or of a whole discourse—usually analyze hypothetical texts constructed to highlight the principles being considered. Although useful for theoretical discussions, these passages do not resemble the writing of our students, nor do they help us discover which coherence conditions students have the most difficulty meeting. Examining the presence or absence of coherence in student texts such as those written for the National Assessment can not only give us insights into students' difficulties in producing coherent texts, but can suggest ways for us to intervene productively in students' writing processes to help them write more coherently.

I had initially intended to compare coherent and incoherent essays using ratings from the National Assessment analysis. The original NAEP analysis consisted of two parts: a holistic general impression score and a detailed description of specific features (particularly grammatical and mechanical errors) known as the "mechanics" scoring. Coherence ratings were given during the mechanics scoring; raters evaluated the coherence of each paragraph according to a set of criteria provided. In a preliminary analysis, I discovered that NAEP's rubric and scoring procedures for coherence rendered many of the coherence ratings invalid. To begin with, the analysts rated the coherence of individual paragraphs, so essay- or discourse-level coherence was not rated unless an essay consisted of a single paragraph. In addition, the coherence scoring guide did not include all coherence features, omitting particularly any consideration of overall structure or form, a feature often critical for coherence through the whole essay, and the guide also confounded coherence with paragraph development.[15] To overcome the limitations of NAEP's mechanics analysis. I developed a new rubric that assessed coherence at both the local (or sentence) and global (or discourse) levels. The rubric asked raters to focus on all textual features that affect coherence and to assign a holistic score for the entire essay, ignoring paragraph indentations and development. Results from these holistic ratings were then used to separate coherent from incoherent essays.[16]

The coherence scale I used to rescore the NAEP essays has the strengths as well as the weaknesses of other holistic scales. Although it reliably rank orders writing according to a set of criteria, it does not identify which features are present or missing in particular essays.[17] To identify specific features that result in perceived incoherence, I analyzed the coherence features in a subset of essays, looking for the presence or absence of linguistic features or rhetorical structures specified in the rubric. Not surprisingly, essays with coherence scores in the lower half lacked coherence between sentences and through the whole discourse:

> He had huge body frame that obtain shock, bumps, cuts, but it is also in some ways powerful, smart, graceful like a dancer; quick on his feet, speed like lightning, a eye for direction and a mind that keep saying push on and fear of anybody. Hand that slap feet that are step, leg that are broken, arm that bend, and a head that get push in the ground, but into all of those thing a person that is determine to push on because glory is at the end.[18]

The perceived absence of local coherence in the essay above is due primarily to mechanical and grammatical errors, a type of miscue not usually considered in theoretical discussions of coherence. However, such errors do interfere with a reader's attempt to construct a text and integrate details into a coherent whole. The writer of the essay above left out thirteen inflectional endings, including five "ed" past tense verb endings, two third-person singular "s" verb endings, and eight noun plural "s" inflections. The writer also omitted words ("had huge body frame," "fear of anybody") and used other unexpected words and phrases—"obtain shocks," "eye for direction," "into all of those." To process the text, readers must backtrack and reread to fill in missing words and grammatical inflections. Not only do the errors interfere with the processing of sentences, but readers' focus on individual words and letters distracts their attention from global cues.

However, editing the essay above to eliminate grammatical and mechanical errors would not make it coherent. The essay above illustrates a problem common even among 17-year-old writers: the writer failed to identify the topic—to tell the reader who or what the essay is about. Readers can infer that the essay is describing a large man ("he," "huge body frame") and find enough details to form some impressions of the man's physical and mental qualities, but they cannot identify him. The description suggests a fighter, but is it a particular fighter—Muhammed Ali or the hero of *Rocky*— is it someone known only to the writer? Writers of incoherent essays often failed to identify their topic even though the instructions for the writing task reminded them to "name what you are describing." These writers apparently assumed that readers shared the information they possessed and that the topic was, therefore, "given" information.[19] Their descriptive details enabled readers to infer a superordinate term—man, building, monument, etc.—but not to identify the topic unless it was a very familiar object or place (i.e., the Statue of Liberty).

Writers of essays with clear topic statements, on the other hand, regarded the topic as new information that should be stated at the beginning of the essay. The most skillful writers not only identified their topic but provided an introduction that oriented the reader to the situation and placed the subject in context by identifying time, place, and circumstance.[20]

> When you cross the Golden Gate Bridge from San Francisco to Sausalito, on your right you see an ominous object in the middle of the bay. It's an island called Alcatraz. Water smashes up against the rocks and gulls fly over this godforsaken, lonely, deserted prison. There are many buildings which now lay crumbling to ruins. A lone water tower juts up from the rest of the building. Once the buildings were white but now only gray buildings sun cracked remain.
>
> It sits out in the middle of the San Francisco Bay by itself crying for it has been the ruin of many men. It was almost inescapable until it was shut down. The Indians took it over and much of it was burned and devastated in the early seventies. The only way to reach it was by small boat. No one was permitted on it unless given special governmental permission. In August 1974 it was opened to the public.

The description of Alcatraz begins successfully because the writer establishes the setting (San Francisco Bay) and the tone ("ominous object") in addition to identifying the topic. More often, writers announced the topic, but expected the reader to fill in the context:

> I am describing an ancient Egyptian statue of the goddess Bastet.
>
> The statue is made of bronze, and is extremely old, dating back to perhaps 1087 bc. The figure of Bastet is slender, with fine contours of the body. The goddess is cat-headed, with large erect ears and slanting eyes. She is wearing a tight-fitting sheath-like garment, which emphasizes her graceful female body and noble carriage. At her feet are several tiny bronze kittens.

The writer of the essay above clearly identifies her topic, even emphasizes it by setting it off as a paragraph, but fails to create a context for the description. A reader must draw on his world knowledge—ancient statues are usually viewed in museums—to construct the context. Whether readers can construct a context will, of course, depend upon their background and their prior knowledge as well as on the information provided by the writer.

The "describe" topic tended to elicit from writers a list of attributes, a more difficult organizational structure for readers to process and recall than structures such as comparison, problem-solution, or cause-effect.[21] When writers failed to arrange these details according to an overall plan, readers often had difficulty integrating the details into a coherent whole. Writers of coherent essays used several different ordering plans to create a global structure. One effective arrangement orders descriptive details according to a plan of movement such as general to particular, whole to part, and container to contained.[22] The essay on Alcatraz begins with such a strategy: the writer first gives general statements describing the whole complex ("This godforsaken, lonely, deserted prison"), then moves to particular details describing parts of the prison ("buildings crumbling to ruins," "a lone water tower"). He does not sustain this order through the essay, however, and the last section simply lists events that occurred after the prison was closed. The writer who described Bastet arranges her description more effectively by sustaining the whole-to-part, general-to-particular plan throughout the essay and by arranging particular details describing the statue in a spatial order from top to bottom. The reader thus sees Bastet much as he might if standing before a glass case in a museum—first the whole statue, then her "cat's head," her "graceful female body," and finally the "tiny bronze kittens" at her feet.

The "riddle" structure was another plan used—with surprising frequency and varying success.[23] In "riddle" essays, the writer deliberately withheld the identity of the subject, listed attributes that would let the reader "guess" the subject, and optionally revealed the "answer" in the final sentence. Generally, riddle essays were judged coherent when the writer finally identified the topic or included enough description details to enable the reader to infer the subject. The most successful riddle essays did both, the final identification confirming the reader's guess.

Other writers organized descriptive details in the form of a "tour." In these essays the writer seemed to be taking the reader on a guided tour of the place being described, a strategy that transformed spatial information into a chronologically organized narrative.[24] In the essay below, the writer first created a context for the reader by narrating the events leading up to a family visit to Pala Dura Canyon and the initial stage of the trip. She began her tour as her family's car entered the canyon:

> As we entered the entrance gates of Pala Dura we could gaze down and look at the tall trees and cliffs which were much lower than we were. The narrow paved road was built on the side of a mountain and the far side was protected by guard railings. Many signs were up warning tourists not to park on this road because of the possibility of falling rocks. As we continued on down the road our ears soon became stopped up because of the rapid decrease in altitude. When we finally reached the bottom of the canyon, we could look up and see what we had seen coming down.

By carefully signaling each stage of the tour through the canyon—"As we entered the entrance gates"; "As we continued on down the road"; "When we finally reached the bottom of the canyon," the writer recreated the visit for readers, thereby providing a narrative sequence into which descriptive details could be woven.

The whole-to-part, riddle, and tour plans used to arrange descriptive details share a common feature: they are structures of knowledge familiar in our experience and are thus ready accessible to both writers and readers. The whole-to-part, general-to-particular and spatial orders reflect the way we normally perceive places or objects—first grasping the gestalt, then observing particulars, usually in a systematic spatial order. Riddles and tours, both part of the typical elementary school child's world, are well practiced and familiar patterns by age seventeen. Writers who failed to draw on these or other ordering strategies produced essays that were essentially lists of unordered details:

> It is a exciting place with characters such as Mickey Mouse or Donald Duck running around.
>
> The rides are fun, but the lines can become quite long. The rides all seem to be real. And in the president's Hall of Fame, the presidents actually breathe. When Lincoln is giving a speeches, two other president's turn toward each other and start whispering.
>
> The grounds are always clean. There are boys and girls who go around with a tray on a handle and brooms and pick up everything even cigerate butts.
>
> When you first go in, you buy a book of tickets. And when you ride something, you give them a ticket. Also, when you leave your motel, you ride on a monorail.
>
> The motels are nice. They both have heated pools and you can rent boats (peddle) and ride in the lagoon.
>
> The experience is well worth your time and your money. But it is better to go during school, so it won't be as crowded.

Although many readers can probably infer that the essay above is describing Disneyland, they will find no structure to help them organize the details. Even though each paragraph indentation signals a different set of descriptive details (the rides, the grounds, the motels, etc.), the details follow no logical, spatial, or temporal order. Placing them in separate paragraphs gives readers little help in integrating them into a coherent whole.

The failure of 17-year-olds to achieve coherence because of incomplete announcement of the topic, failure to establish a context, and/or selection of an inadequate organizational plan may seem surprising, particularly since the topic makes relatively low-level cognitive demands.[25] Essays on more complex topics often lack global or overall coherence because writers have not yet discovered the main point they wish to make about their subject or have not yet fully understood the relationships among their ideas. In most of the essays in this study, however, writers simply failed to give readers necessary information about the topic or to organize the details adequately.

Writers (students and others) may have difficulties in focusing on topic and selecting a plan of organization, or in creating a context for their readers, because they continue to struggle with the production of words and sentences. Fear of error can halt the flow of discourse and cripple a writer's attempts to project and sustain plans.[26] However, many essays lacking discourse-level coherence were not particularly error-ridden. (See, for example, the essay above that describes Disneyland.) These essays fit Linda Flower's description of "writer-based" prose: retaining an egocentric focus, ordering ideas with a narrative framework or merely listing them randomly in survey form, and relying on general "code" words or phrases that draw their meaning from the writer's individual experience and are, therefore, not accessible to readers. Flower views the composing of "writer-based" prose as a functional strategy because it allows writers to avoid overloading the short-term memory, lets them concentrate on retrieving information from memory, and postpones the task of forming complex concepts or considering the reader's needs. Flower argues that "writer-based" prose should be seen as a "half-way place," writing that can later be transformed into reader-based prose that takes into account the reader's needs and purpose in reading.[27] Accordingly, impromptu essays such as these should be regarded as first drafts, not as the best writing that students can produce.

Nevertheless, the writing elicited by the topic illustrates a full range of writing skills among 17-year-olds. The better writers were able to take the reader's perspective from the beginning and produced well-structured, coherent essays. This ability seems to be a consequence of both the writer's skill and experience and the relative lack of difficulty in the writing task. Based on the holistic ratings of coherence, the percentage of students able to write coherent or partially coherent first drafts on this topic increased from 39% to 51% between ages 13 and 17, a reflection of the writers' developing control over written discourse. However, some writers of coherent first drafts on this topic would almost certainly be unable to duplicate their success if given a conceptually more demanding topic. The National Assessment's first analysis of mechanics found that essays written in 1974 contained fewer coherent paragraphs than those written in 1969,[28] and some "back-to-the-basics" critics interpreted these results as further justification for more instruction in grammar and in production of correct sentences. But another look at the failures of coherence in these essays indicates that the most serious coherence problems occurred over the whole discourse.

The difficulties students experienced in writing coherent essays for the National Assessment give us a starting point for identifying ways in which we can intervene in students' composing processes to help them produce more coherent texts. Essays that have only local coherence problems can often be improved by careful editing or proofreading—adding words and phrases to make relationships between sentences more explicit or correcting mechanical errors that interfere with the reading process. However, essays that are incoherent overall almost always require major restructuring and rewriting to provide the unity, organization, and identification of context needed by a reader.

Writers cannot always take the reader's perspective during their initial planning and drafting, but they can revise their first efforts into coherent texts if they know what makes a text coherent and know how to revise so that a text meets those conditions for coherence. However, research on revision indicates that most student writers do not revise effectively. They revise primarily sentences or words, making minor adjustments that are largely cosmetic or have a minimal effect on the text. Others, especially weaker writers, edit their work prematurely and are unable to sustain their focus on a topic or maintain a plan of organization. Only a few seem able to make the substantive changes that would convert writer-based to reader-based prose.[29]

If producing writer-based prose is to be for students a functional goal of composing, we must be able to teach them to revise effectively. Finding effective teaching strategies, however, is not easy. Peer group reading of essays in progress, one of the most frequently recommended techniques derived from research on the writing process, promotes effective revision by helping students internalize the needs of readers. It not only gives them responses to their writing from a real audience, but also makes them aware of the needs of that audience as readers when they respond to essays written by their fellow students. Peer readers are particularly good at pointing out places where more detail or information is needed in order to orient readers or to fill in gaps in the text, where terms are unclear, where connections between sentences need to be more explicit, and where digressions or shifts of topic occur. But although peer readers can often identify poor organization as a problem, they are less often able to propose a plan or overall design that will eliminate the difficulty.

Both composition teachers and textbook writers recognize the importance of organization. But, like peer readers, both groups are often unable to help students find satisfactory designs for their essays. Perhaps the best known attempt to propose an essay structure which students can start with has resulted in the Procrustean formula for the five-paragraph essay, a prescription rightly rejected as too rigid and limiting. Nevertheless, the most successful NAEP essays were those in which writers projected and sustained an overall design—such as the whole-to-part and tour plans—that controlled the entire essay. But even though these plans successfully organize descriptive details, they are likely to have limited applicability to other types of writing. They could not, for example, serve as adequate designs for the more analytic expository and persuasive discourse commonly demanded by universities and businesses. Moreover, the NAEP essays were quite short, and longer essays attempting more complex tasks may need to draw at various times on several different plans to organize their information. Writers need to learn practical and flexible strategies that will help them organize the information in their essays—even when these are fairly short—and to learn ways to help readers remain aware of these plans.[30]

When we look at coherence in its broadest sense, we become aware that almost any feature—whether seen locally or over the whole discourse—has the potential to affect a reader's ability to integrate details of a text into a coherent whole. But although effective writing will be coherent at both levels, attention to overall coherence must precede most concerns about local coherence. First drafts are likely to have global or overall coherence only when the writing task is routine or when it makes relatively low-level cognitive demands. Our goal as writing teachers must be to create a classroom setting that enables students to understand what makes a text coherent and to teach them ways of revising their writing to meet those conditions.

NOTES

1. Bain's six paragraph rules first appeared in the 1866 edition of *English Composition and Rhetoric*, a manual designed for his classes at the University of Aberdeen. All six rules, adapted from the 1866 and 1887 editions, are restated in Ned A. Shearer, "Alexander Bain and the Genesis of Paragraph Theory," *Quarterly Journal of Speech*, 58 (December, 1972), 413. For a discussion of these rules and the development of paragraph theory in the second half of the nineteenth century, see Paul C. Rodgers, Jr., "Alexander Bain and the Rise of the Organic Paragraph," *Quarterly Journal of Speech*, 51 (December, 1965), 399–408.
2. *Writing With a Purpose, Short Edition* (Boston: Houghton Mifflin Company, 1980), pp. 104–110.
3. National Assessment of Educational Progress, *Writing Mechanics 1969–1974*, Writing Report No. 05-W-01. (Washington, D.C.; U.S. Government Printing Office, 1975).
4. *Cohesion in English* (London: Longman, 1976), pp. 1–30.
5. "Coherence, Cohesion, and Writing Quality," *College Composition and Communication*, 32 (May, 1981), 189–204.
6. See van Dijk's discussion in *Macrostructures* (Hillsdale, NJ: Lawrence Erlbaum Associates, 1980), pp. 32–46. Local coherence differs from cohesion in that, for local coherence, logical relationships between sentences need not be explicitly stated. In this essay, I am using Van Dijk's more inclusive term "local coherence" rather than Halliday and Hasan's term "cohesion."
7. Teun A. van Dijk, *Text and Context: Explorations in the Semantics and Pragmatics of Discourse* (London: Longman, 1977). p. 149.
8. Roger Schank and Robert Abelson, *Scripts, Plans, Goals and Understanding* (Hillsdale, NJ: Lawrence Erlbaum Associates, 1977).
9. "The Transformation of Experience in Narrative Syntax" *Language in the Inner City: Studies in the Black English Vernacular* (Philadelphia: University of Pennsylvania Press, 1972), pp. 354–396. One of the earliest and best known story grammars is David Rumelhart, "Notes on a Schema for Stories," in D. Bobrow and A. Collins, ed., *Representation and Understanding* (New York: Academic Press, 1975), pp. 237–272. For a recent summary of this research see Teun A. van Dijk, "Story Comprehension: An Introduction," *Poetics* 9 (June, 1980), 1–21.
10. Marcel Just and Patricia Carpenter, eds., *Cognitive Processes in Comprehension* (Hillsdale, NJ.: Lawrence Erlbaum Assoc., 1977).

11. "Rethinking Coherence: A Conceptual Analysis and Its Implications for Teaching Practice," in Marilyn Sternglass and Douglas Buttruff, ed., *Building the Bridge Between Reading and Writing* (Conway, AR: L&S Books, in press).
12. "Reading: A Psycholinguistic Guessing Game," in Doris V. Gunderson, ed., *Language and Reading* (Washington, D.C.: Center for Applied Linguistics, 1970), pp. 107–119.
13. Frank Smith, *Understanding Reading* (New York: Holt, Rinehart & Winston, 1971).
14. Marilyn Adams and Allan Collins, "A Schema-Theoretic View of Reading," in Roy O. Freedle, ed., *New Directions in Discourse Processing, Vol.* 2 (Norwood, NJ: Ablex Publishing Co., 1979), pp. 1–21.
15. In the "1974 Mechanics Scoring Guide" (mimeo, 12 pp., n.d.), paragraph coherence was defined as "the interconnectedness among sentences and among the ideas of those sentences." The scoring guide listed four major ways of achieving coherence: (1) consistency in time, voice, person, number, subject; (2) clear pronoun reference; (3) use of transitional markers; and (4) use of rhetorical strategies such as lexical repetition, parallel structure, antithesis. Paragraphs were both coherent and developed if, in addition to meeting the above criteria, they had an expressed or implied topic sentence that "identifies and limits the central area of concern in the paragraph" with each subsequent sentence adding to or explaining something about the main idea in an orderly manner. Paragraphs which were "neither coherent nor developed" according to the criteria above, along with most one-sentence paragraphs, were grouped into a category labeled "Paragraph Used." This amorphous term allowed NAEP to group together paragraphs that lacked coherence and paragraphs in which the indentation was essentially a graphic device. The number of paragraphs in this last category was used by the National Assessment to estimate the level of coherence in National Assessment essays. A short form of the scoring guide may be found in *Writing Mechanics 1969–1974,* 1975.
16. Essays meeting the following criteria were rated "fully coherent" (4) on the four-point holistic coherence rubric: writer identifies the topic; writer does not shift topics or digress; writer orients the reader by describing the context or situation; writer organizes details according to a discernible plan that is sustained throughout the essay; writer skillfully uses cohesive ties such as lexical cohesion, conjunction, reference, etc. to link sentences and/or paragraphs together; writer often concludes with a statement that gives the reader a definite sense of closure; writer makes few or no grammatical and/or mechanical errors that interrupt the discourse flow or the reading process. Essays that were partially coherent (3) met enough of the criteria above so that a reader could make at least a partial integration of the text. Essays were rated incoherent (2) when some of the following prevented a reader from integrating the text into a coherent whole: writer does not identify the topic and the reader would be unlikely to infer or guess the topic from the details provided; writer shifts topics or digresses frequently from the topic; writer assumes the reader shares his/her context and provides little or no orientation; writer has no organizational plan in most of the text and frequently relies on listing; writer uses few cohesive ties such as lexical cohesion, conjunction, reference, etc. to link sentences and/or paragraphs together; writer creates no sense of closure; writer makes numerous mechanical and/or grammatical errors, resulting in interruption of the reading process and a rough or irregular discourse flow. Essays receiving the lowest score (1) were literally incomprehensible because missing or misleading cues prevented readers from

making sense of the text. Inter-rater reliability on the holistic rescoring was .85. Although the holistic scores and original NAEP coherence ratings overlapped, almost 40% of the 17-year-olds' essays containing one or more paragraphs not given a "coherent" rating by NAEP were reclassified as coherent by the holistic scoring. Most of these essays contain brief one- or two-sentence paragraphs that were on the topic and fit into the overall organization of the essay but were excluded from NAEP's "coherent" paragraph category because of their brevity.

17. For a discussion of holistic and other types of evaluation scales, see Lee Odell and Charles Cooper, "Procedures for Evaluating Writing: Assumptions and Needed Research," *College English,* 42 (September, 1980), 35–43.

18. This and all subsequent essays used as examples were written by 17-year-olds for the 1974 National Assessment. Essays are transcribed exactly, including all grammatical and mechanical errors. Essays from the *Writing Mechanics Analysis* are available on computer tape from the Education Commission of the States, Suite 700, 1860 Lincoln Street, Denver, Colorado 80203.

19. Herbert Clark and Susan Haviland, "Comprehension and the Given-New Contract," in Roy O. Freedle, ed., *Discourse Production and Comprehension, Vol. I* (Norwood, NJ: Ablex Publishing Co., 1977), pp. 1–39.

20. Teun A. van Dijk discusses state descriptions (descriptions of places or static objects) and the importance of creating a context in *Macrostructures*, p. 35.

21. Bonnie J. Meyer, "What is Remembered From Prose: A Function of Passage Structure," in Roy O. Freedle, ed., *Discourse Production and Comprehension,* Vol. I (Norwood, NJ: Ablex Publishing Co., 1977), pp. 307–336.

22. Van Dijk, *Macrostructures*, p. 35.

23. Colleen Aycock and Kevin O'Connor, two graduate students at the University of Southern California, first identified the riddle plan in these essays.

24. My use of this term is taken from a study by Charlotte Linde and William Labov, "Spatial Networks as a Site for the Study of Language and Thought," *Language,* 51 (December, 1975), 924–939. Almost all (97%) of the New Yorkers asked to describe the layout of their apartment used a tour plan. Readers of transcribed apartment tours often found them confusing and hard to follow, perhaps because of the complex spacial relationships. In the NAEP essays the tour plan was usually an effective organizational structure.

25. In *The Development of Writing Abilities* (11–18) (London: Macmillan Education Ltd., 1975), James Britton divides transactional writing into seven categories according to level of abstraction. Within his divisions, most of the "describe" essays would be classified at the second level, report, and a few at the next level up, generalized narrative.

26. Mina Shaughnessy, *Errors and Expectations* (New York: Oxford University Press, 1977) and Sondra Perl, ""The Composing Processes of Unskilled College Writers," *Research in the Teaching of English,* 13 (December, 1979), 317–336, document this phenomenon from different perspectives.

27. "Writer-Based Prose, A Cognitive Basis for Problems in Writing," *College English,* 41 (September, 1979), 19–37.

28. *Writing Mechanics Report,* 1975.

29. For research on students' revision strategies see Richard Beach, "Self-Evaluation Strategies of Extensive Revisers and Nonrevisers," *College Composition and Communication,* 27 (May, 1976), 160–164; Nancy Sommers, "Revision Strategies

of Student Writers and Experienced Adult Writers," *College Composition and Communication* 31 (December, 1980), 378–388; and Lillian Bridwell, "Revising Strategies in Twelfth Grade Students' Transactional Writing," *Research in the Teaching of English,* 14 (October, 1980), 197–222.

30. In "Toward a Linear Rhetoric of the Essay," *College Composition and Communication* (May, 1971), 140–146, Richard Larson illustrates a method of essay analysis that focuses on writers' purposes as a way of perceiving their organizational plans. He suggests that this procedure may help students construct plans for their own writing, In a recent paper "Pragmatics of Form: In This Paper I Will Assert, Dispute, Confirm, Recount, and Recommend," presented at the Conference on College Composition and Communication, Dallas, March 1981, Marilyn Cooper links a writer's purposes to specific speech acts and discusses the conditions for their successful performance. She argues that a writer's illocutionary intentions can be used to create a pragmatic form—that is, form conceived as a series of purposes to be achieved rather than simply a series of topics to be discussed.

Teaching Style

Edward P. J. Corbett

The study and teaching of style was a central concern of Edward P. J. Corbett throughout his career. In his book Style and Statement, *co-authored with Robert J. Connors, and in many of the articles collected by Connors in* Selected Essays of Edward P. J. Corbett, *Corbett explores classical and 18th-century rhetoric as well as recent studies for effective approaches to analyzing and teaching style. In this article, first published in Donald A. McQuade's 1986 book,* The Territory of Language: Linguistics, Stylistics, and the Teaching of Composition, *Corbett describes pedagogies past and present that develop students' styles through analysis and imitation. Close analysis of another's style, Corbett claims, teaches students to use language self-consciously as they read and write and provides them with a vocabulary to help them analyze their sentences and make informed stylistic decisions.*

If your educational experience in any way resembled mine, you have been uncertain about what style is. *Style* was a familiar enough word for you, but your concept of style was probably vague. You sensed that certain authors had a distinctive style, but you were not quite sure what it meant to say that an author "has style" and even less sure about what made a style distinctive. In reading a piece of prose, you experienced an undeniable effect, but you could not designate just what it was in that collection of sentences that caused that effect. Consequently, you still may not know how to analyze style or how to talk about it in any meaningful way.

Style may be a vague concept to us because our own teachers spent little or no time talking about style. They may have used such general terms as "lucid," "elegant," "labored," "Latinate," "turgid," or "flowing" in commenting on an author's style, but they never bothered to analyze the features or the constituents of the styles that bore those epithets. Those were largely impressionistic labels, and if we too regarded a certain authors style as, say, "turgid"—whatever *that* was—then we agreed with our teacher's classification of the style. But if we felt that this same author had a "lilting style" we knew no way of describing a "lilting style" or no way of refuting our teacher's judgment. So we dutifully copied down in out notebooks the appropriate

Edward P. J. Corbett. "Teaching Style" from *Selected Essays of Edward P. J. Corbett,* edited by Robert J. Connors, Southern Methodist University Press, 1989.

epithets for each author we read and discussed in class, and we delighted in moving on to talk about more determinable matters, like the content or the structure of the piece of literature. If we listed ourselves as members of that post-World War II generation of students who regularly practiced the Brooks and Warren method of close analysis, we could talk about the linguistic features of a poem with great specificity. Yet we may well have been stymied when we wanted to talk about the linguistic features of a prose text.

If you could put these questions concerning style (what is it? what effects does it produce in a reader? what does one look for in studying it?) to a Renaissance schoolboy, he could give you satisfactory answers. His education was predominantly language-oriented. From the beginning to the end of the school day, he was steeped in words—English words, Latin words, sometimes even Greek words. He had to recite the grammatical rules that he had memorized the night before; he had to paraphrase sentences; he had to translate Latin sentences into English sentences or English sentences into Latin sentences; he had to be able to write original sentences according to a prescribed pattern; he had to paraphrase sentences in a variety of ways; he had to be able to recognize, classify, and define the schemes and tropes in a passage being studied (and there were more than a hundred of those listed in the Renaissance rhetoric texts). T.W. Baldwin's *William Shakespere's Small Latine & Lesse Greeke,* or Sister Miriam Joseph's *Shakespeare's Use of the Arts of Language,* or Donald L. Clark's *John Milton at St. Paul's School will* give you a generous sense of the language-arts regimen that the Tudor school boy was subjected to in the grammar schools.[1] If we required of our students what Renaissance schoolmasters demanded of theirs, we would no doubt face a general revolt.

This rigorous regimen, however, produced students who really learned grammar and rhetoric and who knew not only the meaning of style but also the procedures for analyzing someone else's style and improving their own. They could tell you that style represented the choices that an author made from the lexical and syntactical resources of the language. Style represented a curious blend of the idiosyncratic and the conventional. The more idiosyncratic a style, the more distinctive it became; the more conventional, the more bland it likely became—although not necessarily less serviceable for being bland. In one sense, then, "Style was the man," because it represented the characteristic way in which a person expressed his or her thoughts and feelings.

For that reason, everyone can be said to "have a style." But some styles are more pleasing, more distinctive, more effective than others. Some writers can command several styles—a range of styles into which they can readily shift as the subject matter, the occasion, or the audience necessitates. There are high styles and low styles and middle styles. In his book *The Five Clocks,* Martin Joos compares these various styles to what he calls the five registers—the frozen, the formal, the consultative, the casual, and the intimate.[2] Joos also notes that sophisticated language-users can shift into and out of these registers as the occasion demands.

Some people do not command the full range of styles or registers, simply because they have not yet acquired the full repertory of diction and syntax needed for stylistic versatility. As the philosophers would say, they have the command *potentially* but not *actually*. Our task as teachers is to turn the *potency* into *act*.

If we as teachers want to engage our students in the study of style, the first point that needs to be made is that the circumstances in which we teach may not allow us to deal with style at all. Many of us teach in a curriculum so crowded that there simply is not enough time to deal adequately with style. And the study of style does take time. The Renaissance schoolmaster had the same group of pupils for the full academic year, often had them six days a week for six to eight hours a day. That generous allotment of time allowed for relentless recitation, rigorous drill, and reinforcing repetition. And the curriculum then was not as cluttered as it is now. If you cannot devote at least two weeks to the study of style, either in a concentrated period or in scattered sessions throughout the semester, you had better not deal with style at all.

The relative sophistication of your students in language matters may also determine whether you can deal with style in the classroom. I can imagine some teachers saying, "Good heavens, I have all I can do just to get my students to the point where they can consistently write sentences that parse. My students have to learn how to walk before I can teach them how to run." There is no question that a minimal grammatical competence is a *sine qua non* for stylistic studies. If style represents the choices one makes from the available grammatical options, then students must have at least a basic awareness of what the grammatical options are if they are to profit from stylistic studies. But a deficiency in conscious knowledge of grammar is not an insuperable disqualification for studying style. Many students can learn their grammar while studying style. I have found that students are invariably fascinated by style—not only because it offers something new and different but also because it provides an element of fun in changing words and shifting parts. And in such a positive and creative atmosphere, students may well be more inclined to develop an interest in grammar or at least to absorb grammar subconsciously.

Studying style in English courses can have two focuses or objectives: to learn either how to analyze someone else's style or how to improve our own. These two objectives are ancillary rather than countervailing. As teachers, we can pursue either or both, but we should determine our main objective for the course at the outset. Learning how to analyze someone else's style belongs primarily to the literature class; learning how to improve one's own style belongs primarily to the composition class. But there is no reason why both kinds of learning cannot take place in both classes. In fact, learning how to analyze someone else's style in the composition class is almost a necessary prelude for learning how to improve one's own style. By analyzing an accomplished writer's style, we can recognize the marks of effective style, and then we can begin, either consciously or unconsciously, to incorporate some of those features into our own style. The process works in reverse too. By deliberately working on our own style to refine it, we learn what to look for in analyzing someone else's style.

Studying style begins with some awareness of what we should look at or look for. In the chapter on style in my *Classical Rhetoric for the Modern Student* and in my "A Method of Analyzing Prose Style, with a Demonstration Analysis of Swift's 'A Modest Proposal,'" I outline the features that can be observed and analyzed.[3] I divide these features into four main categories: diction, sentence patterns, figures of speech, and paragraphing. But my designating those main categories may not be very helpful to you. What about diction? What about sentence patterns? Just what aspects of diction and sentence patterns are significant?

Let me be a little more specific here. A writer's choice of words contributes to the effects that style has on readers. If we think about it for a moment, we must acknowledge that choosing a big word or a little word, a general word or a specific word, an abstract word or a concrete word does make a difference in what the text conveys to us either explicitly or implicitly. And when we observe that certain kinds of words are recurrent, when we observe that sets of words exemplify certain motifs, these words become even more significant because of what they tell us about an author's characteristic way of saying things. A writer's working vocabulary—the stock of words that a writer actually uses in a piece of writing rather than the words that he or she can recognize in someone else's writing—reflects the range of a writer's knowledge and interests. The larger one's working vocabulary, the more likely it is that one can choose precise diction. Shakespeare's working vocabulary of over 21,000 words was an extraordinary lexicon—and not only for his time.

The study of the lexical element of style involves fewer objectively observable items than the study of any other stylistic element. By the term "objectively observable item," I mean an item which can be definitely classified by observation rather than by judgment. For instance, one can decide whether a particular word is monosyllabic or polysyllabic by simply looking at the word. The decision, however, about whether a word is abstract or concrete, general or specific, often involves a judgment, because those dichotomies are more relative than absolute. Consider, for example, a sentence like "The wealthy Texan owned huge herds of cattle." Is the word *cattle* general or specific? It is more specific than *livestock* but less specific than *steers.* Because of the relativity of the general-specific dichotomy, the classifier has to make an arbitrary judgment about the word *cattle* in this particular context. In this respect, it is worth remembering that any tabulating of percentages of words in a text according to whether the words are abstract or concrete, general or specific, formal or informal, denotative or connotative is likely to be somewhat less than precise, simply because in many instances the yes-no decision represents someone's arbitrary judgment.

When we move on to study collocations of words in sentences, we find not only more objectively observable items but more significant features of writing habits. Most of the stylistic features of sentences are objectively observable items:

length of sentences (in number of words); grammatical types of sentences (simple, compound, complex, compound-complex); rhetorical types of sentences (loose, periodic, balanced, antithetical); functional types of sentences (statement, question, command, exclamation); types and frequency of sentence-openers; methods and location of expansions in sentences; amount of embedding. Analysis and classification of features like those tell us a great deal about the level of a writer's "syntactic fluency."

Syntactic patterns also tell us something about the way a writer structures his or her thoughts, about a writer's "epistemic orientation," to use Richard Ohmann's term.[4] The frequent occurrence, for instance, of balanced or antithetical patterns in Dr. Johnson's sentences suggests that he tended to structure his thinking in terms of parallel or opposing dichotomies. The many levels of subordination in John Henry Newman's prose suggests that he tended to see things in terms of hierarchies. The stringing together of independent clauses in Hemingway's prose, often with redundant use of coordinating conjunctions, indicates that Hemingway tended to view the phenomenal world as a flux of discrete, coordinate elements. Henry James's heavy use of parenthetical elements reflects a mind disposed to meticulous qualifications. And so on.

The gathering of data about syntactic patterns involves a lot of tedious counting and tabulating. Data of that sort were not previously available because the counting and measuring had to be done by hand and took hours and weeks. When Edwin Lewis and L.A. Sherwin did their studies in the 1890s of sentence and paragraph length in the works of several British writers, they did all their counting by hand.[5] Today, the computer facilitates such tedious data-gathering, and as a result, stylistic studies of large corpuses of prose and poetry have proliferated.

Collecting data—once tedious and time-consuming—still must be done. We are much more impressed when someone pronounces that a certain writer strings together unusually long sentences and supports that claim with the empirically derived evidence that the writer's average sentence length is 37.8 words. And we are further impressed by the disclosure that 18 percent of that writer's sentences are ten or more words longer than that average.

How much of a corpus has to be studied before valid generalizations can be made about someone's style? I have told undergraduate students studying style—either their own or some professional writer's—that they must analyze somewhere between 1000 and 1500 words of a piece of prose. That is not very much really at most four double-spaced typescript pages, maybe two pages of printed text. But it is substantial enough to allow for some valid inferences to be drawn. Students writing a dissertation or a scholarly article on someone's prose style should be reminded not only that they would have to study a much larger corpus but also that they would have to study several specimens of a writer's prose, pieces written at different periods and on different subject matters for different audiences. As in any inductive study, the larger and the more representative the sampling, the safer the conclusions will be.

The gathering of data is a necessary stage but should not be the stopping point. Necessary as the gathering of the data is, what one does with the data matters more. Data—even raw statistical data—can convey some illuminating information. But often the full or the most salient significance of the data depends upon interpretation. The act of interpretation calls upon all of one's intellectual and imaginative powers; it requires that one shift from the role of a mere counter to the role of a critic.

Critical interpretation demands that one be able to detect the relevance or the relationship of the data to the exigencies of the rhetorical situation—to the occasion, purpose, subject matter, audience, or author of the discourse. We may find, for instance, that in a particular discourse, the author used an unusually high percentage of interrogative sentences—let us say 18 percent, almost one out of every five sentences. Why? A question like that poses a real challenge for the critic. The critic may find the answer by relating the statistical fact to the nature of the subject matter that the author addressed. The writer may have been writing on a subject about which he was uncertain. He was exploring the subject, probing for answers. So he frequently resorted to questions, knowing that sometimes asking the right questions can be as illuminating as proposing hesitant answers. Or the critic might relate the statistical fact to the disposition of the audience for this piece of discourse. The author, let us say, knew that his audience harbored a certain hostility to the position he was espousing. He knew that he could exacerbate that hostility if he were dogmatic in his pronouncements. So he decided that it would be a prudent strategy to soften his assertiveness by frequently resorting to the tentativeness of questions. But looking closely at his questions might reveal, for example, that many of them are framed as rhetorical questions in which the writer has subtly implied the answers he wants to elicit from his audience.

That kind of interpretation, that kind of relating of fact to function, may be beyond the capacity of some students in basic writing courses. After all, that kind of interpretation requires a great deal of linguistic and rhetorical sophistication. Some students may not be mature enough to make such connections and to come forth with anything more than the most superficial interpretation. But the present incapacity of some students for such critical insights is not the issue. They have learned something valuable about the text simply from gathering the data. They have learned something too from the mere *attempt* to interpret the data. Inadequate as their interpretation may be, they have grown a few inches in the attempt.

In addition to diction and syntax, there are other aspects of style that we might have our students look at: the incidence of figures of speech, the rhythms of sentences, the manner of paragraphing.

A figure of speech may be defined as any artful deviation from the ordinary way of speaking or writing. The classical rhetoricians commonly divided the *figura* into two main groups: schemes and tropes. A scheme involves a deliberate deviation from the ordinary pattern or arrangement of words. In addition to common patterns like parallelism and antithesis, schemes include such artistic patterns as the inversion of the natural or normal word order *(anastrophe),* deliberate omission of the normally expected conjunctions in a series of related words, phrases, or clauses *(asyndeton),* repetition of the same word or group of words at the beginning of successive clauses *(anaphora),* repetition of initial consonants in two or more adjacent words *(alliteration),* and reversal of the grammatical structures in successive clauses *(chiasmus* or *crisscross*). Tropes, the second main kind of figurative language, are deliberate deviations from the ordinary *meaning* of words and include such familiar figures as metaphor, simile, hyperbole, synecdoche, metonymy, oxymoron, and irony.

In the schools of rhetoric, pupils were expected to be able to identity, define, and illustrate the figures they encountered in the texts they read and to be able to invent similar figures. Their task was complicated by the fact that the number of schemes and tropes had proliferated enormously. *Rhetorica ad Herennium,* an influential Roman rhetoric text, listed 65 figures; the 1577 edition of Henry Peacham's *The Garden of Eloquence* identified 184. Undoubtedly, the proliferation of the figures resulted from overly subtle anatomizing, but amazingly, once students were made aware of the many kinds of artful deviations from the normal meanings or arrangements or words, they readily found the figures in the prose and poetry they read. In the second edition of my *Classical Rhetoric for the Modern Student,* more than half of the schemes and tropes illustrated there were supplied to me by two classes of freshman students who, over a six-week period, searched for examples in their reading. They found a surprising number of examples in magazine advertisements and television commercials. Once students become familiar with a wide range of schemes and tropes, they find them everywhere, even where authors were not conscious that they were creating figures.

What should teachers encourage students to look for when studying the figures, and what does the occurrence of figures tell them about an author's style? First of all, we ought to ask them simply to look for the schemes and tropes. When they find them, they ought to identify and tabulate them and perhaps draw up some statistical information about them. If there are many schemes and tropes, they can begin to classify them into groups or clusters. A particular author, let us say, uses mainly schemes of repetition. Most of this author's metaphors are based on agricultural analogies. Certain patterns or motifs begin to emerge that tell students something about a particular author's mind-set. The presence—or the absence—of figures tells students something about the texture and flavor of an author's prose.

In the modern classroom, teachers rarely, if ever, consider prose rhythms, but our forebears in Greek and Latin schools regularly engaged their pupils in analyzing and composing various prose rhythms. The Greeks and the Romans, of course, had developed elaborate prosodies for their synthetic languages, and since a good deal of their formal communication took place in the oral medium, they were much more conscious than we of the sounds and rhythms of words when they composed their orations. We have only to read sections of Cicero's rhetoric texts or his orations to find out the careful attention this rhetorician gave to the composition of euphonious prose.

English-speaking people probably lost their ear for verbal rhythms when written or printed documents superseded oral discourse as the primary mode of communication. In the late eighteenth century, the elocutionary movement in England, fostered by former actors like Thomas Sheridan, tried to revive interest in the sounds of prose.[6] Although English teachers continued to teach students how to scan lines of poetry, they began to lose all interest in the aural dimensions of prose early in the twentieth century, along about 1915, when teachers of speech formally divorced themselves from the National Council of Teachers of English and formed their own speech association.

But at a time when the aural element has become dominant again and music is the favorite medium of young people, perhaps we should revive the study of prose rhythms in the classroom. Literateurs like George Saintsbury have shown us that there is an elaborate prosody for scanning prose rhythms,[7] but I would not recommend that we spend valuable time in the classroom exploring the technicalities of that system. If we would revive the practice of reading prose aloud, we might be able to cultivate our students' ears for the harmonies of prose. In the February 1977 issue of *College Composition and Communication,* Thomas Kane published an engaging article about what teachers might do in the classroom to cultivate a sense for the ring and rhythm of well-constructed sentences.[8] Prose, of course, is most often read silently, but curiously enough, euphonious sentences somehow disclose their meanings more easily than awkwardly constructed sentences do, even when read silently. Rhythm is a neglected area of stylistic study, but the classical rhetoricians were right when they preached that the harmonies of prose did make a positive contribution to the conveyance of a message.

For the classical rhetoricians, stylistic study rarely extended beyond the limits of the sentence. Maybe the reason for that neglect was that the concept of paragraphing had not yet developed, even in their writing system. The typographical device of paragraphing was largely the invention of printers, and it was not until the late nineteenth century that a systematic rhetoric of the paragraph was developed by Alexander Bain.[9] Recently, however, such rhetoricians as Francis Christensen, Alton Becker, Paul C. Rodgers, and Frank D'Angelo have convinced us that there is such a thing as a "style" of paragraphing.[10]

What should teachers and students look for in studying the "style" of paragraphing? They can, for example, examine the length of paragraphs, measured in number of words or sentences per paragraph. Information about the average length of paragraphs reveals whether an author tends to break up the discourse into small units or into large units and whether an author tends to develop topics elaborately or minimally. Teachers and students can also note whether an author uses explicit topic sentences and where those topic sentences are placed in the paragraph. Moreover, they can observe the coherence devices that an author uses to articulate sequences of sentences within and between paragraphs. Using Francis Christensen's system, they can diagram the levels of coordination and subordination in paragraphs. They can also catalogue the methods of development that an author uses. Indeed, the kinds of choices that an author makes in composing a paragraph are comparable to, if not identical with, the kinds of choices an author makes in composing a sentence. There is, then, a style of paragraphing.

Each aspect that teachers and students can look at when studying someone else's style can be applied to studying specimens of their own prose. And I would strongly urge teachers to analyze their own style. They can take a paper of 1000 to 1500 words that they wrote for one of their college classes or a paper that they have published and subject it to some of the kinds of counting and measuring that I outlined. They will find the investigation fascinating, and they will discover some surprising features about their style—some felicitous characteristics and some regrettable mannerisms.

Improving our students' analytical skills is a proper concern of English teachers, but improving our students' synthetical skills should be our main concern as teachers of composition. And let me suggest, although in the broadest terms, the kinds of exercises that can help our students refine their style and enhance their stylistic virtuosity.

In my own rhetoric texts, I have suggested a number of imitative exercises that have proven fruitful for me and for my students. Let me just mention those exercises, without elaborating on them. (1) Simply copying verbatim admired passages of prose. (2) Copying a passage but changing one element in it—for instance, changing all the past-tense verbs to present-tense verbs. (3) Composing a sentence on the pattern of a sentence written by some admired author. (4) Taking a sentence that someone else has written and seeing in how many different ways one can say essentially what the model sentence says. (5) Taking a group of isolated kernel sentences and combining them into a single sentence.

You can get more details about these exercises by consulting the chapters on style in my two rhetoric texts, in Francis Christensen's article "A Generative Rhetoric of the Sentence," in the two NCTE monographs on sentence-combining by John Mellon and Frank O'Hare, in Walker Gibson's *Tough, Sweet, and Stuff,* in Winston Weathers and Otis Winchester's *Copy and Compose,* in Joseph Williams' *Style: Ten Lessons in Clarity and Grace,* or in Thomas Whissen's A *Way With Words.*[11]

Perhaps the classroom practices I have suggested here are wholly impracticable for your situation. With all the requirements—and time constraints—of a composition course, the study of style may be more than you can handle. Or some of your students may be so minimally literate that engaging them in any of the analyses or exercises I have proposed would prove futile. But even if your students are not ready to engage in stylistic studies, you can do so yourself. Such a regimen promises to help you grow immeasurably in your awareness of the remarkable richness and variety of our language and in your resourcefulness as a teacher of language, literature, and composition.

NOTES

1. T.W. Baldwin, *William Shakespeare's Small Latine Lesse Greeke, 2 vols.* (Urbana, IL: Univ. of Illinois Pr., 1944); Sister Miriam Joseph, *Shakespeare's Use of the Arts of Language* (New York: Columbia Univ. Pr., 1947); Donald L. Clark, *John Milton at St. Paul's School: A Study of Ancient Rhetoric in Renaissance Education* (New York: Columbia Univ. Pr., 1948).
2. Martin Joos, *The Five Clocks* (New York: Harcourt, Brace, and World, Harbinger Books, 1962), p. 11.
3. Edward P.J. Corbett, "Style," in *Classical Rhetoric for the Modern Student,* 2nd ed. (New York: Oxford Univ. Pr., 1971), pp. 414–593; Edward P.J. Corbett, "A Method of Analyzing Prose Style, with a Demonstration Analysis of Swift's *A Modest Proposal,"* in *The Writing Teacher's Sourcebook,* ed. Gary Tate and Edward P.J. Corbett (New York: Oxford Univ. Pr., 1981), pp. 333–52.
4. Richard Ohmann, *Shaw, the Style and the Man* (Middletown, CT. Wesleyan Univ. Pr., 1962).
5. Edwin H. Lewis, *History of the English Paragraph* (Chicago: Univ. of Chicago Pr., 1894); L.A. Sherman, *Some Observations upon Sentence Length in English Prose* (Lincoln, NB: Univ. of Nebraska Pr., 1892).
6. See Wilbur Samuel Howell, "The British Elocutionary Movement," in his *Eighteenth-Century British Logic and Rhetoric* (Princeton, NJ: Princeton Univ. Pr., 1971), pp. 145–256.
7. George Saintsbury, *A History of Prose Rhythm* (London, 1912; re-issued Bloomington, IN: Indiana Univ. Pr., 1965).
8. Thomas S. Kane, "'The Shape and Ring of Sentences,'" *College Composition and Communication,* 28 (February 1977), 38–42.
9. Paul C. Rodgers, Jr., "Alexander Bain and the Rise of the Organic Paragraph," *Quarterly Journal of Speech,* 50 (December 1965), 399–408.
10. Francis Christensen, "A Generative Rhetoric of the Paragraph," in his *Notes Toward a New Rhetoric* (New York: Harper and Row, 1967), pp. 74–103; Alton L. Becker, "A Tagmemic Approach to Paragraph Analysis," *College Composition and Communication* 16 (December 1965), 237–42; Paul C. Rodgers, Jr., "A Discourse-Centered Rhetoric of the Paragraph," *College Composition and Communication,* 17 (February 1966), 2–11; Frank D'Angelo, "Style as Structure," *Style,* 8 (Spring 1974), 322–64.
11. Edward P. J. Corbett, "Style," in *Classical Rhetoric,* pp. 414–593; Edward P.J. Corbett, "Expressing What You Have Discovered, Selected, and Arranged," in *The Little Rhetoric and Handbook,* 2d ed. (Glenview, IL: Scott, Foresman, 1982), pp. 70–120; Francis Christensen, "A Generative Rhetoric of the Sentence," in his *Notes Toward a New Rhetoric* pp. 23–44; John C. Mellon, *Transformational Sentence Combining: A Method for Enhancing the Development of Syntactic Fluency* (Urbana, IL: National Council of Teachers of English, 1969); Frank O'Hare, *Sentence Combining: Improving Student Writing Without Formal Grammar Instruction* (Urbana, IL: National Council of Teachers of English, 1973); Walker

Gibson, *Tough, Sweet, and Stuffy* (Bloomington, IN: Indiana Univ. Pr., 1966); Winston Weathers and Otis Winchester, *Copy and Compose: A Guide to Prose Style* (Englewood Cliffs, NJ: Prentice-Hall, 1969); Joseph Williams, *Style: Ten Lessons in Clarity and Grace,* 2nd ed. (Glenview, IL: Scott Foresman, 1984); Thomas Whissen, *A Way with Words: A Guide for Writers* (New York: Oxford Univ. Pr., 1982).

ADDITIONAL READINGS

Those interested in pursuing the study of style may consult the following selected readings, as well all the books and articles cited in the notes.

Bennett, James R., et al. "The Paragraph: An Annotated Bibliography." *Style,* 11 (Spring 1972), 107–18.

Corbett, Edward P.J. "Approaches to the Study of Style." Teaching *Composition: 10 Bibliographical Essays.* Ed. Gary Tate. Fort Worth: Texas Christian University Press, 1976, pp. 73–109.

Corbett, Edward P.J. "Ventures in Style." *Reinventing the Rhetorical Tradition.* Ed. Aviva Freedman and Ian Pringle. Ottawa, Ontario: Canadian Council of Teachers of English, 1980, pp. 79–87.

Davidson, Donald. "Grammar and Rhetoric: The Teacher's Problem." *Quarterly Journal of Speech,* 39 (December 1953), 425–36.

Fleishauer, John. "Teaching Prose Style Analysis: One Method." *Style,* 9 (Winter 1975), 92–102.

Graves, Richard. "A Primer for Teaching Style." *College Composition and Communication* 25 (May 1974),186–90.

Love, Glen A. and Michael Payne. eds. *Contemporary Essays on Style: Rhetoric, Linguistics, and Criticism.* Glenview, IL: Scott, Foresman, 1969.

Milic, Louis T. "Theories of Style and Their Implications for the Teaching of Composition." *College Composition and Communication,* 16 (May 1965), 66–69, 126.

Milic, Louis T. *Style and Stylistics: An Analytical Bibliography.* New York: Free Press, 1967. Since 1967, the journal *Style* has been publishing the annual bibliographies on style and also several special bibliographies on style.

Price, Marian. "Recent Work in Paragraph Analysis: A Bibliography." *Rhetoric Society Quarterly,* 12 (Spring 1982), 127–31.

Secor, Marie J. "The Legacy of Nineteenth-Century Style Theory. " *Rhetoric Society Quarterly,* 12 (Spring 1982), 76–94.

Vitanza, Victor J. "A Comprehensive Survey of Course Offerings in the Study of Literary Style in American Colleges and Universities." *Style,* 12 (Fall 1978), 342–82.

Weathers, Winston. "Teaching Style: A Possible Anatomy." *College Composition and Communication,* 21 (May 1970), 144–149.

Weaver, Richard M. "Some Rhetorical Aspects of Grammatical Categories." In his *The Ethics of Rhetoric.* Chicago: Henry Regnery, 1953, pp. 115–127.

Where's the Action?

Richard A. Lanham

Richard A. Lanham, professor emeritus of English at UCLA, has written about style, classical rhetoric, literacy, computers, and literature, always in an engaging and lively style. Some of his books are Style: An Anti-Textbook, Revising Business Prose, A Handlist of Rhetorical Terms, *and* The Electronic Word: Democracy, Technology, and the Arts, *as well as* Revising Prose, *the source of the following selection. In this essay Lanham introduces the Paramedic Method, a simple procedure for analyzing and revising sentences to avoid the tangled prose of the Official Style and give one's writing life and vigor.*

THE PARAMEDIC METHOD

1. Circle the prepositions.
2. Circle the "is" forms.
3. Ask, "Where's the action?" "Who's kicking who?"
4. Put this "kicking" action in a simple (not compound) active verb.
5. Start fast—no slow windups.
6. Write out each sentence on a blank sheet of paper and mark off its basic rhythmic units with a "/".
7. Read the passage aloud with emphasis and feeling.
8. Mark off sentence lengths in the passage with a "/".

Since we all live in a bureaucracy these days, it's not surprising that we end up writing like bureaucrats. Nobody feels comfortable writing simply "Boy meets Girl." The system requires something like "A romantic relationship is ongoing between Boy and Girl." Or "Boy and Girl are currently implementing an interactive romantic relationship." Or still better, "It can easily be seen that an interactive romantic relationship is currently being implemented between Boy and Girl." Contrived examples? Here are some real ones. A businessman denied a loan does not suffer but instead says that "I went through a suffering process." A teacher does not say, "If you use a calculator in class, you will never learn to add and subtract," but instead, "The fact is that the use of the calculator in the classroom is negative for the learning process." An undergraduate wants to say, "Lungsick Inc. and other companies have spent years trying to find a substitute for asbestos." But it comes out, "Identification of an acceptable substitute for asbestos in asphalt mastics has been the subject of research by Lungsick Inc. and other manufacturers for several years." A politician "indicates his reluctance to accept the terms on which the proposal was offered" when he might have said "No." A teacher of business writing tells us not that "People entering business today must learn to speak effectively," but "One of these factors is the seemingly increasing awareness of the idea that to succeed in business, it is imperative that the young person entering a business career possess definite skill in oral communication."

The Official Style comes in many dialects—government, military, social scientific, lab scientific, MBA flapdoodle—but all exhibit the same basic attributes. They all build on the same central imbalance, a dominance of nouns and an atrophy of verbs. They enshrine the triumph, worshipped in every bureaucracy, of stasis over action. This basic imbalance is easy to cure, if you want to cure it-and this book's Paramedic Method tells you how to do it. But when do you want to cure it? We all sometimes feel, whatever setting we write in, that we will be penalized for writing in plain English. It will sound too flip. Unserious. Even satirical. In my academic dialect, that of literary study, writing plain English nowadays is tantamount to walking down the hall naked as a jaybird. Public places demand protective coloration; sometimes you must write in The Official Style. And when you do, how do you make sure you are writing a good kind of Official Style—if there is one—rather than a bad one? What can "good" and "bad" mean when applied to prose in this way?

Revising Prose starts out by teaching you how to revise The Official Style. But after you've learned that, we'll reflect on what such revision is likely to do for, or to, you in the bureaucratic world of the future—and the future is only going to get more bureaucratic. You ought then to be able to see what "good" and "bad" mean for prose, and what you are really doing when you revise it. And that means you will know how to socialize your revisory talents, how to put them, like your sentences, into action.

PREPOSITIONAL-PHRASE STRINGS

We can begin with three examples of student prose:

> This sentence is in need of an active verb.
>
> Physical satisfaction is the most obvious of the consequences of premarital sex.
>
> In strict contrast to Watson's ability to control his mental stability through this type of internal gesture, is Rosalind Franklin's inability to even conceive of such "playing."

What do these examples have in common? They have been assembled from strings of prepositional phrases glued together by that all-purpose epoxy "is." In each case the sentence's verbal force has been shunted into a noun, and its verbal force has been diluted into "is," the neutral copulative, the weakest verb in the language. Such sentences project no life, no vigor. They just "are." And the "is" generates those strings of prepositional phrases fore and aft. It's so easy to fix. Look for the real action. Ask yourself, who's kicking who? (Yes, I know, it should be *whom*, but doesn't *whom* sound stilted?)

In "This sentence is in need of an active verb," the action obviously lies in "need." And so, "This sentence needs an active verb." The needless prepositional phrase "in need of" simply disappears once we see who's kicking who. The sentence, animated by a real verb, comes alive, and in six words instead of nine.

Where's the action in "physical satisfaction is the most obvious of the consequences of premarital sex"? Buried down there in "satisfaction." But just asking the question reveals other problems. Satisfaction isn't really a consequence of premarital sex, in the same way that, say, pregnancy is. And, as generations of both sexes will attest, sex, premarital or otherwise, does not always satisfy. Beyond all this, the contrast between the clinical phrasing of the sentence, with its lifeless "is" verb, and the life-giving power of lust in action makes the sentence seem almost funny. Excavating the action from "satisfaction" yields "Premarital sex satisfies! Obviously!" This gives us a lard factor of 66% and a comedy factor even higher. (You find the lard factor by dividing the difference between the number of words in the original and the revision by the number of words in the original. In this case, 12 - 4 = 8; 8 ÷ 12 = .66. If you've not paid attention to your own writing before, think of a lard factor (LF) of one-third to one-half as normal and don't stop revising until you've removed it. The comedy factor in prose revision, though often equally great, does not lend itself to numerical calculation.)

But how else do we revise here? "Premarital sex is fun, obviously" seems a little better, but we remain in thrall to "is." And the frequent falsity of the observation stands out yet more. Revision has exposed the empty thinking. The writer makes it even worse by continuing, "Some degree of physical satisfaction is present in almost all coitus." Add it all together and we get something like, "People usually enjoy premarital sex" (LF 79%). At its worst, academic prose makes us laugh by describing ordinary reality in extraordinary language.

The writer discussing James Watson's *The Double Helix* sleepwalks into the standard form of absent-minded academic prose: a string of prepositional phrases and infinitives, then a lame "to be" verb, then more prepositional phrases and infinitives. Look at the structure:

In strict contrast
to Watson's ability
to control his mental stability
through this type

of internal gesture,
is Rosalind Franklin's inability
to even conceive
of such "playing."

Notice how long this laundry list takes to get going? The root action skulks down there in "ability to control." So we revise:

> Watson controls himself through these internal gestures; Rosalind Franklin does not even know such gestures exist.

I've removed "in strict contrast" because the rephrasing clearly implies it; given the sentence two simple root verbs—"controls" and "knows"; and, to make the contrast tighter and easier to see, used the same word—"gestures"—for the same concept in both phrases. We've reduced seven prepositional phrases and infinitives to one prepositional phrase, and thus banished that DA-da-da, DA-da-da monotony of the original. A lard factor of 41% but, more important, we've given the sentence *shape*, and some life flows from its verbs.

The drill for this problem stands clear. Circle every form of "to be" ("is," "was," "will be," "seems to be," "have been") and every prepositional phrase. Then find out who's kicking who and start rebuilding the sentence with that action. Two prepositional phrases in a row turn on the warning light, three make a problem, and four invite disaster. With a little practice, sentences like "The mood Dickens paints is a bleak one" will turn into "Dickens paints a bleak mood" (LF 35%) almost before you've written them.

Undergraduates have no monopoly on that central element in The Official Style, the string of prepositional phrases. Look at these strings from a lawyer, a scientist, and a critic:

> Here is an example *of* the use *of* the rule *of* justice *in* argumentation.

> One *of* the most important results *of* the presentation *of* the data is the alteration *of* the status *of* the elements *of* the discourse.

> *In* the light *of* the association *in* the last quarter *of* the sixteenth century *of* wit *with* the means *of* amplification, which consist mainly *of* the processes *of* dialectical investigation, this definition probably has more validity than has generally been accorded it.

The *of* strings are the worst of all. They seem to reenact a series of hiccups. When you try to revise them, you can feel how fatally easy the "is" plus prepositional phrase Official Style formula is for prose style. They blur the central action of the sentence—you can't find out what is really going on. Let's try revising.

Here *is* an example *of* the use *of* the rule *of* justice *in* argumentation.

"Rule of justice" is a term of art, so we must leave it intact. After we have found an active verb—"exemplify"—buried in "is an example of the use of," the rest follows easily.

This passage exemplifies argumentation using the rule of justice.

Now, how about the second sentence. It represents a perfect Official Style pattern: string of prepositional phrases + "is" + string of prepositional phrases. Let's diagram it for emphasis:

One

of the most important results
of the presentation
of the data
is the alteration

of the status
of the elements
of the discourse.

See the formulaic character? The monotonous rhythm? The blurred action? I'm not sure what this sentence means, but the action must be buried in "alteration." Start there, with an active, transitive verb—"alter." How about "Presentation of the data alters the status of the discourse elements"? Or less formally, "The status of the discourse elements depends on how you present the data." Or it may mean, "You don't know the status of the elements until you have presented the data." At least two different meanings swim beneath the formulaic prose. To revise it you must *rethink* it.

Now, the third sentence:

In the light
of the association
in the last quarter
of the sixteenth century
of wit
with the means
of amplification,
  which consist mainly
of the processes
of dialectical investigation,

> this definition probably has more validity than has generally been accorded it.

Here, the prepositional phrases have been assembled into a gigantic preparatory fanfare for a central action which does not come until the end—

> this definition probably has more validity.

These slow-motion openings, a sure sign of The Official Style, drain all the life from the sentence before we ever get to the verb, and hence the action. I'll revise to get off to a faster start, using my knowledge of what the writer—behind the infarcted prose—was trying to say:

> This definition holds true more than people think, especially considering what wit meant around 1600. (15 words instead of 42; LF 64%)

"BLAH BLAH *IS THAT*" OPENINGS

The formulaic slo-mo opening often provides your first taste of The Official Style. And it is a fatally easy habit to fall into. Let's look at some typical examples of what we will call the "Blah blah *is that*" opening from students, professors, and writers at large:

> What I would like to signal here *is that* . . .

> My contention *is that* . . .

> What I want to make clear *is that* . . .

> What has surprised me the most *is that* . . .

> The upshot of what Heidegger says here *is that* . . .

> The first *is that* . . .

> The point I wish to make *is that* . . .

> What I have argued here *is that* . . .

> My opinion *is that* on this point we have only two options . . .

> My point *is that* the question of the discourse of the human sciences . . .

> The fact of the matter *is that* the material of this article is drawn directly from . . .

> The one thing that Belinda does not realize *is that* Dorimant knows exactly how to press her buttons.

Easy to fix this pattern; just amputate the mindless preludial fanfare. Start the sentence with whatever follows "Blah blah *is that. . . .*" On a word processor it couldn't be simpler: do a global search for the phrase "is that" and revise it out each time. For example:

> The upshot of what **Heidegger says** here is that . . .

> My opinion is that on this point **we have only two options . . .**

> My point is that the question of **the discourse of the human sciences . . .**

> The fact of the matter is that **the material of this article is drawn directly from . . .**

We can even improve my favorite from this anthology:

> The one thing that **Belinda does not realize** is **that Dorimant knows exactly how to press her buttons.**

By amputating the fanfare, you *start fast*, and a fast start may lead to major motion. That's what we're after. Where's the *action*?

Writers addicted to the "blah blah *is that*" dead rocket often tie themselves in knots with it. One writes: "The position **we are at is this.**" Another: "The traditional opposite notion **to this is that there are. . . .**" And a third, a university professor, in an article accurately titled "On the Weakness of Language in the Human Sciences," offers this spasmodic set of **thises, thats** and **whats**:

> Now **what** I would like to know specifically **is this**: **what is** the meaning of **this** "as" **that** Heidegger emphasizes so strongly when he says **that "that** which is explicitly understood"—**that is, that** which is interpreted—"has the structure of something as something"? My opinion **is that** what Heidegger means **is that** the structure of interpretation (*Auslegung*) is figural rather than, say, intentional. (Emphasis mine.)

In escaping from this Houdini straitjacket, a couple of mechanical tricks come in handy. Besides eliminating the "is's" and changing every passive voice ("is defended by") to an active voice ("defends"), you can squeeze the compound verbs hard, make every "are able to" into a "can," every "seems to succeed in creating" into "creates," every "cognize the fact that" (no, I didn't make it up) into "think," every "am hopeful that" into "hope," every "provides us with an example of" into "exemplifies," every "seeks to reveal" into "shows," and every "there is the inclusion of" into "includes." Then, after amputating those mindless *fact that* introductory-phrase fanfares, you'll start fast. After that fast start, "cut to the chase," as they say in the movies, as soon as you can. Instead of "the answer is in the negative," you'll find yourself saying "No."

THE PARAMEDIC METHOD

We now have the beginnings of the Paramedic Method (PM):

1. Circle the prepositions.
2. Circle the "is" forms.
3. Ask, "Where's the action?" "Who's kicking who?"
4. Put this "kicking" action in a simple (not compound) active verb.
5. Start fast—no slow windups.

Let's use the PM on a more complex instance of blurred action, the opening sentences of an undergraduate psych paper:

> The history of Western psychological thought has long been dominated by philosophical considerations as to the nature of man. These notions have dictated corresponding considerations of the nature of the child within society, the practices by which children were to be raised, and the purposes of studying the child.

Two actions here—"dominate" and "dictate"—but neither has fully escaped from its native stone. The prepositional-phrase and infinitive strings just drag them down.

> The history
> *of* Western psychological thought . . .
> *by* philosophical considerations
> *as* to the nature
> *of* man.
> . . .
> *of* the nature
> *of* the child
> *within* society . . .
> *by* which children . . .
> *to* be raised . . .

of studying . . .

In asking, "Where's the action?" "Who's kicking who?" we next notice all the actions fermenting in the nouns: *thinking* in "thought," *consider* in "considerations, " more *thinking* somewhere in "notions." They hint at actions they don't supply and thus blur the actor-action relationship still further. We want, remember, a plain active verb, no prepositional-phrase strings, and a natural actor firmly in charge.

> The **actor** must be: "philosophical considerations as to the nature of man."
>
> The **verb**: "dominates."
>
> The **object** of the action: "the history of Western psychological thought."

Now the real problems emerge. What does "philosophical considerations as to the nature of man" really mean? Buried down there is a question: "What is the nature of man?" The "philosophical considerations" just blur this question rather than narrow it. Likewise, the object of the action—"the history of Western psychological thought"—can be simply "Western psychological thought." Shall we put all this together in the passive form that the writer used?

> Western psychological thought has been dominated by a single question: What is the nature of man?

Or, with an active verb:

> A single question has dominated Western psychological thought: What is the nature of man?

Our formulaic concern with the stylistic surface—passives, prepositional phrases, kicker and kickee—has led here to a much more focused thought.

The first sentence passes its baton very awkwardly to the second. "Considerations," confusing enough as we have seen, becomes "these notions" at the beginning of the second sentence, and these "notions," synonymous with "considerations" in the first sentence, dictate more but different "considerations" in the second. We founder in these vague and vaguely synonymous abstractions. Our unforgiving eye for prepositional phrases then registers "*of* the nature *of* the child *within* society." We don't need "within society"; where else will psychology study children? And "the nature of the child" telescopes to "the child." We metamorphose "the practices by which children were to be raised" into "child rearing," and "the purposes in studying the child" leads us back to "corresponding considerations of the nature of the child within society," which it seems partly to overlap. But we have now a definite actor, remember, in the first sentence—the "single question". "So a tentative revision:

> This basic question leads to three others: What are children like? How should they be raised? Why should we study them?

Other revisions suggest themselves. Work out a couple. In mine, I've used "question" as the baton passed between the two sentences because it clarifies the relationship between the two. And I've tried to expose what real, clear action lay hidden beneath the conceptual cotton wool of "these notions have dictated corresponding considerations."

> A single question has dominated Western psychological thought: What is the nature of man? This basic question leads to three others. What are children like? How should they be raised? Why should we study them?

This two-sentence example of student academic prose rewards some reflection. First, the sentences boast no grammatical or syntactical mistakes. Second, they need not have come from a student. Any issue of a psychology journal or text will net you a dozen from the same mold. How else did the student learn to write them? Third, not many instructors reading this prose will think anything is wrong with it. Just the opposite. It reads just right; it sounds *professional.* The teacher's comment on this paper reads, in full: "An excellent paper—well conceived, well organized, and well written—A+." Yet a typical specimen sentence from it makes clear neither its main actor nor action; its thought consistently puffs into vague general concepts like "considerations," "notions," and the like; and its cradle-rocking monotonous rhythm puts us to sleep. It reveals a mind writing in formulas, out of focus, above all a mind putting no pressure on itself. The writer is not thinking so much as, on a scale slightly larger than normal, filling in the blanks. You can't build bridges thinking in this muddled way; they will fall down. If you bemuse yourself thus in a chemistry lab, you'll blow up the apparatus. And yet the student, obviously very bright, has been invited to write this way and rewarded for it. He or she has been doing *a stylistic imitation,* and has brought if off successfully. Chances are that the focused, plain-language version I've offered would get a lower grade than the Official Style original. Revision is always perilous and paradoxical, but nowhere more so than in the academic world. Not so perilous, though, as bridges that fall down or lab apparatus that blows up. In the long run, it is better to get your thinking straight and take your chances.

SUGGESTED READINGS: FORM AND STYLE

Bishop, Wendy, ed. *Elements of Alternate Style: Essays on Writing and Revision.* Portsmouth, NH: Boynton/Cook, 1997.

Braddock, Richard. "The Frequency and Placement of Topic Sentences in Expository Prose." *Research in the Teaching of English* 8 (1974): 287–302.

Christensen, Francis. *Notes Toward a New Rhetoric.* New York: Harper & Row, 1967.

Coe, Richard M. "If Not to Narrow, Then How to Focus: Two Techniques for Focusing." *CCC* 32 (1981): 272–77.

Coe, Richard M. *Toward a Grammar of Passages.* Carbondale: Southern Illinois UP, 1988.

Daiker, Don, Andrew Kerek, and Max Morenberg, eds. *Sentence Combining: A Rhetorical Perspective.* Carbondale: Southern Illinois UP, 1985.

D'Angelo, Frank J. *A Conceptual Theory of Rhetoric.* Cambridge: Winthrop, 1975.

D'Angelo, Frank J. "The Topic Sentence Revisited." *CCC* 37 (1986): 431–41.

Faigley, Lester. "Names in Search of a Concept: Maturity, Fluency, Complexity, and Growth in Written Syntax." *CCC* 31 (1980): 291–300.

Joos, Martin. *The Five Clocks.* New York: Harcourt, Brace and World, 1961.

Lanham, Richard A. *Style: An Anti-Textbook.* New Haven: Yale UP, 1974.

Markels, Robin Bell. *A New Perspective on Cohesion in Expository Paragraphs.* Carbondale: Southern Illinois UP, 1984.

McQuade, Donald A., ed. *The Territory of Language: Linguistics, Stylistics, and the Teaching of Composition.* Carbondale: Southern Illinois UP, 1986.

Moran, Michael G. "The English Paragraph." *Research in Rhetoric and Composition: A Bibliographic Sourcebook.* Ed. Michael G. Moran and Ronald F. Lunsford. Westport, CT: Greenwood, 1984. 425–50.

Podis, Joanne M., and Leonard A. Podis. "Identifying and Teaching Rhetorical Plans for Arrangement." *CCC* 41 (1990): 430–42.

Podis, Leonard A. "Teaching Arrangement: Defining a More Practical Approach." *CCC* 31 (1980): 197–204.

Popken, Randell L. "A Study of Topic Sentence Use in Academic Writing." *Written Communication* 4 (1987): 209–28.

The Sentence and the Paragraph. Urbana, IL: NCTE, 1963.

Smith, Rochelle. "Paragraphing for Coherence: Writing as Implied Dialogue." *College English* 46 (1984): 8–21.

Stotsky, Sandra. "Types of Lexical Cohesion in Expository Academic Discourse." *CCC* 34 (1983): 430–46.

Strunk, William, Jr., and E. B. White. *The Elements of Style*. 3rd ed. Boston: Allyn & Bacon, 1979.

Vande Kopple, William J. "Something Old, Something New: Functional Sentence Perspective." *Research in the Teaching of English* 17 (1983): 85–99.

Weathers, Winston. *An Alternate Style: Options in Composing*. Rochelle Park, NJ: Hayden, 1980.

Williams, Joseph M. *Style: Ten Lessons in Clarity and Grace*. 5th ed. New York: Addison Wesley Longman, 1996.

Witte, Stephen P., and Lester Faigley. "Coherence, Cohesion, and Writing Quality." *CCC* 32 (1981): 189–204.

Grammar, Grammars, and the Teaching of Grammar

Patrick Hartwell

Decades of studies that challenge the usefulness of teaching formal grammar to improve student writing have not settled the issue of how to instruct students to edit their texts and avoid violating conventions of standard American English. In this frequently reprinted article that originally appeared in College English *in 1985, Patrick Hartwell reviews this debate and applies linguistic theory and research to the understanding of error. Hartwell argues that most errors are not "conceptual errors" that disappear with the study of formal rules of grammar. Most errors are "performance errors" that can stem from any number of causes.*

For me the grammar issue was settled at least twenty years ago with the conclusion offered by Richard Braddock, Richard Lloyd-Jones, and Lowell Schoer in 1963.

> In view of the widespread agreement of research studies based upon many types of students and teachers, the conclusion can be stated in strong and unqualified terms: the teaching of formal grammar has a negligible or, because it usually displaces some instruction and practice in composition, even a harmful effect on improvement in writing.[1]

Indeed, I would agree with Janet Emig that the grammar issue is a prime example of "magical thinking": the assumption that students will learn only what we teach and only because we teach.[2]

But the grammar issue, as we will see, is a complicated one. And, perhaps surprisingly, it remains controversial, with the regular appearance of papers defending the teaching of formal grammar or attacking it.[3] Thus Janice Neuleib, writing on "The Relation of Formal Grammar to Composition" in *College Composition and Communication* (23 [1977], 247–50), is tempted "to sputter on paper" at reading the quotation above (p. 248), and Martha Kolln, writing in the same journal three years later ("Closing the Books on Alchemy," *CCC*, 32 [1981], 139–51), labels people like me "alchemists" for our perverse beliefs. Neuleib reviews five

---

experimental studies, most of them concluding that formal grammar instruction has no effect on the quality of students' writing nor on their ability to avoid error. Yet she renders in effect a Scots verdict of "Not proven" and calls for more research on the issue. Similarly, Kolln reviews six experimental studies that arrive at similar conclusions, only one of them overlapping with the studies cited by Neuleib. She calls for more careful definition of the word grammar—her definition being "the internalized system that native speakers of a language share" (p. 140)—and she concludes with a stirring call to place grammar instruction at the center of the composition curriculum: "our goal should be to help students understand the system they know unconsciously as native speakers, to teach them the necessary categories and labels that will enable them to think about and talk about their language" (p. 150). Certainly our textbooks and our pedagogies—though they vary widely in what they see as "necessary categories and labels"—continue to emphasize mastery of formal grammar, and popular discussions of a presumed literacy crisis are almost unanimous in their call for a renewed emphasis on the teaching of formal grammar, seen as basic for success in writing.[4]

An Instructive Example

It is worth noting at the outset that both sides in this dispute—the grammarians and the anti-grammarians—articulate the issue in the same positivistic terms: what does experimental research tell us about the value of teaching formal grammar? But seventy-five years of experimental research has for all practical purposes told us nothing. The two sides are unable to agree on how to interpret such research. Studies are interpreted in terms of one's prior assumptions about the value of teaching grammar: their results seem not to change those assumptions. Thus the basis of the discussion, a basis shared by Kolln and Neuleib and by Braddock and his colleagues—"what does educational research tell us?"—seems designed to perpetuate, not to resolve, the issue. A single example will be instructive. In 1976 and then at greater length in 1979, W.B. Elley, I.H. Barham, H. Lamb, and M. Wyllie reported on a three-year experiment in New Zealand, comparing the relative effectiveness at the high school level of instruction in transformational grammar, instruction in traditional grammar, and no grammar instruction.[5] They concluded that the formal study of grammar, whether transformational or traditional, improved neither writing quality nor control over surface correctness.

> After two years, no differences were detected in writing performance or language competence; after three years small differences appeared in some minor conventions favoring the TG (transformational grammar) group, but these were more than offset by the less positive attitudes they showed towards their English studies. (p. 18)

Anthony Petrosky, in a review of research ("Grammar Instruction: What We Know," *English Journal,* 66, No. 9 [1977], 86–88), agreed with this conclusion, finding the study to be carefully designed, "representative of the best kind of educational research" (p. 86), its validity "unquestionable" (p. 88). Yet Janice Neuleib in her essay found the same conclusions to be "startling" and questioned whether the findings could be generalized beyond the target population, New Zealand high school students. Martha Kolln, when her attention is drawn to the study ("Reply to Ron Shook," *CCC*, 32 [1981], 139–151), thinks the whole experiment "suspicious." And John Mellon has been willing to use the study to defend the teaching of grammar; the study of Elley and his colleagues, he has argued, shows that teaching grammar does no harm.[6]

It would seem unlikely, therefore, that further experimental research, in and of itself, will resolve the grammar issue. Any experimental design can be nitpicked, any experimental population can be criticized, and any experimental conclusion can be questioned or, more often, ignored. In fact, it may well be that the grammar question is not open to resolution by experimental research, that, as Noam Chomsky has argued in *Reflections on Language* (New York: Pantheon, 1975), criticizing the trivialization of human learning by behavioral psychologists, the issue is simply misdefined.

> There will be "good experiments" only in domains that lie outside the organism's cognitive capacity. For example, there will be no "good experiments" in the study of human learning.
>
> This discipline ... will, of necessity, avoid those domains in which an organism is specially designed to acquire rich cognitive structures that enter into its life in an intimate fashion. The discipline will be of virtually no intellectual interest, it seems to me, since it is restricting itself in principle to those questions that are guaranteed to tell us little about the nature of organisms. (p. 36)

Asking the Right Questions

As a result, though I will look briefly at the tradition of experimental research, my primary goal in this essay is to articulate the grammar issue in different and, I would hope, more productive terms. Specifically, I want to ask four questions:

1. Why is the grammar issue so important? Why has it been the dominant focus of composition research for the last seventy-five years?

2. What definitions of the word *grammar* are needed to articulate the grammar issue intelligibly?

3. What do findings in cognate disciplines suggest about the value of formal grammar instruction?

4. What is our theory of language, and what does it predict about the value of formal grammar instruction? (This question—"what does our theory of language predict?"—seems a much more powerful question than "what does educational research tell us?")

In exploring these questions I will attempt to be fully explicit about issues, terms, and assumptions. I hope that both proponents and opponents of formal grammar instruction would agree that these are useful as shared points of reference: care in definition, full examination of the evidence, reference to relevant work in cognate disciplines, and explicit analysis of the theoretical bases of the issue.

But even with that gesture of harmony it will be difficult to articulate the issue in a balanced way, one that will be acceptable to both sides. After all, we are dealing with a professional dispute in which one side accuses the other of "magical thinking," and in turn that side responds by charging the other as "alchemists." Thus we might suspect that the grammar issue is itself embedded in larger models of the transmission of literacy, part of quite different assumptions about the teaching of composition.

Those of us who dismiss the teaching of formal grammar have a model of composition instruction that makes the grammar issue "uninteresting" in a scientific sense. Our model predicts a rich and complex interaction of learner and environment in mastering literacy, an interaction that has little to do with sequences of skills instruction as such. Those who defend the teaching of grammar tend to have a model of composition instruction that is rigidly skills-centered and rigidly sequential: the formal teaching of grammar, as the first step in that sequence, is the cornerstone or linchpin. Grammar teaching is thus supremely interesting, naturally a dominant focus for educational research. The controversy over the value of grammar instruction, then, is inseparable from two other issues: the issues of sequence in the teaching of composition and of the role of the composition teacher. Consider, for example, the force of these two issues in Janice Neuleib's conclusion: after calling for yet more experimental research on the value of teaching grammar, she ends with an absolute (and unsupported) claim about sequences and teacher roles in composition.

> We do know, however, that some things must be taught at different levels. Insistence on adherence to usage norms by composition teachers does improve usage. Students can learn to organize their papers if teachers do not accept papers that are disorganized. Perhaps composition teachers can teach those two abilities before they begin the more difficult tasks of developing syntactic sophistication and a winning style. ("The Relation of Formal Grammar to Composition," p. 250)

(One might want to ask, in passing, whether "usage norms" exist in the monolithic fashion the phrase suggests and whether refusing to accept disorganized papers is our best available pedagogy for teaching arrangement.)[7]

But I want to focus on the notion of sequence that makes the grammar issue so important: first grammar, then usage, then some absolute model of organization, all controlled by the teacher at the center of the learning process, with other matters, those of rhetorical weight—"syntactic sophistication and a winning style"—pushed off to the future. It is not surprising that we call each other names: those of us who question the value of teaching grammar are in fact shaking the whole elaborate edifice of traditional composition instruction.

The Five Meanings of "Grammar"

Given its centrality to a well-established way of teaching composition, I need to go about the business of defining grammar rather carefully, particularly in view of Kolln's criticism of the lack of care in earlier discussions. Therefore I will build upon a seminal discussion of the word *grammar* offered a generation ago, in 1954, by W. Nelson Francis, often excerpted as "The Three Meanings of Grammar."[8] It is worth reprinting at length, if only to re-establish it as a reference point for future discussions.

> The first thing we mean by "grammar" is "the set of formal patterns in which the words of a language are arranged in order to convey larger meanings." It is not necessary that we be able to discuss these patterns self-consciously in order to be able to use them. In fact, all speakers of a language above the age of five or six know how to use its complex forms of organization with considerable skill; in this sense of the word—call it "Grammar 1"—they are thoroughly familiar with its grammar.
>
> The second meaning of "grammar—call it "Grammar 2"—is "the branch of linguistic science which is concerned with the description, analysis, and formulization of formal language patterns." Just as gravity was in full operation before Newton's apple fell, so grammar in the first sense was in full operation before anyone formulated the first rule that began the history of grammar as a study.
>
> The third sense in which people use the word "grammar" is "linguistic etiquette." This we may call "Grammar 3." The word in this sense is often coupled with a derogatory adjective: we say that the expression "he ain't here" is "bad grammar. " ...
>
> As has already been suggested, much confusion arises from mixing these meanings. One hears a good deal of criticism of teachers of English couched in such terms as "they don't teach grammar any more."

> Criticism of this sort is based on the wholly unproven assumption that teaching Grammar 2 will improve the student's proficiency in Grammar 1 or improve his manners in Grammar 3. Actually, the form of Grammar 2 which is usually taught is a very inaccurate and misleading analysis of the facts of Grammar 1; and it therefore is of highly questionable value in improving a person's ability to handle the structural patterns of his language. (pp. 300–301)

Francis' Grammar 3 is, of course, not grammar at all, but usage. One would like to assume that Joseph Williams' recent discussion of usage ("The Phenomenology of Error," *CCC*, 32 [1981], 152–168), along with his references, has placed those shibboleths in a proper perspective. But I doubt it, and I suspect that popular discussions of the grammar issue will be as flawed by the intrusion of usage issues as past discussions have been. At any rate I will make only passing reference to Grammar 3—usage—naively assuming that this issue has been discussed elsewhere and that my readers are familiar with those discussions.

We need also to make further discriminations about Francis' Grammar 2, given that the purpose of his 1954 article was to substitute for one form of Grammar 2, that "inaccurate and misleading" form "which is usually taught," another form, that of American structuralist grammar. Here we can make use of a still earlier discussion, one going back to the days when *PMLA* was willing to publish articles on rhetoric and linguistics, to a 1927 article by Charles Carpenter Fries, "The Rules of the Common School Grammars" (42 [1927], 221–237). Fries there distinguished between the scientific tradition of language study (to which we will now delimit Francis' Grammar 2, scientific grammar) and the separate tradition of "the common school grammars," developed unscientifically, largely based on two inadequate principles—appeals to "logical principles," like "two negatives make a positive," and analogy to Latin grammar; thus, Charlton Laird's characterization, "the grammar of Latin, ingeniously warped to suggest English" *(Language in America* [New York: World, 1970], p. 294). There is, of course, a direct link between the "common school grammars" that Fries criticized in 1927 and the grammar-based texts of today, and thus it seems wise, as Karl W. Dykema suggests ("Where Our Grammar Came From," *CE*, 22 [1961], 455–465), to separate Grammar 2, "scientific grammar," from Grammar 4, "school grammar," the latter meaning, quite literally, "the grammars used in the schools."

Further, since Martha Kolln points to the adaptation of Christensen's sentence rhetoric in a recent sentence-combining text as an example of the proper emphasis on "grammar" ("Closing the Books on Alchemy," p. 140), it is worth separating out, as still another meaning of *grammar,* Grammar 5, "stylistic grammar," defined as "grammatical terms used in the interest of teaching prose style." And, since stylistic grammars abound, with widely variant terms and emphases, we might appropriately speak parenthetically of specific forms of Grammar 5—Grammar 5

(Lanham); Grammar 5 (Strunk and White); Grammar 5 (Williams, 9 *Style*); even Grammar 5 (Christensen, as adapted by Daiker, Kerek, and Morenberg).[9]

The Grammar in Our Heads

With these definitions in mind, let us return to Francis' Grammar 1, admirably defined by Kolln as "the internalized system of rules that speakers of a language share" ("Closing the Books on Alchemy," p. 140), or, to put it more simply, the grammar in our heads. Three features of Grammar 1 need to be stressed: first, its special status as an "internalized system of rules," as tacit and unconscious knowledge; second, the abstract, even counterintuitive, nature of these rules, insofar as we are able to approximate them indirectly as Grammar 2 statements; and third, the way in which the form of one's Grammar 1 seems profoundly affected by the acquisition of literacy. This sort of review is designed to firm up our theory of language, so that we can ask what it predicts about the value of teaching formal grammar.

A simple thought experiment will isolate the special status of Grammar 1 knowledge. I have asked members of a number of different groups—from sixth graders to college freshmen to high-school teachers—to give me the rule for ordering adjectives of nationality, age, and number in English. The response is always the same: "We don't know the rule." Yet when I ask these groups to perform an active language task, they show productive control over the rule they have denied knowing. I ask them to arrange the following words in a natural order:

French the young girls four

I have never seen a native speaker of English who did not immediately produce the natural order, "the four young French girls." The rule is that in English the order of adjectives is first, number, second, age, and third, nationality. Native speakers can create analogous phrases using the rule—"the seventy-three aged Scandinavian lechers"; and the drive for meaning is so great that they will create contexts to make sense out of violations of the rule, as in foregrounding for emphasis: "I want to talk to the French four young girls." (I immediately envision a large room, perhaps a banquet hall, filled with tables at which are seated groups of four young girls, each group of a different nationality.) So Grammar 1 is eminently usable knowledge—the way we make our life through language—but it is not accessible knowledge; in a profound sense, we do not know that we have it. Thus neurolinguist Z.N. Pylyshyn speaks of Grammar 1 as "autonomous," separate from common-sense reasoning, and as "cognitively impenetrable," not available for direct examination.[10] In philosophy and linguistics, the distinction is made between formal, conscious, "knowing about" knowledge (like Grammar 2 knowledge) and tacit, unconscious, "knowing how" knowledge (like Grammar 1 knowledge). The importance of this distinction for the teaching of composition—it provides a powerful theoretical justification for mistrusting the ability of Grammar 2 (or Grammar 4) knowledge to affect Grammar 1 performance—was pointed out in this journal by Martin Steinmann, Jr., in 1966 ("Rhetorical Research," *CE*, 27 [1966], 278–285).

Further, the more we learn about Grammar 1—and most linguists would agree that we know surprisingly little about it—the more abstract and implicit it seems. This abstractness can be illustrated with an experiment, devised by Lise Menn and reported by Morris Halle, about our rule for forming plurals in speech. It is obvious that we do indeed have a "rule" for forming plurals, for we do not memorize the plural of each noun separately. You will demonstrate productive control over that rule by forming the spoken plurals of the nonsense words below:

thole   flitch   plast

Halle offers two ways of formalizing a Grammar 2 equivalent of this Grammar 1 ability. One form of the rule is the following, stated in terms of speech sounds:

a. If the noun ends in /s z s z c j/, add /Iz
b. otherwise, if the noun ends in /p t k f o/, add /s/;
c. otherwise, add /z/.[11]

This rule comes close to what we literate adults consider to be an adequate rule for plurals in writing, like the rules, for example, taken from a recent "common school grammar," Eric Gould's *Reading into Writing: A Rhetoric, Reader, and Handbook* (Boston: Houghton Mifflin, 1983):

> *Plurals* can be tricky. If you are unsure of a plural, then check it in the dictionary.
> The general rules are
> Add *s* to the singular: *girls, tables*
> Add *es* to nouns ending in *ch, sh, x or s: churches, boxes, wishes*
> Add *es* to nouns ending in *y* and preceded by a vowel once you have changed *y* to *i*: *monies, companies.* (p. 666)

(But note the persistent inadequacy of such Grammar 4 rules: here, as I read it, the rule is inadequate to explain the plurals of *ray* and *tray,* even to explain the collective noun *monies,* not a plural at all, formed from the mass noun *money* and offered as an example.) A second form of the rule would make use of much more abstract entities, sound features:

a. If the noun ends with a sound that is [coronal, strident], add /Iz/;

b. otherwise, if the noun ends with a sound that is [non-voiced], add /s/;
C. otherwise, add /z/.

(The notion of "sound features" is itself rather abstract, perhaps new to readers not trained in linguistics. But such readers should be able to recognize that the spoken plurals of *lip* and *duck*, the sound [s], differ from the spoken plurals *sea* and *gnu*, the sound [z], only in that the sounds of the latter are "voiced"—one's vocal cords vibrate—while the sounds of the former are "non-voiced.")

To test the psychologically operative rule, the Grammar 1 rule, native speakers of English were asked to form the plural of the last name of the composer Johann Sebastian *Bach*, a sound [x], unique in American (though not in Scottish) English. If speakers follow the first rule above, using word endings, they would reject a) and b), then apply c), producing the plural as /baxz/, with word-final /z/. (If writers were to follow the rule of the common school grammar, they would produce the written plural *Baches*, apparently, given the form of the rule, on analogy with *churches.)* If speakers follow the second rule, they would have to analyze the sound [x] as [non-labial, noncoronal, dorsal, non-voiced, and nonstrident], producing the plural as /baxs/, with word-final /s/. Native speakers of American English overwhelmingly produce the plural as /baxs/. They use knowledge that Halle characterizes as "unlearned and untaught" (p. 140).

Now such a conclusion is counterintuitive—certainly it departs maximally from Grammar 4 rules for forming plurals. It seems that native speakers of English behave as if they have productive control, as Grammar 1 knowledge, of abstract sound features (± coronal, ± strident, and so on) which are available as conscious, Grammar 2 knowledge only to trained linguists—and, indeed, formally available only within the last hundred years or so. ("Behave as if," in that last sentence, is a necessary hedge, to underscore the difficulty of "knowing about" Grammar 1.)

Moreover, as the example of plural rules suggests, the form of the Grammar 1 in the heads of literate adults seems profoundly affected by the acquisition of literacy. Obviously, literate adults have access to different morphological codes: the abstract print *-s* underlying the predictable /s/ and /z/ plurals, the abstract print *-ed* underlying the spoken past tense markers /t/, as in "walked," /ed/, as in "surrounded," /d/, as in "scored," and the symbol /Ø/ for no surface realization, as in the relaxed standard pronunciation of "I walked to the store." Literate adults also have access to distinctions preserved only in the code of print (for example, the distinction between "a good Ku" and "a good sailor" that Mark Aranoff points out in "An English Spelling Convention" (*Linguistic Inquiry,* 9 [1978], 299–303). More significantly, Irene Moscowitz speculates that the ability of third graders to form abstract nouns on analogy with pairs like *divine::divinity* and *serene::serenity,* where the spoken vowel changes but the spelling preserves meaning, is a factor of knowing how to read. Carol Chomsky finds a three-stage developmental sequence in the grammatical performance of seven-year-olds, related to measures of kind and variety of reading;

and Rita S. Brause finds a nine-stage developmental sequence in the ability to understand semantic ambiguity, extending from fourth graders to graduate students.[12] John Mills and Gordon Hemsley find that level of education, and presumably level of literacy, influence judgments of grammaticality, concluding that literacy changes the deep structure of one's internal grammar; Jean Whyte finds that oral language functions develop differently in readers and non-readers; José Morais, Jésus Alegria, and Paul Bertelson find that illiterate adults are unable to add or delete sounds at the beginning of nonsense words, suggesting that awareness of speech as a series of phones is provided by learning to read an alphabetic code. Two experiments—one conducted by Charles A. Ferguson, the other by Mary E. Hamilton and David Barton—find that adults' ability to recognize segmentation in speech is related to degree of literacy, not to amount of schooling or general ability.[13]

It is worth noting that none of these investigators would suggest that the developmental sequences they have uncovered be isolated and taught as discrete skills. They are natural concomitants of literacy, and they seem best characterized not as isolated rules but as developing schemata, broad strategies for approaching written language.

Grammar 2

We can, of course, attempt to approximate the rules or schemata of Grammar 1 by writing fully explicit descriptions that model the competence of a native speaker. Such rules, like the rules for pluralizing nouns or ordering adjectives discussed above, are the goal of the science of linguistics, that is, Grammar 2. There are a number of scientific grammars—an older structuralist model and several versions within a generative-transformational paradigm, not to mention isolated schools like tagmemic grammar, Montague grammar, and the like. In fact, we cannot think of Grammar 2 as a stable entity, for its form changes with each new issue of each linguistics journal, as new "rules of grammar" are proposed and debated. Thus Grammar 2, though of great theoretical interest to the composition teacher, is of little practical use in the classroom, as Constance Weaver has pointed out (*Grammar for Teachers* [Urbana, Ill.: NCTE, 1979], pp. 3–6). Indeed Grammar 2 is a scientific model of Grammar 1, not a description of it, so that questions of psychological reality, while important, are less important than other, more theoretical factors, such as the elegance of formulation or the global power of rules. We might, for example, wish to replace the rule for ordering adjectives of age, number and nationality cited above with a more general rule—what linguists call a "fuzzy" rule—that adjectives in English are ordered by their abstract quality of "nouniness": adjectives that are very much like nouns, like *French* or *Scandinavian,* come physically closer to nouns than do adjectives that are less "nouny," like *four* or *aged* But our motivation for accepting the broader rule would be its global power, not its psychological reality.[14]

I try to consider a hostile reader, one committed to the teaching of grammar, and I try to think of ways to hammer in the central point of this distinction, that the rules of Grammar 2 are simply unconnected to productive control over Grammar 1. I can argue from authority: Noam Chomsky has touched on this point whenever he has concerned himself with the implications of linguistics for language teaching, and years ago transformationalist Mark Lester stated unequivocally, "there simply appears to be no correlation between a writer's study of language and his ability to write."[15] I can cite analogies offered by others: Francis Christensen's analogy in an essay originally published in 1962 that formal grammar study would be "to invite a centipede to attend to the sequence of his legs in motion,"[16] or James Britton's analogy, offered informally after a conference presentation, that grammar study would be like forcing starving people to master the use of a knife and fork before allowing them to eat. I can offer analogies of my own, contemplating the wisdom of asking a pool player to master the physics of momentum before taking up a cue or of making a prospective driver get a degree in automotive engineering before engaging the clutch. I consider a hypothetical argument, that if Grammar 2 knowledge affected Grammar 1 performance, then linguists would be our best writers. (I can certify that they are, on the whole, not.) Such a position, after all, is only in accord with other domains of science: the formula for catching a fly ball in baseball ("Playing It by Ear," *Scientific American*, 248, No. 4 [1983], 76) is of such complexity that it is beyond my understanding—and, I would suspect, that of many workaday centerfielders. But perhaps I can best hammer in this claim—that Grammar 2 knowledge has no effect on Grammar 1 performance—by offering a demonstration.

The diagram below is an attempt by Thomas N. Huckin and Leslie A. Olsen *(English for Science and Technology* [New York: McGraw-Hill, 1983]) to offer, for students of English as a second language, a fully explicit formulation of what is, for native speakers, a trivial rule of the language—the choice of definite article, indefinite article, or no definite article. There are obvious limits to such a formulation, for article choice in English is less a matter of rule than of idiom ("I went to college" versus "I went to a university" versus British "I went to university"), real-world knowledge (using indefinite "I went into a house" instantiates definite "I looked at the ceiling," and indefinite "I visited a university" instantiates definite "I talked with the professors"), and stylistic choice (the last sentence above might alternatively end with "the choice of the definite article, the indefinite article, or no article").

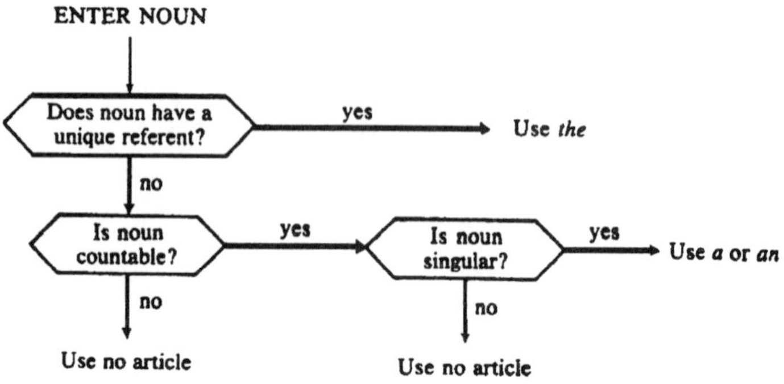

Huckin and Olsen invite non-native speakers to use the rule consciously to justify article choice in technical prose, such as the passage below from P.F. Brandwein *(Matter: An Earth Science* [New York: Harcourt Brace Jovanovich, 1975]). I invite you to spend a couple of minutes doing the same thing, with the understanding that this exercise is a test case: you are using a very explicit rule to justify a fairly straightforward issue of grammatical choice.

> Imagine a cannon on top of _____ highest mountain on Earth. It is firing _____ cannonballs horizontally. _____ first cannonball fired follows its path. As _____ cannonball moves, _____ gravity pulls it down, and it soon hits_____ground. Now_____velocity with which each succeeding cannonball is fired is increased. Thus, _____ cannonball goes farther each time. Cannonball 2 goes farther than _____ cannonball 1 although each is being pulled by _____ gravity toward the earth all _____ time. _____ last cannonball is fired with such tremendous velocity that it goes completely around _____ earth. It returns to_____mountaintop and continues around the earth again and again. _____ cannonball's inertia causes it to continue in motion indefinitely in _____ orbit around earth. In such a situation, we could consider _____ cannonball to be _____ artificial satellite, just like _____ weather satellites launched by _____ U.S. Weather Service. (p. 209)

Most native speakers of English who have attempted this exercise report a great deal of frustration, a curious sense of working against, rather than with, the rule. The rule, however valuable it may be for non-native speakers, is, for the most part, simply unusable for native speakers of the language.

Cognate Areas of Research

We can corroborate this demonstration by turning to research in two cognate areas, studies of the induction of rules of artificial languages and studies of the role of formal rules in second language acquisition. Psychologists have studied the ability of subjects to learn artificial languages, usually constructed of nonsense syllables or letter strings. Such languages can be described by phrase structure rules:

S => VX
X => MX

More clearly, they can be presented as flow diagrams, as below:

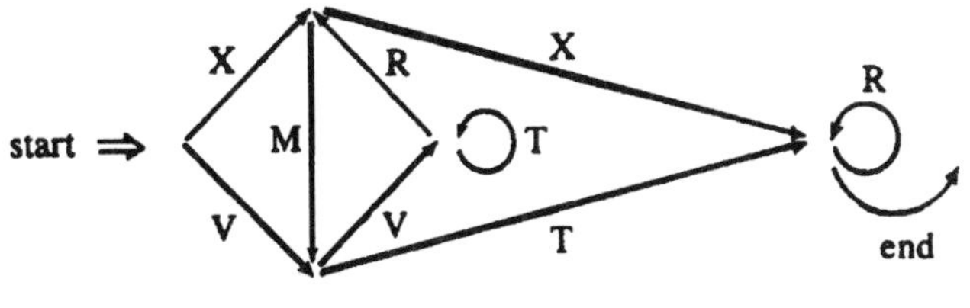

This diagram produces "sentences" like the following:

VVTRXRR.	XMVTTRX.	XXRR.
XMVRMT.	VVTTRMT.	XMTRRR.

The following "sentences" would be "ungrammatical" in this language:

*VMXTT. *RTXVVT. *TRVXXVVM.

Arthur S. Reber, in a classic 1967 experiment, demonstrated that mere exposure to grammatical sentences produced tacit learning: subjects who copied several grammatical sentences performed far above chance in judging the grammaticality of other letter strings. Further experiments have shown that providing subjects with formal rules—giving them the flow diagram above, for example—remarkably degrades performance: subjects given the "rules of the language" do much less well in acquiring the rules than do subjects not given the rules. Indeed, even telling subjects that they are to induce the rules of an artificial language degrades performance. Such laboratory experiments are admittedly contrived, but they confirm predictions that our theory of language would make about the value of formal rules in language learning.[17]

The thrust of recent research in second language learning similarly works to constrain the value of formal grammar rules. The most explicit statement of the value of formal rules is that of Stephen D. Krashen's monitor model.[18] Krashen divides second language mastery into acquisition-tacit, informal mastery, akin to first language acquisition—and formal learning—conscious application of Grammar 2 rules, which he calls "monitoring" output. In another essay Krashen uses his model to predict a highly individual use of the monitor and a highly constrained role for formal rules:

> Some adults (and very few children) are able to use conscious rules to increase the grammatical accuracy of their output, and even for these people, very strict conditions need to be met before the conscious grammar can be applied.[19]

In *Principles and Practice in Second Language Acquisition* (New York: Pergamon, 1982) Krashen outlines these conditions by means of a series of concentric circles, beginning with a large circle denoting the rules of English and a smaller circle denoting the subset of those rules described by formal linguists (adding that most linguists would protest that the size of this circle is much too large):

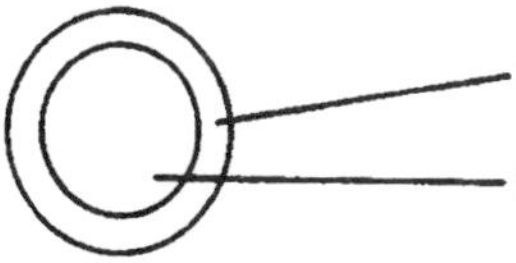

(p. 92)

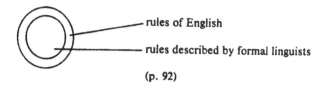

Krashen then adds smaller circles, as shown below—a subset of the rules described by formal linguists that would be known to applied linguists, a subset of those rules that would be available to the best teachers, and then a subset of those rules that teachers might choose to present to second language learners:

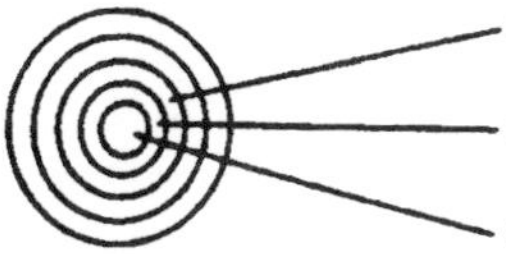

(p. 93)

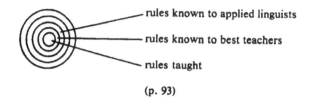

Of course, as Krashen notes, not all the rules taught will be learned, and not all those learned will be available, as what he calls "mental baggage" (p. 94), for conscious use.

An experiment by Ellen Bialystock, asking English speakers learning French to judge the grammaticality of taped sentences, complicates this issue, for reaction time data suggest that learners first make an intuitive judgment of grammaticality, using implicit or Grammar 1 knowledge, and only then search for formal explanations, using explicit or Grammar 2 knowledge.[20] This distinction would suggest that Grammar 2 knowledge is of use to second language learners only after the principle has already been mastered as tacit grammar 1 knowledge. In the terms of Krashen's model, learning never becomes acquisition *(Principles,* p. 86).

An ingenious experiment by Herbert W. Seliger complicates the issue yet further ("On the Nature and Function of Language Rules in Language Learning," *TESOL Quarterly,* 13 [1979], 359–369). Seliger asked native and non-native speakers of English to orally identify pictures of objects (e.g., "an apple," "a pear, "a book," "an umbrella"), noting whether they used the correct form of the indefinite articles *a* and *an.* He then asked each speaker to state the rule for choosing between *a* and *an.* He found no correlation between the ability to state the rule and the ability to apply it correctly, either with native or non-native speakers. Indeed, three of four adult non-native speakers in his sample produced a correct form of the rule, but they did not apply it in speaking. A strong conclusion from this experiment would be that formal rules of grammar seem to have no value whatsoever. Seliger, however, suggests a more paradoxical interpretation. Rules are of no use, he agrees, but some people think they are, and for these people, assuming that they have internalized the rules, even inadequate rules are of heuristic value, for they allow them to access the internal rules they actually use.

The Incantations of the "Common School Grammars"

Such a paradox may explain the fascination we have as teachers with "rules of grammar" of the Grammar 4 variety, the "rules" of the "common school grammars." Again and again such rules are inadequate to the facts of written language; you will recall that we have known this since Francis' 1927 study. R. Scott Baldwin and James M. Coady, studying how readers respond to punctuation signals ("Psycholinguistic Approaches to a Theory of Punctuation," *Journal of Reading Behavior,* 10 [1978], 363–83), conclude that conventional rules of punctuation are "a complete sham" (p. 375). My own favorite is the Grammar 4 rule for showing possession, always expressed in terms of adding -'s or -s' to nouns, while our internal grammar, if you think about it, adds possession to noun phrases, albeit under severe stylistic constraints: "the horses of the Queen of England" are "the Queen of England's horses" and "the feathers of the duck over there" are "the duck over there's feathers." Suzette Haden Elgin refers to the "rules" of Grammar 4 as "incantations" *(Never Mind the Trees,* p. 9: see footnote 3).

It may simply be that as hyperliterate adults we are conscious of "using rules" when we are in fact doing something else, something far more complex, accessing tacit heuristics honed by print literacy itself. We can clarify this notion by reaching for an acronym coined by technical writers to explain the readability of complex prose—COIK: "clear only if known." The rules of Grammar 4—no, we can at this point be more honest—the incantations of Grammar 4 are COIK. If you know how to signal possession in the code of print, then the advice to add *-'s* to nouns makes perfect sense, just as the collective noun *monies* is a fine example of changing *-y* to *-i* and adding *-es* to form the plural. But if you have not grasped, tacitly, the abstract representation of possession in print, such incantations can only be opaque. Worse yet, the advice given in "the common school grammars" is unconnected with anything remotely resembling literate adult behavior. Consider, as an example, the rule for not writing a sentence fragment as the rule is described in the best-selling college grammar text, John C. Hodges and Mary S. Whitten's *Harbrace College Handbook,* 9th ed. (New York: Harcourt Brace Jovanovich, 1982). In order to get to the advice, "as a rule, do not write a sentence fragment" (p. 25), the student must master the following learning tasks:

Recognizing verbs.
Recognizing subjects and verbs.
Recognizing all parts of speech. *(Harbrace* lists eight.)
Recognizing phrases and subordinate clauses. *(Harbrace* lists six types of phrases, and it offers incomplete lists of eight relative pronouns and eighteen subordinating conjunctions.)
Recognizing main clauses and types of sentences.

These learning tasks completed, the student is given the rule above, offered a page of exceptions, and then given the following advice (or is it an incantation?):

> Before handing in a composition, ... proofread each word group written as a sentence. Test each one for completeness. First, be sure that it has at least one subject and one predicate. Next, be sure that the word group is not a dependent clause beginning with a subordinating conjunction or a relative clause. (p. 27)

The school grammar approach defines a sentence fragment as a conceptual error—as not having conscious knowledge of the school grammar definition of *sentence.* It demands heavy emphasis on rote memory, and it asks students to behave in ways patently removed from the behaviors of mature writers. (I have never in my life tested a sentence for completeness, and I am a better writer—and probably a better person—as a consequence.) It may be, of course, that some developing writers, at some points in their development, may benefit from such advice—or, more to the point, may think that they benefit—but, as Thomas Friedman points out in "Teaching Error, Nurturing Confusion" (*CE*, 45 [1983], 390–399), our theory of language tells us that such advice is, at the best, COIK. As the Maine joke has it, about a tourist asking directions from a farmer, "you can't get there from here."

Redefining Error

In the specific case of sentence fragments, Mina P. Shaughnessy *(Errors and Expectations* [New York: Oxford University Press, 1977]) argues that such errors are not conceptual failures at all, but performance errors—mistakes in punctuation. Muriel Harris' error counts support this view ("Mending the Fragmented Free Modifier," *CCC*, 32 [1981], 175–182). Case studies show example after example of errors that occur *because of* instruction—one thinks, for example, of David Bartholmae's student explaining that he added an *-s* to *children* "because it's a plural" ("The Study of Error," *CCC*, 31 [1980], 262). Surveys, such as that by Muriel Harris ("Contradictory Perceptions of the Rules of Writing." *CCC*, 30[1979], 218–220), and our own observations suggest that students consistently misunderstand such Grammar 4 explanations (COIK, you will recall). For example, from Patrick Hartwell and Robert H. Bentley and from Mike Rose, we have two separate anecdotal accounts of students, cited for punctuating a *because*-clause as a sentence, who have decided to avoid using *because.* More generally, Collette A. Daiute's analysis of errors made by college students shows that errors tend to appear at clause boundaries, suggesting short-term memory load and not conceptual deficiency as a cause of error.[21]

Thus, if we think seriously about error and its relationship to the worship of formal grammar study, we need to attempt some massive dislocation of our traditional thinking, to shuck off our hyperliterate perception of the value of formal rules, and to regain the confidence in the tacit power of unconscious knowledge that our theory of language gives us. Most students, reading their writing aloud, will correct in essence all errors of spelling, grammar, and, by intonation, punctuation, but usually without noticing that what they read departs from what they wrote.[22] And Richard H. Haswell ("Minimal Marking," *CE,* 45 [1983], 600–604) notes that his students correct 61.1% of their errors when they are identified with a simple mark in the margin rather than by error type. Such findings suggest that we need to redefine error, to see it not as a cognitive or linguistic problem, a problem of not knowing a "rule of grammar" (whatever that may mean), but rather, following the insight of Robert J. Bracewell ("Writing as a Cognitive Activity," *Visible Language,* 14 [1980], 400–422), as a problem of metacognition and metalinguistic awareness, a matter of accessing knowledges that, to be of any use, learners must have already internalized by means of exposure to the code. (Usage issues—Grammar 3—probably represent a different order of problem. Both Joseph Emonds and Jeffrey Jochnowitz establish that the usage issues we worry most about are linguistically unnatural, departures from the grammar in our heads.)[23]

The notion of metalinguistic awareness seems crucial. The sentence below, created by Douglas R. Hofstadter ("Metamagical Themas," *Scientific American,* 235, No. 1 [1981], 22–32), is offered to clarify that notion; you are invited to examine it for a moment or two before continuing.

> Their is four errors in this sentance. Can you find them?

Three errors announce themselves plainly enough, the misspellings of *there* and *sentence* and the use of *is* instead of *are.* (And, just to illustrate the perils of hyperliteracy, let it be noted that, through three years of drafts, I referred to the choice of *is* and *are* as a matter of "subject-verb agreement.") The fourth error resists detection, until one assesses the truth value of the sentence itself—the fourth error is that there are not four errors, only three. Such a sentence (Hofstadter calls it a "self-referencing sentence") asks you to look at it in two ways, simultaneously as statement and as linguistic artifact—in other words, to exercise metalinguistic awareness.

A broad range of cross-cultural studies suggest that metalinguistic awareness is a defining feature of print literacy. Thus Sylvia Scribner and Michael Cole working with the triliterate Vai of Liberia (variously literate in English, through schooling; in Arabic, for religious purposes; and in an indigenous Vai script, used for personal affairs), find that metalinguistic awareness, broadly conceived, is the only cognitive skill underlying each of the three literacies. The one statistically significant skill shared by literate Vai was the recognition of word boundaries. Moreover, literate Vai tended to answer "yes" when asked (in Vai), "Can you call the sun the moon and the moon the sun?" while illiterate Vai tended to have grave doubts about such metalinguistic play. And in the United States Henry and Lila R. Gleitman report quite different responses by clerical workers and Ph.D. candidates asked to interpret nonsense compounds like "house-bird glass": clerical workers focused on meaning and plausibility (for example, "a house-bird made of glass"), while Ph.D. candidates focused on syntax (for example, "a very small drinking cup for canaries" or "a glass that protects house-birds").[24] More general research findings suggest a clear relationship between measures of metalinguistic awareness and measures of literacy level.[25] William Labov, speculating on literacy acquisition in inner-city ghettoes, contrasts "stimulus-bound" and "language-bound" individuals, suggesting that the latter seem to master literacy more easily.[26] The analysis here suggests that the causal relationship works the other way, that it is the mastery of written language that increases one's awareness of language as language.

This analysis has two implications. First, it makes the question of socially nonstandard dialects, always implicit in discussions of teaching formal grammar, into a non-issue.[27] Native speakers of English, regardless of dialect, show tacit mastery of the conventions of Standard English, and that mastery seems to transfer into abstract orthographic knowledge through interaction with print.[28] Developing writers show the same patterning of errors, regardless of dialect.[29] Studies of reading and of writing suggest that surface features of spoken dialect are simply irrelevant to mastering print literacy.[30] Print is a complex cultural code—or better yet, a system of codes—and my bet is that, regardless of instruction, one masters those codes from the top down, from pragmatic questions of voice, tone, audience, register, and rhetorical strategy, not from the bottom up, from grammar to usage to fixed forms of organization.

Second, this analysis forces us to posit multiple literacies, used for multiple purposes, rather than a single static literacy, engraved in "rules of grammar." These multiple literacies are evident in cross-cultural studies.[31] They are equally evident when we inquire into the uses of literacy in American communities.[32] Further, given that students, at all levels, show widely variant interactions with print literacy, there would seem to be little to do with grammar—with Grammar 3 or with Grammar 4—that we could isolate as a basis for formal instruction.[33]

Grammar 5: Stylistic Grammar

Similarly, when we turn to Grammar 5, "grammatical terms used in the interest of teaching prose style," so central to Martha Kolln's argument for teaching formal grammar, we find that the grammar issue is simply beside the point. There are two fully-articulated positions about "stylistic grammar," which I will label "romantic" and "classic," following Richard Lloyd-Jones and Richard E. Young.[34] The romantic position is that stylistic grammars, though perhaps useful for teachers, have little place in the teaching of composition, for students must struggle with and through language toward meaning. This position rests on a theory of language ultimately philosophical rather than linguistic (witness, for example, the contempt for linguists in Ann Berthoff's *The Making of Meaning: Metaphors, Models, and Maxims for Writing Teachers* [Montclair, N.J.: Boynton/Cook, 1981]); it is articulated as a theory of style by Donald A. Murray and, in somewhat different grounds (that stylistic grammars encourage overuse of the monitor), by Ian Pringle. The classic position, on the other hand, is that we can find ways to offer developing writers helpful suggestions about prose style, suggestions such as Francis Christensen's emphasis on the cumulative sentence, developed by observing the practice of skilled writers, and Joseph Williams' advice about predication, developed by psycholinguistic studies of comprehension.[35] James A. Berlin's recent survey of composition theory (*CE*, 45 [1982], 765–777) probably understates the gulf between these two positions and the radically different conceptions of language that underlie them, but it does establish that they share an overriding assumption in common: that one learns to control the language of print by manipulating language in meaningful contexts, not by learning about language in isolation, as by the study of formal grammar. Thus even classic theorists, who choose to present a vocabulary of style to students, do so only as a vehicle for encouraging productive control of communicative structures.

We might put the matter in the following terms. Writers need to develop skills at two levels. One, broadly rhetorical, involves communication in meaningful contexts (the strategies, registers, and procedures of discourse across a range of modes, audiences, contexts, and purposes). The other, broadly metalinguistic rather than linguistic, involves active manipulation of language with conscious attention to surface form. This second level may be developed tacitly, as a natural adjunct to developing rhetorical competencies—I take this to be the position of romantic theorists. It may be developed formally, by manipulating language for stylistic effect, and such manipulation may involve, for pedagogical continuity, a vocabulary of style. But it is primarily developed by any kind of language activity that enhances the awareness of language as language.[36] David T. Hakes, summarizing the research on metalinguistic awareness, notes how far we are from understanding this process:

> the optimal conditions for becoming metalinguistically competent involve growing up in a literate environment with adult models who are themselves

> metalinguistically competent and who foster the growth of that competence in a variety of ways as yet little understood. ("The Development of Metalinguistic Abilities," p. 205: see footnote 25)

Such a model places language, at all levels, at the center of the curriculum, but not as "necessary categories and labels" (Kolln, "Closing the Books on Alchemy," p. 150), but as literal stuff, verbal clay, to be molded and probed, shaped and reshaped, and, above all, enjoyed.

The Tradition of Experimental Research

Thus, when we turn back to experimental research on the value of formal grammar instruction, we do so with firm predictions given us by our theory of language. Our theory would predict that formal grammar instruction, whether instruction in scientific grammar or instruction in "the common school grammar," would have little to do with control over surface correctness nor with quality of writing. It would predict that any form of active involvement with language would be preferable to instruction in rules or definitions (or incantations). In essence, this is what the research tells us. In 1893, the Committee of Ten *(Report of the Committee of Ten on Secondary School Studies* [Washington, D.C.: U.S. Government Printing Office, 1893]) put grammar at the center of the English curriculum, and its report established the rigidly sequential mode of instruction common for the last century. But the committee explicitly noted that grammar instruction did not aid correctness, arguing instead that it improved the ability to think logically (an argument developed from the role of the "grammarian" in the classical rhetorical tradition, essentially a teacher of literature—see, for example, the etymology of *grammar* in the *Oxford English Dictionary*).

But Franklin S. Hoyt, in a 1906 experiment, found no relationship between the study of grammar and the ability to think logically; his research led him to conclude what I am constrained to argue more than seventy-five years later, that there is no "relationship between a knowledge of technical grammar and the ability to use English and to interpret language" ("The Place of Grammar in the Elementary Curriculum," *Teachers College Record,* 7 [1906], 483–484). Later studies, through the 1920s, focused on the relationship of knowledge of grammar and ability to recognize error; experiments reported by James Boraas in 1917 and by William Asker in 1923 are typical of those that reported no correlation. In the 1930s, with the development of the functional grammar movement, it was common to compare the study of formal grammar with one form or another of active manipulation of language; experiments by I.O. Ash in 1935 and Ellen Frogner in 1939 are typical of studies showing the superiority of active involvement with language.[37] In a 1959 article, "Grammar in Language Teaching" *(Elementary English,* 36 [1959], 412–421), John J. DeBoer noted the consistency of these findings.

> The impressive fact is ... that in all these studies, carried out in places and at times far removed from each other, often by highly experienced and disinterested investigators, the results have been consistently negative so far as the value of grammar in the improvement of language expression is concerned. (p. 417)

In 1960 Ingrid M. Strom, reviewing more than fifty experimental studies, came to a similarly strong and unqualified conclusion:

> direct methods of instruction, focusing on writing activities and the structuring of ideas, are more efficient in teaching sentence structure, usage, punctuation, and other related factors than are such methods as nomenclature drill, diagramming, and rote memorization of grammatical rules.[38]

In 1963 two research reviews appeared, one by Braddock, Lloyd-Jones, and Schorer, cited at the beginning of this paper, and one by Henry C. Meckel, whose conclusions, though more guarded, are in essential agreement.[39] In 1969 J. Stephen Sherwin devoted one-fourth of his *Four Problems in Teaching English: A Critique of Research* (Scranton, Penn.: International Textbook, 1969) to the grammar issue, concluding that "instruction in formal grammar is an ineffective way to help students achieve proficiency in writing" (p. 135). Some early experiments in sentence combining, such as those by Donald R. Bateman and Frank J. Zidonnis and by John C. Mellon, showed improvement in measures of syntactic complexity with instruction in transformational grammar keyed to sentence combining practice. But a later study by Frank O'Hare achieved the same gains with no grammar instruction, suggesting to Sandra L. Stotsky and to Richard Van de Veghe that active manipulation of language, not the grammar unit, explained the earlier results.[40] More recent summaries of research—by Elizabeth I. Haynes, Hillary Taylor Holbrook, and Marcia Farr Whiteman—support similar conclusions. Indirect evidence for this position is provided by surveys reported by Betty Bamberg in 1978 and 1981, showing that time spent in grammar instruction in high school is the least important factor, of eight factors examined, in separating regular from remedial writers at the college level.[41]

More generally, Patrick Scott and Bruce Castner, in "Reference Sources for Composition Research: A Practical Survey" (*CE*, 45 [1983]: 756–768), note that much current research is not informed by an awareness of the past. Put simply, we are constrained to reinvent the wheel. My concern here has been with a far more serious problem: that too often the wheel we reinvent is square.

It is, after all, a question of power. Janet Emig, developing a consensus from composition research, and Aaron S. Carton and Lawrence V. Castiglione, developing the implications of language theory for education, come to the same conclusion: that the thrust of current research and theory is to take power from the teacher and to give that power to the learner.[42] At no point in the English curriculum is the question of power more blatantly posed than in the issue of formal grammar instruction. It is time that we, as teachers, formulate theories of language and literacy and let those theories guide our teaching, and it is time that we, as researchers, move on to more interesting areas of inquiry.

NOTES

1. *Research in Written Composition* (Urbana, Ill.: National Council of Teachers of English, 1963), pp. 37–38.
2. "Non-magical Thinking: Presenting Writing Developmentally in Schools," in *Writing Process, Development and Communication,* Vol. II of *Writing: The Nature, Development and Teaching of Written Communication,* ed. Charles H. Frederiksen and Joseph F. Dominic (Hillsdale, N.J.: Lawrence Erlbaum. 1980). pp. 21–30.
3. For arguments in favor of formal grammar teaching, see Patrick F. Basset, "Grammar— Can We Afford Not to Teach It?" *NASSP Bulletin,* 64, No. 10 (1980), 55–63; Mary Epes, et al., "The COMP-LAB Project: Assessing the Effectiveness of a Laboratory-Centered Basic Writing Course on the College Level" (Jamaica, N.Y.: York College, CUNY, 1979) ERIC 194 908; June B. Evans, "The Analogous Ounce: The Analgesic for Relief," *English Journal,* 70, No. 2 (1981), 38–39; Sydney Greenbaum. "What Is Grammar and Why Teach It?" (a paper presented at the meeting of the National Council of Teachers of English, Boston, Nov. 1982) ERIC 222 917; Marjorie Smelstor, A *Guide to the Role of Grammar in Teaching Writing* (Madison: University of Wisconsin School of Education, 1978) ERIC 176 323; and A.M. Tibbetts, *Working Papers: A Teacher's Observations on Composition* (Glenview, Ill.: Scott, Foresman, 1982).

   For attacks on formal grammar teaching, see Harvey A. Daniels, *Famous Last Words: The American Language Crisis Reconsidered* (Carbondale: Southern Illinois University Press, 1983); Suzette Haden Elgin, *Never Mind the Trees: What the English Teacher Really Needs to Know about Linguistics* (Berkeley: University of California College of Education, Bay Area Writing Project Occasional Paper No. 2. 1980) ERIC 198 536; Mike Rose, "Remedial Writing Courses: A Critique and a Proposal," *College English,* 45 (1983), 109–128; and Ron Shook, "Response to Martha Kolln," *College Composition and Communication,* 34 (1983), 491–495.
4. See, for example, Clifton Fadiman and James Howard, *Empty Pages: A Search for Writing Competence in School and Society* (Belmont, Cal.: Fearon Pitman, 1979); Edwin Newman, *A Civil Tongue* (Indianapolis, Ind.: Bobbs-Merrill, 1976); and *Strictly Speaking* (New York: Warner Books, 1974): John Simons, *Paradigms Lost* (New York: Clarkson N. Potter, 1980); A.M. Tibbets and Charlene Tibbets, *What's Happening to American English?* (New York: Scribner's, 1978); and "Why Johnny Can't Write," *Newsweek,* 8 Dec. 1975, pp. 58–63.
5. "The Role of Grammar in a Secondary School English Curriculum," *Research in the Teaching of English,* 10 (1976), 5–21; *The Role of Grammar in a Secondary School Curriculum* (Wellington: New Zealand Council of Teachers of English, 1979).

6. "A Taxonomy of Compositional Competencies," in *Perspectives on Literacy,* ed. Richard Beach and P. David Pearson (Minneapolis: University of Minnesota College of Education, 1979). pp. 247–272.
7. On usage norms, see Edward Finegan, *Attitudes toward English Usage: The History of a War of Words* (New York: Teachers College Press, 1980), and Jim Quinn, *American Tongue in Cheek: A Populist Guide to Language* (New York: Pantheon, 1980); on arrangement, see Patrick Hartwell, "Teaching Arrangement: A Pedagogy," *CE,* 40 (1979), 548–554.
8. "Revolution in Grammar," *Quarterly Journal of Speech,* 40 (1954), 299–312.
9. Richard A. Lanham, *Revising Prose* (New York: Scribner's, 1979); William Strunk and E.B. White, *The Elements of Style,* 3rd ed. (New York: Macmillan, 1979); Joseph Williams, *Style: Ten Lessons in Clarity and Grace* (Glenview, Ill.: Scott, Foresman, 1981); Christensen, "A Generative Rhetoric of the Sentence," *CCC,* 14 (1963), 155–161; Donald A. Daiker, Andrew Kerek, and Max Morenberg, *The Writer's Options: Combining to Composing,* 2nd ed. (New York: Harper & Row, 1982).
10. "A Psychological Approach," in *Psychobiology of Language,* ed. M. Studdert-Kennedy (Cambridge, Mass.: MIT Press, 1983), pp. 16–19. See also Noam Chomsky, "Language and Unconscious Knowledge," in *Psychoanalysis and Language: Psychiatry and the Humanities,* Vol. III, ed. H. Smith (New Haven, Conn.: Yale University Press, 1978), pp. 3–44.
11. Morris Halle, "Knowledge Unlearned and Untaught: What Speakers Know about the Sounds of Their Language," in *Linguistic Theory and Psychological Reality,* ed. Halle, Joan Bresnan, and George A. Miller (Cambridge. Mass.: MIT Press, 1978), pp. 135–140
12. Moscowitz, "On the Status of Vowel Shift in English," in *Cognitive Development and the Acquisition of Language,* ed. T.E. Moore (New York: Academic Press, 1973), pp. 223–60; Chomsky, "Stages in Language Development and Reading Exposure," *Harvard Educational Review,* 42 (1972), 1–33; and Brause, "Developmental Aspects of the Ability to Understand Semantic Ambiguity, with Implications for Teachers," *RTE,* 11 (1977), 39–48.
13. Mills and Hemsley, "The Effect of Levels of Education on Judgments of Grammatical Acceptability," *Language and Speech,* 19 (1976), 324–342; Whyte, "Levels of Language Competence and Reading Ability: An Exploratory Investigation," *Journal of Research in Reading,* 5 (1982), 123–132; Morais, et al., "Does Awareness of Speech as a Series of Phonemes Arise Spontaneously?" *Cognition,* 7 (1979), 323–331; Ferguson, *Cognitive Effects of Literacy: Linguistic Awareness in Adult Non-readers* (Washington, D.C.: National Institute of Education Final Report, 1981) ERIC 222 857; Hamilton and Barton, "A Word Is a Word: Metalinguistic Skills in Adults of Varying Literacy Levels" (Stanford, Cal.: Stanford University Department of Linguistics, 1980) ERIC 222 859.
14. On the question of the psychological reality of Grammar 2 descriptions, see Maria Black and Shulamith Chiat, "Psycholinguistics without 'Psychological Reality, '" *Linguistics,* 19 (1981), 37–61; Joan Bresnan, ed., *The Mental Representation of Grammatical Relations* (Cambridge, Mass.: MIT Press, 1982); and Michael H. Long, "Inside the 'Black Box': Methodological Issues in Classroom Research on Language Learning," *Language Learning,* 30 (1980), 142.

15. Chomsky, "The Current Scene in Linguistics," *College English,* 27 (1966), 587–595; and "Linguistic Theory." in *Language Teaching: Broader Contexts,* ed. Robert C. Meade, Jr. (New York: Modern Language Association, 1966), pp. 43–49; Mark Lester, "'The Value of Transformational Grammar in Teaching Composition," *CCC,* 16 (1967), 228.
16. Christensen, "Between Two Worlds," in *Notes toward a New Rhetoric: Nine Essays for Teachers,* rev. ed., ed. Bonniejean Christensen (New York: Harper & Row, 1978), pp. 1–22.
17. Reber, "Implicit Learning of Artificial Grammars," *Journal of Verbal Learning and Verbal Behavior,* 6 (1967), 855–863; "Implicit Learning of Synthetic Languages: The Role of Instructional Set," *Journal of Experimental Psychology: Human Learning and Memory,* 2 (1976), 889–94; and Reber, Saul M. Kassin, Selma Lewis, and Gary Cantor, "On the Relationship Between Implicit and Explicit Modes in the Learning of a Complex Rule Structure," *Journal of Experimental Psychology: Human Learning and Memory,* 6 (1980), 492–502.
18. "Individual Variation in the Use of the Monitor," in *Principles of Second Language Learning,* ed. W. Richie (New York: Academic Press, 1978), pp. 175–185.
19. "Applications of Psycholinguistic Research to the Classroom," in *Practical Applications of Research in Foreign Language Teaching,* ed. D.J. James (Lincolnwood, Ill.: National Textbook, 1963), p. 61.
20. "Some Evidence for the Integrity and Interaction of Two Knowledge Sources," in *New Dimensions in Second Language Acquisition Research,* ed. Roger W. Andersen (Rowley, Mass.: Newbury House, 1981), pp. 62–74.
21. Hartwell and Bentley, *Some Suggestions for Using Open to Language* (New York: Oxford University Press, 1982), p. 73; Rose, *Writer's Block: The Cognitive Dimension* (Carbondale: Southern Illinois University Press, 1983), p. 99; Daiute, "Psycholinguistic Foundations of the Writing Process," *RTE,* 15 (1981), 5–22.
22. See Bartholmae, "The Study of Error"; Patrick Hartwell, "The Writing Center and the Paradoxes of Written-Down Speech," in *Writing Centers: Theory and Administration,* ed. Gary Olson (Urbana, Ill.: NCTE, 1984), pp. 48–61; and Sondra Perl, "A Look at Basic Writers in the Process of Composing," in *Basic Writing: A Collection of Essays for Teachers, Researchers, and Administrators* (Urbana, Ill.: NCTE, 1980), pp. 13–32.
23. Emonds, *Adjacency in Grammar: The Theory of Language-Particular Rules* (New York: Academic, 1983); and Jochnowitz, "Everybody Likes Pizza, Doesn't He or She?" *American Speech,* 57 (1982), 198–203.
24. Scribner and Cole, *Psychology of Literacy* (Cambridge, Mass.: Harvard University Press, 1981); Gleitman and Gleitman, "Language Use and Language Judgment," in *Individual Differences in Language Ability and Language Behavior,* ed. Charles J. Fillmore, Daniel Kemper, and William S.Y. Wang (New York: Academic Press, 1979), pp. 103–126.
25. There are several recent reviews of this developing body of research in psychology and child development: Irene Athey, "Language Development Factors Related to Reading Development," *Journal of Educational Research,* 76 (1983), 197–203; James Flood and Paula Menyuk, "Metalinguistic Development and Reading/Writing Achievement," *Claremont Reading Conference Yearbook,* 46 (1982), 122–132; and the following four essays: David T. Hakes, "The Development of Metalinguistic Abilities: What Develops?" pp. 162–210; Stan A. Kuczaj, II, and Brooke Harbaugh,

"What Children Think about the Speaking Capabilities of Other Persons and Things," pp. 211–227; Karen Saywitz and Louise Cherry Wilkinson, "Age-Related Differences in Metalinguistic Awareness," pp. 229–250; and Harriet Salatas Waters and Virginia S. Tinsley, "The Development of Verbal Self-Regulation: Relationships between Language, Cognition, and Behavior," pp. 251–277; all in *Language, Thought, and Culture,* Vol. 11 of *Language Development,* ed. Stan Kuczaj, Jr. (Hillsdale, N.J.: Lawrence Erlbaum, 1982). See also Joanne R. Nurss, "Research in Review: Linguistic Awareness and Learning to Read," *Young Children,* 35, No. 3 (1980), 57–66.

26. "Competing Value Systems in Inner City Schools," in *Children in and Out of School: Ethnography and Education,* ed. Perry Gilmore and Allan A. Glatthorn (Washington, D.C.: Center for Applied Linguistics, 1982), pp. 148–171; and "Locating the Frontier between Social and Psychological Factors in Linguistic Structure," in *Individual Differences in Language Ability and Language Behavior,* ed. Fillmore, Kemper, and Wang, pp. 327–340.

27. See, for example, Thomas Farrell, "IQ and Standard English," *CCC*, 34 (1983), 470–484; and the responses by Karen L. Greenberg and Patrick Hartwell, *CCC*, 35(1984), 470–484.

28. Jane W. Torrey, "Teaching Standard English to Speakers of Other Dialects," in *Applications of Linguistics: Selected Papers of the Second International Conference of Applied Linguistics,* ed. G.E. Perren and J.L.M. Trim (Cambridge, Mass.: Cambridge University Press, 1971), pp. 423–428; James W. Beers and Edmund H. Henderson, "A Study of the Developing Orthographic Concepts among First Graders," *RTE,* 11 (1977), 133–148.

29. See the error counts of Samuel A. Kirschner and G. Howard Poteet, "Non-Standard English Usage in the Writing of Black, White, and Hispanic Remedial English Students in an Urban Community College," *RTE,* 7 (1973), 351–355; and Marilyn Sternglass, "Close Similarities in Dialect Features of Black and White College Students in Remedial Composition Classes," *TESOL Quarterly,* 8 (1974), 271–283.

30. For reading, see the massive study by Kenneth S. Goodman and Yetta M. Goodman, *Reading of American Children Whose Language Is a Stable Rural Dialect of English or a Language other than English* (Washington, D.C.: National Institute of Education Final Report, 1978) ERIC 175 754; and the overview by Rudine Sims, "Dialect and Reading: Toward Redefining the Issues," in *Reader Meets Author/Bridging the Gap: A Psycholinguistic and Sociolinguistic Approach,* ed. Judith A. Langer and M. Tricia Smith-Burke (Newark, Del.: International Reading Association, 1982), pp. 222–232. For writing, see Patrick Hartwell, "Dialect Interference in Writing: A Critical View," *RTE,* 14 (1980), 101–118; and the anthology edited by Barry M. Kroll and Roberta J. Vann, *Exploring Speaking-Writing Relationships: Connections and Contrasts* (Urbana, Ill.: NCTE, 1981).

31. See, for example, Eric A. Havelock, *The Literary Revolution in Greece and its Cultural Consequences* (Princeton, N.J.: Princeton University Press, 1982); Lesley Milroy on literacy in Dublin, *Language and Social Networks* (Oxford: Basil Blackwell, 1980); Ron Scollon and Suzanne B.K. Scollon on literacy in central Alaska, *Interethnic Communication: An Athabascan Case* (Austin, Tex.: Southwest Educational Development Laboratory Working Papers in Sociolinguistics, No. 59.

1979) ERIC 175 276; and Scribner and Cole on literacy in Liberia, *Psychology of Literacy* (see footnote 24).

32. See, for example, the anthology edited by Deborah Tannen, *Spoken and Written Language: Exploring Orality and Literacy* (Norwood, N.J.: Ablex, 1982); and Shirley Brice Heath's continuing work: "Protean Shapes in Literacy Events: Ever-Shifting Oral and Literate Traditions," in *Spoken and Written Language,* pp. 91–117; *Ways with Words: Language, Life and Work in Communities and Classrooms* (New York: Cambridge University Press, 1983); and "What No Bedtime Story Means," *Language in Society,* 11 (1982), 49–76.

33. For studies at the elementary level, see Dell H. Hymes, et al., eds., *Ethnographic Monitoring of Children's Acquisition of Reading/Language Arts Skills in and Out of the Classroom* (Washington, D.C.: National Institute of Education Final Report, 1981) ERIC 208 096. For studies at the secondary level, see James L. Collins and Michael M. Williamson, "Spoken Language and Semantic Abbreviation in Writing," *RTE,* 15 (1981), 23–36. And for studies at the college level, see Patrick Hartwell and Gene LoPresti, "Sentence Combining as Kid-Watching," in *Sentence Combining: A Rhetorical Perspective,* ed. Donald A. Daiker, Andrew Kerek, and Max Morenberg (Carbondale: Southern Illinois University Press, 1985).

34. Lloyd-Jones, "Romantic Revels—I Am Not You." *CCC,* 23 (1972), 251–271; and Young, Concepts of Art and the Teaching of Writing," in *The Rhetorical Tradition and Modern Writing,* ed. James J. Murphy (New York: Modern Language Association, 1982), pp. 130–141.

35. For the romantic position, see Ann E. Berthoff, "Tolstoy, Vygotsky, and the Making of Meaning," *CCC,* 29 (1978), 249–255; Kenneth Dowst, "The Epistemic Approach," in *Eight Approaches to Teaching Composition,* ed. Timothy Donovan and Ben G. McClellan (Urbana, Ill.: NCTE, 1980), pp. 65–85; Peter Elbow, "The Challenge for Sentence Combining"; and Donald Murray, "Following Language toward Meaning," both in *Sentence Combining: A Rhetorical Perspective* (see footnote 33); and Ian Pringle, "Why Teach Style? A Review-Essay," *CCC,* 34 (1983), 91–98. For the classic position, see Christensen's "A Generative Rhetoric of the Sentence"; and Joseph Williams' "Defining Complexity," *CE,* 41 (1979), 595–609, and his *Style: Ten Lessons in Clarity and Grace* (see footnote 9).

36. Courtney B. Cazden and David K. Dickinson, "Language and Education: Standardization versus Cultural Pluralism," in *Language in the USA,* ed. Charles A. Ferguson and Shirley Brice Heath (New York: Cambridge University Press, 1981), pp. 446–468; and Carol Chomsky, "Developing Facility with Language Structure," in *Discovering Language with Children,* ed. Gay Su Pinnell (Urbana, Ill.: NCTE, 1980), pp. 56–59.

37. Boram, "Formal English Grammar and the Practical Mastery of English," Diss. University of Illinois, 1917; Asker, "Does Knowledge of Grammar Function?" *School and Society,* 17 (27 January 1923), 109–111; Ash, "An Experimental Evaluation of the Stylistic Approach in Teaching Composition in the Junior High School," *Journal of Experimental Education,* 4 (1935), 54–62; and Frogner, "A Study of the Relative Efficacy of a Grammatical and a Thought Approach to the Improvement of Sentence Structure in Grades Nine and Eleven," *School Review,* 47 (1939), 663–675.

38. "Research on Grammar and Usage and its Implications for Teaching Writing," *Bulletin of the School of Education,* Indiana University, 36 (1960), pp. 13–14.

39. Meckel, "Research on Teaching Composition and Literature," in *Handbook of Research on Teaching,* ed. N.L. Gage (Chicago: Rand McNally, 1963), pp. 966–1006.
40. Bateman and Zidonis, *The Effect of a Study of Transformational Grammar on the Writing of Ninth and Tenth Graders* (Urbana, Ill.: NCTE, 1966); Mellon, *Transformational Sentence Combining: A Method for Enhancing the Development of Fluency in English Composition* (Urbana, Ill.: NCTE, 1969); O'Hare, *Sentence-Combining: Improving Student Writing without Formal Grammar Instruction* (Urbana, Ill.: NCTE, 1971); Stoisky, "Sentence-Combining as a Curricular Activity: Its Effect on Written Language Development," *RTE,* 9 (1975), 30–72; and Van de Veghe, "Research in Written Composition: Fifteen Years of Investigation," ERIC 157 095.
41. Haynes, "Using Research in Preparing to Teach Writing," *English Journal,* 69, No. 1 (1978), 82–88; Holbrook, "ERIC/RCS Report: Whither (Wither) Grammar," *Language Arts,* 60 (1983), 259–263; Whiteman, "What We Can Learn from Writing Research," *Theory into Practice,* 19 (1980), 150–156; Bamberg, "Composition in the Secondary English Curriculum: Some Current Trends and Directions for the Eighties," *RTE,* 15 (1981), 257–266; and "Composition Instruction Does Make a Difference: A Comparison of the High School Preparation of College Freshmen in Regular and Remedial English Classes," *RTE,* 12 (1978), 47–59.
42. Emig, "Inquiry Paradigms and Writing," *CCC,* 33 (1982), 64–75; Carton and Castiglione, "Educational Linguistics: Defining the Domain," in *Psycholinguistic Research: Implications and Applications,* ed. Doris Aaronson and Robert W. Rieber (Hillsdale, N.J.: Lawrence Erlbaum, 1979), pp. 497–520.

Explaining Grammatical Concepts

Muriel Harris and Katherine E. Rowan

Muriel Harris and Katherine E. Rowan are colleagues at Purdue University. Harris is the longtime director of Purdue's Writing Center and editor of the Writing Lab Newsletter. Her publications include Teaching One-to-One: The Writing Conference, Tutoring Writing: A Sourcebook for Writing Labs, *and* The Prentice Hall Reference Guide to Grammar and Usage. *Rowan and Harris originally published this article in the* Journal of Basic Writing *in 1989, explaining an approach to teaching grammar consistent with the implications of Hartwell's article. For Harris and Rowan, editing is not a simple one-step process but an activity of detection, diagnosis, and revision that requires critical thinking. Instead of lectures and drills on grammar rules, Harris and Rowan suggest teaching grammatical concepts at the student's point of need, when the student is grappling with an editing problem. Such instruction should focus on the elements of the concept that are crucial for the student to understand and correct the error, presenting the student with a range of examples. Conferences with the student should help the student form questions that build on his or her innate knowledge of language to guide the editing.*

Although editing for grammatical correctness rightly begins when composing is basically complete, editing is—at least for unpracticed writers—almost as demanding as composing. Editing for grammatical errors is not a one-step process, but a complete series of steps which involve detecting a problem (finding a mistake), diagnosing the error (figuring out what's wrong), and rewriting (composing a more acceptable version). Skilled writers don't always consciously need to move through all of these steps, but most students do. As writing lab instructors, we are acutely aware of situations when students are able to detect sentence-level problems but have few clues for resolving them. "That sentence isn't right—should I take it out?" a student will mumble as we sit with them. "This needs something, but I don't know what," another will say. Or, "I know I should be checking for commas, so maybe I

Muriel Harris and Katherine E. Rowan. "Explaining Grammatical Concepts," *Journal of Basic Writing*, Fall 1989.

should put some in this sentence." Anxiety, frustration, and even anger surface as they flail around knowing that something should be done—if they only knew what.

Certainly no one needs prescriptive grammar to generate grammatically complete oral sentences: everyone masters this mysterious skill before the age of four. And as those opposed to the teaching of grammar are quick to point out, many people can rely on their competence as native speakers to "sense" a fragment or agreement error and correct it without resorting to conscious knowledge of grammar. But this detection skill does little or nothing to help many students edit their papers. Admittedly, these students don't need to be able to spout grammatical *terminology* (e.g., "That's a participial phrase"). But they do need to understand fundamental grammatical *concepts* so that they can successfully edit their writing. And grammatical concepts, effectively taught, can be learned. However, despite the hype of textbook salesmen, the glossy packages of supplements, and the stacks of free review copies of books that inundate our mailboxes, it is not particularly obvious how grammatical concepts can best be learned. As Patrick Hartwell notes, many tried-and-true explanations of grammar are COIK—clear only if known (119).

Hartwell has identified a core issue: too much of what passes for explanation of grammar may be perfectly clear to the teacher or textbook writer but leaves the student groping for help. To address this problem, we draw on concept learning research, a field which identifies the reasons why students generally have difficulties learning concepts and which offers tested strategies for overcoming these problems. Support for this approach comes from recent reviews of research on the teaching of grammar (Hillocks 140) and in the field of concept learning. What concept learning research offers is not some heretofore unknown approach or miracle cure but an affirmation of the need to combine a variety of interlocking strategies for success. Any standard textbook will illustrate some of these strategies or partial use of some approaches, but concept learning research emphasizes the need for thoroughness in our presentations. As we shall point out, using a few misleading examples to support a flawed explanation can cause confusion or misperceptions that may thwart a student's attempts to edit for years to come.

The term "concept," as used here and in concept learning research, refers to those mental abstractions that represent a class (or set) of entities which share certain essential characteristics. The names of these concepts (for example, the terminology traditionally used in grammar instruction) are merely conveniences for communicating about the concept. Although terminology can facilitate talking about grammatical concepts, a focus on learning terminology may cause problems because learners can mistakenly think that knowing the name means knowing all the critical features of the concept. Being able to identify ten (or two hundred) restrictive clauses in no way ensures that the student knows all the critical features of the concept. The broad definition of concepts helps us to see that concept learning principles are meant for all disciplines. While some of the research in concept learning is conducted with lessons in other fields, many projects include instruction in grammatical and poetic concepts, which researchers have successfully taught to students in junior high through college. These studies are not often cited in composition research, perhaps because the work appears in journals that composition teachers don't normally think of as being in their domain, e.g., *Educational Technology and Communication Journal*, *The Journal of Educational Psychology*, and *Review of Educational Research*.[1] Our purpose in this essay is to show how insights and strategies from concept learning literature can make the teaching of grammatical concepts efficient and effective. Throughout, we use instruction in the grammatically complete sentence as an example of how the principles of concept learning can facilitate understanding of grammatical concepts.[2] We've chosen sentence completeness because it is one of the writer's basic tools for clear, correct writing. In addition, a shaky concept of the sentence can inhibit writers from composing sentences they might otherwise construct. In a study of sentence errors, Dona Kagan describes the fragment as "among the most prevalent and irremediable errors" found in student writing (127).

Research in concept learning shows that a basic criterion for good explanations of difficult ideas is that they address students' most frequent misunderstandings. Hence, to identify our students' notions of the complete sentence, we first examined and categorized fragments that they wrote. We then altered a student essay slightly so that each of these characteristic fragments was represented (see Appendix A). To see what information students call upon while editing for fragments, we asked 179 students to identify each of thirty items in the essay as either a sentence or a fragment and to explain, in writing, why they made each choice. The students were enrolled in nine classes at our university, classes ranging from freshman composition to advanced writing, business writing, technical writing, and journalism. This gave us a sample of students about half of whom were juniors or seniors who had completed one or more college writing courses and another half of whom were completing their first semester of freshman composition. The tabulations of the students' responses (Table 1) show that while no item was correctly identified by all the respondents, some were more confusing to them than others.[3]

More important for our purposes than the matter of correct identifications are the reasons the students offered for their decisions. These responses open a window into student conceptions—and misconceptions—of the sentence. We use examples of these student responses to illustrate what concept learning researchers have identified as problems in learning concepts in nearly any field. After describing each problem, we offer strategies from concept learning research which overcome the particular difficulty. These strategies, as we illustrate, are found to some degree in contemporary grammar textbooks and programmed learning guides. However, concept learning research has shown that no one of these strategies can be truly effective if used alone. Instead, concept learning strategies are interlocking and reinforcing and achieve their purpose only in combination. In short, partial explanations, examples, and practice too often produce, at best, partial learning.

Learning Concepts: Key Difficulties and Effective Strategies in Overcoming Them

1. Recalling Background Knowledge

Evidence of the Difficulty:

The work of learning theorists like Robert Gagne shows that learning a new concept usually involves building on other, more basic, concepts. If these other concepts are not familiar to a student, any explanation of the new concept can be a classic case of COIK, clear only if known. This is obvious to a teacher trying to explain the sentence to students who lack knowledge of subjects and predicates. To understand the concept of subjects, students have to know not only what nouns and pronouns are but, ultimately, phrases and clauses too, since all can exist as subjects. They may have some partial knowledge of these concepts, but it is necessary that at some point they have access to complete knowledge of all forms that can act as subjects. Otherwise, as we saw among the students we studied, the inability to consistently recognize subjects and predicates causes frequent errors in distinguishing sentences from fragments. For example, some of the students who identified the complete sentences #22, 23, and 27 in the test essay (Appendix A) as fragments did so because they said that there was no subject, an indication that the pronouns in these sentences weren't recognized as subjects. Even more confusion appears to exist for the student who identified a fragment (#16) as a sentence because it contains a verb, "perfect," and a noun, "his." Other students labeled item #19 as a fragment, saying "it has no subject or verb." (It has both, though in dependent clauses.)

Students also revealed their difficulties in distinguishing dependent from independent clauses. As a typical example, one student incorrectly identified item #4 as a fragment "because each clause cannot stand by itself," and another student incorrectly labeled item #13 as a fragment "because it is a prepositional phrase." This small, but representative sampling of the students' comments could be extended, but it is clear that these students' background knowledge is inadequate and that there is no point in expecting them to understand a definition of a fragment which assumes an understanding of the subject, verb, phrase, and clause.

Strategy for Overcoming the Difficulty.

Meeting this difficulty by providing background knowledge may seem to lead to an endless regression, but this is not the case. In their studies of concept learning, Tennyson and his associates have demonstrated the effectiveness of presenting background information at the point that the student seems to need help (Tennyson and Cocchiarella 62–63). For example, this technique is used to teach the sentence in the opening pages or "frames" of Joseph Blumenthal's *English 2200, 2600,* and *3200,* a venerable and widely used—but not unflawed—series of self-instructional texts.[4] Included in Blumenthal's definition of a complete sentence are the concepts of subject and predicate which are defined as the "naming" and "telling" parts of the sentence. Practice is then offered for identifying the "naming" and "telling" parts of several sentences. In Lynn Quitman Troyka's *Simon and Schuster Handbook for Writers,* the sentence fragment is also defined and illustrated. Then, as the definition is extended, the concept of "verb" is introduced, explained, and illustrated, and the subject is explained next. Then, with this background information provided, the handbook explains dependent and independent clauses, beginning with an explanation of subordinating conjunctions (260–263). Thus at each step, background information is provided as needed.

2. Controlling All the Critical Features of a Concept

Evidence of the Difficulty:

Another problem faced by students learning new concepts is that of internalizing all the concept's critical (or essential) attributes, that is, of building a mental representation which includes every one of these necessary attributes. In the classic view of concept learning, recognizing a list of critical features was viewed as sufficient. But research on applied problems of concept learning has shown that people learn concepts by forming a mental prototype, that is, a clear case or best example (Reitman and Bower; Tennyson, Chao, and Youngers; Tennyson, Youngers, and Suebsonthi). In learning a specific concept, the more of its critical features our prototype includes, the fuller and more complete our grasp of this concept is. Nevertheless, what we store in memory is not a list of a concept's critical features but a prototype, an abstraction derived from *examples* of the concept that we've encountered.

The chief difficulty in forming a prototype is that of identifying the particular cluster of attributes which are truly critical and of distinguishing this cluster from the variable attributes, those that can and do occasionally or frequently appear, but aren't necessary. We can thus mistakenly include in the cluster of critical features attributes that are really only variables or omit a critical feature because we wrongly think it is a variable. For example, we can understand the source of confusion experienced by the child who, watching a kilted Scottish bagpiper in full regalia, says, "Why does that lady have a beard?" Skirts may be most frequently associated with women, but it is not a critical attribute of skirts that they be worn only by women. Assuming a variable to be a critical attribute is also a common source of humor, particularly with stereotypes: "Why did Adam remain happy when he left the Garden of Eden?" "Because he *still* had no mother-in-law."

Unpleasantness, despite the vast repertoire of jokes on the subject, is a variable, not a critical attribute of mothers-in-law.

In our study we noticed numerous problems in students' prototypes of sentences which resulted from their confusion or misperceptions about critical and variable features. For example, in our pilot work, Teresa told us that the sentence, "John went to the store," was not a complete thought because it did not say what John bought at the store. For Teresa, the semantic feature "fully informative" was a critical attribute of all sentences rather than a variable attribute. (Sentences in context in paragraphs are not always fully informative.) Thus, we found students labeling as fragments complete sentences such as items #26, 27, and 30 because these items contained references to previous sentences by means of pronouns such as "he" and "that" and were therefore somehow "incomplete." Transition words (at the beginning of items #7, 13, and 15) and the phrase "on the other hand" in item #9 also provoked this sense of incompleteness. Among the students who said that the transitional phrase "to sum up" (item #25) marked a sentence as a fragment, one explained that it was incomplete by noting "To sum up what?" To prove the point that "first" (items #7 and 15) causes incompleteness, one student wrote, "What's second?" Another student wrote, "If there's a first, there needs to be a second thought to complete the sentence." These misperceptions raise the question of whether some students avoid the connectives we encourage for coherence because they see these as making a word group not "able to stand alone" (another commonly used definition of the sentence that students were unable to operationalize successfully). The conjunctions "and" and "but" are also definitely forbidden as sentence openers in the minds of many students. They noted that "and" as the first word of item #18 and "but" as the first word of item #26 identified these sentences as fragments. Said one student, "After putting in a subject and verb I allow a sentence to do almost anything it wants except begin with a conjunction." This misconception is most probably due to advice that students mistakenly store as a fixed rule.

The problem of viewing variable attributes of sentences as critical caused other difficulties as well. For example, sentence length, a variable attribute, exists as a critical attribute in the minds of those students who incorrectly labeled items #5 and 21 as fragments with explanations such as "it's too short" and a lengthy fragment (#28) as a sentence with explanations such as "it has enough words." The criterion of word length was given for other items as well. (Kagan's study documents the same misconception, that complete sentences need to exceed a certain number of words.) This raises the question of whether some students don't vary the word length of their sentences because they fear violating some rule they think applies to complete sentences. We found internal punctuation within the sentence included in many students' concepts of the sentence as well. For example, students incorrectly said that items #2 and 9 were fragments because of internal punctuation problems. Item #1 was incorrectly identified as a fragment because of "missing punctuation before the quote," item #12 was incorrectly marked as a fragment because "it needs punctuation after 'patience,'" and item #26 was also incorrectly identified as a fragment because "it needs commas." For other students, usage errors caused a word group to be a fragment. Thus, for item #22, a reason given by several students for incorrectly identifying it as a fragment was their discomfort with the phrase "fast and easy." Another student noted that item #27 (a sentence) was a fragment because "something is wrong with 'both very much.'"

In all this confusion we can see either ignorance of what constitutes the critical features of a sentence or elaborate but dysfunctional representations of the sentence. As Shaughnessy has argued, the problem is not that students are novices with a "lack" of knowledge but rather that from their bits of knowledge, they have constructed some elaborate, convoluted, and misleading conceptions. Kagan reaches a similar conclusion when she notes that "poor writers may simply have misperceived examples of written language and thus have abstracted incorrect rules regarding the structure of complete sentences" (127). Behind many of the students' comments in the responses we read, we heard echoes of familiar, overly brief, incomplete definitions such as "a sentence is a group of words with a subject and a verb," "a sentence tells who and what," "a sentence expresses a complete thought." Such inadequate definitions, accompanied by a few examples carefully chosen to support the definitions, leave students thinking they understand what a sentence is. However, such definitions also leave students without any way to think about sentences where the "who" or "what" is less than obvious (as in the sentence, "What she did to him is wrong") or about sentences which make sense only in context of other sentences (e.g., "They did it again"). The problem here is that students mistakenly apply the notion of "completeness" to the semantic meaning of the sentence and think that sentences must be fully informative. However, in realty, many grammatically complete sentences are not fully informative or "complete thoughts" outside the context of other surrounding sentences. In many of the mistaken student responses in our study, we observed a great deal of confusion when the students used semantic completeness as a test for a sentence rather than grammatical completeness. The weakness of the "tells who or what" definition is particularly evident in the frequency with which it turned up in student responses as justification for incorrectly identifying dependent clauses as complete sentences.

Strategy for Overcoming the Difficulty:

In the discussion of student perceptions—and misperceptions—of the sentence, we noted that definitions help students mentally represent the critical attributes of a concept. Evidence for the usefulness of definitions comes from C.S. Dunn's study of six methods of teaching science concepts. She found that the least effective was a "discovery" approach in which students were not given definitions. Instead, they were asked to discern the critical attributes of a concept from a set of diverse examples. Since the purpose of a definition is to highlight the critical attributes of a concept, the definition should contain a list of these critical features with each feature graphically highlighted.

Along with definitions, clear, typical, and varied examples also help students to master a concept's critical attributes. Grammar handbooks, intended primarily to be used as references rather than as programs of instruction, do not generally have space to include all the typical examples that are needed, but they often have quite adequate definitions. For example, the definition in Troyka's handbook is helpful in that it includes, among several definitions from various perspectives, a grammatical one: "Grammatically, a sentence contains an independent clause, a group of words that can stand alone as an independent unit" (154). Troyka then goes on to discuss the structure of a sentence and also presents a range of clear, typical examples. Initially, there are also five examples of fragments. The first three are phrasal fragments (no verb, no subject, no verb or subject) which, as we and Kagan found in our studies, students are most likely to recognize. The last two are clausal fragments (dependent clause and a subject with a dependent clause), the ones which students have more trouble recognizing and are more likely to produce (Harris). The discussion in Troyka's book then builds up to more complex examples of typical fragments. Other widely used handbooks such as the *Harbrace College Handbook* or the *Random House Handbook* tend to have a more limited number and range of examples, and the difficulty of attempting a brief, easily grasped (but incomplete) definition can be seen in the popular workbook, *Grassroots.* Here students are told: "For a sentence to be complete, it must contain a *who* or *what* word." Further down the page in *Grassroots,* the subject is defined as the "*who* or *what* word" (4), thus failing to distinguish subjects from objects. Such a definition can create further confusion in that it does not allow for subjects which consist of more than one word. In sum, then, good definitions list all of the critical features of a concept and are accompanied by a range of clear, typical examples.

3. Recognizing New Instances of a Concept

Evidence of the Difficulty:

Another problem in learning a concept, as suggested in the examples cited above, is that of recognizing newly encountered instances of the concept. In fact, researchers such as Homa, Sterling, and Trepel; and Tennyson, Chao, and Youngers say that this is one of the most frequent problems learners have. Certainly it is familiar to teachers: students can recite a definition of a sentence, but they have difficulty identifying new examples of sentences or fragments, or examples in unfamiliar contexts. People struggle to recognize concepts in context because, first, some of the guises or forms in which a concept appears are easier to spot than others and, second, to identify a new instance of a concept one must recognize all of its critical attributes. For example, some of the students who incorrectly labeled items

#18 and 26 as fragments did so because they noted that these items "lacked verbs." What they did not recognize were verbs which are manifested in contractions ("he's" and "that's"). However, other examples of fragments were easy for students in our study to recognize. For example, most students recognized short, phrasal fragments such as those in items #6, 11, 16, and 29. But a dependent clause (in item #19) was harder to recognize. Kagan also found that students had difficulty recognizing as fragments verbs followed by various structures, particularly objects modified by prepositional phrases. From the perspective of concept learning research, then, some students either may not understand all of the forms in which subjects and predicates can appear, or they may not understand that fragments can be either phrases or dependent clauses.

Strategy for Overcoming the Difficulty:

To help students recognize new instances of a concept, it is particularly important to use examples, more examples, and even more examples if possible, though they have to be carefully constructed and ordered. As already noted, we need to start with clear, typical cases that accompany definitions so that students can form and encode a prototype in memory. After that, students need an extended presentation of various kinds of examples, displayed in matched sets and discussed in easy-to-difficult order. The sets of examples should illustrate a wide range of critical and variable attributes. Highlighting for visual emphasis, particularly in explaining the examples, is very helpful.

- **Matched Sets.** Examples should be in matched sets of examples and nonexamples to help students discriminate between critical and variable features. Examples and nonexamples are matched when all the irrelevant or variable attributes of the set are as similar as possible. For example, because students may have trouble realizing that some contractions may include verbs, matched sets of examples and nonexamples could be used to illustrate this fact:

Concept: verb in a contraction

Matched sets:
Example: She ***is*** lovely.
Example: She***'s*** lovely.
Nonexample: She lovely.

Example: When cotton shirts are old, they ***are*** more comfortable.
Example: When cotton shirts are old, they***'re*** more comfortable.
Nonexample: When cotton shirts are old, they more comfortable.

> *Explanation:* Some verb forms can be present in contractions. In the matched sets above, the word groups that can stand alone as sentences (examples) contain complete verbs. The nonexamples lack verbs.

The use of nonexamples may seem to contradict a currently popular approach, offering instruction which is described as "nonerror based." The assumption in nonerror based instruction is that students should avoid seeing examples of errors. However, a number of studies indicate the power of the nonexample in effective concept formation (Markle and Tiemann; Tennyson 1973; Tennyson and Park; Tennyson, Woolley, and Merrill).

For example, since some students think that a pronoun cannot be the subject of a sentence (perhaps because a pronoun as the subject would cause the sentence to be less than fully informative), an effective sequence of instruction would present a sentence with a pronoun as a subject and an accompanying fragment with the same pronoun as a subject. An explanation of the pair would point out that both the sentence and the fragment have a pronoun as a subject. (Putting the sentence in the context of other sentences would help the student see that sentences refer to each other.) This kind of matching is helpful because the purpose of the nonexample is to have students see that a variable feature is indeed irrelevant.

Because the irrelevant or variable features to present are those likely to cause confusion, we can look at our students' writing to determine which variable attributes to illustrate. For example, since 20% of the students we studied labeled sentence #8 (a fragment containing a subject with a lengthy dependent clause modifying it) as a complete sentence, the following example/nonexample pair might be presented and discussed:

> ***Six*** of the players who had poor grades on their mid-semester exams ***are sitting*** on the bench.
>
> > (This is an example of a sentence because it has a subject, "six," with a lengthy word group describing it and then the verb "are sitting" which tells what the six are doing.)
>
> ***Six*** of the players who had poor grades on their mid-semester exams.
>
> > (This is not a sentence because it has a subject, "six," with a word group describing it but no verb. The word group after the subject describes only the subject.)

Given the confusions about sentence length that we found, another matched pair should contain only a few words while a third should be lengthy to emphasize that length is not a critical feature of the sentence.

The *English 2200, 2600, 3200* books make considerable use of this kind of matching. When these texts offer examples of new concepts, the examples are usually paired with matched nonexamples. For instance, in *3200,* Blumenthal offers the following advice and matched sets:

> Remember, too, that the length of a word group has nothing to do with its being a sentence or not. Two words may form a sentence provided that they are a subject and verb and make sense by themselves.
>
> a. (The) ***Neighbors objected*** b. The ***neighbors.***
> Which is a complete sentence?—
>
> (33, frame 1367)

To further show that length is a variable and irrelevant feature of sentences, Blumenthal offers another matched set:

> [a.] The ***neighbors,*** who were annoyed by Joanne's practicing her trombone at all hours of the day and night. (37, frame 1369) [versus]
> [b.] The ***neighbors,*** who were annoyed by Joanne's practicing her trombone at all hours of the day and night, ***complained.*** (41, frame 1371)

By using these and many more matched sets, Blumenthal illustrates the irrelevance of length as a feature of sentences and highlights the critical importance of subjects and verbs.

- **Easy-to-difficult order.** Researchers have also found that students benefit when matched pairs are discussed in "easy-to-difficult" order. Easy examples have variable attributes that students make fewer mistakes with, and the progression should be to variable attributes that are more and more likely to cause students difficulties. To determine whether examples and nonexamples are easy or difficult, instructors can examine students' own writing or give diagnostic tests. In their work, Tennyson, Woolley, and Merrill found that when students are exposed only to easy items, they either fail to recognize all of the critical attributes of a concept, or they fail to recognize the full range of guises in which these attributes may appear. (Of course, this range will vary as students mature and become more proficient writers.)

- **Divergence between sets.** There should also be divergence between sets of examples. This helps students in discriminating a variety of apparent from real instances of a concept when they encounter new examples. Thus, for instance, when teaching sentences, we would include some matched sets of sentences/fragments beginning with the conjunctions, transitional words, and phrases that too many students think indicate fragments and other sets without such beginnings. Students would see, for example, both a sentence and a fragment starting with "but" and another matched set lacking this initial term. Other variable attributes would also be drawn from the lists of problems and confusions students have.

- **Highlighting.** Another characteristic that increases the effectiveness of presentations, particularly in discussing examples, is the use of "attribute isolation," that is, the use of typographical or graphic highlighting such as underlining, italics, and/or white space to call attention to the critical features of a concept (Tennyson "Pictorial Support"). A text that uses attribute isolation particularly effectively is Troyka's handbook which, in the discussion of fragments, uses boldface lettering, shaded boxes, contrasting colors of print (red and black), and generous use of white space to highlight important points. In the classroom, with homegrown materials, we are not likely to have at our disposal such elegant type features, but we can make use of underlining, circling, arrows, and white space.

Accompanying the examples should be explanations, to call attention to the various critical features that we want students to notice. For the sentence, we might present examples and nonexamples and note: "This is an example of a sentence because it has both a subject and a predicate, which constitute an independent clause," or "This is not an example of a sentence because it has only a dependent clause." These examples and accompanying explanations ("expository presentations") perform a necessary and important function in concept learning, for it is here that students see what Tennyson and Cocchiarella call the "dimensionality or richness of the conceptual knowledge" (61). Presenting only simple sentences with clear subjects and predicates sidesteps all the elaborations and variety of real sentences (and fragments) that occur when students actually write.

For examples of good expository presentations in current texts, see the discussion of fragments in the *Harbrace College Handbook*—which uses matched sets, divergence across sets, and some highlighting—or Troyka's extended expository presentation on fragments (260–64) which makes good use of nonexamples in matched sets, divergence across sets, easy-to-difficult order, and highlighting. Although *Grassroots* has very short expository presentations or discussions of concepts, it does illustrate the use of practice exercises in easy-to-difficult order and uses some highlighting to emphasize key words. An example of a presentation which omits nonexamples, matched sets, divergence across sets, and easy-to-difficult ordering can be seen in the *Random House Handbook.*

4. Discriminating Apparent from Real Instances of a Concept

Evidence of the Difficulty:

A fourth aspect of learning difficult concepts is that of discriminating apparent from real instances of the concept's application. Students develop this discriminatory ability only with time, practice, and feedback (Dunn). In our study, we did not explore the history of our subjects' attempts to master the sentence-fragment distinction; however, the study does show that even as juniors and seniors, many students had fuzzy notions of the sentence which did little to help them master this distinction. Those who reported using the "complete thought" definition often seemed to use this in some vague semantic sense. Those who used the "who or what does the action" criterion failed to understand that their notion of the sentence did not include predication. For example, one student incorrectly identified item #24 as a sentence because it "gives who or what." Perhaps such students have inaccurate notions because they never practiced the sentence-fragment distinction in a context where they received continual feedback which explained why their answers were correct or incorrect.

Strategy for Overcoming the Difficulty:

To distinguish between apparent and real instances of a concept, students continually need reminders about the features that are truly critical to it. Tennyson and his associates found that students are more likely to classify concepts correctly and recall them better when they not only have a chance to read expository presentations of examples but also have the chance to work through "inquisitory practice sessions" (Dunn; Tennyson, Chao, and Youngers). These are exercises in which students are presented with new examples and nonexamples and are asked to identify them by working through a list of questions. After they give both correct and incorrect answers, students receive feedback which reminds them of the basis on which they should have made their identification (i.e., whether or not a given item had or didn't have all critical attributes of the concept). By working through these questions (which ask students to think about a concept's critical attributes) and by receiving feedback (which discusses the presence or absence of a given critical attribute in a particular item), students gradually learn to look for these critical attributes on their own. For an example of inquisitory practice, see Figure 1.

Similar strategies can be seen elsewhere in Troyka's handbook where, for example, at the beginning of the first exercise on fragments, students are told: "Check each word group according to the Test for Sentence Completeness on p. 261" (264). Students have to flip back and forth between the test and the exercises, but they are reminded of how they should proceed in determining whether or not a word group is a sentence or a fragment. *Grassroots* does not phrase the critical attributes of fragments as questions, but it does remind students of at least some of these critical attributes by beginning an exercise with the following instructions: "All of the following are *fragments;* they lack either a subject or a verb or both. Add either a subject or verb or both in order to make the fragments into sentences" (17). Unfortunately, this fails to help students whose fragments are primarily dependent clauses, but it is more helpful than the instructions in the *Harbrace College Handbook*, which tells students: "Eliminate each fragment below by including it in the adjacent sentence or by making it into a sentence" (29).

Tennyson, Chao, and Youngers have demonstrated the importance of providing students with both expository presentations and inquisitory practice in a study which contrasted three learning situations. In the first, students were given only an expository presentation with examples. In the second, they were given only the inquisitory practice, while in the third, they were given both. The students in all three situations were able to recall the concept's critical attributes and some examples. However, the students who worked through both the expository presentation and the inquisitory practice had significantly higher scores than the other two groups in identifying new examples of the concept in context and in discriminating between instances of the concept and entities that appeared to be instances. In Dunn's replication of this study, once again it was the combination of explanations of matched examples and nonexamples and inquisitory practice that increased performance in every aspect of concept attainment.

Inquisitory Practice

Concept: Fragment
Definition: A fragment is one word or a group of words that cannot pass Troyka's Test for Sentence Completeness

(Troyka's) Test for Sentence Completeness
1. Is there a verb? If no, there is a sentence fragment.
2. Is there a subject? " If no, there is a sentence fragment.
3. Do the subject and verb start with a subordinating word—and lack an independent clause to complete the thought? If yes, there is a sentence fragment. (Troyka 261)

Applying the Test—1

Directions: Identify all the sentence fragments incorrectly punctuated as sentences in the passage below. To do so, examine each numbered item by asking the three questions in Troyka's test.

The Change in Our Family

(1) When I was sixteen. (2) My father died. (3) Our family, my mom, me, and my two sisters, struggled to make ends meet. (4) We decided to move to an apartment because we couldn't afford our house any more (5) The apartment, a big adjustment for us all. (6) For we had always seen ourselves as middle class. (7) The move made us wonder if we still were. (8) We have adjusted over the years and learned to be more realistic, I think. (9) It's not been easy. (10) But maybe we're a more honest family now.

Applying the Test-2

Directions: Using Troyka's Test to guide your decisions, punctuate the following passage.

Passage: To celebrate the opening of his theater the owner decided to give a television set to the person holding the lucky ticket when the number was called seventy-two people flocked to the box office each having the lucky number the printer had made a slight mistake. (Blumenthal 71, frame 1386)

Figure 1. "Applying the Test" exercises are examples of inquisitory practice. The first exercise (#1) should be easier than the second (#2) because it requires students to make fewer decisions. The second exercise is more difficult but more realistic, requiring students to detect, diagnose, and edit.

Conclusion

In all of the information that concept learning research has to offer, one point stands out: students do not learn difficult concepts when presented with any single technique. What works is a *combination* of techniques:

- Providing background information when and where it is needed
- Offering definitions that list critical attributes and that are not overly simple or misleading
- Using a wide array of examples and nonexamples, chosen to reflect students' actual difficulties, and discussing the examples
- Including practice sessions, with feedback, that help students turn a concept's critical attributes into questions they ask themselves.

As we have seen, some of these principles are at work in our textbooks, but not as consistently or thoroughly as concept learning research would urge. But we can keep these guidelines in mind when choosing workbooks and textbooks and when offering instruction—both in classrooms and in tutoring sessions. And we can supplement, where necessary, adequate but not entirely complete textbook assignments and computer-assisted instruction. (However, spending time on uprooting misconceptions caused by inept textbooks is, like swatting mosquitoes, a frustrating, unending task.) The use of concept learning strategies is not the only way into better explanation of grammatical concepts, but it is a way, one based on sound principles and extensive research. It may appear to involve a great deal of effort, but if our students have convoluted, erroneous concepts that have to be untangled or corrected, we can't give short shrift and expect good results. They come to our classes with the capacity to detect some editing problems. They should leave with their detection, diagnosis, and revision skills enhanced.

Item #	No. (and %) identifying it as a sentence	No. (and%) identifying it as a fragment
1 (sentence)	161 (90%)	17 (9%)
2 (sentence)	144 (89%)	31 (17%)
3 (fragment)	3 (2%)	175 (98%)
4 (sentence)	161 (90%)	17 (9%)
5 (sentence)	165 (92%)	13 (7%)
6 (fragment)	4 (2%)	175 (98%)
7 (sentence)	153 (85%)	24 (13%)
8 (fragment)	36 (20%)	140 (78%)
9 (sentence)	168 (94%)	10 (6%)
10 (sentence)	175 (98%)	3 (2%)
11 (fragment)	4 (2%)	172 (96%)
12 (sentence)	162 (91%)	15 (8%)
13 (sentence)	98 (55%)	79 (44%)
14 (sentence)	174 (97%)	4 (2%)
15 (sentence)	160 (89%)	18 (10%)
16 (fragment)	9 (5%)	168 (94%)
17 (sentence)	164 (92%)	12 (7%)
IS (sentence)	60 (34%)	114 (64%)
19 (fragment)	23 (13%)	152 (85%)
20 (fragment)	75 (42%)	97 (54%)
21 (sentence)	167 (93%)	5 (3%)
22 (sentence)	148 (83%)	25 (14%)
23 (sentence)	156 (87%)	17 (9%)
24 (fragment)	14 (8%)	157 (88%)
25 (sentence)	144 (80%)	28 (16%)
26 (sentence)	54 (30%)	114 (64%)
27 (sentence)	154 (86%)	15 (8%)
28 (fragment)	21 (12%)	150 (84%)
29 (fragment)	3 (2%)	167 (93%)
30 (sentence)	154 (86%)	14 (8%)

Table 1. Tabulation of student responses to the test essay. (Number of students = 179. Because of some omitted responses, totals are not always 100%.)

Appendix A

(Included here is the essay that students in our study were given. They were asked to identify each sentence as either a sentence or a fragment and to explain their responses.)

My Brothers

(1) The phrase I heard only too often when I was younger was 'You're too little to play.' (2) Whatever my older brothers did I wanted to do, wherever they went I wanted to go. (3) Pat being two years older than myself and allowed to hang out with Randy, being four years older. (4) Since there was such a difference in age. I developed different and unique relationships with each.

(5) My brothers have clashing identities. (6) Total opposites of each other. (7) First, Pat is the kind of brother you see on television. (8) The kind that would help you with your homework and your problems. (9) Randy, on the other hand, isn't the smartest brother in the world but, he's been around and knows a lot. (10) The best summary of Randy is that he's the Mr. Hyde of Pat. (11) Not exactly bad, though a lot different. (12) He has no patience especially when he gets angry. (13) Then he goes on apologizing for days.

(14) There are traits in both of my brothers that I dislike. (15) First, Pat is too perfect. (16) Much too perfect for his own good. (17) The biggest annoyance is that he gets great grades. (18) And he's also nice to people that bother him. (19) Because he thinks it's important to be polite. (20) Not to mention his mannerisms are good at all times. (21) Randy likes to move around a lot. (22) He gets bored with a job fast and easy. (23) He just can't stay in the office very much. (24) Which makes him a very good salesman.

(25) To sum up, we have our differences. (26) But that's just like any other family. (27) 1 still like them both very much. (28) Any differences that I may have because of age or size which wasn't resolved or will be through time. (29) For a final note to this assignment. (30) 1 would never say any of this to their faces, just on paper.

NOTES

1 In such journals one can find the work of Robert Tennyson and his associates, e.g., Johansen and Tennyson; Merrill and Tennyson; Tennyson, Welsh, Christensen, and Hajovy; and Tennyson, Woolley, and Merrill. An accessible summary for teachers of this work is M. David Merrill and Robert Tennyson's *Teaching Concepts: An Instructional Design Guide*. Reviews of more recent research in concept learning can be found in an article by Tennyson and Park and another by Tennyson and Cocchiarella.

2 We should note that the "grammar" being referred to here is that set of school grammar conventions labeled "grammar 4" by Patrick Hartwell, to distinguish it from other grammars, such as the descriptive grammar of linguists, stylistic grammar, or the internal grammar which guides all of our language use.

3 While it was not our purpose to look for developmental gains as students progress through writing courses, we should note here that the students in the upper level writing courses did not perform appreciably better than the freshmen in distinguishing complete sentences from fragments.

4 The books we use as examples in this paper are among those frequently used to teach grammar at the college level, according to sales information from major publishers.

Works Cited

Blumenthal, Joseph C. *English 3200: A Programmed Course in Grammar and Usage,* 3rd ed. New York: Harcourt, 1981.

Crews, Frederick and Ann Jessie Van Sant. *The Random House Handbook,* 4th ed. New York: Random, 1984.

Dunn, C.S. "The Influence of Instructional Methods on Concept Learning." *Science Education* 67 (October 1983): 647–56.

Fawcett, Susan and Alvin Sandberg. *Grassroots: The Writer's Workbook,* 3rd ed. Boston: Houghton, 1987.

Gagne, Robert. *Essentials of Learning for Instruction.* Hinsdale, IL: Dryden, 1974.

Harris, Muriel. "Mending the Fragmented Free Modifier." *College Composition and Communication* 32 (May 1981): 175–82.

Hartwell, Patrick. "Grammar, Grammars, and the Teaching of Grammar." *College English* 47 (February 1985): 105–27.

Hillocks, George Jr. *Research on Written Composition: New Directions for Teaching.* Urbana, IL: ERIC Clearinghouse on Reading and Communication Skills, 1986.

Hodges, John C., Mary E. Whitten, with Suzanne S. Webb. *Harbrace College Handbook,* 10th ed. New York: Harcourt, 1986.

Homa, D., S. Sterling, and L. Trepel. "Limitations of Exemplar-Based Generalizations and the Abstraction of Categorical Information." *Journal of Experimental Psychology: Human Learning and Memory* 7 (November 1981): 418–39.

Johansen, Keith J. and Robert D. Tennyson. "Effects of Adaptive Advisement on Perception in Learner-Controlled, Computer-Based Instruction Using a Rule-Learning Task." *Educational Communication and Technology Journal* 31 (Winter 1983): 226–36.

Kagan, D. M. "Run-on and Fragment Sentences: An Error Analysis." *Research in the Teaching of English* 14 (May 1980): 127–38.

Markle, S.M. and P.W. Tiemann. "Some Principles of Instructional Design at Higher Cognitive Levels." *Control of Human Behavior.* Eds. R. Ulrich, T. Stocknik, and J. Mabry. Vol. III. Glenview, IL: Scott, 1974.

Merrill, M. David and Robert D. Tennyson. *Teaching Concepts: An Instructional Design Guide.* Englewood Cliffs, NJ: Educational Technology Publications, 1977.

Reitman, J.S. and G.H. Bower. "Structure and Later Recognition of Exemplars of Concepts." *Cognitive Psychology* 4 (March 1973): 194–206.

Tennyson, Robert D. "Effect of Negative Instances in Concept Acquisition Using a Verbal-Learning Task." *Journal of Educational Psychology* 64 (April 1973): 247–60.

——. "Pictorial Support and Specific Instructions as Design Variables for Children's Concept and Rule Learning." *Educational Communication and Technology* 26 (Winter 1978): 291–99.

Tennyson, Robert D., J.N. Chao, and J. Youngers. "Concept Learning Effectiveness Using Prototype and Skill Development Presentation Forms." *Journal of Educational Psychology* 73 (June 1981): 326–34.

Tennyson, Robert D. and Martin J. Cocchiarella. "An Empirically Based Instructional Design Theory for Teaching Concepts." *Review of Educational Research* 56 (Spring 1986): 40–71.

Tennyson, Robert D. and O. Park. "The Teaching of Concepts: A Review of Instructional Design Literature." *Review of Educational Research* 50 (Spring 1980): 55–70.

Tennyson, Robert D., M.W. Steve, and R.C. Boutwell. "Instance Sequence and Analysis of Instance Attribute Representation in Concept Acquisition." *Journal of Educational Psychology* 67 (December 1975): 821–27.

Tennyson, Robert D., James C. Welsh, Dean L. Christensen, and Halyna Hajovy. "Interactive Effect of Information Structure, Sequence of Information, and Process Learning Time on Rule Learning Using Computer-Based Instruction." *Educational Communication and Technology Journal* 33 (Fall 1985): 213–23.

Tennyson, Robert D., F.R. Woolley, and M. David Merrill. "Exemplar and Nonexemplary Variables Which Produce Correct Concept Classification Behavior and Specified Classification Errors." *Journal of Educational Psychology* 63 (April 1972): 144–52.

Tennyson, Robert D., J. Youngers. and P. Suebsonthi. "Acquisition of Mathematical Concepts by Children Using Prototype and Skill Development Presentation Forms." *Journal of Educational Psychology* 75 (April 1983): 280–91.

Troyka, Lynn Quitman. *Simon and Schuster Handbook for Writers.* Englewood Cliffs, NJ: Prentice Hall, 1987.

SUGGESTED READINGS: GRAMMAR

Bartholomae, David. "The Study of Error." *CCC* 31 (1980): 253–69.

D'Eloia, Sarah. "The Uses—and Limits—of Grammar." *Journal of Basic Writing* 1 (1977): 1–20.

Gilyard, Keith. *Voices of the Self: A Study of Language Competence*. Detroit: Wayne State University, 1991.

Hairston, Maxine. "Not All Errors Are Created Equal: Nonacademic Readers in the Professions Respond to Lapses in Usage." *College English* 43 (1981): 794–806.

Harris, Jeanette. "Proofreading: A Reading/Writing Skill." *CCC* 38 (1987): 464–66.

Hunter, Susan, and Ray Wallace, eds. *The Place of Grammar in Writing Instruction: Past, Present, Future*. Portsmouth, NH: Boynton/Cook, 1995.

Kolln, Martha. "Closing the Books on Alchemy." *CCC* 32 (1981): 139–51.

Labov, William. *Language in the Inner City: Studies in the Black English Vernacular*. Philadelphia: U of Pennsylvania P, 1972.

McAlexander, Patricia J., Ann B. Dobie, and Noel Gregg. *Beyond the "SP" Label: Improving the Spelling of Learning Disabled and Basic Writers*. Urbana, IL: NCTE, 1992.

Noguchi, Rei R. *Grammar and the Teaching of English: Limits and Possibilities*. Urbana, IL: NCTE, 1991.

Smitherman, Geneva. *Talkin and Testifyin: The Language of Black America*. Detroit: Wayne State UP, 1986.

Students' Right to Their Own Language. *CCC* 25. Urbana, IL: NCTE, 1974.

Weaver, Constance. *Grammar for Teachers: Perspectives and Definitions*. Urbana, IL: NCTE, 1979.

Williams Joseph M. "The Phenomenology of Error." *CCC* 32 (1981): 152–68.

Improving Our Responses to Student Writing: A Process-Oriented Approach

Leonard A. and Joanne M. Podis

Leonard A. Podis and Joanne M. Podis describe a process-oriented approach to responding to student writing based on the principles of error analysis in this 1986 article, first published in Rhetoric Review. *Instead of product-centered comments that judge student papers against an "Ideal Text" in the instructor's head, Podis and Podis state that teachers should engage in a close reading of a student's text to try to understand the writer's intentions and mental processes. Problems in a paper normally signal difficulties that the writer has had working through his or her "process of discovery" or in "negotiating a particular rhetorical situation."*

"Awk!" "Frag." "Unity?" "Coh." Such are the response symbols on which composition instructors have traditionally been reared. Of course many writing teachers have come to reject such responses and the evaluative approach to commentary they bespeak, viewing them as useless (Knoblauch and Brannon, "Teacher Commentary" 285–88), if not downright harmful (Hartwell 9). In recent years a significant number of instructors have adopted more thoughtful, enlightened attitudes in commenting on student writing, in some cases not merely eschewing the strictly evaluative response, but going so far as to "deconstruct" drafts in order to perceive student intentions so that these may be "mapped onto later drafts" (Comprone). It is just such a "deconstructionist" approach that we would like to set forth in this essay; although our method rather than consciously drawing on post-modernist literary theory, we emphasize the attitude of the error analyst in responding to writing (Shaughnessy; Kroll and Schafer; Bartholomae). We hope the essay will also constitute a step toward taxonomizing some of the more process-oriented responses to student writing.

A brief survey of recent literature on responding to student writing indicates that the dominant model for instructors' comments is still the traditional evaluative response. In their first of several statements on the subject, for example, Knoblauch and Brannon reported that product-centered, judgmental responses have overwhelmingly remained the norm; they noted, "Our assumption has been that evaluating the product of composing is equivalent to intervening in the process" ("Teacher Commentary" 288). Even less flattering to our profession was Nancy Sommers' "Responding to Student Writing" (148–56). In the responses of the

Leonard A. Podis and Joanne M. Podis. "Improving Our Responses to Student Writing: A Process-Oriented Approach," *Rhetoric Review,* Vol. 5, No. 1, Fall 1986, pp. 90–98. Reprinted with permission.

instructors whose work she studied, Sommers found "hostility and meanspiritedness" (149). Moreover, she judged most comments to be confusing to students because they failed to differentiate between low-level and high-level textual problems. In a follow-up to their earlier article, Brannon and Knoblauch concluded that instructors tended in their responses to appropriate students' texts, devaluing them in relation to some "Ideal Text" the instructor had in mind ("On Students' Rights" 158–59). Knoblauch and Brannon's most recent treatment of the subject discusses at length the type of "facilitative commentary" that might profitably replace the traditional evaluative response *(Rhetorical Traditions* 126–30). They appear to endorse Sommer's belief that "We need to develop an appropriate level of response for commenting on a first draft..." (155).

In our approach, instructors encourage student potential by identifying draft weaknesses and interpreting them in the light of recent findings about the composing process. Specifically, we propose that, by analogy to the work of those who practice error analysis, writing instructors routinely undertake close readings of student drafts in order to pinpoint rhetorical or structural problems that might signal legitimate intentions rather than simple failure or inadequacy. Although draft weaknesses are not technically "errors" in the same sense as syntactic or grammatical problems, we believe that the attitude involved in error analysis—the desire to comprehend the mental process that underlies some evidence of difficulty in creating a discourse—is appropriate in reading and responding to the writing of learners. We have recognized that many textual weaknesses represent useful stages in the writer's composing process. Such an approach seems particularly valid in light of the work of process advocates and researchers, who tell us that normal composing often includes the production of incomplete or flawed drafts (Murray; Hairston 85–86). Our method, then, calls for instructors to approach draft difficulties as potential keys to understanding student writers' intentions, and in some cases as keys to helping the writers better define their intentions in their own minds.

We have chosen three examples to illustrate our method and to provide the beginnings of a taxonomy for this kind of response. In addition, in our conclusion we briefly identify several more kinds of draft weaknesses and suggest appropriate responses. Each of the three main examples was selected because we believed it represented some issue that teachers of writing may face while responding to student drafts and because we were successful in guiding revision by first identifying a draft weakness and then interpreting it as resulting from a healthy difficulty in composing. In each case we explain what the initial problem was, how we interpreted it as signifying a potentially legitimate difficulty in composing, how we responded, and what happened in subsequent revisions.

Our first example begins with a paragraph written in a basic writing course, addressing the topic of "an unreasonable assignment made at school or work." We can see that the student began with the intention of discussing unreasonable math assignments but then moved away from that idea:

> I had a math teacher in junior high named Mr. Douglas that I thought gave a lot of homework. Maybe it was because I didn't like math

> that much. I feel as you get older you start to realize that you have to have some sort of responsibility. In a way I think homework is a form of responsibility. In my first year of high school I hardly ever did any homework and barely passed. In my junior year I did a little better because I started realizing that homework was important. At the end of my junior year I told myself that I was going to put homework first on my priority list as far as schoolwork went. I never really had an unreasonable assignment made at school. I think I was blessed with some good teachers in my first 12 years of school.

If we evaluate this paragraph according to traditional standards, we must judge it as disorganized and uncertain in focus, particularly in relation to the assignment it was addressing. It is the type of writing that can all too easily lead a composition instructor to resort to the "mean-spirited" marginal comments that Nancy Sommers found so prevalent in her study. However, a closer look at the paragraph's major flaw shows that the rambling organization and uncertain focus, while they make for a weak text, do appear to be leading the student to some kind of understanding about his school career. Starting with sentence three, we can detect a group of sentences that apparently leads the writer toward the realization that his attitude about assignments changed.

Sensing this possibility, the instructor decided not to concentrate on the paragraph's weakness as a sign of failure, but rather as a potential reflection of a healthy difficulty in composing, as the messy residue that can accompany writing as discovery. In so doing, the instructor decided against urging the student to revise in order to create her own "Ideal Text"—one that would discuss "an unreasonable assignment made at school." Instead, she responded by noting that the paragraph suggested the student had learned something important about assignments while in school, and that the writing seemed to be helping him to discover what it was he had learned.

The instructor's response, then, was not a negative evaluation of the paragraph but an assurance to the student that the paragraph was indeed a good way to have *begun* his composing, though it was not necessarily a good finished product. Instead of strongly criticizing the paragraph, she conveyed a positive message about it and emphasized the new awareness the student had reached through the act of writing it. She concluded by asking the student to revise. The following is his second draft:

> I guess I never really had an unreasonable assignment made at school, although sometimes they seemed unreasonable to me. In junior high school I did think my ninth-grade math teacher gave an awful lot of homework, but maybe it was because I didn't like math that much and didn't understand the importance of school work. Over the years I realized that homework is important and should be put on the priority list as far as school goes. It's no coincidence that I started getting better grades once I changed my attitude.

> Now that I'm older I can look back and say none of my assignments was unreasonable. They helped teach me a sense of responsibility.

The second version is better organized and has a clearer focus. It could, of course, be improved further. However, it shows that the student, having been encouraged to view his original paragraph as a promising draft rather than a flawed text, has begun to understand how he can improve both his writing and his awareness of the process that effective writers often follow.

Our second example focuses on another common student text weakness, plot summary in the critical essay on literature. It can perhaps be most usefully understood as a manifestation of what Linda Flower and John Hayes call "writer-based" prose, prose which uses patterns borrowed, in the case of plot summary, "from a structure inherent in the material the writers examined" (459).

This student's initial text was laden with sections in which she retold parts of Faulkner's "The Bear," adding few interpretive remarks and seemingly allowing the story to speak for itself. In this case the instructor's initial response was more traditional. He had disparaged the paper as a poor critical essay that substituted plot summary for interpretation.

Bringing her marked paper with her to her conference, the student expressed her frustration with comments in the margin about the need to avoid summarizing the plot. That advice, she said, is what her English teachers had always given her, but she couldn't understand how it was possible to do what they told her to. How, she asked, could she write any generalizations about the story when she didn't know what they were until she worked through some of the important parts of the plot on paper? Her method had been to choose instinctively the events she felt to be important and to let her discussion of them lead her to an understanding of them. By writing down exactly what happened, in the order it happened, she clarified, even discovered, the meaning of the material. What she had not realized was that her weak "finished papers" might be legitimate discovery drafts. For her, the chief effect of the instructor's plot-summary comment was to make her doubt the value of the *way she was composing* as much as the text she composed.

Reconsidering her paper, the instructor attempted to understand how its chief weakness might reflect some legitimate problem of composing. For this writer, it occurred to him, retelling the plot was apparently a necessary stage in invention. Thus she was perplexed by responses that criticized her own approach and enjoined her to "put generalizations first." She apparently needed a response that initially *valued* her plot summarizing as a useful drafting technique, but then recommend a revision in which the plot summary, having served its heuristic purpose, would be condensed or eliminated to create a more presentable finished paper.

In her revision she was in fact able to pare down her retelling of the story and to add more interpretive generalizations about the importance of the episodes she did discuss. The problem finally did not rest in her inability to interpret the story or to express herself. It rested in her inability to function well within the traditional single-submission, evaluative-response system, for given only one chance at drafting, she had an inability to distinguish between the written record of an invention technique and an acceptable finished text.

Writer-based prose such as plot summary may be a natural stage in the process of learning to write more effectively, but both students and instructors need to be aware of this before students can improve. Moreover, the nature of the instructor's response is often crucial in determining whether a student such as the one just discussed will come to recognize the distinction between a discovery draft and a completed paper.

Our final extended example is somewhat similar to the first one we discussed in that the student apparently failed to do the assignment requested of her. But the reasons in this instance were much different. In such a case we've found it's important for the instructor to tailor a response by first attempting to determine the writer's intentions. Whether the assignment is completed unsatisfactorily because of an honest misunderstanding, because of ineptitude, or because of chicanery, for instance, should make a big difference in the instructor's response to it. In our example the instructor learned that the student's first draft signified her attempt to negotiate a rhetorical situation complicated enough that she could not accomplish her aim without some further guidance.

The following paragraph is the introduction to a four-page draft in which the student apparently failed to respond adequately to the assignment her women's studies instructor had given her. She was to interview an older working woman and then write an essay analyzing the pressures that woman had faced during her career. The opening paragraph reflects the content or the draft:

> Mrs. Thelma Morton Arnold has worked for Oberlin College for thirty years. In December of 1981, she was promoted from the position of dormitory custodian to that of supervisor of dorm custodians on the north end of campus. Last week, Mrs. Arnold talked with me about her life.

Essentially, the paper that followed was a straight biography of Mrs. Arnold with no apparent analysis of any pressures she had encountered. Significantly, there were passages in the draft that could be construed as bearing on career pressures, but the writer herself didn't seem to recognize their relevance. The instructor noted these points in his initial response.

In conference, the student confided that she in fact knew her draft had evaded the issue. Apparently she had avoided explicitly analyzing the pressures in Mrs. Arnold's career because she had promised to let Mrs. Arnold read the paper that would result from the interview. Mrs. Arnold was such a trusting, pleasant woman that the student could not bring herself to do what she regarded as a "cold, clinical analysis" of her life. She was so uncomfortable with this notion, in fact, that she was willing to accept a low grade in her women's studies course to avoid displeasing Mrs. Arnold and embarrassing herself.

In this case the student had written the paper mainly to one audience—Mrs. Arnold—because she assumed that writing more to her other audience—her women's studies instructor—would ruin the paper for Mrs. Arnold. Her composition instructor attempted to convince her that it was possible for her to juggle the expectations and demands of both audiences, to please both Mrs. Arnold and the women's studies instructor. If she could see herself at some point in the role of the *lab-coated clinician*, but at other points in the role of, say, the *main speaker at a testimonial dinner* for Mrs. Arnold, she might be able to satisfy both audiences. Here is the opening paragraph of her revision:

> Mrs. Thelma Morton Arnold has worked for Oberlin College for thirty years. In December of 1981, she was promoted from the position of dormitory custodian to that of supervisor of dorm custodians on the north end of campus. As a black working woman, she has faced discriminatory pressures in choosing her occupation, as well as in her attempts to earn promotions and equal pay. She has fought to overcome these pressures and gain just treatment for herself and others.

While the first two sentences of this paragraph are the same as in the earlier version, the third sentence of the earlier version—"Last week, Mrs. Arnold talked with me about her life"—has been replaced with two sentences, each of which represents a nod toward one of the two competing audiences. Sentence three of the new version is aimed at the instructor, for it encapsulates the analysis of pressures which is to come in the paper. Sentence four, on the other hand, prefigures the tone of praise which will also characterize the paper to come.

Having conferred with her composition instructor, the student was able to revise in such a way that her dilemma was solved. Her first draft represented her view of a problem which she was unsure of handling. In one sense her attempt reflected a genuine strength: she had chosen a single audience toward which to write, a legitimate intention underlying the weakness in her draft. To make the most helpful response in this instance, the instructor needed to recognize another facet of the composing process, one also stressed by proponents of the new pedagogy: that writing does in fact occur in the context of a rhetorical situation.

In our examples we have examined three types of draft weaknesses: uncertainty of focus, plot summary in the critical essay, and lack of attention to some aspect of the assignment. In all cases, the weaknesses in the initial drafts resulted either from difficulties related to writing as a process of discovery, or from an inability to negotiate a particular rhetorical situation. In each instance we were able to respond most helpfully to our students by interpreting their difficulties as evidence of legitimate attempts to deal with the complexities of composing.

We want to suggest some other possible situations in which our approach would help students revise their work. For example, the student narrative, whether written about historical events for a history class or about personal experiences for a composition class, will often feature an overabundance of short, simple sentences and a lack of subordination and complicating modification. Rather than simply indicating a weak style or even an inability to interpret the material, such writing often stems from the student's respect for reporting the verifiable facts related to a given event. In other words, some students produce flat, deadpan narratives, not because of limited verbal ability or inadequate analytic powers, but because they believe they are doing the right thing in producing what they consider to be a camera-copy of reality. Probably the most helpful response in such a case is to correct the student's view of the purpose of such writing, to clarify what the audience's demands and expectations really are, as opposed to what the student supposes them to be.

Similarly, consider the case of the student paper which is written in overblown generalities and which makes use of pompous academese. Typical responses to such writing urge the use of more concrete details and specific examples, which is certainly fine advice. Yet the most effective response may be the one which recognizes that the student's writing has resulted from a belief that his or her audience values overblown generalities, and which then attempts to clarify the student's picture of the audience.

The often artificial nature of the classroom setting may also create difficulties in students whose concern for the form of an assignment may override any considerations of what they actually have to say. They then produce writing which employs the required "comparison-contrast" or "descriptive" modes, as the case may be, but which is woefully inadequate in terms of content and style. We have found that by discussing with students their motivations for choosing, for example, a given pattern of development, we can determine whether students made their selections after following sound invention strategies, or whether they selected on the basis of pressure to turn in papers which fit the required form. If the latter is true, then an effective revision may result after the student is counseled to follow better heuristics for invention.

Digressions are another common text weakness, the exploration of which may lead to an improved product. In our experience digressions sometimes signal that a writer's thinking has moved in a potentially more interesting or valuable direction. Discussing with students the way in which writing can encourage thinking, and suggesting that perhaps that is why a particular digression occurred, may lead them to realize that they are just beginning the writing process for a paper they assumed was completed. In short, the apparent digression may actually represent a fruitful line of inquiry stimulated by the composing process itself. We have seen many cases where students have successfully revised their work by refocusing it on ideas initially thought to be "digressions."

Finally, students who produce drafts with repetitive ideas couched in somewhat different terms have generally been criticized for producing texts weak in both structure and content. But is their repetition always the sign of a tenuous grasp of exposition and a paucity of ideas, or might it reflect a more positive attempt to try out different ways of saying something in an effort to achieve greater clarity or effect? Might not a repetitive discourse sometimes reflect a healthy attempt to achieve a fuller command of style and substance?

Certainly for some instructors this method of interpreting draft difficulties in order to understand the mental processes that gave rise to a writer's problems is not completely new. Particularly those instructors who teach process-oriented courses featuring multiple drafts and revisions may already be reading and responding to drafts in ways similar to those we have recommended. Still, the findings of Sommers and Brannon and Knoblauch suggest that our profession as a whole is far from adopting such "facilitative" approaches to commentary. We believe that, with further attempts to identify and codify various categories of draft weaknesses matched with the kind of comments we have recommended above, our profession can make successful inroads against the domain of the evaluative response.

Works Cited

Bartholomae, David. "The Study of Error." *CCC* 31 (1980): 253–69.

Brannon, Lil, and C.H. Knoblauch. "On Students' Rights to Their Own Texts: A Model of Teacher Response." *CCC* 33 (1982): 157–66.

Comprone, Joseph J. "Recent Literary and Composition Theory: Readerly and Writerly Texts." Presented at the Conference on College Composition and Communication, Minneapolis, 21 March 1985.

Flower Linda, and John Hayes. "Problem-Solving Strategies and the Writing Process." *CE* 39 (1977): 449–61.

Hairston, Maxine. "The Winds of Change: Thomas Kuhn and the Revolution in the Teaching of Writing." *CCC* 33 (1982): 76–78.

Hartwell, Patrick. "Paradoxes and Problems: The Value of Traditional Textbook Rules." *Pennsylvania Writing Project Newsletter* 3 (1983): 7–9.

Knoblauch, C.H., and Lil Brannon. "Teacher Commentary on Student Writing: The State of the Art." *Rhetoric and Composition: A Sourcebook for Teachers and Writers.* 2nd ed. Ed. Richard L. Graves. Upper Montclair, NJ: Boynton/Cook, 1984: 285–91.

——. *Rhetorical Traditions and the Teaching of Writing.* Upper Montclair, NJ: Boynton/Cook, 1984.

Kroll, Barry M., and John C. Schafer. "Error Analysis and the Teaching of Composition." *CCC* 29 (1978): 243–48.

Murray, Donald C. "Internal Revision: A Process of Discovery." *Research on Composing: Points of Departure.* Ed. Charles R. Cooper and Lee Odell. Urbana, IL: NCTE, 1978.

Shaughnessy, Mina. *Errors and Expectations.* New York: Oxford UP, 1977.

Sommers, Nancy. "Responding to Student Writing" *CCC* 33 (1982): 148–56.

Reflective Reading: Developing Thoughtful Ways to Respond to Students' Writing

Chris M. Anson

Chris M. Anson, a professor at the University of Minnesota, has focused on teacher responses to student writing in much of his scholarship, including Writing and Response: Theory, Practice, and Research *and* Scenarios for Teaching Writing: Contexts for Discussion and Reflective Practice. *In this 1999 article first published in Charles Cooper and Lee Odell's* Evaluating Writing: The Role of Teachers' Knowledge about Text, Learning, and Culture, *Anson describes many of the circumstances that can affect a teacher's response to a paper, from the teacher's pedagogical goals, personal beliefs, and knowledge of the student to the teacher's mood and the time of day. Anson's article hopes to help teachers comment more reflectively on student writing, with greater awareness of how circumstances affect their responses and of how students respond to their responses.*

Writers improve by *being read.* Hearing other people's response to their work helps writers to develop a kind of internal monitor, a "reading self," that informs their decisions as they enter new and more sophisticated worlds of writing. By experiencing a range of responses to their work—from teachers, peers, and others—young writers gain a sense of their own authorship, learn how their composing choices affect their readers, and become more able to assess the effectiveness of their syntax, diction, and organization.

Early research and scholarship on response to student writing aimed to develop principles and methods that teachers could use more or less uniformly to help students improve their writing in different settings. However, more recent scholarship, which is well demonstrated in the contributions to this collection, has been exploring response and evaluation in complex and multifaceted ways that take into account issues of gender, culture, and personality (see also Elbow 1993; Hake 1986; Sperling 1993; Straub and Lunsford 1995; McCracken 1993). In practice, as much of this work suggests, response to writing is richly complex, highly context-dependent, and widely varied in method, style, and focus both within and across classrooms. Our stated beliefs about teaching and our descriptions of our response styles are not always reflected in what we write on students' papers, which may vary depending on our mood, context, or knowledge of specific students and their writing. In many cases, such variation takes place so tacitly that we may not be aware of the differences between our beliefs and the different roles we play as readers (see Purves 1984). The self-confessed grammarian, for example, finds himself so thoroughly engaged in a paper that he stops reading with, as Mina Shaughnessy put it, "a lawyer's eyes, searching for flaws" (1977, 7). He unconsciously overlooks several errors that he would have identified for a student with less engaging material. The response or evaluation then displays a greater enthusiasm for the captivating material, and the proportion of identified errors goes down. Similarly, a teacher who claims that she always tries to render her comments as questions for revision might become so frustrated with a student who changes very little between drafts that she starts writing specific, controlling directions. Her response might look authoritative (and certainly inconsistent) next to her stated practices, but she is using her best intuitions as a teacher to guide this particular student.

Faced with discrepancies in our response practices, many teachers become frustrated or anxious, as if we have been made aware of some small but annoying hypocrisy. We don't like to think of ourselves reading students' writing subjectively, messily. The hope for uniformity and consensus becomes a way to remove such feelings of instability or inconsistency. In the practice of response to student writing, we like to think that if we can discover some key method, informed by theory and predictable in outcome, its application will lessen some of the bewildering complexity that reading students' work inevitably calls into play.

But given the influence of context on our responses, we need to reconsider this prevailing attitude toward inconsistency. As Straub and Lunsford (1995) have shown in their study of the differences in response styles among twelve "expert" composition scholar-teachers, it seems problematic to develop a unified set of practices for responding to students' writing. Response is so rooted in context and human temperament that accepting diverse and even contradictory approaches or rhetorical styles may be more useful than searching for a single method supported by empirical research. It may be entirely appropriate, in other words, to use quite different response strategies as long as we know how to choose and apply them constructively. This is not to suggest that we don't bring to our responses an overarching disposition or educational theory that guides our choices and sometimes makes us do similar things with different pieces of writing. But it allows us to admit some flexibility with which we can make informed choices about the strategies to employ for a specific piece of writing.

Such a shift in priorities mirrors new theories of teaching effectiveness which place the locus of teachers' improvement not on the accumulation of research findings but on developing a higher consciousness, a kind of "thoughtfulness," often captured in the phrase "reflective practice" (Schön 1983, 1987). In the area of response to writing, such an approach assumes that developing a greater awareness of how our context influences the way we read students' writing can help us to make more informed decisions—and to become more able to adapt our responses to specific situations.

This chapter looks first at an interesting and troubling student essay in order to describe some of the contextual factors that influence our response practices in classroom settings. What external conditions shape our responses? How might situations change the way we look at a piece of student writing? The chapter then turns to some practical ways in which we can become more thoughtful readers of students' writing, developing the strategic knowledge that allows us to adapt our response methods to various students, classrooms, and institutions in educationally productive ways.

Some Varieties of Response and their Possible Sources

As an illustration of how we might begin to explore the ways in which our responses may be contextually influenced, consider an unusual essay, written by Leang, a young Cambodian refugee who was a first-year college student enrolled in a regular section of an introductory composition course.[1]

My Message

> Thanks God for let me have my life still, also thanks for let me have my little brother too, plus my older one and sisters. But I still can't forget my others. My parents and the people of Cambodia. What a past! I miss my family so very much and my country too. I wished I had my family back. The family of ten brothers and sisters stood side by side with my parents plus my nieces, nephews and grand nephews running all over the house. What had happened to my family and every family in the whole country? Who had created that problem???
>
> April, 17, 1975, It was the day that Cambodia had collapsed into communism. In that day every thing in my country had changed. It was the disastrous day for my people. All school, hospitals, shops and markets and any business were closed. A lot of city people were killed by communist sodiers. And the rest were force to leave the cities to the country side. The jungle where no one live before. There was no more freedom. It was "THE COMMUNISM." The regime that all the properties were belong to the government alone. That was under the leader of Pol Pot. Imagine, Phenom Phen, the capital city of Cambodia used to be noisy with the sound of cars, trucks, radio, T.V., school children and everything, had been turned into the city of graveyard. The new rules and regulation had been set to people by the communist. It said "There are no more rich, no more people. We are all equal. No more religion, and no more believe in anything, but there is one to believe in "FARMING". My family the same as the rest of the city

[1] Leang graciously allowed me to use his essay in faculty workshops as well as to reproduce and comment on it here. Because his essay is so much a part of this chapter, I offered him an honorarium for his contribution and invited him to write a response to be included in the chapter, but he declined both, simply glad, he said, that his essay was being put to use.

people were forced to leave the city with bare hands to work in the farm. Over there, there were no buildings, no houses, no street-shops or market, but there were trees, forest far away in the country side. At first, my dad had started with to cut the trees branches and leaves to make hut ourselve. We ran out of food, medicine clothing and lack of others consumer goods that we needed. Because the fierce Goverment would not let us so. The communists starved to give people very little of food, almost nothing day by day. But, they forced us to work so damn hard, at list 12 to 16 hours every day. We worked like slave. We worked without enough food. When we got sick, the fierce communists ignored us and gave us no medicine. They used the forces on people. They said all kind of bad words and even killed someone just to show the rest not to do the same. "You'll must work in the farm! You'll must obey the communist's Rules! And must do whatever the communists have said, other wise, you people are known as the enemy of the communist Goverment! The enemy must dead!!!" The rule had set.

Three years and eight months living in communism was a trash. Life was really a tragic. In my family alone, first one of my sisters was dead, six months later, one of my brother was dead. Then my Aunts, uncles, nieces, nephews, my other brothers plus sister-in-laws. And at last when the communist ground our people so bad, my parents passed away. My parents died only one week apart. My family, my people, the whole couple millions of cambodian died one after others because of the starvation and the killing. I still rememberd how my dad died. He died because he was sick. He could not go to work for them (communist Goverment) and they starved him for weeks to die. My mom too, if they kindly gave my mom only a tea spoon of sugar to make home made medicine, probably she still suvive till today. I had seen every movement of my parents before they died because I was living with them.

In communism, actually we lived seperatly in the group of age. Children must lived differented from adults, adults lived differently from older adults and elderly. The reason that I could live with my parents and my four years old brother because I took a risk of my own life. I ran away from my group. There was nothing hurt more than seeing family, parents and a little brother laying sick side by side on a dirty mat at home with out food, medicine and water and had not a thing around. At that time I was about 12 years old, I myself was so weak too because I had malaria for months. I was so skinny with all my body turned pale; my eyes was kind of blue and yellow. But I had no more thinking of myself. I had tried all my best to find out the things that my family needed. I was became a thif. I stole foods from people. I disobeyed the rules of the communism and running around to find helps. I even prayed to God to take my life or killed me first before he took my parents and my little brother. But that was impossible, not very long later my parents died. God did not accepted my pray neither. Any way. I still have my mom's last words before she died.

> Her word remind me all the time I think of them. She said in a very weak sound that she wanted me to stay alive; do not give up no matter what. She wanted me grown up to be a man with mercy. A man that knew right and wrong. A man that knew clearly between war-killing and peace. A man that knew the difference between communism and freedom. And before she met the end of her life she called me in name, wispered and looked at me in the eyes and turned to look at my ennicent brother sitting quietly on the dirty clothe near the fire wood that I had made. My mom's eyes were full of tear. It seem like she had million of words to say. Then she passed away and left us behind in the middle of no where.
>
> When I think of "The War" I alway think of my country, my family and my people. I think the way they were destroyed . . . . then, I turned to get angry, sad and even more frustrate. I still miss my family and country so much. I love them always. I used to live with comfortable when they're around.

After reading this essay, many teachers have strong feelings. The content moves some to tears. Others are shocked to think the student is enrolled in a standard first-year college composition course. Still others become immersed in the underlying politics of Leang's "message," and reflect on their attitudes toward communism, human rights, the Vietnam War, or whether Leang should be more radical and proactive than his essay suggests. The variety of readings prompted by this essay whenever it is presented without any context—and the even greater range of suggestions about what we might say to Leang about his writing—illustrate some of the many sources of our response practices.

The Influence of Curricular Timing

Our choice of what to say to a student about his or her writing is heavily influenced by the point at which we read the writing in its development. Before the process movement began to pressure more traditional teaching practices, response was heavily evaluative; it was almost entirely summative, measuring the student's text against some established standards. Comments aimed at improving the writing (or the writer) looked toward the next occasion for practice; but comments on the next paper were again judgmental, coming from sometimes new and different sets of standards.

In the contemporary, process-oriented classroom, response may vary depending on when it is given in the development of a piece of writing. In such classes, response typically serves to motivate revisions (and encourage learning and further writing practice). A common response to Leang's essay, for example, locates the paper early in the process and treats it as a draft:

> Leang's story is *so* dramatic that it would be a great piece of writing if he could reorganize it, cut some material, expand some material, and clean up all the errors. I'd put him to work identifying as much of this as he could so that he could end up with a really first-rate paper.

Implied in this response is a vision of the classroom as a workshop, but one still very much focused on finished products. For both teacher and student, success is measured by the number of good papers produced, and the very best quality control (instruction, response, and evaluation) yields papers that can even be circulated or entered into contests. Although revision may play an important role in the course, it is directed toward the improvement of specific papers, without being generalized as a set of strategies for other and perhaps quite different tasks.

Some newer curricular approaches offer interesting and complicated varieties of this focus on the production of polished texts, requiring an even greater repertoire of response strategies. In some courses, a greater focus on the student shifts attention away from products alone and toward their writers, who will eventually move from site to site (into, say, a biology class or, later, a corporation or small business). In other courses in which students create portfolios of their work (see Belanoff and Dickson 1991), teachers may comment on students' in-process writing by playing the role of a (later) evaluator. This strategy involves first reading from the perspective of some institutionalized standards for the portfolio assessment, and then translating this reading into comments that recognize the progress of the student's work and its improvement. Some teachers who use a portfolio method, for example, would advise Leang that his narrative comes nowhere near the portfolio standards already established. The result may be a comment that invokes both the evaluator's and the teacher's different roles:

> I think as this essay stands that it won't be judged as ready for entry into Leang's portfolio. But I find it a really moving and interesting narrative, one that with some more revision and editing might just get there. I would say so to Leang, and then suggest that we sit down together so I can explain in more detail what he needs to do to get this ready for the portfolio assessment.

Some teachers may also be mindful of the entire process a student goes through in readying a piece for an external assessment; the response given on one occasion, then, plays a role in a later assessment of the student's overall performance on a writing project or in a course.

These potentially complicated readings of student writing suggest the need to identify and refine response strategies that are sensitive to issues of *timing and purpose.* While it may seem obvious that a response to a draft-in-progress will not look like a response to a final, graded paper, we must become more aware of how our choice of comments affects students at various points during this process. A teacher who "reads for meaning, not for errors," might not see the need to switch strategies between an in-progress draft and a final text submitted for a grade. But unless we are subverting an institutional grading system, differences must exist between these two occasions—differences in our roles as guides and coaches vs. gatekeepers and evaluators. Knowing what these differences are, and how they govern our choice of strategies, offers us the kind of higher-level knowledge that leads to more principled practice.

The Influence of Institutional Standards

As Mina Shaughnessy suggested in her discussion of the reaction to open admissions policies in the late 1960s at CUNY (1977), one response to students who don't seem to exhibit the appropriate skills necessary to survive in an academic setting is to quietly eliminate those students through failure. This strategy almost always involves a sorting and ranking process. Typically, a teacher will make expert decisions about a student's ability relative to the available program of instruction:

> It's clear that Leang is misplaced. Something went wrong in the diagnostic or advising system. He belongs in an ESL class, where he would get the kind of help he needs as a non-native speaker, especially with the surface mechanics and grammar.

This has traditionally been called text-based response because it measures the student's writing against a preexisting, often institutionalized standard. Such response strategies involve at least some gatekeeping: The student's paper is "owned" by the system, rather than by the student (cf. Knoblauch and Brannon 1982). The teacher's role—often requiring considerable training, expertise, and knowledge of alternative curricula available in the system—is to accurately assess ability against the standards set at the gate.

Standards for judging the quality of writing come to us from many sources at many levels—cultural, institutional, disciplinary, departmental, and personal (Anson and Brown 1991, 257–66). At the highest level, a "cultural ideology" of writing often influences how we think about and respond to students' work. Schools, while maintaining their autonomy and academic freedom within the larger culture, often reflect and amplify "larger sets of social and cultural values in the emphases they give to kinds and ways of knowing" (Piché 1977, 17). Nationally sponsored "writing report cards," speeches by the secretary of education or other high-ranking officials, reportage and editorials in newspapers and periodicals, and other commentaries on the state of education all subtly influence our values. Some teachers confess to using response practices that invoke much tougher standards in the wake of such commentaries, which may leave some students confused or frustrated as they try to figure out why there has been a sudden shift in the language or focus of the response.

In the case of recommending Leang to a different curriculum, the ranking takes place at an *institutional* level that focuses on the necessary skills and preparation of a college student, ignoring the kind of intellectual and emotional "preparation" that Leang brings into that setting from a regime in which he experienced atrocities that many American students can hardly imagine. Teachers comfortable with such an institutionalized ranking system will not feel as conflicted in their responses as those who may be opposed to it; but it is the very relationship between the two systems—institution and classroom—that guides our responses (see, for example, Mary Traschel's [1992] study of the role of college entrance examinations in the teaching of English).

Discipline-specific norms and standards may also influence our response to students' writing. When students enter an academic discipline as novices or outsiders, they may not be familiar with these norms. In such contexts, it is important for teachers to learn how to respond both as a representative of the discipline (gatekeeper) and as one who helps students to learn the information and strategies needed to pass through the gate. A response from the former position alone may be entirely unhelpful in enculturating students into the field.

Occasionally an individual *department* may have collective practices that are somewhat different from those expected professionally. Teachers in technical or scientific fields who tolerate or even encourage students to write from a highly subjective position may respond in ways antithetical to the goals of more traditional colleagues. In such situations, response to writing might come entwined with commentary about the discipline's received paradigm: "I really like the way you've placed yourself at the center of your case study, Peter. You know, of course, that many scientists would insist on a kind of clinical objectivity that your paper resists."

Some teachers may entirely avoid imposing institutional standards on students in a particular class, perhaps because they have more context-specific goals for their instruction than those that are generally expected across the campus. For example, in dislodging the emphasis on error hunting or pushing student writing into the synthetic mold of the five-paragraph theme, reader-response advocates have for several decades championed a less criterion-based way of responding to students' writing that deliberately avoids the didactic effluence of the red pen. This practice, in its further extension, may downplay the role of response and evaluation; the writing is produced in what Peter Elbow calls an "evaluation-free zone" (1993). The following often-heard reaction to Leang's essay illustrates this approach to the issue of standards:

> I'm incredibly moved by this account. In fact, the story is so authentic that cleaning up the errors makes it too Anglo, too fake. There is something compelling about the voice, the voice of a real refugee. I want to react in all my original horror, to be moved, because the story is moving and Leang should know it.

The strategy implied by such a response is to help Leang develop by focusing on function and meaning—a strategy strongly and elegantly advocated in much of the work of Russell Hunt (see Hunt 1986 and 1989 for representative accounts). Theoretically, literate activities are by nature purposeful, meaning-rich, and contextual (Bleich 1989; Brandt 1991). It follows that literacy improves mainly through meaningful literate experiences, not the practice of isolated skills or the production of artificial, readerless texts.

Yet approaches that deliberately avoid error hunts or red-ink corrections may seem puzzling to students who are already socialized into a system where their lived experience is subjugated to the goal of perfecting the linguistic features of their writing. From the student's perspective, this strategic withholding of response often appears deliberately, sometimes playfully, sometimes even unfairly evasive—the teacher's attempt to push the relativism of multiple rhetorical choices (see Perry 1970; Anson, 1989a). After working so hard to acquire English, Leang may be fully expecting to have his errors identified even in the context of so moving a personal account. An important strategy is knowing in advance when a student is ready for what may be an unfamiliar kind of response.

An extension of this meaning-focused response relates readerly reactions more closely to the process of revision:

> I wouldn't grade Leang's paper or invoke any kind of textual standards whatsoever. What he doesn't need right now are criteria; he needs a real, natural, reader-based response, one that can connect with him on the basis of his meaning. I'd say how moved I was. I'd also indicate some places where I was confused or wanted more information, or where I stumbled over his expression. But I'd keep the focus pretty much on Leang's experience and my experience, and hope that my reaction would lead him to identify places he could improve.

Here, the goal is to use the reading process (usually characterized as "natural") to encourage the student to explore other options. It relies, in other words, on the social construction of meaning to create the dissonance that will lead to revision.

While reader-based response supports a purposeful, meaning-centered curriculum, it is wrong to assume that such reading is any more "natural" than hunting for errors. It is, after all, a kind of pedagogical strategy. Our position as educators is already inscribed by our context. Behind the apparently simple donning of an armchair-reader's perspective lies an elaborate set of theories about what might help students to develop their writing in just a few weeks. That development is not purely rhetorical and linguistic; it involves creating in students' own thinking the same underlying beliefs about writing being modeled in our response. (Much of the literature on peer groups suggests that students can learn to respond to each other's writing as we do, even though the conditions of their response are altogether different from ours.)

The Influence of Personal Belief

What specific beliefs do we bring to our reading, relative to its content, that might influence our response? Teachers reading Leang's essay sometimes respond in ways apparently designed to pressure him into thinking about the underlying political implications of his autobiographical account. When they take the form of typical academic consciousness-raising, such responses may place the teacher in a fairly neutral position, perhaps by invoking a reader who might not agree with the writer. When they take the form of a more direct challenge, however, such comments demonstrate a political critique designed to make the student intellectually uncomfortable. At its strongest, "contestatory" response admits that all texts (and all reactions to them) must be political and ideological. Instead of veiling this fact beneath the discourse of feigned neutrality, contestatory response tries to pressure students into becoming more aware of their political and personal conditions and how their writing and the writing of their culture can either reveal or hide such realities. As illustrated in the following paraphrase, the teacher can use this strategy to reflect a particular bias or position, very strongly deciding for the writer what intellectual journey he or she should travel:

> I don't think Leang goes far enough in trying to understand what Communism is, so he ends up simply endorsing (by default) an American system that has its own share of atrocities both national and international. He is almost blind to the ways in which he has been oppressed twice, and the second case is in some ways more insidious than the first because the oppression is less visible. I'd want to tell him so, and get him to critique his material conditions now, to examine what has really changed, and who is really in control in the midst of his newfound freedom.

Because it is sometimes emotionally charged, such a response strategy can be very difficult to apply. Unconsciously, we may praise some students for making assertions with which we agree, but then engage our strategy of contestation for students whose thinking we want to reform. The former students remain complacent in their views while the latter are challenged.

At a time when many teachers are actively challenging students' attitudinal complacencies, understanding the relationship between response, personal belief, and the development of writing abilities has never been more important. Many tensions now arising between teachers and students owe to mismatches of political and cultural attitudes expressed in student writing and teachers' own often strongly held beliefs. Better awareness of the sometimes tacit ways in which belief systems influence response can help us to develop strategies that do not condemn while they contest, strategies that are sensitive to the goals of particular courses, as well as the backgrounds and dispositions of particular students and their own intentions for their papers. We can then more ably translate personal reactions into the kinds of comments that help students to see multiple perspectives and not feel as if they are being forced to accept particular views.

The Influence of Rhetorical and Situational Goals

Knowledge of the complicated relationships between the rhetorical goals of an assignment and the student's interpretation of those goals in her own rhetorical plans can strongly influence our response. Typically, response is shaped by the extent to which a paper (as a text) conforms to the implicit rhetorical standards of the assignment. Yet students' own goals and plans offer a rich source of information about a piece of writing that can completely change a teacher's response strategy. Jeffrey Sommers (1989), for example, has described a technique in which students write a memo about their paper to help their teacher decide how to respond. The response is shaped by the student's own expressed needs. Similar strategies involve short, tape-recorded narrative commentaries from the student describing his or her goals for a paper and calling attention to things the student wants to work on. In collections of students' work, the reflective "cover statement" accomplishes a similar objective—to provide teachers with the student's own "review and consideration and narration and analysis and exploration of what learning is occurring in writing" (Yancey 1992, 16). Response that expects students to articulate their own intentions, as illustrated in the following paraphrase, also helps to move students beyond what Sharon Crowley calls the "distressing fact that students' intentions may amount to little more than getting a passing grade on an assignment, or pleasing us by demonstrating their ability to observe the formal strictures we have laid down in class" (1989, 108):

> My response would be a set of questions to Leang. I want to know what he wants to do with this paper, who he's talking to, what his purpose is in sharing this piece. Does he want us to think differently about refugees or Cambodians? Does he want us to feel the tension between his love of his country and people and his hatred of the oppressive regime under which he suffered? Or is this therapeutic, a venting of his life woes, a completely self-directed text shared with us only through his educational circumstances?

Here the teacher is simply unable to talk to Leang without more complete knowledge of his purposes. Extended a bit further, this response can become a nonresponse, not in the sense of an "evaluation-free zone" (Elbow 1993), but an inability to respond until the student himself has helped the teacher to choose the most useful strategy for the student's needs.

Sometimes response may be influenced by imagined situational goals that extend beyond students' expressed needs, as shown in the following comment which has surfaced in discussions of Leang's paper at several schools:

> I've seen this sort of paper before. Such papers are all too common to people who work in writing labs. While I don't doubt the authenticity of Leang's account, many students who have had shocking experiences in other countries try to use these to get an emotional response from a teacher, softening the grammatical blow. Sometimes they'll use the same paper or experience several times because they know it works. It's a kind of unsinister ploy. I wouldn't play into it.

This response practice tries to take into account the student's subsidiary motives for choice of topic, writing style, or use of detail. It may come from thinking about the circumstances of the student's writing beyond the classroom (that the student is on an athletic team, or is trying to get into law school, or is the daughter of the department chair) or from imagining more general aspects of student "underlife" to which most of us have little direct access (see Brooke 1987; Anderson et al. 1990). Attitudes toward students in general or toward the particular kinds of students that attend our school can profoundly influence our response. In this case, the teacher simply guesses, perhaps in a less than charitable way, what nonnative speakers like Leang try to do with their writing.

In the absence of information from students about their intentions, we usually invoke instructional goals often deeply embedded in our teaching, such as the need to avoid generalizations, entertain a reader, or give evidence for assertions:

> I assume that in this kind of writing it is always important to use details and images to embellish and support more general claims. Under these circumstances, I would want Leang to go back over the piece and identify places where he could add detail or sharpen our image of the events.

This response practice comes from a more highly goal-driven pedagogy; specific papers are occasions to learn specific skills, sometimes in isolation. Narratives, for example, are used to work on "showing versus telling"; or five-paragraph themes are used to practice logical and argumentative structures. Such practices often owe to what Peter Mosenthal calls a "utilitarian ideology" that stresses the nature of tasks and the passing on of knowledge necessary to survive in real-world settings 1983, 40). Tasks are often organized in increasing complexity, using writing for their practice and acquisition. Assuming that Leang's assignment is designed to help students practice effective paragraphing techniques, the teacher might focus on various moments in his essay where such technique is lacking.

Bringing students' needs together with implied and expressed goals of particular assignments can lead to a more strategic, tailored response. The decision to focus on a particular rhetorical issue such as paragraph development, for example, can also be informed by a higher sense of what is appropriate given the content of the text, as well as Leang's personality, his interaction in class and in small groups, his office visits, the nature of his previous writing, and the amount of time already spent in class working on the skills being applied. Without knowledge of these often intricate details, we have no basis on which to cast a negative judgment on a response that puts aside Leang's meaning in favor, for this moment, of calling attention to errors.

The Influence of Readers' Circumstances

Most of the time, we respond to writing without reflecting consciously on the influence of our personal circumstances. We may be aware that we read four (of twenty-five) student papers early in the morning on a train or bus, ten more later in our office (with coffee), three during the evening news, and the final eight late at night after a long day. While such considerations may seem trivial, developing strategies for response in quite different circumstances can help us to avoid trying to use the wrong strategy at the wrong time. Some teachers aware of this issue split their response process into different readings. "First reading" can be done anywhere—it is an occasion to get a holistic impression of an entire text. "Second reading," however, is accompanied by careful response and must be done without distraction and in time blocks conducive to reflection.

Another external circumstance is the order in which papers are read. Most of us have experienced the curious phenomenon of searching for the paper of a "good" student when we are tired and want to respond just to one or two more pieces of writing. In such cases, we may be choosing a different strategy for response, one that acknowledges our readings of students' past work or class performance. The reading may seem easier because we expect fewer errors, organizational problems, or weaknesses in content. Our focus shifts to other, more meaning-centered issues, issues that may require less translation of our reactions into directed commentary for revision or assessment. Similarly, one paper in a group of essays may influence our subsequent judgments. Six papers all displaying the same lack of paragraph development may have a profound effect on the reading of the seventh, which is judged to be very strong when it might have been judged problematic if preceded by six superb essays. In Leang's case, the content of the essay may be so rich and culturally interesting on the heels of half a dozen bland accounts of minor car accidents and summer jobs that its quality improves by virtue of its location in a string of essays.

The "pace" or "tempo" of reading students' work can also influence the nature and focus of the response (see Himley 1989). Reading students' writing first requires a complicated, rich internal response, much of it never shared with the writer. Of this response, we then select relevant ideas and translate them into an external commentary, using appropriate, student-centered language. In most cases, the internal response is more elaborate and less strictly pedagogical than external response. Good teaching requires a highly complex process as we read, collect impressions, formulate an internal response, choose which of the many impressions and ideas the student should receive, and then decide what form the commentary should take, how long it should be, and what language and style it should be rendered in.

Developing expertise in response relies on a higher awareness of the "tempo" of this translation. Novice teachers sometimes experience little lag time between an internal reaction and an external written comment, time when a more experienced teacher might pause to reflect on the internal reaction and translate it into a comment that will carry more weight or be more instructive. Unable to slow their reading to the molasses-like pace that could yield a really full response for each of fifty (or 150) student papers, expert teachers learn to trade off external response time (marginal comments) against time to reflect internally, knowing that a single well-chosen and articulated comment can ripple through an entire paper and, for the right student, harvest a major and fortuitous revision. In other words, the teacher writes less but says more.

There are several reasons for disparities in the amount of reflection between internal and external response. Newer teachers often feel that quantity shows diligence: The more they can say or write, the more their students will improve. Some teachers may also suffer from conditions that work against reflection—150 papers begging for response, or large classes of blurred faces in a mechanical curriculum. Under these less-than-ideal circumstances, however, a changed tempo and a more reflective response may actually lessen a teacher's burden and offer students more useful feedback. Furthermore, some kinds of writing may require less time for reflection and translation of internal response than others. If a teacher is modeling the process of reading, then writing down internal responses as they occur may be more appropriate than reading the entire text, reflecting on it, and translating and distilling many impressions into a carefully worded summary.

Many other dimensions of our situations as educators affect our response to students' writing. The few I have touched on here represent some useful starting points for discussions of what we do when we respond and, given the great variety in our focus and styles, how we can make the best use of these in particular circumstances. Doing so, as I have argued, is helped by reflection—by sharing strategies and by developing as much consciousness of our practices as we can. The next section considers some of the ways in which, as teachers, we can practice such reflection, both individually and collectively.

Toward Reflective Practice in Response and Evaluation

As a kind of discourse, response to students' writing is carried out in an often-personal domain between teacher and student—necessarily personal, we might argue, because of the expert-novice relationship that ensues in most educational settings. Yet this privacy not only blocks the chance for collaborative inquiry into our practices, but, perhaps as a result, relegates response to a more tacit domain of instruction, unexamined and undiscussed. Unlike the course syllabus, which teachers develop with conscious attention to various educational principles and which is often seen and even responded to by other colleagues, response remains curiously shielded from collective view (Anson 1989b). Clearly, we need more effective approaches for drawing to the surface, in both personally meaningful and collectively useful ways, the complexities involved in reading, responding to, and evaluating students' writing. Several such approaches—including "authentic" faculty-development workshops, teaching portfolios, and deep cases—are promising ways to begin such individual and collaborative reflections on response.

Authentic Workshops on Response

In spite of the ultimately personal nature of response, the most productive methods for improving this area of teaching take place, not surprisingly, in collaborative settings involving sustained dialogue and exchanges among trusting peers. While any such group activities must adjust to local circumstances, they offer participants the chance to share and study the complex interactions between teachers and individual students.

Samples of students' work, such as the essay written by Leang, can help us to talk about and analyze our methods for response and evaluation. While the resulting discussion can be enlightening, most of the time it is set in motion by generalized "response schemas" based on typical educational settings. The discussion may also lead to remarks *about* the essay, not comments directed to the student who wrote it.

More useful for developing response strategies are workshops that invite participants to bring in actual samples of students' writing from their own classes, on which they have made either formative or summative evaluative comments. In such "authentic" workshops, teachers can take turns describing the context of the paper(s) they have brought, which inevitably calls into play descriptions of the student, assignment, curriculum, preceding classroom work, school, and other important information. Once the context of the writing is clear, the group can discuss the teacher's commentary in detail, focusing on the appropriateness of the remarks, their style, focus, length, and effectiveness. Reflection can be prompted by comparisons of the teacher's and other participants' internal responses; by careful analyses of the language the teacher chose, relative to his or her purposes in the context described; by discussions of the participants' impressions of specific comments, especially their attempts to understand the teacher's underlying purpose or rationale for the comment and its placement; and by conclusions about the relationship between the teacher's system of beliefs and the response he or she made. Sharing such reflections not only exposes us to different response strategies (perhaps ones we have never used or seen used), but also helps us to formulate theoretical and practical justifications for the decisions we make. What results from such discussions is at once a larger repertoire of response strategies and a clearer, more informed understanding of how to use such strategies in the classroom.

Teacher Portfolios as a Context for Reflection

Workshops that bring teachers together to share their ideas, observations, and practices provide a social context for faculty development, but individual teachers need time to reflect on their instruction and then try out new methods in their classrooms. As Centra (1993) points out, teachers "become experts in part by the lessons they learn through their own inquiries and insights" (111). The "teaching portfolio," a widely heralded method for instructional development, is ideally suited for encouraging such reflective inquiry.

Teaching portfolios have gained national attention, especially in higher education, as useful tools both for improving teaching through greater reflection and for evaluating teaching effectiveness through richer forms of documentation than student evaluations or peer-review notes (see Anson 1994; Edgerton, Hutchings, and Quinlan 1991; Seldin 1991). As repositories of documents that demonstrate sustained reflection on important teaching issues, portfolios give us a space in which to examine critically our own response practices and develop new strategies.

Portfolio entries to be shared in draft form during inservice meetings or faculty workshops could reflect on specific features of response, such as the balance of positive, negative, and constructive commentary, or even on the definition of such terms as "positive," "negative," and "constructive." In development programs for pre-service teachers or teaching assistants, participants might work through several such features of response, each in a different portfolio entry (choice of language; choice of focus; clarity of explanations; amount of annotation; percentage of questions vs.

command statements; balance of comments on surface features vs. matters of meaning; and so on). Teachers with more background in rhetoric or composition research could supplement their discussions with references to the theories that inform their practices. Over time, teachers could revisit samples of writing to which they responded years before and chart the course of their own development as readers of students' writing, along the lines of various developmental schema of teaching (e.g., Shaughnessy 1976; Anson 1989b).

"Deep Cases" of Response

In the absence of real samples of students' writing, "deep cases" may give enough context to enrich group discussions of student writing. Deep cases are real or highly realistic scenarios that invite readers to imagine themselves in the situation and often pose some problem or set of problems to solve. Such cases often take the form of narratives with various characters—teacher, students, supervisors, colleagues—and involve complicated, unresolved conflicts that lead teachers into long, involved conversations about the issues, problems, and potential solutions or courses of action in the case. Cases of student writing, for example, could offer rich, detailed background information about many of the factors that we have already examined in this chapter. Participants could then respond to the writing (in its draft or final form) and discuss, analyze, or rationalize their commentary in light of the deep background information provided. Cases could be created to highlight certain aspects of the response process or the teaching situation (see Anson et al. 1993; Hutchings 1993).

Collaborative Teaching

As teachers we should be actively experimenting with response methodology and sharing the results with colleagues. Portfolio programs for student writing, for example, have led to creative new teaching situations involving multiple readings of students' work (see Elbow and Belanoff 1986). Several experiments in which teachers team up to offer the same version of a course, but read and anonymously grade the work of each other's students, have offered interesting anecdotal information about the interpersonal dynamics of response (in one case, for example, students felt hopelessly cheated because their evaluator was not privy to their visible hard work and earnestness in the classroom—aspects of response and evaluation that beg for much more exploration).

Various institutionally sponsored initiatives can encourage teachers to pair or team up in ways that directly affect the way they respond to students' writing. Linked courses, for example, can bring teachers of English or writing together with teachers in discipline-specific courses such as psychology, history or science to create joint-enrollment courses. Teachers linked in such ways can design writing assignments together and then work out creative ways to read and respond to them. Constantly comparing their impressions and judgments can help them to reflect on the relationship between the students' work and the many other contextual issues influencing their decisions.

New Media for Response

In light of the electronic revolutions taking place in education at all levels, we must begin to explore more fully various alternative media for response. Although tape-recorded responses have been discussed in the literature sporadically for decades, few scholars or teachers have looked carefully into this alternative to handwritten marginalia (see Anson 1997). Computer programs are now available that allow teachers to deposit icons in the margins of their students' on-screen work; these icons turn on a computer tape recorder to record the teacher's verbal comments. A second click of the icon turns off the recording device until the next comment is desired. The student, opening her paper on her own computer screen later on, can click on the marginal icons and hear her teacher's voice commenting on her text. Such programs were once thought futuristic, but now they are being supplemented by video boxes that appear in the corner of the screen to give the verbal message a visual accompaniment.

Interactive computer technology, e-mail response, chat lines, virtual writing labs with tutors who telecommute, programs that pretend to read and analyze texts—all such systems and more will characterize the response environment of the next few decades. While many such alternatives seem exciting and novel, we must also be prepared to assess them from the perspective of the new awareness encouraged by deeper thought about our more conventional, traditional methods.

Response in Classroom-based Research

Most of us have little occasion to study the effects of our response and evaluative practices on our students or to test out new strategies. Such information usually comes to us in the form of successful or unsuccessful revisions of drafts on which we have commented, or when students are puzzled or upset by what we write or say about their work. A more systematic investigation of response and evaluation, however, can lead to many new insights about the teaching and learning processes. Questions teachers can explore without the need for much sophisticated apparatus or complicated research designs might include these:

1. What sorts of responses do students like and dislike the most, and why?
2. Which forms of response do they find most helpful? How are they judging what is "helpful"? What kinds of revision are prompted by the response?
3. How do the conditions of our response affect us?
4. What do we typically do with student writing when we respond to it?
5. How do we respond to different kinds of writing (short or long, basic or advanced) or by different kinds of students (men or women, native or nonnative speakers, majors or nonmajors, upper- or working-class)?
6. How do we vary our responses in light of our knowledge about the

writer or the circumstances of the writing?

7. How do we change our response between in-progress work and final texts?
8. How do institutional or departmental standards affect our practices?

Studying such questions in the context of our own teaching not only forms higher-level awareness of our practices but also encourages improvement by giving us at least some quasi-empirical basis for our understandings and beliefs.

In this chapter I have claimed that multiple strategies for response may be more instructionally useful to us than aiming for a single, unified method. My belief is supported by my faith in the power of reflection to help us understand and justify our diverse practices, so that we do not fall into the trap that Richard Fulkerson (1979) documented in his analysis of unprincipled shifts in response styles. To adapt our practices to meet our increasingly diverse educational settings, we must become more reflective of the many complicated influences on our behavior. Those reflections, finally, will lead us to educational practices that are informed by thoughtfulness, balance, and clarity of method.

Yet, clearly, much more inquiry is needed into the relationship between teacher reflection and the practice of responding to students' writing. We do not know, for example, what effects a strong focus on reflective practice could have on the success of teachers' responses. Furthermore, the focus of reflective practice has remained steadily on teachers, largely ignoring the ways in which students' own reflections might provide information that facilitates both learning and teaching in specific classrooms. We need much more inquiry into what students bring to the response process—how they read our comments, and how, in turn, they develop new ways of reading their own and others' writing. In an interesting analysis of students reading and commenting on each other's writing, Lee Odell (1989) asks a number of questions about how students develop the ability to respond to other people's texts and to interpret the responses they receive. In addition to developing strategies for responding to students' writing based on fuller analyses of our situations, we need to be investigating and reflecting on how students interpret and act on these responses.

With the new knowledge such investigations yield, and with more attention to the ways in which we can think about and develop our teaching and responding methods, we will be in a better position to play out our roles as expert readers in a context where many people are growing in different ways.

Works Cited

Anderson, Worth, Cynthia Best, Alycia Black, John Hurst, Brandt Miller, and Susan Miller. 1990. "Cross-Curricular Underlife: A Collaborative Report on Ways with Academic Words." *College Composition and Communication* 41: 11–36.

Anson, Chris M. 1989a. "Response Styles and Ways of Knowing." In *Writing and Response: Theory, Practice, and Research,* ed. Chris M. Anson, 332–66. Urbana, IL: National Council of Teachers of English.

——. 1989b. "Response to Writing and the Paradox of Uncertainty." In *Writing and Response: Theory, Practice, and Research,* ed. Chris M. Anson, 1–11. Urbana, IL: National Council of Teachers of English.

——. 1994. "Portfolios for Teachers: Writing Our Way to Reflective Practice." In *New Directions in Portfolio Assessment: Reflective Practice, Critical Theory, and Large-Scale Scoring,* ed. Laurel Black, Donald Daiker, Jeffrey Sommers, and Gail Stygall, 185–210. Portsmouth, NH: Boynton/Cook-Heinemann.

——. 1997. "In Our Own Voices: Using Tape-Recorded Commentary to Respond to Student Writing." In *Assigning and Responding to Writing in the Disciplines,* ed. Peter Elbow and Mary Deane Sorcinelli, 105–13. San Francisco: Jossey-Bass.

Anson, Chris M., and Robert L. Brown, Jr. 1991. "Large-Scale Portfolio Assessment: Ideological Sensitivity and Institutional Change." In *Portfolios: Process and Product,* ed. Pat Belanoff and Marcia Dickson, 248–69. Portsmouth, NH: Boynton/Cook-Heinemann.

Anson, Chris M., Joan Graham, David A. Jolliffe, Nancy Shapiro, and Carolyn Smith. 1993. *Scenarios for Teaching Writing: Contexts for Discussion and Reflective Practice.* Urbana, IL: National Council of Teachers of English.

Belanoff, Pat, and Marcia Dickson, eds. 1991. *Portfolios: Process and Product.* Portsmouth, NH: Boynton/Cook-Heinemann.

Bleich, David. 1989. "Reconceiving Literacy: Language Use and Social Relations." In *Writing and Response: Theory, Practice, and Research,* ed. Chris M. Anson, 15–36. Urbana, IL: National Council of Teachers of English.

Brandt, Deborah. 1991. *Literacy as Involvement: The Acts of Readers, Writers, and Texts.* Carbondale: Southern Illinois University Press.

Brooke, Robert. 1987. "Underlife and Writing Instruction." *College Composition and Communication* 38: 141–53.

Centra, John A. 1993. *Reflective Faculty Evaluation: Enhancing Teaching and Determining Faculty Effectiveness.* San Francisco: Jossey-Bass.

Cooper, Charles R. 1977. "Holistic Evaluation of Writing." In *Evaluating Writing: Describing, Measuring, Judging,* ed. Charles R. Cooper and Lee Odell, 3–32. Urbana, IL: National Council of Teachers of English.

Crowley, Sharon. 1989. "On Intention in Student Texts." In *Encountering Student Texts: Interpretive Issues in Reading Student Writing,* ed. Bruce Lawson, Susan Sterr Ryan, and W. Ross Winterowd, 99–110. Urbana, IL: National Council of Teachers of English.

Edgerton, Russell, Patricia Hutchings, and Kathleen Quinlan. 1991. *The Teaching Portfolio: Capturing the Scholarship in Teaching.* Washington, DC: American Association for Higher Education.

Elbow, Peter. 1993. "Ranking, Evaluating, and Liking." *College English* 55: 187–206.

Elbow, Peter, and Pat Belanoff. 1986. "Portfolios as a Substitute for Proficiency Examinations." *College Composition and Communication* 37: 336–39.

Fulkerson, Richard P. 1979. "Four Philosophies of Composition." *College Composition and Communication* 30: 43–56.

Hake, Rosemary. 1986. "How Do We Judge What They Write?" "In *Writing Assessment: Issues and Strategies,* ed. Karen L. Greenberg, Harvey S. Wiener, and Richard A. Donovan, 153–67. White Plains, NY: Longman.

Himley, Margaret. 1989. "A Reflective Conversation: 'Tempos of Meaning.'" In *Encountering Student Texts: Interpretive Issues in Reading Student Writing,* ed. Bruce Lawson, Susan Sterr Ryan, and W. Ross Winterowd, 5–19. Urbana, IL: National Council of Teachers of English.

Hunt, Russell A. 1986. "Could You Put In a Lot of Holes? Modes of Response to Writing."

Language Arts 64: 229–32.

——. 1989. "A Horse Named Hans, a Boy Named Shawn: The Herr von Osten Theory of Response to Writing." In *Writing and Response: Theory, Practice, and Research,* ed. Chris M. Anson, 80–110. Urbana, IL: National Council of Teachers of English.

Hutchings, Pat. 1993. *Using Cases to Improve College Teaching: A Guide to More Reflective Practice.* Washington, DC: American Association of Higher Education.

Knoblauch, Cy, and Lil Brannon. 1982. "On Students' Rights to Their Own Texts: A Model of Teacher Response." *College Composition and Communication* 33: 157–66.

Lees, E. O. 1979. "Evaluating Student Writing." *College Composition and Communication* 30: 370–74.

McCracken, Nancy. 1993 (November). "Toward a Conversational Theory of Response." Paper presented at the Annual Convention of the National Council of Teachers of English, Pittsburgh, PA.

Mosenthal, Peter. 1983. "On Defining Writing and Classroom Writing Competence." in *Research on Writing: Principles and Methods,* ed. Peter Mosenthal, Lynne Tamor, and Sean S. Walmsley, 26–71. New York: Longman.

Murray, Patricia Y. 1989. "Teachers as Readers, Readers as Teachers." In *Encountering Student Texts: Interpretive Issues in Reading Student Writing,* ed. Bruce Lawson, Susan Sterr Ryan, and W. Ross Winterowd, 73–85. Urbana, IL: National Council of Teachers of English.

Odell, Lee. 1989. "Responding to Responses: Good News, Bad News, and Unanswered Questions." In *Encountering Student Texts: Interpretive Issues in Reading Student Writing,* ed. Bruce Lawson, Susan Sterr Ryan, and W. Ross Winterowd, 221–34. Urbana, IL: National Council of Teachers of English.

Perr, William G., Jr. 1970. *Forms of Intellectual and Ethical Development in the College Years: A Scheme.* New York: Holt, Rinehart & Winston.

Piche, Gene L. 1977. "Class and Culture in the Development of the High School Curriculum, 1880–1900." *Research in the Teaching of English* 11: 17–27.

Polanyi, Michael. 1966. *The Tacit Dimension.* Garden City, NY: Doubleday.

Purves, Alan C. 1984. "The Teacher as Reader: An Anatomy." *College English* 46: 259–65.

Schön, Donald A. 1983. *The Reflective Practitioner: How Professionals Think in Action.* New York: Basic.

——. 1987. *Educating the Reflective Practitioner.* San Francisco: Jossey-Bass.

Seldin, Peter. 1991. *The Teaching Portfolio.* Boston: Ankara.

Shaughnessy, Mina P. 1976. "Diving In: An Introduction to Basic Writing." *College Composition and Communication* 27: 234–39.

——. 1977. *Errors and Expectations: A Guide for the Teacher of Basic Writing.* New York: Oxford University Press.

Sommers, Jeffrey. 1989. "The Writer's Memo: Collaboration, Response, and Development." In *Writing and Response: Theory, Practice, and Research,* ed. Chris M. Anson, 174–86. Urbana, IL: National Council of Teachers of English.

Sperling, Melanie. 1993 (November). "Response to Writing Multiply Construed." Paper presented at the Annual Convention of the National Council of Teachers of English, Pittsburgh, PA.

Straub, Richard, and Ronald F. Lunsford. 1995. *Twelve Readers Reading.* Cresskill, NJ: Hampton Press.

Traschel, Mary. 1992. *Institutionalizing Literacy: The Historical Role of College Entrance Examinations in English.* Carbondale: Southern Illinois University Press.

Yancey, Kathleen Blake. 1992. "Teachers' Stories: Notes Toward a Portfolio Pedagogy." In *Portfolios in the Writing Classroom,* ed. Kathleen Blake Yancey, 12–19. Urbana, IL: National Council of Teachers of English.

Ranking, Evaluating, and Liking: Sorting Out Three Forms of Judgment

Peter Elbow

Peter Elbow has written many influential books and articles on teaching writing, including Writing without Teachers, Writing with Power, Embracing Contraries, *and* What Is English? *A professor of English at the University of Massachusetts at Amherst, he has long argued for approaches to teaching and assessing writing that are sensitive to the individual voices and circumstances of students. In this influential article, first published in* College English *in 1993, Elbow argues that the grading or ranking of individual papers is unreliable and incommunicative, encouraging students to write more for a grade than for their own purposes. Elbow suggests several methods, such as portfolios, contract grading, and analytic grids, for teachers to assign a course grade that emphasize thoughtful written and spoken evaluation of student writing over ranking. Yet he also argues that teachers should provide students with "evaluation-free zones," opportunities such as freewriting to write without being ranked or evaluated.*

This essay is my attempt to sort out different acts we call assessment—some different ways in which we express or frame our judgments of value. I have been working on this tangle not just because it is interesting and important in itself but because assessment tends so much to drive and control *teaching*. Much of what we do in the classroom is determined by the assessment structures we work under.

Assessment is a large and technical area and I'm not a professional. But my main premise or subtext in this essay is that we nonprofessionals can and should work on it because professionals have not reached definitive conclusions about the problem of how to assess writing (or anything else, I'd say). Also, decisions about assessment are often made by people even less professional than we, namely legislators. Pat Belanoff and I realized that the field of assessment was open when we saw the harmful effects of a writing proficiency exam at Stony Brook and worked out a collaborative portfolio assessment system in its place (Belanoff and Elbow; Elbow and Belanoff). Professionals keep changing their minds about large-scale testing and assessment. And as for classroom grading, psychometricians provide little support or defense of it.

THE … HE BENEFITS OF EV…

…dgment of a performance or person … every time we give a grade or holistic … ntinuum or dimension along which all

… act of expressing one's judgment of a … ut the strengths and weaknesses of different … every time we write a comment on a paper or … ue. Evaluation implies the recognition of different … implication different contexts and audiences for the san… on requires going *beyond* a first response that may be nothin… king ("I like it" or "This is better than that"), and instead looking ca… n at the performance or person to make distinctions between parts or featu… iteria.

It's ob… ious, thus, that I am troubled by ranking. But I will resist any temptation to argue that we can get rid of all ranking—or even should. Instead I will try to show how we can have *less* ranking and *more* evaluation in its place.

I see three distinct problems with ranking: it is inaccurate or unreliable; it gives no substantive feedback; and it is harmful to the atmosphere for teaching and learning.

(1) First the unreliability. To rank reliably means to give a fair number, to find the single quantitative score that readers will agree on. But readers don't agree.

This is not news—this unavailability of agreement. We have long seen it on many fronts. For example, research in evaluation has shown many times that if we give a paper to a set of readers, those readers tend to give it the full range of grades (Diederich). I've recently come across new research to this effect—new to me because it was published in 1912. The investigators carefully showed how high school English teachers gave different grades to the same paper. In response to criticism that this was a local problem in English, they went on the next year to discover an even greater variation among grades given by high school geometry teachers and history teachers to papers in their subjects. (See the summary of Daniel Starch and Edward Elliott's 1913 *School Review* articles in Kirschenbaum, Simon, and Napier 258–59.)

We know the same thing from literary criticism and theory. If the best critics can't agree about what a text means, how can we be surprised that they disagree even more about the quality or value of texts? And we know that nothing in literary or philosophical theory gives us any agreed-upon rules for settling such disputes.

Students have shown us the same inconsistency with their own controlled experiments of handing the same paper to different teachers and getting different grades. This helps explain why we hate it so when students ask us their favorite question, "What do you want for an A?": it rubs our noses in the unreliability of our grades.

Of course champions of holistic scoring argue that they get *can* get agreement among readers—and they often do (White). But they get that agreement by "training" the readers before and during the scoring sessions. What "training" means is getting those scorers to stop reading the way they normally read—getting them to stop using the conflicting criteria and standards they normally use outside the scoring sessions. (In an impressive and powerful book, Barbara Herrnstein Smith argues that whenever we have widespread inter-reader reliability, we have reason to suspect that difference has been suppressed and homogeneity imposed—almost always at the expense of certain groups.) In short, the reliability in holistic scoring is not a measure of how texts are valued by real readers in natural settings, but only of how they are valued in artificial settings with imposed agreements.

Defenders of holistic scoring might reply (as one anonymous reviewer did), that holistic scores are not perfect or absolutely objective readings but just "judgments that most readers will agree are the appropriate ones given the purpose of the assessment and the system of communication." But I have been in and even conducted enough holistic scoring sessions to know that even that degree of agreement doesn't occur unless "purpose" and "appropriateness" are defined to mean acceptance of the single set of standards imposed on that session. We know too much about the differences among readers and the highly variable nature of the reading process. Supposing we get readings only from academics, or only from people in English, or only from respected critics, or only from respected writing programs, or only from feminists, or only from sound readers of my tribe (white, male, middle-class, full professors between the ages of fifty and sixty). We *still* don't get agreement. We can sometimes get agreement among readers from some subset, a particular community that has developed a strong set of common values, perhaps one English department or *one* writing program. But what is the value of such a rare agreement? It tells us nothing about how readers from other English departments or writing programs will judge—much less how readers from other domains will judge.

(From the opposite ideological direction, some skeptics might object to my skeptical train of thought: "So what else is new?" they might reply. "Of *course* my grades are biased, 'interested' or 'situated'—always partial to my interests or the values of my community or culture. There's no other possibility." But how can people consent to give grades if they feel that way? A single teacher's grade for a student is liable to have substantial consequences—for example on eligibility for a scholarship or a job or entrance into professional school. In grading, surely we must not take anything less than genuine fairness as our goal.)

It won't be long before we see these issues argued in a court of law, when a student who has been disqualified from playing on a team or rejected from a professional school sues, charging that the basis for his plight—teacher grades—is not reliable. I wonder if lawyers will be able to make our grades stick.

(2) Ranking or grading is woefully uncommunicative. Grades and holistic scores are nothing but points on a continuum from "yea" to "boo"—with no information or clues about the criteria behind these noises. They are 100 percent evaluation and 0 percent description or information. They quantify the degree of approval or disapproval in readers but tell nothing at all about what the readers

actually approve or disapprove of. They say nothing that couldn't be said with gold stars or black marks or smiley-faces. Of course our first reactions are often nothing but global holistic feelings of approval or disapproval, but we need a system for communicating our judgments that nudges us to move beyond these holistic feelings and to articulate the basis of our feeling—a process that often leads us to change our feeling. (Holistic scoring sessions sometimes use rubrics that explain the criteria—though these are rarely passed along to students—and even in these situations, the rubrics fail to fit many papers.) As C.S. Lewis says, "People are obviously far more anxious to express their approval and disapproval of things than to describe them" (7).

(3) Ranking leads students to get so hung up on these oversimple quantitative verdicts that they care more about scores than about learning—more about the grade we put on the paper than about the comment we have written on it. Have you noticed how grading often forces us to write comments to justify our grades?—and how these are often not the comment we would make if we were just trying to help the student write better? ("Just try writing several favorable comments on a paper and then giving it a grade of D" [Diederich 21].)

Grades and holistic scores give too much encouragement to those students who score high—making them too apt to think they are already fine—and too little encouragement to those students who do badly. Unsuccessful students often come to doubt their intelligence. But oddly enough, many "A" students also end up doubting their true ability and feeling like frauds—because they have sold out on their own judgment and simply given teachers whatever yields an A. They have too often been rewarded for what they don't really believe in. (Notice that there's more cheating by students who get high grades than by those who get low ones. There would be less incentive to cheat if there were no ranking.)

We might be tempted to put up with the inaccuracy or unfairness of grades if they gave good diagnostic feedback or helped the learning climate; or we might put up with the damage they do to the learning climate if they gave a fair or reliable measure of how skilled or knowledgeable students are. But since they fail dismally on both counts, we are faced with the striking question of why grading has persisted so long.

There must be many reasons. It is obviously easier and quicker to express a global feeling with a single number than to figure out what the strengths and weaknesses are and what one's criteria are. (Though I'm heartened to discover, as I pursue this issue, how troubled teachers are by grading and how difficult they find it.) But perhaps more important, we see around us a deep *hunger to rank*—to create pecking orders: to see who we can look down on and who we must look up to, or in the military metaphor, who we can kick and who we must salute. Psychologists tell us that this taste for pecking orders or ranking is associated with the authoritarian personality. We see this hunger graphically in the case of IQ scores. It is plain that IQ scoring does not represent a commitment to looking carefully at people's intelligence; when we do that, we see different and frequently uncorrelated *kinds* or *dimensions* of intelligence (Gardner). The persistent use of IQ scores represents the hunger to have a number so that everyone can have a rank. ("Ten!" mutter the guys when they see a pretty woman.)

Because ranking or grading has caused so much discomfort to so many students and teachers, I think we see a lot of confusion about the process. It is hard to think clearly about something that has given so many of us such anxiety and distress. The most notable confusion I notice is the tendency to think that if we renounce ranking or grading, we are renouncing the very possibility of judgment and discrimination—that we are embracing the idea that there is no way to distinguish or talk about the difference between what works well and what works badly.

So the most important point, then, is that *I am not arguing against judgment or evaluation.* I'm just arguing against that crude, oversimple way of *representing* judgment—distorting it, really—into a single number, which means ranking people and performances along a single continuum.

In fact I am arguing *for evaluation.* Evaluation means looking hard and thoughtfully at a piece of writing in order to make distinctions as to the quality of different features or dimensions. For example, the process of evaluation permits us to make the following kinds of statements about a piece of writing:

- The thinking and ideas seem interesting and creative.

- The overall structure or sequence seems confusing.

- The writing is perfectly clear at the level of individual sentences and even paragraphs. There is an odd, angry tone of voice that seems unrelated or inappropriate to what the writer is saying.

- Yet this same voice is strong and memorable and makes one listen even if one is irritated.

- There are a fair number of mistakes in grammar or spelling: more than "a sprinkling" but less than "riddled with."

To rank, on the other hand, is to be forced to translate those discriminations into a single number. What grade or holistic score do these judgments add up to? It's likely, by the way, that more readers would agree with those separate, "analytic" statements than would agree on a holistic score.

I've conducted many assessment sessions where we were not trying to impose a set of standards but rather to find out how experienced teachers read and evaluate, and I've had many opportunities to see that good readers give grades or scores right down through the range of possibilities. Of course good readers sometimes agree—especially on papers that are strikingly good or bad or conventional, but I think I see difference more frequently than agreement when readers really speak up.

The process of evaluation, because it invites us to articulate our criteria and to make distinctions among parts or features or dimensions of a performance, thereby invites us further to acknowledge the main fact about evaluation: that different readers have different priorities, values, and standards.

The conclusion I am drawing, then, in this first train of thought is that we should do less ranking and more evaluation. Instead of using grades or holistic scores—single number verdicts that try to sum up complex performances along only one scale—we should give some kind of written or spoken evaluation that discriminates among criteria and dimensions of the writing—and if possible that takes account of the complex context for writing: who the writer is, what the writer's audience and goals are, who we are as readers and how we read, and how we might differ in our reading from other readers the writer might be addressing.

But how can we put this principle into practice? The pressure for ranking seems implacable. Evaluation takes more time, effort, and money. It seems as though we couldn't get along without scores on writing exams. Most teachers are obliged to give grades at the end of each course. And many students—given that they have become conditioned or even addicted to ranking over the years and must continue to inhabit a ranking culture in most of their courses—will object if we don't put grades on papers. Some students, in the absence of that crude gold star or black mark, may not try hard enough (though how hard is "enough"—and is it really our job to stimulate motivation artificially with grades—and is grading the best source of motivation?).

It is important to note that there are certain schools and colleges that do *not* use single-number grades or scores, and they function successfully. I taught for nine years at Evergreen State College, which uses only written evaluations. This system works fine, even down to getting students accepted into high quality graduate and professional schools.

Nevertheless we have an intractable dilemma: that grading is unfair and counterproductive but that students and institutions tend to want grades. In the face of this dilemma there is a need for creativity and pragmatism. Here are some ways in which I and others use *less ranking* and *more evaluation* in teaching—and they suggest some adjustments in how we score large-scale assessments. What follows is an assortment of experimental compromises—sometimes crude, seldom ideal or utopian—but they help.

(a) Portfolios. Just because conventional institutions oblige us to turn in a single quantitative course grade at the end of every marking period, it doesn't follow that we need to grade individual papers. Course grades are more trustworthy and less damaging because they are based on so many performances over so many weeks. By avoiding frequent ranking or grading, we make it *somewhat* less likely for students to become addicted to oversimple numerical rankings—to think that evaluation always translates into a simple number—in short, to mistake ranking for evaluation. (I'm not trying to defend conventional course grades since they are still uncommunicative and they still feed the hunger for ranking.) Portfolios permit me to refrain from grading individual papers and limit myself to writerly evaluative comments—and help students see this as a positive rather than a negative thing, a chance to be graded on a body of their best work that can be judged more fairly. Portfolios have many other advantages as well. They are particularly valuable as occasions for asking students to write extensive and thoughtful explorations of their own strengths and weaknesses.

A midsemester portfolio is usually an informal affair, but it is a good occasion for giving anxious students a ballpark estimate of how well they are doing in the course so far. I find it helpful to tell students that I'm perfectly willing to tell them my best estimate of their course grade—but only if they come to me in conference and only during the second half of the semester. This serves somewhat to quiet their anxiety while they go through seven weeks of drying out from grades. By midsemester, most of them have come to enjoy not getting those numbers and thus being able to think better about more writerly comments from me and their classmates.

Portfolios are now used extensively and productively in larger assessments, and there is constant experimentation with new applications (Belanoff and Dickson; *Portfolio Assessment Newsletter; Portfolio News).*

(b) Another useful option is to make a strategic retreat from a wholly negative position. That is, I sometimes do a *bit* of ranking even on individual papers, using two "bottom-line" grades: H and U for "Honors" and "Unsatisfactory." I tell students that these translate to about A or A- and D or F. This practice may seem theoretically inconsistent with all the arguments I've just made, but (at the moment, anyway) I justify it for the following reasons.

First, I sympathize with a *part* of the students' anxiety about not getting grades: their fear that they might be failing and not know about it—or doing an excellent job and not get any recognition. Second, I'm not giving *many* grades; only a small proportion of papers get these H's or U's. The system creates a "non-bottom-line" or "non-quantified" atmosphere. Third, these holistic judgments about best and worst do not seem as arbitrary and questionable as most grades. There is usually a *bit* more agreement among readers about the best and worst papers. What seems most dubious is the process of trying to rank that whole middle range of papers—papers that have a mixture of better and worse qualities so that the numerical grade depends enormously on a reader's priorities or mood or temperament. My willingness to give these few grades goes a long way toward helping my students forgo most bottom-line grading.

I'm not trying to pretend that these minimal "grades" are truly reliable. But they represent a very small amount of ranking. Yes, someone could insist that I'm really ranking every single paper (and indeed if it seemed politically necessary, I could put an OK or S [for satisfactory] on all those middle range papers and brag, "Yes, I grade everything.") But the fact is that I am doing *much less sorting* since I don't have to sort them into five or even twelve piles. Thus there is a huge reduction in the total amount of unreliability I produce.

(It might seem that if I use only these few minimal grades I have no good way for figuring out a final grade for the course—since that requires a more fine-grained set of ranks. But I don't find that to be the case. For I also give these same minimal grades to the many other important parts of my course such as attendance, meeting deadlines, peer responding, and journal writing. If I want a mathematically computed grade on a scale of six or A through E, I can easily compute it when I have such a large number of grades to work from—even though they are only along a three-point scale.)

This same practice of crude or minimal ranking is a big help on larger assessments outside classrooms, and needs to be applied to the process of assessment in general. There are two important principles to emphasize. On the one hand we must be prudent or accommodating enough to admit that despite all the arguments against ranking, there are situations when we need that bottom-line verdict along one scale: which student has not done satisfactory work and should be denied credit for the course? Which student gets the scholarship? Which candidate to hire or fire? We often operate with scarce resources. But on the other hand we must be bold enough to insist that we do far more ranking than is really needed. We can get along not only with fewer occasions for assessment but also with fewer gradations in scoring. If we decide what the *real* bottom-line is on a given occasion—perhaps just "failing" or perhaps "honors" too—then the reading of papers or portfolios is enormously quick and cheap. It leaves time and money for evaluation-perhaps for analytic scoring or some comment.

At Stony Brook we worked out a portfolio system where multiple readers had only to make a binary decision: acceptable or not. Then individual teachers could decide the actual course grade and give comments for their own students—so long as those students passed in the eyes of an independent rater (Elbow and Belanoff, Belanoff and Elbow). The best way to begin to wean our society from its addiction to ranking may be to permit a tiny bit of it (which also means less unreliability)—rather than trying to go "cold turkey."

(c) Sometimes I use an analytic grid for evaluating and commenting on student papers. An example is given in Figure 1. I often vary the criteria in my grid (e.g. "connecting with readers" or "investment") depending on the assignment or the point in the semester.

Figure 1.

Strong	OK	Weak	
			CONTENT, INSIGHTS, THINKING, GRAPPLING WITH TOPIC
			GENUINE REVISION, SUBSTANTIVE CHANGES, NOT JUST EDITING
			ORGANIZATION, STRUCTURE, GUIDING THE READER
			LANGUAGE: SYNTAX, SENTENCES, WORDING, VOICE
			MECHANICS: SPELLING, GRAMMAR, PUNCTUATION, PROOFREADING
			OVERALL [Note- this is not a sum of the other scores.]

Grids are a way I can satisfy the students' hunger for ranking but still not give in to conventional grades on individual papers. Sometimes I provide nothing but a grid (especially on final drafts), and this is a very quick way to provide a response. Or on midprocess drafts I sometimes use a grid in addition to a comment: a more readerly comment that often doesn't so much tell them what's wrong or right or how to improve things but rather tries to give them an account of what is *happening to me* as I read their words. I think this kind of comment is really the most useful thing of all for students, but it frustrates some students for a while. The grid can help these students feel less anxious and thus pay better attention to my comment.

I find grids extremely helpful at the end of the semester for telling students their strengths and weaknesses in the course—or what they've done well and not so well. Besides categories like the ones above, I use categories like these: "skill in giving feedback to others," "ability to meet deadlines," "effort," and "improvement." This practice makes my final grade much more communicative.

(d) I also help make up for the absence of ranking—gold stars and black marks—by having students share their writing with each other a great deal both orally and through frequent publication in class magazines. Also, where possible, I try to get students to give or send writing to audiences outside the class. At the University of Massachusetts at Amherst, freshmen pay a ten dollar lab fee for the writing course, and every teacher publishes four or five class magazines of final drafts a semester. The effects are striking. Sharing, peer feedback, and publication give the best reward and motivation for writing, namely, getting your words out to many readers.

(e) I sometimes use a kind of modified *contract grading.* That is, at the start of the course I pass out a long list of all the things that I most want students to do—the concrete activities that I think most lead to learning—and I promise students that if they do them *all* they are guaranteed a certain final grade. Currently, I say it's a B—it could be lower or higher. My list includes these items: not missing more than a week's worth of classes; not having more than one late major assignment; *substantive* revising on all major revisions; good copy editing on all final revisions; good effort on peer feedback work; keeping up the journal; and substantial effort and investment on each draft.

I like the way this system changes the "bottom-line" for a course: the intersection where my authority crosses their self-interest. I can tell them, "You have to work very hard in this course, but you can stop worrying about grades." The crux is no longer that commodity I've always hated and never trusted: a numerical ranking of the quality of their writing along a single continuum. Instead the crux becomes what I care about most: the *concrete behaviors* that I most want students to engage in because they produce more learning and help me teach better. Admittedly, effort and investment are not concrete observable behaviors, but they are no harder to judge than overall quality of writing. And since I care about effort and investment, I don't mind the few arguments I get into about them; they seem fruitful. ("Let's try and figure out why it looked to me as though you didn't put any effort in here.") In contrast, I hate discussions about grades on a paper and find such arguments fruitless. Besides, I'm not making fine distinctions about effort and investment—just letting a bell go off when they fall palpably low.

It's crucial to note that I am not fighting evaluation with this system. I am just fighting ranking or grading. I still write evaluative comments and often use an evaluative grid to tell my students what I see as strengths and weaknesses in their papers. My goal is not to get rid of evaluation but in fact to emphasize it, enhance it. I'm trying to get students to listen *better* to my evaluations—by uncoupling them from a grade. In effect, I'm doing this because I'm so fed up with students *following* or *obeying* my evaluations too blindly—making whatever changes my comments suggest but doing it for the sake of a grade, not really taking the time to make up their own minds about whether they think my judgments or suggestions really make sense to them. The worst part of grades is that they make students obey us without carefully thinking about the merits of what we say. I love the situation this system so often puts students in: I make a criticism or suggestion about their paper, but it doesn't matter to their grade whether they go along with me or not (so long as they genuinely revise in some fashion). They have to think, to decide.

Admittedly this system is crude and impure. Some of the really skilled students who are used to getting A's and desperate to get one in this course remain unhelpfully hung up about getting those A's on their papers. But a good number of these students discover that they can't get them, and they soon settle down to accepting a B and having less anxiety and more of a learning voyage.

THE LIMITATIONS OF EVALUATION AND THE BENEFITS OF EVALUATION-FREE ZONES

Everything I've said so far has been in praise of evaluation as a substitute for ranking. But I need to turn a corner here and speak about the *limits* or *problems* of evaluation. Evaluating may be better than ranking, but it still carries some of the same problems. That is, even though I've praised evaluation for inviting us to acknowledge that readers and contexts are different, nevertheless the very word *evaluation* tends to imply fairness or reliability or getting beyond personal or subjective preferences. Also, of course, evaluation takes a lot more time and work. To rank you just have to put down a number; holistic scoring of exams is cheaper than analytic scoring.

Most important of all, evaluation harms the climate for learning and teaching—or rather *too much* evaluation has this effect. That is, if we evaluate *everything* students write, they tend to remain tangled up in the assumption that their whole job in school is to give teachers "what they want." Constant evaluation makes students worry more about psyching out the teacher than about what they are really learning. Students fall into a kind of defensive or on-guard stance toward the teacher: a desire to hide what they don't understand and try to impress. This stance gets in the way of learning. (Think of the patient trying to hide symptoms from the doctor.) Most of all, constant evaluation by someone in authority makes students reluctant to take the risks that are needed for good learning—to try out hunches and trust their own judgment. Face it: if our goal is to get students to exercise their own judgment, that means exercising an immature and undeveloped judgment and making choices that are obviously wrong to us.

We see around us a widespread hunger to be evaluated that is often just as strong as the hunger to rank. Countless conditions make many of us walk around in the world wanting to ask others (especially those in authority), "How am I doing, did I do OK?" I don't think the hunger to be evaluated is as harmful as the hunger to rank, but it can get in the way of learning. For I find that the greatest and most powerful breakthroughs in learning occur when I can get myself and others to *put aside* this nagging, self-doubting question ("How am I doing? How am I doing?")—

and instead to take some chances, trust our instincts or hungers. When everything is evaluated, everything counts. Often the most powerful arena for deep learning is a kind of "time out" zone from the pressures of normal evaluated reality: make-believe, play, dreams—in effect, the Shakespearian forest.

In my attempts to get away from too much evaluation (not from all evaluation, just from too much of it), I have drifted into a set of teaching practices which now feel to me like the *best* part of my teaching. I realize now what I've been unconsciously doing for a number of years: creating "evaluation-free zones."

(a) The paradigm evaluation-free zone is the ten minute, nonstop freewrite. When I get students to freewrite, I am using my authority to create unusual conditions in order to contradict or interrupt our pervasive habit of always evaluating our writing. What is essential here are the two central features of freewriting: that it be private (thus I don't collect it or have students share it with anyone else); and that it be nonstop (thus there isn't time for planning, and control is usually diminished). Students quickly catch on and enter into the spirit. At the end of the course, they often tell me that freewriting is the most useful thing I've taught them (see Belanoff, Elbow, and Fontaine).

(b) A larger evaluation-free zone is the single unevaluated assignment—what people sometimes call the "quickwrite" or sketch. This is a piece of writing that I ask students to do—either in class or for homework—without any or much revising. It is meant to be low stakes writing. There is a bit of pressure, nevertheless, since I usually ask them to share it with others and I usually collect it and read it. But I don't write any comments at all—except perhaps to put straight lines along some passages I like or to write a phrase of appreciation at the end. And I ask students to refrain from giving evaluative feedback to each other—and instead just to say "thank you" or mention a couple of phrases or ideas that stick in mind. (However, this writing-without-feedback can be a good occasion for students to discuss the *topic* they have written about—and thus serve as an excellent kick-off for discussions of what I am teaching.)

(c) These experiments have led me to my next and largest evaluation-free zone—what I sometimes call a "jump start" for my whole course. For the last few semesters I've been devoting the first three weeks *entirely* to the two evaluation-free activities I've just described: freewriting (and also more leisurely private writing in a journal) and quickwrites or sketches. Since the stakes are low and I'm not asking for much revising, I ask for *much more* writing homework per week than usual. And every day we write in class: various exercises or games. The emphasis is on getting rolling, getting fluent, taking risks. And every day all students read out loud something they've written—sometimes a short passage even to the whole class. So despite the absence of feedback, it is a very audience-filled and sociable three weeks.

At first I only dared do this for two weeks, but when I discovered how fast the writing improves, how good it is for building community, and what a pleasure this period is for me, I went to three weeks. I'm curious to try an experiment with teaching a whole course this way. I wonder, that is, whether all that evaluation we work so hard to give really does any more good than the constant writing and sharing (Zak).

I need to pause here to address an obvious rejoinder: "But withholding evaluation is not normal!" Indeed, it is *not* normal—certainly not normal in school. We normally tend to emphasize evaluations—even bottom-line ranking kinds of evaluations. But I resist the argument that if it's not normal we shouldn't do it.

The best argument for evaluation-free zones is from experience. If you try them, I suspect you'll discover that they are satisfying and bring out good writing. Students have a better time writing these unevaluated pieces; they enjoy hearing and appreciating these pieces when they don't have to evaluate. And I have a much better time when I engage in this astonishing activity: reading student work when I don't have to evaluate and respond. And yet the writing improves. I see students investing and risking more, writing more fluently, and using livelier, more interesting voices. This writing gives me and them a higher standard of clarity and voice for when we move on to more careful and revised writing tasks that involve more intellectual pushing—tasks that sometimes make their writing go tangled or sodden.

THE BENEFITS AND FEASIBILITY OF LIKING

Liking and disliking seem like unpromising topics in an exploration of assessment, They seem to represent the worst kind of subjectivity, the merest accident of personal taste. But I've recently come to think that the phenomenon of liking is perhaps the most important evaluative response for writers and teachers to think about. In effect, I'm turning another corner in my argument. In the first section I argued against ranking—with evaluating being the solution. Next I argued not *against* evaluating—but for no-evaluation zones in *addition* to evaluating. Now I will argue neither against evaluating nor against no-evaluation zones, but for something very different in addition, or perhaps underneath, as a foundation: liking.

Let me start with the germ story. I was in a workshop and we were going around the circle with everyone telling a piece of good news about their writing in the last six months. It got to Wendy Bishop, a good poet (who has also written two good books about the teaching of writing), and she said, "In the last six months, I've learned to *like* everything I write." Our jaws dropped; we were startled—in a way scandalized. But I've been chewing on her words ever since, and they have led me into a retelling of the story of how people learn to write better.

The old story goes like this: We write something. We read it over and we say, "This is terrible. I *hate* it. I've got to work on it and improve it." And we do, and it gets better, and this happens again and again, and before long we have become a wonderful writer. But that's not really what happens. Yes, we vow to work on it—but we don't. And next time we have the impulse to write, we're just a *bit* less likely to start.

What really happens when people learn to write better is more like this: We write something. We read it over and we say, "This is terrible. ... But I *like* it. Damn it, I'm going to get it good enough so that others will like it too." And this time we don't just put it in a drawer, we actually work hard on it. And we try it out on other people too—not just to get feedback and advice but, perhaps more important, to find someone else who will like it.

Notice the two stories here—two hypotheses. (a) "First you improve the faults and then you like it." (b) "First you like it and then you improve faults." The second story may sound odd when stated so baldly, but really it's common sense. Only if we like something will we get involved enough to work and struggle with it. Only if we like what we write will we write again and again by choice—which is the only way we get better.

This hypothesis sheds light on the process of how people get to be published writers. Conventional wisdom assumes a Darwinian model: poor writers are unread; then they get better; as a result, they get a wider audience; finally they turn into Norman Mailer. But now I'd say the process is more complicated. People who get better and get published really tend to be driven by how much *they* care about their writing. Yes, they have a small audience at first—after all, they're not very good. But they try reader after reader until finally they can find people who like and appreciate their writing. I certainly did this. If someone doesn't like her writing enough to be pushy and hungry about finding a few people who also like it, she probably won't get better.

It may sound so far as though all the effort and drive comes from the lonely driven writer—and sometimes it does (Norman Mailer is no joke). But, often enough, readers play the crucially active role in this story of how writers get better. That is, the way writers *learn* to like their writing is by the grace of having a reader or two who likes it—even though it's not good. Having at least a few appreciative readers is probably indispensable to getting better.

When I apply this story to our situation as teachers, I come up with this interesting hypothesis: *good writing teachers like student writing* (and like students). I think I see this borne out—and it is really nothing but common sense. Teachers who hate student writing and hate students are grouchy all the time. How could we stand our work and do a decent job if we hated their writing? Good teachers see what is only *potentially* good; they get a kick out of mere possibility—and they encourage it. When I manage to do this, I teach well.

Thus, I've begun to notice a turning point in my courses—two or three weeks into the semester: "Am I going to like these folks or is this going to be a battle, a struggle?" When I like them everything seems to go better—and it seems to me they learn more by the end. When I don't and we stay tangled up in struggle, we all suffer—and they seem to learn less.

So what am I saying? That we should like bad writing? How can we see all the weaknesses and criticize student writing if we just like it? But here's the interesting point: if I *like* someone's writing it's *easier* to criticize it.

I first noticed this when I was trying to gather essays for the book on freewriting that Pat Belanoff and Sheryl Fontaine and I edited. I would read an essay someone had written, I would want it for the book, but I had some serious criticism. I'd get excited and write, "I really like this, and I hope we can use it in our book, but you've got to get rid of this and change that, and I got really mad at this other thing." I usually find it hard to criticize, but I began to notice that I was a much more critical and pushy reader when I liked something. It's even fun to criticize in those conditions.

It's the same with student writing. If I like a piece, I don't have to pussyfoot around with my criticism. It's when I don't like their writing that I find myself tiptoeing: trying to soften my criticism, trying to find something nice to say—and usually sounding fake, often unclear. I see the same thing with my own writing. If I like it, I can criticize it better. I have faith that there'll still be something good left, even if I train my full critical guns on it.

In short—and to highlight how this section relates to the other two sections of this essay—liking is not same as ranking or evaluating. Naturally, people get them mixed up: when they like something, they assume it's good; when they hate it, they assume it's bad. But it's helpful to uncouple the two domains and realize that it makes perfectly good sense to say, "This is terrible, but I like it." Or, "This is good, but I hate it." In short, I am not arguing here *against* criticizing or evaluating. I'm merely arguing *for* liking.

Let me sum up my clump of hypotheses so far:

- It's not improvement that leads to liking, but rather liking that leads to improvement.

- It's the mark of good writers to like their writing.

- Liking is not the same as evaluating. We can often criticize something better when we like it.

- We learn to like our writing when we have a respected reader who likes it.

- Therefore, it's the mark of good teachers to like students and their writing.

If this set of hypotheses is true, what practical consequences follow from it? How can we be better at liking? It feels as though we have no choice—as though liking and not-liking just happen to us. I don't really understand this business. I'd love to hear discussion about the mystery of liking—the phenomenology of liking. I sense it's some kind of putting oneself out—or holding oneself open—but I can't see it clearly. I have a hunch, however, that we're not so helpless about liking as we tend to feel.

For in fact I can suggest some practical concrete activities that I have found fairly reliable at increasing the chances of liking student writing:

(a) I ask for lots of private writing and merely shared writing, that is, writing that I don't read at all, and writing that I read but don't comment on. This makes me more cheerful because it's so much easier. Students get *better* without me. Having to evaluate writing—especially bad writing—makes me more likely to hate it. This throws light on grading: it's hard to like something if we know we have to give it a D.

(b) I have students share lots of writing with each other—and after a while respond to each other. It's easier to like their writing when I don't feel myself as the only reader and judge. And so it helps to build community in general: it takes pressure off me. Thus I try to use peer groups not only for feedback, but for other activities too, such as collaborative writing, brainstorming, putting class magazines together, and working out other decisions.

(c) I increase the chances of my liking their writing when I get better at finding what *is* good—or *potentially* good—and learn to praise it. This is a skill. It requires a good eye, a good nose. We tend—especially in the academic world—to assume that a good eye or fine discrimination means criticizing. Academics are sometimes proud of their tendency to be bothered by what is bad. Thus I find I am sometimes looked down on as dumb and undiscriminating: "He likes bad writing. He must have no taste, no discrimination." But I've finally become angry rather than defensive. It's an act of discrimination to see what's good in bad writing. Maybe, in fact, this is the secret of the mystery of liking: to be able to see potential goodness underneath badness.

Put it this way. We tend to stereotype liking as a "soft" and sentimental activity. Mr. Rogers is our model. Fine. There's nothing wrong with softness and sentiment—and I love Mr. Rogers. But liking can also be hard-assed. Let me suggest an alternative to Mr. Rogers: B.F. Skinner. Skinner taught pigeons to play ping-pong. How did he do it? Not by moaning, "Pigeon standards are failing. The pigeons they send us these days are no good. When I was a pigeon ..." He did it by a careful, disciplined method that involved close analytic observation. He put pigeons on a ping-pong table with a ball, and every time a pigeon turned his head 30 degrees toward the ball, he gave a reward (see my "Danger of Softness").

What would this approach require in the teaching of writing? It's very simple ... but not easy. Imagine that we want to teach students an ability they badly lack, for example how to organize their writing or how to make their sentences clearer. Skinner's insight is that we get nowhere in this task by just telling them how much they lack this skill: "It's disorganized. Organize it!" "It's unclear. Make it clear!"

No, what we must learn to do is to read closely and carefully enough to show the student little bits of *proto*-organization or *sort of* clarity in what they've already written. We don't have to pretend the writing is wonderful. We could even say, "This is a terrible paper and the worst part about it is the lack of organization. But I will teach you how to organize. Look here at this little organizational move you made in this sentence. Read it out loud and try to feel how it pulls together this stuff here and distinguishes it from that stuff there. Try to remember what it felt like writing that sentence— creating that piece of organization. Do it some more." Notice how much more helpful it is if we can say, "Do *more* of what you've done here," than if we say, "Do something *different* from anything you've done in the whole paper."

When academics criticize behaviorism as crude it often means that they aren't willing to do the close careful reading of student writing that is required. They'd rather give a cursory reading and turn up their nose and give a low grade and complain about failing standards. No one has undermined behaviorism's main principle of learning: that reward produces learning more effectively than punishment.

(d) I improve my chances of liking student writing when I take steps to get to know them a bit as people. I do this partly through the assignments I give. That is, I always ask them to write a letter or two to me and to each other (for example, about their history with writing). I base at least a couple of assignments on their own experiences, memories, or histories. And I make sure some of the assignments are free choice pieces—which also helps me know them.

In addition, I make sure to have at least three conferences with each student each semester—the first one very early. I often call off some classes in order to keep conferences from being too onerous (insisting nevertheless that students meet with their partner or small group when class is called off). Some teachers have mini-conferences with students during class—while students are engaged in writing or peer group meetings. I've found that when I deal only with my classes as a whole—as a large group—I sometimes experience them as a herd or lump—as stereotyped "adolescents"; I fail to experience them as individuals. For me, personally, this is disastrous since it often leads me to experience them as that scary tribe that I felt rejected by when *I* was an eighteen-year-old—and thus, at times, as "the enemy." But when I sit down with them face to face, they are not so stereotyped or alien or threatening—they are just eighteen-year-olds.

Getting a glimpse of them as individual people is particularly helpful in cases where their writing is not just bad, but somehow offensive—perhaps violent or cruelly racist or homophobic or sexist—or frighteningly vacuous. When I know them just a bit I can often see behind their awful attitude to the person and the life situation that spawned it, and not hate their writing so much. When I know students I can see that they are smart behind that dumb behavior; they are doing the best they can behind that bad behavior. Conditions are keeping them from acting decently; something is holding them back.

(e) It's odd, but the more I let myself show, the easier it is to like them and their writing. I need to share some of my own writing—show some of my own feelings. I need to write the letter to them that they write to me—about my past experiences and what I want and don't want to happen.

(f) It helps to work on my own writing—and work on learning to *like* it. Teachers who are most critical and sour about student writing are often having trouble with their own writing. They are bitter or unforgiving or hurting toward their own work. (I think I've noticed that failed Ph.D.s are often the most severe and difficult with students.) When we are stuck or sour in our own writing, what helps us most is to find spaces free from evaluation such as those provided by freewriting and journal writing. Also, activities like reading out loud and finding a supportive reader or two. I would insist, then, that if only for the sake of our teaching, we need to learn to be charitable and to like our own writing.

A final word. I fear that this sermon about liking might seem an invitation to guilt. There is enough pressure on us as teachers that we don't need someone coming along and calling us inadequate if we don't *like* our students and their writing. That is, even though I think I am right to make this foray into the realm of feeling, I also acknowledge that it is dangerous—and paradoxical. It strikes me that we also need to have permission to hate the dirty bastards and their stupid writing.

After all, the conditions under which they go to school bring out some awful behavior on their part, and the conditions under which we teach sometimes make it difficult for us to like them and their writing. Writing wasn't meant to be read in stacks of twenty-five, fifty, or seventy-five. And we are handicapped as teachers when students are in our classes against their will. (Thus high school teachers have the worst problem here, since their students tend to be the most sour and resentful about school.)

Indeed, one of the best aids to liking students and their writing is to be somewhat charitable toward ourselves about the opposite feelings that we inevitably have. I used to think it was terrible for teachers to tell those sarcastic stories and hostile jokes about their students: "teacher room talk." But now I've come to think that people who spend their lives teaching *need* an arena to let off this unhappy steam. And certainly it's better to vent this sarcasm and hostility with our buddies than on the students themselves. The question, then, becomes this: do we help this behavior function as a venting so that we can move past it and not be trapped in our inevitable resentment of students? Or do we tell these stories and jokes as a way of staying stuck in the hurt, hostile, or bitter feelings—year after year—as so many sad teachers do?

In short I'm not trying to invite guilt, I'm trying to invite hope. I'm trying to suggest that if we do a sophisticated analysis of the difference between liking and evaluating, we will see that it's possible (if not always easy) to like students and their writing—without having to give up our intelligence, sophistication, or judgment.

Let me sum up the points I'm trying to make about ranking, evaluating, and liking:

- Let's do as little ranking and grading as we can. They are never fair and they undermine learning and teaching.

- Let's use evaluation instead—a more careful, more discriminating, fairer mode of assessment.

- But because evaluating is harder than ranking, and because too much evaluating also undermines learning, let's establish small but important evaluation-free zones.

- And underneath it all—suffusing the whole evaluative enterprise—let's learn to be better likers: liking our own and our students' writing, and realizing that liking need not get in the way of clear-eyed evaluation.

WORKS CITED

Diederich, Paul. *Measuring Growth in English.* Urbana: NCTE, 1974.

Belanoff, Pat, and Peter Elbow. "Using Portfolios to Increase Collaboration and Community in a Writing Program." *WPA: Journal of Writing Program Administration* 9.3 (Spring

1986): 27–40. (Also in *Portfolios: Process and Product.* Ed. Pat Belanoff and Marcia Dickson. Portsmouth, NH: Boynton/Cook-Heinemann, 1991.)

Belanoff, Pat, Peter Elbow, and Sheryl Fontaine, eds. *Nothing Begins with N: New Investigations of Freewriting.* Carbondale: Southern Illinois UP, 1991.

Bishop, Wendy. *Something Old, Something New: College Writing Teachers and Classroom Change.* Carbondale: Southern Illinois UP, 1990.

——. *Released into Language: Options for Teaching Creative Writing.* Urbana: NCTE, 1990.

Elbow, Peter. "'The Danger of Softness." *What Is English?* New York: MLA, 1990. 197–210.

Elbow, Peter, and Pat Belanoff. "State University of New York: Portfolio-Based Evaluation Program." *New Methods in College Writing Programs: Theory into Practice.* Ed. Paul Connolly and Teresa Vilardi. New York: MLA, 1986. 95–105. (Also in *Portfolios: Process and Product.* Ed. Pat Belanoff and Marcia Dickson. Portsmouth, NH: Boynton/Cook-Heinemann, 1991.)

Gardner, Howard. *Frames of Mind: The Theory of Multiple Intelligences.* New York: Basic, 1983.

Kirschenbaum, Howard, Simon Sidney, and Rodney Napier. *Wad-Ja-Get? The Grading Game in American Education.* New York: Hart Publishing, 1971.

Lewis, C.S. *Studies in Words.* 2nd ed. London: Cambridge UP, 1967.

Portfolio Assessment Newsletter. Five Centerpointe Drive, Suite 100, Lake Oswego, Oregon 97035.

Portfolio News. c/o San Dieguito Union High School District, 710 Encinitas Boulevard, Encinitas, CA 92024.

Smith, Barbara Herrnstein. *Contingencies of Value: Alternative Perspectives for Critical Theory.* Cambridge: Harvard UP, 1988.

White, Edward M. *Teaching and Assessing Writing.* San Francisco: Jossey-Bass, 1985.

Zak, Frances. "Exclusively Positive Responses to Student Writing." *Journal of Basic Writing* 9.2 (1990): 40–53.

What Grades Do for Us, and How to Do without Them

Marcy Bauman

This selection, by Marcy Bauman of the University of Michigan-Dearborn, appeared in Alternatives to Grading Student Writing, *edited by Stephen Tchudi, Chair of the NCTE Committee on Alternatives to Grading Student Writing. This book was published in 1997 in response to an NCTE resolution to discourage traditional grading of student writing and to investigate alternatives. Bauman describes many of the problems created by traditional grading, especially in providing useful feedback to students and in getting students to take responsibility for their writing. But without the motivation of grades, Bauman writes, teachers must develop assignments and situations that encourage students to work hard at writing, finding real audiences and purposes for students' writing.*

I have chosen not to grade students' writing any longer for a very simple reason: I have found that grading just doesn't work in helping people to learn to write more effectively. In my experience, no matter how much I try to make the assignments "real," no matter how I try to encourage students to write for their own purposes and to make their own discoveries, no matter how easy I make it for students to take risks, as long as I'm the one grading their papers, students tend to understand the writing situation as one in which their task is to please me so that they get a better grade. When I give grades, they tend to ask questions like "How can I make this paper better? Why didn't it get an A? What do you want me to revise?"—all questions that indicate to me that they haven't seen the writing of that paper to be a communicative act, but rather a demonstrative one. They have written to produce what Anne Freadman might call "an example of" something, rather than the something itself.

I see several problems with this state of affairs. The first is that it portrays what is to me a false notion of what writing is and what purpose it serves, because it obscures writing's communicative function (sometimes beyond recognition). The cycle of write, revise, get a grade, write, revise, get a grade tells students that writers write primarily for the purpose of being evaluated, not for the purpose of conveying information or attitudes about a subject that they care about, and certainly not to change anyone's mind, or to move anyone, or to make them angry, or to get them to laugh; that writing is typically produced and evaluated in a vacuum, divorced from

---

genuine communicative intent or function or a genuine real-life situation to prompt it; that the purpose of writing is to produce fixed texts which serve no function beyond providing the writer with occasions to produce them; and that the end point of writing is for the writer to receive varying degrees of approval or disapproval. This is a bit like suggesting that the point of growing vegetables is to win prizes at the county fair. Prizes are (arguably) nice, but they don't put food on the table.

Furthermore, if students are concentrating on their grades at the expense of thinking about their writing as a communicative act, they are being given a false model of how people actually develop as writers. They are laboring under the delusion that learning to write is simply a matter of being told what to do and then doing it, that if the teacher could but only provide the necessary bits of information (or if they could only manage to learn all the right rules), they could generate flawless texts every time. If students are intent on getting a grade, they don't see much of the necessary cognitive work involved with learning to write; they don't come to understand that to a large degree, they will have to learn by trial and error—and that they themselves, not some outside authority, will have to determine where the error lies, that they themselves will have to determine what to do to correct it. They may come to think of learning to write as a process with an end point which the teacher has achieved and they have not. Or worse, they may think of learning to write as something only a few people can accomplish; and they will never develop the habits of mind which will enable them to continue to grow as writers for as long as they care to. This is really my chief objection to using grades and teacher-generated assessment and evaluation to teach writing: It denies the cognitive work about assessment and evaluation that has to become part of every writer's repertoire. What's important isn't that *the teacher* thinks that a student has done well, but that *the student* knows how to determine if she's done what she set out to do in a particular piece of writing (which may or may not include getting a good grade on it).

Finally, a grade-driven model of writing prevents students from engaging a great deal of what they already have learned about communication and language and how they function in the world. Students come to school with a number of years of rhetorical experience. They come to us with a host of language-learning behaviors that have served them since infancy. While I would not claim that learning to write is identical to learning to speak, I would argue that the two are similar enough that we ought to apply what we know about language learning in general to the classroom in particular. I would also argue that by not doing so, we deprive ourselves and our students of rich resources for learning to write—and that our students' development of writing skills is considerably hampered as a result. But explicit correction or evaluation of the kind provided by grades plays an extremely limited role in natural language-learning situations, which instead provide intricate, multilayered avenues of feedback and support for the language learner.

How Not to Grade?

I have tried many different arrangements for arriving at grades without my actually having to grade students' work. I have used various kinds of portfolio assessment methods; I have had people evaluate each other's work; and I have used contract-grading schemes. At this point, I have arrived at a method which suits me and which seems to allow for more of the kinds of learning I value than do the other methods I've used.

My approach is two-pronged: I try to create writing situations that simulate natural, out-of-school language-learning situations as closely as possible, and I shift the tasks of assessment and evaluation to the writers themselves in as many ways and as many different contexts as possible. What I actually do to determine students' final grades is really quite simple: I assign grades solely on the basis of the amount of work that a person does. Thus, in the freshman writing class that I taught in the fall of 1995, for example, I required that students

- read and annotate about 200 pages' worth of articles, culled (by them) from popular periodicals for the first half of the term and from scholarly sources for the second half;
- write one-page article recommendations (whose purpose is to convince others in the class to read the article they recommended) about once every other week (a total of five);
- write one-page responses to articles which had been recommended by others (they wrote six of these in all);
- produce a draft and final copy of a five- to seven-page type-written, double-spaced midterm report;
- produce a draft and final copy of a five- to seven-page type-written, double-spaced final report;
- write one-page responses for the authors of five to seven other midterm reports;
- write one-page responses for the authors of five to seven other final reports;
- write five 150–200-word "colleague acknowledgments": statements about the writing of classmates whose writing they respected;
- write a three- to five-page self-evaluation at the end of the semester.

Anyone who did all of those assignments to the length requirements specified got an A. Anyone who did 80 percent of the work (counted as total numbers of pages specified) got a B. Seventy percent of the work got a person a C, and so on. Missing a major assignment (I defined the midterm and final reports, the colleague acknowledgments, and the self-evaluation as major assignments) got a student's grade lowered by a whole letter.

Let me elaborate a bit. The scheme above called for 200 pages of reading and a minimum of thirty-six pages of writing. If students did at least 90 percent of that—80 pages of reading and thirty-two pages of writing—they were assured of getting an A in the course, assuming they'd not missed a major assignment.

This sort of grading plan creates a lot of paperwork; it's necessary to inform people early and often about where they stand. It also involves a lot of discussion, particularly at the beginning of the semester, about matters such as what constitutes a page, and so on. Sometimes those discussions get tedious—but they are no more tedious than the discussions I used to have about what makes a "substantive" revision, or what "better" means, or why certain changes haven't improved a piece of writing.

Actually arriving at the students' final grades for the course is only the tip of the iceberg, though; it doesn't take much work or thought to devise a scheme and to keep track of who has done what. Anybody could do this, once they'd decided to; it's pathetically easy to determine a final grade on the basis of quantity instead of quality. That's not the interesting part. The real trick is to create contexts where people are motivated to work and learn—where they take the work of the classroom seriously—in spite of the lack of grades on papers.

What Do Grades Do for Us?

As I have experimented with different ways of not grading writing, I've developed a healthy respect for the myriad functions that grades serve for both teachers and students in our classrooms—functions that relate to a student's performance and behavior in the classroom, even as they have little to do with that student's mastery of the subject of the class—and for the difficulty of replicating those functions in the current context of American schooling. It is not enough simply to take the specter of grading away and then to expect that students, liberated, will soar into new realms of language development and risk taking in their writing, and that teachers, released from the burden of evaluating and grading, will become coaches, mentors, and friends. Take away grades and you also take away the traditional means whereby students are motivated to work hard; you take away the chief mechanism through which they get feedback about their writing; you take away the means through which they learn how successfully they write compared with their classmates and others; and you take away their sense of accomplishment and reward. Similarly, when you take away grades, you take away the familiar lens through which teachers are accustomed to viewing students, themselves, and everyone's respective roles in the classroom-even what goes on in the classroom. If we choose not to grade student writing, that choice sets in motion a chain of causation that necessitates a number of other decisions as well.

If we take away the prop of grades, then, we need to see to it that the functions served by grades (albeit poorly served, for many people) are met in other ways. In the rest of this essay, I want to discuss those functions and the other means by which I've been trying to meet them. I also want to provide a small glimpse into how my role in the classroom has changed because I am no longer grading students' writing.

Motivation

It is undeniable that grades motivate many people. The problem, as I see it, lies in what grades motivate *for*. Grades provide people with extrinsic rewards, which work at cross-purposes with intrinsic motivations. There are numerous studies which show that extrinsic rewards severely inhibit intrinsic motivation (summarized in Kohn).

Furthermore, extrinsic motivation doesn't lead to intrinsic motivation. Once the extrinsic reward is removed, people do not generally continue to engage in the behavior for which they were rewarded. Extrinsic reward doesn't lead to long-term, lasting changes in behavior (Kohn).

And long-term, lasting changes in behavior are precisely what I want to foster in my writing classroom. I not only want people to get response and feedback from their peers for the fourteen weeks in which they are enrolled in my course, I want them to continue to see getting a reader's response as a valuable addition to their repertoire of writerly tools. I not only want people to engage in extensive reading and research when they write papers in my class, I want them to come to understand that research really means extended engagement with the academic conversation, not finding five sources to quote for a paper. I want people in my classes to find reasons to be motivated to read, write, and research—and I want them to be able to find those reasons when they write for other classes later on (even if those classes are graded traditionally).

As I have experimented with different ways of not grading in my classrooms, I've come to see motivation as the result of a complex interrelation between activities and reasons. Paris and Turner argue that it is misleading to think of motivation as a "characteristic of people or a property of events" (213). Instead, they propose that "analyses of motivation should consider the characteristics of individuals in specific situations because a person's motivational beliefs and behavior are derived from contextual transactions" (213–4). They identify four characteristics of academic tasks which motivate learning:

- choice ("the ability to choose among different courses of action, or, at least, the freedom to choose to expend varying degrees of effort for a particular purpose") (222);
- challenge ("success without effort is a cheap reward and quickly loses its value in the classroom") (224);
- control ("Once students have chosen personally interesting and challenging tasks, they must exhibit control and autonomy to reach those goals in classrooms.... Despite... [the] benefits of student control and autonomy, teachers often provide little genuine freedom in classrooms") (225); and
- collaboration ("Social guidance and cooperation in classrooms have now been recognized as fundamental for motivation") (226).

Setting up situations where students have motivated reasons to write without grades is tricky and risky. It requires second-guessing the sorts of tasks that will interest students and being willing to change or modify expectations in midstream if interest is waning. It requires setting up mechanisms whereby people are held accountable for doing their work. It requires giving students as much control as possible over the circumstances in which they write, while at the same time providing enough structure so that they can get help if and when they need it.

At first, engineering a classroom that provides students with choice, challenge, control, and collaboration seems like a dizzying, impossible task. One imagines a room full of twenty-five students pursuing twenty-five different agendas—with a teacher writing twenty-five lesson plans, twenty-five sets of feedback, and going home each day to twenty-five nervous breakdowns. Happily enough, I've found, creating such situations is largely a matter of "less is more." You start with one or two organizing principles or overarching pedagogical goals and move out from there. In my case, I am determined that all the writing my students do will be dialogic—they will write to people who will answer their writing, either by writing back, or by using it as the basis for further research, or by trying to do what it asks, or whatever—because I believe that those uses of writing illustrate most clearly what writing is for and why people do it. I want my students to perceive that they are writing out of their own genuine need to communicate something to someone who really wants to know what they have to say. A writing classroom without grades cannot function without this condition being present; otherwise, students will know that there is no reason (real or otherwise) for them to do the required work, and they will become bored and frustrated.

My task, then, initially becomes to find real audiences for my students' writing, or to make the situation in the classroom real enough that students care about reading what their classmates have to say. I try to find one large task, encompassing many smaller tasks, that will engage people for the duration of the semester-in short, I try to find what Frank Smith calls "enterprises." In the past, I have had freshman writers collaboratively investigate Henry Ford, the auto industry, and their impact on the southeast Michigan region where I teach; I have had technical writing students create discipline-specific Internet guides for humanities faculty; I have had technical writing students create World Wide Web pages for departments on campus; and I have had ESL students write a booklet designed to tell students new to the U.S. and to our campus about strange or baffling customs and university procedures. In each of these cases, the primary audience for the writing was someone other than me and someone outside the classroom, but I have also had success with having students work in groups to investigate specific topics and present the results of their research to their classmates by means of a class book.

If students' anonymous and confidential end-of-semester evaluations are any guide, the enterprises work at motivating people:

> I liked the way we were assigned to write documents that were actually going to be used. This not only helped to motivate me in doing the work, but it also gave me a sense of accomplishment knowing that what I was spending so much time writing wasn't going to be read by the instructor, graded, and then thrown out.

> The freedom that we had during this class's [electronic] discussion also motivated me. It would be easy to say that my personal involvement in my writing has taught me that what I write has great meaning and it created a passion to write rather than a boring and bland analytical writing assignment where I am struggling and just jumbling words onto paper to

> reach the professors' requirements. I wanted to write, I wanted to send email messages, I wanted to make my point, I wanted people to notice and understand my writing. The freedom to choose our own research topic also pushed me to write with a definite goal and an absolute interest to make my point.

When I read those self-evaluations, I hear the voices of students who did find motivation in the situations I created for them.

Such is not always the case, though, and those other circumstances are troubling. The flip side of grading as a motivator for students is that grading can be a means of punishment, or at least of control, for a teacher. Giving a low grade can be a way (a not very specific way, to be sure, and hence not very threatening to the teacher) of signaling to a student that she needs to buckle down and work harder. Not giving grades on writing means that instructors have to find other means of informing students that their work is substandard and that they need to pay attention to it. I hope that the enterprises I've constructed will create means whereby a student will become publicly embarrassed if she does not complete her work on time and correctly-the need to fulfill an obligation made to group members or to other faculty on campus often does keep students more conscientious than simply completing an assignment for me.

Feedback

Grading is a crude substitute for many of the mechanisms that provide feedback in naturally occurring language-learning situations, and yet, as feedback mechanisms, grades are extremely poor. Even when teachers (or peers) offer extensive commentary in addition to grades, the presence of grades distorts the feedback, influencing the way the writer hears it. Giltrow and Valiquette, for example, showed that while students in their writing center recognized that instructors' comments on their papers constituted a specific genre which it was important for them to understand, the actual comments themselves confused and sometimes angered the students, who didn't know what they were supposed to do on the basis of them. Giltrow and Valiquette found that students most often read the comments as justifications for the grade on the paper, rather than as specific suggestions for improvement.

Other research, too, shows the dubious value of teacher comments on students' papers. Summarizing the research, Sperling writes that

> The emphasis on response has motivated much research on the comments written by teachers on students' papers. A large number of investigators examining the effects of such comments on students' writing have concluded that comments alone do not affect students' work (see review by Hillocks, 1986). One study of college teachers' comments showed them to be so facile and vague as to be mere "rubber stamps," interchangeable from text to text (Sommers, 1982). Other studies have shown comments to carry meaning for the teacher but not for the student, to be ignored by students

> and thrown away, and to be discounted by students who see in such comments their teachers' "confused readings" of their papers rather than their own writing weaknesses (e.g., Butler, 1980; Hahn, 1981). (66)

Sperling further notes that most of those studies were conducted on the basis of analyzing comments apart from instruction; there is evidence that comments may function best when embedded in process-based instruction. Even here, though, Sperling issues a caution, pointing to research that suggests that "student writers and teacher readers abide by complex and context-bound assumptions about one another that comments may not help to mediate.... When students read teachers' responses to their writing, they may face, in part, the task of unpacking this complex of orientations" (67).

By contrast, in natural language situations, feedback is inherently easier to understand because the language always is intended to *do* something, to provoke some sort of a response in a hearer or reader. In such situations—a toddler asking her father for a glass of juice, for example—there is no need for grades; the person making the utterance knows if it succeeds by whether or not her hearer acts in the way she intended for him to act. Actions, of course, need not be restricted to physical movements; it is often the case that people talk to each other in order to evoke emotional reactions in their hearers, or to get others to share their point of view on a particular topic. Much research (Polanyi; Labov) shows that the point of a conversation is, in fact, to negotiate the meaning of the conversation, to settle on an interpretation of the facts and events being discussed. Thus, in the normal course of language-learning events, the ability to cause a specific action or to negotiate a certain meaning with our hearers provides feedback about the success of our efforts at communicating.

Naturally occurring language-learning situations also provide feedback to the learner specifically about particular utterances. For example, children learn the grammar and syntax of their native language largely by trial and error, and explicit correction from adults is comparatively rare. (Usually, in fact, it is restricted to specific formulaic situations—"Say thank you for the gift"—or to a small percentage of a child's utterances—"Don't say 'ain't.'") When correction occurs, though, it almost always occurs subtly and in the context of a meaningful discussion. If, for example, a child's utterance is unclear or ambiguous, a listener will ask for clarification, possibly offering alternatives, as in the following example:

> *Child* [looking at a car in a parking lot]: Mom, look at how that one's shaped.
> *Mother:* Shaped?
> *Child:* Yeah. It's all banged up. Look. It has rust.
> *Mother:* Oh, what shape it's in.
> *Child:* Yeah, what shape it's in.

In situations where an ungrammatical utterance does not interfere with meaning, usually no explicit correction is given. However, adults will sometimes repeat the structure of the utterance in a later utterance of their own.

Grades alone, of course, come nowhere near to offering this kind of subtle example or reinforcement to learners. Grades only tell students whether or not their work has met an acceptable level of competence, without helping them to know in what ways their communication has failed or succeeded and without providing alternatives which might have worked better. As a result, students come to believe that all that really matters is a sort of crude acceptable/sort of acceptable/not acceptable rating; they lose interest in the finer distinctions about performance.

Furthermore, grades teach people not to care much about what linguists, in reference to spoken language, call "repair"—about modifying or expanding on their work so as to clear up any initial confusion that resulted from it. For most people, once the grade is given, the transaction is concluded. Even in writing-process classrooms, the opportunity to revise for a higher grade is often seen by students as an opportunity to raise a grade, not to clarify the communication.

In the classroom, again, enterprises help to structure situations that provide for a fuller and more meaningful range of feedback for writers. As a result of structuring situations where written language will actually be used—to persuade or inform readers, who will use the information or arguments to carry out further tasks or to construct counterarguments—writers' and readers' feedback is always embedded within a context where the writing is expected by everybody to be immediately meaningful and pertinent. In such cases, the ways in which the reader uses the information that the writer has presented, or the sorts of counterarguments that readers advance, tell students the ways in which their written discourse is effective or ineffective. For example, if the enterprise in the class is to teach faculty members how to use the Internet, a guide that is incomprehensible to the faculty member for whom it was written is clearly ineffective. The situation provides the feedback; the faculty member clearly cannot follow the instructions the student has written because the faculty member is doing the wrong thing at the wrong time. The writers are pushed to clarify their statements and to find other ways of expressing their thoughts. The communication is not finished until a successful negotiation has occurred.

The standard set by negotiating understanding is at once more demanding and satisfying than working for an A. As one student put it:

> At the start of the semester the only thing I was looking forward to was the end of class.... But with the group work.. .1 notice that from reading other people's materials and just actively listening to what is being said amongst the groups that the quality of my work is improving. When I can look at my work and honestly tell that it is getting better, I try to dig deeper to get more facts or look at the topic from a different viewpoint to make it more interesting. Also, when I see people actively discussing my paper and arguing it vigorously, it is sometimes hard for me to believe that I wrote it.

And in an anonymous, end-of-semester evaluation another student said:

> I learned to be persuasive with my writing. The class discussions on the e-mail were very helpful. Not only did I get to express myself but often times

students questioned my opinion and I had to explain in more depth the exact meaning of my statement. Which skilled me with the technique of persuasive and supportive writing.

Evaluation and Reward

Perhaps most obviously, grades are also a crude way of evaluating a person's performance and rewarding people for a job well done. Grades enable students to know where they stand in relation to others in the class, and they (theoretically) are supposed to give outsiders—employers or graduate school admissions committees, most likely—an objective measure of how an individual ranks in comparison with some Platonic standard.

This notion of standards is problematic. On the one hand, we want students to be aware that there *are* standards, and yet their understanding too often takes the form of wanting precise rules. If there's a standard way of doing things, why don't we simply tell them about it, so they can get on with it? A too-rigid conceptualization of standards reinforces a cookbook-style approach to writing: Follow the recipe and you'll succeed. Even though we as teachers know that blindly following recipes for good writing almost always leads to disaster, students are more often than not resentful at our refusal to provide recipes because they think we're holding out on them.

In the same way, although we might promote the idea that standards are really quite flexible (by saying, for example, that there are many types and kinds of good writing, or that there are many ways to approach a particular assignment) and that they are negotiated within a particular community (and thus, not really a product of a particular teacher's whims), students invariably understand standards as instantiated in particular classrooms at particular times by particular individuals. Thus, they ask, "What do you want on this paper?"—not "What does the academic community at large consider acceptable on this paper?"

Thus, if students are writing primarily to get a decent grade, then their focus must necessarily be on writing in a way that conforms to the standards held by the grade giver. To the degree to which they are writing in accordance with what the grade giver thinks of as good writing, they are denied the opportunity to learn to make their own value judgments about writing. Grades deprive students of the need to do the cognitive work involved in figuring out what constitutes appropriate writing in a given genre or discourse community. I want to be clear that this state of affairs applies simply because of the presence of grades in the classroom, irrespective of what any particular teacher does or does not do. As long as the teacher is passing judgment, the teacher's judgment will matter more than the student's.

But it is neither possible nor desirable to sidestep judgment altogether. In a class where grades are not given in the traditional manner, students still need to know how their performance compares with that of their classmates, to get a sense of how their writing works overall, out in the real world. Rather than provide such evaluations myself, however, I try to construct situations which will enable students to learn to make them. Learning to assess their strengths and weaknesses in comparison with others' is, to my mind, a crucial ability for writers (at any level) to develop and nurture. Good writing starts with the admiration of and respect for others' good writing.

To satisfy the writer's need for evaluation, and also to give people the chance to make their own judgments, I use a process of colleague acknowledgments, which I have borrowed and adapted from Russell Hunt (1993–1996) at St. Thomas University. At several points during the semester, I ask students to write me a note, telling me which (three or four or five) of their classmates' writing is particularly effective. I vary the wording of this assignment, depending on which rhetorical features I want them to think about. I might ask them to explain which pieces of writing have challenged their beliefs or perceptions, I might ask them whose writing is the clearest, or I might ask them whose style they most admire and why. I might ask them to quote specific bits from others' writing in their explanations.

I then redistribute these acknowledgments (anonymously) to the people who have been acknowledged. Thus, students in the class gain an understanding of whether others see their work as valuable, and if they do, what exactly about their writing strikes people as worthwhile. I love distributing the acknowledgments; people usually find them far more affirming than any grade could be—and since the acknowledgments are freely given, they are read by the recipients as being much more sincere than even the sincerest praise coming from a teacher.

The acknowledgments always make for interesting reading, both for me and for the people being acknowledged. I am frequently amazed at the diversity and subtlety of what students notice about each other's writing; I nearly always get a fresh insight into what's really going on in class for the students-what they value about writing and the class, what they're coming to value, as well as what they're not seeing or understanding. Mostly, though, students' acknowledgments are often specific and perceptive as well as complimentary, as the following example shows:

> Jennifer is a very talented writer; she is very expressive and heartfelt in her papers. I especially enjoyed reading the article on corruption in America's PD. She is very persuasive in the presentation of her topic, and doing so on a level that is of interest to us, young college students. I thought that her point-of-view was the same as mine, or vice-versa, in that, "What distinguishes an officer of the law from the average person?" and "We do not need close-minded corrupt police officers taking away individual rights and creating chaos." I admire the fact that she is strong-minded and will put it in her writing. I am always afraid of what other people would think, and tried to avoid any type of controversy. After reading Lisa's papers, however, I realized that your view won't always be like someone else's, but it is a good way to make a discussion. I have learned to be more expressive from Jennifer's example.

Sometimes, even if the acknowledgments are not particularly specific, they display an honesty which is not available to me as a teacher to show:

> Kerri puts a lot of effort into her work; you can tell she doesn't B.S. her way through writing assignments and she does a good job making her topic sound important and meaningful.
>
> Sandy's writing is never confusing; she always gives great detail and gets right to the point. I can read her papers without getting completely bored.
>
> I thought Laurie's topic proposal on stress was very persuasive compared to most of the other proposals. She made a somewhat boring topic sound pretty interesting.

Also, sometimes it is clear that the acknowledger understands that her acknowledgment is written primarily for the writer, although she knows that I read them, too:

> I think that Danny R. is an excellent writer for a variety of reasons. He manages to write casually, without losing the basic sense of grammar or the point of the assignment. I enjoy reading his writings because they are interesting as well as informative. I like what he did to the encyclopedia article. He used his imagination to get around the obstacle the article presented. (He knows what I mean). I respect his writing because he gives his opinion very openly, yet at the same time, it is never offensive. I hope he keeps this writing style because it is persuasive, and I think we will find it beneficial to the group.

It often happens that not everyone in a class will receive acknowledgments. In order to increase the learning that is possible from the acknowledgments, I have used a variety of strategies to make it possible for others to read them. One strategy is to ask people who've been acknowledged to send me, via e-mail, the acknowledgment they value the most, along with a short explanation of why it was meaningful to them. I then reproduce those notes anonymously and pass them out for the whole class to read. At that point, we can discuss in more general terms what makes for effective writing—and what makes for effective acknowledging. People thus have the opportunity to see what kinds of qualities their classmates have acknowledged in others' writing, as well as how others have effectively expressed their admiration; the whole notion of what makes for good writing can thus expand beyond any one person's ideas.

Another strategy that I have begun to use is to ask students to post their acknowledgments anonymously via computer using a World Wide Web-based bulletin-board program called HyperNews. The advantage here is that as the acknowledgments are posted, other students can read them. I'm hoping that being able to read what others have said, just before they post their own acknowledgments, will give students another context for learning strategies for effective writing. I also hope that the ability to read others' acknowledgments will help to develop a classroom climate of appreciation—rather than criticism—for the writing being done in the class.

Replacing Grades with Learning

Finally, then, deciding not to grade students' writing has had a far more profound impact on my classroom than I ever imagined it would. In the process of noticing that removing grades was also removing many positive elements from the classroom, and of trying to replicate those positive elements in other ways, I have had to interrogate many of my longest-practiced teaching techniques in light of my most deeply held assumptions about the nature of teaching and learning. I have begun to question nearly everything that goes on in classrooms—in mine and others'. I think that I'm on the right track with what I am doing now. The kinds of learning I see in my students lead me to believe that if a class is structured to provide the elements that grades supply, not grading students' writing really can free them to take more control over their work.

I'd like to close with comments written by two students on their end-of-semester self-evaluations:

> I think I have reached new heights in self-expression this semester. Sometimes when I write for classes I am afraid of my point of view offending people. This semester I think I have overcome that fear. A lot of what my group was writing about is considered controversial and I was aware of how strong my views are about the topic, but I overcame that and wrote what I felt should be written. It was especially rewarding when people agreed with my strong opinions and enjoyed my writing because of them. In other classes I would have toned it down a bit. I really felt that there would be no negative consequences from writing "from the heart" so I went ahead and did just that. I didn't have to worry about being graded down for offending the professor. Because of the lack of grades, I was able to concentrate completely on my writing and not what I thought the professor wanted to read.
>
> Through high school I had always done well in English but I never really got the opinion of other students on my writing. In this class I found that all those A's in high school didn't really mean anything if other people can't understand your writing, find it boring, or have many questions about what you wrote.

These evaluations, and others like them, let me know that the payoff for upsetting the apple cart is that at least for the space of time that they're in my class, people have the chance to learn what it means to write for themselves.

Works Cited

Freadman, Anne. "'Genre' and the Reading Class." *Typereader: The Journal of the Centre for Studies in Literary Education* 1(1988): 1–7.

Giltrow, Janet, and Michelle Valiquette. "Student Writers and Their Readers: The Conventions of Commentary." Paper presented at the Conference on College Composition and Communication. Mar. 16–20 1994. Nashville, TN.

Hunt, Russell A. Personal correspondence. 1993–1996.

Kohn, Alfie. *Punished by Rewards: The Trouble with Gold Stars, Incentive Plans, A's, Praise, and Other Bribes*. Boston: Houghton, 1993.

Labov, William. *Language in the Inner City: Studies in the Black English Vernacular*. Philadelphia: U of Pennsylvania P, 1972.

Paris, Scott G., and Julianne C. Turner. "Situated Motivation." *Student Motivation, Cognition, and Learning: Essays in Honor of Wilbert J. McKeachie*. Hillsdale: Erlbaum, 1994: 213–37

Polanyi, Livia. "So What's the Point?" *Semiotica* 25.3/4 (1979): 207–41.

Smith, Frank. *Essays into Literacy: Selected Papers and Some Afterthoughts*. London: Heinemann, 1983.

Sperling, Melanie. "Revisiting the Writing-Speaking Connection: Challenges for Research on Writing and Writing Instruction." *Review of Educational Research* 66.1 (1996): 53–86.

SUGGESTED READINGS: DESIGNING, RESPONDING TO, AND EVALUATING WRITING ASSIGNMENTS

Allison, Libby, Lizbeth Bryant, and Maureen Hourigan, eds. *Grading in the Post-Process Classroom: From Theory to Practice*. Portsmouth, NH: Boynton/Cook, 1997.

Anson, Chris M., ed. *Writing and Response: Theory, Practice, and Research*. Urbana, IL: NCTE, 1989.

Anson, Chris M., et al. *Scenarios for Teaching Writing: Contexts for Discussion and Reflective Practice*. Urbana, IL: NCTE, 1993.

Belanoff, Pat, and Marcia Dickson, eds. *Portfolios: Process and Product*. Portsmouth, NH: Boynton/Cook, 1991.

Black, Laurel Johnson. *Between Talk and Teaching: Reconsidering the Writing Conference*. Logan: Utah State UP, 1998.

Burch, C. Beth. *Writing for Your Portfolio*. Boston: Allyn & Bacon, 1999.

Connors, Robert J., and Andrea A. Lunsford. "Teachers' Rhetorical Comments on Student Papers." *CCC* 44.2 (1993): 200–23.

Cooper, Charles R., and Lee Odell, eds. *Evaluating Writing: The Role of Teachers' Knowledge about Text, Learning, and Culture*. Urbana, IL: NCTE, 1999.

Flynn, Thomas, and Mary King. *Dynamics of the Writing Conference: Social and Cognitive Interaction*. Urbana, IL: NCTE, 1993.

Harris, Muriel. *Teaching One-to-One*. Urbana, IL, NCTE, 1986.

Hashimoto, Irvin Y. *Thirteen Weeks: A Guide to Teaching College Writing*. Portsmouth, NH: Boynton/Cook, 1991.

Heller, Dana A. "Silencing the Soundtrack: An Alternative to Marginal Comments." *CCC* 40 (1989): 210–15.

Horvath, Brooke K. "The Components of Written Response: A Practical Sythesis of Current Views." *Rhetoric Review* 2 (1984): 136–56.

International Reading Association and National Council of Teachers of English. *Standards for the Assessment of Reading and Writing*. Newark, DE: IRA; Urbana, IL: NCTE, 1994.

Knoblauch, Cy, and Lil Brannon. "On Students' Rights to Their Own Texts: A Model of Teacher Response." *CCC* 33 (1982): 157–66.

Lawson, Bruce, Susan Sterr Ryan, and W. Ross Winterowd, eds. *Encountering Student Texts: Interpretive Issues in Reading Student Writing*. Urbana, IL: NCTE, 1989.

Moffett, James. *Active Voice: A Writing Program across the Curriculum*. 2nd ed. Portsmouth, NH: Boynton/Cook, 1992.

Ponsot, Marie, and Rosemary Deen. *Beat Not the Poor Desk*. Upper Montclair, NJ: Boynton/Cook, 1982.

Rubin, Donnalee. *Gender Influences: Reading Student Texts*. Carbondale: Southern Illinois UP, 1993.

Sommers, Nancy. "Responding to Student Writing." *CCC* 33 (1982): 145–56.

Tchudi, Stephen, ed. *Alternatives to Grading Student Writing*. Urbana, IL: NCTE, 1997.

White, Edward M. *Teaching and Assessing Writing*. 2nd ed. San Francisco: Jossey-Bass, 1994.

Yancey, Kathleen Blake. *Portfolios in the Writing Classroom: An Introduction*. Urbana, IL: NCTE, 1992.

Yancey, Kathleen Blake, and Irwin Weiser, eds. *Situating Portfolios: Four Perspectives*. Logan: Utah State UP, 1997.

Zak, Frances, and Christopher C. Weaver, eds. *The Theory and Practice of Grading Writing: Problems and Perspectives*. Albany: SUNY P, 1998.

FURTHER SUGGESTED READINGS

JOURNALS

academic.writing: Interdisciplinary Perspectives on Communication Across the Curriculum

The ACE Journal: The Journal of the NCTE Assembly on Computers in English

Assessing Writing

College Composition and Communication

College English

Composition Chronicle

Composition Forum

Composition Studies

Computers and Composition

Dialogue

English Journal

Journal of Advanced Composition

Journal of Basic Writing

Journal of Teaching Writing

Journal of Technical Writing and Communication

Journal of Writing Program Administration

Kairos (online)
Language and Learning Across the Disciplines

Pre/Text

Research in the Teaching of English

Rhetoric Review

Teaching English in the Two-Year College

Writing Center Journal

The Writing Instructor

Writing Lab Newsletter

Writing on the Edge

Written Communication

BIBLIOGRAPHIES ON TEACHING COLLEGE COMPOSITION

CCCC Bibliography of Composition and Rhetoric: 1987– . Carbondale: Southern Illinois UP, 1988– .

ERIC: Educational Resources Information Center. National Institute of Education. US Department of Education.

Hillocks, George, Jr. *Research on Written Composition.* Urbana, IL: NCTE, 1986.

Horner, Winifred Bryan, ed. *The Present State of Scholarship in Historical and Contemporary Rhetoric.* Rev. ed. Columbia: U of Missouri P, 1990.

Moran, Michael G., and Ronald F. Lunsford, eds. *Research in Composition and Rhetoric: A Bibliographic Sourcebook.* Westport, CT: Greenwood, 1984.

Tate, Gary, ed. *Teaching Composition: Twelve Bibliographic Essays.* Fort Worth: Texas Christian UP, 1987.

COLLECTIONS OF READINGS

Brooks, Charlotte K., ed. *Tapping Potential: English and Language Arts for the Black Learner*. Urbana, IL: NCTE, 1985.

Caywood, Cynthia L., and Gillian R. Overing, eds. *Teaching Writing: Pedagogy, Gender, and Equity*. Albany: SUNY P, 1987.

Chappell, Virginia A., Mary Louise Buley-Meissner, and Chris Anderson, eds. *Balancing Acts: Essays on the Teaching of Writing in Honor of William F. Irmscher*. Carbondale: Southern Illinois UP, 1991.

Bazerman, Charles, and David R. Russell, eds. *Landmark Essays on Writing Across the Curriculum*. Davis, CA: Hermagoras, 1995.

Cope, Bill, and Mary Kalantzis, eds. *The Powers of Literacy: A Genre Approach to Teaching Writing*. Pittsburgh: U of Pittsburgh P, 1993.

Corbett, Edward P. J. *Selected Essays of Edward P. J. Corbett*. Ed Robert J. Connors. Dallas: Southern Methodist UP, 1989.

Ede, Lisa, ed. *On Writing Research: The Braddock Essays 1975-1998*. Boston: Bedford/St. Martin's, 1999.

Farmer, Frank, ed. *Landmark Essays on Bakhtin, Rhetoric, and Writing*. Davis, CA: Hermagoras, 1998.

Gilyard, Keith, ed. *Race, Rhetoric, and Composition*. Portsmouth, NH: Boynton/Cook, 1999.

Graves, Richard L., ed. *Rhetoric and Composition: A Sourcebook for Teachers and Writers*. 3rd ed. Portsmouth, NH: Boynton/Cook, 1992.

Hurlbert, C. March, and Michael Blitz, eds. *Composition and Resistance*. Portsmouth, NH: Boynton/Cook, 1991.

Lunsford, Andrea A., Helene Moglen, and James Slevin, eds. *The Right to Literacy*. New York: MLA, 1990.

Murphy, James J., ed. *The Rhetorical Tradition and Modern Writing.* New York: MLA, 1982.

Odell, Lee, ed. *Theory and Practice in the Teaching of Writing: Rethinking the Discipline.* Carbondale: Southern Illinois UP, 1993.

Petrosky, Anthony R., and David Bartholomae, eds. *The Teaching of Writing.* Chicago: NSSE, 1986.

Reynolds, Mark, ed. *Two-Year College English: Essays for a New Century.* Urbana, IL: NCTE, 1994.

Smith, Louise Z., ed. *Audits of Meaning: A Festschrift in Honor of Ann E. Berthoff.* Portsmouth, NH: Boynton/Cook, 1988.

Tate, Gary, Edward P. J. Corbett, and Nancy Myers, eds. *The Writing Teacher's Sourcebook.* 3rd ed. New York: Oxford UP, 1994.

Villanueva, Victor, Jr., ed. *Cross-Talk in Comp Theory: A Reader.* Urbana, IL: NCTE, 1997.

Wiley, Mark, Barbara Gleason, and Louise Weatherbee Phelps, eds. *Composition in Four Keys: Inquiring into the Field.* Mountain View, CA: Mayfield, 1996.

Winterowd, W. Ross, and Vincent Gillespie, eds. *Composition in Context: Essays in Honor of Donald C. Stewart.* Carbondale: Southern Illinois UP, 1994.

Witte, Stephen P., Neil Nakadate, and Roger D. Cherry, eds. *A Rhetoric of Doing: Essays on Written Discourse in Honor of James L. Kinneavy.* Carbondale: Southern Illinois UP, 1994.

Yancey, Kathleen Blake, eds. *Voices on Voice: Perspectives, Definitions, Inquiry.* Urbana, IL: NCTE, 1994.

TEACHING INTERNATIONAL STUDENTS

Ferris, Dana, and John S. Hedgcock. *Teaching ESL Composition: Purpose, Process, and Practice.* Mahwah, NJ: Lawrence Erlbaum, 1998.

Hamp-Lyons, Liz. *Assessing ESL Writing in Academic Contexts*. Norwood, NJ: Ablex, 1992.

Johnson, Donna M., and Duane H. Roen, eds. *Richness in Writing: Empowering ESL Students*. New York: Longman, 1989.

Kroll, Barbara, ed. *Second Language Writing: Research Insights for the Classroom*. New York: Cambridge UP, 1990.

Leki I. *Understanding ESL Writers: A Guide for Teachers*. New York: St. Martin's, 1992.

Li, Xiao-Ming. *"Good Writing" in Cross-Cultural Context*. Albany: SUNY P, 1996.

Nelson, Marie Wilson. *At the Point of Need: Teaching Basic and ESL Writers*. Portsmouth, NH: Boynton/Cook, 1991.

Purves, Alan, ed. *Writing Across Languages and Cultures: Issues in Contrastive Rhetoric*. Newbury Park, CA: Sage, 1988.

Ruetten, Mary K. "Teaching ESL Students in Regular Classes." *Journal for College Writing* 1 (1994): 15–20.

Severino, Carol, Juan C. Guerra, and Johnnella E. Butler, eds. *Writing in Multicultural Settings*. New York: MLA, 1997.

TEACHING STUDENTS WITH LEARNING DISABILITIES

Dunn, Patricia A. *Learning Re-abled: The Learning Disability Controversy and Composition Studies*. Portsmouth, NH: Boynton/Cook, 1995.

Graham, Steve, Shirley S. Schwartz, and Charles A. MacArthur. "Knowledge of Writing and the Composing Process, Attitude Toward Writing, and Self-Efficacy for Students With and Without Learning Disabilities." *Journal of Learning Disabilities* 26 (1993): 237–49.

O'Hearn, Carolyn. "Recognizing the Learning Disabled College Student." *College English* 51 (1989): 294–304.

Scott, Sally S. "Determining Reasonable Academic Adjustments for College Students with Learning Disabilities." *Journal of Learning Disabilities* 27 (1994): 403–12.

WRITING CENTERS

Gillespie, Paula, and Neal Lerner. *The Allyn & Bacon Guide to Peer Tutoring*. Boston: Allyn & Bacon, 2000.

Harris, Muriel, ed. *Tutoring Writing: A Sourcebook for Writing Labs*. Glenview, IL: Scott, Foresman, 1982.

Maxwell, Martha, ed. *When Tutor Meets Student*. 2nd ed. Ann Arbor: U of Michigan P, 1994.

Meyer, Emily, and Louise Z. Smith. *The Practical Tutor*. New York: Oxford UP, 1987.

Mullin, Joan A., and Ray Wallace, eds. *Intersections: Theory-Practice in the Writing Center*. Urbana, IL: NCTE, 1994.

Murphy, Christina, and Joe Law, eds. *Landmark Essays on Writing Centers*. Davis, CA: Hermagoras, 1995.

Murphy, Christina, Joe Law, and Steve Sherwood. *Writing Centers: An Annotated Bibliography*. Westport, CT: Greenwood, 1996.

North, Stephen M. "The Idea of a Writing Center." *College English* 46 (1984): 433–46.

Olson, Gary A., ed. *Writing Centers: Theory and Administration*. Urbana, IL: NCTE, 1984.

Silk, Bobbie Bayliss, ed. *The Writing Center Resource Manual*. Emmitsburg, MD: NWCA P, 1998.

Wallace, Ray, and Jeanne Simpson, eds. *The Writing Center: New Directions*. New York: Garland, 1991.

NOTES

NOTES

NOTES

NOTES

NOTES

ECONOMIC ISSUES

FOR CONSUMERS

Fourth Edition